MANAGING PUBLIC SERVICES – IMPLEMENTING CHANGES

The work of a manager in a service organization is not the same as the work of a manager in an organization that manufactures goods. *Managing Public Services – Implementing Changes* is for students and managers who intend to work in a service organization, whether it is owned publicly or privately. This book concentrates on how managers can change things for the better. It explains 'why' as well as 'how'.

Management of people, finance, information and operations are considered separately, then integrated through chapters on managing change, managing projects, managing learning and managing personal development.

The emphasis is on the thinking and learning skills which managers need to implement changes. Key skills are developed through extensive thinking, learning and assessment activities at the end of each chapter. Students develop learning skills that enable them to transfer their learning from one situation to another and thinking skills that enable them to adapt the way that they apply their learning as circumstances change. Case studies and interviews with public service managers working in Europe, Asia, Australia and the US are incorporated.

Managing Public Services – Implementing Changes begins by predicting the changes that will affect public services over the next 20 years and ends with a critique of the way in which management values are undermining ethics, efficiency and effectiveness. The last chapter argues that unless there is a more thoughtful approach to management education, additional resources will not lead to improved management practice. The book answers the question, 'How can public services be improved without wasteful injections of public money?'

Tony L. Doherty, St Martin's College, is an author, academic, researcher and public sector consultant. As well as a wide variety of management subjects, he has taught religious studies and theology, and has worked for the European Commission. He has 15 years' experience of managing public services in the voluntary sector, local government and the Home Office, working with police, probation, youth, social, education, urban regeneration and health services.

Terry Horne, Lancashire Business School, is an author, academic and general management consultant with a special interest in public service organizations. His clients have included the BBC, the NHS, the Crown Agents, local government, colleges of further and higher education, ICI, Pfizer pharmaceuticals, British Gas, The Children of Russia Foundation and the Institute of Management. He was formerly a director of BTR, owners of Dunlop, and Colt International, owners of Pratt & Whitney Aerospace.

MANAGING PUBLIC SERVICES – IMPLEMENTING CHANGES

A thoughtful approach to the practice of management

Tony L. Doherty and Terry Horne

London and New York

First published 2002
by Routledge
11 New Fetter Lane, London EC4P 4EE

Simultaneously published in the USA and Canada
by Routledge
29 West 35th Street, New York NY 10001

Routledge is an imprint of the Taylor & Francis Group

Typeset in Garamond by Wearset Ltd, Boldon, Tyne and Wear
Printed and bound in Great Britain by St Edmundsbury Press,
Bury St Edmunds, Suffolk

British Library Cataloguing in Publication Data
A catalogue record for this book is available from the British Library

Library of Congress Cataloging in Publication Data
Doherty, Tony L., 1957–
Managing public services—implementing changes : a thoughtful approach to the
practice of management / Tony L. Doherty & Terry Horne.
p. cm.
Includes bibliographical references and index.
1. Public administration. 2. Government business enterprises—Management.
I. Horne, Terry. II. Title.
JF1351 .D59 2002
658—dc21
2001041858

ISBN 0–415–18027–9 (hbk)
ISBN 0–415–18028–7 (pbk)

DEDICATION

This book is dedicated to Carolyn Horne. She was a Quaker. She was a lovely wife, an inspired teacher, a loving mother and a successful manager. She had a thoughtful approach to management. She greeted those who worked with her as individuals and held genuine conversations with them. She tried to learn something every day. She tried to improve something every week. She committed random acts of gratuitous kindness. The world is a better place for her having lived in it.

THE STRUCTURE OF THE BOOK

First thoughts
Managing in context

Role one
Managing change

Managing resistance to change	Managing strategy continuity and change

Role two
Managing operations

Managing markets	Managing quality

Role three
Managing people

Managing groups	Managing motivation	Managing individuals

Role four
Managing resources

Managing budgets	Managing resources	Managing performance

Role five
Managing information

Managing communication	Managing decisions

Role six
Managing learning

Managing learning	Managing personal development

Final thoughts
Managing values
Managment as Religion

CONTENTS

PREFACE

Read not to contradict and confute,
Nor to believe and take for granted . . .
But to weigh and consider.
(Francis Bacon, *Essays*, no. 50, 'Of Studies')

This book will help readers to perform routine management procedures efficiently and to develop a thought-ful approach to the complex issues that face managers of public services, whether publicly or privately owned. The book helps readers to implement changes, provided the changes are for the better. It explains 'why' as well as 'how'. Managing People, Managing Operations, Managing Resources and Managing Information are considered separately. These roles are integrated through chapters on Managing Change, Managing Commu-nication, Managing Learning, Managing Personal Development and Managing Projects. The book draws on more than 2,000 conversations with people who worked in public services in Eastern Europe, Western Europe, Asia, India, Pakistan, Africa, South America, Australia, Fiji, Madagascar, the United States and the United Kingdom. There are controversial findings on strategy, stakeholding, team working and workplace learning. There are new approaches to overcoming resistance, managing motivation, dealing with poor per-formers and managing difficult people.

The material on each topic is sequenced in ascending order of the academic demands it makes on the reader. There is material needed by supervisory and junior management at NVQ level 3. The material for middle managers is presented at undergraduate level 4. The Final Thoughts of each chapter are at postgradu-ate level 5. The whole book is suitable as an introduction to general management for MBA students who have no previous experience of practical management education. For practising managers it will be an endur-ing source of reference. This book will support them throughout their careers.

The book emphasizes the thinking skills and conversational skills which managers need in order to imple-ment changes. These skills can be developed through a carefully scaffolded sequence of thinking and learning activities. The thinking and learning activities are included in a separate section at the end of each chapter. Readers can choose to work alone or in pairs (sometimes in groups). Readers can develop key cognitive and social skills. The cognitive skills will help them to transfer their learning to new situations as their circum-stances change. A wide range of thinking skills is developed, including recollection, reflection, prediction, imagination and calculation, as well as ethical, creative and critical thinking.

The book begins with a prediction of the changes that will affect public services over the next 20 years. It ends with a critique of the way managers can damage the economy, efficiency, effectiveness and the ethics of public services – the dangers of management as religion.

ACKNOWLEDGEMENTS

This study spans 32 years. During that period over 2,000 managers, and the people they manage, took time to hold conversations with us or our research workers. Only 14 of those conversations are formally acknowledged in the text – one in each chapter. The rest of you will find your influence throughout the text, in the thinking and learning activities, and in the case studies at the end of each chapter. Some of you worked with us on public service projects for over 20 years. The projects were diverse, sometimes exciting. Many made a difference, sometimes in spite of management! Thanks to you all. Geoff Woodhall, our accountant, gave us specialist help with public service finance. The University Department of Journalism helped with the section on managing the media. Gilly McHugh, Peter Knock, Dr Muckthiar Zammen, Kay Kent, Jim Mehan, John Harrison and Ian Hathornethwaite, all postgraduate students at Lancashire Business School, did the research on environmental analysis, local government, transcultural management, private finance initiatives workplace learning and the process of thinking and learning. The research on thinking and learning profited from 7 years' research and development projects with Simon Wootton and Roger Armstrong. The original research on relationship formation was done by Anne Girardot at Lancaster University. We have benefited from Sue Bloxham's thoughtful approach to the development of public service managers at St Martin's College. St Martin's has a long tradition of preparing managers and professionals for work in public services. The ethos of St Martin's College supported the emergence of many of the ideas in this book.

A project spanning 32 years cannot be brought to a successful conclusion without the help of many people. We diminish nobody by acknowledging especially the patience and forbearance which we have shown each other, and which has been shown to us, by our families and friends and by Elaine Bradley. In particular, we want to say thank you to Anne Girardot and Sue Doherty. Sue is an excellent example of a thoughtful public service manager. Aidan and Luke Doherty have grown from children into mature young men during the writing of this book! Thank you both for your patience!

FIRST THOUGHTS

1

MANAGING IN THE CHANGING CONTEXT OF PUBLIC SERVICES

Since changes are going on anyway, the great thing is to learn enough about them. Conditions and events are neither to be fled from nor passively acquiesced in; they are to be utilised and directed.

(John Dewey (1920) *Reconstruction in Philosophy*)

LEARNING OUTCOMES

This chapter will enable the reader to:

- Understand what is meant by a public service organization.
- Analyse the impact of external changes on public service organizations.
- Consider the potential for conflict between managers and professionals.
- Examine 'new public service management' from an international perspective.
- Understand what is meant by the organizational structure of a public service.
- Decide whether new forms of organization have replaced traditional bureaucracy.
- Consider the implications for public service managers of the changes that are likely to take place in the next 20 years.

INTRODUCTION

Managers need to adapt the way they manage to suit their present context. Public service organizations have a history. It is helpful for managers to understand that history when they are trying to implement changes. Public service organizations have a relationship with the users of their services which is quite different from the relationship between a factory and its customers. Even when we adapt our management thinking to accommodate what is different about public services, we find that the public services are themselves changing in the face of technological, economic, political, legal and social forces. These forces have produced changing forms of ownership, changing forms of organization and changing roles for managers and professionals. This is not new. From their origins in defence, taxation and law enforcement, in most countries public service organizations underwent rapid change after the Second World War. The period 1980–2000 saw changes in patterns of ownership and in forms of organizational structure. It is these developments that we wish to consider in this chapter.

DEFINING PUBLIC SERVICES

In the nineteenth century, the industrial revolution in Northern Europe and North America brought wealth and change. New urban environments were created and with them new social needs. A mixture of philanthropy and vested interest encouraged the state to provide services for the well-being of its citizens. Adam Smith, an economist, defined public services as:

> those public institutions and those public works which, though they may be in the highest degree advantageous to a great society, are of such a nature, that the profits could never repay their expenses to any individual or small number of individuals and which it cannot be expected, therefore, that any individual or small number of individuals, would ever erect or maintain.[1]

Many public service organizations started life as charitable or religious organizations. Their work was taken over by publicly funded bodies, many of which are now privately owned. Others started life as privately owned companies which are now publicly owned. Originally, private companies owned many roads, bridges and railways. In most countries these were taken into public ownership, along with water, gas, electricity and telephone services. In the UK, the iron, steel and coal industries were included. In many Eastern European countries, public ownership was extended to agriculture and most industries. Although these organizations were publicly owned, they were not public services, because they manufactured consumable and industrial goods. In the period 1980–2000, many public services returned to private ownership, albeit with varying degrees of public subsidy and regulation.

The function of a public service is often defined by law. Law and order, environmental health and national defence services are almost always provided by central government. In 1997 Flynn[2] pointed out that distinctions between privately and publicly owned public service organizations were no longer clear. Private companies sometimes use state-owned assets to provide public services. The state sometimes leases assets owned and managed by private companies. In the UK, for example, schools draw up business plans, market themselves to attract pupils, devise innovative funding schemes, maximize revenues, minimize costs and develop 'strategic approaches' to gaining 'competitive advantage'. In 1999 Lawton and Rose[3] concluded that it was unhelpful to adopt hard and fast definitions of public service management. The most important differences between public and private ownership occur in resourcing and accountability. These are discussed in Chapters 9, 10 and 11. The competencies required to manage any organization providing services to the public are similar, whether the organization is privately owned or publicly owned.

A Spectrum of Public Services

Tomkins[4] sees public services as a spectrum. Within this spectrum, public services range from those that are fully owned by private shareholders, to those that are fully in public ownership (Table 1.1).

Public service organizations may move both up and down this spectrum of ownership. Railway services in the UK, for example, have moved from wholly private to wholly public to partly private again. In Pakistan, some hospitals have moved from wholly public to jointly public and privately financed. It is useful for managers to understand the implications for them when the nature of the ownership changes.

Table 1.1 A spectrum of public services

Organization	Example
Charity	Oxfam
Fully private	Care homes for the elderly
Joint private and public ventures	Railway from London to the Channel Tunnel
Private but publicly regulated	Some electricity and water companies
Contracted out	Refuse collection
Public with managed competition	The UK Prison Service
Public without competition	National Mail Services

Public versus Private Ownership in Public Services

There are a number of distinctions between publicly and privately owned organizations. Publicly owned organizations, for example, usually have politically defined goals, whereas privately owned organizations are more likely to follow 'free market forces'. Charles Handy[5] argued that if society were always to follow market forces, then people who could not create enough personal wealth to cover their own costs would be discarded, exported or condemned to death. This illustrates the difficulty of leaving some public services to the mercy of unregulated market forces. We shall return to this problem in Chapter 4 and again in our final chapter on the clash between 'management masters and public servants'.

Many public services are financed through taxation rather than through the direct charging of customers. Even where there is a charge, which there is for most health services in most countries in Europe, services are still supplied to people who cannot afford them. How managers charge for services will depend on whether the public service is being provided by an organization that is owned by a charity, a local community, a national government or private shareholders.

The Size and Scale of Public Services

Table 1.2 illustrates the scale of local public expenditure to pay for public services.

Table 1.2 Local government expenditure in England, 1995–96

Examples	£M
Education and Employment	20,118
Social Services	11,235
Law and Order	8,189
Local Health	7,327
Environment	5,056
Transport	2,475
Heritage	1,246
Housing	343

Source: HM UK Treasury (1996)

In addition to the local expenditure shown in Table 1.2, there is expenditure on activities that are accountable to a government minister. In the UK, for example, this includes:

- the Civil Service
- the Armed Forces
- the National Health Service
- non-departmental agencies

Non-departmental agencies have terms of reference determined by statute. For example, the UK Equal Opportunities Commission and the Commission for Racial Equality are agencies that are responsible for monitoring compliance with laws dealing with discrimination. Public services are also provided by regional governments and other authorities that have power to raise local taxes to finance public services. California, for example, levies its own sales tax. There are also many public corporations, like Audit Commissions or Her Majesty's Stationery Office. Although the boards of public corporations are normally appointed through the Civil Service, they usually manage their affairs without strict supervision by politicians.

Quangos

The statistics in Tables 1.2 and 1.3 understate UK expenditure on public services. Many public services

Table 1.3 Central government spending in the UK, 1995–96

Examples	£M
Department of Social Security	72,962
National Health Service	33,134
Local government	30,311
National defence	21,221
Education	14,900
Scotland	14,472
Wales	7,823
Housing	6,685
Home Office	6,574
Transportation	4,757
Trade and Industry	3,727
Agriculture, Fisheries	2,904
European Community	2,900

Source: HM UK Treasury (1996)

are provided by Quasi-Autonomous Non-Governmental Organizations (QUANGOS). Many quangos are private companies which carry out functions previously carried out by government departments. In 1996 there were 325 executive bodies, 814 advisory bodies, 71 tribunals and 135 boards of visitors.[6] Quangos spend public money but are not directly accountable to the public for the way in which they spend it.

Challenging the Postwar Consensus

In 1992 the UK National Audit Office (NAO) called for a revolution in the way that publicly owned public service organizations were run and in the way that public servants acted.[7] The so-called 'New Right' had been developing a rationale for this revolution since the early 1970s. The ideas were not new, even then, but their time had come. In the UK, these ideas were seized upon by Mrs Thatcher. She challenged the postwar consensus that government should fund services to fight 'the evils of want, squalor, disease, ignorance and idleness' (Beveridge Report 1942). Policies based on the notion that the 'state will provide' were pursued with considerable success until the international oil crisis in 1973. In western countries, the postwar period had been characterized by sustained economic growth, full employment and a burgeoning growth in public services funded by public expenditure. Economic policies were based on the ideas of Maynard Keynes.[8] By and large, Keynesian economic policies worked successfully, despite the cost of the Vietnam War and the cost of Lyndon Johnson's 'Great Society' reforms in the United States.

The Oil Crisis and Inflation

The blow that signalled a dramatic slowdown in the rate of growth of publicly financed public services, fell on 16 October 1973. Representatives of five Arab countries met with a representative of Iran and raised the price of oil to $5.12 a barrel. In December 1973 they raised it again, this time to $11.65 – a fourfold increase in three months! The resultant inflation caused unemployment in western countries to rise to levels unseen for 40 years. In 1979 the overthrow of the Shah of Persia (now Iran) precipitated another oil price shock. Inflation in the US hit 10 per cent. The US sold its gold reserves and President Carter was forced to seek support from the International Monetary Fund (IMF). Wage and price controls failed to contain inflation. Paul Volker was appointed chairman of the US Federal Reserve with a brief to control inflation. Within weeks, 30 years of Keynesian full employment was out and the monetarist policies of Milton Friedman were in. Monetarists attribute inflation to an excess of money. If there is too much money in the economy, there will be too much spending. Governments should therefore concentrate on controlling the money supply. Otherwise government should leave the economy alone, except to remove things that might hinder the efficient running of the market, such as restrictive practices by trades unions or professional bodies. Increased public service expenditure was out. Increased exposure to the market was in.

Faced with inflation caused by the high price of oil, western governments reassessed their taken-for-granted assumption that expenditure on public services could grow in line with growing needs. When Margaret Thatcher was elected in 1979, she inherited a level of public expenditure that was not sustainable. Even her left-wing predecessor, James Callaghan, had been forced to cut public expenditure, as a condition for receiving a loan from the International Monetary Fund (IMF).[9]

Rolling back the Welfare State

James Callaghan had been forced to take this course of action for economic reasons. To this economic imperative, Mrs Thatcher added an ideological commitment to 'roll back the welfare state'. In this she was influenced by Friedrich Hayek who saw the European concept of the socialist state as a 'Road to Serfdom'. After the Second World War, western governments had been anxious to avoid a return to the high levels of poverty and unemployment experienced in the 1930s.[10] They had intervened by rationalizing many public services and introducing subsidies and price controls in others. Friedrich Hayek, Milton Friedman and others saw this type of intervention as a threat to individual freedom. In 1947 they met in Switzerland and founded the Mont Pelerin Society[11] which sought to promote free-market economics and the rights of individuals. They warned against the dangers of socialism. Underlying Mrs Thatcher's campaign to 'roll back the welfare state' was her own belief that state intervention created a 'dependency culture'. To this she added a personal hostility to trades unions which she saw as dominating public service organizations. She thought that publicly owned organizations were riddled with restrictive practices.

If monetarist and market-led policies were an appropriate response to the upward movement in the price of oil in the 1970s, what should have been the response when oil prices moved back down to the level they were at before the oil price crisis? Figure 1.1 shows that during the 1990s oil prices had returned to their pre-crisis levels. Deflation – not inflation – threatened Japan and the 'Tiger' economies of Southeast Asia. So why did monetarist and market-led policies persist well beyond the

point where their economic necessity seemed to have passed? The new millennium held the prospect of a return to Keynesian policies of full employment and of increases in public expenditure sufficient to fund an expansion in public services.

Monetarists, like Friedman, argued that publicly owned public service organizations should be exposed to market forces, because competition would cause public resources to be allocated more efficiently than if resources continued to be allocated by professional bureaucracies. Flynn suggested that there had been a hidden agenda:

> The motive for establishing markets, whatever the rhetoric, was not to improve the allocation of resources or efficiency. One motive was to distance politicians from decisions which would prove unpopular.[12]

Throughout the world, between 1980 and 2000, the 'invisible hand of the market' was blamed for politically unpopular decisions such as the closure of libraries, schools or hospitals. 'Inefficient managers' became the scapegoats, instead of politicians. Public service managers were put under increasing pressure to manage their organizations more efficiently. Another argument used in favour of a market

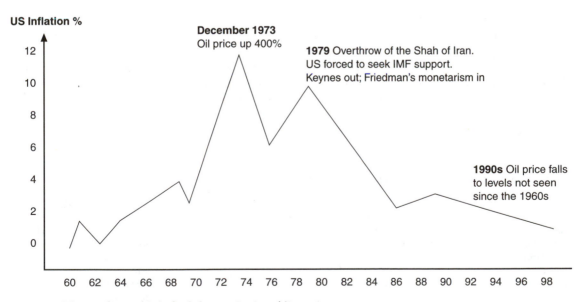

Figure 1.1 The case for a publicly funded expansion in public services

approach was that it would make professionally dominated and unresponsive public services more responsive. This brought public service managers into active conflict with public service professionals.

From Professionalism to Managerialism

Up until the early 1980s, many public services were dominated by professional workers who knew 'what was best' for service users. According to Exworthy and Halford, writing in 1999:

> Managers were traditionally seen as conformist, self-interested and career motivated; whereas professionals were seen as creative, altruistic and driven by an ethical commitment, or at least, by commitment to their profession as a way of securing status and privilege.[13]

Managers were seen as entrepreneurial and driven by the needs of the market, while professionals were supposed to be more concerned with their technical expertise and with the needs of service users. Even when professionals such as doctors, teachers and socials workers took up managerial roles, they often held on to the core values of their profession (see Chapter 15). Their managerial power base enabled them to resist change and led to calls for the introduction of generic managers.[14] Farnham and Horton[15] argued that the introduction of a new managerialism – often called New Public Management – would be a way of challenging the power of professionals in public services. In the UK, following the Griffiths Report in 1983, general managers were introduced into the NHS partly to challenge the vested interests of its professional groups.[16] Table 1.4 polarizes the conflicts between managers and profes-

sionals. In reality the relationship between managers and professionals is more complex than this.

A Marxist Perspective

So far, we have analysed the forces affecting public service organizations from a liberal perspective. A Marxist might see things differently. A Marxist analysis might begin from the premise that one purpose of public services is to support the owners of wealth by defending their property and by providing them with a healthy, educated, mobile and socialized workforce. Public services must deal with the damage caused by the owners of wealth to members of their workforce. A Marxist might argue that much of the damage caused to members of the workforce is the direct consequence of the inequality, discrimination and poverty that often characterize the lives of those who work for those who own the wealth. Capitalist economies experience economic cycles of boom and bust. In boom periods public services grow, because the increased earning of workers can be taxed to fund an expansion in the public services which they need. When the economy goes into a cycle of decline – paradoxically when the need for public services may be greater – there is less taxation available to pay for them and public services are often cut! During economic downturns, professionals are likely to want to expand public services to meet the increased needs of the public. If cuts are needed, the professionals have to be replaced by managers. Managers then use other criteria, such as economy and efficiency, in order to make the cuts in services. Managers legitimize these cuts by citing market

Table 1.4 Polarized conflicts between managers and professionals

	Managerialism	Professionalism
Goals	Efficiency/profit	Effectiveness/technical ability
Regulation	Hierarchical	Collegial/self-regulation
Legitimacy	Hierarchical authority	Technical expertise
Control	Trust/compliance	Trust/dependency
Allegiance	The Bureaucracy	Their Profession
Clients	Corporate	Individual

forces, while professionals continue to cite public need.

If we accepted this analysis, we would expect the relationship between managers and professionals to be dominated by conflict. But this is only one way of understanding the relationship between professionals and managers in public services. It is possible to develop new patterns of collaboration and compromise between professionals and managers. There is an increasing recognition that career development for professionals is dependent not only on updating professional expertise but also on developing managerial competence and qualifications. In 1999 Exworthy and Halford found evidence that professionals in healthcare, education and social services were becoming more comfortable in managerial roles.[17] Perhaps, as Clarke and Stewart suggest, we need a better balance between professionals and managers in public services: 'Managers in education, social work or environmental health need to be sensitive to the particular concerns of those disciplines, but should not allow them to get in the way of the broader view.'[18]

'Rolling Back the Welfare State' and other Myths

Despite the rhetoric of 'rolling back the welfare state' and numerous interventions to alter the structure of public service organizations and their management arrangements, expenditure on the welfare state in the UK was *not* reduced during the Thatcher years (see Table 1.5). Flynn discovered that the majority of people valued public services and objected to cuts in public expenditure that affected them. In a democracy, this undermines political will for reform:

> The reason for the failure to greatly reduce the role of the state in the welfare field is the same as the reason for its establishment: most people benefit from health, education and social security provisions and only a small minority can afford or wish to make their own arrangements.[19]

It could be argued that without Thatcher's political will to reduce 'dependency', expenditure might have risen even more than it did. The number of elderly people in the population increased by 30 per cent during this period and the elderly have above-average needs for public services. Table 1.5 compares public spending as a percentage of GDP for the UK in 1981–82 and 1995–96. The figures indicate little reduction despite the rhetoric. If the figures for defence and trade are excluded, the proportion of national budget spent on so-called 'welfare dependency' items actually increased slightly during the Thatcher years!

The Enabling State

From Table 1.5 it can be seen that in the 'dependency' areas of health and social services, public expenditure – as a proportion of UK GDP – actually grew by 8 per cent. This was despite putting local government and health and social service managers under great pressure to ensure that public expenditure was not squandered on the undeserving poor. Voluntary and private sector organizations were encouraged to share the burden of addressing social needs. Government pump primed new developments, by offering to match funding raised from

Table 1.5 Reducing dependency – the myth

Sector	1981–82 % GDP	1995–96 % GDP
Public Health and Social Services	6.2	6.9
Other Environmental Services	1.5	1.4
Health and Social Security	17.7	18.9
Agriculture and Fisheries	0.6	0.6
Law and Order	1.8	2.2
Overseas Aid	0.6	0.5
Education	5.4	5.1
Defence	5.0	3.0
Trade	2.5	1.3
Transport	1.9	1.3
Housing	1.6	0.7
Heritage	0.5	0.4
Miscellaneous	1.3	1.3

Source: Public Expenditure Analysis – 7, Cm 3201, HM Treasury (March 1996)

private sources. The idea of an 'enabling state' was subject to different interpretations: a partnership of private, public and voluntary sectors to deliver public services; a blight on the functions and responsibilities of local government; a development of community governance or the empowering of individuals to be less passive consumers of services.[20] Clarke and Stewart[21] saw the concept of the enabling state as a means of improving public services, strengthening local democracy and encouraging individuals to become more active citizens. Some of the enabling methods suggested by Clarke and Stewart included:

- Contracting out work to other organizations
- Giving grants to agencies to provide services
- Entering into partnerships with other agencies
- Contracting work to the voluntary sector
- Contracting work to the private sector

PRIVATIZATION AND CHANGING PATTERNS OF OWNERSHIP

The main area where a truly 'new right' agenda was achieved was in the transfer of public service organizations into private ownership. Throughout the world, public services as various as air transport, ferries, electricity, water, ship building, telecommunications and bus services were increasingly delivered by privately owned public service organizations. The privatizations were linked to the espoused virtues of a free market. Bishop and Kaye argued that it was really a strategy to curb the power of trades unions.[22] Various other reasons were given: reducing the public sector borrowing requirement, creating wider share ownership, increasing efficiency and improving value for money in public services. However, the temptation to use the proceeds of privatization to reduce taxation prior to elections was not always resisted. During the 1990s the proceeds of privatization in the UK were running at £7 billion per annum.

The urge to privatize public services encompassed the developing world as well as the industrialized world. The driving force was the belief that privati-

zation and the application of private sector management practices would raise performance. These beliefs proved ill founded. Cook and Kirkpatrick catalogued the damaging effects of privatization in Pakistan and in Thailand.[23]

From State Monopoly to Private Monopoly

Often state monopolies became private monopolies. 'Customers' for water services, for example, cannot move easily from one water company to another. Some governments tried to set up regulatory bodies to monitor the new private owners of the old public services. Contractual agreements were made, specifying the standards of public service expected. This reflected a rise in consumerist expectations on the part of people using public services. It also provoked the rise in expectations. Isaac-Henry suggested that people using public services had started to behave more like customers.[24] They had become more sophisticated, more discriminating, more assertive and less subservient to public officials. They expected more services and they expected those services to be of better quality (see Chapter 5). A survey commissioned in 1993 by the Public Management Foundation found that the majority of people thought that privatized public service organizations were failing to meet their expectations: 'The message from the public is clear, the work that has gone into quality improvement has been important, but it needs to be improved and opened up to much broader local consultation.'[25]

Even though many of the changes were originally made in the name of political rhetoric, or in the name of free market values, the same underlying forces continue to drive a need to implement changes in public services and in the way that they are managed (Box 1.1).

We talked to Hilton Dawson, UK Member of Parliament and formerly social service manager (Box 1.2). As a social worker and as a manager of a social services department, Hilton Dawson talks about what it was like to be on the receiving end of a 'new managerialism' – to be forced to work within

---

Box 1.1

FORCES FOR CHANGE – A SUMMARY

- Cuts in public expenditure in some areas and increases in others
- An emphasis on the public as customer and on customer choice
- The replacement of public service professionals by managers
- A blurring between private and public

- Demographic changes such as ageing
- The introduction of performance management
- Advances in information technology
- A more discerning public
- Increased self-reliance
- Internal markets
- Privatization

---

structures that were not compatible with his 'professionalism'. He hopes that politicians will encourage the involvement of young people and 'active citizens' in the management of public services. He hopes for a 'learning society' and a 'third way' that is not polarized by the politics of the left or the right, or by arguments about public or private ownership, or by the conflicting values of managers and professionals. In the UK, these ideas found support from the Audit Commission and from the National Audit Office (see Chapter 12). In 1998 Keen and Scase[26] concluded that the election of a Labour government had not heralded a return to the routinized bureaucracy of the past. The third way rejected both Mr Callaghan's corporate ethos and Mrs Thatcher's neo-liberalism.[27] Public service managers needed to develop their ability to understand and implement changes. They could not stall hoping that a change of government would make change unnecessary. Were things any different elsewhere in the world?

NEW MANAGERIALISM: AN INTERNATIONAL PERSPECTIVE

Australia and New Zealand

In 1996 Ferlie *et al.*[28] reported on the increasing role of managers in public services throughout the world. The managers' roles varied, depending on local history, culture and political leadership. The style of management did not appear to be related in any consistent way to any one political ideology. We cautioned earlier against assuming that the 'new' management of public services would go away when the political climate changed. The evidence does not support that assumption. The 'new' management of public services reflects changes that go beyond politics. In both New Zealand and Australia the introduction of a managerial approach to running public services was implemented by left-wing governments. Barton[29] analysed the New Zealand Labour Party's quest for improved efficiency and accountability. This involved separating commercial and non-commercial activities, a move from centralized to locally based services and, in some cases, the introduction of performance-related pay (PRP). Zifcack[30] compared the 'Next Steps' changes in the Civil Service in Whitehall UK with changes that were implemented in Australia under the Financial Management Improvement Initiative. He concluded that Mr Hawke in Australia and Mrs Thatcher in the UK had pursued similar aims. Hawke's approach was judged to be more collaborative and consensual. Zifcack thought that this was the reason why the reforms of the Civil Service in Australia were more considered, better crafted and more transparent than was the case in the UK.

Box 1.2

EXTRACT FROM A CONVERSATION WITH HILTON DAWSON MP: 'A THIRD WAY FOR PUBLIC SERVICES?'

Tony: How have things changed for public services?

Hilton: I began as a social services manager during the 'reforms' in the early 1980s. I had over 300 staff involved in children's services. My organization was very benign. I was given a lot of space to develop ideas and take new initiatives. There was a lot of goodwill and commitment which helped to overcome some poor practice. By and large, people gave their all. They worked in their own time. They had a sense of vocation. They wanted to do a good job. Then came devolved budgets and then spending cuts. Management thinking was driven by an overriding concern for economy and efficiency. Nobody bothered about effectiveness as long as we kept within budget.

Tony: You said that you studied Management?

Hilton: Yes. I remember the ideas about flatter organizations, less hierarchy and less bureaucracy. They appealed to me. They were exciting ideas. But in public services things became even more centralized and even more coercive. We wanted to make the service better as well as more efficient but we were not allowed to. The only way to make changes was to go through lots of committees.

Tony: What was the quality of the service like?

Hilton: Very professional. Good quality social work continued despite 'new' management. The changes did not improve the quality of the services to children. They were only about budgets.

Tony: What about privatized public service organizations?

Hilton: I see nothing wrong in using private sector management techniques. There are many privately owned companies whose business is providing public services. I don't have a problem with that as long as the values of the private companies are right. They must be concerned about quality and about decent pay and working conditions for their staff. Flexibility must be achieved without exploiting employees.

Tony: What is the relationship between politics and public services?

Hilton: Politicians can help to change the culture of a public service. Our 1997 White Paper on Health Services was well received because it reflected good practice rather than vague managerial thinking about reducing costs. Our White Paper emphasized partnerships and co-operation, rather than competition. Our aim was to make services more responsive. We wanted to emphasize long-term relationships. In our 1998 White Paper on the Modernization of Local Government, we stressed that decision-making should involve the public. That public service organizations must be open to public scrutiny. We need more direct democratic control. More than just voting politicians in or out of office every 5 years! Public service managers will have to encourage interaction between service users and service providers. They must help people to learn together.

Tony: What do you mean by more interaction?

Hilton: For example, I have a special interest in young people. I often feel inspired listening to young people talking about public services. Managers need to encourage people from all sections of the community to get involved with social services, education and the police for example. The Government's Best Value initiative requires that public service organizations get the public's views on how well they are performing. Once you get a conversation going, people have lots of good ideas about how public services should be managed.

Tony: Thank you Hilton.

The United States

In the early 1990s, Pollitt[31] was able to demonstrate that public service reforms in the USA predated the Republican presidency of Reagan. Some went back to the Democratic presidency of Carter in 1978. Many of President Clinton's reforms were based on the work of Osborne and Gaebler.[32] They called for the 'reinvention of government' and emphasized the role of the state as an enabler rather than a provider of public services. Clinton was a Democrat not a Republican, and yet he argued for more entrepreneurial, decentralized and flexible public services with a strong customer orientation. He wanted this to be combined with traditional public service values, such as probity and accountability (see Chapter 11). The following extract could easily be mistaken for a Republican speech. It is taken from the work of Osborne and Gaebler – policy advisors to President Clinton:

> Most entrepreneurial governments promote *competition* between service providers. They *empower* citizens by pushing control out of the bureaucracy, into the community. They measure the performance of their agencies by focusing not on inputs but on *outcomes*. They are driven by their goals – their *missions* – not by their rules and regulations. They redefine their clients as *customers* and offer them choices. . . . They decentralize authority, embracing participatory government. They prefer *market* mechanisms to bureaucratic mechanisms. And they focus not simply on providing public services, but on *catalysing* all sectors – public, private and voluntary – into action to solve their community problems. [Italics added].[33]

This call, for more entrepreneurial government, reflected disillusion with traditional public administration and a call for new approaches to public service management in the USA. The call echoed around Europe.

The Netherlands, Sweden, France, Germany, Austria and Switzerland

In 1996 Flynn and Strehl[34] carried out a comparative study of how public services were managed in the UK, The Netherlands, Sweden, France, Germany, Austria and Switzerland. While they noted that many features of 'new' public management could be identified (improved accountability, more autonomous decentralized services, performance measures and targets, cost reduction and competition), they cautioned against assuming that the management practice was homogeneous. Differences in the way the state was perceived to operate, and differences in politics and culture, generated a diversity of approaches to managing public services. Management practice was very dependent on local context. For example, Germany, Austria and Switzerland operated public services through classic centralized bureaucracies, which carried out functions defined by law. In Switzerland, the Federal government is constitutionally forbidden to take on functions that can be performed regionally.

Developing Countries

Up until the late 1980s the public services of most developing countries were characterized by traditional models of public administration. In many cases this was a colonial inheritance. After independence, in countries like India, Kenya and Zimbabwe, the inheritance was perpetuated because many lower-level civil servants became senior officers. In China bureaucratic styles of public administration go back 2,000 years to the teachings of Confucius. According to Hughes,

> Features which worked in the West, notably political neutrality and incorruptibility, were not followed in the Third World. The bureaucracy, while maintaining the appearance and institutions of traditional bureaucracy, served particular elite or ethnic, or religious interests. Above all it served itself![35] [Exclamation mark added]

Following the end of the Cold War in the mid-1980s, most countries in the developing world rejected socialism and started to adopt approaches to the management of public services that were similar to the new public management in the west. Market economies were introduced and participation in the world trade system was encouraged. The World Bank and the International Monetary Fund favoured the privatization of public assets and reductions in public expenditure. In Malaysia, for example, Total

---

Box 1.3

AN INTERNATIONAL COMPARISON – EMERGING THEMES[36]

Decentralization: The degree of decentralization varied. Where governments were concerned to maintain uniformity and equality of access to services, as in the education services in France and Austria, for example, strong central control was maintained and local autonomy was limited.

Accountability: Flynn and Strehl reported widespread concern and confusion as to who is accountable to whom, for what and when. In The Netherlands, for example, it was not clear who would be responsible for the deterioration of services at a municipal level, if nationally devolved funds proved insufficient.

Personnel management: In all the countries examined there was evidence of increased investment in development and training. An increasing customer service orientation was identified. Not all training was about business management and customer orientation; for example, training to aid the development of active citizenship was common (see Chapter 13).

Financial management: A focus on budgeting was common. In particular there was a move away from traditional incremental budgeting. Changes in financial management in all countries emphasized the importance of business planning and the measurement of performance (see Chapters 9 and 11).

Competition to collaboration: As foreshadowed in our conversation with Hilton Dawson MP in 1998, Chris Ham[37] found evidence that public services were becoming disenchanted with market forces in many countries. In New Zealand, The Netherlands and Sweden, policy-makers were exploring non-competitive ways of improving organizational performance. From country to country, different reasons are given. In the UK, it has been attributed to a change of government. Elsewhere it appears to be due to the failure of markets to deliver promised improvements. In New Zealand and Sweden there were objections to the high levels of costs involved in drawing up and administering contracts.

Quality Management and Client Charters were introduced (see Chapter 5).

While not advocating a return to colonial styles of public administration, Hughes shared our concern about the wisdom of moving western models of management into public services in the developing world.

Some changes in the processes of management were associated with changes in the design of organization structures. In the next section we examine how organizational structures have changed in public services.

THE DESIGN OF ORGANIZATIONAL STRUCTURES

Classical Approaches

In classical approaches, universal principles were assumed to exist and to inform the design of organizations. The classical approaches emerged from the works of Taylor, Fayol, Urwick and Mooney.[38] They were concerned with the running of large-scale, predominantly industrial organizations. Classical approaches have an overarching concern with improving efficiency. They place a strong emphasis on the planning of work. They assume that behaviour in organizations is rational.

W. F. Taylor,[39] a Quaker, was regarded as a progressive reformer in his time. He is sometimes referred to as the father of scientific management. He considered that management was a science, resting on clearly defined laws, rules and principles. According to Taylor, all activity was subject to scientific laws and therefore all activity could be scientifically managed. He proposed that every job be broken down into its routine parts and that each task be completed in the most efficient way possible (Box 1.4).

Fayol[40] developed these ideas further (Box 1.5).

The classical approach to organizational design has provoked adverse reactions from employees and trades unions. Following the introduction of some of Taylor's methods at the Watertown Arsenal in the United States, the workforce went on strike. In 1912 the House of Representatives investigated the incident. As a result, Taylor's time studies were banned from defence establishments in the USA. The report acknowledged the benefits of Taylor's ideas but it was critical of the way production managers used them. Taylor believed that workers were entitled to clear instructions and to be told in advance about disciplinary codes and procedures for appealing against them. Workers were entitled to expect management to specify how work was to be carried out. Rose,[41] however, thought that the barbarities to which Taylor's ideas had led invited denunciation. Drucker[42] was kinder to Taylor and suggested that Taylor's main concerns were not with efficiency, but with improving conditions and remuneration for workers and with the elimination of ineffectual management. It is hard to argue with many of Taylor's ideas. Many workers are motivated by being rewarded financially and do respond well to managers who are clear about tasks and procedures. However, Taylor's ideas have been abused. Power does corrupt. What starts as legitimate control often becomes coercive and even bullying as a style of management. Some of the changes that have occurred in public services – particularly the moves from professionalism to managerialism – have been criticized on the grounds that they represent an inappropriate application of Taylor's ideas.

Neo-Taylorism in Public Services

In many public services throughout the world, the term 'administration' has been replaced by the term

---

Box 1.4

PRINCIPLES OF SCIENTIFIC MANAGEMENT

- The specification of work to be done
- The division of the specified work into routine tasks
- The motivation of the workers by reward and incentive
- The selection and training of workers to carry out the routine tasks
- The allocation of clear responsibilities for the achievement of the routine tasks

---

Box 1.5

FAYOL'S APPROACH

- Division of labour
- Punitive discipline
- Specialization of tasks
- Centralization of power
- Subordination of individual needs
- A fair day's pay for a fair day's work
- Unity of command – one worker, one boss
- Earning money as the main motivation
- Definitions of roles and responsibilities
- Equal treatment of workers
- Encouragement of initiative
- Stability of tenure
- 'Esprit de corps'

'management'. According to Isaac-Henry,[43] 'new managerialism' in public services consisted of three components: a businesslike approach, more internal accountability and performance management. The first component, a 'businesslike' approach, has sometimes come to mean a 'tough minded' approach characterized by the ability to implement unpopular changes and reduce costs. The second component – internal accountability – is designed to make public service employees more answerable to their managers within their organizations.[44] The third component of new managerialism in public services is performance management. This involves setting objectives with well-defined performance indicators in relation to the three E's of economy, efficiency and effectiveness. In Chapter 12 we argue for the addition of a fourth E for ethics, to embrace a concern for equity, empathy and ecology. Under performance management, performance is appraised and in some cases related to pay.

Pollitt,[45] in a survey of new managerialism in the UK and America, noted a 'striking uniformity' in the way new management manifested itself, whether in health services, education services or civil services. In all cases he found tight cash limits, staff cuts, staff appraisal and devolved budgets. He found a type of management training which emphasized short-term

goals. He discovered much rhetoric about the need to be 'more responsive to customers'. Because of its similarities to Taylor's ideas on scientific management, Pollitt[46] described 'new managerialism' as 'Neo-Taylorism'. Neo-Taylorism and new managerialism are not a perfect fit. For example, the emphasis on training belongs more to a human relations approach (see Chapter 8).

Bureaucracy

Traditionally, public services have been managed through bureaucratic structures. It is unfortunate that the term 'bureaucracy' is often used in a derogatory manner. Bureaucracy is a form of organization that is well suited to many activities, especially activities such as education and criminal justice, which rely on the keeping of accurate records. The term 'bureaucracy' has its origins in the work of the German sociologist Max Weber.[47] He considered bureaucracies to be the most rational and potentially the most efficient means of public administration. The term literally means 'rule by office or by official'.

In 1980 Haynes[48] reported that local governments were almost universally organized as bureaucracies, with a vertical hierarchy for communication and control. They were characterized by an emphasis on

---

Box 1.6

CHARACTERISTICS OF BUREAUCRACIES

- **Hierarchical**. Authority is based on a chain of command. Each lower position is supervised by and accountable to a higher position.
- **Job specialization**. Jobs are broken down into routine and well-defined tasks. Authority and responsibility are clearly defined.
- **Formal rules**. To ensure uniformity, operations are carried out according to transparent rules which are applied and monitored consistently.

- **Career structure**. Managers are professional officials and work for fixed salaries. Promotion is based on seniority and merit.
- **Formal selection**. Employees are selected on the basis of qualifications, training, education or formal examination.
- **Impersonality**. Rules and controls apply so that everyone is treated with parity.
- **Controlled access**. Information is stored in files and all transactions are recorded.

staff rights, duties and qualifications, with clear career development paths and standardized procedures. Such systems have much to commend them. Bureaucracies, however, have come under attack from a number of quarters.

Bureaucracies under Attack

In 1940 Merton[49] demonstrated how bureaucratic rules can become ends in themselves, resulting in the loss of their original meaning and purpose. The rigid application of rules often fails to address the requirements of individual clients in specific situations. Weber himself was well aware of the limitations of bureaucracy and its potential to interfere with democratic processes.

Niskanen[50] argued that bureaucrats have a personal interest in the growth of budgets and resources, because rewards like salary and status are related to the scale of their responsibilities. He advocated more competitive forms of bureaucracy in which different offices and departments competed with one another to provide the most efficient services. Under attack from both academics and politicians – not to mention a fairly hostile public – the period 1980–2000 saw the reform of bureaucracy high on the agendas of most senior managers in public service organizations.

Beyond Bureaucracy – The Contingency Approach

Burns and Stalker[51] asserted that in order to understand how organizations worked, it was necessary to take into account the contexts in which they operate. They concluded that there were two main types of organization, each suited to different contexts. The two main types of organization were mechanistic and organic (see Boxes 1.7 and 1.8).

Burns and Stalker suggested that bureaucracies were mechanistic and that they would perform best in relatively stable environments.

Organic organizations adapt themselves more readily and so perform better than mechanistic organizations in uncertain and turbulent environments. Bennis argued that most organizations did not have a choice about what organizational structures to adopt, because nearly all faced turbulent, unstable environments. He concluded that every organization will have to become an

> adaptive, rapidly changing, temporary system … the organization will be arranged on an organic rather than a mechanical model, it will evolve in response to a problem rather than a programmed role expectation … this is the organizational form that will gradually replace bureaucracy as we know it.[52]

Bureaucracy was to be replaced by 'adhocracy', with an emphasis on responsiveness and flexibility.

Box 1.7

CHARACTERISTICS OF MECHANISTIC ORGANIZATIONS

- Upward flow of information and downward flow of decision
- Hierarchical systems of control and communication
- Functional specialisms and defined jobs
- Loyalty and obedience

Box 1.8

CHARACTERISTICS OF ORGANIC ORGANIZATIONS

- Flexible job descriptions
- Lateral as well as vertical communications
- Less formal authority, dependent on expertise rather than position
- An emphasis on participation not control; on information not instruction

---

Box 1.9

PERIODS IN THE HISTORY OF HUMAN ORGANIZATIONS

- **First-wave pre-industrial organizations** developed in order to meet society's need to sow and harvest food.
- **Second-wave industrial organizations** evolved to address the needs of a largely urban, industrialized society. They were characterized by standardization and central-

ization. Managers divided work into simple functions which they controlled through punitive authority. Bureaucracies are second-wave organizations.

- **Third-wave decentralized organizations** were characterized by reduced hierarchy and increased flexibility.

Toffler[53] suggested that post-industrial society was moving towards what he called 'third-wave' organizations. According to Toffler, there have been three great 'waves' in the history of human organizations (see Box 1.9).

Hecksher argued that,[54] the fundamental problem with second-wave organizations was that people were only responsible for doing their own jobs. Second-wave hierarchical organizations were based on the assumption that the top layer of the hierarchy could think rationally and decide what was best for the rest of the organization. However, the thinking power and the learning power of the rest of the organization also need to be developed (see Chapters 13 and 14). Rational bureaucracy drives many informal transactions underground. Throughout this book we seek ways to harness the potential energy of these informal transactions.

Old Ways in New Waves

There are problems when managers rehearse the rhetoric of changing to third-wave organizational structures, while clinging to second-wave ways of managing. Schroder[55] noted three negative consequences of the clash between third-wave organization structures and second-wave management styles. We have characterized these three negative consequences as: 'digging the same hole deeper', 'battening down the hatches' and 'rebadging'.

Digging the same hole deeper

Schroder observed that when forces for change were perceived as a threat, this resulted in increased commitment to the familiar features of second-wave bureaucratic organizations. Managers dug their second-wave holes deeper. They exercised even more authority and more control and became even more restrictive, in order to protect their own sphere of operation. According to Schroder, this ego-protecting behaviour centralized the manager's power base but isolated their departments.[56] Such behaviour often kept their own departments looking good, while damaging other interdependent departments.

Battening down the hatches

Schroder observed that other managers scaled down their departments – battening down the hatches in the face of economic storms. They curried favour by 'downsizing', 'flattening', 'right sizing', 'delayering' or other flavour-of-the-month ideas. Although these measures could have been the first steps towards creating a third-wave organization, they were not followed through. The principles on which third-wave organizations were based were ignored. There was no follow-through to reduce centralization, or to build cross-functional teams, or to allocate responsibility downwards. According to Schroder, one of the reasons why attempts to create scaled-down, third-wave structures did not work in public services was because of a shortage of managers with the competencies to work effectively within them:

> [F]lattening, in the absence of competent managers and without the development of people to take on more responsibility, will lead to a negative climate, failure to change the structures and lower organisational effectiveness.[57]

Rebadging

Sometimes, instead of re-engineering a car, a vehicle manufacturer will make cosmetic alterations to the appearance, add a few new features and then rebadge the car as a new model. Under its rebadged body shell it is still the same old car. Sometimes second-wave managers stick third-wave badges on to their organizations – quality circles, team briefings, customer focus groups. But underneath the new third-wave badges the same old second-wave managers remain unchanged – hierarchical, controlling and punitive. Schroder concluded that:

> in such organizations the members of the organizations quickly feel the gap between what they are asked to do and what they are able to do in practice, given the culture of the organization. This will produce a negative, distrusting climate and the abandonment of innovation.[58]

How then can people responsible for changing public service organizations get beyond digging the same hole deeper, battening down the hatches and rebadging?

CHANGING ORGANIZATIONAL STRUCTURES

The Span of Control

There is evidence that the structures of public services organizations are changing in response to the forces we discussed earlier.[59] Clear organizational structures can help to determine how the work of an organization is divided and co-ordinated. Clear organizational structures make it easier to answer questions such as 'what am I supposed to do?' and 'to whom am I accountable?' Traditional public service

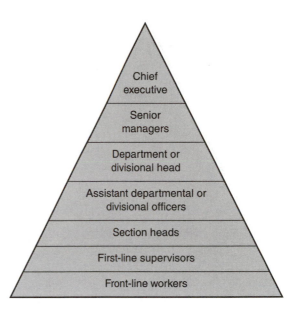

Figure 1.2 A pyramid structure of a traditional public service organization

organizations have a pyramid structure with clear chains of command (Figure 1.2).

A key characteristic of an organizational structure is the span of control. Span of control refers to how many subordinates on average are being managed by each manager. The span is generally smaller at the top of the organization. At the bottom of the hierarchy, where tasks are carried out by employees who have no subordinates, a larger span of control is possible. The average span of control will determine how many layers there are in the structure. If the average span is small, the structure will be tall. Figure 1.2 illustrates the hierarchical structure of a traditional public service organization. An average span of control of four would result in five layers of management to run an organization employing 4,000 people (Figure 1.3), whereas an average span of control of ten would need only three layers of management to run an organization more than twice that size (Figure 1.4). It is easy to see why restructuring is favoured by senior managers who need to save money. By merging two traditional organizations, each employing around 5,000 people, 1,600

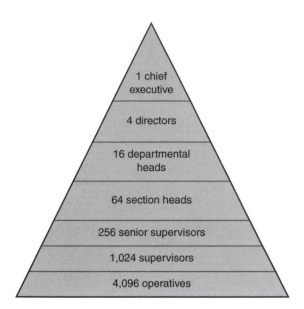

Figure 1.3 A tall organizational structure with a span of control of four

Figure 1.4 A flat organizational structure with a span of control of ten

less middle managers might be needed! As a bonus, the speed of communications from the top to the bottom of the organization should be improved, because there are two less layers of management. Speed of response and customer service quality should also be better. Assuming the average manager costs twice as much as the average front-line worker, in the traditional pyramid structure in Figure 1.2 nearly half the salary bill was spent on managers and only half on people working with the clients. In the hypothetical merged structure, the proportion spent on clients increased by 60 per cent, thereby improving the quality of service and increasing numbers of people benefiting from it.

Improved information technology (see Chapter 12) makes mergers and 'delayering' feasible, but, as we shall see later, it is not always that simple.

Even in the new merged and delayered structure, the salary bill for the 1,000 first-line managers seems a likely target in any attempt to reduce spending on management and move it to front-line services. This, amongst other things, fuels interest in 'team working' and in 'self-managed' teams. Both are

fraught with difficulties (see Chapter 6). Table 1.6 describes some of the factors that must be considered when designing an organizational structure. In Chapter 3 we will consider how redesigning an organizational structure can contribute to the management of change.

We have looked at different forms of organizational structure that might have been appropriate to the changing contexts of public services in the period 1980–2000. What evidence is there that any of these new organizational forms were ever adopted? Certainly, there was much talk of replacing bureaucratic and mechanistic second-wave organizations with more organic third-wave forms of organization. The rhetoric of 'empowered teams' and flexible, responsive, organic organizations was widely rehearsed (see Chapter 6). In 1982 Peters and Water-mann[60] gave the impression that self-empowered teams and flexible structures were about to sweep the board. Twelve years later, in 1994, Hecksher reported that the use of self-empowered teams in public companies was 'only in its infancy ... the truth is that although many companies have joined in the anti-bureaucratic rhetoric, few have actually moved more than a step or two from traditional structures'.[61]

Narrowing the Gap between Rhetoric and Reality

In 1993 Buchanan and Boddy,[62] while acknowledging that their evidence was incomplete, claimed to

Table 1.6 Designing a public service organization – some considerations

Function	Role
Control	Communicate the organization's objectives, take decisions and ensure that they are carried out. (Chapters 8, 11)
Technical	Design and maintain systems and procedures for obtaining market information, carrying out developments, maintaining quality, keeping accounts, ensuring legal compliance, keeping up-to-date. (Chapters 4, 5, 9, 11, 13)
Operational	Recruit, induct, train, develop, motivate and take care of the operational staff who perform the work directly related to the service. (Chapters 7, 8, 13, 14)
Management	Provide, organize, develop and motivate middle and first-line managers who co-ordinate and communicate objectives and decisions to the operational staff. (Chapters 7, 8)
Support	Train, develop and motivate those who support the operation. (Chapters 7, 13, 14)
Culture	Develop appropriate culture and values. (Chapters 3, 15)

have found a tendency towards third-wave structures in some public service organizations. They quoted research carried out by the Ashridge Management Centre and the British Institute of Management which supported their view. The Institute identified the emergence of 'responsive organizations' and 'networked organizations' and 'flexible organizations'. All of these forms of organizational structure correspond closely to third-wave organizations. Also in 1993, Morley[63] argued that the UK government's 'Next Steps' programme was moving the Civil Service from bureaucratic second-wave to progressive third-wave structures. He said that these third-wave Civil Service organizations were characterized by a focus on long-term strategic planning, rather than the day-to-day maintenance of operations. According to Morley, they were more decentralized, and unity was achieved through commitment to shared values (see also Chapters 3 and 15). People were seen as valuable assets. Creativity and innovation were highly valued and management style was reported to be supportive. According to the report *Making the Most of Next Steps*, this third-wave progressive form of Civil Service organization had achieved renewed enthusiasm and had increased commitment to improving value for money and quality of service.[64] The report acknowledged that there remained a gap to be bridged between those Civil Service departments that still

retained second-wave structures and those that had adopted a progressive third-wave model. According to Morley, the trend was still convincingly in the direction of the third-wave organization.

By 1998 Keen and Scase[65] had found further evidence of both the rhetoric and the reality of change in the structures of public service organizations. They found evidence of a move from hierarchical to decentralized, market-oriented organizations. However, despite the rhetoric of entrepreneurship and empowerment, many officers complained that they had not been given commensurate decision-making powers. Overall, the findings of Morley, Keen and Scase indicate that both the rhetoric and the reality were moving convincingly in the direction of the post-bureaucratic, third-wave forms of organization. Hecksher thought that these third-wave post-bureaucratic organizations were likely to perform better in the turbulent environments which he believed public service organizations would continue to face. We do not agree with Hecksher's analysis and we do not share his enthusiasm for the idea that all public service organizations should move towards post-bureaucratic structures. We maintain that for public organizations such as health, education, immigration and criminal justice services, for example, bureaucracy remains an appropriate form of organization.

Do New Owners and New Structures Require New Managers?

Do the forces for change which arose in the 1980s and 1990s and the new forms of ownership and the new forms of organization to which they gave rise, require a 'new' type of management? We think not. Managers will require the same core competencies that managers have always needed – competencies in managing activities, managing people, managing resources, managing information, managing change and managing personal development. These are the competencies which internationally recognized management qualifications have always aimed to develop. 'New' management is a cloudy concept. It changes with the prevailing winds, mainly political and economic. If you stare at a cloud for long enough you can see in it what you want to see. In an effort to make sense of 'new' management, Ferlie *et al.*[66] described four types of public service management: Efficiency Management, Post-Fordist Management, Excellence Management and Public Service Orientation Management.

Efficiency Management

Efficiency models of management assume that public service organizations should become more businesslike. This is the type of management that Hilton Dawson MP talked about when he described his experience of managing a children's service. This is the type of management which Pollitt[67] described as Neo-Taylorist. Managers of this type emphasize economy and efficiency at the expense of effectiveness and ethics (see Chapter 11). In the UK, the 1997 Labour government tried to temper this tendency by introducing the concept of Best Value (see Chapter 5).

Post-Fordist Management

Post-Fordist management appeared in both privately owned and publicly owned public service organizations. It was a reaction against the bureaucratic forms of organization commonly associated with the mass production of motor cars. Post-Fordist managers decentralize and create flexible, semi-autonomous units and sub-units and move away from 'command and control' management styles. Post-Fordist management is the type of management that would be best suited to what we earlier described as third-wave, post-bureaucratic organization structures.

Excellence Management

The excellence approach to management had a significant impact on the rhetoric in both publicly and privately owned organizations. 'Excellent' managers emphasized strong leadership, shared values, clear vision and cultural change. Peters and Watermann[68] studied successful American corporations and identified the ten commandments of managerial excellence which they believed had led to the success of 43 US corporations (see Box 1.10).

Many of these 'commandments' are highly plausible taken separately. They are also platitudinous, inconsistent and mutually contradictory. They have often been cited in support of a more 'businesslike' approach to managing public services.[69] The attributes of excellence might have been a correlation but they could not have been a cause of the success of the 45 organizations studied by Peters and Watermann. Within five years of the study, the performance of two-thirds of the companies had deteriorated. This highlights the danger of following 'management fads' about 'how' without understanding 'why'. In this book we try to explain 'why' as well as 'how' to manage public services.

Public Service Orientation: Learning Organizations for a Learning Society

Public Service Orientation (PSO) management is the application of private sector management techniques in accordance with the traditional values of public service. PSO managers are sceptical about market-based approaches to distributing resources (see Chapter 4). Concern about quality is paramount (see Chapter 5). Public discourse and public participation are important – particularly participation that

---

Box 1.10

THE TEN COMMANDMENTS OF MANAGERIAL EXCELLENCE

1 **Stick to the knitting**
   Excellent companies stick to what they know and do best.

2 **Stay close to the customer**
   Excellent companies respond to customer needs.

3 **Productivity through people**
   Excellent companies care about the feelings and views of their staff.

4 **Autonomy and entrepreneurship**
   Excellent companies encourage initiative and risk-taking. They empower people.

5 **Value driven**
   Excellent companies have a strong culture, epitomized by values that reflect a compelling vision, vigorously espoused and consistently practised.

6 **Vision**
   Excellent companies have managers who provide clear direction and vision.

7 **Hands-on**
   Excellent companies have managers who are involved in daily operations.

8 **Bias for action**
   Excellent companies take action on new ideas.

9 **Simple structure and lean staffing**
   Excellent companies are distinguished by a small headquarters. Authority is devolved to decentralized business units. Rigid job descriptions are the exception.

10 **Loose/tight control mechanisms**
   Excellent companies encourage high levels of autonomy, empowerment and risk-taking. They also apply strict financial control and have clear performance targets.

---

involves citizens in making decisions about public services. Accountability is stressed and traditional values of probity and good stewardship are emphasized (see Chapter 11). According to Ferlie *et al.*[70] another characteristic of a PSO manager is support for the idea of a 'learning organization'. Management theories in the 1990s coalesced around the notion of a learning organization that had the capacity to implement continuous change based on the continuous personal development of the individuals who worked within it.[71] Ranson and Stewart[72] went even further, suggesting that public service organizations that were learning organizations might become vehicles for a 'learning society'. We are critical of these ideas and of the attempts that have been made to operationalize them through workplace learning (see Chapter 13).

An important task for public service managers is to bring a public service orientation to public service management. Public service managers have to do this while maintaining the day-in-day-out delivery of public services to increasing numbers of people, demonstrating competence in at least six different roles: managing resistance and change; managing operations and activities; managing finance and resources; managing communication and information; managing learning and personal development; and managing groups and individuals.

Having explored the changing context of public services during the 20 year period 1980–2000, we will consider the likely context for the work of public service managers over the next 20 years.

THE NEXT 20 YEARS

If accounting is about the past and administration is about the present, then one concern of management is surely about the future. Reviews of past results and present performance are valuable because they can inform a manager's decisions about what to preserve and what to change. The future is a continuation of the past. We have looked at the last 20 years; we are now in a position to make some assumptions about what is likely to affect public services in the next 20 years.

Managers of public services need knowledge and understanding which can underpin their functional competence in managing resistance, change, operations, activities, people, finances, resources, communication, information, people, learning and personal development. Managers need to be able to transfer their knowledge and understanding to different contexts, as the contexts change. We want to look at the kind of thinking skills that public service managers will need in order to adapt their approach from one type of organization to another and from one occasion to the next. The contexts in which public services are delivered will change, in response to the technological, economic, market, political, legal, ethical and social forces which we have been exploring in this chapter.

Future Challenges to Public Services: the Thinking Skills Required

In the next 20 years we have assumed that strategic thinking and managing change will not be monopolized by top management. Managers at all levels will need to think reflectively about information, think predictively about imagined futures, think creatively about innovative developments, think empathetically about the consequences for others, and think critically in evaluating options for change. When managers implement changes, they need the thinking skills of the 'conversational manager' (see Figure 1.5).

In looking forward 20 years, we have made ten assumptions about the context in which public service managers will need to exercise their thinking and conversational skills.

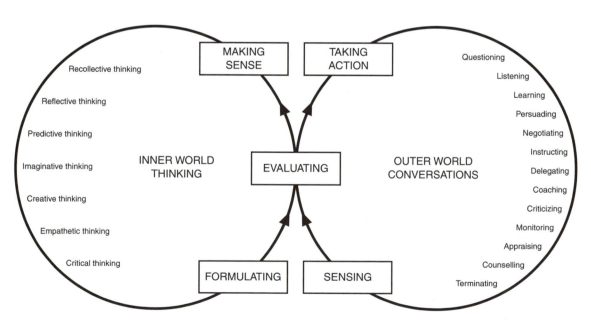

Figure 1.5 The thinking skills of the conversational manager

The Next 20 Years – Ten Assumptions

1 We have assumed that collaborative bidding will oblige managers to work together (but in competition) with other managers! Managers will be expected to work in collaboration with people from organizations whose values and perceptions challenge their own (Chapter 3). Working in multi-agency teams is discussed in Chapter 6.

2 We have assumed that local services will be squeezed between a central assessment of their performance according to official criteria and local citizens who will become vociferous critics of service quality. Managing quality and value for money is addressed in Chapters 5 and 11.

3 We have assumed that national and international comparisons of performance will continue to be made, pressurizing managers to improve quality and to attain specific measures of performance. A manager's ability to motivate, to be entrepreneurial, to manage stress, and to assess risk will become more important. We discuss this in Chapters 7, 8 and 10.

4 We have assumed that the demand for locally provided services will increase and that the per capita resources available to meet this growing demand will decrease. Whatever political parties are in power, money will be kept within tight limits. Budgeting skills and the ability to quantify will be at a premium. We examine these topics in Chapters 9 and 12.

5 We have assumed the need for an outward-looking role. Increasingly, managers will become involved in the creation and maintenance of active networks of stakeholders. Good political thinking will be essential. Public service managers will conduct their work under conditions of increasing openness and scrutiny. We deal with these issues in Chapters 4, 11 and 15.

6 We have assumed that social trends will adversely affect traditional patterns of family life and that crime will continue to rise. All this will make increasing demands on social, education, police and community services. Ethical thinking will be needed to make choices and to resolve conflicts. This will be discussed in Chapter 11.

7 We have assumed that the ability to manage and to make sense of ambiguous, uncertain and conflicting information will become increasingly valuable. We discuss information management and decision-making in Chapter 12.

8 We have assumed that unemployment will persist, despite employment-led policies. Predictive, creative and imaginative thinking will be required of public service managers working as agents of local economic development and as supporters of communities sorely afflicted by unemployment. Not only will managers themselves need new learning skills, they will also need to develop them in others – in the community and in the workplace. We discuss this in Chapters 13 and 14.

9 We have assumed that uncertainty about careers and about the continued existence of some public service organizations will cause public service managers to feel insecure. The ability to learn, relearn and swap careers will help them to combat their insecurity. Thinking and learning skills will be at a premium. Each chapter has activities designed to develop thinking and learning skills and Chapter 14 is devoted to managing one's career and personal development.

10 Finally, we anticipate that managers will increasingly be required to manage the culture and values of their organizations. In Chapters 3 and 15 we examine how to clarify organizational values and to manage culture, continuity and change.

'Stand and Deliver!'

The research underpinning this book spanned 30 years. The need to write it became pressing as we foresaw disastrous consequences for democratic governments that tried to stand for election on a platform of well-intentioned promises to improve public services. Even if their economies prospered and permitted politicians to honour their well-intentioned pledges of better funding, it became clear to us that politicians would fail to deliver their promise of improved public services – unless the majority of public service managers acquired the thinking skills and conversational skills that would be needed to implement changes. We were concerned that politicians who failed to deliver promises to improve public services might be punished at the ballot box, or even worse, in the streets. When we considered what alternative appeals might be made to a disappointed and frustrated electorate, we feared the possible consequences for public servants and the public good. When politicians promise the electorate improved health, education and transport; freedom from fear of crime; safer water, food and farming; more reliable gas, electricity and telecommunications, then public service managers hold the fate of governments in their hands. Yet public service managers often do not know how to manage major capital projects without being distracted from the day-in-day-out vigilance that is needed to maintain the standard of the existing services for which they are responsible.

In 2001 the UK, Prime Minister Blair was accosted in the streets by members of the public who angrily recounted examples of deteriorating public services. Yet 5 billion pounds which he had given to public service managers in the previous two years remained unspent. Money alone was not the answer to the improvements to public services that Mr Blair's government had promised.

Mr Blair aimed to improve the performance of public services by recruiting managers from the private sector. As we have seen in this chapter, importing managers from the private sector does not work. Providing public services is not the same as manufacturing products, commanding troops or running a supermarket. Yet our evidence is that public service managers can learn how to raise the performance of their organizations. Managers need alternatives to discredited approaches to team working and work-based learning. Their staff need to be treated individually. People need to be motivated as individuals, through one-to-one conversations. Given the numbers of managers commonly employed in public service organizations, this is not difficult to achieve. Managers need to manage. This is what they are paid to do. They can learn how to do it better. A more conversational approach is needed

to implementing changes. Much of the jargon of strategic management needs to be debunked (Chapter 15). A more thoughtful approach is needed to the practice of management in public services.

Developing the Thinking Skills of the Public Service Manager

Chapter 1 has provided information about the changing context in which public service managers need to carry out their work. The following 13 chapters provide information on *how* to carry out this work. The chapters are grouped under six roles:

1 Managing change
2 Managing operations and activities
3 Managing people
4 Managing finances and resources
5 Managing information
6 Managing learning and personal development

Under each role, readers will find information on relevant management techniques. Because it is important to understand *why* as well as *how*, readers will also find information on the concepts that underpin each management technique. Your understanding of why things work as well as how to do them will enable you to transfer your management knowledge from one situation to another. Your understanding will be developed through numerous examples taken from public services in Eastern and Western Europe, Asia, America, India, Pakistan, Africa, South America, Australia, New Zealand, Fiji, Madagascar and the United States, as well as in the United Kingdom.

At the end of each chapter there are activities to carry out either on your own, in pairs or in groups – either inside or outside the workplace. By carrying out these activities you will not only deepen your understanding of the knowledge that underpins your competence, but also develop the learning skills you will need in order to keep your knowledge up to date. You will also develop a repertoire of thinking skills. These thinking skills will help you to transfer your learning, apply your knowledge and adapt your skills as circumstances change.

SUMMARY

- We considered the definition and development, the scope and the scale of public services. We discovered that throughout the world public services are provided by a wide spectrum of types of public service organizations.
- We learned about the way in which economic, market, political, legal, ethical and social forces cause change in public service organizations throughout the world. These forces lead to changes in the structure of public service organizations and to changes in the approaches that managers adopt in order to manage them. There was evidence of changing roles for both managers and professionals.
- We evaluated the strengths and weaknesses of bureaucracies. New forms of organization are emerging. We described these as post-bureaucratic or 'third-wave' organizations. 'Third-wave' organizational structures do not appear to be compatible with 'second-wave' approaches to managing them.
- We looked at Efficiency, Post-Fordist and Excellence models of management and at the development of a public service orientation.
- We made predictions about the ways that global changes over the next 20 years might impact on the work of public service managers.
- Public services depend on the functional competence of managers in managing resistance and change, managing operations and activities, managing finance and resources, managing information and communication, managing learning and personal development and managing people. The knowledge and understanding that underpin these functional competencies and the thinking and learning skills required are identified.

NOTES

1 Smith, A. (1876) *The Wealth of the Nations*. Book V, Chapter 1, Part III.
2 Flynn, N. (1997) *Public Sector Management*. Prentice Hall, p. 11.
3 Lawton, A. and Rose, A. (eds) (1999) *Public Services Management*. FT/Prentice Hall.
4 Tomkins, C. R. (1987) *Achieving Economy, Efficiency and Effectiveness in the Public Sector*. Kegan Paul.
5 Handy, C. (1997) *The Hungry Spirit*. Ransom House, p. 18.
6 Flynn, op. cit., p. 16.
7 National Audit Office (1992) *Annual Report*, p. 4.
8 Pollard, S. (1992) *The Development of the British Economy 1914–1990*. Edward Arnold, p. 43.
9 Worthington, I., cited in Lawton and Rose, op. cit.
10 Sloman, J. (1991) *Economics*. Harvester Wheatsheaf, p. 408.
11 *The Sunday Times* (1997), 13 April .
12 Flynn, op. cit., p. 34.
13 Exworthy, M. and Halford, S. (1999) *Professionals and the New Managerialism in the Public Sector*. Open University Press, p. 1.
14 Ibid., p. 2.
15 Farnham, D. and Horton, S. (1996) *Managing the New Public Services*. Macmillan.
16 Exworthy and Halford, op. cit., p. 88.
17 Ibid., p. 79.
18 Clarke, M. and Stewart, J. (1990) *General Management in Local Government: Getting the Balance Right*. Longman, p. 6.
19 Flynn, op. cit., p. 36.
20 Isaac-Henry, K. *et al.* (1993) *Management in the Public Sector. Challenge and Change*. Chapman & Hall, p. 21.
21 Clarke and Stewart, op. cit., p. 32.
22 Bishop, K. and Kaye, J. (1988) *Does Privatisation Work? Lessons from the UK*. London Business School.
23 Cook, P. and Kirkpatrick, C. (1995) *Privatisation Policy and Performance. International Perspectives*. Harvester Wheatsheaf, p. 21.
24 Isaac-Henry, K. *et al.*, op. cit., p. 12.
25 Foster, A. (1993) Controller of the Audit Commission and G. Parston, chief executive of the OPM.
26 Keen, L. and Scase, R. (1998) *Local Government Management. The Rhetoric and Reality of Change*. Open University Press, p. 162.
27 Harrup, K., cited in Lawton and Rose, op. cit.
28 Ferlie, E., Ashbourner, L., Fitzgerald, L. and Pettigrew, A. (1996) *The New Public Management in Action*. Oxford University Press, p. 27.
29 Barton, J. (1987) 'Transforming New Zealand's Public Sector. Labour's Quest for Improved Efficiency and Accountability'. *Public Administration*, no. 65, Winter.
30 Zifcack, S. (1994) *New Managerialism. Administrative Reform in Whitehall and Canberra*. Oxford University Press, p. 172.
31 Pollitt, C. (1993) *The New Managerialism in the Public Services: the Anglo-American Experience*. Basil Blackwell.
32 Osborne, D. and Gaebler, T. (1992) *Reinventing Government. How Entrepreneurial Spirit is Transforming the Public Sector*. Addison-Wesley.
33 Ibid., p. 20.
34 Flynn, N. and Strehl, L. (1996) *Public Sector Management in Europe*. Prentice Hall.

35 Hughes, P. (1998) *Public Management and Administration. An Introduction.* 2nd edn. Macmillan, p. 214.

36 Flynn and Strehl, op. cit., pp. 264–66.

37 Chris Ham, Director of Health Services Management. Birmingham University. Cited in the *Guardian* (18 February 1998).

38 Mullins, L. (1999) *Management and Organisational Behaviour.* 5th edn. FT/Pitmans.

39 Taylor, W. F. (1947) *Principles of Scientific Management.* Harper & Row.

40 Fayol, H. (1949) *General and Industrial Management.* Pitman.

41 Rose, M. (1978) *Industrial Behaviour.* Penguin, p. 31.

42 Drucker, P. F. (1981) 'The Coming Rediscovery of Scientific Management' in *Towards the Next Economics and Other Essays.* Heinemann.

43 Isaac-Henry, K. *et al.* (1993) *Management in the Public Sector. Challenge and Change.* Chapman and Hall.

44 Day, P. and Klein, R. (1987) *Accountabilities. Five Public Services.* Tavistock, p. 21.

45 Pollitt, op. cit., p. 21.

46 Ibid., p. 65.

47 Weber, M. (1964) *The Theory of Social and Economic Organisation.* Macmillan.

48 Haynes, R. J. (1980) *Organisational Theory and Local Government.* Allen & Unwin.

49 Merton, R. K. (1940) 'Bureaucratic Structure and Personality'. *Social Forces*, no. 18.

50 Niskanen, W. A. (1971) *Bureaucracy and Representative Government.* Aldine-Atherton.

51 Burns, T. and Stalker, G. M. (1961) *The Management of Innovation.* Tavistock.

52 Bennis, W. (1969) *Organizational Development, Its Nature, Origins and Prospects.* Addison Wesley, p. 19.

53 Toffler, A. (1973) *Future Shock.* Pan Books.

54 Hecksher, C. (1994) *The Post Bureaucratic Organization. New Perspectives on Organizational Change.* Sage, p. 20.

55 Schroder, H. M. (1989) *Managerial Competence: the Key to Excellence.* Kendall/Hunt.

56 Ibid., p. 45.

57 Ibid., p. 47.

58 Ibid., p. 49.

59 Furnham, A. (1997) *The Psychology of Behaviour at Work. The Individual in the Organisation.* Psychology Press, p. 604.

60 Peters, T. J. and Watermann, R. H. (1982) *In Search of Excellence.* Harper & Row.

61 Hecksher, op. cit., p. 76.

62 Buchanan and Boddy, op. cit., p. 81.

63 Morley, D. (1993) 'Strategic Direction in British Public Services'. *Journal of Long Range Planning*, vol. 26.

64 HMSO (1991) *Making the Most of the Next Steps.*

65 Keen and Scase, op. cit., p. 82.

66 Ferlie *et al.*, op. cit., p. 16.

67 Pollitt, op. cit.

68 Peters and Watermann, op. cit.

69 Ferlie *et al.*, op. cit.

70 Ibid., p. 32.

71 Starkey, K. (1996) *How Organisations Learn.* ITP Business Press, p. 2.

72 Ranson, S. and Stewart, J. (1994) *Management for the Public Domain. Enabling the Learning Society.* Macmillan, p. 246.

ROLE ONE

MANAGING CHANGE

In Chapter 1 we examined some of the major changes that were taking place at the turn of the century. We found evidence of changes in approaches to management and changes in the design of organization structures. In Role One we examine the manager's role in implementing changes.

In Chapter 2, we explore the nature of change. We argue for a balance between the need to manage continuity and the need to manage change. We examine different responses to change and ask who is likely to oppose change, why and how. We explore ways in which managers can anticipate and overcome resistance to the implementation of changes in public service organizations. In Chapter 3 we direct atten-

tion to ways in which managers can implement changes. We evaluate rational prescriptive approaches and experimental emergent approaches. We propose a conversational approach to integrating prescriptive and emergent approaches. We consider how project management techniques can be used. Manual and computer-based techniques for planning projects and evaluating changes – such as Gantt charts, critical path analysis and programme evaluation and review techniques – are described in detail. It is important to manage the emotions that are generated during change. Finally, we explore the difficulties faced by managers who attempt to change the culture of public service organizations and we suggest ways in which these difficulties can be overcome.

2

MANAGING RESISTANCE TO CHANGE IN PUBLIC SERVICES

All things come into being through opposition, all are in flux like a river ... you can't step into the same river twice.

(Heraclitus c. 580)

LEARNING OUTCOMES

This chapter will enable the reader to:

- Consider the nature of organizational change.
- Understand theories of change and that not all change is for the better.
- Understand how to anticipate and prepare for resistance to change.
- Empathize with a chief executive whose Civil Service department has been privatized.
- Understand who might resist change, why and how.
- Evaluate the roles of coercion, manipulation, persuasion, negotiation, delegation, facilitation, participation and learning, in moving from resistance to implementing changes.
- Consider changing ideas about change.

INTRODUCTION

We are not used to seeing change described as ordinary. We are more used to seeing change described as radical, complex, accelerating, dramatic or transformational. But change is part of ordinary life. We manage it all the time. It gives us problems to solve and opportunities to do something different. We experience it physically, mentally and emotionally. Usually it is subtle and slow but it can be sudden – disrupting our work, dislocating our relationships or ruining our leisure time. Sometimes we can discern a pattern, sometimes not. Sometimes we can explain it, sometimes not. Change involves the unfamiliar, sometimes the unknown. Many of us prefer what is familiar. Rather than seek change, we continue to live with our old familiar feelings, even when our old familiar feelings are not very good. Managers who can learn to embrace the unknown, and to relish uncertainty, will thrive in organizations where these attributes are in short supply. Generally, people prefer advance warnings of change. They prefer to be given reasons, preferably in person. This is not true for everybody. It is dangerous to assume that people who do not want to be involved in the process of planning change will not resist it. They may volunteer to be involved in order to be better placed to resist the change. Managers should welcome the conflict that this will generate. Objections need to be surfaced if they are to be overcome. Individuals need to be helped to deal with shock and denial. Managers should expect to achieve at least acceptance.

Managers need to know when change is for the better. This means understanding when not to change – when to manage continuity. Do not assume that your ideas have no merit, just because they plough into the sand. Be prepared for anti-climax, hiatus, lead balloons and postnatal depression. You may need to keep your idea alive, until it is ready to assume a life of its own.

In Chapter 1 we looked at the changes caused by privatization, the pressure to provide value for money, new managerialism and new organization structures. We have chosen to start with managing change as Role One because implementing change is integral to all of the roles in which managers are expected to demonstrate competence. Each management role is discussed separately. We look at the need to change in response to stakeholders and the marketing activities of competitors (Chapter 4). Improving quality requires the continuous implementation of incremental changes (Chapter 5). In Chapter 6 we see how working in groups and teams can impede change. In Chapter 7 we question the role of transformational leadership in implementing change. A motivated workforce is a powerful aid to implementing changes. Recruiting, inducting, training and disciplining individuals often play an important part in implementing changes (Chapter 8). Implementing change requires additional resources. We look at how these resources can be obtained and how to check that they are used economically, effectively, efficiently and ethically (Chapters 9, 10 and 11). Making decisions about change and communicating them requires systems to manage the flow of information. We find that information technology not only enables change but also forces other changes in its wake (Chapter 12). We look at the beneficial relationship between change and learning (Chapter 13). We then switch our focus from managing change to changing managers when we look at managing personal development (Chapter 14). Finally, in Chapter 15, we look at how surfacing the assumptions and beliefs of managers can help to balance the need for continuity against the need for change.

THE NATURE OF CHANGE

A change is a 'difference, a variation or a substitution of one state for another'. Changing is 'becoming or making different'. To change is 'to become or make different'. The common thread is difference. It could be a little difference or a big difference. It could occur slowly or quickly (Figure 2.1).

For centuries information was recorded and stored on scrolls and kept in religious libraries. By 1800 any literate person could record information on a writing pad. By 1900 manual typewriters were available. By 1960 these were electric. By 1980 word processors were commonplace. By 1990 laptop computers had audio input. By 1995 they were hand held. By the year 2000 people could use their TV or cell phone to record, send or access information instantly from anywhere on the world wide web. All of these changes were relatively small – one to another. All of them helped to shape the way public and private organizations operated. Although, historically, change has had different immediate drivers, ultimately most changes have been driven by changes in technology. Technological change has powered economic change and brought political and social change in its wake. Although technology might have been the ultimate driver, the immediate drivers can be growth, regulation, competition, changing markets, rising costs or new managers needing to make their mark on the organization (Figure 2.2).

None of these drivers is new. Changes of all four types shown in Figure 2.1 – emergent, incremental,

Speed \ Difference	LITTLE	BIG
SLOW	Emergent	Transitional
FAST	Incremental	Transformational

Figure 2.1 Types of change

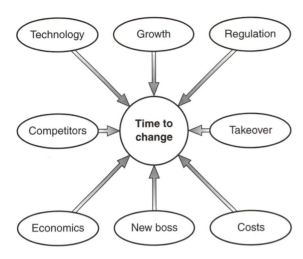

Figure 2.2 Time to change – the drivers

transitional and transformational – have been occurring for a long time. New technologies have always
altered work. Organizations have always reorganized.
Social attitudes, including attitudes to work, have
been changing worldwide, since 1945. It is the speed
of change rather than the scale of change that sometimes causes it to warrant special management. Even
a 30 per cent reduction in staff may be achievable
through thoughtful management, given 3–5 years in
which to accomplish it. Moaning about change is
futile. Managers are paid to manage change. This
does not mean leaping into action the moment a
change is proposed. Even when under direct instruction to implement a change, it is important how we
do it. The working lives of people for whom we are
responsible depend on our doing it well. Skill in
implementing changes is a matter of empathy as
well as efficiency. Implementing change requires
explanation, preparation, control and commitment.
Often it involves the use of specific techniques such
as project management (Chapter 3). We will need to
communicate, persuade, negotiate, delegate and
coach and to deal sensitively with individuals, as
well as trades unions and employee representatives.
Finally, we will need to evaluate and learn from the
changes that we have made.

THEORIES OF CHANGE

Energy Theories of Change

Newton's second law of thermodynamics states
that in any random transaction, the entropy will
increase. Entropy is a measure of how random things
are – how chaotic. This implies that throughout the
universe, any random change, will be in the direction of increasing variety and complexity. This
implies that if a manager does nothing, the organization will change anyway. The behaviours of the
people in the organization will change from day to
day in small and random ways, adding up, over time,
to significant non-compliance with systems and
procedures. Vigilant visiting, attentive listening
and a watchful eye are needed if managers are
to sense what is happening and intervene when,
and only when, the effect of the random change is
detrimental.

Mathematical Theories of Change

Mathematical models of life and the universe often
predict steady states that will persist over very
extended periods until the combination of certain
variables causes the overall state 'to step' or take a
'quantum leap'. At this point an overall value may
plummet to zero (break down) or may start growing
at an ever accelerating rate (go critical). This is what
causes an atomic explosion when a critical mass is
attained or a critical temperature is reached. According to mathematical catastrophe theories, these functions predict the inevitability of catastrophes like
earthquakes, volcanoes, tornadoes and slumps in the
economy. Complex mathematical models underpin
the forecasts issued daily by Meteorological Offices
throughout the world. Simpler mathematical models
of human bio-rhythms have been used to predict
physical, mental and emotional crises for individuals.
When 'triple low bio-rhythms' are predicted, people
are prevented from driving taxis in Japan or from
flying aircraft in the US Navy. Mathematical models
developed by Niels Bohr even predicted that the
very act of observing something would change it.

Almost any manager who has been involved in an organizational audit could have told him that! Computerized mathematical models have been used to warn of the likelihood of riots in jails, gridlock in city centres, or epidemic threats to public health. They are the basis of war games used to simulate the effect of changes in the balance of power or fear or deterrence.

Economic Theories of Change

Economic theories of change claim that people will make changes in favour of their own economic advantage. More sophisticated models even put a cost on the need to accommodate personal conscience. Everyone is thought to have their price! The cost of not changing can also be calculated. Goods or services inevitably move along price gradients, causing major changes in investment and the migration and emigration of whole populations, from rural to urban, or from the Southern to the Northern Hemisphere. According to economic theorists, if markets are left unrestricted then new suppliers will continue to appear until competition between them results in costs and prices that are so low that it is uneconomic for another supplier to enter the field. If, on the other hand, goods or services are supplied free, then demand will continue to rise to take up the increase in supply until the demand is exhausted. The problem with this approach to health services, for example, is that the demand is virtually inexhaustible for the foreseeable future.

Biological Theories of Change

According to Dawkins,[1] people organize themselves, their behaviour or their environments so as to maximize the chances that their genes will survive, perpetuate and dominate those of other people. The implication is that if an organization does not change and adapt as the environment changes, it too will become extinct. This is a process that Darwin described as natural selection. According to Darwin, times of rapid environmental change favour the survival of the fittest. Organizations with the best outwardly focused, long distance vision will have the earliest warning of impending changes. They will have more time to prepare and more chance of adapting and surviving, especially if they have well-rehearsed contingency plans.

Systems Theories of Change

In systems thinking,[2] human activity systems are assumed to be part of a universal hierarchy of wider systems and subsystems. One property of these systems is that they regulate themselves by making changes that ensure their continuity. They are sensitive to changes in their environments and have feedback mechanisms through which they automatically adjust their inputs, their cross boundary flows, their internal processes and their outputs (Chapter 5). Political parties carry out routine polls of public opinion and adjust their policies. Public service organizations use focus groups to anticipate reactions to proposed service developments. Transport services passenger groups provide feedback on service quality. Universities ask students to take part in satisfaction surveys by filling in questionnaires. Such feedback can be used to predict reaction to planned changes and provoke proposals for further change.

Psychological Theories of Change

Psychologists use the idea of cognitive dissonance to explain why people try to change from their existing state to another state which they think is more desirable. When the grass is greener on the other side of the river, people try to cross. Hence the need for immigration services and armed forces. Cognitive dissonance is used to explain the drive behind learning, the success of advertising, the pressure behind economic migration and the motivation of staff. The 'shared vision' in transformational change is an attempt to get large numbers of people to desire the same new state, to pull in the same 'strategic direction' (Chapter 7).

Psychoanalytic Theories of Change

Jung's[3] idea of a 'collective unconsciousness' is invoked to explain why some changes are inevitable and why others will be resisted, whenever people are brought together in groups or organizations. Freud and researchers like Bowlby[4] thought that the response of adults to change was determined by their childhood experiences of birth, suckling, sibling rivalry, attachment, separation and loss. They concluded that for many adults the prospect of change might re-stimulate their separation anxiety and their fear of loss. They predicted a pattern of shock, denial, grieving, catharsis, insight and adaptation. For Kurt Lewin[5] this meant that resistance to organizational change was inevitable. Lewin thought that resistance to change could be tackled by managers through a process which he called Force Field Analysis.

Political Theories of Change

For political theorists, change will usually be explicable in terms of the desire of the powerful to retain and increase their power. Some tenets are that people with power rarely surrender it willingly; that people with power tend to make changes that increase their power; that power corrupts; and that absolute power corrupts absolutely. Feelings of powerlessness in the face of change can provoke feelings of sadness (expressed as depressive illness, absenteeism, tokenism, withdrawal, passivity or low morale) or feelings of anger (expressed as resistance, non co-operation, working to rule, industrial action, espionage, sabotage, desertion or betrayal). Token consultation and nominal participation can be used to preserve the power of the powerful. Even 'employee empowerment' can be part of a strategy to 'divide and rule'. In bureaucratic organizations, or in Fordist organizations where the work has been so proceduralized that it is devoid of emotionally engaging content, a power game can become the only game in town! In public services power games are often played by middle managers and senior civil servants.

Sociological Theories of Change

When people come together in groups, communities, cities or nations, levels of confusion and anxiety rise. Attempts are made to manage this anxiety by creating structure, rules and legislation. As we saw in Chapter 1, Mrs Thatcher's call for less government legislation resulted in the creation of 1,345 agencies to audit, control and regulate the activities of UK citizens!

Cultural Theories of Change

Organizations can be viewed as mini societies in which changes are driven or resisted in accordance with the beliefs that are deeply held by the members of that society. The beliefs may not be articulated explicitly. They may be conveyed symbolically, through such things as stories, myths, rituals and ceremonies. According to cultural theories, people are likely to change their behaviour in response to symbolic actions by managers. The more senior the manager, the more powerful the signal. If senior managers break with a traditional way of doing things, they signal the direction in which they want the organization's culture to shift. If they consult clients or front-line staff before putting proposals to the board, they send out a very different message than if they always consult a member of the board before they do anything (Chapter 3).

Developmental Theories of Change

To developmental theorists, curiosity and a search for stimulus are innate. To them this explains the drive to explore, to learn, to push back boundaries, to break new records – in short, to change things. An innate drive to discover things makes scientific discoveries inevitable. Historically, advances in science and technology have been the prime drivers of change. A constant search for stimulation can lead to a constant search for entertainment or distraction (or shopping!). In the absence of real distractions, some people can develop fantasies about an external enemy or a suspected competitor. They constantly make changes as they prepare to defend themselves. At a national level, rehearsal for war (national defence against enemies known and unknown) drives the development of new weapons and new technologies. It drives the development of the public services that provide military and economic intelligence. Secret services plot against unseen enemies – terrorists, spies and others who are seen as a potential threat. In some countries the factories that manufacture warships, military aircraft and conventional nuclear and biological weapons are owned by the state. These are not public service organizations. Many of the problems facing managers of service organizations are not the same as the problems facing managers of manufacturing organizations, even if the latter are publicly owned. Some people appear to make changes just for the sake of making changes. Change for change's sake satisfies the curiosity of wondering what would happen if . . . It provides stimulation and it relieves boredom. Speculating what management will do next and exploring the implications of the latest grapevine rumours about impending changes helps many people to pass the time. They while their present lives away – immersed in hopes and fears about the future. Actual changes, on the other hand, can be the object of reflection: 'I won't do that again in a hurry.' Whether changes are internal or external, real or imagined, for better or for worse, to the developmentalist they are the inevitable product of an innate search for stimulation and novelty. Managers of supermarkets know that one key to successful marketing is increased variety, more choice, new options. Management 'fads' are popular with those who are looking for a change (Chapter 15).

Many theories of change seem to imply that change is inevitable. Not all of them imply that resistance to change is inevitable. In most organizations it is possible to find some people who welcome change. They can be recruited as change agents – supporters of change who can help managers to overcome resistance to change. Often as many as one third of the organization will be supportive. Whether or not change is inevitable, the most important thing is that its implementation is well prepared. It is to this that we now turn.

PREPARING FOR CHANGE

Anticipating Readiness to Change

People's ability to adapt and to deal with external volatility are two key variables in determining how they will respond to change. Figure 2.3 models the likely reaction of people faced with a change that affects them.

Implementing changes is obviously easier when people are nearer the right-hand side of the model. As we saw in Chapter 1, external volatility is usually high for most public service organizations. In 1994 Brookes and Bates[6] argued that public services, such as the UK Civil Service, were staffed by people who preferred stable environments and well-structured ways of doing things. Their work implied that managers could expect considerable resistance when trying to implement changes in public services. It is useful to anticipate the likely phases of resistance and pessimism (Figure 2.4).

As we can see from Figures 2.4 and 2.5, most people – even those favourably disposed to a change – are likely to have adverse reactions at some stage. They may not see the point of a particular step or they may temporarily 'lose the plot'. They may be very busy with other things and suffer temporary overload or 'change fatigue'. They may perceive themselves incorrectly to be threatened by some

External volatility \ Adaptability	LOW	HIGH
LOW	Resistant	Co-operative
HIGH	Fatalistic	Proactive

Figure 2.3 Likely reactions to change

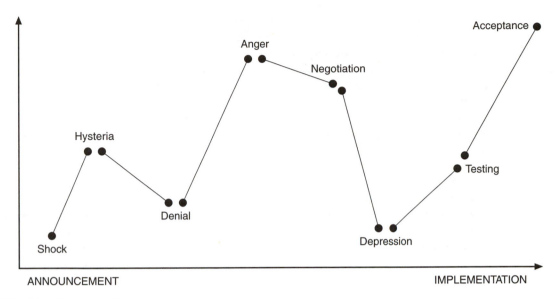

Figure 2.4 The phases of resistance to change

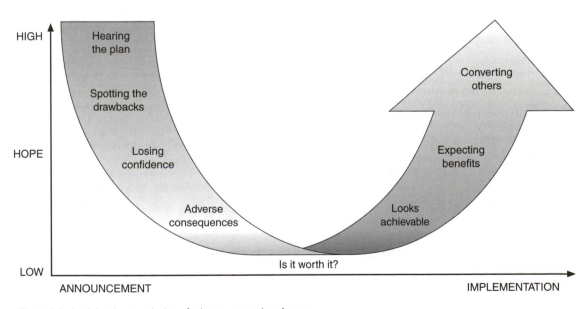

Figure 2.5 Anticipating pessimism during co-operative change

aspect of the change. They may perceive themselves quite correctly to be threatened by some aspect of the change. They may be feeling anxious or aggrieved at the prospect of having to negotiate. They may be psychologically or politically averse to the change. The change may involve a culture clash – threatening strongly held beliefs or values. Whether people's initial response is resistant or co-operative, they are likely to need support and information to help them manage the various stages in their response to change. At each stage people will need to know what is happening and why. They are entitled to be given good reasons for what is happening, or at least the best reasons that management can give. The good reasons given will not necessarily prove acceptable to all the people to whom they are given.

Preparing People for Change: A Conversational Approach

People need to be spoken to face-to-face by their line manager and they need to know that this will happen regularly, when and where – 'the last Friday of every month from 4.30 to 5.00 pm, in the main office'. At least 15 out of 20 minutes should be spent on information about how the change affects them. Five minutes only should be spent on general rationale and background information. Ten minutes should be left for questions. Chapter 12 deals with the way briefing groups can be planned and improved. The main points of a briefing should be written down to avoid contradictions. As near as possible, briefings should be given at the same time to all groups affected by the change. This minimizes the time wasted correcting grapevine rumours. If you find that your briefings tend to overrun, increase their frequency but not their length. Twenty to 30 minutes exceeds the concentration span of most people receiving verbal information. The purpose of the briefing is to keep them 'on board'. If they get bored, they may jump ship! Although we have emphasized the importance of interpersonal conversations, at a time of change you should check that all channels of communication are working well. You will need to think about who, what, when, and where. Who will need to be told what, by whom and where this will take place. Who are the people likely to be affected by the change? Tell them three things: what you plan to do, what you have done so far, and what you plan to do next. Where you tell them depends on how many people there are and where they normally spend their time. Wherever possible, communicate face to face. Communicate frequently so that it never takes more than 20 minutes to recap and get all the new information across. Whenever possible – and it is not always possible – aim to gain and keep the commitment of about 30 per cent of the people involved in the change. Gaining the commitment of at least 30 per cent of those affected by the change is an important determinant of the speed, accuracy and durability of the change. Table 2.1 helps to assess your chances of success.

Consultation and Target-setting

To conclude this section on preparing for change, it is important to consider the role of consultation, communication and setting targets. If there is time, consult those affected. It need not take long. It is not a search for compromise or consensus. Listen actively to the views of those affected. Accept them or reject

Table 2.1 Change – the chances of success

Support of Top Management	Initial reaction			
	Resistant	Fatalistic	Co-operative	Proactive
Helping	Hard work	Good chance	Good chance	Good chance
Allowing	Forget it	Hard work	Good chance	Good chance
Grudging	Forget it	Forget it	Forget it	Hard work

them, with good reason. You may learn something that had not occurred to you. In any event, people prefer to have had a say, even if their ideas are not taken up or accepted. Deal promptly with grievances. Strive for equality of pain or reward. Attach deadlines to physical changes that will occur. Make sure that people see these tangible products of their work. Publicize their work to as wide an audience as possible. In Chapter 12 we deal with the use of the media. Finally, check the checklist (Box 2.1).

Despite a manager's best efforts to anticipate reactions to change and to prepare the ground, resistance is likely from at least 70 per cent of the workforce. In the next section we shall consider why people resist change, how to anticipate resistance, and how to overcome resistance to implementing changes. First, a conversation with a senior manager who had a leading role in implementing changes in the UK Civil Service. David Maclaren is the chief executive officer of an 'Agency'. The agency had been set up by his government under statutory powers to take over and run public services that were formerly run by ministerial departments.

David talks about many problems related to managing change in a public service. These are problems that arise when the real world gets in the way of strategic plans, the need to change organizational culture and the way individuals think. We deal with these types of problem in the following chapter. David also talks about a 'boggy centre' who bog down his efforts to implement changes. What might David have done to anticipate and overcome the resistance he encountered when implementing changes in public services?

Box 2.1

PREPARING FOR CHANGE: THE AVOCADOS CHECKLIST

A = Assistance	Has anyone else ever done this? Do not re-invent the wheel. Seek advice. Use a consultant.
V = Vision	Could someone paint a picture – literally or in words – of what things will look like afterwards?
O = Optimism	How do we create a presumption – an expectation – of success? What emotions will be released when we succeed? How can we harness them now?
C = Communication	Whose job will it be to sell and keep selling the benefits of the change? Where is the intended communication plan?
A = Analysis	Is there a 'rich picture' or 'map' of the existing organization?
D = Decisions	Whose decisions will be crucial to the success of the change? Are they signed up?
O = Owners	Who owns the change? Does the owner or head of the organization support it?
S = Stakeholders	What do other key stakeholders think about the change?

Box 2.2

EXTRACTS FROM A CONVERSATION WITH DAVID MACLAREN

'CHANGING THE CIVIL SERVICE'

Tony: What's it like trying to manage civil servants?

David: Some of my civil servants are blinkered by blind obedience to rules and procedures. This can stifle initiative and frustrate those who see the need for change. The administrative class can be arrogant and out of touch with reality. They often lack the 'big picture' and sometimes get lost in detail. They tend to look after their own. Even when they can see the need for change they don't usually do anything. Their most common excuse is 'But it has financial implications' – as though financial matters can be divorced from operations!

Tony: Can you give me an example?

David: Yes. We have to order equipment from central procurement. I have to provide incredibly detailed technical information so that equipment can be purchased by someone who knows nothing about it. We often get poor quality, out-of-date equipment and usually pay over the odds for it! Because we cannot vire money between budgets, we buy more machines than we need, but cannot pay anyone to run them!

Tony: How did you decide what to change?

David: I listened to politicians. They talked increasingly about objectives, budgets and measures of performance. I wanted to speak their language, so I devolved budgets.

Tony: How did that work out?

David: Many good things came from it, but it was foolish to pretend that we were like a private business. We are not guided by the 'bottom line' of profitability. We cannot opt out of providing certain services because they are too costly or because demand is low. Nor can we develop new products or go for new markets. In fact, we cannot do most of the things that most businesses do! Yet we have to have a strategic plan, which sets out our aims and objectives, describes our intended allocation of resources, and provides the basis of performance targets. Producing a strategic plan was difficult. We could not have done it without the help of outside consultants. We did not know the difference between a success criterion and a performance indicator. We couldn't set sales targets and then measure actual sales against them, as you might in a private business. Our business is to respond to the unexpected – an overseas conflict or a sudden epidemic, for example.

Tony: How has change been resisted?

David: Some of my fellow CEOs continue to seek advice before deciding what to do, even though they are paid handsomely to make decisions. I also experience problems with my middle managers. I call them my 'Boggy Centre'. They have the ability to get things well and truly 'bogged down'. For example, I issued an instruction to a member of my staff the other day and a few days later I asked him how things were going. He said 'I've asked permission to do what you told me to do and I'm waiting for a reply'. He still does not accept that the only person he needs permission from is me.

Tony: Looking back over the change, what thoughts occur to you?

David: Looking back, change was a bit haphazard. My ministers seemed to be making up strategy as they went along! There was never any consistent direction. However, I enjoyed it and so did most of the CEOs. We met together regularly and our meetings were full of enthusiasm. We felt our way together. There was no blueprint. The main drift was to 'be more businesslike'. People are slowly becoming more imaginative. They are beginning to act on their own initiative. Getting people to change the way they think is the most difficult. CEOs have learned to get out more and talk to people. Things would have gone much better if I had spent more time talking to my middle managers – my 'boggy centre'. I should have persuaded people at all levels that it really was OK to make decisions and not always to refer them or wait for me. My personal view was 'give me the opportunity to make changes and if I make big mistakes too often, sack me'. I am a bit out on my own with that one!

Tony: I bet! Thank you for your time David.

ANTICIPATING AND OVERCOMING RESISTANCE TO CHANGE

In Chapter 1 we discussed the difference between mechanistic and organic organization structures. We concluded that organic structures aid organizational change. Despite evidence of some moves towards organic structures, most public service organizations still tend to be mechanistic and resistant to change. McConkey[7] explores why (Box 2.3).

Our conversation with David Maclaren, the senior civil servant, seems to echo some of McConkey's findings. It confirmed, for example, that even when decision-making is devolved, staff find it hard to break the habit of passing decisions back to the top. The delays that this creates are exacerbated because it is not clear where the top is. It might be the highest level of administration or the highest level of political representation. If the latter, staff may find politicians reluctant to agree to the change, especially if it is likely to upset people in marginal constituencies. Politicians often prefer to be in a position to disown, or even criticize, decisions that prove to be unpopular. Senior managers, on the other

---

Box 2.3

REASONS FOR RESISTANCE TO CHANGE IN PUBLIC SERVICES

- Adherence to bureaucratic 'habits' related to delegation, legalism, procedural regulation; the need for caution and security: scepticism – often legitimate – about management.
- Difficulties due to multiple levels of authority, accountability and reporting.
- Tendency to push decision-making upwards. This conflicts with approaches that seek to increase self-control and self-direction.

- Relationships are guided by the interests of many stakeholders (Chapter 4).
- Conflicting interests, agendas, alliances, reward structures and values.
- Financial support for change management programmes is difficult to obtain. Funding for consultants is limited because many people have to agree spending.

hand, sometimes want to exaggerate the impact of popular changes they have championed.[8] According to McConkey,[9] organizational change initiatives in publicly owned public services are more likely than in privately owned public services to be small scale, involving only single departments rather than whole organizations. We will return to the difficulty of managing large-scale changes in the following chapter, when we discuss changing the culture of an organization.

Anticipating Resistance

When preparing for change, managers need to predict the likely levels of resistance, anticipate what forms that resistance might take, and plan how that resistance might be overcome. In 1993 Buchanan and Boddy[10] produced a useful model for anticipating levels of resistance (Figure 2.6).

- **Quadrant 1** refers to relatively easy changes, such as the introduction of e-mail or the rearrangement of an open plan office. These changes are likely to produce relatively low levels of resistance because they are peripheral to the primary task. They will still produce some resistance and this will need to be managed carefully.
- **Quadrant 2** changes pose more of a problem because although the changes are peripheral to core activities, they are large in scale. More people are involved and likely to become stressed by uncertainty, disruption and loss of what has become familiar to them. An example could

involve the introduction of a new system for recording client details.

- **Quadrant 3** change has greater implications because it affects the core of the organization's activity. It will be difficult to reverse such changes and the penalties for failure will be high. Resistance will be higher, especially on the part of the managers, who will be exposed to criticism if it goes wrong. An example would be the introduction of interdisciplinary working in a multi-union situation. A multi-disciplinary youth offending team, for example, might combine professionals from probation, education, social services and the police (Chapter 6). The consequences of failures can be serious and are likely to be very visible.
- **Quadrant 4** changes pose the greatest challenge because such changes will be large scale and will affect the core of the service. An example would be replacing an existing service with a new one. Stakes are likely to be high in terms of the career development of the managers and other professionals involved.

Our primary interest in Buchanan and Boddy's work has been to seek help in anticipating the level of resistance to change. We share also their concern for the manager's own vulnerability. We recognize the manager's understandable instinct for self-preservation. The resistance of managers is likely to take the form of risk aversion. Change will challenge the manager's capacity for emotional resilience (Chapter 3). Having anticipated the level of resistance to change, we need to anticipate what form that resistance might take.

Centrality / Scale	SMALL	LARGE
PERIPHERAL	(1) Low	(2) Moderate
CENTRAL	(3) Moderate	(4) High

Figure 2.6 Predicting resistance to change

Forms of Resistance

Outright opposition is rare. Extreme cases might necessitate disciplinary action (Chapter 8). We are concerned here with more common forms of resistance (Box 2.4).

Resistance sometimes involves what seem like supportive suggestions, e.g. offers to set up a working party. Tread carefully. These may be intended to

Box 2.4

TEN COMMON FORMS OF RESISTANCE

- Apathy
- Lateness
- Sabotage
- Sick leave
- Absenteeism
- Procrastination
- Working-to-rule
- Working slowly ('Going Slow')
- Embarrassing leaks to press and media
- Undermining behind-the-back criticism

thwart the implementation of change rather than to support it. It can be hard to spot the difference between a positive desire to participate and a negative intention to delay and obstruct. In any case, the creation and use of groups should be avoided where possible (Chapter 6). One-to-one conversations are preferable. Bringing a group together is time consuming; it involves a lot of 'storming' before the group gets around to 'performing' (Figure 2.7). It can

be hard to separate the difficulties that groups are having in coming together, from the difficulties they are having with the proposed changes.

If you wish to reduce resistance, it is useful to understand it.

REASONS FOR RESISTANCE

Not all people resist change. For some it is a source of excitement or a welcome break from the tedious routine of life. The majority do resist change. Even small changes, introduced incrementally, may be resisted – especially if they break up valued informal groups, or if people fear they might look foolish in the changed situation. Rapid, big-step, transformational change provokes fears of redundancy. The first stage in trying to reduce resistance is trying to understand it. Hussey's[11] idea of a psychological contract may help.

A Psychological Contract

Apart from the terms and conditions spelled out in a formal contract of employment, there are unwritten assumptions that form an important part of an employee's relationship with an organization. This psychological contract governs *how* employees expect to work, as well as what they are expected to achieve. Some people expect to work on their own initiative, or to use and develop certain skills, or to enjoy the companionship of others. In return, managers might assume that employees will volunteer extra effort in times of crisis and apply their skills beyond the strict confines of their job description. If proposed changes appear to break their psychological contract, feelings of injustice, resentment and even betrayal are not uncommon. One way to find whether employees are likely to perceive a proposed change as a breach of their psychological contract is to talk to them. Box 2.5 suggests some questions to ask.

If employees answer yes to any of these questions, they may be experiencing the change as a breach in their psychological contract. They may be feeling resentful or fearful. In either case resistance is to be

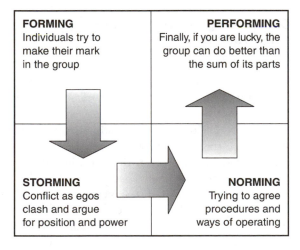

Figure 2.7 Group resistance to change

Box 2.5

DETECTING PSYCHOLOGICAL CONTRACTS: 12 QUESTIONS

Do you think that this change might cause you to have:

1 Less pay?
2 Less skill?
3 Less status?
4 Less respect?
5 Less holiday?
6 Less pension?
7 Less training?
8 Less security?
9 Less authority?
10 Less satisfactory work?
11 Less scope for initiative?
12 Less opportunity to socialize?

Box 2.6

WHO MIGHT RESIST CHANGE?

- Check out employees who are older – they may fear that they are too old to learn.
- Check out the less well educated – they may doubt their self worth, or their value to the organization, or their ability to benefit from retraining.
- Check out the junior staff – they may be the least informed and the most vulnerable to rumour and to cynicism from older staff who have 'seen it all before' and may advise junior staff to keep their heads down and wait for the change to go away.

---

expected. If the fear or resentment is based on a mis-apprehension, then correcting the mistaken impression on the spot can help to reduce resistance. Delay in clearing up doubts and misunderstandings can damage trust and lead to paranoid suspicion. In particular it might increase resistance from older or less well-educated employees (Box 2.6).

Whether or not staff belong to one of the groups in Box 2.6, most changes bring real threats. News of change strikes fear into the hearts of most employees and realistically so. When British Telecom, for example, talked about a 'culture change', employees knew that there would be casualties. The more confident staff feared that senior management was 'making a big mistake' because they had failed to take into account some technical and marketing information which was held lower down in the hierarchy. They waged guerrilla warfare, resisting the proposed changes in an attempt to 'save senior management from its own folly'. Whether resistance is based on reality or misunderstanding, it is intensified

if too little notice of the change is given. Failure to give good reasons for change will further intensify resistance. Intensified resistance is further exacerbated by careless or clumsy communication which reduces confidence in management and increases cynicism about managers' motives. None of these things helps when trying to overcome resistance to change.

Overcoming Resistance to Change: Force Field Analysis

Force field analysis was developed by Kurt Lewin.[12] Force field analysis enables managers to identify the forces that are likely to restrain a particular change (Figure 2.8).

In Figure 2.8 the size of the arrows reflects the strength of the forces they represent. Force field analysis is sometimes used with groups in order to structure an open discussion about what is blocking a change. Having identified the potential sources and levels of resistance, Lewin suggested that managers should act so as to reduce the restraining forces, rather than to intensify the forces driving the change. Lewin, like Newton, argued that to every

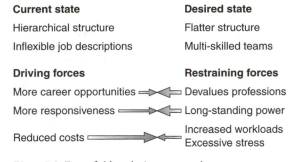

Current state	Desired state
Hierarchical structure	Flatter structure
Inflexible job descriptions	Multi-skilled teams

Driving forces	Restraining forces
More career opportunities	Devalues professions
More responsiveness	Long-standing power
Reduced costs	Increased workloads Excessive stress

Figure 2.8 Force field analysis: an example

action there was an equal and opposite reaction. Increasing the forces for change increases the forces resisting it.

FROM DEFIANCE THROUGH COMPLIANCE AND TO ALLIANCE

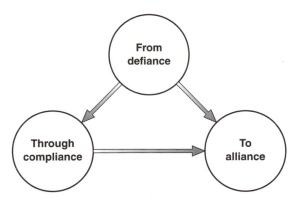

Figure 2.9 Overcoming resistance

Overcoming resistance was characterized by Russell-Jones[13] as a movement from defiance, through compliance to alliance (Figure 2.9).

CONVERSATIONAL APPROACHES TO OVERCOMING RESISTANCE

Central to the effectiveness of any approach to managing resistance is the quality of the relationships that managers develop with people in the organization. We look at conversational approaches to

developing closer relationships with people in Chapter 8 and again in our 'Carolyn' case study in Chapter 15. Other types of conversation are not uncommon (Figure 2.2).

1 Coercive Conversations

This involves threatening people, for example, with the loss of their jobs, limited career prospects, or transfer. Short-term contracts which are only renewed if employees comply are a form of coercion. We think that coercive approaches can inhibit change. As one senior civil servant put it:

> A three-year contract makes you feel less secure and more wary. It discourages you from putting all your cards on the table and it encourages staff to believe that they can sit tight and resist your ideas until your contract is over.[14]

Some three-year contracts are 'rolling contracts'. Rolling contracts are reviewed every year and are not rolled out for the third year when employees displease their managers. This makes managers reluctant to initiate change. They are nervous about provoking conflict in their departments, lest it reflect badly on the extension of their own contract. The Oughton Report[15] noted that short-term contracts tended to destabilize organizations. People on short-term contracts tend to look around for new posts well before their contracts expire. Coercion can also be detected in the monitoring of performance (Chapter 11). Measures of performance are set which can only be met if changes are implemented. If measures of performance are not met, then contracts may not be renewed.

2 Manipulative Conversations

Managers sometimes seek to overcome resistance through covert manipulation of key individuals. Buchanan and Boddy[16] insist that manipulative conversation must be part of the repertoire of the change agent. This approach is often used when key stakeholders have the power to block change. Key stakeholders can be compromised by conversations during which they are given privileged information in strict

Table 2.2 Eight conversational approaches to managing resistance

Approach	Situation	Advantage	Drawbacks
1 Coercion	Where the change is urgent and the change initiator is powerful	Speed	Risky when it creates enemies
2 Manipulation	Where all else fails	Quick and inexpensive	Causes resentment
3 Persuasion	Where the change initiator is in a strong position and people are easily persuaded	Quick and inexpensive	At later stages those who have been persuaded may claim they were pressurized
4 Negotiation	Where a group may lose out	Relatively easy	Can be expensive.
5 Delegation	Where there is support for the change and people know that they can benefit	Shares work and responsibility. Can empower and develop	Time consuming. Requires close monitoring. May depend on training or coaching
6 Facilitation	Where individuals have problems	Best method for dealing with problems of adjustment	Can be time consuming, expensive and still fail
7 Participation	Where information is missing or there is strong opposition	Gains commitment, and relevant information	Time consuming. Agreed changes may not be enough
8 Learning	Where new information or competence needed	Motivation, involvement, new ideas, commitment	Time consuming. Involves many people. (Can be costly)

confidence, or which implicate them in the design of the change. The object is to get the potential resister 'on board' without giving them a serious role in the decision-making. It is made to look like participation but it is not genuine. Appealing to the emotions, distorting information, exaggerating benefits and understating problems are all manipulation. In the short term, manipulative conversations are a cheap way of overcoming resistance. However, if a manager develops a reputation for being manipulative, this may generate resistance to any future changes with which the manager is associated. Manipulative conversations can destroy the trust on which persuasion, for example, may depend.

3 Persuasive Conversations

To understand how attitudes to change can themselves change, it is necessary to understand the process of persuasion. In the past experts such as scientists, doctors and lawyers were thought of as persuasive. By the turn of the century they were viewed with some scepticism and even suspicion in many western countries. Attractiveness also plays an important part in persuasion. Attractive people are used in advertising to persuade consumers to buy products. Ability is important too. Managers who are perceived to be capable, trustworthy and good at their job will have an edge when it comes to persuading others. Unconfident people with low self-esteem are easier to persuade than confident people with high self-esteem. According to Mackie and Worth,[17] individuals who hold extreme positions are more resistant to persuasion. People who are in a good mood are easier to persuade. Managers need to recognize that individuals differ in their susceptibility to persuasion. When managers are required to implement unpopular policies at work, they are

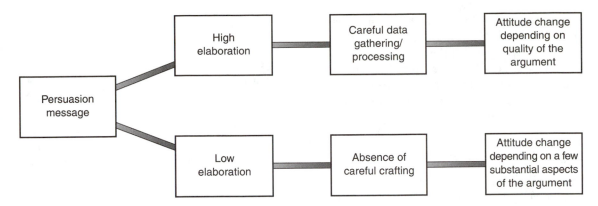

Figure 2.10 The elaboration model of persuasion

Source: After Campbell Quick (1996)

sometimes tempted to mention only positive aspects of the change. But their employees may be aware already of some of the negative aspects of the change. Managers will be more persuasive if they acknowledge these negatives, while still emphasizing the preponderance of good things that will result from the change.

Campbell Quick[18] offers a high/low elaboration model of persuasion (Figure 2.10). High elaboration is only necessary when the issue is highly relevant to individuals who are likely to think carefully about the issue. In this case carefully crafted arguments, often supported by statistics, will be more likely to prevail. When the issue is not seen as personally relevant, individuals will be persuaded more by the characteristics of the persuaders than the contents of their arguments. For example, by their expertise, trustworthiness, attractiveness or ability.

Persuasive Conversations: A Seven-Step Model

Step 1: Generalize

Before turning to the way a particular change might affect the person with whom you are having the conversation, talk generally around the way other people are accepting or even enjoying change – other departments, other organizations, people in the news, people generally accepting the need for change. Try to get nodding agreement to three or four general statements about the need for change and the need to find good ways to implement it.

Step 2: Probe

Ask open questions – 'why?' 'how?' and 'what about . . . ?' Confirm your understanding with closed questions requiring only 'yes' or 'no' replies. 'So, if I understand you correctly, you think that . . . is that so?' or 'So, you don't think that . . . ?' Listen actively. Give clear, non-verbal indications that you are listening attentively. Try not to interrupt. Try not to break any awkward silences by revealing your own opinions at this stage. You are trying to gather as much information as you can about the person you are hoping to persuade. What are their interests, motives, values? How could they benefit from the change you are going to propose? What benefits might they value, enjoy, or get excited about? Probe to find out what matters to them – what might get them to accept your idea?

Step 3: Introduce the benefits

When you have confirmed at least three ideas about the benefits which the proposed change might give the other person, introduce the proposed change as a way of giving the person these benefits which you believe they will value. If all these benefits of the change appear to be accepted, go directly to Step 6 and ask for acceptance. If the person doubts that the proposed change will deliver a particular benefit, go to Step 4 and deal with doubt. If the person raises an objection to the proposed change, go to Step 5 and handle the objection.

Step 4: Deal with doubt

Start by clarifying the exact nature of the doubt: 'So you are not yet sure that this change will result in Benefit A for you?' or 'You see that this change will give you B and C, but you are not yet sure that it will give you A?' Adjourn to gather evidence, statistics, case studies of other organizations, expert testimony, or to arrange for the other person to visit an installation, a supplier or a pilot study group. Meet again to summarize the benefits accepted in your previous conversation and present your evidence dealing with any remaining doubts. Conclude by restating the benefits that will flow from the change. 'And so you see that you will, in fact, get Benefit A'. Try always to maintain a confident presumption that the change will be accepted and that it will deliver the benefits that you have confirmed will be valued by the person you are persuading. Probe to confirm that their doubt is dispelled. If there are no objections, proceed to Step 6 and ask for acceptance.

Step 5: Handle objections

First clarify the objection: 'So you are worried that X will happen when the change is implemented?' If the objection is based on a mistaken impression, a false premise, or misinformation, correct the mistaken impression and conclude by summarizing all the benefits that will flow when the change is implemented, perhaps moving directly to Step 6 and asking for acceptance. If the objection is valid, do not pretend otherwise. As straightforwardly as possible show how, on balance, the benefits greatly outweigh the admitted drawbacks. If no doubt is expressed, go to Step 6 and ask for acceptance.

Step 6: Ask for acceptance

Strike a note of confidence that the proposal for change has been accepted and summarize the benefits which the other person has accepted will follow, when the proposed change is accepted. 'So, when X [the change] is in place, we have worked out that you will have A and gain B with the potential for C – What do you think we should do next?' 'What's the next step?' 'When would be a good time?' 'Are you free on Friday, or would Saturday be a better time?'

Step 7: Confirm the conversation

At the end of the conversation, record the time and place of the conversation. Write a brief summary of the main benefits that the other person agreed would flow, as a result of the change. Confirm what was agreed to be the next step, by whom and by when. Send an e-mail, or a hand-written note, or postcard. Photocopy onto A4 for easy filing. The seven steps of persuasion are summarized as an algorithm in Figure 2.11.

4 Negotiating Conversations

Negotiation is not persuasion. It is getting the best agreement that is possible when agreement must be reached. Failure to agree is a failure to negotiate successfully. When stakeholders with significant power (such as trades unions or politicians) resist change, negotiation is particularly appropriate. On the other hand, making it clear that some things are not negotiable can avoid having to make concessions which negate the desired effect of the changes. The following seven steps can be taken in steering a negotiating conversation.

Negotiating Conversations: A Seven-Step Model

Step 1: Decide your own maximum and minimum positions

The most you might hope for. The least you would accept.

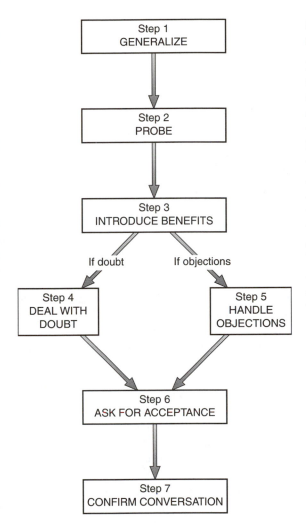

Figure 2.11 The seven steps of persuasive conversations

Step 2: Set up hypotheses

Speculate on your opposite number's minimum and maximum position.

Step 3: Compare 1 and 2 in order to assess common ground

If there is overlap, i.e. common ground, negotiation is possible. If there is no overlap, i.e. no common ground, then negotiation is not possible.

Step 4: Probe to determine their minimum and maximum positions

Probe by asking questions, preferably 'open' rather than 'closed' questions. For example, 'What do you mean exactly when you say you won't . . . ?' or 'How do you come to that conclusion?' Watch for non-verbal, as well as verbal, responses: eye movements, body positions, tone of voice. Try to determine what they convey (Chapter 8). If negotiating teams are involved, adjourn frequently to compare notes with members of your team. During this step you are trying to gain as much information as possible about the other person's 'wish list', while revealing as little as possible about your own. Resist the temptation to break awkward silences. Better to adjourn and think of more questions to ask. If you cannot think of another question to ask, summarize their position. Take notes, or have a trusted colleague do so. Use note-taking to give yourself time to structure your thinking. If you need more time, adjourn. Hurrying to save minutes in a negotiation can lose days or weeks, if negotiations break down.

Step 5: Test your hypotheses

Offer hypothetical concessions in your position in return for concessions that you believe lie within your opposite number's range of negotiation. For example, 'If we were by any chance able to find a way to get our team to agree to Y, might your team agree to X?' X and Y could be such things as times, places, schedules, guarantees, undertakings, conditions, options, training, support or contingencies. Try to keep your mind open to what might be negotiable. Think creatively about what they might want, or need, even before they do, but do not offer it unless you need to trade in order to secure agreement. Do not make unilateral concessions. 'I'm sure we can help, is there anything else that you want to mention? Nothing at all?' Adjourn.

Step 6: Summarize areas for a tentative agreement

When, and only when, you think you have identified things which you and your opposite number are

Table 2.3 Making sense of what you hear

Hearing . . .	May mean . . .
'I can't say I'm happy about . . .'	'I agree, but there's just one more thing'
'That's way beyond our remit'	'That's quite acceptable, provided you make it clear what we will get out of it'
'I am prepared to discuss that'	'We can discuss that, but not now'
'I never negotiate on costs'	'But if you insist, you start'
'It's not our normal practice to . . .'	'But I will make an exception if pushed'
'I do not have any authority to . . .'	'But I could get it if I needed to'
'We are not set up to . . .'	'You'll owe me one if I agree to do it'

willing to give and take, offer a tentative verbal summary of what appears to be a basis for agreement. This should be reiterated, clarified and repeated – always verbally – before anything is committed to paper. Build a sense of expectant inevitability that agreement will be good for everyone – 'OK', 'good', 'right', 'that'll work', 'that's fair', 'that's a good idea', 'good suggestion', 'OK, let's do that'. During this stage you may need to use your eyes as well as your ears to 'make sense' of what you hear. (Table 2.3).

Do not introduce new issues. Adjourn to discuss with colleagues what they heard, as opposed to what was said. Be sure that you really understand what was really meant.

Step 7: Accept agreement

Prepare a written summary of what has been agreed verbally. If the negotiation has been carried out skilfully, signing up should be a formality. Do not introduce new issues or demands. In general, during negotiation conversations beware of allowing your objectives to drift, so as to become more demanding. Many a negotiation has tragically broken down at the end over points that would have been readily accepted at the beginning – what a waste.

5 Delegating Conversations

Managers who think that they have to implement every change themselves are likely to be ineffective as change agents. One way of getting others to implement changes and to overcome resistance to change is through delegation. Managers delegate when they deliberately choose to give subordinates authority to carry out work which the managers could do themselves. Delegation requires careful thought about responsibility, authority and accountability:

- **Responsibility** for tasks.
- **Authority** that gives the power to make decisions and to take necessary actions.
- **Accountability** for decisions taken and for the resources used in achieving the tasks.

The authority needs to be commensurate with the responsibility. For example, if someone is given responsibility for improving the new appraisal system but is not given the authority to change existing practices, then the delegated task is unlikely to be accomplished. Some managers are reluctant to delegate because they fear that the task will not be carried out well and that ultimately they will be held accountable for poor performance. Alternatively, some managers fear that the task will be carried out too well and that this will lead to a subordinate being favoured in a promotion. Delegation can be experienced as feeling out of control. This can be difficult for managers who have been attracted to management because they like to feel in control. Finally, some managers find it hard to delegate tasks which they enjoy. Staff quickly resent the feeling that they are only given the 'dirty work' to do. Despite these difficulties, there are good reasons for delegation. Delegation enables managers to focus on the jobs that require their experience or position. Good delegation empowers employees. It can lead to improved morale and improved performance (Chapter 11). Delegation can be a source of training and personal development (Chapter 14). It can enable employees to demonstrate that they are ready for promotion. Managers may have more time for their own work and at the same time they can see their subordinates develop. Managers need to ask:

- What tasks could a subordinate perform?
- How could performance be monitored?
- What opportunities are there for learning?

Figure 2.12 summarizes a conversational approach to delegation.

Where individuals are reluctant to accept additional responsibility, the need for some sort of facilitative conversation may be required.

6 Facilitative Conversations

This approach is most helpful when individuals resist change because they are fearful or over-anxious. By offering support in the form of listening, training and more relaxed procedures, resistance to change can often be overcome. Workplace counsellors can be employed. Sometimes the work is carried out under contract by independent counsellors or by an outside organization. They provide support for staff experiencing difficulties with new structures, or suffering from 'change fatigue' or 'burn out'. This approach can be costly, but so too can be the damages awarded by courts and tribunals to staff deemed to have suffered stress as a result of lack of due care by employers (Chapter 8). If the time, money and patience required to offer qualified counselling support are not forthcoming, it should not be offered. Poor counselling can do harm. Stress generated by change is exacerbated for some individuals when they feel 'helpless' i.e. at the mercy of events that they cannot

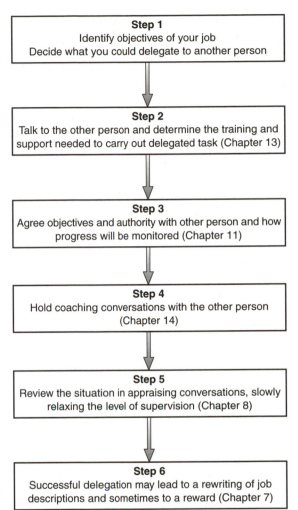

Figure 2.12 A conversational approach to delegation

control. Sometimes this is eased when they feel they are participating in the change process.

7 Participative Conversations

Buchanan and Boddy[19] suggested that if you asked any management group what they regard as the preconditions for effective change in organizations, the terms involvement, ownership, communication, commitment, trust and participation invariably emerge. Pettigrew[20] has referred to this approach as the 'truth, trust, love and collaboration' approach to organizational change. This approach has a long pedigree stretching back to the classic studies of Coch and French[21] in the 1940s. They demonstrated how resistance to change at a pyjama manufacturers was reduced by involving and consulting staff. Their work started a movement towards participative management that had several incarnations. These included Hertzberg's[22] job enrichment in the 1960s and 1970s and quality circles in the 1980s (Chapter 5). In the 1990s Peters and Watermann[23] and Kanter[24] added the concept of self-managing teams and employee empowerment (Chapters 6 and 7). Clearly, the participative movement has been influential. The benefits are less clear. The limitations of participative processes, in both publicly and privately owned organizations, are well documented. Child[25] pointed out that participation may be inappropriate when, for example, there is widespread agreement, or when management is in a position to implement the change without much resistance. In such cases, consultation wastes time. When there is little chance of agreement about change, the use of consultation may again be inappropriate. Consensus may only be possible if the change is diluted to the point where it no longer yields the benefits originally sought. The disruptive costs of proposing change are hard enough to justify in the first place, without defeating their object. Where resistance is implacable, inviting participation seriously risks derailing the whole process. Following studies made in America, Child concluded that it is unrealistic to hope for consensus in large bureaucracies.[26] Australian researchers Dunphy and Stace[27] found that participation was irrelevant where choices were limited. Where rapid change was necessary, they reported that directive and coercive approaches had proved more effective.

The notion that people should be involved in changes that affect their lives reflects western political, religious and social values, such as freedom of choice and individual liberty. Such values are not universal. Change raises issues that challenge personal values and ethical standards. Change impacts directly on people's lives, livelihoods and well-being. The participative approach, with its underlying logic of establishing ownership of change, prioritizes the need to be sensitive to different stakeholders (Chapter 4). People may resist change that is in their best interests – especially if they do not understand it. They may resist it simply because they dislike being told what to do. They may resist it because they dislike not feeling in control of their lives. This feeling is highly correlated with stress-related illnesses (Chapter 8). Involving people in the process of change can help to reduce the build-up of stress in some individuals, but may exacerbate it in others. Using speedy and appropriate communication processes (Chapter 12) may help to avoid resistance building up in the first place and perhaps enable change to be viewed as a 'learning experience'.

8 Learning Conversations

In Chapter 13 we discuss the role of learning conversations not only as a means of learning, but also as a means of motivating people and of improving organizational performance. Learning is also an important part of change. Learning bridges the gap between 'managing change and changing managers' (Chapter 14). Some organizations use learning workshops to help bring changes about. When the electricity industry in the UK was being privatized, employees had workshops on politics, economics and technology, to help them understand why the electricity industry needed to change. When managing quality, learning why something is not working well, and then taking action to improve it, automatically generates change. For effective managers, change is the normal outcome of learning and learning is the normal consequence of change. Ideally, all change should be a learning experience. As well as developing new understanding, learning from change may enable employees to acquire new and transferable skills which they will be able to use to implement other changes. By identifying the skills that employees need in order to perform effectively in changing situations, managers can reduce resistance to new ways of working. During the 1990s, the notion of developing 'learning organizations' as a means of overcoming resistance to change was widely canvassed. However, as Pedler[28] and his colleagues acknowledge, creating such an organization is easier said than done. We return to this in Chapter 13.

Having looked at the nature of change, who resists it, why it is resisted, what form that resistance can take and how that resistance might be managed, we turn, in Chapter 3, to the manager's role in implementing the change. But first, some final thoughts on changing ideas about change.

FINAL THOUGHTS: CHANGING IDEAS ABOUT CHANGE

Changing ideas about change implies changing the way people think about the world. We try to avoid the idea that there is *one* right way to think about the world. Our implicit assumption has been that there may be as many views of the world as there are individuals viewing it. Some might describe our assumption as postmodernist – no one best way, only different ideas about how best to make sense of a changing world. We want to explore two of these ideas. These two ideas may help to explain why some managers prefer prescriptive rational approaches to implementing changes and why other managers prefer emergent experimental approaches to implementing changes. Both ideas began their journey in Greece, before the birth of Socrates. A question that challenged the minds of philosophers then was 'What is real and how do we know?' We began this chapter with a quotation from Heraclitus. He taught that reality is in a constant state of flux: 'You cannot step into the same river twice'. When we step into the river for a second time, it is different as a result of our having stepped into it before.

While Heraclitus was proposing that reality was in a permanent state of flux, another group of philosophers was saying the opposite. They argued that reality was characterized by permanence, tangibility and unity. One proponent of this way of thinking was Parmenides. His way of viewing the world came to dominate western thought. It still underpins much that is written about organizations and how they should be managed. It is characterized by:

- An assumption that the world is stable, i.e. that managers can stand back and analyse organizations because the organisations will not change while the managers analyse them.
- Credence is given to cause and effect.
- Credence is given to what we can see and measure – if you can't count it, it doesn't count!

Parmenidian thinking was sometimes referred to as 'atomistic' thinking. It underpinned physical science until the early part of this century. The mind was viewed as a mirror which could reflect outside reality. The greatest minds were highly polished mirrors which could provide the most accurate reflections of reality. During the twentieth century, a number of developments led to doubts about this way of sensing and making sense of the world. Heisenberg and Niels Bohr challenged simple notions of causality. Bohr claimed that we could not observe reality without changing it in some way, since any observation would necessarily involve an interaction with the observer.[29] We think that these ideas undermine many assumptions that managers commonly make about the extent to which they can observe and analyse their organizations. The questions managers ask and the ways in which they ask them will change the very things they seek to know. Charles Handy[30] sided with Heisenberg and Bohr. An important step in Handy's own journey towards 'uncertainty' was his rejection of the idea that everything could be understood, predicted and managed:

> [T]he success stories of yesterday may have little relevance to the problems of tomorrow. They might even be damaging. The world at every level has to some extent to be reinvented. Certainty is out and experiment is in.[31]

According to Handy, we are coming closer to the world of Heraclitus who gave primacy to the continuous changing and becoming of things, rather than to the static, causal world of Parmenides. Rational thinking alone tends to oversimplify the issues that managers face when trying to implement change. Theories about organizational change may need to start by assuming that there is no such thing as a real organization.[32] An organization might be viewed as a fictional construct, built up in the minds of at least three groups: people who work in the organization; people who belong to the society in which the organization operates; and managers who seek to be well paid for managing the organization. It is as though in each person's head there is a cinema projector. Out of their eyes they project on to the screen of their outer world an image that is based on their inner world thinking about outer world events. When many such images are projected by different people on to the same outer world screen and they roughly coincide, then some sort of consensual picture of reality can emerge. If there is little coincidence amongst the projected images, then the collective picture of the organization is fuzzy and unfocused. This might account for the difficulties of managing change within it.

Theories about the social changes that drive organizational change need to be able to explain the occurrence of sudden dislocations – quantum leaps – like the dramatic changes that occurred in Eastern Europe, China, Kosovo and Southeast Asia between 1980 and the year 2000. The ongoing probability that such disruptive events will continue to occur creates uncertainty. Our conversational approach to taking action in the world (Figure 2.13) seeks to emphasize the importance of linking inner world thinking to the actions which can be taken in the outer world in order to implement changes.

In our model (Figure 2.13) the taking of action in the outer world is part of the process of thinking more deeply about the outer world and the options for changing it. The act of trying to change the outer world is part of the thinking needed to deepen our understanding of it.[33] Our emerging thoughts about possible changes can be tested through conversations of different types, with the people in the outer world who are potential beneficiaries, or victims, of our proposed changes. When we hold conversations about the implementation phase of change, we seek to understand the other person's unspoken beliefs, implicit values and taken-for-granted practices. The thinking skills needed to formulate changes are

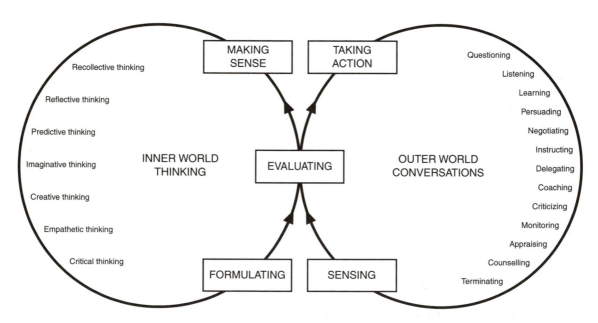

Figure 2.13 A conversational approach to taking action in the world

inseparable from the social skills needed to implement them. By holding conversations, people can not only change their outer worlds, they can also change their own thinking and when their 'thinking changes, they change'.[34] In other words, interpersonal outer world change is followed by intrapersonal inner world change. This can be intensified through the practice of certain thinking skills.[35] These ideas on personal change resonate with a different way of viewing intelligence[36] which we develop in Chapters 13 and 14.

In this book we invite readers to try things out for themselves. We invite readers to look beyond simplification and to reject any 'quick fix' techniques which appear to distort their problems to fit our proposed solutions. Many problems are far from simple. Sometimes they can be solved by using reason and logic, but managers should be aware of the ambiguity, inconsistency and incompleteness of the data on which their reasoning is based. Managers can learn to use their intuition, but in a disciplined way. Managers can learn to live with the paradox that organizational life is a river into which they can never step twice.

responsible for implementing major organizational change in a privatized agency.

- We discovered that mechanistically structured public services resist change.
- We have learned who might resist change; why they might resist change; what forms their resistance might take; and how this resistance might be reduced.
- We have evaluated conversational ways in which resistance might be reduced, namely coercion, manipulation, persuasion, negotiation, delegation, facilitation, participation and learning.
- In our Final Thoughts, we explored the way our views on change are intimately related to the way we view the relationship between our inner and outer worlds.

SUMMARY

- We learned that we need to distinguish between emergent, transitional, incremental and transformational change. Each change poses different levels of difficulty.
- We learned that there are many theories that could be used to explain the nature of change. These theories are derived from disciplines such as mathematics, economics, biology, psychology, politics and sociology. Not all point to change being inevitable or inevitably revisited.
- Some theories help us to understand why change is sometimes resisted.
- We have listened to the difficulties facing a former senior civil servant, now CEO,

THINKING AND LEARNING ACTIVITIES

Activity 1 Self-assessment

1 Distinguish between emergent, transitional, incremental and transformational change.
2 What difficulties might be posed by each of these types of changes?
3 How might a mathematician view change? How could mathematical models of change be used?
4 How might an economist view change? What are the implications of the economist's view?
5 What might be learned by viewing an organization as though it were a biological system?
6 How might a psychologist view change? How could a manager make use of these ideas?
7 How might a sociologist view change? How could a manager use the sociologist's ideas?

8 If you viewed an organization as an arena in which power games were played, what insights would that give you into changes in any organization with which you are familiar?

9 Which theories help to explain resistance to change?

10 Who, in an organization, is most likely to resist change and why?

11 What forms can resistance take?

12 Briefly describe eight conversational ways to overcome resistance.

Activity 2 Individual or Paired Learning: Recollective Thinking

Remembering change

Consider a time when you went through a significant change in your life; something that was important to you and about which you can now think without upset.

- What did you handle well and why was this?
- What did you find difficult? Why was this?

Activity 3 Individual Learning: Reflective Thinking

Evaluating change

Refer back to the personal change that you considered in the previous activity.

- Can any of the theories of change or resistance help you to explain any reactions to that change?
- Which theory best explains what you experienced?
- Explain why you have come to this conclusion.

Activity 4 Individual or Paired Learning: Reflective Thinking

Predicting resistance

Revisit our model 'Predicting Resistance to Change' (Figure 2.6). Think back over your experience of changes in organizations with which you are familiar (home, school, religious, college, sports club or work organization). Find four examples, one to illustrate each quadrant. Explain why you think each example is appropriately categorized.

Activity 5 Individual, Paired or Group Learning: Creative Thinking

Do it for a change

The task is to design an A4 poster containing 10 suggestions that you think would help managers to reduce resistance to change. You can give it a new title. Start by working alone and making notes and sketches. Find a partner, compare notes. Each pair finds another pair and organizes to produce a final design and display it at an agreed time in an agreed place.

Activity 6 Individual or Paired Learning: Predictive Thinking

Force field analysis

Working alone or with a partner, think of an organization with which you are familiar. Imagine you were the chief executive officer. Think of a change you would like to introduce in the organization. Construct a force field analysis of the likely driving forces and the restraining forces. Use the text to help you. Brainstorm some ideas for reducing each restraint.

Activity 7 Individual Learning: Visual and Creative Thinking

Breaking the mould

Draw a square. Place one dot or blob at each corner of the square and one in the centre of each side. Finally place a dot or blob exactly in the middle of the square.

You should have nine dots or blobs on your paper. Try to connect the nine dots with four straight lines without lifting your pen off the paper and without going through the same dot or blob more than once. What are you assuming about this activity? When you have solved the problem, think about what you had to do in order to solve it. You probably had to change the way that you assumed that you were supposed to look at the problem? Now that you have changed your dominating assumption – your paradigm – you can join the dots or blobs with only three lines, or only two, or, in fact, with only one!

Activity 8 Individual or Paired Learning: Unconscious Thinking

Psychological contracts

Re-read the section on psychological contracts. Working alone, write down what you think might be the main points of your psychological contract with your employer or your institute of education. Compare notes with someone else.

Activity 9 Paired or Group Learning: Visual and Analytic Thinking

Mapping causation

In the centre of a large piece of paper write a concrete description of a situation that you would like to change. Draw a balloon or bubble around it. Brainstorm ideas for the things that are the direct cause of the problem situation. Put each in separate balloons, arranging them in an inner ring around the central balloon. Do not spend time detailing any of the suggested causes. Aim for at least five. Stop at 12. Take 5–10 minutes only.

Visit each inner ring cause in turn and write down what you think are the main causes of each of the inner ring causes. Complete each one at a time, before moving systematically to the next inner ring cause. Repeat until the root causes of the problem have been identified. For the problem 'No Community Spirit' a causation map might look like Figure 2.14.

Activity 10 Paired or Group Learning: Predictive Thinking

Mapping consequence

Explore the consequences (*not* the causes this time) of something you would like to change, e.g. 'increasing reliance on cars'. Proceed as in Activity 10, creating an inner ring of consequences in balloons arranged around the thing you would like to change. As before, work outwards until you have exhausted all the consequences you can think of. A completed map of consequences can provide arguments in favour of your proposed change and reveal sometimes unlikely allies to help you achieve it. The process of producing maps, e.g. groups working on the floor around a large sheet, can help to get a new group of people to know each other. If individuals make a suggestion that is not a direct consequence of the particular balloon being considered, write it down on a separate sheet and make it clear that you will come back to it and try to fit it in later. Coloured pens or chalks can be used to divide up the overall map for further thought and action planning, by people working on their own, or in pairs. A consequence map of 'increasing reliance on cars' is shown in Figure 2.15.

Activity 11 Group Work: Empathetic Thinking

Me and my shadow

One person will persuade another to change or make a particular change. During their conversation each person will be partnered with a 'shadow' who will place his or her hand on the partner's shoulder. The shadow watches the body language and breathing and listens to the tone and speed and volume of the dialogue and occasionally adds audibly to what their partner is saying, sentences

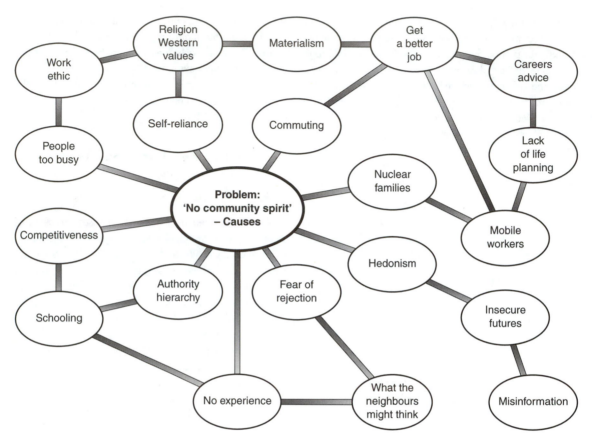

Figure 2.14 Drawing a causation map

like 'and I am also thinking that...' and 'I am feeling...' The shadow tries not to disturb the flow of the dialogue which should proceed as though the shadow were not there. Ten minutes is long enough. The purpose is to practise empathizing with other people and to reveal the opinions and feeling that often underlie resistance to change. Choose another topic and reverse roles with your shadow. The exercise is very revealing.

Activity 12 Individual or Paired Learning: Reflective Thinking

Redesigning a management course

Members of a university Management Department were called together by the Head of Department as a con-

sequence of a conversation with a disgruntled first-year, part-time MBA student. The conversation took place at 9.30 pm, after the tired student had been at work all day before attending a three-hour evening seminar. Further investigation revealed that the Managing Change Module, which has been designed to integrate the work done on the finance, marketing and operations modules, was experienced by the students as a needless repetition of material they had already covered. It was a waste of their precious time. The MBA course team considered their options:

● Carry on with the existing design and hope that students would eventually accept its usefulness
● Scrap the dedicated change management module and introduce change management as a 'theme' in the other modules

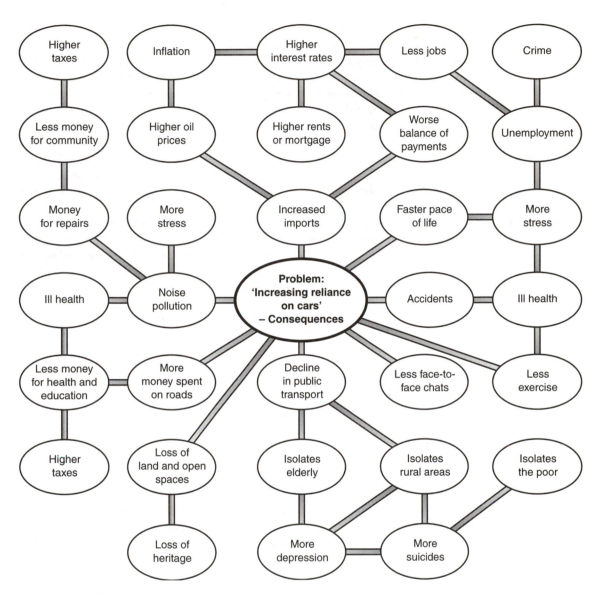

Figure 2.15 Drawing a consequence map

- Make attendance optional
- Offer it as an optional revision weekend
- Make the change management module the vehicle for the whole of the first year teaching, introducing finance, marketing and operations as needed.

The latter would avoid disintegrating management into discrete areas that then had to be integrated again. This was appealing. The team had always believed that management was holistic and had only accepted subject-based teaching in the first case because subject colleagues were resistant to the idea of team teaching. Reducing duplication could free up teaching time for more skill development and thus address another source of student dissatisfaction. The Head of Department was convinced. Course development away-days were timetabled for staff. Money was offered to fund an outdoor management residential and an international exchange visit if teaching costs could be reduced as a result of the redesign. The staff away-day was a great success. The walls were festooned with causation maps, consequence maps, task analysis lists and action plans. Enthusiasts were designated to follow up.

Consider the Ten Commandments of Change in Box 2.7. To what extent did this management department practise what these Ten Commandments preached? Under each commandment, record what you recall from reading this chapter.

Box 2.7

THE TEN COMMANDMENTS

1 Change must be fun
2 Change is everywhere
3 Change is never-ending
4 Change is about success
5 There is no one best way
6 Change is only about people
7 Change must start from the top
8 Change needs skilled change agents
9 Change must be 'owned' by those affected
10 Change must involve groups of people

Activity 13 Paired Learning: Empathetic and Predictive Thinking

Case Study – casualties of change

Jane, Libby, Bill, Paul and Jacqueline were all affected by different types of change in their places of work.

Read each of their mini case studies and then think empathetically about what their initial reactions to the change might have been. In particular, consider what they might have felt and thought while the change was going on. How might they have resisted the change, if at all? Then think predictively about their likely reactions to change. What do you think were the eventual outcomes of their responses to the change? Complete the matrix (Figure 2.16) and discuss your conclusions.

Jane joined her company 20 years ago straight from school at the age of 16. She has worked her way up to become head of the communications pool. She has a staff of 36, including three supervisors who are all family friends in the small town where they all live. The communications pool is to be disbanded. She has been told that her salary will be protected and that she is certain to be found a job to do.

Libby, aged 29, had been the personal secretary to the Estates Director for eight years, when he was summarily dismissed. He left the same day. Little was said about the reasons for his dismissal. She felt her boss had been treated unfairly. He was not replaced. For the last few months she has been asked to cover for people on holiday or off sick in almost every department.

Bill has worked his way up to section head in the drawing office by going to night classes. Each year he passed more exams towards membership of the Institute of Draughtsmen. The year he became a full member of the Institute, the head of the department left. The head's job was advertised. Bill was annoyed that it had gone out to advert because everyone agreed that he was the natural successor, and deservedly so. After the selection interviews, he was astonished when they gave the job to an outsider – a graduate engineer, ten years younger than Bill. The new graduate manager was obsessed with supervisory control and paper work.

Jacqueline ran the library and resource centre for the whole of the departmental headquarters. She cut out, indexed and filed articles on anything that might come in handy for anyone who worked there. She knew from long experience what information she was likely to be asked for at short notice. She prided herself on never being caught out. She liked working on her own, in her

Name	Thinking empathetically		Thinking predictively	
	Likely thoughts and feelings	Likely forms of resistance	Likely reactions	Likely outcomes
Jane				
Libby				
Bill				
Jacqueline				
Paul				

Figure 2.16 Empathetic and predictive thinking matrix

own little library, in her own way. When they divided the region into six 'self-managed' area units, some of them had their own library, or a research centre. They said she could choose which unit she wanted to work in. They were all quite a distance away from the city centre where she lived. They said she could reclaim her travel expenses for two years and relocation expenses if she preferred to move. They were not sure what she would do. She would need to define her own role.

Paul, aged 38, was a senior computer programmer and systems designer. Originally an accounts technician, Paul installed his organization's first mainframe computer. The new technology that is now being introduced is unfamiliar to him, but it is very familiar to his junior staff. The consultants handling the installation will provide contract staff for at least the first two years.

Activity 14 Individual Learning Review: Reflective Thinking

Inner world thinking

What inner world thinking skills can you identify in the manager's work described in this chapter? Have any of the thinking skills you have identified emerged for the first time in this chapter? If so, add them to your accumulating model of the kinds of thinking skills that you

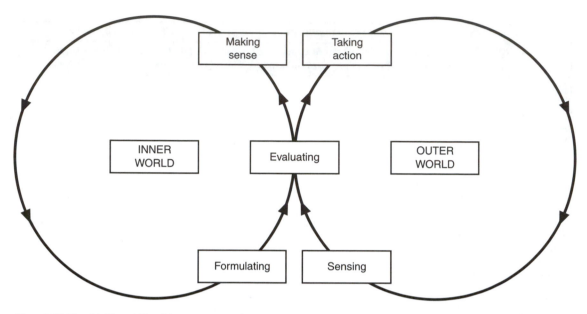

Figure 2.17 The thinking skills of the conversational manager

consider to be useful to managers of public services (Figure 2.17). What things could you do to develop any of the thinking skills that you have just added to your model? What would be the first step?

Outer world conversations

What outer world conversational skills can you identify in the manager's work described in this chapter? Have any of the types of conversational skills you have identified emerged for the first time? If so, add them to your accumulating model of the kinds of conversational skills you think are useful to managers of public services.

What things could you do to develop any of the conversational skills which you have just added to your model? What would be the first step?

Activity 15 Individual Learning: Metacognitive Thinking

Metacognition

Look back through the thinking and learning activities you have been asked to carry out in this chapter. What

thinking skills were involved in each of these activities? For each type of thinking, write down how you were learning when you were learning to think in each of the different ways.

NOTES

1 Dawkins, R. (1997) *The Selfish Gene.* Macmillan.
2 Checkland, P. (1981) *Systems Thinking and Systems Practice.* John Wiley & Sons.
3 Jung, C. (1953) *The Integration of Personality.* Farrah & Ruckhart.
4 Bowlby, J. (1981) *Attachment, Separation and Loss*, vols I, II and III. Penguin.
5 Lewin, K. (1951) *Force Field Analysis.* Harper & Row.
6 Brookes, I. and Bates, P. (1994) 'The Problems of Effecting Change within the British Civil Service: a Cultural Perspective'. *British Journal of Management*, vol. 5, no. 3, pp. 177–90.
7 McConkey, D. D. (1993) 'Organisation Development in the Public Sector' in Cummings, T. and Worley, C. G. (eds) *Organisation Development and Change.* 5th edn. West Publishing Co., pp. 634–42.
8 Lawton, A. and Rose, A. (1999) *Public Services, Management.* FT/Prentice Hall, p. 293.
9 McConkey, op. cit.
10 Buchanan, D. and Boddy, D. (1993) *The Expertise of the Change Agent. Public Performance and Backstage Activity.* Prentice Hall.
11 Hussey, D. E. (1995) *Organisational Change.* Kogan Page, p. 25.

12 Lewin, op. cit.

13 Russell-Jones, N. (1995) *Management Pocket Book*. Alresford Press.

14 HMSO (1986) *Career Progression in the Civil Service* [The Oughton Report].

15 Ibid.

16 Buchanan and Boddy, op. cit.

17 Mackie, D. M. and Worth, L. T. (1989) 'Processing Deficits and the Mediation of Positive Affect in Persuasion'. *Journal of Personality and Social Psychology*, no. 57, pp. 27–40.

18 Campbell Quick, J. (1996) *Organisation Behaviour. The Essentials*. West Publishing Company.

19 Buchanan and Boddy, op. cit., p. 4.

20 Pettigrew, A. (ed.) (1987) *The Management of Strategic Change*. Basil Blackwell.

21 Coch, L. and French, J. R. P. (1948) 'Overcoming Resistance to Change'. *Human Relations*, vol. 1, pp. 512–32.

22 Hertzberg, F. (1966) *Work and the Nature of Man*. Staples Press.

23 Peters, T. and Watermann, H. (1982) *In Search of Excellence. Lessons from America's Best Run Companies*. Harper & Row.

24 Kanter, R. M. (1983) *The Change Masters*. Allen & Unwin.

25 Child, L. (1994) *Organizations – A Guide to Problems and Practice*. Harper & Row.

26 Ibid.

27 Dunphy, D. C. and Stace, D. A. (1990) *Under New Management. Australian Organisations in Transition*. McGraw-Hill. Sydney.

28 Pedler, M., Burgoyne, J. and Boydell, T. (1986) *The Learning Company. A Strategy for Sustainable Development*. McGraw-Hill.

29 Plotnitsky, A. (1994) *Complementarity: Anti-epistemology after Bohr and Derrida*. Durham University Press, pp. 66–7.

30 Handy, C. (1995) *Beyond Certainty: The Changing Worlds of Organisations*. Hutchinson, p. 16.

31 Ibid.

32 Giddens, A. (1984) *The Constitution of Society: Outline of the Theory of Structuration Polity*. Polity.

33 Argyris, C. and Schon, D. (1974) *Theory in Practice: Increasing Professional Effectiveness*. Jossey-Bass.

34 Antonio de Mello, S. J. (1985) *The Sadhanna – A Way to Truth*. Diaz Del Rio.

35 Brotherton, C. (1990) *New Development in Adult Cognition*. Nottingham University Department of Adult Education.

36 Egestrom, Y. (1989) *Developing Thinking in the Workplace – Towards a Redefinition of Expertise*. University of California: Centre for Human Information Processing.

3

MANAGING STRATEGY AND CHANGE IN PUBLIC SERVICES

If you want to make enemies, change something, because doing things differently involves thinking.

(Woodrow Wilson)

LEARNING OUTCOMES

This chapter will enable the reader to:

- Consider the role of strategic management in identifying the need for strategic changes in public services.
- Consider the advantages and disadvantages of prescriptive and emergent approaches to managing strategic changes.
- Understand how a conversational approach can be used to 'craft' the integration of prescriptive and emergent approaches to identifying and defining the need for operational changes.
- Understand how to use project management to implement operational changes.
- Consider how to manage the emotions released during the process of change.
- Understand what is meant by the culture of an organization.
- Consider how managers might help to change the culture of an organization.
- Understand the role of symbolic literacy in managing cultural change.

INTRODUCTION

In Chapter 2 we looked at the way that change can be resisted – who resists, why they resist and how they resist change. Anticipating and managing resistance is important preparation for the implementation of change and it is to this that we now turn. Our conversation in the previous chapter with David Maclaren, the Civil Service CEO, gave us some insights into what the implementation of change looks like and feels like from the top – from the strategic apex of a large, privately owned, public service organization. In this chapter we will explore what is meant by strategy and what is involved in implementing strategy. The ability to put yourself in the place of the people affected by change is called empathy. The ability to empathize with the boss is as important as the ability to empathize with other people affected by change. We will look at the rise of strategic management and consider the benefits it held out and the problems it has brought to public services. We will describe a conversational approach to strategic change and a project management approach to operational change. We consider the feasibility and the desirability of changing the culture of public service organizations. Many approaches involve analysis, design, planning and action. Their general form is shown in Table 3.1. The sequence of tasks described in Table 3.1 is common to most rational approaches to implementing change. The structure of the chapter is shown in Figure 3.1.

Table 3.1 Implementing change: task analysis and methods used

Aspects	Purpose	Jobs	Methods	Outputs
Analyse	Understand Organization Culture	Temples Analysis Values audit 10 M audit	Reports Workshops One-to-one conversations	Rich picture Stakeholders Likely resistance
Design	Agree vision Recruit help	Consult Iterate Refine Fine tune	Workshops Presentations Consultations	Vision Team support
Plan	Details of who will do what, when and how	Specify tasks times resources contingencies	Research Gantt charts PERT	Documents IT control Agreed budgets
Implement	Install change	Communicate Role out Monitor Modify plan	Meetings Conversations Projects Communication	Physical changes Improved performance Durable change

DEFINING STRATEGY

There is no universally acknowledged definition of strategy.[1] Clearly it is concerned with identifying the aim of an organization and the specific actions that need to be taken in order to realize it. Johnson and Scholes[2] think that strategy is that which describes how an organization will match its resources to its environment so as to meet the expectations of its stakeholders (see Box 3.1).

The aim of a strategy is its ultimate purpose. Strategic aims are usually stated in one or two sentences. Strategic aims are usually stated in positive terms – as something which is desired. For example: 'The village shall be a safe and mutually supportive place in which to bring up children.' Strategic goals are realistically achievable steps towards those strategic aims. For example: 'We will have a self-sustaining community centre.' Strategic goals are achieved by setting and achieving tactical objectives. For example: 'We will apply for planning permission for a community centre in December.' The implementation of tactical objectives takes a relatively short time. They require a few well-defined actions – tactics – for which the resources already exist. For

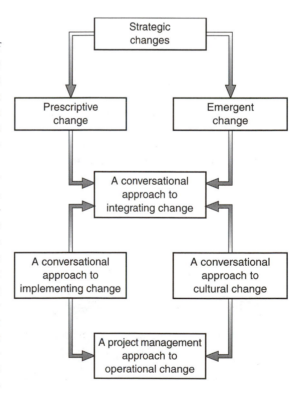

Figure 3.1 A conversational approach to change

Box 3.1

DEFINING STRATEGIC CHANGE

Strategic Analysis

Identifying the technological, economic, market, political, legal, ethical and social changes that impact on the organization and assessing the opportunities and threats they pose.

Strategic Formulation

Identifying, selecting and evaluating strategic options, taking into account their desirability to stakeholders and the feasibility and risk of implementing them.

Strategic Implementation

Planning and allocating resources, considering organizational design and structure, defining operational roles and procedures and managing change.

(*Source*: Horne and Wootton 1997)[3]

---

example: 'We will talk to the planning department next Tuesday.' A plan that connects aims, goals, objectives and tactics is called a strategic plan. It is the means by which the actions of people and the deployment of resources can be co-ordinated (Figure 3.2).

The tactics chosen (the means) must be in harmony with the spirit and intention of the aims (the ends). When the means contradict the ends, the ends are destroyed. Thinking about change in this way is called strategic thinking. It involves connecting and recombining many of the basic thinking skills that will be developed in the thinking and learning activities in this book. Strategy has been much written about and much mystified. It is demystified in this book and also in *Strategic Thinking* by Wootton and Horne (2001 Kogan Page).

The Strategic Paradigm

Paradigms are collections of basic assumptions. Sometimes these basic assumptions are made clear and explicit. For example, the notion of strategic management carries with it assumptions about the rights and powers of managers; views on how organizations should be structured and for whose benefit; views on what sort of people should be employed and how decisions should be taken. Such assumptions affect the meaning that people give to what they hear and see; their view about what is acceptable around here and the degree of importance that they attach to rules and procedures. When we look later at cultural changes, we shall see that a very particular approach to managing change is needed when it involves a 'paradigm shift'. Since a 'paradigm shift' involves changing the way people think, i.e. changing the mindset of the ways of thinking that they ordinarily employ, it is not surprising that it is difficult. The Thinking and Learning Activities in this book help to raise awareness of the kinds of

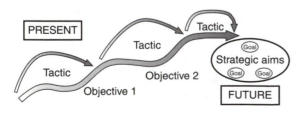

Figure 3.2 Visualizing strategy

thinking skills that are involved. There is further information in *Thinking Skills for Managers* by Horne and Wootton.[4]

The Origins of Strategic Management

People retiring from military service imported the notion of strategy into the business and management community. It brought with it a paradigm that esteemed logistics and planning. This was a 'paradigm clash' with the opportunism and entrepreneurship that dominated private manufacturing industry. The strategy paradigm found a more ready home in bureaucratic organizations that provided public services, or ran public utilities. It took root and blossomed into the dominant paradigm in many public service organizations. Despite being more than 25 years old, many of the original manifestations and techniques of strategic management are still important features of the management of public services. Table 3.2 illustrates a slowdown in the rate of development of management thinking since it coalesced into strategic management. Since that time, a gush of books and articles on strategy has supported a heavy investment by academic institutions in MBAs and in strategic consultancy. 'Strategy speak' created and maintained the legitimacy of many senior management positions in public services. Such a heavy

---

Box 3.2

THE MAIN FEATURES OF STRATEGIC MANAGEMENT

Environmental Analysis	See Chapter 1
Stakeholder Analysis	See Chapter 4
Management Audit	See Chapter 5
Planning and Budgeting	See Chapter 9
Resource Allocation	See Chapter 10
Performance Management	See Chapter 11
Organization Control	See Chapter 11
Information Control	See Chapter 12

---

investment, by such a powerful constituency, may help to explain the persistency of the strategic paradigm. As we saw in Chapter 2, those with power are reluctant to give it up. They seek to defend it and to extend it. One way to do this in senior management is through the colonizing power of language, deploying jargon and terminology that few other people understand. In Chapter 15 we suggest that by the 1990s it had become tantamount to heresy to challenge the underlying beliefs and values that came

---

Table 3.2 Strategic management: a case of arrested development?

Year	Development	
1940	Functional analysis	Management process
	Manpower planning	Work study
	Facilities management	Budgetary control
1950	Training needs analysis	Corporate planning
1960	Management development	Management by objectives
1970	Systems analysis	Strategic business units
	Environmental analysis	Internal audit
	SWOT analysis	Business planning
1975	Strategic management	Strategic management
2000	?	?

with the strategy paradigm. We think that management is a social process involving the deployment of thinking and conversational skills. This view frees managers from some aspects of strategic management that are hard to reconcile with the management of public services.

Chapters 6, 7 and 8 are on managing individuals and Chapters 13, 14 and 15 are on learning and values. These chapters attempt to step outside the strategic paradigm and explore the implications of managing people as individuals. Some of the benefits of strategic management are summarized in Box 3.3.

Strategic Management – The Problems

Organizational success is not about predicting and following trends. It is about anticipating imminent deviations from trends and taking pre-emptive action. In any event, a strategy can only be as good as the information on which it is based (Chapter 12). Unless the environment is stable, the usefulness of the information on which the strategy is based is questionable and the value of the strategy diminishes. Even under circumstances which make the possibility of strategic management propitious, it is still costly. It is difficult to demonstrate that there are benefits commensurate with the costs. For a start, it is hard to agree on what would be the right measure of performance. Annual reports and accounts often reflect public relations and the likely impact on funding bodies and taxation authorities. Consequently, they might not provide an accurate description of performance. Even if we had a reliable report that the performance of the organization was good, it would be hard to say that it was good owing to strategic management. A correlation is not necessarily a cause. If we had a reliable report that the performance was bad, it may have been the fault of poor management practice rather than poor management strategy. Even if the cost of producing and implementing strategies could be justified, strategies could still prove to be a handicap if the organization were faced with the need to react quickly to an unexpected event, such as a war, a poor harvest, a flood, a natural disaster or an infectious disease.

In a turbulent world, organizations are likely to survive if they react quickly to changes, learn from mistakes, and reverse immediately any policy that does not appear to be working. A strategy to be flexible involves deciding in advance that you are prepared to alter organization structures, procedures for decision-making, services offered, client groups served, suppliers used and the jobs that individuals are expected to do. Old partners can be dropped and new alliances formed. Principles can be abandoned and values ignored. Expediency and pragmatism rule.

Box 3.3

THE BENEFITS OF STRATEGIC MANAGEMENT

- **Holistic**: Decisions are only taken in the light of full information about the likely impact on the whole organization.
- **Long termism**: Avoids short termism – the taking of decisions without regard for their long-term consequences.
- **Co-ordination**: It is never easy to co-ordinate departments, units and other agencies.
- **Preparedness**: Strategy formulation forces empathetic and predictive thinking about threats to client groups and resources and encourages contingency planning.
- **Evaluation**: It is easier to produce criteria by which performance can be measured.
- **Creativity**: Speculation about the future encourages the use of imagination and may result in creative thinking about services or new methods of delivery.

Evaluating Strategic Management: Strategic Fit and Strategic Capability

Good results do not necessarily mean that a strategy is working. It might just be good luck. Likewise, poor results do not necessarily reflect poor strategy – the results might have been worse without it. One approach to evaluation is to assess the 'fit' between the strategic aims, goals, objectives and tactics of the organization and its internal resources (Chapter 5). For a good 'strategic fit', resources must be deployed in relation to the future mission of the organization. This might imply closing down some departments and retraining their staff to provide a new service, or to work in a new place. A question then asked is whether the redeployed resources – usually people – have the 'strategic capability' to carry out the tactical actions needed to achieve the tactical objectives that will further the strategic aim of the organization. If the environment is stable, then strategies can be written down. They should be clear, concise and coherent. The actions required to implement them should be **SMART**, i.e. **S**pecific, **M**easurable and **A**greed to be **R**ealistically achievable in the **T**ime allowed. If the environment is not stable, we prefer to use Bennett's[5] idea of a 'map' that shows escape routes, road blocks and bridges. Strategies are fallible. History shows that about half of military strategies failed! The vagaries of technology and the morale of soldiers often thwart the strategists.

An alternative to waiting to see which way the political wind will blow, or for your strategy to be torpedoed by technology, is to seek out changes to make every day, every week, every month, every year. We look now to the management of those changes in public services.

STRATEGIC CHANGE IN PUBLIC SERVICES

At first sight the strategic aim of a public service may seem obvious. But water companies have dabbled in water sports and leisure services, tele-phone companies in mail order shopping services and cable television, and electricity companies have provided information services using optic fibres wrapped around their overhead cables. Is the purpose of higher education, for example, to pass on the knowledge, culture and values of previous generations, or to generate new knowledge, culture and values? Is it to teach students or to get students to learn for themselves? Is it to equip students for leadership or to provide the brain fodder for global capitalism? We cannot assume that things will be the same in the future as they were in the past. As Heraclitus said, 'You cannot step in the same river twice' (Chapter 2). An inner city centre school, which sees opportunities for survival by specializing in information technology, sport, art, dance or music, must be sure to have the specialist resources and technical skills to pursue such opportunities. Lancaster University was brought almost to bankruptcy by an over-ambitious expansion programme.[6] Figure 3.3 demonstrates the interlinked components of strategic thinking and strategic action.

Carrying out the strategic analysis in Figure 3.3 will help us to decide who are the stakeholders. When public services are provided by a privately owned organization, the stakeholders consist largely of shareholders, staff, suppliers and customers. When public services are provided by a publicly owned organization, stakeholders often include a much wider range of individuals and bodies. These might include service users, taxpayers, political representatives, public auditors, members of regulatory bodies, licensing bodies, voluntary bodies and a wide range of pressure groups and lobbyists. These stakeholders usually have different interests and expectations. As Ranson and Stewart suggest: 'Strategic management in the public domain has to be grounded in a richer political process which involves the public in debating, bargaining and balancing, as conflicting interests are weighted and judged.'[8] In Chapter 4 we look at stakeholder analysis in public services in more detail.

In privately owned organizations, a central plank of strategy is striving to gain advantage over competitors and another is making it difficult for new

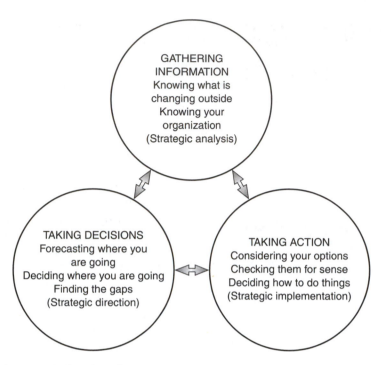

Figure 3.3 Interlinking strategic thought and action

Source: Wootton and Horne (1997)[7]

competitors to enter the market. Where public services are provided by a publicly owned organization, this is not always appropriate. Ranson and Stewart[9] go on to argue that managing strategic change in publicly owned public services is not the same as in privately owned organizations. First, publicly owned services do not face market choices – often the reason why they are providing services is because of market failures. Second, they do not respond to the demands of a market – they respond to the demands of the public, often raised through political processes. Third, publicly owned services have little choice about their location, or the clients they serve – they cannot relocate easily, or drop old clients in favour of new ones. We consider these matters in more detail in Chapter 4, where we examine the market for public services.

A number of techniques can be used to analyse the external environment in which public service organizations operate. Often PEST analysis is used. **PEST** is a mnemonic which reminds us to consider Political, Economic, Social and Technological influences. We prefer **TEMPLES** analysis which reminds us to consider Technological, Economic, Market, Political, Legal, Ethical and Social influences. Another simple tool is SWOT analysis. **SWOT** stands for Strengths, Weaknesses, Opportunities and Threats. As we demonstrate in Chapter 4, a SWOT analysis can easily be integrated with a TEMPLES analysis by asking, under each heading: 'Is there a threat or an opportunity?' For example, under T for Technology, opportunities might be identified to bid for money to set up Learning Access Centres, threats might be seen in the cost of training staff to use new technology. Other techniques for carrying out strategic analysis are detailed in Chapter 4.

Box 3.4

PRESCRIPTIVE OR EMERGENT APPROACHES TO MANAGING CHANGE?

Prescriptive Approaches

These are so called because they assume that ways of managing change can be prescribed through a logical process which involves defining aims and objectives in a sequential manner and delineating the necessary steps to implement them.

Emergent Approaches

These are based on the belief that there is limited value in prescribing rigid, long-term strategies for change in an organization, because the organization is subject to forces that are far too complex to be reduced to a predictable sequence of events. To deal with complexity and unpredictability an emergent approach would be experimental and iterative. Strategies can only be seen retrospectively to have been successful.

Prescriptive or Emergent Approaches to Managing Strategic Change?

Possible approaches to strategic management approaches have been characterized as prescriptive by Ansoff[10] and emergent by Mintzberg.[11] Box 3.4 summarizes the differences.

Prescriptive Approaches

Prescriptive approaches are favoured when the environment is stable and predictable. A variety of prescriptive approaches have been prevalent since the early 1980s. They were often extolled as 'excellence' theories.[12] The McKinsey '7S' model was widely accepted as a framework for change analysis (Box 3.5).

The key strength of the 7S framework is its simplicity. The model captured the various elements that should be considered but it did not elaborate on the many relationships between them (Figure 3.4). The framework might have been better with an eighth element: S for Synergy, representing how well all the elements worked together.

Charles Handy[13] prescribed organizational change as a formula 'one half of three times two' $(1/2 \times 3 \times 2)$, i.e. change needed to result in half the workforce doing three times the work, for twice the pay! Handy believed that one way to achieve this was to dispense with traditional pyramidal organizational structures. In attacking the gap between what organizations say they do and what they

Box 3.5

THE MCKINSEY 7S FRAMEWORK

1 **Structure**: the structure of the organization (Chapter 1)
2 **Strategy**: the general direction the organization has chosen (Chapters 3, 4)
3 **Systems**: the procedures that enable the organization to function (Chapters 5, 11)
4 **Style**: the approach taken by the organization and its leaders (Chapter 7)
5 **Staff**: employees and their needs for development and motivation (Chapters 7, 8)
6 **Skills**: the competencies needed within the organization (Chapters 13, 14)
7 **Superordinate Goals**: express organizational values and vision (Chapter 15)

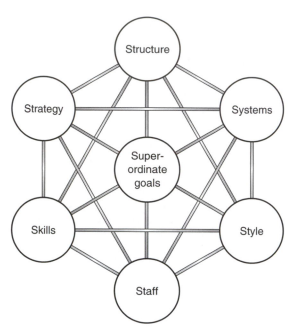

Figure 3.4 Relating the McKinsey 7 elements

actually do, Handy built directly on the work of Chris Argyris.[14] His prescription of responsiveness was echoed by Kanter.[15]

Richard Pascale, in his book *Managing on the Edge*,[16] emphasized that there were forces, such as 'contention', that drove change. He prescribed cultural change. However, as we shall see later in this chapter, it is not easy to change the culture of an organization. Done in the way that Pascale prescribes, one might not like what grows in the new culture. It may be necessary to guide or even force change in a particular direction. The idea of forcing change was taken up by Beer *et al.*[17] They argued that a pivotal aspect of the change process was the altering of the structure of the organization. Beer argued that behavioural change would follow structural change and that people's attitudes would change to accommodate their new reality. Beer *et al.*[18] claimed that if structural and cultural changes were not in place, then other changes were likely to fail. They reported that making small local changes was more effective than making large-scale, centrally

driven changes. As a result of his study of General Electric, Welch[19] proposed simple processes to get the changes implemented. Schaffer and Thompson[20] prescribed building infrastructures that would make sure that the changes stuck. They pointed out that a strategic vision was needed that was strong enough to avoid fragmentation when implementing change incrementally. Box 3.6 summarizes features of prescriptive approaches to managing change.

Emergent Approaches

The emergent school of thought highlights the importance of understanding how the change process actually works, as opposed to prescribing how it ought to work. Prescriptive approaches emphasize the importance of clear goals, delegated responsibilities and effective control mechanisms. Prescriptive approaches assume that change in organizations unfolds as a sequence of logically sequenced activities. Following his study of change in the UK National Health Service, Pettigrew[21] found that this assumption was not valid. He found that change did not move forward in a direct linear way, nor through easily identifiable phases – quite the reverse. The pattern was much more iterative and uncertain. According to Pettigrew, the pattern of change, which he uncovered, defied straightforward logic because of the conflicting personal and professional agendas of the individuals involved. He concluded that: 'The process of strategic change cannot be likened to a linear, sequential ordered production line ... A more faithful analogy would be with the process of fermentation, with its connotation of volatility.'[22]

So managing strategic change is not like managing a production line, it is more like brewing beer! Change is a heady, cumulative process of trial and error – of experiment, sometimes with reflection and sometimes with learning. The emergent approach emphasizes the political and cultural dimensions of change and argues that the whole of the change process cannot be captured by a rational linear logic. The rational dimensions of change are not denied. Rather, they are seen as intertwined with cultural and political processes involving the victims and beneficiaries of the proposed changes. According to Pettigrew, every change decision involves three elements that interact continuously with each other. These three elements are the context, the content and the process of change:

● The **context** refers to the environment: *why* is this change necessary?
● The **content** answers the question: *what* actions will be required?
● The **process** answers the question: *how* are these actions to be implemented?

The why, the what and the how of change interact continuously and must be managed simultaneously by the change manager (Figure 3.5).

Quinn[23] argued that strategic change was an evolutionary rather than revolutionary process. These ideas contrast strongly with those of the prescriptive 'designer' strategists such as Porter[24] and Ansoff.[25] Designing long-term strategies for change may be an interesting but vain distraction from the need to make short-term, everyday changes that make things a little better every day. This is not nearly as dramatic or glamorous as plotting long-term change. But it is hard to outguess the market in the long term. Grandiose long-term schemes are easily telegraphed and copied, depriving them of many intended advantages. It may be better to start many short-term initiatives and then prune ruthlessly those

that do not take root or bear fruit. Those who argue for an emergent approach to managing change probably consider that the natural selection of the market is more telling than the 'strategic choices' of the would-be manager of prescriptive strategic change.

Crafting Change

Despite the apparent differences between emergent and prescriptive approaches to managing change, they are not mutually exclusive. Public service organizations may use both at different times. Mintzberg captures the essence of the complementary nature of emergent and prescriptive approaches in his writing about 'crafting change':

> The popular view sees the strategist as either a planner or as a visionary; someone sitting on a pedestal dictating brilliant strategies for everyone else to implement. While recognising the importance of thinking ahead and especially the need for creative vision in this pedantic world, I wish to propose an additional view of the strategist – as a pattern recogniser, a learner, if you will – who manages a process in which strategies (and visions) can emerge, as well as be deliberately conceived.[26]

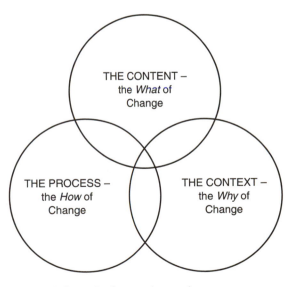

Figure 3.5 Strategic change – integrating context, content and process

Source: Pettigrew (1987)

In reality, according to Mintzberg, strategic change was 'crafted' rather than planned. The challenge is to operationalize Mintzberg's call for a 'crafting' approach which combines the prescriptive and emergent approaches to managing change. We suggest a conversational process for achieving this integration.

A CONVERSATIONAL APPROACH TO MANAGING CHANGE

We have seen strategic management described earlier in impressive language. The different kinds of conversation that managers can learn to use are summarized in Figure 3.6.

The types of conversations shown in Figure 3.6 are introduced in separate chapters. At the end of each chapter there are Thinking and Learning Activities which enable managers to acquire or to develop the conversational skills they will need in order to implement changes. Some senior managers in public

services use 'strategy speak' not only to impress but also to intimidate others. It shrouds their work in mystery. We favour a more ordinary view of the work of managers. Much of the work of managers can be carried out through ordinary conversations. We think that prescriptive and emergent approaches to managing change can be integrated through a 'conversational approach' to managing change. Our conversational approach recognizes Pettigrew's[27] experience that changes do not move forward in linear ways, through easily defined stages. We agree with Pettigrew that implementing changes in public services is complicated by the personal agendas and by the conflicting goals of the managers and professionals affected by the changes. We see managing change as moving between inner world thinking and outer world conversations. The key skills needed in the inner world are thinking skills. The key skills needed in the outer world are conversational skills (Figure 3.6).

In Chapter 2 we introduced conversational approaches to overcoming resistance, e.g. persuasion,

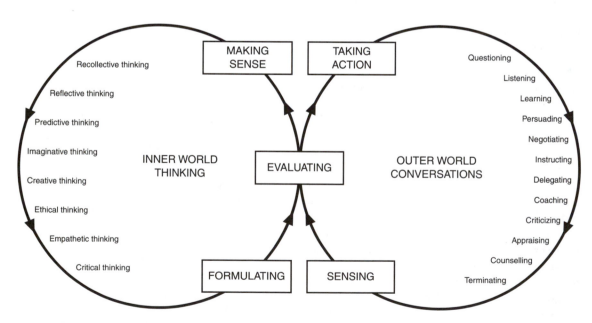

Figure 3.6 A conversational approach to managing change

delegation and counselling. The initial conversations involved information gathering and checking, developing empathetic predictions of how other people are likely to think and feel, and then thinking aloud with them about possible solutions. As possible ways of implementing changes become clearer, the conversations become more persuasive, delegating or counselling. Ideas for the types of conversations needed, and with whom are gained by asking questions – of yourself, as well as others. Useful questions to ask yourself or others can be grouped under:

1 Managing the Motives
2 Sensing and Probing
3 Preparing the Ground
4 Finding some Friends
5 Managing the Outsiders
6 Managing the Insiders
7 Managing the Bosses
8 Managing the Results
9 The Opening Moves
10 The Closing Moves

Asking the questions grouped under these ten headings prompts thinking that is personal and empathetic as well as political. First, what's in it for them – finding and managing the motives for change.

1 Managing the Motives

It is much easier to make effective use of conversations designed to persuade, sell or negotiate if people have some idea of 'what's in it for them' – or what could be. Up to 30 per cent of people can be motivated to help you to overcome the resistance of the 70 per cent who will probably resist your ideas initially.

- Why are we attempting this change anyway and what kind of change is it?
- Whose positions have already been compromised and what was traded?
- Who originally initiated this change idea?
- What has triggered the need for this change now?

- Who championed it when it was first mooted?
- Who accepted the change and why?
- Who supported it and why?
- Who fought it and lost?
- Are they resentful?

When you have asked yourself these questions and noted down your answers, you are ready to plan your first round of questioning and intelligence-gathering conversations.

2 Sensing and Probing

When you find stakeholders who are likely to be affected by the change, get them to imagine the change proceeding. Tell them what they will see and hear. Ask them what they are feeling and thinking as they imagine the change proceeding.

- Who are the interest groups?
- Who will be the key stakeholders?
- Who will be supportive of this change?
- Are you in a position yet to map the forces?
- How can you find out what each resistance is really about?
- Put yourself, in turn, into the shoes of all the key stakeholders.
- Ask yourself how you can gather facts, figures, opinions and attitudes.
- How could you draw a map of all the relationships between the stakeholders?
- What will you do when blockages, poor performance or external changes, indicate a possible threat to the progress of your change?
- To what warning signals will you be alert?
- What are your contingency plans?

By answering these questions you can begin to prepare the ground for change.

3 Preparing the Ground

Imagine that the change is already installed.

- What will people notice?
- What will be physically different?
- How will you publicize successes?

- How will the change be experienced?
- What contingency plans do you have?
- What slack will you need to deal with snags?
- What will it really look like, sound like, feel like?
- Can you create a picture or 'vision' of the change?
- How could you share your vision with those likely to be interested?
- What new roles and structures will you create to signal serious intent?
- What will you do to create wide recognition of the need for the change?
- What will you do to create broad acceptance of the method of implementation?
- If there will be a new building or a new vehicle, what shape or colour will it be?
- How could you keep checking that you are keeping to your communication plan?
- Can you draw a visual representation of the steps involved in your plan for communicating with other key stakeholders?

However well thought out your plans and your back-up plans, you will probably need a friend or two to help you get them into place.

4 Finding Some Friends

Friends are allies – they are individuals who will support your ideas, stick up for you and champion your change. If someone else decides that you must make use of groups – interdisciplinary teams, inter-agency working parties or interdepartmental support groups – then prepare yourself for the fact that such groups are not always friendly (Chapter 6).

- Which groups are worth the difficulties that will arise when working with them?
- Do the benefits of working with each group outweigh the difficulties?
- If you use groups, what will you watch for?
- Has the group got the role skills and thinking skills it needs?
- How will you manage the inevitable anxieties?

- How will you encourage leadership roles to rotate as the task changes?
- How will you decide the frequency and duration of each group meeting?
- How will you guide groups through forming, storming, norming to performing?

Now look outwards.

5 Managing the Outsiders

By now you should have a list of significant external stakeholders and interest groups that can influence your change plans for better or worse.

- How will you monitor the attitudes of key stakeholders and interest groups?
- What events, associated with your change, could alter their views?
- What will you do to be alert to the possibility of such events?
- How realistic are the expectations of outsiders likely to be?
- What will you do to manage expectations?
- Who might be stakeholders whose interests will only be apparent later?
- What benefits could you offer to each key stakeholder or interest group?
- What options will you have if blockages or attitudes threaten your progress?

If you think outsiders are difficult, what about the insiders?

6 Managing the Insiders

Consult your growing list of people who will be affected by the change. Staff will be anxious about their abilities, training needs, security, status, quality of working life, or loss of self-determination.

- How can you find out what relevant skills and experiences people might have?

- Which staff might be willing to contribute their thinking about the changes?
- Who is there on your list that has power comparable to your own?
- What benefits can you offer to stakeholders and interest groups?
- How will you address the needs of your staff?
- What steps will you take to win their acceptance?
- How will you gather their ideas and suggestions?
- For what danger signals will you watch?
- How will you monitor their attitudes?
- What might be in it for them?

By this time your growing action list should highlight the things that you need to do to keep the change moving. A common wildcard is your boss.

7 Managing the Bosses

In some instances your boss's direct involvement will be crucial to making the change happen. You need to consider which other senior managers are also key to this change. They are likely to involve your boss if you don't. How will you influence them? You should consider whether there are even more senior managers who might suddenly take an interest in what you are doing and whether their interest is likely to be welcome by your boss. How can their involvement be pre-empted or harnessed? You need to watch your boss's back as well as your own.

- Are there ways you could anticipate or reduce the risks described above?
- What might be early warning signs that a senior intervention is likely?
- What do you need to do to be alert to such signs?
- What will you do if you get a sign?
- Who are their 'gate keepers'?
- Can you draw a visual representation of the steps you need to take and the communications you need to make with all the senior people?

If you can keep staff and colleagues 'on board' and your boss 'on message', you are on your way to managing the results.

8 Managing the Results

You will need to think about your own performance as well as that of your staff.

- What will constitute acceptable performance?
- How will performance be appraised?
- Might the desired outcomes of the change alter?
- Will you involve teams or groups in reviewing their own effectiveness?
- How will you get people to agree on *how* they are going to work together?
- What rewards will be offered, or sanctions threatened, to encourage support?
- Work processes are often as important as end results, especially if you are likely to need these people to work with you again.

It is time to make a start. Like chess, the opening moves are all-important.

9 Opening Moves – A Pawn Sacrifice?

'White opens pawn to king 4 and his game is in its last throes!' You may need to signal a change in culture. You will want your opening move to result in as much new information as possible, especially about likely sources of resistance. You will want to avoid revealing too much detail about your still tentative plans for implementing changes. Try 'flying a kite', 'casting bread on the water' or 'making a pawn sacrifice'.

- Are all your agents and sensors in place to monitor the initial reactions?
- What risks are associated with the first move you are planning to make?
- Is more covert intelligence needed before you make your first move?
- To whom should you talk before making your first move?
- Whose initial reactions would be useful?
- With whom can you rehearse and think aloud?

- What needs to be in place before you go public?
- Who should make the first move?

During opening moves do not involve your best players. If your opening move goes wrong, it may cause your best players to become discredited. If you were forced to withdraw, would you be able to do so gracefully, with your reputation intact? If forced to beat an undignified retreat, what are your escape routes?

10 Closing Moves

In your emergency planning think about all the things that could be terminal for your change. What will be your exit strategy if failure looms?

- How might damage be limited?
- How will you monitor progress?
- Who could authorize its termination?
- How would you cope if the changes failed?
- What can you do to recognize warning signs?
- What are the other possible areas of damage?
- How will you publicize success and to whom?
- Whose success will it be important to publicize?
- What will you do to capture more learning?
- To whom would it be of interest or value?
- Have you already made contact with them?
- Will you have a helpline, a complaints line or a grouse box?
- Who will maintain the change and monitor its continued success?

Using the questions to structure your thinking about managing motives, sensing and probing, finding friends, managing outsiders, managing insiders and managing the boss, will help you to hold the types of conversations that are needed to get you from your opening moves through to managing results. These conversations will help you to define, resource, plan, implement and evaluate operational changes that will be needed to get you from your opening moves to your closing moves. It is to the management of these operational changes that we now turn.

MANAGING OPERATIONAL CHANGE

In this section we look at the role of project management in implementing operational changes. According to Senior,[28] project management involves the achievement of a carefully defined series of objectives in a logical sequence over an extended period of time. Sometimes project managers can find it easier to implement changes than line managers. Line managers have to live with the consequences of their mistakes. It may be more important to a line manager to preserve close working relationships with staff, colleagues and clients on whom they remain dependent, rather than to keep a project on time or within budget. After traumatic change projects, project managers – often external consultants – can take the blame (and any bad feelings) away.

According to Buchanan and Boddy,[29] projects should be unique ventures with a distinct beginning and end. They should meet specific goals within parameters of cost, time and quality. The content will normally be an agreed list of the tasks to be completed. Control is the essence of a contract to manage a project. Tight control of project activities is essential; any deviations from the original project specification should be agreed formally. A typical sequence of activities is shown in Box 3.7.

The use of Gantt charts is common. They are particularly easy to use. They are helpful in areas such as time management (Chapter 14). A Gantt chart identifies who is responsible for specific actions and states when those actions must be started and completed. Gantt charts are particularly useful because they identify the time by which activities must be completed in order that subsequent activities can go ahead. Figure 3.7 demonstrates how a Gantt chart could be used by a couple – Steven and Gillian (S & G) – to plan the buying of a house within 12 weeks. The first forward slash against an activity indicates the week in which that activity must start. The last forward slash indicates the week by which the activity must be completed. When the activity is started, the forward slash is crossed through. When the activity is completed, the last

Box 3.7

**PROJECT MANAGEMENT:
TYPICAL ACTIVITIES**

1 Identifying problems and needs
2 Gathering and analysing data
3 Setting aims and objectives
4 Identifying a list of tasks
5 Assigning responsibilities
6 Agreeing deadlines
7 Initiating actions
8 Monitoring progress
9 Solving problems
10 Completing key stages on time
11 Evaluating processes and outcomes

Some public service organizations have their own customized approach to managing operational change. In the UK, British Telecom has specified a five-stage approach to managing quality improvement projects. This is summarized in Box 3.8.

Project managers often assume that tasks will unfold in a rational sequence of well-planned activities and that groups will behave in rational ways. People, however, often behave irrationally in organizations and if organizational priorities change, project goals can become dysfunctional. So how, then, are projects to be managed?

MANAGING PROJECTS

Why do projects need managing? The variety of meanings of the word 'project' might provide a clue. To project is to predict; to propose; to throw forward; to imagine that other people are feeling the same as you are; to cause one's voice to be heard over a wide area! Project managers need to be able to keep lots of people doing lots of different things simultaneously. It's more like conducting an orchestra than barking orders at a squad of soldiers! You need to get everybody reading the same line on the same

forward slash is crossed through. If the project is proceeding to plan, all activities before the current week should be crossed through. By week 3 Gillian and Steve already have a problem. They need to pay more attention to the Bank and Building Society and less to finding a window cleaner!

Who	What/Week	1	2	3	4	5	6	7	8	9	10	11	12
S&G	Select lender	X											
S	Qualify for mortgage		/	/									
S&G	House hunt	X	X	X	/	/							
S&G	Win bid					/	/						
S	Obtain survey						/	/	/				
S	Obtain mortgage						/	/	/	/			
S&G	Close on house								/	/	/		
S	Find window cleaner											X	X
S&G	Move in												/

Figure 3.7 Gantt chart for buying a house

Box 3.8

BT'S APPROACH TO MANAGING OPERATIONAL CHANGE

Stage 1: Change Proposal

Identify:

- Problems
- Ownership
- Requirements
- Measurements
- Targets and milestones
- Plans for communicating intended change, training and quality improvement

Stage 2: Change Analysis

Identify:

- Sub-projects
- Measurements
- Possible solutions
- Resource requirements
- Problem costs and benefits
- Planned actions, stages and duration

Stage 3: Communicating Change

- Promote understanding and involvement of all those effected by changes

Stage 4: Detailed Change Planning

- Action plans
- Commitment
- Involvement

Stage 5: Implementing Changes

- Measure, assess and report on results
- Report to a steering/monitoring committee

---

the same score at the same time. You need to bring them into play at exactly the right time and then keep them working in harmony. You need players with different skills to play the different instruments. Different players with different skills will dominate different movements of the project symphony. Unfortunately, project managers are not given time to rehearse! Project managers with a reputation for getting things 'right first time' are highly sought after.

Effective project management is not just about getting the project finished on time. It has a broader perspective. An effective project manager will clarify the overall purpose of the project, address the resource requirements, and plan in detail a timetable of key tasks. The implementation can then be monitored. Regular review and occasional reschedul-ing may be needed. Finally, the project will need to be evaluated. This evaluation will measure how well the purpose of the project has been achieved and identify better ways to manage future projects. Figure 3.8 summarizes the project management process:

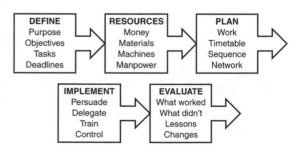

Figure 3.8 The project management process

We will discuss each of these five stages in turn, first defining the project.

Defining the Project

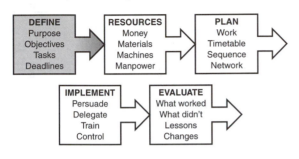

The goals of a strategic change are often broad and ill defined, e.g. to enable people to pay municipal taxes on-line, or to upgrade the housing stock. In order to translate these goals into actions that can be project managed, they need to be broken down into clear objectives. During the defining phase, the project manager relies on people who can define, agree and agree SMART objectives – that is, objectives that are Specific, Measurable, Agreed, Realistic and Timetabled.

Resourcing the Project

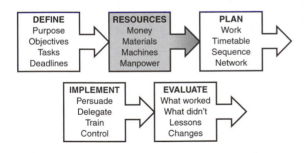

During the resourcing phase, the project manager will be check-listing four of the 10 M's (see Chapter 5):

- **Money** (the budget, cashflow, bonus payments, penalty clauses, contingency funds)

- **Materials** (including buildings, equipment)
- **Machines** (computers, mobile phones, vehicles)
- **Manpower** (skills, experience, motivation, sanctions and rewards)

Chapters 9 and 10 deal in detail with the way that resources are obtained and their use planned and co-ordinated.

Planning the Project

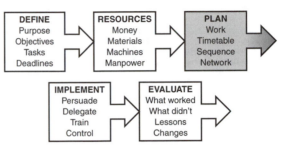

The plan will need to detail: How much? To what standard? By when? How long will it take? How will we know when it is done? The plan must detail the tasks involved and the order in which work must be carried out. Plans will be needed for communication, for engendering support and for reducing resistance (Chapter 2). For example, the project manager might need to plan visits to places where the proposed change is already working. Arrangements for temporary overtime, weekend working, interim bonus schemes and funding away-days might need to be authorized and put in place. Having listed all the tasks, the next job is to allocate times to each. Which tasks are most urgent? How much time will be available each day or each week? Which tasks can be carried out in parallel? Which tasks have to be completed before others? Is there a necessary sequence? One of the best ways to record this information is on the type of Gantt chart we discussed earlier. Figure 3.9 and Table 3.3 show the construction of Gantt charts for the content and process work involved in the replacement of a temporary UNESCO building with a new rural health centre in Pakistan, close to the border with Afghanistan.

Tasks \ Month	J	F	M	A	M	J	J	A	S	O	N	D
Communication plan agreed	/											
Communicate	/	/	/	/	/	/	/	/	/	/	/	/
Recruit team			/	/								
Team away-day					/							
Team training						/	/	/				
Evaluate plan												/
Evaluate team working										/		
Install IT								/				
IT pre-training						/	/	/				
Investigate IT		/	/	/								
Agree budget	/											
Modify budget							/					
Content work starts												/
Progress reports		/			/							

Figure 3.9 Afghan rural health centre – process work – emerging Gantt chart

Actual building work cannot start until next January but there is much process work to be done during the year running up to next January (Table 3.3). When milestones are completed, they can be crossed through. When reports have been sent off, they too can be crossed through with an X. As an activity begins, the first forward slash can be crossed to show that it started on time. If it starts late, a cross is entered when it did start. At the end of the project an analysis of the discrepancies will help to improve future planning. A quick visual check at the end of each month, should show all activities to the left of the month, started or completed. If not, catch-up action is needed.

The beauty of Gantt charts is that you don't have to think of the tasks in sequence and all at once. Tasks you have overlooked (e.g. job no. 16) or never thought about, can easily be inserted and entered on your emerging, chart (Table 3.3).

In the above example (Figure 3.10), we found that using week numbers was better than using actual dates because funds never come through in time for building to be started in the dry season! Week 1 was

Table 3.3 Afghan rural health project: task analysis

Task	Estimated duration (weeks)	Allocated job no.
Start project	0	1
Draw and submit plans	15	2
'Convince' tribal leaders	16	3
Create foundations	5	4
Timber frame for roof	5	5
Secure building	5	6
Make watertight	1	7
Paint exterior	10	8
Electrics	3	9
Air conditioning	10	10
Insulation	5	11
Plaster	5	12
Internal joinery	5	13
Decorating	5	14
Cleaning	3	15
Flooring	3	17
Rehearse opening	2	18
[Whoops!] the internal electrics	2	16
Opening doors	2	19
Total weeks	**100**	

Weeks	1–15	16–30	31–46	47–60	61–78	79–96	97–104
1							
2	/ / /						
3		/ / /					
4			/				
5			/				
6			/				
7			/ /				
8			/	/			
9				/ /			
10			/	/			
11				/			
12				/ /			
13				/			
14					/ /		
15					/ /		
16						/ /	
17						/	
18						/	
19							/

Figure 3.10 Afghan rural health centre – project content – emerging Gantt chart

the first week after February that it was dry enough to start.

If there are a lot of tasks that cannot be started until others are finished, it may be useful to create a network of the activities. The network can then be analysed to see what is the longest route. This is called Critical Path Analysis. It enables us to see what is the shortest possible time in which the project can be completed on the basis of the current plan. If that does not hit your deadlines, you either need to revise your plan or renegotiate your deadline. One of the most popular ways to draw the network is to use a **PERT** programme (Programmed Evaluation and **R**eview Technique). This programme is widely available as computer software. You simply enter the task, its prerequisites and their likely duration. The software then draws the network, finds the critical path and the completion date with a degree of lati-

tude that reflects the leeway you have indicated on the task duration times. Figure 3.11 is the PERT network for the Afghan border rural health centre. The network is made up of arrows. Each arrow has a number at the beginning of its shaft, a number on the length of its shaft, and a number at the arrowhead. The number at the beginning of the shaft is the number of the task that must be completed before the task at the sharp end can be started. The number along the shaft is the estimated time to complete the task at the sharp end of the arrow. (Sometimes three numbers are shown – Best Hope, Most Likely and Worst Estimate.) The arrowheads represent the completion of the tasks to which they point. A task cannot be started until all the tasks on its incoming arrows have been completed. The solid arrows lie on the critical path. Any delay in completing tasks on this path will delay the final completion

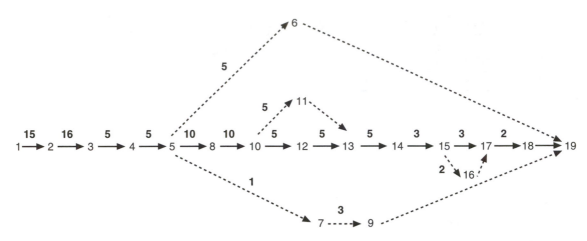

Figure 3.11 PERT network for Afghan border (rural) health centre

time. Dotted arrows do not lie on the critical path. They must still be completed before any succeeding jobs can be started but there is some slack time in getting them done.

The Afghan rural border health centre critical path analysis in Figure 3.11 reveals that although the total work content is 100 weeks, the project can, in fact, be completed in 84 weeks ($15 + 16 + 5 + 5 + 10 + 10 + 5 + 5 + 5 + 3 + 3 + 2 = 84$), providing there is no slippage in the time taken to complete any of the tasks which lie on the path formed by the solid arrows. This is called the critical path.

Implementing the Project

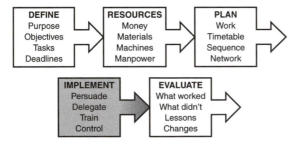

This involves persuading and delegating. A conversational approach to persuasion and delegation was developed in the previous chapter. The role of training

and a conversational approach to coaching and mentoring and learning are developed in Chapters 13 and 14. Control is one of the keys to project management. During the implementation phase the project manager will be much occupied with control processes. The key to control is anticipation – ensuring that the activities needed to complete the SMART objectives start on time and do not overrun their estimated durations. Figure 3.12 shows four problem areas where things commonly go out of control.

In a participative approach to implementation, the matrix in Figure 3.12 would be completed in advance by all involved in the project. Box 3.9 shows a typical agenda for a meeting to review progress. Collective reviews increase the chances that all

	Likely problem	How would I know?	What would I do?
Quantity			
Cost			
Time			
Quality			

Figure 3.12 Matrix for controlling projects

Box 3.9

AGENDA FOR A PROJECT REVIEW MEETING

- Develop a 'no-blame' culture
- Write action notes in the meeting
- Encourage the reporting of bad news
- Written progress reports should be short
- Allow 5 minutes only for verbal reports
- Limit the meeting to 30 minutes
- If it is not long enough increase the frequency but not the length of the meetings
- Spend the last 5 minutes of the meeting evaluating 'how are we working together?'

members of the project group will be 'on message' and 'singing from the same songsheet' when they are talking to others about the project and its progress, but there are problems in getting people together in groups (Chapter 6). Keep the meetings to 30 minutes. Do the analysis away from the group, working with individuals. Formulate the questions to be put to the group and the message to be communicated. Take away questions and problems raised by the group to think about on your own, or with one other person. Report back to the group at your next 30-minute review meeting.

Evaluating the Project

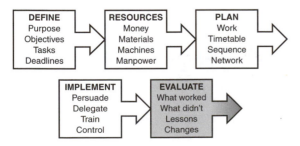

In relation to each of the first four stages – defining, resourcing, planning and implementing – ask the following questions:

- What went well?
- What did not go well?
- What can we learn from this experience?
- What would we do differently another time?

The answers can be summarized as in Figure 3.13.

As we have seen, project management assumes that change can be managed in a rational and objective manner. However, organizations are often far from rational places, especially when changes generate strong emotions.

The Management of Emotions

Pettigrew's work in 1987[30] provided confirmation of the irrational and emotional world of change which we explored in Chapter 2. In 1994 Dawson[31] published work on the content, process and context of change. Dawson's context included the law, economics and the politics of the society in which the organization was operating and the politics and culture of the organization itself. Dawson showed that personal and professional motives had a decisive effect on what was changed, when it changed and how it changed. This brought welcome recognition of our view that change management was more complex than many models of change had assumed. During the 1980s and 1990s, models of change began to be reviewed. Goodman,[32] Burnes,[33] Wilson[34] and Schein[35] all produced reviews. Schein categorized change processes as adaptive, evolutionary, coercive, managed or therapeutic. It is to this last category that we now turn.

Therapeutic processes accept that managing emotion is an important aspect of managing change. Therapeutic processes hold out the possibility of working with the emotions generated during change, rather than cooling them through logic or controlling them through project management. For the moment, we are interested in the 'soft' side of managing change. It is an interest that has been

Project phase	What went well?	What didn't go well?	What can we learn from this experience?	What would we do differently the next time?
Defining				
Resourcing				
Planning				
Implementing				
Evaluating				

Figure 3.13 Matrix for evaluating a change management project

shared with others such as Hirschhorn,[36] Diamond,[37] Fineman[38] and Vince.[39] Vince's interest, in what happens at the boundary between managers and the individuals they manage, is consistent with our view of managing as a social process. While we accept that powerful economic and political forces shape structures of organizations, managers are primarily concerned with the relationships that take place within those structures. Clearly, wider environmental systems impact on the systems within the organizations, but we will return to this later, when we look at systems thinking in Chapter 5. For the moment we assume that managing change is about having 'the grace to accept the things you cannot change, the courage to change the things you can, and the wisdom to know the difference'. Few managers can change the economic and political forces that shape the structures of their organizations, but they can change what happens in the space between themselves and another person. According to Smith,[40] when organizational change is emotionally charged, the idea of maintaining interpersonal boundaries is helpful. We envisage each person as able to inflate around themselves a personal boundary – a bit like blowing up a bubble with yourself

inside. Social relationships take place between these personal boundaries. These boundaries can be thought of as being like the boundary walls of the cells of your body. Cell walls are not rigid and impermeable. If they were, the cell would die. The cell walls permit the absorption or diffusion of liquids and vapours, in and out of the cell, so that it can maintain the balance it needs to survive. Likewise, the boundary around you should permit the controlled absorption of emotions, as well as ideas. The boundary should help you to pause for thought, before you diffuse your own feelings and ideas back into the interpersonal space. In this way you can observe your own emotions as well as those of the other person. Accept them for what they are. They are part of the situation. As Jung said,[41] we cannot change anything unless we first accept it. Judgement does not liberate, it oppresses.

Our personal boundary intersects also with the political boundaries of the organization.[42] This helps us to accept that organizational politics comes into the space between other people and ourselves. The emotions that you observe in those spaces will give you important clues about the way that people are relating to your ideas and to the ideas of others.

Exploring those relationships can provide you with the energy to understand them and to consider how the relationships might need to change.[43] In the space between you and other people, you can discover creative ways of changing how to relate to others and to the organization as a whole. According to Stacey,[44] it is often a waste of time to plan a series of specific changes too far in advance. Vince[45] is cautious about approaches to change based on long lists. He cites Ramone's '10 Critical Factors',[46] Reynold's '4 Distinct Phases',[47] Kyle's '10 Key Principles'[48] and Conner's '5 Common Causes'[49] as examples. These writers assume that change can be strategically prescribed and strategically managed. We have aired already our misgivings about that assumption. What matters, surely, is what is on the 'lists' – i.e. what steps are being suggested.

Complexity beyond Lists

'Lists' can be constructed to help managers think about what might be relevant. Much of what needs to be thought about occurs in the spaces between individuals. One difficulty with project management 'lists' is that they can oversimplify complex problems. But complexity is inevitable when trying to change organizations. Emotions contribute to that complexity. Project managers, hired for their strengths in strategic analysis, task focus and cost control, can sometimes find emotions difficult to sense, let alone articulate, observe or express. They can find it difficult to observe or tolerate the expression of emotion by others. But psychoanalysts claim that expression of feelings often needs to precede the insight necessary for change to take place. In which case, the expression of emotion might be a prerequisite of change. That is why our lists include activities to discern feelings as well as opinions. That is why we seek to develop empathetic thinking alongside analytic thinking. Empathetic thinking is the ability to think for yourself as though you were the other person affected by the change. Exploring the stress and discomfort that other people might be feeling, helps to uncover what might seem contradictory or paradoxical. Exploring apparent contradictions often opens up the possibility of resolving them.

When some managers become anxious at the prospect of strong emotions being felt or expressed, they take flight. They resort to logical processes and ritualized procedures. This is a way of defending themselves against their anxieties. As defence mechanisms, techniques such as project management can be an asset or a liability, depending on why they are used and how frequently they are used. If they are used habitually, and without deliberate consideration as to why they are being used, then they are a liability. At the level of the individual, covering up, denying or distracting oneself from one's anxieties can cause stress and possibly ill health. At the level of the organization, unconscious defence against anxiety can result in unhelpful levels of competition – 'Let's rally around the flag!'; or competition between professions, e.g. between doctors and nurses; or competition between departments, e.g. accountants and everybody else! Lack of unity is denied – 'Let's make sure that we are all singing from the same song sheet'. Internal conflict is avoided. Eggshell walking is elevated to an art form!

In his book on the relationship between change and loss, Morris[50] sees change as a process of forcing people to let go of things. But the things that people need to let go of may be important to them in defining their self-concept – the way that they see themselves. This can have an effect way beyond the loss of material possessions. For example, for many people, relationships play an important part in defining who they are. When people are forcibly detached from things that help them to define who they are, they can panic and become desperate – suicidal even. They may react by blaming others, by blaming themselves or by feeling guilty, unworthy or insignificant. Their behaviour might seem self-destructive and in reality it might be so. In a desperate bid to regain some control over themselves and their lives, they might abandon normal processes – they might demand an interview with the chief executive, or an audience with the president. They might gatecrash meetings, or whistle-blow, or talk to the press. Better that their feelings are explored in the space between them and their manager, than in the space between them and a microphone, telephone, TV camera or an Internet site!

Thinking about the emotions provoked by change prompts a shift in our focus on managing change. We have looked critically at the role of strategy and strategic management in identifying changes that an organization might seek to implement. We have tried to 'craft' a conversational approach to integrating prescriptive and emergent approaches to implementing changes. We have detailed the way that project management can be used to implement operational changes. The case for adopting a strategic approach to managing change seems plausible, but there is little hard evidence to support its plausibility. Indeed, there is some evidence which challenges the value of prescriptive approaches to strategy, from studies of corporate failure and survival (Chapter 15). There does appear to be some value in learning to think strategically.[51]

Our last section on managing emotions contains some clues as to why, even when changes are successful, they sometimes fail to stick. As we saw in Chapter 2, there is a battle for hearts as well as minds when implementing changes. If we reject the idea that organizational change is a rational process, then an approach that relies on first changing the culture of an organization might have more appeal. The notion is that rather than bring about a change in the culture of an organization by forcing people to change their behaviour, we can change the culture first and then hope that the behaviour we seek will grow in the new culture. However, bad things as well as good things can grow in a new culture! Lack of predictability and lack of control are feared by most managers (Chapter 15). None the less, we have decided to include cultural change because cultural change is a challenge that faces many managers of public services. In an attempt to bring greater predictability and control to the process of cultural change, we have decided to devote considerable space to explaining how managers can do it. The Thinking and Learning Activities at the end of the chapter create opportunities to explore some approaches that may be unfamiliar.

MANAGING CULTURAL CHANGE

Project management and some prescriptive approaches to strategic management are underpinned by a rational problem-solving approach to setting aims and objectives and controlling their implementation. They are approaches concerned with the formal structures and working of the organization. However, as we saw earlier in this chapter, management thinkers such as Pettigrew recognize that change management is an iterative, experimental process, which is likely to be driven by a mix of rational and irrational factors. The informal workings of organizations have a powerful influence on how people react. If aspects of the informal organization such as values, beliefs, norms and assumptions are ignored during the change process, then there is a danger that the hoped for benefits of change projects will be delayed, diluted or just deleted! Managers can use the concept of organizational culture to influence the informal aspects of organizations. In the next section we consider how managers can surface and realign organizational culture with new organizational directions. But first let us consider Rosie Wakely's experience of culture change at the English National Opera (Box 3.10).

What is Organizational Culture?

Lundberg[55] suggested that familiarity with the culture in which we are immersed makes it difficult for us to define the concept. Lundberg suggested that culture

- Endures over time.
- Is modifiable, but not easily so.
- Is a shared, taken-for-granted, frame of reference.
- Helps denote the organization's uniqueness.
- Has a symbolic dimension manifested in language and behaviour.
- Is socially learned and transmitted and provides meaning for those involved.

In short, it is 'the way we do things around here'. Box 3.11 gives some different perspectives on organizational culture.

Box 3.10

EXTRACTS FROM A CONVERSATION WITH ROSIE WAKELY

(Manager at the English National Opera):

'PHANTOMS AT THE OPERA'

Tony: How has the culture of the ENO changed?

Rosie: We have to be more responsible and accountable for the large sums of public money invested here. We now have 'senior managers' to rein in the excesses of the 'artists'. This has resulted in a values clash because we cannot ever make a profit and in any case, most of us didn't come here to make a profit. We can't 'compete' with other suppliers of 'entertainment'. We cannot hope to compete with television, video or even cinemas as a medium for opera. This notion of 'competing' would result in the closure of the majority of regional theatres as well as Covent Garden, The National Theatre and The Royal Shakespeare Company.

Tony: So where do we go from here?

Rosie: The reality is that live opera costs a lot of money. It is difficult to support a profit-making mentality in an organization which does not exist for that purpose. Our raison d'être is more to do with 'Art for Art's sake' and idealism about serving the community. In the last ten years, the constant drive for efficiency savings has weakened us to a point where artists are leaving. To understand why artists are leaving, you have to understand why they joined in the first place. They joined to indulge their love of their particular art form. Once here they are quickly indoctrinated into a culture of 'The show must go on!' This produces a highly motivated and dedicated workforce.

Tony: So how is this a problem?

Rosie: The demands on individuals in terms of time and energy and initiative are enormous. Most people think that working in the theatre is glamorous and fun. In fact it is extremely hard work. Although the hours are long and the pay is generally low, the effort of an individual can make a huge difference to the show. That is why there is such a high level of job satisfaction. That is why people who would be better off elsewhere would rather work in the Arts. Until now, that is! What is happening now is that management values have polluted our arts values. Previous team leaders – who were usually masters of their crafts – have been placed behind doors labelled 'Manager' and given management training to help with their metamorphosis.

Tony: How do these new 'managers' cope?

Rosie: A stream of 'strategic initiatives' descend from a great height onto their shoulders. They are expected to implement changes which they know are irreconcilable with day-to-day operations. For example, a senior manager took over responsibility for compliance with health and safety regulations. His method of managing was to pass down edict-like memos saying that certain practices must cease immediately. When new middle managers protested that to comply would mean that the show would *not* go on, they were told to sort it out because it was the law. Knowing that to follow the edict would close down the show, the middle managers ignored it. This was not because they were cavalier about health and safety, but because it was operationally impossible to meet the requirements. These middle managers were being conscientious, but they found their situation stressful and de-motivating. When you combine clashes like these, with senior managers who try to measure things that can't be measured, you begin to understand why there is a mass exodus of artists from 'well managed' arts organizations.

Tony: Thank you Rosie.

Box 3.11

CULTURE – THE WAY WE DO THINGS AROUND HERE

- **Culture as metaphor**: Machines, organisms and theatres have also been used as metaphors to describe organizations. Morgan[56] suggested that culture is just another metaphor to describe organizations.
- **Culture as objective reality**: Some management writers see organizational culture as objectively real. Pachanowsky and O'Donnel-Trujillo[57] suggested that organizational culture is everything about the organization as a whole.
- **Culture as a psychological phenomenon**: According to Schein,[58] organizational culture is the psychological predispositions or assumptions which lead people to think and act in certain ways.

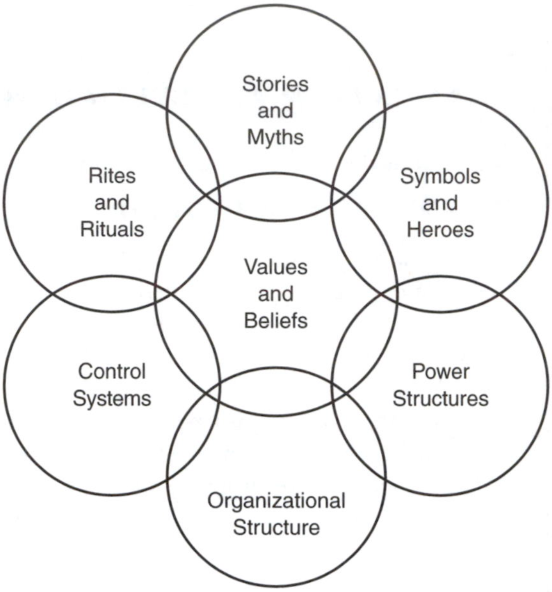

Figure 3.14 Johnson's cultural web
Source: After Johnson (1992)

Mapping Culture

An organization's culture can be characterized by:

- Ethical codes
- Basic assumptions
- Norms of behaviour
- Beliefs, values and attitudes
- Artefacts, symbols and symbolic action
- Rites, rituals, ceremonies and celebrations
- Jokes, metaphors, stories, myths and legends
- The history of the organization and its heroes

Schein[59] suggested that things such as stories, jokes, rites and rituals were surface manifestations of culture, whereas basic assumptions reflected the deepest levels of organizational culture. Following his extensive study of Australian and UK Civil Service reforms, Zifcack[60] posed the question 'Why do the reforms so often fail?' The answer, Zifcack suggested, lay in the fact that organizations (or the individuals who compose them) cling with great tenacity to the ideologies, myths, metaphors and symbols which give their existence meaning. Johnson[61] used the metaphor of a web to describe organizational culture (Figure 3.14). His cultural web is one of stories and myths, symbols and heroes, rites and rituals, control systems and power structures. The strands of Johnson's cultural web have in common that they are all manifestations of the organization's underlying paradigm – the way things are seen, interpreted, given meaning. A paradigm is the 'way we see things around here'. Cultures reflect paradigms. Paradigms, as we saw earlier, when thinking about the strategy paradigm, reflect deeply held beliefs and values.

THE STRANDS OF A CULTURAL WEB

Shared Language and Shared Meaning

To think of culture as a web is to think metaphorically. Organizational metaphors help to develop a shared language. Metaphors such as mushroom farming or sailing in turbulent waters are often used to describe what it is like to work in organizations. Parker and Lorenzini[62] suggest that it is useful to determine at what level a metaphor has penetrated an organization. They suggest that a metaphor has penetrated to a psychological level when individuals use the metaphor to describe how they feel or how they see their organization. For example, 'I feel like a cog in a machine'. The metaphor has penetrated to a social level when it is used consistently across an organization. In one organization in which we worked, senior managers were frequently referred to as 'The Thought Police'.

The adaptation and widespread use by managers of a new metaphor can be a powerful way of signalling and effecting cultural change. Organizational metaphors help to develop a shared language in an organization. Developing a shared language is an essential prerequisite to developing shared meaning. For example, when there is no shared understanding of what is meant by quality, then it is very difficult to maintain quality standards in public services. Similarly, a shared meaning of 'equal opportunity' is a prerequisite to the development of policies on discrimination.

Spiders' webs are very hard to destroy. If even a wisp of the sticky gossamer is left, the web can quickly be reconstructed. The new reconstructed web is often stronger than the original. Even if the trees or brambles to which it clings are blown down, the web usually survives. Similarly the cultural web of an organization is resilient whichever way the managerial wind blows. That is what makes the cultural web so hard to change. All strands of the web must change.

The easiest strands of the cultural web to change are the shaded ones shown in Figure 3.15 – those strands concerned with authority, control and structure. We saw that project management was dominated by the need for control, yet change management projects often unravel, even as the consultant project managers are packing their bags to leave for their next assignment. Trying to change things by reorganizing the structure is as

old as the Roman Empire, which rose only to fall again. To paraphrase Gaius Petronius Arbiter (AD 50):

> No sooner did we begin to form than we would be reorganized. I was to learn later in life that we tended to meet any new problem by reorganizing. And what a wonderful method this is for creating the illusion of progress, while producing low morale, inefficiency and confusion.

Some things hardly change at all! The failure of changes based on changing, systems of control and organization structures may be due in part to lack of attention to the four unshaded areas in Figure 3.15, namely Stories and Myths; Rites and Rituals; Symbols and Heroes; Values and Beliefs. It is to these that we now turn.

Stories and Myths

All the public service organizations that we have worked in have their own stories. The same demons,

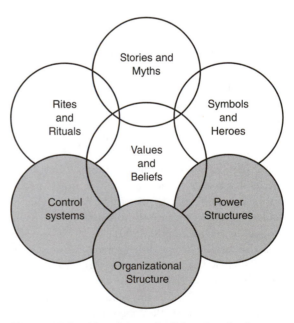

Figure 3.15 Breaking the strands of the cultural web

jokers and heroes who usually appear in well-told folk tales often make an appearance in these stories. Sometimes the stories can be related to specific events, such as the story of how the organization was born. Stories can be indicators and the perpetuators of important beliefs. Martin *et al.*[63] identified the types of questions which stories can answer:

- Is the boss human?
- Can employees break rules?
- Can subordinates get to the top?
- What do I have to do to lose my job?
- How will superiors react to my mistakes?
- How will the organization deal with obstacles?

Stories can evoke values, signal power relationships and communicate feelings. For example, historical tales associated with health services usually stress miraculous recoveries or miracle cures. There are very few stories about preventative medicine or health promotion. Similarly, in the police force, the story is often of detectives working out 'who dunnit' or brave officers 'getting their man'. Stories about crime prevention and community policing are less common.

Myths are often distinguished from stories on the basis of truth. Brown,[64] for example, suggests that myths are stories the basis for which is wholly fanciful. Brown misses the point. The point is that myths are believed to be true. It is the fact that the myth is believed that makes it a revealing characteristic of the culture of the organization. While many stories may circulate around the grapevine of organizations, relatively few have the status of myths. Myths tend to be *the* stories – stories against which the likely truths of other stories are judged. Owen[65] thought of myths as vantage points from which other organizational truths could be discerned. For example, it could be argued that one of the important myths in UK public services, in the 1980s and 1990s, was the idea that private sector management practices were best. What was important about this idea was not whether or not it was true, but that it was widely believed to be true. Having acquired the status of myth, it dominated thinking about UK public service management until the late 1990s.

Rites and Rituals

Ceremonies are usually associated with collective celebration, for example, ceremonies that mark the anniversaries of important events – like the founding of the organization. These ceremonies have an important function in reinforcing cultural values. Trice and Beyer[66] define rites and rituals as relatively elaborate, dramatic activities, which consolidate various forms of culture. Ceremonies, rites and rituals take on a variety of forms in organizations. For example, in many public services there is a ritual feeding frenzy near the end of the financial year as people attempt desperately to gobble up all the remaining financial food, lest it be deducted from next year's budget! (See Chapter 9.) Other rituals are identified in Box 3.12.

Ceremonies, rites and rituals can provide a means of pointing out 'rising stars' as well as labelling the 'old guard' as the 'old guard'. They can signal 'who's in' and 'who's out'. Ritualized behaviour is important not just for the message it communicates to individuals in the organization but also for the power it wields over them.[67] The rich tapestry of organizational myths, stories and rituals can impede or accelerate the implementation of change.

Box 3.12

COMMON RITUALS IN ORGANIZATIONS

- **Ritual renewals**: reorganizations and regrading of jobs
- **Ritual questioning**: audits, tribunals and committees of enquiry
- **Ritual passages**: induction, probation and passing-out parades
- **Ritual evaluations**: annual inspections, reviews and ministerial visits
- **Ritual degradations**: sideways moves, resignations and forced retirements

Symbols and Heroes

Symbols are words, objects, conditions or actions that signify something in addition to their face value. Dandridge et al.[68] identify three uses of symbols:

1 **Descriptive symbols**: They say something about what it is like to work here
2 **Energizing symbols**: They have the effect of motivating or demotivating
3 **Maintenance symbols**: They legitimize procedures, structures or actions

These types of symbols are summarized in Table 3.4.

Peters and Watermann[69] drew attention to the role of corporate heroes and their importance as benchmarks of excellence and motivation. Common roles for heroes are:

- They can motivate others.
- They can set high standards.
- They can provide role models.
- They can encourage commitment.
- They can reinforce cultural values.
- They can convey what is best about us.

As we will see in Chapter 7, heroic leaders are in short supply in public services and can be liabilities. For example, when they have excessive levels of power, they may resist changes that might reduce their power or expose their weaknesses.

Values and Beliefs

According to Kirschbaum[70] a value is a deeply held belief that has been consciously adopted. Values are

concerned with what 'ought' to be done. Values are often enshrined in professional codes of conduct or formal statements of the kind shown in Boxes 3.13 and 3.14. While a value is a deeply held belief that has been consciously chosen, a belief is concerned with what is regarded to be true or false. Beliefs differ from values because they may have been inherited, and may never have been questioned, let alone adopted. Beliefs are taken-for-granted aspects of organizational life which people may find hard to explain. They may not even be aware that they hold the beliefs. Beliefs can become values by being made explicit – by being clarified and then by being formally adopted, as illustrated in the formal values statement of the Community Drug and Alcohol team shown in Box 3.14. This is a helpful distinction because, over time, deeply held beliefs, like rituals, may become meaningless or irrelevant. It is a good idea to revisit a statement of values from time to time and to rearticulate those values in the context of contemporary experience. This is likely to generate conflict, because values are often cherished and help people to make sense of their lives. To question their continued relevance is risky.

Social Values

The beliefs of organizations tend to reflect the beliefs of the wider society to which their staff and their clients belong. Beliefs change over time, albeit slowly. Surfacing these beliefs and adopting them as organizational values forms an important part of implementing cultural change. By managing the process by which beliefs are surfaced and adopted as values, a manager can increase the chances that cultural change will take place in a direction that is consistent with other changes which the manager wishes to implement. Values that are espoused but which are then contradicted by the behaviour of managers are unlikely to be widely accepted and the culture of the organization will not change. There has been much debate regarding the feasibility and even the desirability of managing cultural change in organizations. For the most part there is agreement that culture can

Table 3.4 Symbols in organizations

Uses	Types		
	Verbal	Behavioural	Material
Descriptive	Myths	Celebrations	Logos
Energizing	Jokes	Questioning	Posters
Maintenance	Stories	Training	Manuals

Box 3.13

JOHNSON & JOHNSON: OUR CREDO

We believe that our first responsibility is to the doctors, nurses and patients,
to mothers and all others who use our products and services.
In meeting their needs everything we do must be of high quality.
We must constantly strive to reduce our costs
in order to maintain reasonable prices.
Customers' orders must be serviced promptly and accurately.
Our suppliers and distributors must have an opportunity
to make a fair profit.

We are responsible to our employees,
the men and women who work with us throughout the world.
Everyone must be considered as an individual.
We must respect their dignity and recognise their merit.
They must have a sense of security in their jobs.
Compensation must be fair and adequate,
and working conditions clean, orderly and safe.
Employees must feel free to make suggestions and complaints.
There must be equal opportunity for employment and development
and advancement for those qualified.
We must provide competent management,
and their actions must be just and ethical.

We are responsible to the communities in which we live and work
and to the world community as well.
We must be good citizens – support good works and charities
and bear our fair share of taxes.
We must encourage civic improvements and better health and education.
We must maintain in good order
the property we are privileged to use,
protecting the natural environment and natural resources.

Our final responsibility is to our shareholders.
Business must make a sound profit.
Research must be carried out, innovative programs developed
and mistakes paid for.
New equipment must be purchased, new facilities provided
and new products launched.
Reserves must be created to provide for adverse times.
When we operate according to these principles,
the stockholders should realise a fair return.

Box 3.14

A VALUE STATEMENT BY A COMMUNITY DRUG TEAM

- **Accessibility**: We try to create a welcoming environment in which individuals are respected and made to feel at ease. We will strive to make our service relevant to under-represented groups.
- **Individual care planning**: We aim to respond rapidly and to provide treatment tailored to the needs of individuals.
- **The chance to change**: We believe that service users can make positive changes in lifestyles and stabilize their substance misuse.
- **Commitment to a learning culture**: We

acknowledge the uncertainty and unpredictability of the environment in which we work and the need to be flexible and open to change. We will reflect on what we do and why, and learn from what we do.

- **Respect for our clients**: We aim to ensure that our clients' confidentiality, dignity, cultural beliefs and rights are respected and that our clients have our service contract and confidentiality policy explained to them.

(*Source*: Doherty 1998)

---

be changed. There is a spectrum of views about how easy it is to effect the change. At one end of the spectrum there are writers who emphasize the ease with which culture can be managed and at the other end there are those who tend to stress the difficulties. Brown[71] suggests that cultural change is desirable and achievable – relatively easily and without coercion. Anthony,[72] on the other hand, sees cultural change as a difficult process involving an alternation of crisis and learning, which needs constant reinforcement through strong leadership. Gagliari's[73] three-phase process for changing organizational values reflects both these themes (Box 3.15).

We do not subscribe to a 'culture-busting' approach to organizational change. A spectrum of possible changes in organizational values can be developed. In this way some new values can be incorporated progressively while maintaining continuity with the past. Once the new values are seen to be associated with success, they will be idealized and internalized. They will become part of the value system of the organization. A 'culture-busting' model of organizational change tends to destroy both

the wanted and the unwanted aspects of an organization's culture.

A MODEL FOR CULTURAL CHANGE

Our model for managing cultural change in public service organizations applies when services that are offered by private companies are taken into public ownership. This happened extensively throughout the world in the period 1910–60. The model is equally applicable when services previously supplied through publicly owned organizations are taken into private ownership. The model has three stages: Surfacing, Interpreting and Signalling.

1 Surfacing Cultural Information

Surfacing cultural information involves the collection of information that can reveal the beliefs and assumptions that underlie the culture of the organization. This can be done through surveys, workshops or focused interviews (Box 3.16).

Box 3.15

CHANGING VALUES

- **Phase** 1: A leader can help develop a vision which is based on a set of beliefs which can provide a basis for setting objectives and orienting the organization. Initially not all members of the organization will accept these beliefs. The leader has some power to influence others into accepting them, but the beliefs will only be adopted as values if they prove to be the basis of actions that prove successful.
- **Phase** 2: The second phase occurs when those involved assert that their beliefs have helped the organization to achieve desirable results. For example, 'It was because we believed in continuous quality improvement that our results improved so much last year.' Such beliefs may then be adopted as organizational values.
- **Phase** 3: In the final phase of the process, these values become assimilated at an unconscious level. Gagliari calls it a process of 'idealization', whereby values come to be held emotionally rather than logically.

(*Source*: After Gagliari 1986)

Box 3.16

CULTURE-SURFACING CONVERSATIONS

1 What messages do you think are given by the physical features of the organization, e.g. the front door, the reception area, the colour scheme, the notice boards etc.?
2 Are there events that take place every day? Every week? Every month? Every year? What do they tell you about the organization?
3 Can you think of any stories that are regularly passed around the organization? What messages do they convey?
4 What animals might people choose to represent your organization and why?
5 What incidents or jokes are often retold? What messages do they convey?
6 What words would you use to describe the culture of your organization?
7 Does the organization have any formal or informal rituals?
8 Does the organization have any traditions or practices?
9 Does the organization have any heroes or villains?

2 Interpreting Cultural Information

It can be useful to have a model to help interpret the information surfaced during the previous step. We have selected two, one put forward by Charles Handy,[74] the other by Parker and Lorenzini.[75]

Handy's model

Handy's model is based on earlier work by Harrison.[76] Handy's model classifies culture into four types each represented by a figure in Greek mythology: Zeusian power cultures; Apollonian role cultures; Athenian task cultures; and Dionysian person cultures.

Zeus was the leader of the Greek gods. All power emanated from him. Power cultures have a single source from which power radiates. There are few bureaucratic rules and procedures. Control is maintained via patronage through the advancement of individuals who use interpersonal power to get things done. The problem with this type of culture is that it may be difficult to find such people in public services. Their attributes can be hard to develop through conventional training. Control through interpersonal power used to be hard to

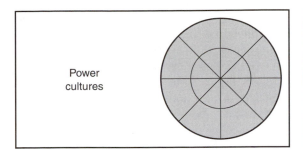

Figure 3.16 Zeusian power cultures

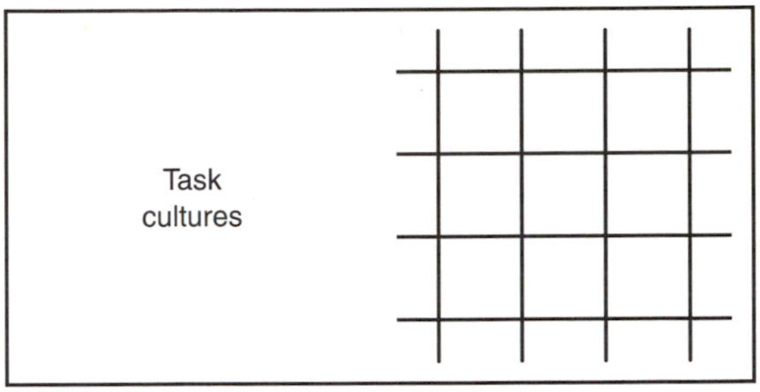

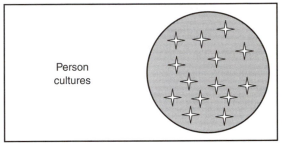

Figure 3.18 Athenian task cultures

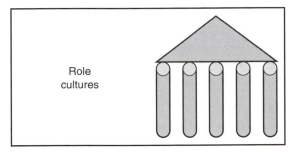

Figure 3.17 Apollonian role cultures

Figure 3.19 Dionysian person cultures

exercise at a distance, but improvements in transport and communications technology are favouring its increased use in many parts of the world.

Apollo was the Greek God of reason. Role cultures are organized through rational rules and procedures. Specialist functions such as finance, personnel and marketing are likened to the pillars of a temple. Each function is controlled by a small group of senior executives. Continuity and stability are highly valued. The main problem with role cultures is that they may be slow to react to a need for change. Ambitious employees may be frustrated by the formality of promotion procedures.

Athena was the Greek goddess of wisdom. It is not clear why she was chosen to symbolize task cultures. In task cultures, project teams with specific tasks are the norm. Team working, innovation, flexibility and individual autonomy are valued. Ability rather than status or position is respected. These cultures are most suited to highly competitive environments that require quick responses.

Dionysus was a Greek god known for his self-

interest. Person cultures develop when groups of individuals decide to work together for their own benefit. For example, solicitors and doctors. The workload is shared but individuals have a high degree of autonomy.

The Parker and Lorenzini model

Parker and Lorenzini[77] suggest three ways of 'framing' an organization's culture as integrative, diverse or polarized. In an integrative culture all the cultural manifestations – rites and rituals, stories and myths, symbols and ceremonies, structures and controls – are coherent. They reinforce one another. They do not contradict the core beliefs and values of the organization. They are consistent with the cultural paradigm. For example, 'equality – we are equal to our staff' – is reinforced by the ritual presence of a high-profile senior manager at ceremonies for awarding staff training certificates to junior staff. Managers whose actual behaviour is inconsistent with espoused values readily wreck the coherence of the culture.

In a diverse culture, no single culture is valued. Suggestions for 'new ways of doing things around here' are the norm. When some of the diverse cultural manifestations clash, the culture may be framed as 'polarized'. As when, for example, a flat non-hierarchical organizational structure is espoused but is contradicted by rituals that reinforce hierarchy and privilege (Chapter 1). In public services, a common clash is between competitive cultures and collaborative cultures. The process of surfacing cultural information and interpreting it may lead automatically to recognition of the need for cultural change.

3 Signalling Cultural Change

La Monica[78] argued that attempts that had been made to shift the culture of the UK NHS from a role culture to a task culture had failed. She concluded that this failure was rooted in a lack of clarity about its purpose. The NHS did not know whether it was supposed to be preventative, palliative or holistic. The service, she said, was made up of different 'tribes', including midwives, nurses, doctors and other professional groups. The 'tribes' had different beliefs about what constituted effective healthcare and valued different things in their relationships with their clients. What was needed was clear signalling of the intended direction of the cultural change. Two possible roots present themselves – leadership by senior management (Chapter 7) or personnel management (Chapter 8).

Personnel management has great potential for influencing organizational culture. It can legitimately invent new rites and rituals. It controls rites of initiation, such as induction, and rites of degradation, such as disciplinary procedures. Performance appraisal and upgrading schemes can involve rites of passage. The training function can be used to promote the value of learning. In the wake of learning can come a culture in which it is OK to take risks and admit mistakes. Senior managers, as leaders, can play an important role in establishing a vision for the organization. The ways senior managers spend their time, and their apparent priorities, are interpreted symbolically by their staff. Even the

way managers dress sends a message about the type of culture they favour. By referring constantly to quality, or by themselves attending training events and refusing to be interrupted, managers signal what is valued and in what direction the culture of the organization should consolidate or move. By choosing to be a member of a particular project team, they affirm the value of the project. When they offer to meet at the client's home, or when they choose to 'walk-the-job' to another manager's office, the word soon gets around. Managers must be prepared to enact as well as espouse the values that they wish to underpin the culture of the organization. Box 3.17 summarizes the main processes involved in managing cultural change in public service organizations.

FINAL THOUGHTS: 'MANAGING MEANING'

In many public service organizations, a key dilemma is how to balance the need for change against the benefits of continuity. Surfacing beliefs, interpreting their cultural assumptions and adopting new values, can be a useful way of orchestrating a debate about continuity and change. In our experience of working in public services, polarized cultures can result in the inadvertent loss of the values and beliefs that have been traditional in public services. By surfacing these beliefs and valuing the continued relevance of many of them, we have been able to reduce the demotivation which otherwise accompanies the indiscriminate discrediting of past practices. This involves attributing meaning to symbolic attributes of the organization. There are three features of symbolic literacy: symbolic thinking, symbolic language and symbolic actions.

Symbolic Thinking

Symbolic thinking is the ability to think by manipulating not only words but also symbols such as models, frameworks, analogies, metaphors and images. For example, in one organization a particular department was referred to as a 'leaky bucket'. The bucket symbol was used to think about other aspects

---

Box 3.17

CHANGING ORGANIZATIONAL CULTURE: A SUMMARY

1 **Understand culture**
   - Manage the tangible and the intangible, the formal and the informal.
2 **Surface cultural information**
   - Use the cultural web to structure workshops, questionnaires and interviews.
3 **Interpret cultural information**
   - Is it a power, role, task or person culture?
   - Is it integrated, diverse or polarized?
4 **Evaluate the appropriateness of the culture**
   - What values are conveyed by the culture?
   - Do these values support or inhibit the aims of the organization?

- Do values support or inhibit changes that need to be made?
- Can they be rearticulated to make them more supportive?
- Do new values need to be adopted?
- Do some values need to be rejected?

5 **Signalling cultural change**
   - Identify the actions needed to convey the direction of cultural change.
   - Enable things that convey the desired culture and its underlying values.

---

of the organization. Its symbolic meaning was extended. People were encouraged to think aloud. It wastes resources; what causes the holes – rust, accident, sabotage? How can holes in a bucket be repaired – by a temporary patch or by welding up the hole? Is it better to keep plugging the holes or is it better in the long run to throw away the bucket and get a new one? Why do we need a bucket anyway, now that we have running water? We could fill it full of sand in case of fire. Its always useful to have somewhere to put rubbish when you can't think of anywhere else to put it. But visitors don't like to see an old department treated like a rubbish bin. The bucket is only leaky because it's old and it has done a lot of hard work. It has been around ever since the organization was first started. It's familiar; people who pop back expect to see it. Perhaps we should polish it up and use it to grow indoor plants? OK, why don't we make it a museum or an exhibition centre or a training centre? Now there's an idea . . .

Using images to communicate involves a different part of the brain than using logic. It extends your head space! It increases the chances of thinking creatively. Thinking symbolically develops symbolic fluency and your ability to interpret the meaning of symbols. Symbolic language is dense and rich in meaning; this can be useful when dealing with complex issues like cultural change. Stories can be used to alter the perceptions of large numbers of people relatively quickly. This can be useful in organizations employing large numbers of staff, or serving a large population. Stories can be formal (based on well-documented case histories) or informal (an anecdote about a particular client or well-known member of staff).

It is useful not only to be able to think and talk in the symbolic language of an organization but also to be able to create new symbols. New symbolic language can help to 'unfreeze' the organization. New symbols can legitimize new action and consolidate change. Changing the name of a department, or changing a person's job title, can signal major cultural change. We once arrived as guests at a University Business School located in a prestigious office block rented in the town centre. On the impressive front door it said:

XYZ University Business School
No entrance for undergraduates
Undergraduates use the rear entrance

Not long into our consultancy time, we were not surprised to learn from one of the undergraduate course leaders that the university was having trouble with its undergraduate programmes generally. On the way out, rather mischievously, we suggested to the course leader that she cross through the word undergraduate and above it write the word customers, so that it read 'No entrance for customers – Customers please use the rear entrance'. Within a week one of the university governors had seen the notice and ordered that it be removed. Similar notices around the campus were removed. A culture change was underway.

SUMMARY

- We looked at the role of strategy and strategic management in identifying necessary changes in public services. We expressed some reservations about the efficacy of strategic management.
- We considered the advantages and disadvantages of rational, prescriptive approaches and incremental, emergent approaches to managing change and concluded that they are not mutually exclusive.
- We proposed a conversational approach to 'craft' the integration of prescriptive and emergent approaches to implementing change.
- Specific operational changes could be implemented via project management.
- A project is a unique venture with a beginning and an end, normally conducted by people to meet goals within parameters of cost, time and quality.
- We learned how 'SMART' objectives might be controlled using Gantt charts, PERT networks, critical path analysis and project review and evaluation.
- We considered how emotions generated during change might be managed.

- The cultural web of an organization is composed of a rich tapestry of myths and stories, rites and rituals, symbols and ceremonies that can provide shared meaning and which can also contradict each other.
- Values and beliefs are the hub around which the cultural web is spun. As the beliefs in society change, so will the beliefs of different stakeholders.
- Managers should stay tuned to the changing beliefs of stakeholders, periodically adopting some beliefs as organizational values. Surfacing and interpreting cultural information, clarifying and adopting new values, and taking symbolic action to signal new directions, facilitates cultural change.
- Finally, we considered how symbolic thinking, symbolic language and symbolic action can be used to manage meanings.

THINKING AND LEARNING ACTIVITIES

Activity 1 Self-assessment

1 What are: strategy, strategic management, strategic change and strategic thinking?
2 What is a strategic aim, a strategic goal, a strategic objective and an operational tactic? Give an example of each.
3 Give examples of strategic analysis, strategic formulation and strategic decision-making.
4 What is the difference between an emergent and a prescriptive approach to managing and implementing change?
5 What are the strengths and weaknesses of the McKinsey 7S framework when used for managing strategic change?

6 What did Mintzberg suggest as a 'crafting' approach to integrating prescriptive and emergent approaches to implementing change?

7 Describe a 10-step 'crafting' methodology for integrating prescriptive and emergent approaches to managing change.

8 How would you define a project?

9 When is a project management approach to managing change likely to be successful and when is it likely to fail?

10 What factors do managers need to consider when resourcing a project?

11 Describe a Gantt chart. How can the use of Gantt charts be helpful to managers?

12 Describe Critical Path Analysis. How can it help project managers?

13 If you were a project manager, how would you try to control the project to ensure that it was being implemented according to plan?

14 How would you evaluate a change project? Why is project evaluation important?

15 What emotions are likely to be released or provoked during change?

16 Which emotions are most likely to be present at what stages of the change?

17 What steps can be taken by managers to increase awareness of and expression of strong emotions?

18 How might insight, understanding and acceptance of emotion aid the implementation and maintenance of change?

19 Why do you think that there is a growing interest in organizational culture?

20 What are beliefs? How can they become organizational values?

21 How are organizational values related to the culture of an organization?

22 How might the values in a non-profit-making public service organization differ from the values in a privately owned profit-making organization?

23 How can cultural information be collected? How can cultural information be interpreted? How can cultural change be signalled in the right direction?

24 What are the main difficulties a manager might face in attempting to change organizational culture?

Activity 2 Individual Learning: Imaginative and Empathetic Thinking

The politics of change

Think of a major change that you would love to make in an organization with which you are familiar. It must be such a major change that it is likely to be beyond your capacity, personally, to implement it. Use your imagination, think of something really big! Refer back to the integrative model in the text and try to answer the questions posed under each of the ten headings:

1 Managing the Motives
2 Sensing and Probing
3 Preparing the Ground
4 Finding Some Friends
5 Managing Outsiders
6 Managing Insiders
7 Managing the Boss
8 Managing Results
9 Opening Moves
10 Closing Moves

Activity 3 Individual Learning: Reflective Thinking

Project management

Consider a change that has occurred in an organization with which you are familiar. Refer to the five stages of project management described in the text – defining, resourcing, planning, implementing and evaluating.

Can you identify any of these stages in the change you are recalling? Where – if at all – did the change encounter problems? How might a project management approach have addressed these problems?

Activity 4 Paired Learning: Metaphorical Thinking

Gardening, fishing or learning to fly?

Managing a change project has been compared to conducting an orchestra. Different groups of people have different skills and need to be brought in, on time, at different times, and kept to the same tempo. All need to be playing parts of the same symphony. Harmony is valued and preparation and rehearsal are invaluable. This is called metaphorical thinking. Use the following metaphors to describe the process of managing a change project.

- Managing projects is like gardening . . .
- Managing projects is like going fishing . . .
- Managing projects is like learning to fly . . .

Jot down your thoughts. If possible discuss them with someone else. What insights does each metaphor bring? Can you think of a metaphor that sums up what project management means to you?

Activity 5 Individual or Group Learning: Numerical Thinking

Charting SMART objectives

Think of a project in which you are or will be involved. The project could be a work-based activity, or a leisure time pursuit. It would be useful to choose something that you actually needed to plan, for example, a holiday, or a house move, or a party. Translate any broad aims into SMART objectives. Attach names to all the objectives and translate them into tasks. Make a list of all the things that need to be done to achieve each task. Estimate how long each will take. Now devise a Gantt chart that identifies who will do what and when they will do it. How could you control the implementation of the activities you have plotted on the Gantt chart?

Activity 6 Individual or Paired Learning: Predictive Thinking

What might go wrong?

Use the matrix in Figure 3.20 opposite to try to think about what might go wrong when trying to implement the change you thought about using the ten-step integrative approach to managing change (Activity 2).

Activity 7 Individual or Paired Learning: Predictive Thinking

'The best laid schemes of mice and men . . .'

Use the matrix in Figure 3.20 to think about what might go wrong when you prepared plans using the project management approach outlined in the text, i.e. defining, resourcing, planning, implementing and evaluating.

	What might happen?	How would I know?	What would I do?
Quantity			
Quality			
Time			
Cost			

Figure 3.20 Matrix: what might go wrong

Activity 8 Individual, Paired or Group Learning: Symbolic Thinking

The way we do things around here

Consider a public service organization with which you are familiar, for example, a place of education or a hospital. Describe a myth, a symbol or a ceremony, which you believe conveys the culture of the organization. How would you characterize the culture of this organization? If possible, compare notes with someone else or feed back to a group who are familiar with the organization you are considering.

Activity 9 Paired or Group Learning: Creative Thinking

It's a myth . . .

Think of a favourite story from a book, a play or one that was once told to you. Why was it so powerful for you? If possible, discuss your answer with a colleague. Does it matter whether or not the story was true? Try to come up with a story that is often told about a particular public service organization. It does not matter if the story is true or just a myth (a story not based on objective reality). What is the message of this story? What does it reveal about the culture of the organization? If possible, tell the story to a group and ask them what they think it signifies about the organization (this often releases a lot of humour and laughter).

Activity 10 Individual or Paired Learning: Ethical thinking

Credos and value statements

The values statement of a Community Drugs and Alcohol team and the Credo of Johnson & Johnson can be found in the text (Boxes 3.13 and 3.14). Refer back to them and answer the following questions:

1 What are the main differences between the two texts?
2 What do you find surprising or interesting about the two texts?
3 What do you infer about the values espoused by the two organizations from these two texts?
4 Give examples of how you might expect the values conveyed by these texts to be expressed in the operational management of the two organizations.
5 How might these values impact on the survival of each organization?

Activity 11 Individual or Paired Learning: Ethical Thinking

'By their deeds ye shall know them'

- Make a list of the values that underpin the organization where you work or study.
- Are any of these values contradicted by what the managers do?
- Is there any conflict between the values you have identified and the values implied by any recent changes – actual or proposed?
- Are any of your own beliefs challenged by these changes?

- If you answer yes, explain why. If you answer no, imagine changes that would threaten your beliefs.

Activity 12 Individual or Paired Learning: Analytical Thinking

Animal, vegetable or mineral?

Using the questions in Box 3.16 in the main text of this chapter, undertake a cultural audit of an organization with which you are familiar. It could be the organization where you work, a voluntary organization or the educational institution at which you are studying.

Activity 13 Individual or Paired Learning: Reflective Thinking

The Gods of Management

Use either Handy's Gods of Management or Parker and Lorenzini's Integrative, Diverse or Polarized Model to make sense of the cultural information you collected in Activity 12. Is there one dominant culture? If so, describe it. If there is more than one culture, are there any areas where the cultures clash?

Activity 14 Individual or Paired Learning: Symbolic Thinking

Judging by appearances – managing meaning

There are two parts to the management of meaning. One is interpreting existing meanings, the second is signalling new meanings. Think about yourself, your dress, your hobbies, your office, your procedures, your ornaments, your home, your entrance way and the way you like to be addressed. What symbolic messages is each of these things likely to convey to others? If you can, check out your ideas with other people. Do any of these messages conflict? What different messages would you like people to receive about you? What could you do, buy, send, wear or change, to convey symbolically a different message about yourself? Make the changes and say nothing about it. Wait and be alert for reactions. Now, what could you do next? Choose one thing and do it!

Activity 15 Individual or Group Learning: Analytical and Projective Thinking

CASE STUDY: Forces for change in healthcare

The year had ended as it had begun, with hospitals closing their doors to patients. The impression remained that the UK National Health Service (NHS), after five years of continuous reform and large increases in the volume of resources available to it, was unable to cope with the pressures created by changes in technology, economy, patient expectations, politics, the law and social attitudes.

Advances in Science and Technology

Advances in the understanding of genetics are having huge implications for healthcare. The Human Genome Project has mapped the genetic blueprint of human life. This has increased doctors' ability to predict and manage health problems, including the eradication, prevention and reductions in the incidence of some life-threatening diseases. These developments are raising profound ethical questions. Expensive technology has until recently only been available at a limited number of specialized centres. According to Langley and Warner:

> Falling costs, information transfer and miniaturization may allow greater decentralisation of services ... increased medical specialisation is also likely and new technologies may erode existing boundaries between specialities.[79]

At the same time there is an increasing need to manage a proliferation of expensive services. Information technology could potentially transform the way clinicians treat patients:

> It could offer support to clinicians by allowing distance diagnosis and fast retrieval, digitised imaging data and offering expert systems. It could also strengthen the power of the public by giving easy access to fuller information on health issues and allowing patients much more control over their own care.[80]

Cost benefit analysis of the introduction of new technologies is becoming essential before their introduction, including the cost of staff training. In a rapidly changing environment, skills are rapidly becoming redundant. Managers must anticipate future training needs.

Changing Population, Lifestyles and Patterns of Disease

Population projections for the year 2010 indicate a 75 per cent increase in those aged 85 years and over. More than one in three marriages are ending in divorce and this often results in impoverishments which have a serious effect on health. There will be fewer adults to care for elderly relatives. The Internet and education are increasing knowledge and understanding of personal health, but they are also leading to demands for more and better healthcare. Health promotion services are advocating the adoption of healthier lifestyles. However, there is no change in the numbers of young people who smoke. Employment continues to become more desk-bound. These factors could have implications for heart disease and osteoporosis (weakening of the bones) in later life. Paradoxically, successful health promotion will not necessarily reduce demands on health services, because those who may have died prematurely as a result of unhealthy lifestyles may now live longer and require more healthcare. Some major life-threatening diseases have declined but new diseases are emerging and old ones are re-emerging, for example, AIDS, TB, diabetes and asthma amongst the young. Fractures in senior citizens are increasing. There is no evidence that the overall demand for healthcare will decline.

Developments in the Economy and Working Conditions

Standards of living can affect health. Studies have shown that unemployment, poor housing and disparities in income and poor working conditions all have a negative impact on health. The strength of the economy will affect resource levels in the health service. For example, Professor Chris Ham, Director of the Health Services Management Centre at the University of Birmingham, argued that more resources would be needed simply to enable the NHS to stand still.[81] In Wales, between 1987 and 1992 there was an increase of 19 per cent in hospital admissions and waiting lists (Welsh Office 1992). Private healthcare continues to expand and, in a climate of increasing cost and demand, the issue of whether some forms of insurance or private sources of healthcare should be increased is being debated. It was thought that some services should move closer to home and some services should be more centralized. Rationalization necessitates the closure of some hospitals. This is proving unpopular. Without careful management, changes in government policy could cause massive disruption and consequent deterioration of service. Where existing resources were being improperly managed, throwing money at the problem simply made it worse. Better management of existing resources must precede increasing resourcing.

Questions

1 List ways in which advances in science and technology affect health services. How might new technology affect the structure of health service organizations?
2 In what ways might a post-bureaucratic organizational structure enable health services to meet the challenges of the early twenty-first century?
3 Identify factors that increase the demand for health services. How could health services be organized to reduce these demands?
4 How would you set about persuading public meetings to accept changes to the health service which may be resisted but which make sound financial sense?

Activity 16 Individual Learning Review: Reflective Thinking

Inner world thinking

What inner world thinking skills can you identify in the manager's work described in this chapter? Have any of the thinking skills you have identified emerged for the first time in this chapter? If so, add them to your accumulating model of the kinds of thinking skills that you consider to be useful to managers of public services.

What things could you do to develop any of the thinking skills that you have just added to your model? What would be the first step?

Outer world conversations

What outer world conversational skills can you identify in the manager's work described in this chapter? Have any of the types of conversational skills you have identified emerged for the first time? If so, add them to your accumulating model of the kinds of conversational skills you think are useful to managers of public services.

What things could you do to develop any of these conversational skills which you have just added to your model? What would be the first step?

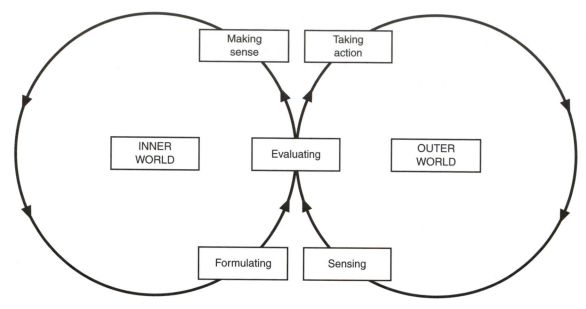

Figure 3.21 The thinking skills of the conversational manager

Activity 17 Individual Learning: Metacognitive Thinking

Metacognition

Look back through the Thinking and Learning Activities you have been asked to carry out in this section. What thinking skills were involved in each of these activities? For each type of thinking, write down how you were learning what you were learning, when you were learning to think in each of these different ways.

NOTES

1 Quinn, J. B. (1980) *Strategies for Change: Logical Incrementalism.* Irwin Homewood.
2 Johnson, G. and Scholes, K. (1993) *Exploring Corporate Strategy.* Prentice Hall.
3 Wootton, S. and Horne, T. (1997) *Strategic Thinking: the Nine Step Programme.* Kogan Page.
4 Wootton, S. and Horne, T. (2001) *Thinking Skills for Managers.* Kogan Page.
5 Bennett, J. (1999) *Corporate Strategy.* FT Management.
6 Rowe, P. (1997) *The University of Lancaster: Institutional Lessons to be Learned, 1994–1996.* Lancaster University.
7 Wooton and Horne (1997), op. cit.
8 Ranson, S. and Stewart, J. (1994) *Management for the Public Domain.* Macmillan.
9 Ibid.
10 Ansoff, I. (1961) *The Practice of Management.* Mercury.
11 Mintzberg, H. (1997) 'Patterns in Strategy Formation'. *Management Science*, May, p. 34.
12 Peters, T. and Watermann, H. (1982) *In Search of Excellence. Lessons from America's Best Run Companies.* Harper & Row.
13 Handy, C. (1989) *The Age of Unreason.* Business Books.
14 Argyris, C. (1991) 'Teaching Smart People How to Learn'. *Harvard Business Review*, Mar.–April.
15 Kanter, R. M. (1983) *The Change Masters.* Allen & Unwin.
16 Pascale, R. T. (1990) *Managing on the Edge.* Penguin.
17 Beer, M., Eisenstaat, R. A., Spector, B. (1990) 'The Critical Path to Corporate Renewal'. *Harvard Business Review*, Mar.–April.
18 Ibid.
19 Welch, J. (1989) 'Speed, Simplicity and Self Confidence'. *Harvard Business Review*, Sept.–Oct., pp. 112–20.
20 Schaffer, R. H. and Thompson, H. A. (1992) 'Successful Change Programmes Begin with Results'. *Harvard Business Review*, Jan.–Feb.
21 Pettigrew, A. *et al.* (1991) *Managing Change for Competitive Success.* Basil Blackwell Business.
22 Ibid.
23 Quinn, op. cit.
24 Porter, M. E. (1985) *Competitive Advantage.* Free Press.
25 Ansoff, op. cit.
26 Mintzberg, H. (1987) 'Crafting Strategy'. *Harvard Business Review*, July–Aug., p. 65.

27 Pettigrew, A. (1987) *The Management of Strategic Change*. Basil Blackwell.

28 Senior, B. (1997) *Organisational Change*. Pitman, p. 232.

29 Buchanan, D. and Boddy, D. (1993) *The Expertise of the Change Agent. Public Performance and Backstage Activity*. Prentice Hall.

30 Pettigrew (1987), op. cit.

31 Dawson, P. (1994) *Organisational Change. A Processual Approach*. Paul Chapman.

32 Goodman, P. (1982) *Change in Organizations*. Jossey-Bass.

33 Burnes, B. (1992) *Managing Change*. Pitman.

34 Wilson, D. C. (1992) *A Strategy of Change*. Routledge.

35 Schein, E. H. (1985) *Organizational Culture and Leadership*. Jossey-Bass.

36 Hirschhorn, L. (1990) The Workplace within. *Psychodynamics of Organizational Life*. MIT Press.

37 Diamond, M. A. (1993) *The Unconscious Life of Organisations*. Quorum.

38 Fineman, S. (1993) *Emotions in Organisations*. Sage.

39 Vince, R. (1996) *Managing Change. Reflections on Equality*. Policy Press.

40 Smith, K. K. (1982) 'Philosophical Problems in Thinking about Change', in Goodman, op. cit.

41 Jung, C. (1990) *Psychological Reflections*, Jacobi, H. and Hall, S. (eds). Macmillan.

42 Fineman, op. cit.

43 Vince, op. cit.

44 Stacey, R. (1993) *Strategic Management and Organisational Dynamics*. Pitman.

45 Vince, op. cit.

46 Ramone, J. (1993) 'Resistance to Change is Natural'. *Supervisory Management*, vol. 38, no. 10, p. 10.

47 Reynolds, L. (1994) 'Understanding Employees' Resistance'. *Human Resource Focus*, vol. 11, no. 6, p. 17.

48 Kyle, N. (1993) 'Staying with the Flow'. *Journal of Quality and Participation*, vol. 4, p. 32.

49 Conner, D. R. (1993) 'Managing Change'. *Business Quarterly*, vol. 58, no. 2, p. 88.

50 Morris, P. (1986) *Loss and Change*. Routledge.

51 Wootton and Horne (2001), op. cit.

52 Peters and Watermann, op. cit.

53 Brown, A. (1995) *Organisational Culture*. Pitman.

54 Leach *et al.* (1994) *The Changing Organisation and Management of Local Government*. Macmillan, p. 58.

55 Lundberg, C. C. (1991) 'Surfacing Organisational Culture'. *Journal of Management Psychology*, vol. 3, pp. 78–90.

56 Morgan, G. (1986) *Images of Organisation*. Sage.

57 Pachanowsky, M. and O'Donnel-Trujillo, N. (1982) 'Communication and Organisational Culture'. *The Western Journal of Speech Communication*, no. 46, pp. 23–39.

58 Schein, V. (1985) 'How Culture Forms, Develops and Changes'. In Kilmann, K. H. *et al.* (eds). *Gaining Control over Corporate Culture*. Jossey-Bass.

59 Ibid.

60 Zifcack, A. (1996) *Civil Service Reforms in Whitehall and Canberra*. Oxford University Press.

61 Johnson, G. N. (1992) 'Managing Strategic Change, Culture and Action'. *Journal of Long Range Planning*, vol. 25 (Feb.), pp. 23–38.

62 Parker, L. and Lorenzini, N. (1993) 'Social Navigation: Interpretation and Influence in the Change Process'. *Journal of Strategic Change*, Feb., p. 35.

63 Martin, J., Feldman, M. S., Hatch, M. J. and Sitkin, S. B. (1983) 'The Uniqueness Paradox in Organisational Stories'. *Administrative Science Quarterly*, vol. 28, pp. 54–63.

64 Brown, op. cit., p. 150.

65 Owen, H. (1987) *Spirit, Transformation and Development in Organization*. Abbot Publishing, p.12.

66 Trice, H. M. and Beyer, J. M. (1984) 'Studying Organizational Cultures through Rites and Ceremonials'. *Academy of Management*, vol. 9.

67 Brown, op. cit., p. 17.

68 Dandridge, T. C. *et al.* (1980) 'Organisational Symbolism: A Topic to Expand Organisational Analysis'. *Academy of Management Review*, vol. 5, no. 1, pp. 77–82.

69 Peters and Watermann, op. cit.

70 Kirschbaum, S. (1986) *Values Clarification*. McGraw-Hill.

71 Brown, op. cit.

72 Anthony, P. (1994) *Managing Culture*. Open University Press.

73 Gagliari, P. (1986) 'The Creation and Change of Organizational Cultures: A Conceptual Framework'. *Organizational Studies*, vol. 7, no. 2, pp. 117–34.

74 Handy, C. (1992) *The Gods of Management*. Penguin.

75 Parker and Lorenzini, op. cit.

76 Harrison, R. (1972) 'How to Describe your Organization'. *Harvard Business Review*, vol. 50, May/June.

77 Parker and Lorenzini, op. cit.

78 La Monica, E. L. (1990) *Management in Health Care. A Theoretical and Experiential Approach* (British adaptation by P. Morgan 1994). Macmillan.

79 Langley, E. and Warner, P. (1990) 'Challenges Facing Health Services'. *Journal of Management Decision Making*, vol. 4, pp. 23–42.

80 Ibid.

81 Chris Ham (1997) *Guardian*, May 7.

ROLE TWO

MANAGING OPERATIONS AND ACTIVITIES

In Chapter 1 – First Thoughts – we examined the likely contexts in which public service managers will have to manage their operations and activities. In Role One – Managing Change – we described practical ways in which managers can manage resistance to change and implement the projects to which change gives rise. Of course managers will need to implement changes in other areas of operation and activity. We chose to devote separate chapters to change management because what we say about change management applies equally to the managers' work in other roles, namely: Role Three – Managing People; Role Four – Managing Finances and Resources; Role Five – Managing Communication; and Role Six – Managing Learning and Personal Development.

Here in Role Two – Managing Operations and Activities – we look at two areas of management activity that give rise to changes that an organization needs to implement. In Chapter 4 – Managing Markets – we look at the activities than an organization needs to implement in order to satisfy the needs and wants of customers and clients. These are activities that take place in relation to the external environment of the organization. For example, market research, competitor analysis, portfolio analysis and the marketing mix. In Chapter 5 – Managing Quality – we look at activities that take place mainly inside the organization. For example, activities such as quality control and quality assurance. Bringing together these externally and internally focused activities underpins successful organizational performance.

4

MANAGING THE MARKET FOR PUBLIC SERVICES

The Agora in Athens was the marketplace where the philosophers debated. They thought that to be a citizen and to be a
good person were one and the same thing. Only by working
with other people in your own community could you learn
how to live a valuable life. The civic virtue of co-operation
helped not only to enrich the life of the community but it also
helped you to unfold your own character. In the marketplace
people were encouraged to take responsibility not only for
themselves but for the development of a 'good society'.

(T. L. Doherty 2001)

LEARNING OUTCOMES

This chapter will enable the reader to:

- Understand the concept of marketing.
- Learn about marketing techniques such as
  market research, environmental scanning,
  marketing management, competitor analysis and the marketing mix.
- Understand how to write a service level
  agreement (SLA).
- Evaluate the usefulness of service life
  cycles, service vulnerability appraisals and
  service risk assessments.
- Consider how stakeholder analysis and
  relationship marketing might contribute
  to the management of public services.
- Consider how far the economic, social,
  political and ethical assumptions that
  underpin marketing are consistent with
  the idea of a 'good society'.

INTRODUCTION

In Chapter 1 we saw how public services can come
under pressure to become responsive to the needs of
the public. We agree with Walsh[1] that some marketing techniques can help managers to get closer to
the people who use public services and that marketing skills can play a part in the design and development of services that are user-friendly. However,
many marketing techniques are inappropriate, irrelevant and inapplicable to public services. We only
describe in detail the marketing techniques that we
think are helpful – market research for example. Box
4.1 shows the components of a marketing plan. As
we suggested in Chapter 3, marketing is closely
allied to strategy. Mission statements set out
what an organization is trying to achieve and
for whom. They define priorities. These priorities
are broken down into strategic goals. Objectives
are defined. Tactics are selected in order to
achieve these objectives. These ideas are written
down in a business plan (Chapters 9 and 10). A business plan should be based on a marketing plan.
A marketing plan describes how people in the
organization intend to interact with clients or customers. We will cover the role of organizational
audit in Chapter 5 and financial planning in Chapters 9 and 10.

In this chapter we will focus mainly on market
research. Competitor analysis can also be useful
where public services are provided by privately
owned organizations or by public sector organizations which are being forced to compete with

private sector suppliers. Under portfolio analysis, we describe how service life cycles, vulnerability and risk assessment awareness can be used to review the strengths and weaknesses of a public service in relation to its perceived competition. Under marketing management, we look at concepts like focus, differentiation, cost leadership, market penetration, market development and diversification. We modify the traditional '4P' model of marketing into a '5P' model (see Box 4.1) and look at stakeholder analysis, relationship marketing and the provision of public services through inter-agency working and partnership agreements.

WHAT IS MARKETING?

Arguments about the usefulness or relevance of marketing to public services depend on how you define marketing. There are many definitions of marketing. It is important to resist the temptation to choose a definition that is ill suited to public services in order to dismiss the relevance of marketing to public services — to set up a man of straw in order more easily to knock it down. Drucker[2] sees marketing as encompassing the entire organization — it is the whole organization seen from the point of view of its end purpose. Much of what is written

---

Box 4.1

THE COMPONENTS OF A MARKETING PLAN

Mission Statement

What the organization aims to do,
how it does it and with whom

Vision Statement

Where and what the organization aims to
be in the future

Market Research

- Market Structure
- Market Trends
- Market Segments
- Market Gaps

Organizational Audit

External Audit of Opportunities and Threats
Internal Audit of Strengths and Weaknesses

Competitor Analysis

Porterian Analysis

Portfolio Analysis

Service Life Cycle, Service Vulnerability,
Risk Assessment

Marketing Management

- Marketing Strategy
- Market Penetration
- Diversification
- Service Development

The 5P Model

- Package
- Promotion
- Place
- Price
- People

– Stakeholder Analysis
– Relationship Marketing

The Business Plan

about marketing is written by its practitioners and people committed to the economic, political and social ideas on which marketing is based. Presentation, promotion and persuasiveness are part of their stock in trade. As one would expect, they write good copy in support of the usefulness of marketing! Sometimes we can better understand the importance of present-day ideas by looking at the historical context in which those ideas arose. The present 'marketing era' was preceded by a 'sales era' and the 'sales era' was preceded by a 'production era'.

The Production Era

The 'Production Era' corresponded to the second half of the Industrial Revolution. Mass production was in full swing. As we saw in Chapter 1, mass production was aided by scientific management, emphasizing productivity and payment by results. It was a period in which the relationship between provider and purchaser was characterized as 'we provide – you buy'. Allegedly, Henry Ford said 'my customers can choose any colour they like as long as it's black'! During the production era the term 'marketing', if used at all, referred to the distribution or delivery of goods or services.

The Sales Era

During the 1920s, production began to exceed demand. Managers realized that goods needed to be sold. They knew that once sales exceeded the levels necessary to recover the fixed costs of the business, then all the extra sales contributed directly to increased profits. Once an organization's fixed costs have been covered, adding an extra 10 per cent to its sales revenue can often double its profits. Conversely, as we shall see in Chapter 9, only a small shortfall in sales can precipitate large losses and acute shortages of cash to pay bills, wages and salaries. This creates great pressure to sell everything that the organization has the capacity to deliver. During the 'Sales Era', the term 'marketing' usually meant selling, advertising and promotion.

The Marketing Era

The 'Marketing Era' followed the Second World War. Businesses realized that increasing production and intensifying sales effort did not necessarily guarantee success. *What* was produced became as important as *how much* was produced. Increased competition, more discerning consumers and the increased cost of research and capital equipment meant that businesses had to determine in advance what customers wanted, rather than simply produce goods and services and hope that they would be bought. In order to determine in advance what customers want, organizations must do a number of things. First, they must establish information systems capable of obtaining information about what customers need and want. Second, they must use that information to create goods and services that people want. Third, they must develop a strategy for targeting those goods and services at the customers who want them, at the right price in the right place, using appropriate forms of promotion. Fourth, organizations must structure themselves so that *all activities are aimed at satisfying customer needs in such a way that the organization also achieves its aims.* We have attempted to gather these ideas together into the working definition in Figure 4.1. We will unpack this definition, element by element, during the rest of the chapter.

PUBLIC SERVICE MARKETS

Historically, markets are found in the earliest organized societies. Most villages and towns still specify a time and a place for the local market. The term 'market' means a meeting of people for the purpose of exchange.[3] As in the case of the Agora in Athens, the market can be a place of social, intellectual and commercial exchange. In contemporary usage, the term 'market' usually refers to a process of exchange controlled by supply and demand. Kotler[4] defines a market as a situation in which all those who share a particular need or want make an exchange in order to satisfy these needs or wants. In commercial

Marketing

is the assessment and creation of present and future needs and wants of existing and potential customers

and the auditing and co-ordination

of all the resources of the organization to satisfy those needs and wants

in such a way as to offer sustainable advantage over competitors

so that income of the organization will exceed its expenditure by a planned margin

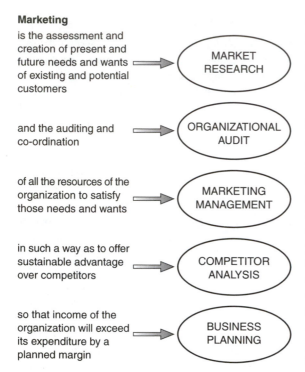

Figure 4.1 A definition of marketing

Source: Horne (1984)

markets the seller exchanges goods and services, usually directly with the purchaser in return for money, which contributes to profit. Competition aims to ensure that producers and suppliers compete for sales and try to establish competitive advantage over rivals by, for example, pricing or quality strategies. For public services, however, the exchange is different. Most public services are involved in distributing benefits on behalf of society in return for revenues provided by taxation. In the public service exchange, the state usually purchases the services needed by clients or service users on behalf of society.[5] For example, people who pay taxes from the proceeds of their employment exchange some of their income in return for social benefits such as education, health and social services.

The market for public sector public services is more constrained than the private market; it is also

difficult to define. In an effort to make sense of public service markets, Ferlie, Cairncross and Pettigrew[6] classified markets as unregulated markets, regulated markets, pseudo markets and relational markets.

Unregulated and Regulated Markets

Unregulated markets follow the assumption that markets allocate resources more efficiently than bureaucratic systems. The problem with this assumption is that the markets for public services are not true markets, in the economist's sense of a place of 'perfect or near perfect competition'. In practice people who use public services are not free to purchase what they choose from whomsoever they choose. There are also artificial barriers which deter competition from entering the marketplace. For example, even when compulsory competitive tendering is used to generate competition between providers of public services, the consumers of those services have no choice, because a purchasing authority chooses who will deliver the service.

Regulated markets attempt to control the market by the imposition of professional and statutory regulations. Regulators attempt to moderate the workings of the market in order to minimize adverse effects on the public. For example, in the UK, private sector organizations can bid to take over the running of a state school. However, the performance of the schools continues to be regulated by OFSTED, a statutory agency responsible for monitoring education services.

Pseudo and Relational Markets

Pseudo markets offer limited competition. According to Ferlie *et al.*[7] they are largely symbolic of new ways of doing things. They are not true markets. Relational markets emphasize the need to maintain long-term relationships between well-established networks of buyers and sellers. The buyers and sellers compete and collaborate according to shared values and accepted rules. This approach goes beyond the economics of the market and introduces a social dimension into the way markets operate. At the end of this chapter we discuss the potential benefits of relationship marketing to public services.

Having examined some of the peculiarities of public service markets, we now examine some specific characteristics of the market environment in which they operate.

The Health 'Market' in the UK

In 1989 a UK White Paper, 'Working for Patients', proposed separating the roles of purchasers and providers of health services. The so-called 'purchaser–provider' split meant that Health Authorities could purchase health services for the communities they served and hospitals, doctors and other community-based providers could contract to provide these services. Some local doctors (to be called GP fund holders), were to be given the opportunity to manage their own budgets and to purchase medical services for their patients. The creation of these 'internal markets' was intended to promote efficiency through competition. In practice there was little competition, especially where patients would have been forced to travel long distances.

Limited market mechanisms were also introduced into social services. For example, the Community Care Act (1989) stated that 85 per cent of certain funds had to be spent on purchasing community care from the private and voluntary sectors. With regard to education, Barnes and Williams[8] claimed that the UK Education Act (1988) created, for individual schools, a climate radically different from that established by the 1944 Education Act. It introduced a system in which survival depends upon the ability of school managers to sell their services in a competitive environment. Barnes and Williams identified a number of assumptions underlying these changes:

- That informed consumer choice would prevail.
- That schools would compete to meet the needs of students and parents.
- That consumer choice would be informed by league tables based on standard attainment tests and on the reports of inspectors from a quality assurance agency.

The 1988 Act provided for schools that failed inspections and re-inspections to be taken over by private companies.

A SPECTRUM OF MARKETS

Internal trading involves deciding who are the customers and who are the suppliers and then drawing up service level agreements (SLAs) between them. Service level agreements stipulate what is expected in terms of the services to be provided. A personnel department, for example, might agree with another department that the maximum lapsed time between receiving a request for new staff and advertising the job would be six weeks. That would constitute an agreed level of service. The document in which that agreed level is noted is called a service level agreement. The cost of providing that agreed level of service is calculated and funds are allocated. Providers have to account for the funds and show that they have provided services to the agreed level. Specifying services in this way opens the possibility of inviting alternative suppliers to say what they would charge for providing the same service. Prices submitted by the other providers can be used as 'benchmarks' against which the economy or the efficiency of a provider is judged. In some cases this comparison may result in whole services being put out to tender. In some countries this is compulsory. At the extreme end of the market spectrum, managers of public services are free to choose when and how they wish to spend their budgets.[9] They have no restrictions in terms of possible suppliers, nor any requirement to put services out to tender.

Is Competition Helpful?

The advantages and disadvantages of competition in public services are debatable. Walsh[10] concluded that Compulsory Competitive Tendering (CCT) had resulted in some cost reductions. In the UK, for example, CCT reduced the cost of refuse collection by 20 per cent. This was achieved by getting fewer staff to do more work. However, it is unlikely that such a saving could be made in services such as education, where the quality of the service is often defined in terms of staff to student ratios. In some cases savings were made by reducing the wages and salaries paid. It is unlikely that such savings could be made, for example, in health services, where quality is often defined by the pay grade of the staff providing the services. Walsh also confirmed that there had been savings in Civil Service departments where new agencies had been established. However, effective managers can achieve comparable savings under existing arrangements. Training managers to be more effective managers is less costly and less time consuming than the disruption caused by introducing competitive tendering or the creation of a new agency.

The Contracting Process

An increasingly important competence required by public service managers is the ability to embody service level agreements into contracts and to monitor whether or not services are being delivered in accord-

ance with the contract. Even if specifications are not used competitively, they will continue to be the basis of inter-agency agreements. Flynn[11] notes that there is a range of different types of contractual agreements in public services. At the most competitive edge, services are put out to tender, inviting sealed bids from possibly unknown suppliers. In most cases the purchasers will know the service providers, since both the purchasers and the providers are employed by the same organization. These internal contracts are not legally enforceable. Failures to agree are resolved by internal administrative processes rather than through recourse to the law. In health services, a commissioning process precedes the contracting process. Commissioning in the NHS means the quantitative and qualitative specification of the healthcare services required to meet the assumed healthcare needs of a given population, over a defined time (usually one year).[12] The contract needs to specify the availability and the value of the services to be provided, and the service level to which the public will be entitled. It might stipulate specific quality indicators, such as waiting times, or the qualifications of the staff who will provide the service. Box 4.2 summarizes the content of a typical service level agreement.

Box 4.2

SERVICE LEVEL AGREEMENTS[13]

Service level agreements should identify:

- The service specification
- A cost for the specified service
- A mechanism for charging for the service
- A mechanism for changing the level
- A mechanism for terminating the agreement
- The level at which the service will be provided, its quantity and quality

In preparing the service level agreement:

- The supplier should involve the customers
- The supplier should provide the customers with a full description of the services

The service level agreement should provide:

- Flexibility in the face of changes
- The processing of SLA transactions
- The amendment of service standards
- A definition of the operation of the agreement
- Mechanisms for customers/clients to control the standards of the service they can expect and to monitor their achievement

Contracting Relationships

The contracting relationship is summarized in Figure 4.2. The purchaser assesses the need and demand for services. A contract is then agreed with a provider of services. The provider may be from the voluntary, private or statutory sector. The provider is required to deliver the services to standards of quality, quantity and value for money that are specified in the contract. Equity and technical aspects of service delivery should also be monitored. Ethical considerations involve empathy with staff, clients and other stakeholders in the community in which services are provided, and acceptance of responsibility for the effects of providing the service (Chapter 11).

Specifying the work that is needed and the processes involved is not always straightforward. The term 'well maintained grounds', for example, is open to interpretation. This could result in a tortuous specification of the length of grass, when it is cut and the numbers of flowers per square metre in a flower bed. There have been some tragic consequences of failures to specify what constitutes a safe level of service for people with mental illness or for people travelling on trains, boats and planes.

Adversarial versus Obligational

Sako[15] identifies two types of contract: obligational and adversarial. Obligational contracts are contracts in which the parties contract to work together for mutual benefit. They share risk and exhibit a high degree of mutual trust. At the other extreme, adversarial contracts are contracts that provide a basis for preventing one partner from gaining at the expense of the other partner. These two extremes provide a useful starting point for analysing possible approaches to contracting in public services. Adversarial contracting, with tight penalty clauses for failure to meet specification, can be expensive and detrimental to the quality of services delivered. For example, deviation from the contract specification is unlikely, even if the original specification was detrimental to the client group. Obligational contracting enables long-term relationships to develop which are based on shared values and a shared concern for the welfare of the services users. Such contracts emphasize an obligation to work together to improve the quality of the service. If the priority is to reduce spending, adversarial contracting may be preferable. Obligational contracting is more consistent with the need to deliver public services that take account of the needs of different stakeholders. We shall return to this issue at the end of this chapter.

Consumers, Customers or Clients?

The terms 'consumer' and 'customer' are not traditionally used in public services. However, they are central to the language of marketing. Stacey struggles with the notion of patients as consumers:

> The concept of the patient as a consumer undervalues the status of the patient. In the ideal of perfect competition, consumers hold high status; the consumers are always right. In monopoly capitalism, in the high bureaucracies of the welfare state, this is no longer true. In these circumstances, the consumer has low status. What else are all the consumers' rights movements about? Only the disadvantaged or threatened develop movements to enhance or defend their rights.[16]

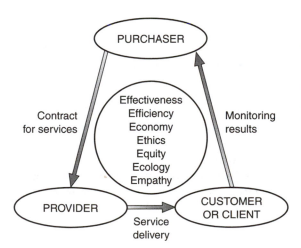

Figure 4.2 Contractual relationship in public services[14]

We would go further. We think that these labels misrepresent the best interests of patients and others for whom public services are provided, such as students! Consumers consume what is offered for consumption. This implies passivity. We do not expect students to be passive consumers of teaching. Patients, like students, need to engage actively with health service providers. In some cases, service users are defined as clients by statute.

The notion of customer, which implies some kind of economic exchange, is also problematic in public services such as primary schools. When choice is limited, or non-existent, the concept of customer seems misleading. It is appropriate, however, when there is a choice and when a direct charge is made for the service. Other terms in common parlance are service user, recipient or beneficiary. No one term seems to capture the complex relationships between providers of public services and those for whom the services are provided.

THE MARKETING PROCESS

In Box 4.3 we define the five key areas of a marketing manager's work, namely market research, organizational audit, marketing management, competitor analysis and business planning.

MARKET RESEARCH

'Assessing the present and future needs and wants of existing and potential customers and clients.'

In public services there is widespread use of market research. Flynn[17] suggests that market research is important in public services because it allows people to express their preferences and assessment of services. Market researchers use surveys, consult focus groups and interview service users. Kotler and Clarke[18] defined marketing research as the systematic collection, analysis and reporting of data relevant to specific situations. They advocated a five-stage model for market research. The first stage calls on the manager to define the problem carefully and to agree objectives for the research. This is usually called the brief. Managers need to be clear about the purpose for which the research will be used. This will determine what type of research is needed. There are three types of market research: exploratory, descriptive and causal. Exploratory market research is used to gather preliminary data to shed light on the nature of the problem and to suggest or refine hypotheses. Descriptive market research is often used to ascertain the key variables. Causal market research, as the name implies, is used to test cause and effect.

Box 4.3

THE MARKETING MANAGER'S JOB – DEFINING FIVE KEY AREAS

Market research is
'the assessment of the present and the future needs and wants of existing and potential customers and clients.'

Organizational audit is
'the auditing of all the resources of the organization.'

Marketing management is
'the co-ordination of all resources so as to satisfy those needs and wants.'

Competitor analysis is
'satisfying needs and wants so as to offer the possibility of sustainable advantage over competitors.'

Business planning is
'planning that the organization's income should exceed its expenditure by a planned margin.'

The second stage of market research is to develop a plan for gathering the needed information. Designing the research plan calls for decisions on data sources, research approaches, research instruments, sampling and control methods. Information can be gained from a variety of sources:

- Information already in the organization
- Local studies that have already been carried out
- National government departments
- The census
- Libraries

The third stage involves collecting information. Researchers must be aware that this stage is the one most liable to error. For example, in the case of surveys, some respondents will be unavailable, others may refuse to co-operate, and some may give biased or dishonest answers. Researchers need to be aware of not influencing the opinions of the participants by their very presence; of administering the instrument of enquiry in a uniform way, and of controlling extraneous factors. Ways of gathering information include public consultations and consumer panels (often called focus groups), telephone surveys, direct observations, using questionnaires, structured or unstructured interviews, postal and telephone surveys.

The fourth stage involves analysing the data. Kotler and Clarke's fifth stage is the presentation of the findings. The researcher should not try to overwhelm others with complicated statistical techniques. Only present major findings that are relevant to the decision that needs to be taken. The study is only useful if it reduces management's uncertainty about the right moves to make. Gilligan and Lowe[19] have amended the model used by Kotler, specifically for research into the market for healthcare services (see Figure 4.3). In this model they suggest primary and secondary sources of data collection, together

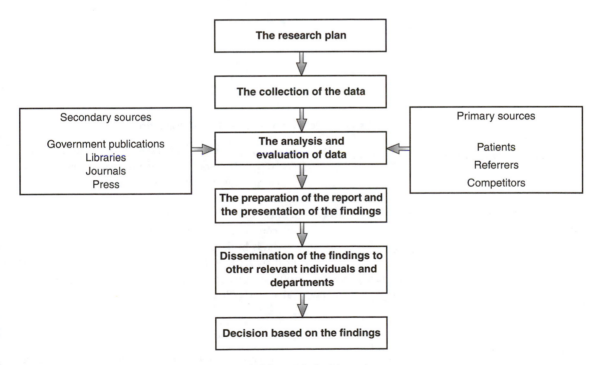

Figure 4.3 The marketing research process amended for public health services

Source: Gilligan and Lowe (1995)

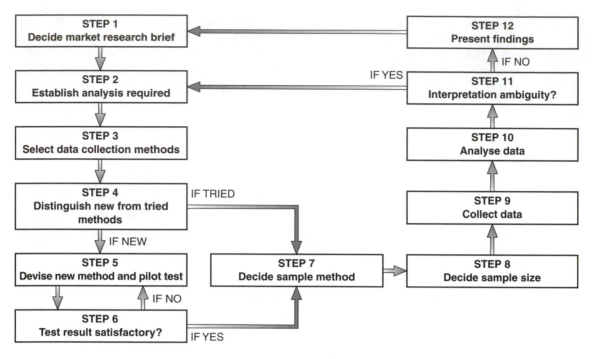

Figure 4.4 The marketing research cycle[20]

with an additional stage where decisions are made on the findings. This model for market research can be further broken down into twelve steps as detailed in Figure 4.4.

A Marketing Research Cycle for Public Services

Step 1: Decide market research brief

What are the decisions public service managers want to take? What do they need to know, by when and how accurately?

Step 2: Establish specific analysis and data

What information is required and in what form – numerical, tabular, summary, quantitative, raw?

Step 3: Select data collection methods

These may include for example, critical incident analysis, one-to-one interviews, focus groups, telephone surveys, patient panels, observation, questionnaires, opinion polling, public meetings, clinical audit, clinical trials, mini case studies or following up complaints. It is very important to design the methods backwards from the format required by the final analysis, especially if advantage is to be taken of software packages readily available for use in statistical analysis (Step 10).

Step 4: Distinguish new from tried methods

Managers can often take short-cuts by adapting data collection instruments already used by other public service organizations.

Step 5: Devise new methods and pilot study

Pilot testing may prolong the wait for results, but can obviate the time wasted when respondents misunderstand questions, replies are inconsistent or response rates are too low to be significant. The sample for the pilot study will need to be representative of the sample to be used in the larger-scale research.

Step 6: Was the pilot successful?

If the design proves unsatisfactory, it may be necessary to interview respondents and non-respondents, in order to rectify problems with the research design.

Step 7: Decide sampling method

Care in the choice of sampling method is essential when seeking representative data. Samples can be:

- Random, using, for example, alphabetic selections or every tenth user.
- Stratified, for example, by age, sex, ethnicity or socio-economic group.
- Quota, for example, a specific number of people with predetermined characteristics.

Step 8: Decide sample size

Consideration should be given to what size of sample would be representative, what size of sample is practically manageable, and what degree of accuracy is required. It is possible to use statistical techniques to determine what sample size is required to provide a given level of reliability.

Step 9: Collect data

If interviews are involved, interviewers will need to be trained and rehearsed. It is very easy, for example, to lead a respondent by the way a question is asked.

Step 10: Analyse data

If the methodology and the data collection are designed by working backwards from the form of analysis intended, analysis should be straightforward. Answers to questions should be in the form required by any software used in the analysis.

Step 11: Interpreting the results

If any results are ambiguous, or contradictory, Steps 2 to 10 may need to be repeated.

Step 12: Present findings

An executive summary should summarize the recommendations and the reasons for these recommendations. The reasons might relate to the market identified or to its size.

MARKET MEASUREMENT

When measuring current market size, a public service organization is likely to want to make four types of estimate: total market demand, area market demand, total market sales and organizational market sales, so that the organization's share of the market can be calculated. Total market demand for a product or service is that total volume that would be bought by a defined consumer group, in a defined geographical area, over a defined time period, in a defined market environment, under a defined marketing programme. The most important thing to realize about total market demand is that it is not a fixed number, but a function of specific conditions. Besides measuring potential demand, a public service organization will want to know the total 'take up' or 'sales' of services in its market. This involves identifying the other organizations serving the same market.

MARKET FORECASTING

Very few public services lend themselves to easy forecasting. Demand tends to rise to take up extensions of free services. Even the asking of market research questions can create a demand for services that people had not previously thought about. The reasons for this and the problems posed by it are discussed later. Poor forecasting can lead to wasteful provision or overstretched services, creating delays and dissatisfaction where none was previously felt. Organizations can use a variety of methods to forecast demand. A forecast can be based on what people say, what people do, or what people have done. The first basis, what people say, involves the systematic determination of the opinion of buyers of services, or those close to them. For example, in the case of education, we could interview the teachers and the parents of the pupils. Basing a forecast on what people do involves market testing. The final basis, what people have done, involves using statistical tools to analyse records of past behaviour.

TEMPLES Analysis of a Public Service

Forecasting involves predicting changes that will impact on the public service being provided. A useful way to review the possible changes that might impact on the future of the service is to use a checklist of the kind developed by Wootton and Horne.[21] In their book on strategic thinking, they describe how changes that might impact on the provision of a particular service can be predicted by asking questions which they group under seven headings which are recalled as the mnemonic TEMPLES:

T TECHNOLOGY
E ECONOMY
M MARKETS
P POLITICS
L LAW
E ETHICS
S SOCIETY

Typical questions that might be asked are:

Changes in technology

- How will improvements in communication systems and methods change the way you work with clients and colleagues?

- What are the implications for training?
- How long before your current technology becomes obsolete?
- Do you still need an office? For how long?

Changes in the economy

- How will changes in key economic indicators such as unemployment, inflation, taxation and public sector borrowing affect your service?
- Is your growth likely to be restricted by skills?
- How will government spending plans affect you?

Changes in the market

- What benefits do your service users obtain from your service?
- Could they obtain these benefits in another way?
- How large is the market for your services?
- How much of it do you currently serve?
- Who are your competitors?
- Are new competitors likely to enter the market?
- How easily could another organization copy what your service provides?

Changes in politics

- What government charters and standards might affect your service?
- What manifesto declarations or policies might affect your service?
- Are government policies a basis for planning?

Changes in the law

- What new or proposed legislation will affect you?
- What is the potential impact on your organization of legislation on employment, the environment, health and safety?
- Are you affected by EU regulations?

Changes in ethics

- What pressure groups are, or might become, interested in your activities?
- Do you look after welfare of employees?
- Do you monitor their stress levels?
- How will 'green' issues affect your organization?

Changes in society

- Are the expectations of your clients changing?
- Do your employees or clients expect to be involved in decisions?
- How will shifts in values, culture and lifestyle affect your organization?
- How will part-time working and short-term contracts affect your service?
- How will concerns over youth crime, community safety, health, education or drug abuse impact?
- How will changes in the population profile, such as the number of elderly people or ethnic composition affect your service?

Problems with Using Market Research in Public Services

The benefit of encouraging managers to look at their work through the eyes of others indicates the need for more, rather than less, market research. Market research requires the researcher to be clear about: 'present and future needs and wants of existing and potential customers and clients'. But what is a need and what is a want for a public service? If a service is free – or feels free – almost everyone may say that they want it. If you try to take it away, people will say that they need it. Powerful pressure groups may form to oppose the withdrawal of a service, even if it is little used. The 'need' for other services may be denied. Few people might agree that there was a need for more traffic wardens, tax inspectors, VAT collectors or court bailiffs. Some people may not see the need for services concerned with the emission of carbon dioxide, the slaughter of cattle, or the approval of genetically modified food. Even the concept of 'customer' is problematic. It brings with it the notion of customer satisfaction and customer dissatisfaction, turning formerly grateful clients into complaining 'customers'. This can demoralize front-line staff. Ambulance drivers, teachers or social workers may have been attracted to their jobs by the idea of providing a service for which people would be grateful.

MARKETING MANAGEMENT

> 'The co-ordination of all the resources of the organization so as to satisfy those needs and wants in such a way as to . . .'

Marketing oriented managers will try to achieve sustainable advantage over competitors and a planned margin of income over expenditure, by co-ordinating all the resources of the organization. Porter[22] suggested that there were three ways to achieve sustainable advantage over competitors: differentiation, focus and cost leadership. The pursuit of these strategies, in different combinations leads to three different marketing strategies: market segmentation, market domination and niche marketing (Figure 4.5).

Marketing oriented managers try to 'segment' their markets and then to 'focus' the efforts of their organization on a few selected segments in order to create

Figure 4.5 Marketing strategies for sustainable advantage

Box 4.4

MARKET SEGMENTATION

- **Geographical**: patterns may vary from one area to another
- **Demographic**: age, ethnicity, religion, sex, social class
- **Lifestyle**: a person's lifestyle may indicate likely needs

service 'niches' in the market. Segmentation is the act of dividing the market into distinct and meaningful groups of service users (Box 4.4). Market segmentation in public services is problematic. The principle of equal access, equal opportunity and equal outcomes underpins many public services. Market segmentation suggests that some people have different needs and wants. Many public service managers see it as their duty to offer the same level of service to everyone. Identifying and serving 'niches' implies discrimination and leaving some people out. To some managers, most doctors, many teachers and, hopefully, all ambulance drivers, this would be inconceivable.

'Focusing' is the selection of one or more of the market segments and the development of a distinctive strategy for each segment. For example, Cost Leadership might be one type of strategy (Box 4.5).

Box 4.5

COST LEADERSHIP – SOME ASSUMPTIONS

- Lower costs make it possible to offer lower prices than competitors
- The message about the lower prices must be communicated to the market
- Low prices are the single most important influence on up-take
- Low price strategies are sustainable

A cost leadership strategy might be followed by a public works department which was doing gardening or landscaping for private sector clients. Focus, on the other hand, might be the strategy preferred by a college which decides to specialize in forestry, or three-dimensional design or perfumery. Differentiation is used when customers can be attracted by things which differentiate the service from that provided by other organizations. Differentiation could be used by a government research centre or by a government security service.

Problems with Marketing Management in Public Services

Some of the ideas involved in marketing management are not problematic in some public services. For example, segmentation and focusing might benefit public services which produce statistics or maps. In the UK, Ordinance Survey maps have been targeted successfully at walkers, cyclists and motorists. Bids for funding for economic development projects and urban regeneration schemes often require market research. The segmentation of communities in terms of such things as ethnicity, age, numbers of single parents or car ownership is part of the everyday work of planning departments. Immigration and Customs and Excise agencies need to forecast the demand for their services, to avoid long queues at border crossings.

Despite these examples of marketing work which readily fits into the work of a public service organization, a market-oriented manager may still face difficulties when trying to co-ordinate the work of professionals, or as we have seen earlier, when trying to apply marketing techniques such as segmentation and focus. Marketing activities often result in a power struggle with the chief executive. The chief executive of a public service may be reluctant to accept the notion that it is the marketing director who should specify what the organization should be doing and that the chief executive's role is to ensure that it gets done. In many public services, chief executives have statutory lines of responsibility and accountability direct to government ministers. This often makes them reluctant to delegate the kind of work which a marketing-oriented manager may see as marketing management. Some chief executives prefer to do this kind of work themselves because they find it more interesting or higher profile than administrative tasks. They may usurp the work of less senior managers who are trying to adopt a more marketing orientation to their work. They can interfere, purporting to have a better 'feel' for the market than most other people in the organization. Direct confrontation is ill advised. The odds too much favour the chief executive.

COMPETITOR ANALYSIS

Porter[23] suggested that the behaviour of competitors was determined, at least in part, by what he called the structure of the market. Porter identified four sources of pressure on organizations which are competing in a particular market: customers, new entrants, substitute services and behaviour of suppliers. We shall explore whether these concepts throw any light on the behaviour of organizations that compete to provide public services. Questions to ask when analysing competition are in Box 4.6.

Box 4.6

COMPETITOR ANALYSIS

- Who are our potential competitors?
- Who are our present competitors?
- What is their current strategy?
- What are their objectives?
- How successful are they?
- What are their strengths?
- What are their weaknesses?
- What will they do in the future?

Free to Compete

Markets for public services, even when privatized, are often not 'free markets'. They may be governed by administrative or regulatory structures. For some public services it is not clear who, if anyone, might be a competitor. The 'barriers to entry' facing a new supplier of electricity or gas or water would be formidable. How much discretion does a purchaser really have to switch from one 'competitor' to another? Significant switching is not common. The market for public services is an imperfect one in which suppliers are often not free to supply customers of their own choosing. In the 1990s in the UK, universities were penalized if they exceeded recruitment targets determined by funding councils. These providers of public services were not allowed to 'grow' their markets. Providers are discouraged from raising expectations which cannot then be met.

Takeovers and Mergers

Privately owned competitors can outgrow each other through takeovers and mergers. This has been happening throughout the world in public utilities and in transport, especially haulage, airline and bus services. Concern is often expressed when control passes to companies that are registered in countries other than the one in which a public service is being provided. This happened when French companies put in a bid to supply water and refuse collection services in the United Kingdom and when an American company bid for a British company supplying electricity. The predatory ambitions of British Airways or British Telecommunications have not always been well received in other countries. The 'global' market for public services is not yet a 'free' market. When competitive mergers are designed to increase efficiency, employees and politicians fear that jobs will be lost and that unemployment will be increased. These fears are well grounded. In public services it is common for up to 70 per cent of the costs of providing the services to be employee costs. Competitive behaviours like mergers and takeovers can be resisted in public services when trades unions, staff associations or professional bodies have members in both organizations and are party to the talks about the merger or takeover. In the UK, members of the Prison Officers Association have resisted proposed takeovers by privately owned security firms. Similarly, the Royal College of Psychiatrists has resisted mergers to create specialist mental health trusts.

Compulsory Competitive Tendering

Governments sometimes offer incentives for privately owned organizations to take over the ownership or at least the management of some public service organizations. This can give rise to concerns about standards. There is public outcry when a privately owned residential care home appears to be abusive or to treat its clients disrespectfully. Systems of licensing, regulation and inspection are then created which absorb some of the hoped for savings in public expenditure. Sometimes the expertise required by both an existing public sector provider and a prospective new private sector supplier is the same. For example, it would take at least five years to train a cohort of educational psychologists. Similar problems would face a new private sector provider of public services which required the expertise of clinical psychologists. Professional bodies can restrict the supply of expertise, thereby preserving their value and power. They could argue, for example, that creating competition duplicates services and the cost of the training needed to support them, i.e. that it is wasteful of the intended savings.

Making Better Use of Capital Assets

One of the arguments in favour of competition is that it leads to more efficient use of capital assets, like buildings. A private sector company that does not fully utilize its land, or fully occupy its buildings, may become an attractive prospect for takeover by another organization which thinks it can make better use of those assets. It must either improve its utilization quickly or dispose of its surplus assets to someone who can. The cash released must then be invested quickly and wisely. If it is not prepared to do either of these things, the company with the under-utilized assets will be prone to takeover by another company who will do it for them. However, in the case of many public services, the disposal of surplus assets is problematic – the disposal of a surplus nuclear power station for example. Many public buildings were originally donated by charities on conditions that restricted their disposal or use. Publicly owned public service organizations, which dispose of under-utilized assets, are rarely free to reinvest the money they raise in order to expand or improve their services. They are often bound by Treasury rules which treat proceeds of capital disposals as revenue, or by Exchequer policies which relate to the management of the national economy. In the UK, money raised by selling publicly owned housing was restricted (Chapter 10).

Values – Competitive or Collaborative?

Finally, many of the people who work in public service organizations might not have been attracted to become public servants, if they had known that it would mean working in a climate characterized by distrust of fellow professionals and permeated by fear of mergers, takeovers and job losses. The pursuit of competitive strategies may be subverted by staff whose ideals run counter to those which underlie competitive behaviour. Jim Mehan, a health service manager, told us about his experience of trying to introduce marketing ideas into a public service (Box 4.7). Let us pick up Jim Mehan's struggle with the idea of a 'marketing mix' and its relevance to public service organizations. Jim's commercial 'marketing cake' is baked by using market research to adjust the product, place, the promotion and the price so as to maximize demand, sales and profits. Jim has suggested the addition of other ingredients when you are trying to bake a 'marketing cake' for public service organizations. We have chosen to add just one more ingredient to his 4Ps for product, promotion, place and price. We have added P for people. So now, we offer a 5P model of the marketing mix.

Box 4.7

EXTRACTS FROM A CONVERSATION WITH JIM MEHAN

(A Health Services Manager)

'THE MARKETING MIX'

Terry: Jim, you used to work in a privately owned organization before becoming a manager in a publicly owned organization. Was it very different?

Jim: At college they said that marketing should apply to all organizations. Personally, I liked the idea that marketing should permeate the whole of an organization. It puts more emphasis on achieving a better match between what our customers want and what we do.

Terry: Go on.

Jim: Well I liked the idea that there were ingredients which an organization could use to bake a marketing cake, ingredients like product, promotion, place and price.

Terry: Are all these things relevant in a health service?

Jim: I must admit it is sometimes difficult for me to relate to all the ingredients. Some belong more to aggressive marketeers in the private sector. Aggression would upset people in the office where I work. However, I can use some of the ideas. Publicising what services I am providing, for example, and especially the benefits that our service provides, so that people will protest to their MPs if anybody tries to cut our funding.

Terry: Who do you see as your customers?

Jim: We have a clearer geographical definition of our customers than a private sector manager of a public service. The idea of 'place' made us take mobile health screening units to do health checks in workplaces. We no longer assume that the public must come to us.

Terry: Is the idea of pricing relevant?

Jim: I admit I do struggle with the idea of pricing a public service. For me the issue is cost not price. I have to get much more out of my budgeted costs than I used to have to do in the private sector. Here there is no scope to make up for overspend by generating extra income. We cannot overspend and that's that.

Terry: Do you think that you should charge for your services?

Jim: This is an ethical issue. Free markets are driven by supply and demand and by the maximum price a customer is willing to pay. If we followed this logic then we could contain demand for healthcare and education and other services by pricing them out of the reach of most people. This would produce a very divided and unhealthy society.

Terry: I'm still not clear whether or not marketing ideas are relevant to your work as a public service manager.

Jim: There are lots of useful things public services managers can learn from marketing people. Perhaps their ideas on relationship marketing are the most applicable to public services. We need to learn to develop better relationships and partnerships with everybody who is concerned with healthcare. For example, I need to build better relationships with education and social services. The days are gone when you could say that education is the sole concern of schools or that the safety of the community is solely the concern of the police. No one service – whether publicly or privately owned – can address the complexity of the problems in these areas. Relationship marketing lends itself well to developing closer working relationships with partner organizations.

Terry: Thank you for taking the time to talk.

A 5P MARKETING MODEL FOR PUBLIC SERVICES

P for Package

According to Dibb et al.[24] the product is a service when it is intangible and has certain other characteristics (Table 4.1).

The delivery of a service cannot be separated from its user. For example, in a doctor's examination, or a social work case conference, or a college seminar, the delivery of the service and the use of the service are simultaneous. The patient, client or student contributes to the quality of the resulting service. Walsh[25] suggested that public services might be better categorized by the benefits which the services were expected to confer. Services could then be analysed to see which characteristics of the service contributed most to the benefits which they were meant to confer. For example, there may be at least three core benefits of a hospital service:

- **The direct benefit** of successful treatment
- **The consequential benefits** that patients and other stakeholders perceive as resulting from successful treatment
- **The convenience benefits** offered by ancillary services, such as appointment systems, reception services, correspondence and co-ordination

Thus, in the case of public services, Kotler's P for Product is really a whole Package of peripheral, as well as, core services. Kotler[26] referred to core product, tangible product and augmented product. In Box 4.8 we have adopted Kotler's ideas to describe a public service.

What are the future prospects of this product. Package – where is it in its life cycle, how vulnerable is it, how much at risk?

Table 4.1 Characteristics of goods and services

Services	Goods
Intangible	Tangible
Cannot be stored	Storable
Cannot be owned	Can be owned
Difficult to standardize	Normally standardized
Produced with the consumer	Produced without the consumer
Quality difficult to guarantee	Quality can be built into product
Do not persist through time	Are persistent through time

Box 4.8

THREE DIMENSIONS OF A SERVICE

- **The Core Service** is that part of the service that delivers core benefits like 'prevention of . . .'; 'elimination of . . .'; 'enhancement of . . .'; 'encouragement of . . .'
- **The Tangible Service** is the visible manifestation of the service – how it is seen and recognized. In the case of teaching, for example, this could include the accommodation and teaching aids. Despite research evidence that undercover policing is more effective in reducing crime rates, the public repeatedly request more visible community policing.
- **The Augmented Service** includes all the add-ons, sometimes called the 'added value' or the 'peripheral value'. For example, the police may provide counselling for victims of crime or housing officers may provide play areas for children so that parents can talk uninterrupted.

The Service Life Cycle

The service life cycle is based on the idea that the market demand for any service has a finite life and that during its life cycle it passes through distinguishable stages. The market for the service needs to be managed in different ways during the different stages of its life. Figure 4.6 represents these changes in the service life cycle.

Once the market for a service has entered the 'maturing' phase, Figure 4.6 implies that you should stop putting new resources – finance, recruitment, research – into the service and begin to think about subcontracting the service to the private sector, or getting a service level agreement with another agency, or contracting it out to a voluntary organization with initial grant aid, or discontinuing it all together. The resources this would release should be put into starting up new services in their 'developing' phase, as shown in Figure 4.6. The 'growth' phase should compensate for the services where the activity level is in the 'declining' phase – so that the overall portfolio of services maintains an even level of demand on the organization.

The Service Vulnerability Matrix

Our Service Vulnerability Matrix is based on the Boston Consulting Matrix which is described in Figure 4.7.

The most attractive products are 'Stars' which have high growth rates and a strong competitive position. They will be deemed to justify the investment needed to develop them and to ensure market dominance. 'Cash Cows' are profitable products which generate cash for the organization. This cash can be used to support the development of other products in the organization. 'Questions' could become very successful, but investment in them is speculative.

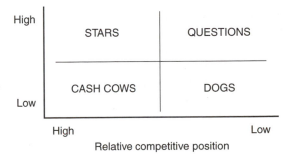

Figure 4.7 The Boston Consulting Matrix

The market is	Developing	Growing	Maturing	Declining
Years				
The buyers are	Few	Increasing	Multiple	Declining
The competitors are	Few	More	Fighting	Retreating
The conditions are	Steep learning curve	Fighting for a share of the market	Emphasis on efficiency, and low	Selective targeting
The market is	Developing	Growing	Maturing	Declining

Figure 4.6 The service life cycle

Source: Wootton and Horne (1997)

	Low vulnerability	High vulnerability
High growth rate	STARS	QUESTIONS
Low growth rate	CASH COWS	DOGS

Figure 4.8 Assessing the vulnerability of a public service

Source: Horne and Riley (1991)

Finally, 'Dogs' are products that should be discontinued, because there is no longer a real market for them. We have adapted the Boston Consulting Matrix for use in public services in Figure 4.8.[27]

The service life cycle model (Figure 4.6) helps managers to think about growth rates and the potential for developments in each of the services being offered. Managers can then try to place each service in one of four quadrants on the Service Vulnerability Matrix (Figure 4.8), by considering which other agencies or private contractors might be invited to compete for the provision of the service, through, for example, compulsory competitive tendering. Managers can then estimate whether they think the service in question is vulnerable.

Having positioned all your services on the Service Life Cycle (Figure 4.6) and then located them on the Service Vulnerability Matrix (Figure 4.8) we can consider the investment of funds released by the discontinuance of 'dog' services. As we shall discover in Chapter 10, new investment requires a risk assessment. A model which can help managers to assess the risk can be found in Figure 4.9. It is based on the work of Ansoff.[28]

Options A carry the lowest risk, involving at most the seeking out of similar users of similar services. These are options for market penetration or service improvement. Following the Z plan, options B are still below average risk because you can pilot your ideas for new developments with existing customers

---

Box 4.9

ASSESSING SERVICE VULNERABILITY

- **Services in Box One** are the most attractive candidates for investment.
- **Services in Box Two** generate cash for the organization which can be used to support the development of other services, providing the organization is not prevented from doing so by financial regulations which restrict reinvestment (see Chapter 10).
- **Services in Box Three** are unlikely to secure financing and other resources unless a private sector partner can be found to share the risk.
- **Service in Box Four** may require strategies for their discontinuation.

---

with whom you have a supportive relationship. The risk is higher for options C. Although these are services which you are well used to supplying, there are always risks when you start to deal with new people or new customers. Still following the Z Plan, it would take the threat of catastrophe to bring forth

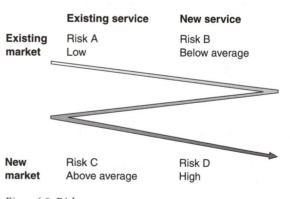

	Existing service	New service
Existing market	Risk A Low	Risk B Below average
New market	Risk C Above average	Risk D High

Figure 4.9 Risk assessment

Source: Horne and Riley (1990)

support for options D. Examples of such threats have been AIDS, 'mad cow' disease (BSE), thalidomide babies, football crowd violence, the sinking of a ferry boat, an unexpected act of terrorism, a sudden rise in drug abuse or the overnight death of all the fish in a Swedish lake.

We have looked at why a public service is not just a single product of an organization's efforts but is a package of peripheral features that determine how it is presented to the public. We have looked at how that package can be reviewed at various points in the life cycle of the service, how vulnerable it might be associated with making any changes to the package. We look now at the way the potential benefits of the package can be communicated. We look at P for promotion.

P for Promotion

Because a service is intangible, services can be harder to promote than industrial goods or consumer durables. Often what is promoted is not the service but the 'image' of the organization providing the service. When people trust an organization, they are attracted to use the services which the organization provides. In Chapter 12 we look at the role of information management in promoting the image of the organization. When promoting a service we consider publicity, persuasion and public relations.

- **Publicity** is the use of media, such as newspapers, TV, radio, direct mail, fax and e-mail
- **Persuasion** is having persuasive conversations with potential users or purchasers of the service. When the overall marketing strategy is working well, it reduces the need for personal persuasion. However, very few services sell themselves without persuasive conversations, usually with front-line staff. We looked at the principles that underpin persuasive conversations in Chapter 2. Keeping a database of people who have used or have contacted the service helps to target publicity materials and can be a source of recommendations or support to new users
- **Public Relations** is about the use of press releases, radio features and TV interviews to communicate information about the service

Historically, publicly owned public service organizations have been reluctant to use publicity, persuasion, public relations, or indeed promotion of any sort, lest they provoke demand that they are unable to meet from cash-limited budgets. This attitude is changing in some western countries and in many international agencies. There is increasing recognition that members of the public are entitled to know what services they are funding when they pay taxes. In Box 4.10 we suggest some conditions under which a manager of a publicly owned public service might consider allocating part of their budget in

---

Box 4.10

WHEN TO PUBLICIZE A PUBLICLY OWNED SERVICE[29]

- When the service is new or has been decentralized to a local office
- When clients are likely to be ignorant of the service, because, for example, they are disabled, illiterate or a marginalized minority
- When eligibility for a service may be unclear, for example, when there is likely to be a poor uptake of benefits, allowances or grants
- When significant changes are being made, for example, when changing the opening times of unemployment centres or post offices
- When effectiveness depends on high usage, for example, in leisure centres or libraries or in programmes to eradicate infectious diseases

order to promote the service to service users. The traditional approach of many public services has been to conceal information about the availability of public services from the public, in case the demand for services should exceed the resources available.

Having considered the way the service package can be composed, developed and then promoted, we look now at where it can be provided. We look at P for place.

P for Place

P for place is concerned with the place where services are delivered. In Pakistan, for example, we are looking at whether health services should be provided in hospitals, or in community centres or in the home. In the UK, we are looking at whether police services should be rooted in the community or in specialist crime squads. Should police officers patrol in cars or on foot? The first year of many undergraduate degrees are now taken in local link colleges. Increasingly, they may be taken at home or in the workplace. Youth service outreach teams contact young people who do not come into youth centres. Health visitors target people at risk from heart disease. Video conferencing for remote diagnosis by a medical consultant is common practice in Australia. Further implications of developments in telecommunications are discussed in Chapter 12. We have looked at P's for package, promotion and place; we turn next to the P for price.

P for Price

Pricing public services is problematic. Walsh[30] pointed out that the very reason why many public services are publicly provided is because they are not amenable to market pricing (Box 4.11). A study of pricing policies in public services by Coopers & Lybrand[31] revealed that:

- There was not one approach
- Rules of thumb were used wrongly
- Copying pricing policies was common
- Invalid reasons are given for not recovering costs

> **Box 4.11**
>
> ## PRICING POLICIES: THE CONSIDERATIONS
>
> - Costs and how to recover them
> - Loans and how to service them
> - Demands and how to maximize them
> - Competitors and how to contain them
> - Profits and how to maximize them

Coopers & Lybrand recommended an increase in the use of direct charges and a reduction in the frequency with which costs were subsidized. Subsequent to that report, in the UK, there was an increase in direct charging for services such as: meals delivered to the homes of the elderly; home cleaning; medical prescriptions; car parking; leisure services; and adult education courses. Because of worldwide concerns about population growth and about the sexual transmission of diseases like AIDS and hepatitis, the prices for condoms, coils, contraceptive pills and abortions have been reviewed. In many countries – particularly in the developing world – these services are now provided free. In some countries men are actually paid if they present themselves for a vasectomy.

We have considered the nature of the package that makes up a service and how it might be reviewed, developed and promoted. We have looked at the place where such services may be found and whether or not a price can be charged for them. Finally, we look at P for the people involved in service delivery.

P for People

People are the major ingredient in the marketing mix for public services. This has implications for staff recruitment, induction, training, appraisal, promotion, discipline and early retirement (Chapter 8). Who are the key players in the marketing game? Who is in play? Who is likely to defend? Who is likely to attack? Who is waiting on the sidelines? Who is coaching from behind the scenes? Who are the rising stars? Who might be dropped? Who could stir up trouble on the terraces? Who owns the club and who chairs the board meetings? These people are all key players; often they are called stakeholders. We turn now to the ways we can identify the stakeholders and the kind of relationships we might need to develop with them.

Stakeholder Analysis and Relationship Marketing in Public Services

Instead of being concerned about individual transactions between suppliers and buyers, the relationship marketing emphasizes the importance of relationships between the organizations.[32] Relationships are developed with 'key accounts', that is, those 20 per cent of accounts who between them account for 80 per cent of revenue. Relationships with these organizations, or key accounts, will usually be handled by a key account executive. In public services the equivalent of a 'key account' is a 'stakeholder agency'. A 'stakeholder agency' is an agency whose work impacts strongly on areas in which the public service is to be provided. Attempts are made to forge alliances through formal agreements. In the UK, for example, alliances have been 'encouraged' by funding bodies that will only consider applications for funding if they are made jointly by the stakeholders between whom the government wishes to see relationships develop. Relationship marketing operates at five levels (Box 4.12).

In the late 1990s, this concept resonated with the UK Labour government which encouraged 'Joined up solutions to joined up problems'.[33] Once stakeholders have been identified, as much as possible is found out about them, including the nature of their expectations and the scope for conflict with them. The strength of a stakeholder is not only vested in their purchasing power. It can be vested in their influence over key decision-makers. Sometimes they are 'gate keepers', who can deny or facilitate access to other key decision-makers. It is important to retain

---

Box 4.12

RELATIONSHIP MARKETING – FIVE LEVELS

Level 1	Basic	'The product or service that we offer is all you need, you're free to buy it when you need it.'
Level 2	Reactive	'Call me if you have any problems, if I can help I will.'
Level 3	Accountable	'I'm checking to see your OK.'
Level 4	Proactive	'I can improve the work of your agency if I understand it better. Let's keep in touch and talk.'
Level 5	Partnership	'I want to help you succeed in every possible way, because I will benefit.'

---

contact with the end users of the service and to inform them about developments affecting their services. There can be problems when the values that underlie different parties to the relationship are not the same. We discussed how these problems might be addressed in Chapter 3. In Chapter 15, we discuss the way stakeholder analysis has been abused.

Developing a Marketing Plan

Having looked at each of the five P's of our 5P model – Package, Promotion, Place, Price and People – a public service organization will need to pull together some form of Plan. Box 4.13 summarizes the key components of a marketing plan.

Box 4.13

THE COMPONENTS OF A MARKETING PLAN

Mission Statement

What the organization aims to do, how it does it and with whom

Vision Statement

Where and what the organization aims to be in the future

Market Research

- Market Structure
- Market Trends
- Market Segments
- Market Gaps

Organizational Audit

External Audit of Opportunities and Threats
Internal Audit of Strengths and Weaknesses

Competitor Analysis

Porterian Analysis

Portfolio Analysis

Service Life Cycle, Service Vulnerability, Risk Assessment

Marketing Management

- Marketing Strategy
- Market Penetration
- Diversification
- Service Development

The 5P Model

- Package
- Promotion
- Place
- Price
- People

– Stakeholder Analysis
– Relationship Marketing

The Business Plan

FINAL THOUGHTS: THE 'GOOD' SOCIETY[34]

The provision of public services in a particular society relies on the assumption that most members of that society want to live in a 'good' society – a society where public services are provided to members of the society in greatest need of them and where the cost of providing these public services is willingly met by the more fortunate members of that society. When belief in the 'good' society crumbles, so does support for public services. Towards the end of the twentieth century, the market was believed by some to be a foundation upon which a good society could be built. Markets swapped information, generated innovation, stimulated economic activity, allowed competition and rewarded enterprise – in short, they created the wealth that was needed to pay for public services. The language of the market pervaded many transactions, even human ones. In a perfect marketing world, each transaction can be costed and should only be allowed to occur if a proper price can be charged for it. But in a good society people do not put a price on human conversation. In a good society we hold many conversations without calculation. We believe that the preparedness to hold conversations unconditionally is one of the characteristics of a good society.

Public service is a conversational process. If you tried to cost all these conversations, you would entirely miss the point of having the public service in the first place. You would have dehumanized the service by putting a price on curiosity, on feelings and on the satisfaction of working with others. According to John Tusa, writing in the *Independent* in January 1997, the BBC Library was asked to set a price on each enquiry made by broadcasters on the BBC world service. There had been a complaint that some broadcasters were using the library more than the average. Ignoring for the moment that it is in the nature of averages that some people must be above them, what is the point of putting a price on a conversation with a librarian, if you risk losing a priceless asset like your reputation for accuracy?

Furthermore, the idea of the individual is damaged. We are no longer individual people; we are members of a market segment. All members of a given market segment are the same, differentiated from other members of other segments by their values, desires and interests. A good society needs good citizens not market segments. The market works against this. The market is not interested in who you are as a whole person. One thing and only one thing matters – what will you buy? A good society must offer a concept of citizenship that sees people as individuals and supports the formation of close one-to-one relationships between them. Markets work in the opposite direction, preferring categories like consumer, purchaser and customer to more humane categories like student, teacher, public servant and citizen.

SUMMARY

- Our definition of marketing involved market research, organizational audit, competitor analysis, marketing management and business planning. We concentrated on market research, competitor analysis and marketing management.
- We analysed differences between marketing goods and marketing public services.
- We explored problems posed by the creation of a contract culture and looked at the role of service level agreements.
- On balance, we thought that market research was useful to managers of public services and a number of techniques were described.
- We demonstrated how service life cycles, service vulnerability appraisals and risk assessment models could be used to maintain and develop a service package.
- When we discussed marketing management, we thought that the concepts of focus, differentiation, cost leadership, market penetration, service development, market development and diversification, could be helpful to privately owned public service organizations.
- We upgraded a 4P model to a 5P model for marketing public services.
- We considered the role of stakeholder analysis and relationship marketing.
- In our final thoughts we wondered whether the political, economic and social values that underlie marketing can ever sit easily with the values that underpin the public provision of many public services, in a 'good' society.

THINKING AND LEARNING ACTIVITIES

Activity 1 Self-assessment

1 Differentiate between the production, selling and the marketing eras.
2 Thinking as a public service manager, identify two or three problematic issues in relation to market research, competitor analysis and segmentation.
3 Which marketing ideas do you think could be useful in public services and why?
4 What problems might public service managers have in using the 4P marketing mix?
5 In what way might a fifth P for people contribute to a public services marketing mix?
6 Explain what stakeholder analysis and relationship marketing mean.
7 What are the elements of a marketing plan? Identify problematic issues related to each of these areas of marketing activity.

Activity 2 Individual or Paired Learning: Empathetic Thinking

Analysing your curriculum

Think about an academic institution you are attending or have attended. Plot the curriculum subjects on offer on the vulnerability matrix in Figure 4.8. (You may wish to apply this exercise to subjects offered in a department of management or business studies. Consult a prospectus or find it on the website). If you were the manager responsible for the prospectus on offer, what would you do? Compare notes with a colleague and come to an agreed strategy. Afterwards, notice the points on which you gave ground. Why did you do that? Make some notes. If you were in the same position again, would you give the same ground?

Activity 3 Individual Learning: Predictive and Visual Thinking

The future of education

Using the questions in the TEMPLES analysis in the main text, think about the way an educational programme with which you are familiar might be affected by changes in technology, economics, markets, politics, law, ethics or society. Assume that the programme adapts to the changes you have predicted. Draw a sketch to represent how the programme might look in 15 years' time. If you find visual sketching difficult, describe in words a day in the life of a student on the programme in 15 years' time.

Activity 4 Individual Learning: Imaginative Thinking

Competition in education

Make a list of the different sorts of competitors and potential competitors facing education institutions.

Activity 5 Paired Learning: Creative and Metacognitive Thinking

Education – the package on offer

Re-read the section on P for package in the main text. Think about the direct, consequential and convenience benefits to you of studying at an institution with which you are familiar. Think about the core, tangible and augmented services which the institution offers. How might the package on offer be improved? Devise a low-risk package improvement plan for the service which would help to protect the service from being taken over by another organization. Make use of the service life cycle model (Figure 4.6), the service vulnerability model (Figure 4.8) and the risk assessment model (Figure 4.2).

If possible, find a partner who has finished the exercise above and discuss the models you have used. Which was the easiest to understand? Which model was the easiest to use and why? Which model provided the most powerful insights that affected your final plan? Can you agree on some criteria for judging the merits of a model?

Activity 6 Paired Learning: Creative and Visual Thinking

Promoting education

If you were the course leader of a course with which you are familiar, how would you promote it? Imagine you were persuading a friend to take the course. What would be your persuasive algorithm? Rehearse the conversation by role playing with your partner. Draft a leaflet to be sent to the careers advisors of local schools. Construct the format by folding an A4 sheet in half by placing the two shortest sides together. This produces an A5 leaflet with four pages. Think about the impact of the cover page; does it encourage the reader to open the leaflet? What information should be on the back page? Will the layout be important? What illustrations, examples, or quotations will you include? Test the leaflet on your intended audience and modify it in the light of their comments. What information on your leaflet would you include on an A3 poster? (Double A4) Sketch out the design for the poster and get some feedback from a colleague. What intriguing information could you fax, phone or e-mail to your local paper or radio station to tempt them to do a story or interview about the course? Make a few notes on your experience of writing and piloting a leaflet and poster.

Activity 7 Individual Learning: Imaginative and Predictive Thinking

There's a place for me, somewhere

Revisit the examples in the TEMPLES analysis in the main text, and the examples you came up with in Activity 3 on predicting changes – especially changes in technology, economics and in society. Think of an educational institution with which you are familiar. What changes do you think it could make immediately in *where* it delivers its

service? (Do not concern yourself, for the moment, with whether it *should* make such changes. We return to that question in Chapter 13 on Learning.) What changes might it be forced to make in the next 20 years? In this, and a number of the activities at the end of this chapter, you have been asked questions based on information that is purely speculative – your own speculations and those of others. Write down how you feel about spending time on questions that are hypothetical, based only on speculation.

Activity 8 Individual Learning: Numerical and Critical Thinking

Who benefits and who pays the price?

What are the arguments for and against institutions charging a price equal to the full cost of education? Who should pay this price – parents, students or the public? What are the arguments for and against each group paying? Think of an educational experience from which you have benefited and decide how, if you had to, you would work out a price for it. What information would you need? Estimate the figures as best you can and arrive at a price. Test out your estimate by asking relevant people whether, if everyone had to pay for education and institutions had to charge, they would regard your price as fair. Afterwards, write some personal notes on the process of trying to arrive at a price.

Activity 9 Individual or Paired Learning: Critical Thinking

Turning ideas into actions

In the case of public services, do you agree that it is better to add a fifth P for people to the marketing mix model? If so, why? If not, why not? If you were the head of an educational institution with which you are familiar, how would you take P for people into account in your market-oriented management of the institution? What would it cause you to do or avoid doing? Discuss your ideas for action with a partner. Afterwards, write some personal notes about the process of moving from ideas and theories into actions.

Activity 10 Individual or Paired Learning: Imaginative Thinking

Contracting out of education

Refer to the main text on contracting and service level agreements. Imagine you were the course leader of any course with which you are familiar. Select part of the course – a module, semester, term, first year – which you are going to invite a nearby college to provide under a licence from your institution. Draw up a draft service level agreement between the institutions. Ask a colleague to play the role of someone in the neighbouring college receiving the draft. Meet to discuss and refine the draft until you would both be happy to sign it. Afterwards, write some notes about the process of drafting and negotiating contracts.

Activity 11 Individual or Group Learning: Predictive Thinking

Action planning in education

The object is to write a marketing plan for an organization – preferably an educational institution – with which you are familiar. Refer to the marketing planning framework in the main text. Sections can be allocated to individuals to write. You will then need to work out how the writing of the sections that are interdependent can be co-ordinated. Finally, you will need a process for pulling it all together. Presentation will need to be thought about (Chapter 12). The business plan may best be left until you have studied Chapters 10 and 11. Choose an audience to whom the plan can be presented for feedback. Afterwards write some personal notes on market planning and, if appropriate, on the experience of involving other people in the process.

Activity 12 Individual or Paired Learning: Critical Thinking

Afterthoughts on the final thoughts

The Final Thoughts section contains many assumptions – some of them implied rather than explicit. What implied assumptions can you spot? Compare notes with a partner. The writer jumps from some of these assumptions to conclusions, without intermediary reasons, support or evidence. Can you spot these jumps? Compare notes with a partner. Could you, in some cases, supply the missing reasoning? In some cases, where reasoning is used, it is open to challenge. Which reasoning would you challenge? Is your counter-reasoning based on logic or can you provide a counter-example? Is there inconsistency in the reasoning which the writer uses in different parts of the argument? Why do you think the writer wrote this piece as a final thought on this marketing chapter? What useful purpose might it serve? Finally, write some bullet points of advice to yourself when presenting your own opinions.

Activity 13 Individual Learning: Evaluative and Visual Thinking

Case study

Before you read the case material (Box 4.14) about the eight public services involved in the stakeholder network, you are forewarned that you will be asked to consider what might be beneficial (B), interesting (I), and questionable (Q) about trying to apply some of the ideas which we have suggested underlie the marketing concept. When you have completed your 'B I Q' review of these ideas in relation to the eight public services, we ask you to form your own view of the helpfulness and relevance of these marketing concepts to public services. You should first give some thought as to how you will record complex views and opinions that are not always complete, as you carry out your 'B I Q' review. You should try to make your record on no more than two sides of A4. You are required to design a matrix, or a table, or a map, or a flowchart, or a Venn diagram, to make a visual record of your thoughts. When you have done this, compare your findings with a colleague and identify areas where you agree, disagree or are simply unable to form a view. Can you help each other? Can you see patterns or themes emerging? Can you summarize which marketing ideas seem applicable here?

Box 4.14

CASE STUDY: PUBLIC HEALTH STAKEHOLDERS[35]

Eight public agency stakeholders form a relational marketing network for the provision of healthcare services in a local community. The reader is now required to consider what might be: *beneficial, interesting* and *questionable* when trying to apply the following marketing ideas to the working of the public service network.

1 **Market Research**
   'the creation of needs and wants of existing or potential customers'
2 **Marketing Management**
   'co-ordinating all the resources' of the network of public services seeking to provide community-based healthcare
3 **Competitor Analysis**
   'satisfying needs and wants' of clients for community-based healthcare more effectively than competitors

There are eight different public services involved in the network which is seeking to provide community-based healthcare.

1 A Public Health Authority

A Public Health Authority is comprised of a chief executive officer, a finance officer and an information department which collects data on health activities relating to local residents. The information department validates and 'cleans' the data and provides reports which monitor the various healthcare contracts held by the authority. A planning and contracting department, uses the information to assess the performance of the current healthcare contracts and to negotiate and re-negotiate contracts accordingly. It also assesses service levels and suggests and develops new specifications as local need or government policy changes. A quality department conducts surveys and uses patient questionnaires to assess the quality of services. It concerns itself with such things as the length of times that patients or the public have to wait for services, or the extent to which waiting areas are perceived as comfortable. There are staff concerned with the routine inspection and control of nursing homes. One recent structural change has resulted in the creation of a 'central agency' which handles all matters relating to general practitioners and community-based care. This 'central agency' deals with such things as payments to doctors and their prescribing habits. This central agency also handles issues to do with computer systems, dental services and many other issues specifically to do with community healthcare. This agency provides services to four other neighbouring Health Authorities. The following seven public service organizations have an interest or can be considered as stakeholders in the work of the authority.

2 Community Health Councils

Typically a Community Health Council (CHC) has 24 members chosen from a wide range of elected representatives and non-elected people nominated by different charities working in the community. The CHC has access to the general public in two ways: by members of the public coming to the CHC with a particular concern, or through a council member's own network of contacts in the community. CHC representatives have access to meetings of the Health Authority and also to meetings of the hospital management boards. CHC representatives also participate in focus groups as users of health services.

3 Council for Voluntary Service

The Council for Voluntary Service (CVS) has direct contact with the public, working through the multitude of voluntary organizations which operate in a community. The work of the CVS involves co-ordination, advice and support for voluntary organizations, the development of new groups, and the representation of the voluntary sector on a variety of bodies such as local authority steering groups, joint consultative groups and community regeneration projects which seek external funding from sources such as the Single Regeneration Budget and the National Lottery. The CVS also provides a channel for communication between different groups and networks particularly to gain support for specific community-based campaigns.

4 Local Government Planning Departments

One of the functions of these departments concerns the use of land, particularly in relation to its suitability for housing, industrial purposes or other institutional, community or commercial use. Planning departments must keep up-to-date records of the number of houses built and the status of local transport provision, in order to facilitate local planning. They have substantial involvement in projects concerned with urban renewal, business land and conservation areas and they have a large input into urban regeneration bids and other projects supported by national government and the European Union. There is some liaison with the voluntary sector and with other charitable bodies.

5 Environmental Health Departments

Environmental health covers five main areas of work: food safety, occupational health and licensing, pollution control, environmental monitoring and building controls. Food safety covers the maintenance of standards of food hygiene, from the small corner shops to large manufacturing plants and from hot dog stands to school kitchens. This involves ensuring that food offered for sale is fit for human consumption and that safe handling procedures are being

used. It includes water quality, infectious disease notification and health issues connected with ports and docks.

The occupational and licensing remit of the Environmental Health Department concerns the enforcement of health and safety at work and other relevant legislation. It also handles complaints relating to nuisances, such as overflowing drains, accumulations of refuse, smoke, dust, fumes, noise and vermin. Environmental monitoring includes a dog warden service, street refuse collection and recycling services and cemetery management. The building control section is responsible for ensuring that new buildings are erected within criteria related to structural safety.

6 Providers of Health Services

Typically hospitals, or community health trusts, provide assessment, diagnosis, treatment and follow-up of patients. There are many departments within a hospital other than those providing clinical and para-medical services. These other departments provide estate management, hotel services and administrative and clerical services.

The management of hospitals is carried out by senior officers and managers who are sometimes called the Executive Board. The Executive Board is joined by a majority of non-executive directors drawn from the local community to form a Trust Board. The chief executive of the Trust has overall responsibility for the work of the Trust and reports to the non-executive chairman of the Trust Board on all issues, including the day-to-day running of the Trust and the development of strategy. This demands qualities of leadership, motivation and vision in order to turn strategic objectives into plans for implementation. The chief executive is also accountable to an independent public accounts committee and an independent Audit Commission concerned with monitoring the economy, the efficiency and effectiveness (the three E's) of all publicly accountable providers of public services. Recently, local health promotion units have come under local NHS Trust providers.

7 The Prison Service

The prison service seeks to provide a safe and secure environment in which to house members of the public sentenced to detention or required by the courts to be remanded in custody awaiting trial. There are a number of different types of prisons, ranging from secure to open prisons, depending on the category of prisoner being detained. A recent report of the Director of Prison Healthcare has stated that the vision of the prison health service is to provide:

> equivalence of healthcare for our patients with that of the National Health Service for the community at large ... to do all within our power to promote and maintain the healthcare of prisoners, irrespective of their offence and independent of their punishment and a clear sense of our moral obligation to safeguard their human rights.[36]

The prison health service is active in recruiting and providing specialist training for all types of healthcare staff such as doctors, nurses, pharmacists and health promotion personnel. Each prisoner is screened for signs of substance abuse, physical disability and mental illness. A 24 hour prison hospital with full-time staff is resourced by the Local Health Authority.

8 Education Services: Universities, Colleges and Schools

Readers of this book will probably be familiar with the work and organization of education services and you are asked to consider how universities, colleges and schools and the public service bodies responsible for their management might be stakeholders in a network of public services concerned with health. You might consider the research and teaching aspects of the university's activities and also their activities concerned with student health and with their responsibilities for the health and safety of large numbers of students and staff. At the other end of the spectrum, what was your own experience of health and social education, school meals, school nursing and dentistry and immunization?

Activity 14 Individual Learning Review: Reflective Thinking

Inner world thinking

What inner world thinking skills can you identify in the manager's work described in this chapter? Have any of the thinking skills you have identified emerged for the first time in this chapter? If so, add them to your accumulating model of the kinds of thinking skills that you think are useful to managers of public services.

What things could you do to develop any of the thinking skills that you have just added to your model? What would be the first step?

Outer world conversations

What outer world conversational skills can you identify in the manager's work described in this chapter? Have any of the types of conversational skills you have identified emerged for the first time? If so, add them to your accumulating model of the kinds of conversational skills you think are useful to managers of public services.

What things could you do to develop any of these conversational skills which you have just added to your model? What would be the first step?

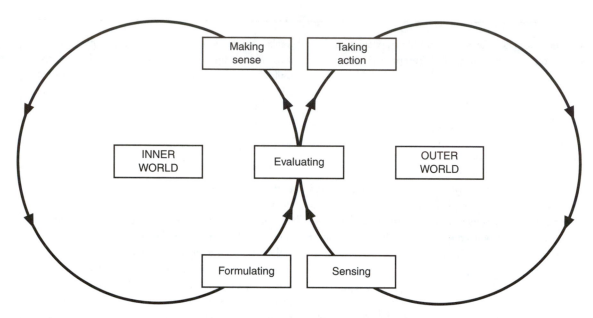

Figure 4.10 The thinking skills of the conversational manager

Activity 15 Individual Learning: Metacognitive Thinking

Metacognition

Look back through the Thinking and Learning Activities you have been asked to carry out in this chapter. What thinking skills were involved in each of these activities? For each type of thinking, write down how you were learning what you were learning, when you were learning to think in each of the different ways.

NOTES

1 Walsh, K. (1993) *Marketing in Local Government.* Longman, p. 5.
2 Drucker, P. (1954) *The Practice of Management.* Harper & Row, p. 56.
3 Chapman, D. and Cowdell, T. (1998) *New Public Sector Marketing.* Financial Times/Pitman.
4 Kotler, P. (1994) *Marketing Management, Analysis, Planning, Implementation and Control.* Prentice Hall International.
5 Chapman and Cowdell, op. cit., p. 37.
6 Ferlie, E., Cairncross, L. and Petigrew, A. (1993) 'Understanding Internal Markets in the NHS', in Tilley, I. (ed.) *Managing the Internal Market.* Paul Chapman.
7 Ibid.
8 Barnes, C. and Williams, K. (1993) 'Education and Consumerism: Managing an Emerging Market Culture in Schools', in Isaac Henry, K. *et al.* (ed.) *Management in the Public Sector. Challenge and Change.* Chapman and Hall.
9 Flynn, N. (1997) *Public Sector Management.* Prentice Hall, pp. 125–7.
10 Walsh, K. (1995) *Public Service Markets Mechanisms: Competition, Contracting and the New Public Management.* Macmillan.
11 Flynn, op. cit., p. 131.
12 Opit, L. (1993) 'Commissioning: An Appraisal of a New Role', in Tilley, I. (ed.) *Managing the Internal Market.* Paul Chapman, p. 83.
13 Blundell, B. and Murdock, A. (1998) *Managing in the Public Sector.* Butterworth-Heinemann.
14 Ibid.
15 Sako, M. (1992) *Prices, Quality and Trust.* Cambridge University Press.
16 Stacey, M. (1976) 'The Health Services Consumer: A Sociological Misconception', in *The Sociology of the NHS.*
17 Flynn, op. cit., p. 157.
18 Kotler, P. and Clarke, D. (1988) *Marketing Management: Analysis, Planning, and Control.* Prentice Hall.
19 Gilligan, C. and Lowe, R. (1995) *Marketing and Health Care Organizations.* Radcliffe Medical Press.
20 Mehan, J. (1997) MBA dissertation, Lancashire Business School.
21 Wootton, S. and Horne, T. (1997) *Strategic Thinking. The Nine Step Programme.* Kogan Page.
22 Porter, M. E. (1980) *Competitive Advantage.* The Free Press.
23 Porter, op. cit.

24 Dibb, S. *et al.* (1994) *Marketing Concepts and Strategies.* Houghton Mifflin, p. 664.
25 Walsh (1993), op. cit., p. 64.
26 Kotler and Clarke (1988), op. cit.
27 See Horne, T. and Riley, D. (1986) 'Market Planning – A Step by Step Approach'. Paper University of Central Lancashire.
28 Ansoff, I. (1966) *Corporate Strategy.* Penguin.
29 Walsh (1995), op. cit., p. 93.
30 Ibid., p. 94.
31 Department of the Environment (1981) Coopers & Lybrand Service Provision and Pricing in Local Government.
32 Dibb *et al.*, op. cit., p. 148.
33 HMSO (1998) *Modernising Local Government.*
34 Based on article by John Tusa, *Independent*, Jan. 1997.
35 Case study based on research undertaken by Jim Mehan in pursuit of a Masters degree at Lancashire Business School, University of Central Lancashire.
36 Report of Director of (Prison) Health April 1993–March 1994. HMSO.

5

MANAGING THE QUALITY OF PUBLIC SERVICES

A person who sees quality and feels it as he works is a person who cares. A person who cares about what he sees and does is a person who is bound to have some characteristics of Quality.

> (Robert Pirsig,
> *Zen and the Art of Motorcycle Maintenance*, 1979)

LEARNING OUTCOMES

This chapter will enable the reader to:

- Understand why the concept of quality is important in public services.
- Distinguish between three approaches to managing quality: quality control, assurance and total quality management.
- Identify characteristics of quality.
- Adopt a '10 M' model for auditing the internal quality of a public service.
- Understand how to improve quality through charters, systems analysis, quality chains, quality circles and benchmarking.
- Adopt a conversational approach to systems mapping in order to assess and improve the quality of inputs, processes and outputs in public services.
- Explore connections between managing quality and quality of life.

INTRODUCTION

At the beginning of the previous chapter we set out to explore what it meant for a public service organization to satisfy the 'needs and wants of customers and clients'. We looked at the merits of broadening our concern from customers to a wider network of stakeholders. In this chapter we will look at ways in which we can 'co-ordinate all the resources of the organization' to meet the needs and wants of its stakeholders, especially those who use the public services. We will look at quality control, quality assurance and quality management and evaluate the usefulness of quality charters, systems analysis, quality chains, quality circles, customer care and benchmarking in public services.

Looking at the management of quality in public services gives us a chance to illustrate the possibility of adopting a conversational approach. Through 'outer world' conversations with key stakeholders, public service managers can obtain hard and soft information about the way key stakeholders are experiencing the performance of the organization and the quality of the service it provides. The types of conversations that will be particularly relevant to the manager's task of managing quality will be questioning, listening and learning conversations. In order to make sense of the hard and soft information gathered through 'outer world' conversations, the manager will need to hold an 'inner world' conversation. The kind of thinking skills that will prove most useful will include recollection, prediction, creative and empathetic thinking and evaluation.

QUALITY – A GROWING CONCERN OR A PROBLEM OF GROWTH?

Prior to the Industrial Revolution, craft workers both produced and inspected the quality of what they produced. Mass production turned the maintenance of quality into a problem. Quality control departments were introduced to inspect samples of what was produced. Statistical approaches to quality measurement were developed. Control charts and sampling techniques were used to measure and report on quality. Deming and Juran[1] convinced Japanese managers that improving quality would open up new markets for the country and lead to economic success. Japanese quality improved at a time when quality levels in the west remained largely unchanged. At the time, western manufacturers had little reason to focus on quality. The USA had a virtual monopoly in manufacturing and consumer demand was booming. US managers were concerned about sales and financial performance. During the 1970s and 1980s, American and European manufacturers began to lose market share to competitors from Japan and they became increasingly interested in the management of quality.

Concerns for Quality in Public Services

Concern for quality also began to emerge in public services. Walsh[2] sees this as an evolutionary development which reflects the growth of public services. In the early years of the postwar welfare state the emphasis was on quantity. There was an obvious need for more housing, more education and more health services. To this was added a search for responsiveness, variation and choice – all elements of quality. Walsh identified four reasons for this (Box 5.1).[3]

In Chapter 1 we traced concern for economy and efficiency in public services to global economic upheavals following the oil crisis of 1973. This drive for economy and efficiency had its limitations. Quality seemed to offer a way to improve public services from the perspective of the service user rather than the accountant. There are also internal reasons for concern about quality in public services (Box 5.2).

Box 5.1

THE QUALITY OF PUBLIC SERVICES: EXTERNAL REASONS FOR CONCERN

- Legislative changes, such as Compulsory Competitive Tendering
- Financial constraints, forcing a rethink about how best to use resources
- Complaints about declining standards in areas such as transport, education and health
- Increasing concern with effectiveness as opposed to economy and efficiency

---

Box 5.2

THE QUALITY OF PUBLIC SERVICES: INTERNAL REASONS FOR CONCERN

- The need for benefits analysis as well as a cost analysis (Chapter 10)
- The rise of internal audit and the concern for quality as well as value for money
- 'Big ideas' such as 'Excellence' and 'Total Quality Management'
- Demotivation of employees by performance management (Chapter 11)

QUALITY, VALUE FOR MONEY AND BEST VALUE

Best Value in the UK

The UK Labour Party introduced the concept of 'Best Value' in 1998. The Best Value initiative emphasized the equal need for public services to provide value for money and high quality.[4] It became a statutory duty for service providers to consult with service users, tax payers and private sector representatives, regarding the costs and quality of public services in their locality.[5] Some quality standards were to be set by central government but other quality standards were expected to be set and measured locally.

Quality in Europe

Pollitt and Bouckaert[6] mapped a complicated picture of diverse quality improvement in public services in Europe. They also noted some common trends including a shift from traditional hierarchical and paternalistic management towards a more participatory approach to the management and delivery of public services. Traditionally, political leaders had determined what services were to be provided, on what terms and to whom. Professional public servants managed and delivered them. Quality standards were defined internally, usually by managers and politicians. Service users tended to be passive consumers. Pollitt noted that across Western Europe, at different speeds and with variances in detail, a new relationship was developing between service users and providers. Citizens were being consulted about quality standards and how they could be implemented. This move from the delivery of public services by a bureaucratic style of management towards a participative, quality-oriented style of management confirms some of the changes in organizational structure which we discussed in Chapter 1.

DEFINING QUALITY

There is no one definition of quality. Definitions include references to conformance, specification, fitness for purpose, or responsiveness to customers or clients.[7] If public services aim to provide what users expect, this implies that managers of public services should concern themselves with managing user expectations as well as designing service provision. Users will have expectations about safety, design and

conformance. People using public services are entitled to assume that they do not place themselves or their dependants at risk by so doing. This places a burden or duty of care on all public servants. Service users are also entitled to expect that services have been designed thoughtfully. Quality also implies that there must be a reasonable match between the intent of the design and the actual service delivered. The training and supervision of staff and the environment in which the service is provided directly affect conformance. For example, in a public library not only should the books be in good condition and easy to find, but the staff should be trained in customer relations and the library buildings should be welcoming. Accessibility to services is essential. We report now on a conversation with Anne who has been trying to access service from a UK social services department. Dean and Evans[8] have suggested that 'quality is meeting or exceeding customer expectations'. In Box 5.3 we look at the way Anne, a UK citizen, perceives these public service departments as 'meeting or exceeding her expectations'.

APPROACHES TO MANAGING QUALITY

Quality Control: Detecting Poor Quality

Quality control is based on inspecting the service after it has been provided and comparing the provision to a pre-existing specification. If the product or service does not come up to specification, sometimes something can be done to put it right after the event. Quality control can help reduce the incidence of poor quality when there is a penalty for failing to meet the quality specifications, or when there is a reward for consistent conformance to the service quality standards. The problem with this approach is that poor quality in the delivery of a public service can often cause damage which is irreparable, for example, when surgery is bungled, serial killers are not caught, rescue services are too late, telephones are jammed, trains are cancelled, mail is lost,

Box 5.3

EXTRACTS FROM A CONVERSATION WITH ANNE
'WELCOME HOME ANNE'

Tony: How did it start?

Anne: In April 1997 I fled from Fiji with my five children. The youngest was only eleven months old. We struggled halfway round the world to get back home to England. Old friends met us at the airport and put us up. On arrival in England I was besieged by a hundred and one new problems. Guilt about running away, fear of being pursued. Where to get food and warm clothes? Coming from a tropical climate, we had only T shirts and shorts. I had 60 Fiji dollars – that's about £15.

Tony: So what happened next?

Anne: I had no money, but I thought I would get help until I could get a job and start providing for my children. I went to a local Department of Employment to register for work but they asked me to go to a Social Benefits office to be interviewed. After phoning every day for two weeks I was given an appointment for the interview. The drabness of the room shocked me. There were panic buttons, security screens, security men, bored children running around screaming, no play area or toys, a drunken man was using foul language. The atmosphere was rank and depressing. My hopes sank. The interview was traumatic. I was asked to relive those terrible last few weeks in Fiji. I was very emotional. The woman behind the desk was very sympathetic. She helped me to complete parts of a form which I did not understand. She told me that it would be a few more weeks before I would hear from the DSS and that I would then receive a benefit cheque.

Tony: How did you manage for five weeks on £15?

Anne: I stayed with different friends and borrowed money from my sister. I counted my pennies and waited. The 'few weeks' passed. I heard nothing. I rang them up. The person on the phone checked my file and only then told me that I was not eligible for benefit because I was not 'habitually resident'. I had lived abroad for too long. I couldn't believe it. I am a UK citizen. My children are British citizens, we all carry British passports, both my parents worked all their lives paying British taxes and yet we were not entitled to any support. I was devastated. They told me that I could appeal. To make an appeal I had to fill in exactly the same forms again. A Citizen's Advice Bureau helped me. They were wonderful people, but nobody in the Department of Social Security would listen to them. My appeal was rejected. The Citizen's Advice Bureau said that this was 'normal procedure'. It was a way they had of making sure that I was not here on holiday.

Tony: What happened next?

Anne: I went back to the Department of Employment who had sent me to the Social Security Office in the first place. They gave me more forms to fill in and asked me to come for an appointment when I had completed them. There were sections of the forms which I simply couldn't understand. I went back and asked for some help to fill in the forms. They said that I would have to make an appointment for an interview. When I went for the interview they told me that I could not have an interview until I had filled in the forms!

Tony: Seems like a vicious circle.

Anne: I panicked. I cried. My baby filled her nappy. There was nowhere for me to change her. In any case, if you lost your place in the queue or came back even a few minutes later they would ask you to make an appointment for another day. They seemed to have no idea what it was like trying to organize five children so that you can come in for an interview. The man who was interviewing me seemed embarrassed by my distress and tried to get rid of me. Finally, he agreed to talk to me and entered my details on their computer. They would not give me any unemployment benefit because I had not been registered for long enough. They were not interested that I had tried to register two months ago. Two weeks later I was supposed to go and see them again. My baby was sick and I couldn't get into town. When I went the next time I was told that all my details had been scrubbed from the computer because I had missed an appointment and that I would have to repeat the whole process of form filling and interviews from the beginning.

Tony: What happened in the end?

Anne: After six months of staying with friends, borrowing money for food and being given clothes so that four of my children could go to school, I won my appeal. I *had* been entitled to their help and service from the beginning. But just look at how I had been treated in the meantime.

Tony: Looking back what do you think now?

Anne: I am amazed at my naïveté, my trust in a romantic notion of a welfare state which was part of a country which I called home. My children and I had experienced not just suffering, but needless suffering – mental stress and physical hunger – because of the administration of a system which, on appeal, was found to be in the wrong. I have never received an apology to this day. Even now, when I see a government brown envelope drop through the letterbox, it fills me with dread. You can see how tears are welling up in my eyes. I can feel again the desperation and the humiliation that I went through at the hands of what I expected to be a caring public service.

Tony: Thank you Anne.

luggage is pilfered, aeroplanes crash, ferries sink, justice is miscarried or drinking water is poisoned. Often the damage caused by these kinds of failures in public services is hard to repair. In the case of Anne in our learning conversation, much could be learned. But the price paid by Anne and her children for this learning is high. As far as we know, there was no quality control. No one collected information from her about the quality of her experience. Nothing was learned and service users may still be experiencing the same poor quality of service.

Quality Assurance: Building in Quality

If quality control is about getting it right second time, then quality assurance is about getting it right first time, i.e. it is about preventing quality problems in the first place. There are a number of quality assurance systems. An internationally recognized quality assurance system is known as ISO 9000. In 1992 Bell and Grover found that 21 per cent of local authorities in the UK had introduced ISO 9000 into at least one department.[9] The cost of meeting the quality criteria defined by these standards is very high. These costs cannot be recovered by local authorities through increased competitiveness or improved profits, as might be the case with public services delivered by a privately owned organization. If ISO 9000 became a prerequisite for bidding for contracts to deliver services, then smaller public service organizations and some voluntary sector organizations could be excluded, because the costs of ISO 9000 certification might be prohibitive.

Building in Bureaucracy

Building in quality often relies on written procedures. These can become overly bureaucratic and prevent the innovation and responsiveness which are the hallmark of many high-quality public services. Where procedures have been written without consulting front-line staff, it may be difficult to motivate staff to comply with them. Service users should be key stakeholders in the process yet they may lack the technical knowledge needed to contribute to the writing of quality standards in areas like pollution control, genetic engineering, highway construction, control of infectious diseases, fire prevention, breaches of patent law or the detection of computer fraud. Pollitt[10] suggests that professionals believe that they alone know best and will usually set standards, which are not necessarily the standards which service users would set. In the UK, the 'Best Value' initiative emphasizes the need for a 'stakeholder' approach to defining quality standards. Quality assurance involves establishing quality standards for individual systems and elements in the delivery of services, but it does not address how these are interconnected. This can give rise to a 'watch your back' culture in which individuals or departments ensure that they meet their quality standards without regard to the impact on the 'total management' of the service. It is to Total Quality Management that we now turn.

Total Quality Management (TQM)

TQM claims to be a system of quality management which includes customer focus, strategic planning, leadership, continuous improvement and team work. It requires organizational and behavioural change. The principal architects of this approach were Edward Deming, Joseph M. Moran and Philip B. Crosby.[11] The most widely known of these is Deming. His approach to quality focuses on improving products and services by continually reducing uncertainty and variability. The aim is 'zero tolerance' of non-conformance. Deming saw TQM as a chain in which higher quality leads to higher output and reduced costs. This can give a competitive advantage to privately owned public service organizations, or enable publicly owned organizations to provide a more extensive public service without increasing public expenditure.

TQM in Public Services: What is Problematic?

Pollitt and Bouckaert[12] note that the language of TQM refers to customers and consumers rather than citizens and citizenship, which are central to the concept of quality in public services. This is not surprising given that TQM was not developed in a public services context. We deal with these issues in detail in Chapter 11, when we consider performance management in public services.

As we saw in Chapter 4, public services are not like manufactured goods; they are intangible and the consumer is intimately involved in their delivery. This makes them more difficult to specify and test for quality. Gaster points out that

> Public services carry out public purposes, balancing the needs and wants of different groups in society, involving the least powerful. They are accountable for public monies and aim not just to meet individual needs, but to improve the quality of life for the whole community.[13]

Public services need to educate people in the community, so that they can make informed and critical judgements about the quality of the service.

Beyond TQM

Stewart and Walsh[14] take the view that to assess quality we should merely ask whether a public service achieves the purpose for which it is designed. We think that it can be useful for public service managers to be concerned about the technical aspects of quality, the quality of the surroundings in which the service is delivered, and the quality of the interpersonal relationships which stakeholders — especially service users — form with members of their organization and with each other (Box 5.5).[15]

The Quality of the Surroundings

Do the surroundings or environment in which the service is provided enhance or detract from the experience of the service user? Are clients made to feel welcome and valued? Environments affect the

Box 5.4

THE ELEMENTS OF TOTAL QUALITY MANAGEMENT

1 **Commitment to quality**. Managers need to take a long-term view. Managers should include commitment to quality in a statement of the mission of the organization (Chapter 3).

2 **Learn the new philosophy**. Managers should abandon notions of management based on numbers, quotas, command and control and adversarial relationships (Chapter 1). Quality is to be a product of co-operation between employees and management (Chapter 8).

3 **Understand inspection**. Managers need to use inspection as a tool for learning how to do things better. Fixing problems after the event reduces output and increases costs. All employees must be responsible for assuring the quality of their own work at all times (Chapter 11).

4 **End cost only decisions**. Managers should not make purchasing decisions based solely on cost. Quality issues should be considered. Long-term relationships should be established with suppliers (Chapters 4 and 10).

5 **Make a difference**. Managers should seek to implement continuous incremental changes, rather than fewer more dramatic changes, in order to improve quality (Chapters 2 and 3).

6 **Institute training**. Managers have a duty to ensure that workers are always learning (Chapters 13 and 14).

7 **Lead and coach**. Managers should assume that guidance and coaching are more effective than policing and supervision (Chapter 13).

8 **Drive out fear**. Managers should not engender fear, such as fear of failure, reprisal or change. Fear encourages adversarial, short-term thinking and a selfish concern for individual performance.

9 **Optimize teams**. Managers should make selective use of team working to surface problems, think creatively about their solutions and implementation (Chapter 6).

10 **Eliminate exhortations**. Rarely can employees be exhorted to improve quality. Assume that they are already doing their best. What may be needed is to change the things that they are doing. A conversational approach may be more helpful than exhortation (Chapter 13).

11 **Eliminate quotas and management by objectives**. Managers should avoid purely quantitative targets. Employees should be encouraged to devise and monitor measures of performance that include quality (Chapter 11).

12 **Remove obstacles to pride**. Deming saw many forms of performance management as a big barrier to pride in the service provided (Chapter 11).

13 **Institute education**. Achieve a balance between training and education. Training focuses on an employee's task-related skills. Education invests in the self-development of the employee (Chapters 13 and 14).

---

way people interpret their experience of the core service (Chapter 4). Waiting and queuing rarely enhance the experience. Many people have short concentration spans and poor tolerance of silence. They may be used to being constantly distracted by a radio or a TV. If so, they may find waiting, especially waiting in their own company, stressful. It is less stressful to be in a queue that keeps moving, however slowly, than it is to be in a short one that involves standing still or feeling that people are watching you. A long queue of people can be amused by a TV screen which can carry income-generating

Box 5.5

A 3D MODEL OF QUALITY IN PUBLIC SERVICES

- **The physical dimension.** The service's attention to the congeniality of its setting
- **The technical dimension.** The service's application of up-to-date technology
- **The social dimension.** The service's ability to form close relationships

advertising or useful public service information, such as is used in some UK postal counter services. Green and pastel colours are better for waiting rooms than strong colours, especially red. Why not involve regular service users in choosing between prospective colour schemes? Parents, like Anne, will be highly stressed if their babies smell because there are no facilities to change them or if their children misbehave because there are no play facilities to distract them. In different cultures, different amounts of 'personal space' are needed to minimize the risk of agitation and conflict (Chapter 8). In some cultures separate waiting facilities are needed for men and women.

The Quality of Relationships

As we shall see in Chapter 8, dress code, initial non-verbal behaviour and behaviour in the first 10 seconds of contact with a client make an abiding impression on that person. Clients filter their subsequent experience of staff and the service through that first impression. The relevance of body language, appropriate language and alignment when dealing with clients will be discussed when we look at a conversational model of relationship formation in Chapter 8.

QUALITY – AN INTERNAL AUDIT

A '10 M' Audit

At the beginning of this chapter we implied that the quality of the service which is provided is limited by the extent to which all the resources of the organization can be co-ordinated so as to satisfy the needs and wants of their clients. It would follow that the quality of the resources themselves might in turn limit the user's experience of the service provided. A '10 M' audit can be carried out (Box 5.6).

Managers who can provide good answers to all the questions posed in the 10 M audit (Box 5.6) will be capable of exercising competence in all six areas of management that we cover in this book, namely: managing resistance and change; managing operations and activities; managing groups and individuals; managing finances and resources; managing communication and information; and managing learning and personal development. The integration of these management competencies and their application in the day-to-day operations of management are central to the management of quality systems in public services.

QUALITY MANAGEMENT SYSTEMS IN PUBLIC SERVICES

Gaster's[17] model for a quality management system for public services emphasizes the relationship between values, objectives and implementation processes. The role of values in public services was discussed in Chapter 3; values will be examined further in Chapter 15. Gaster thinks that the values espoused and lived within an organization will affect how quality is defined. For example, if empowerment, choice, participation and active citizenship are organizational values, then the organization is likely to assume that members of the public should be actively involved in assessing the quality of the organization's work. When quality initiatives fail, it may be because they do not reflect the values that

Box 5.6

A '10 M' FRAMEWORK FOR QUALITY AUDIT[16]

Manpower

- Are all staff multiskilled?
- Is career development training provided?
- Will staff work flexibly across several functions?
- Do staff have a personal development plan?
- Do managers carry out annual appraisals?

Machines

- Is there built-in fax and e-mail?
- Are calls recorded out of office hours?
- Are helpline numbers available for out-of-office hours backup?
- Are all telephone calls diverted so that callers can get an answer?
- Is there newer and better technology available for the core service?

Materials

- Own letterhead?
- Does it look professional?
- Could you benefit from working more closely with one supplier on quality issues?

Mental Agility

- Are employees encouraged to express ideas?
- Do employees have problem-solving skills?
- Are employees flexible?
- Are different ways of thinking introduced?
- Do employees understand the impact on mental agility of: stress, colours, air quality, lighting and odours?

Management

- Can managers handle the public and the media?
- Do managers have coaches and critical friends?
- Can managers develop close relationships?
- Do managers have financial skills?

- Are there sufficient numbers of managers or are there too many?
- Is workplace learning and management development encouraged?
- Are managers aware of how their beliefs and values compare with those of their staff?

Morale

- Do employees feel safe in their jobs?
- Are staff rewarded for good ideas?
- Do employees actively participate in decision-making?
- Do senior managers regularly walk through the places where services are delivered?

Mores

- What beliefs are central to the organization?
- Which beliefs have been adopted as core values?
- How does the organization cope with risk? Does it reject it, accept it or seek it?
- How is decision-making carried out – top down, bottom-up or devolved?

Monitoring

- Are monitoring measures misleading?
- Do managers distinguish between levels of control, e.g. employee self-control, supervisory control or operational control?
- Do managers allow diversity of approach?
- Do managers monitor 'negatively' to identify only performance below plan, or do they monitor both 'negatively' and 'positively'?

Motivation

- What needs do employees meet at work?
- Are there opportunities for employees to feel that they belong?

- Are there opportunities for achievements to be identified and acknowledged?
- Are employees able to control their working environment; their working arrangements; their choice of equipment or office decor?

Movement

- Does the organization own or control its own transport?
- Are transport services always available at the times required by service users?

give rise to the culture of the organization. Quality initiatives often fail when they are perceived as an 'add-on', particularly when they are imposed from above as the latest 'big' idea (Chapter 15).[18] But whose values should underpin quality standards? We think that the values of key stakeholders such as elected representatives, professionals, front-line staff and service users should inform the design of the quality management system in public services. We think that a conversational approach to designing the quality management system will increase the chances that this will happen.

QUALITY CHARTERS

In 1992, in the UK, a Quality Charter scheme was launched to improve the quality of public services. The Charter Mark was well received by the UK National Consumer Council and by the UK Institute for Public Policy Research. To obtain a Charter Mark, organizations which provided direct services to the public had to demonstrate a number of things (see Box 5.7).

Box 5.7

TO OBTAIN A CHARTER MARK

- Give users a choice
- Ensure value for money
- Set challenging standards
- Tell users what the standards are
- Collect evidence of user satisfaction
- Provide friendly complaints procedure
- Plan innovations that improve services
- Tell users what standards are achieved
- Ask users about the services they need
- Ask users how services can be improved
- Collect evidence of quality improvements

A SYSTEMS APPROACH TO IMPROVING QUALITY

If we adopt a systems approach to managing quality in an organization, we assume that quality is best considered as something that emerges from the organization as a whole. It is better to consider the whole organization rather than try to isolate the effect on quality to one or two departments. When we make the assumption that it is advantageous to think about quality in systems terms – to think systemically – we assume that it is useful to view the universe as though it were a hierarchy of wider systems and subsystems. Any organization, viewed as a system, would operate as part of a wider system, such as a local community or a national economy. In turn, the organization itself would be comprised of smaller subsystems, such as technical systems, financial systems or transport systems.

When we think that it is helpful to view something as though it were something else, like an animal or a tree, we are thinking metaphorically (Chapter 3). We do not need to believe that the organization really is an animal – like an elephant or a tiger! All we need to believe is that by examining the characteristics of the elephant or tiger, we can gain insights into the workings of the organization.[19]

Using a System as a Metaphor

What then are the characteristics of a system and what insights into the management of quality in public services can we gain by thinking about an organization as though it were a system? Let us take the case of an adaptive biological system. It has a number of characteristics (Figure 5.1).

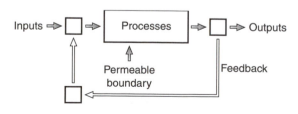

Figure 5.1 Characteristics of a system

The system has a boundary. Inputs cross the boundary. In a biological system these inputs might be food or oxygen. In an organization these might be enquiries, orders or payments of money. Outputs leave the boundary. In a biological system these might be electrical impulses, work done or waste products. In an organization these might be a product, a service, a benefit to a client, a profit to a shareholder or pollution. In biological systems, if the boundary becomes very rigid and impermeable the system may malfunction, become sick or even die. Normally a healthy biological systems boundary is semi-permeable – i.e. it permits the controlled migration of things like water, air or salt across its boundary. If it is too permeable, or if it is ruptured, it may lose internal resources too rapidly or be open to overwhelming invasion by organisms from the outside. Organization boundaries need to be open to external influences and information from their environment but they need to control the rate of movement of staff or people or information across their boundaries, lest they become overrun and disorganized.

The adaptive biological system has some way of sensing conditions that are important to its health and survival and feeding what it senses back into the system. If it senses that all is not what it should be, the system may reduce or increase its inputs, or adjust the transformation processes that are taking place within its boundary, in order to maximize its chances of growth or survival. In organizations the equivalent of sensing feedback and control are provided by subsystems such as market research (Chapter 4), or, importantly for this chapter, by a quality management subsystem. Management writers such as Ackoff[20] have built on earlier work by Bernard, Selznick and Singleton[21] to develop a systems approach to management. For our part we have built on early work by Checkland.[22] For the moment, we could simply consider a public service organization as if it were a system to transform demands from the public into high levels of client satisfaction, political support and success with funding bids and then ask whether the systems functions described above are present in the organization. If they are present, are they working satisfactorily? In the next section we explain how systems mapping can be used to provide answers to questions that can generate a list of possible changes all of which might improve the quality of the service.

Mapping Systems – Improving Quality

In Figure 5.2 you will find a systems map of the laundry system in the author's household. In most cases the quality of the system is acceptable. However, there are certain points where the system breaks down and quality is compromised. This is often due to human error or human fickleness. For example, sometimes washing is not ironed because the family member who is supposed to do this may have other priorities. Colour blindness suddenly afflicts other family members who appear unable to separate white and coloured clothes. The weather may prevent washing from being dried on the outside line – this is not a major problem because an electric dryer can also be used. The electric dryer

may be more efficient than the weather; however, it is less economical.

Although the example in Figure 5.2 is a map of a domestic system, the underlying principles apply to a systems map of any organization. By drawing a systems map we can identify where quality breaks down and identify what may need to be changed in order to improve quality. Box 5.8 suggests some questions that need to be asked when identifying how a system can be improved.

The questions in Box 5.8 can be formulated into a more detailed process for mapping and analysing the quality of a public service organization and identifying where and how quality improvements can be made. One of the benefits of this approach is that, while it views organizations as systems, the approach acknowledges that they are human systems and therefore subject to human error. It is useful to use the process outlined in Box 5.9 to structure conversations between key stakeholders concerned with improving the quality of a public service. A conversational systems-based approach to monitoring the performance of public service organizations is presented in Chapter 11.

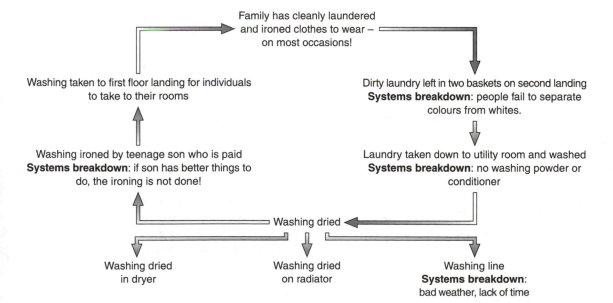

Figure 5.2 Quality breakdown in a domestic laundry system

Box 5.8

IMPROVING SYSTEMS QUALITY: SOME QUESTIONS TO ASK

- Are systems goals clearly defined, appropriate and understood by everyone?
- Do individuals understand how the subsystems relate to bigger systems?
- Are people clear about their tasks and responsibilities within the system?

- How does human fallibility adversely affect the working of the system?
- Are people clear about the consequences of failing to fulfil their tasks?
- What happens when problems arise?
- Do any new systems need to be created?

Quality Chains

A quality chain is a chain that links the different aspects which contribute to the quality of a service. In Chapter 6 we discuss the growing tendency for public service organizations to adopt inter-agency working. This greatly increases the number of links in the quality chain. The UK Audit Commission[23] suggested that managers concerned with the quality of public services should focus on the following links in the quality chain: communication, specification, delivery, people and systems. Anne had to deal with at least five different public services – immigration, social services, a local housing authority, social services and a department of employment and education. However, the combined efforts of a Citizen's Advice Bureau, a doctor and a Member of Parliament could not provide the missing links in the quality chain. Managers concerned with strengthening the links in the quality chain, particularly when different agencies are required to work together, should address the gaps identified in Box 5.10.

Box 5.9

SYSTEMS MAPPING FOR QUALITY IMPROVEMENT

1 Define, in no more than one sentence, the purpose of the system.
2 Identify all the inputs into the system.
3 Identify all the activities needed.
4 Draw a map of the system (see Figure 5.2). Name all the people who are involved and say what they do.
5 Once you have mapped the system, evaluate its quality by answering:
   - Has the system got the right inputs?

   - How efficiently are the inputs transformed?
   - Does the system achieve its purpose?
   - Are the purposes achieved to standard?
6 Identify any changes to inputs, processes and outputs that are needed to improve quality.
7 Redraw the system showing how it would look if improvements were in place.
8 Identify the actions that need to be taken, by whom, in order to make improvements.

Box 5.10

QUALITY CHAINS: GAPS TO ADDRESS

- Gaps between expectations and service
- Gaps between specifications and service
- Gaps between management expectations and what front-line staff do
- Gaps between politicians' views and the views of professionals in the service

---

Quality Circles

The idea of Quality Circles dates from the 1950s and is commonly attributed to Kaoru Ishikawa.[24] These circles usually consist of six to ten people who work in a similar area. They meet voluntarily to identify and analyse problems and propose solutions to them. The members of the circle can implement proposed solutions directly. Sometimes the proposals need to be taken to the managers for implementation. Quality circles take different forms. Sometimes they bring together representatives from different areas, sometimes from different professions or specialisms. The responsibilities are set out in Box 5.11.

The growth in stakeholder networks (Chapters 4 and 11) and inter-agency working (Chapter 6) makes the idea of quality circles tempting in public services. But in our experience they do not always work. Much depends on the culture of the organizations involved. They are not effective when there is little trust between managers and front-line employees, or where only lip-service is paid to empowering employees, or where there is a culture of blaming or passing the buck. Successful quality circles, which become self-regulating and which take action with the delegated authority of senior managers, need special training in how to work and think together. The thinking skills needed for creative problem-solving and the formulation of quality improvement plans are readily disabled by processes that occur naturally in groups that have not been specially trained to avoid them (Chapter 6).

Benchmarking

Benchmarks of quality were established for a whole range of public services in the UK in the 1990s. For example, the Audit Commission produced a study *Seen but not Heard* (1994) which established benchmarks for children's services. Many of these benchmarks related to the quality of the collaboration between different agencies, such as health services, social services and education services, in relation to the needs of children. One benchmark, for example, was that decisions on placing a child into residential care should be taken jointly by health, social services and education services. Box 5.12 sets out a five stage benchmarking process.

A Quality of Life

According to the UK Department of Environment, Transport and the Regions,[25] in 1998 the use of management techniques such as compulsory competitive tendering had produced 'gains in efficiency that were uneven and uncertain'. More importantly, they reported 'significant costs to employees, often leading to ... demotivation' of the very people who were expected to provide the improved quality of life for others. In Chapter 7 Chris Reeve[26] makes a point that

---

Box 5.11

RESPONSIBILITIES OF A QUALITY CIRCLE

- Reviewing and analysing problems
- Making proposals to improve quality
- Developing a detailed plan
- Implementing the plan
- Monitoring the plan
- Reporting results

Box 5.12

BENCHMARKING: A FIVE-STEP PROCESS

1 **Identify Characteristics**. These should focus on characteristics which are of most importance to the public service stakeholders and on which comparable information is available.

2 **Identify Benchmark Partners**. In a large public service organization it is possible to start with internal benchmark partners. An external partner could be the same service provided in another region. This is not usually possible if organizations are competing for the same clients or the same sources of funding. Partners should have a reputation for good quality.

3 **Design Method for Gathering Data**. This could include statistical methods or research into the annual reports of other services. Take care to compare like with like.

4 **Select Framework**. The aim of the framework is to identify which differences in processes are leading to the improved performance.

5 **Implement Changes**. Having identified gaps and why they occur, new standards can be set and the actions planned to meet the new standards.

---

her senior managers ought not to expect her front-line staff to care more about their clients than they themselves felt cared about by their own managers. Front-line staff are people too, with their own lives to lead inside and outside of the workplace (Chapter 7). Certainly it seems an incongruous clash of values to be seeking to improve the quality of life of citizens, if we do so by taking actions that lower the quality of life of those who work in public services. In many countries public service workers make up nearly half the citizens for whom the improved quality of life is intended!

Clearly we need an approach to implementing quality improvements that is thoughtful of the wider consequences of the improvements and which is continuous with the traditional values of public service (Chapter 15). The conversational approach which we propose includes the necessity to think empathetically on behalf of all the stakeholders in the public service and that includes the staff. In Chapter 8 we shall look at the role of questioning, listening and counselling conversations in helping staff to cope with the stress of working in public services. We need to think about the impact of managers' decisions on their quality of life:

It calls for imagination, so that every advance, every change, is not merely a difference but a creative act. Achievement, at any level above the lowest, calls for courage . . . and for exacting discipline.[27]

In our Final Thoughts Robert Pirsig explores what it means to live a 'quality life'.

FINAL THOUGHTS: 'A QUALITY LIFE'

The quotation at the beginning of this chapter is from Robert Pirsig. It introduces a spiritual dimension to the idea of quality. Elsewhere in his book *Zen and the Art of Motorcycle Maintenance* we find that:

Quality is the Buddha. Quality is scientific reality. Quality is the goal of Art. It remains to work these concepts down into a practical, down-to-earth context, and for this there is nothing more practical or down-to-earth than what I have been talking about all along – the repair of an old motorcycle.[28]

For Pirsig, enlightenment could be found as easily in the perfect harmony of smooth running motorcycle parts, as it could be in the delicate symbolism of a lotus flower, or the beautiful isolation of a mountain top. Pirsig is not alone in seeing the pursuit of quality as virtuous. Around 380 BC the Greek

Sophists taught that the main virtue was to put preaching into practice. In a conversational approach to management, theory and practice are explicitly linked. Pirsig complains that Aristotle encouraged the western world to replace virtue with reason and romanticism with classicism. The romantic mode is primarily inspirational, imaginative, creative and intuitive – feeling rather than facts predominate. 'Art', when it is opposed to 'Science', is often romantic: it does not proceed by reason or laws but by feeling, intuition and aesthetic conscience.[29] By contrast the classical mode is concerned with reason and laws. It is straightforward, unadorned, unceremonial, unemotional, economical and carefully proportioned. Its purpose is not to inspire but to bring order out of chaos, to make the unknown known. Motorcycle riding is romantic. Motorcycle maintenance is purely classical. Many approaches to the management of quality are more akin to motorcycle maintenance than motorbike riding.

At the heart of Pirsig's odyssey is a desire to bring about a fusion between the classical and the romantic. If you want to build a factory, or fix a motorcycle, or set a nation right, then classical subject–object knowledge, although necessary, is not enough. You have to have some feeling for the quality of the work. You have to have some sense of what is good. That is what carries you forward. This isn't something you're born with, but it is something you can develop.[30] For Pirsig, the intense care and absorbed concentration of a mechanic whose inner world mind and outer world body are working in harmony is the key to quality. The interweaving of thought, feeling and action then becomes a condition for total quality management.

SUMMARY

- Quality in public services is about meeting or exceeding stakeholder expectations. It has become the object of concern through the pursuit of economy and efficiency at the expense of effectiveness and ethics.
- We found that inspection and control of quality were of limited value in public services, because the putting right of mistakes was difficult, costly and wasteful.
- Quality assurance and the setting of quality standards could be useful in public services, especially if they can be done democratically and without bureaucracy.
- Total Quality Management (TQM) claimed to be a complete system of management. We tabulated Deming's principles.
- We identified the types of questions that need to be asked in order to audit the quality of a public service organization.
- We looked at the properties of a system and used a system as a metaphor for an organization seeking to improve the quality of what it does.
- We demonstrated how systems mapping could be used to assess the quality of public service delivery and to identify how quality could be improved.
- We evaluated the usefulness and relevance of specific techniques such as quality circles, quality chain analysis, customer satisfaction and benchmarking, which can be used to improve the performance of public service organizations.
- Finally, we explored the links between quality, virtue and the good life.

THINKING AND LEARNING ACTIVITIES

Activity 1 Self-assessment

1 Identify the strengths and weaknesses of quality control when applied to public services.
2 Identify the strengths and weaknesses of quality assurance when applied to public services.
3 Identify the strengths and weaknesses of TQM when applied to public services.
4 How can using the metaphor of a system to describe an organization contribute to quality?
5 Summarize the systems approach to improving quality in public services.
6 Describe a quality chain in a public service.
7 What is benchmarking and how can it be used in public services?
8 What is a quality circle and how could it be used to improve quality in public services?
9 Why are values important in developing a quality improvement initiative?
10 What connections can you make between quality management and the quality of life?

Activity 2 Individual Learning: Critical Thinking

Quality chain analysis

Select a public service organization with which you are familiar. Draw a diagram to illustrate both the internal and external links in the quality chain. Assess whether there are gaps in the quality chain and suggest how these gaps can be filled.

Activity 3 Individual Learning: Visual and Evaluative Thinking

Mapping systems changes

Consider a system over which you have some control. It could be a work system (e.g. a system for the disposal of clinical waste), a quality assurance system or a domestic system (e.g. the weekly shopping system, the laundry or the cleaning system). Draw a systems map by following steps outlined in Box 5.9. Identify any changes that might be needed to improve the quality of the system you have mapped. If possible, discuss your systems improvements with a colleague.

Activity 4 Group Learning: Evaluative and Projective Thinking

Auditing a quality system

The educational institution you are attending is likely to have a quality system in place. It will have staff who have a particular responsibility for managing the quality of the education being offered. You are required to arrange an interview with someone concerned with quality in any education institution, preferably not your own, especially if there are a lot of you who need to practise the audit. Plan and carry out an audit interview, preferably working with other students in groups of three. Each group should present their findings back to the larger group. It may be useful to use the following questions in your interview.

1 How is quality defined in the organization?
2 Is the quality system underpinned by values consistent with this definition?
3 Are the objectives of quality improvement clear?
4 How did any quality programme get formulated?
5 Which key stakeholders were involved?
6 Is there evidence of support from the top?

Summarize the main content of the interview and identify any principles that seem to underpin the approach to quality management. Identify any ways that the management of quality in the institution could be improved. Feed these back to the person that you interviewed and consider their response.

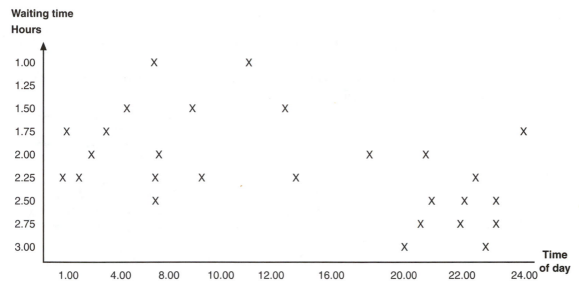

Figure 5.3 Waiting Times target

Activity 5 Individual Learning: Numerical and Evaluative Thinking

A statistical quality control process

1 Identify a quality standard, e.g. a waiting time target.
2 Identify acceptable limits either side of the standard. For example, if the waiting time was 2 hours, then 20 minutes either side of this might be within acceptable limits (see Chapter 11 for how to calculate acceptable limits).
3 Mark acceptable limits on a chart like the chart in Activity 6 below.
4 Plot actual performance in relation to the standard over a period of time.
5 Examine the results and identify those that fall outside the acceptable limits.
6 Recommend action to correct this.

Activity 6 Individual Learning: Numerical and Evaluative Thinking

1 Study the chart in Figure 5.3 and summarize the main problems.
2 Suggest how they could be resolved.
3 Construct a similar graph for any department to which you can gain access.

(Help on interpreting scatter graphs and using them to set targets and quality control limits, can be found at the end of Chapter 12.)

Activity 7 Individual and Group Learning: Evaluative Thinking

CASE STUDY: British Telecom bites the bullet[31]

A commitment to quality is part of the story behind the 13-year transformation of British Telecom (BT) from a bureaucratic, state-owned monopoly to a lean and prominent player in the fiercely competitive global communications market. After privatization in 1984, revenue rose from £6.9 billion to £14.9 billion by 1997. Pre-tax profits rose from £1 billion to £3.2 billion, reflecting a drop in the number of employees from 241,000 to 127,000. Two years after privatization, BT committed itself to TQM – Total Quality Management. Management training and improvement projects quickly followed. Group-wide ISO 9000 certification was awarded in 1994. In both 1996 and 1997 the company won an award from the Brussels-based European Foundation for Quality Management (EFQM).

Peter Docwra, Head of Quality Services at BT, says: 'BT is on a journey of continuous improvement and has been since 1986.' He believes that without the radical transformation from what BT Chairman Sir Ian Vallance called an 'unwieldy telephonic dinosaur', BT would probably be well on its way out of business. BT began self-assessment in 1992, using a model defined by the EFQM, a body that BT helped to found. By January 1997, all 40 BT trading units were carrying out annual self-assessment.

A Consistent Framework

'An assessment provides a consistent framework to identify how you have progressed and where you need to put your energies,' says Peter Docwra, Head of Quality Services at BT. Another important benefit, he says, is that it provides a common management vocabulary for people across the organization. Self-assessment (or assessment, as BT is now making use of external assessors) is a comprehensive, systematic and regular organizational audit. It is not a magic formula. It is a diagnostic tool. A big BT unit produces a self-assessment report of about 75 pages, covering nine criteria. If a unit is small or only just beginning to start assessing itself, it may choose to self-assess by questionnaire or workshop.

The objective is to identify critical issues that need to be addressed. Docwra explains:

> Across BT last year, twenty-five, 75-page documents were written. At least as many units went through some kind of workshop-based assessment. Each workshop requires an assessment team of at least six people and each of those people would have to put in at least four staff days. It is quicker and less resource-demanding to send out questionnaires. However, questionnaires only tell you what people think, not why they think it or how they feel about what they think. Also, many people do not understand the questions.

Scoring System

A scoring or rating system (with a maximum 1,000 points) is incorporated into the assessment. (If you can't count it, it doesn't count – Chapter 11.) Most businesses score between 350–400 on their first assessment. If the feedback is taken seriously and improvements are made, the score should rise by 50–100 points by the next assessment, says Docwra. The best score in Europe is currently 750, though even 500 points is respectable. Docwra emphasizes the aim is not to create a stick with which to beat people. Top-level management commitment, he says is fundamental. 'If they are not committed, then neither will their juniors be – and the process will be a waste of time.' In its corporate submission for the 1997 EFQM awards, BT received feedback identifying 270 strengths and 170 weaknesses – now translated into a seven-point improvement plan. Docwra is confident that the results show 'It comes down to the difference between being a good company and an excellent one.'

Tips for Assessment

As a result of its 1997 assessment, BT offers the following suggestions:

- Be encouraging
- Encourage feedback

- Involve senior management
- Do not attack the assessed
- Be realistic in deciding what action to take
- Be clear how the assessment will be used and followed up
- Do not make assessment an end in itself, it is a means towards an end
- Do not be prescriptive about what must be done, suggest what *could* be done and allow teams to formulate their own action plans

Questions

1 Why do you think that BT's productivity improved after privatization?
2 What do you think Peter Docwra means when he says that a shared management language is important to quality improvement?
3 What do you think are the advantages and disadvantages of using questionnaires and workshops for quality assessment purposes?
4 Identify the factors which you think have made BT's quality programme successful.

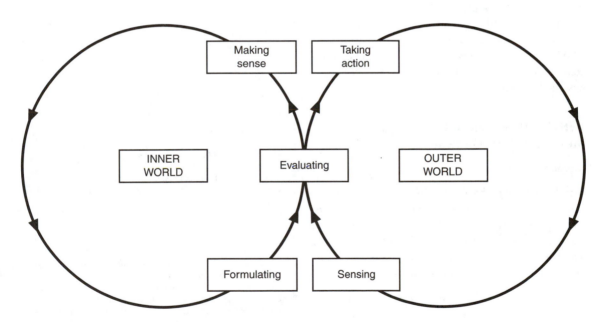

Figure 5.4 The thinking skills of the conversational manager

Activity 8 Individual Learning Review: Reflective Thinking

Inner world thinking

What inner world thinking skills can you identify in the manager's work described in this chapter? Have any of the thinking skills you have identified emerged for the first time in this chapter? If so, add them to your accumulating model of the kinds of thinking skills that you think are useful to managers of public services.

What things could you do to develop any of the thinking skills that you have just added to your model? What would be the first step?

Outer world conversations

What outer world conversational skills can you identify in the manager's work described in this chapter? Have any of the types of conversational skills you have identified emerged for the first time? If so, add them to your accumulating model of the kinds of conversational skills you think are useful to managers of public services.

What things could you do to develop any of these conversational skills which you have just added to your model? What would be the first step?

Activity 9 Individual Learning: Metacognitive Thinking

Metacognition

Look back through the Thinking and Learning Activities you have been asked to carry out in this chapter. What thinking skills were involved in each of these activities? For each type of thinking, write down how you were learning what you were learning, when you were learning to think in each of the different ways.

NOTES

1 See Aguago, R. (1990) *Dr Deming Who Taught the Japanese about Quality.* Simon & Schuster.
2 Walsh, K. (1990) *Management Education and Development*, vol. 21, part 5: *Managing Quality in the Public Service.*
3 Ibid.
4 Dept of the Environment, Transport and the Regions (1998) *Modernising Local Government. Improving Local Service through Best Value.* HMSO, para. 1.2.
5 Ibid, para. 1.7.
6 Pollitt, C. and Bouckaert, G. (1995) *Quality Improvement in European Public Services. Concepts, Cases and Commentary.* Sage.
7 See Juran, J. M. and Gruyner, F. M. (1980) *Quality Planning and Analysis.* McGraw-Hill.
8 Dean, J. W. and Evans, J. R. (1994) *Total Quality Management, Organisation and Strategy.* West Publishing Co., p. 7.
9 Bell, C. H. and Grover, J. (1992) *Quality Management and Local Authorities.* Biennial Symposium. Cranfield School of Management.
10 Pollitt (1987) 'Capturing Quality? The Quality Issue in British and American Health Policies'. *Journal of Public Policy*, vol. 71, no. 1, pp. 71–87.
11 See Oakland, J. S. (1989) *TQM – A Practical Approach.* DTI Enterprise Initiative.
12 Pollitt and Bouckaert, op. cit., p. 6.
13 Gaster, L. (1996) *Managing Quality in Public Services.* Oxford University Press, p. 54.
14 Stewart, J. and Walsh, K. (1989) *The Search for Quality.* Luton Local Govt. Training Board.
15 See also Donabedian, A. (1980) *Explorations in Quality Assessment and Monitoring*, vol. 1: *The Definition of Quality and Approaches to Assessing it.* Michigan Health Administration Press.
16 Wootton, S. and Horne, T. (1997) *Strategic Thinking.* Kogan Page, pp. 22–50.
17 Gaster, op. cit.
18 Ibid.
19 Morgan, G. (1986) *Images of Organization.* Sage.
20 Ackoff, R. L. (1981) *Creating Corporate Futures.* Wiley.
21 Singleton, W. T. (1974) *Man Machine Systems.* Penguin.
22 Checkland, P. B. (1988) 'The Origins and Nature of Hard Systems Thinking'. *Journal of Applied Systems Analysis*, vol. 5, no. 2, p. 99. Also in *Systems Thinking and Practice* (1981) Wiley.
23 Audit Commission (1993) *Their Health, Your Business: the New Role of the District Health Authority.* HMSO, p. 9.
24 Ishikawa, K. (1985) *What is Total Quality Control? The Japanese Way.* Prentice Hall.
25 Department of Environment Transport and Regions, op. cit.
26 Chris Reeve, see Learning Conversation in Chapter 7.
27 Horace Pointing (1946) in *Quaker Faith and Practice.* Published by the Religious Society of Friends.
28 Pirsig, R. (1978) *Zen and the Art of Motorcycle Maintenance.* Black Swan, p. 280.
29 Lessom, R. (1991) *Total Quality Learning.* Basil Blackwell, p. 8.
30 Pirsig, op. cit., p. 291.
31 Based on an interview with Peter Docwra, Head of BT Quality Services. We are grateful to Andrew Draper, telecoms consultant and journalist, who carried out this interview.

ROLE THREE

MANAGING PEOPLE

In Role One, managers implement changes using a conversational approach. In Role Two, they co-ordinate people inside the organization to respond to changes outside it. In Role Three, they need to manage the people involved. Where they must manage people in groups we look at the problems involved and how these might be minimized (Chapter 6). In Chapter 7 we examine what sort of leaders are required, if they are required at all. We explore how the motivation of employees might be managed. We prefer to manage people as individuals. We discuss how and why in Chapter 8. We are concerned with the quality of the relationships which managers form and suggest a conversational approach to developing closer relationships with individuals.

6

MANAGING GROUPS AND LEADING TEAMS IN PUBLIC SERVICES

Insanity in individuals is something rare – but in groups, parties and nations it is the rule.

(Friedrich Nietzsche [1844–1900])

LEARNING OUTCOMES

This chapter will enable readers to:

- Understand formal and informal groups.
- Understand how to manage formal and informal group meetings.
- Understand how groups are formed and consider the roles people play in groups.
- Consider the challenge of managing and developing multi-agency teams.
- Understand why teams fail and what can make groups more effective, especially when the work involves thinking.
- Understand how conflict arises in groups and how to resolve conflict.
- Explore individual differences and their implications for managing groups.
- Manage difficult individuals.
- Analyse conflict between managing people in groups, managing people as individuals and narcissistic individualism.

INTRODUCTION

In public services, managers are frequently encouraged, sometimes obliged, to bring people together in groups. As we discussed in Chapter 1, new organizational structures often emphasize the need to reduce the number of levels in the hierarchy and to devolve responsibility to working groups. Since the 1980s, such groups have increasingly been referred to as teams.[1] Sometimes the teams are semi-permanent, as in multi-disciplinary teams, or more transient, as in project teams which are brought together to implement particular changes (Chapter 3). The use of the term 'working party' has declined, perhaps reflecting an acceptance that little work is done and that attendance at them is no party! With teams comes the idea of a team leader, someone responsible for the performance of the team in a much more managerial way than 'chairing' a committee. With the emergence of 'self-managed teams', the distinction between a team and a group blurs again. In this chapter we are concerned with the work a manager needs to do, whenever people are brought together in groups, whether in departmental meetings, committees, working parties or in teams. We use the term 'managing groups' to distinguish this kind of work from that involved when managers 'manage individuals'. We discuss the work involved in managing individuals in Chapter 8.

Often public service managers have little option but to create and manage groups. Groups may be foisted on them from above, as part of a senior management strategy to make professionals collaborate in bringing about change. The formation of working groups may be driven by legislation, or by the fact that an application for funding must be signed by a multi-agency partnership. Some funding bodies, for example, require the setting up of partnerships which consist of private, public and voluntary sector representatives. Charity commissions often require charities to have a non-executive board as a condition of their tax-free charitable status. Committees, made up of a wide spectrum of professional and lay representatives, often oversee the work of public services. Multi-disciplinary teams are used to co-ordinate work across local government. Customer support units, quality circles, steering groups, learning sets, advisory boards, Internet conferences and 'virtual teams' that never have met in person – all are examples of people trying to work together in groups. They often find that working groups don't work.

INFORMAL AND FORMAL GROUPS

Schein[2] defined a group as any number of people who

- Interact with one another
- Perceive themselves to be a group
- Are psychologically aware of one another

Schein's definition helps us to distinguish between on the one hand a collection of individuals who may have come together randomly – a crowd for instance – and on the other a group in which members see themselves as people who belong to an identifiable unit, who relate to each other in a meaningful way and who have some form of shared identity. Any aggregate of individuals can become a group. People waiting for a train are not usually a group. But if they decide to complain about the train always being late, they can become a group. Group formation can be brought about by a common external threat, such as neighbourhood crime or proposed highway development, school closure, environmental damage or a mooted change in working conditions. Even where there is a common external threat, a group may not crystallize unless the situation is seeded by a critical incident, like the death of a child.

The Adverse Effects of Informal Groups

The Hawthorne experiment[3] demonstrated how people in groups can choose to make their work performance better or worse. The findings of the Hawthorne experiment contributed to the human relations approach to management. This approach emphasized the importance of managing groups in organizations. In the Hawthorne experiment, workers were sometimes more responsive to informal group pressure than to management controls and incentives. For example, informal groups often emerge within organizations to meet the unmet personal and social needs of employees. In public service offices where smoking is banned, it is common to see people meeting outside the back door of a building. Often the same people meet. They can become an informal group that develop shared interests beyond smoking cigarettes. Buchanan and Huczynski[4] defined an informal group as a collection of individuals who were interdependent, influenced each other, and helped to meet mutual needs (Box 6.1).

Informal groups may work against organizational objectives. In the Hawthorne experiments, informal groups deliberately kept their work rates low because they were afraid that if they increased their work rate, then management would simply raise the targets which they had to hit in order to earn bonus.

Box 6.1

CHARACTERISTICS OF INFORMAL GROUPS

- Leaders of informal groups have charisma
- Informal groups meet the social needs of their members
- Group relations are more important than organizational roles
- Their norms are determined by the group, not by external authorities
- The group becomes a more important point of reference than the organization

The group used ridicule and exclusion as a sanction against workers who were tempted to raise their work rate in order to earn themselves more bonus. Elton Mayo[5] referred to informal groups as the 'natural groups' which managers should seek to nurture. In his view, managers were more like gardeners than engineers. Their role was to create a formal organization which corresponded closely to the informal organization.

Formal Groups – Managing Committees

Many public services have some sort of committee structure to oversee the work of departments or services. The managers report to the committee. The members of these committees are usually selected to represent the interests of other groups, or because they can provide expertise which will help the work of the committee. Committee members often include representatives of political parties, volunteers, members of the public, professionals and technical experts. People on committees often have roles such as chairperson and secretary. The chairperson guides the discussion and orchestrates the debate. The chairperson must ensure that all members of the committee are given the opportunity to present their views and that any one person or interest group does not dominate the discussion. The chairperson must have the ability to summarize, to move the discussion forward, and to ensure that relevant issues are addressed. Paperwork associated with the working of the committee must be completed (Chapter 12). The minutes secretary records what is discussed, notes decisions that are made and any tasks that are delegated and to whom. Committees need an agenda, minutes, papers and procedures:

- **Agenda**. The agenda sets out the items to be discussed at the committee meeting. This is sent out to members prior to the committee meeting so that they can prepare their contributions.
- **Minutes**. Minutes of meetings are kept to provide a record of what has been discussed at previous committee meetings. Committee members start by checking that the minutes of the

previous meeting are an accurate record of what took place. If they are not, then alterations are made until everyone agrees the minutes.
- **Papers**. These may be presented to committee members to inform them about particular issues and to assist them in decision-making. Administrative staff, other sub-committees, or internal or external advisors can provide papers. It is common practice in western democracies for heads of departments to present reports on services for which they are responsible (Chapter 12).
- **Procedures**. These are meant to ensure that committee members conduct themselves in an orderly manner and act fairly within the powers ascribed to them. Procedures include formal decision-making (Box 6.2). A more detailed exploration of decision-making is found in Chapter 12.

The decision-making process in a public service committee usually involves voting. Normally a simple majority of an agreed number of members will secure a decision. The agreed number of members is called a quorum. If insufficient members are present, the meeting cannot take decisions. Some decisions may require agreement by more than half the members. A two-thirds majority may be needed to change the committee's membership or its procedures. In some cases, only unanimous decisions are valid. There are advantages to using committees (Box 6.3). All this assumes that decision-making in committees is a rational process that is open to public view.

Box 6.2

FORMAL DECISION-MAKING IN COMMITTEES

- Agree the agenda
- Define parameters of each issue
- Collect information relevant to each
- Generate a range of possible responses
- Assess the consequences of responses
- Select the best response

Box 6.3

ADVANTAGES OF COMMITTEES

- The views of all those interested can be represented
- Decisions are made after the relevant issues have been debated

- Committees can deal with more complex issues than informal groups
- Committees can call on the services of other groups for information and advice

---

Disadvantages of Committees

In committees, behind the scene power and influence determine what is put on or kept off the agenda. The order of discussion, the time allowed, acceptance of papers that no one has had time to read – these kinds of decisions are often taken by the chairperson or the secretary. Excessive time allocated to earlier items can ensure perpetual deferment of unwanted issues. Decisions can be swayed by who is allowed to open and close the discussion and by a strong lead from the chair. Many public service committees have neither the power, the time nor the expertise to question complex decisions. In annual budget rounds key players behind the scenes usually hammer out the most important decisions. The committee is the stage for 'public performance'; the real work goes on 'backstage'. The 'public performance' usually emphasizes rational discourse; the 'backstage activity', on the other hand, is less rational. It may involve power games and horse trading, negotiation and compromise.[6]

MANAGING MEETINGS

Besides committees, public service managers are likely to be called upon to manage other formal meetings (Box 6.4).

Box 6.4

MANAGING MEETINGS

Before the Meeting

State the purpose

- e.g. information giving, consultation, decision-making, legal, educational, support

Plan the agenda

- Complete the agenda
- Send all members a copy
- Can it be completed in time?
- Identify what decisions must be made
- Decide how much time for each item

Make arrangements

- Venue. Refreshments
- Who will take minutes?
- Who will arrange room and seating?
- Who will sort heating and ventilation?
- Who will introduce each item on the agenda?

During the Meeting

Open the meeting

- Welcome people. State the purpose
- Introduce new members. Set out decisions to be made

- Clarify any ground rules
- Agree time the meeting will end. Agree time allocated to each item

Manage the discussion

- Prevent people from hogging the debate
- Involve everyone. Keep discussion to the point
- Make decisions and record them
- Summarize who will do what by when
- Thank everyone for their attendance and contribution and close the meeting

After the Meeting

- Inform people about decisions immediately
- Confirm agreed actions in writing
- Write up and circulate minutes well before the next meeting

GROUP FORMATION

A multi-agency project group or a new committee may be convened, but it does not come into existence fully formed (Figure 6.1). The Tuckman and Jenson[7] model helps to explain why some groups work well and why some groups do not work at all. It also explains why some projects fail. Not all groups get through all of the stages. Some groups never get to the 'storming' phase. They remain inefficient and ineffective. Discussions about what is to be included in the work of the group can be a useful occasion for early 'storming'. Tuckman and Jenson regarded all five stages, including the 'storming', as necessary stages in the development of working groups that work (Box 6.5).

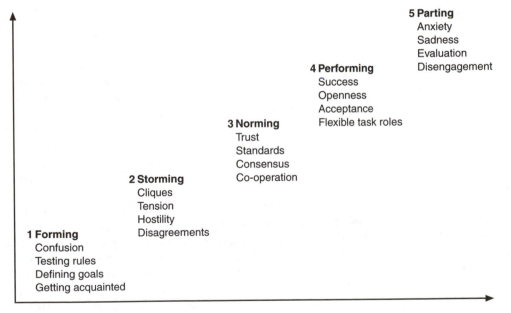

Figure 6.1 Increasing group work effectiveness over time

Box 6.5

FIVE STAGES IN THE LIFE OF A GROUP

1 **Forming** refers to the initial formation of the group. Tasks to be carried out are discussed. Members get to know one another. The resources available to the group are identified. The group seeks reassurance about what is required of them. Groups often develop high dependency on a leader.

2 **Storming** occurs when group members question the task and challenge the way of doing things. The conflict is uncomfortable. Individuals may be confronted and emotive issues raised. Leadership challenges may occur.

3 **Norming** represents a settling down of the group following upheavals in stage 2. Conflicts are resolved and shared norms and values are established. Roles are ascribed to group members and working rules are agreed. Group members begin to co-operate. The group becomes more cohesive.

4 **Performing** describes the group becoming productive and getting on with achieving its objectives. By this stage its members may be happy working alone, in pairs, or in sub-groups as well as in the large group.

5 **Parting** marks the final stage in the life of the group, when the group is about to disband. Before they part, the group members reflect on their time together. They should allow sufficient time for proper leave taking and saying goodbye to each other.

DEVELOPING GROUPS

Multi-disciplinary Teams

Team building is a process which helps team members to understand their own team roles more clearly and to improve their interaction and collaboration. Belbin's[8] approach to understanding team roles has been used extensively. Belbin developed a questionnaire which enabled team members to identify the roles they played in teams. If roles are duplicated, some group members can be asked to work towards developing roles which are under-represented in the team. Other approaches to team building involve asking group members to rate their team's performance under a number of headings, such as clarity of purpose, openness to new ideas, time-keeping or willingness to listen to others. By assessing and analysing these data, problems are raised and addressed.

Team-building programmes based on outdoor activities, such as orienteering or raft building, have been widely used by public service organizations, especially those needing to develop multi-disciplinary working. By the 1990s, in the UK, Action Zones were set up in deprived urban areas. Local authorities were required to set up multi-agency teams to tackle problems of deprivation, crime and disorder. These teams included community development services, the police, social services and different educational departments. The different groups had different values, different norms and different ways of working. They had misconceptions and prejudices about each other. Box 6.6 has some useful questions to ask when getting a group together.

The different groups are invited to exchange their answers to these questions and then to explore their similarities. Differences may be caused by incorrect assumptions, stereotyping, prejudices and ignorance. Different perceptions can be explored with the help of a facilitator. Misconceived ideas about roles, norms and expectations can be identified. The chances of effective intergroup work can be increased.

Box 6.6

GETTING IT TOGETHER: QUESTIONS TO ASK

- What are you like?
- What do you expect from us?
- What do you imagine we expect from you?
- If you had one single success criterion for our working together, what would it be?

GROUP STRUCTURES AND GROUP PROCESSES

Group structures are identifiable patterns of relationships (Box 6.7).

Box 6.7

THE SIX MAIN DIMENSIONS OF GROUP STRUCTURE[9]

- The status of the members
- The quality of communication
- The relative power of the members
- The liking of the members for each other
- The roles played by the different members
- The style and the quality of the leadership

Status and Power in a Group

Status is concerned with ranking within a group. Most groups have leaders and subordinates. Informal groups bestow status on members who meet the expectations of the group. In formal groups, status is often based on hierarchy. As we saw in Chapter 1, staff in bureaucratic organizations have positions which are arranged in an order of increasing authority. The trappings of authority – office size, parking spaces, the quality of furnishings – all inform members of the organization where someone stands in order of authority. The power which a person has is linked to their status. There are different forms of power within a group. French and Raven[10] define power in terms of the potential influence a person has over others. They identified five different types of power exercised in groups: reward power, coercive power, referent power, legitimate power and expert power (Chapter 7). Power is not the same as authority. A manager may have the right to expect subordinates to carry out instructions but may lack the ability to make them do it. They are powerless. On the other hand, a person without formal authority may have the ability to get people to do things. They are powerful.

Likes and Dislikes in a Group

The clustering of people who like each other and who do not like each other, within a group, is sometimes called the affective structure of the group. Identifying affective structure can reveal the roots of particular problems within the group. Moreno[11] invented a technique called sociometry to reveal the affective structure of a group. A sociogram is produced by asking group members a number of questions concerning their preferences regarding the members within a group. For example, with whom would they like to work or spend time or study? These preferences are then mapped by linking lines which determine different people's popularity (Figure 6.2). A sociogram can quickly reveal patterns of relationships within a group, for

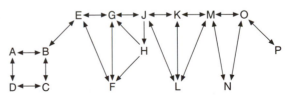

A, B, C and D are a sub-group linked to the main group by B

G, J and M are the most liked members and are likely to have leadership roles

P and H are the least liked members and are likely to be isolated from the main group.

Figure 6.2 A sociogram mapping group structure

example, who is isolated and who is popular and unpopular. It can also identify sub-groupings within a group or team.

Playing Roles in a Group

The role of someone within a group is the set of behaviours that are expected of them. Bales[12] attempted to understand the different roles that people play in groups and the obstacles that this presents to group working. Bales identified two problems facing groups: intra-group communication and group maintenance. Intra-group communication helps to address the uncertainty and confusion that people feel when they come together as a group. Group members need to exert influence on each other in order to reach agreements. Bales asserts that unconscious needs feed the group's desire for leadership and for the adoption of different roles. Bales thinks that leadership and hierarchy are needed by every group in order to maintain itself and survive. Leadership and hierarchy bring problems of their own (Chapter 7). Researchers have sought to charac-

terize the roles that people play in groups. This book is organized around six functional roles: managing change, managing operations, managing people, managing resources, managing information and managing learning. Meredith Belbin[13] identified nine roles based on the way people behaved and thought: company worker, chairman, shaper, plant, resource investigator, monitor-evaluator, team worker, completer finisher and specialist (Table 6.1).

Belbin acquired a good reputation for his work by accurately predicting the failure of teams in which there was nobody to play some of the key roles. Belbin's questionnaire enabled people to self-assess the roles they preferred to play in groups. It was widely used in public services but it is not clear how useful it was. Public service managers rarely had much say over the composition of their groups or teams. Belbin's team profiles draw attention to weaknesses and gaps that might need to be addressed. It is a popular activity and a good icebreaker for new teams. It has the advantage of getting the group to think about processes, before it begins to think about tasks. There may be a

Table 6.1 Nine roles for a successful team

Team role	Main characteristics	Allowable weaknesses
Company worker	Conservative, dutiful, predictable	Inflexible, slow to respond to new ideas
Chairman	Self-confident, controlled, clarifies goals	Can be seen as manipulative
Shaper	Challenging, dynamic. Thrives on pressure	Provokes others, can hurt people's feelings
Plant	Individualistic, creative problem-solver, highly intelligent	Ignores detail, poor communicator
Resource investigator	Extrovert, enthusiastic, inquisitive	Over-optimistic, loses interest easily
Monitor–evaluator	Sober, prudent, cautious, discerning	Lacks drive, doesn't motivate others, critical
Team worker	Sociable, diplomatic, averts friction, listens	Indecisive, easily swayed
Completer–Finisher	Orderly, conscientious, anxious	A worrier, reluctant to delegate, nit-picky
Specialist	Single-minded, self-motivated expert	A narrow contribution, misses the 'big picture'

'Hawthorne effect', i.e. the group's performance may be raised just by thinking itself special enough to merit a Belbin assessment. Belbin's tests are psychological tests of personality and we have discovered some links to thinking style to which we will return later. There are enthusiasts for another set of tests developed by Myers Brigg. These are psychometric tests based on Jungian ideas.[14] They are widely used in management selection and in assessment centres. Their main merit seems to be in developing a group language – a vocabulary of shared meanings. The development of this shared language seems to make it legitimate for members to discuss each other's behaviour in the group. This helps with group iden-tity and cohesiveness. Given how little control public service managers generally have over the size and composition of working groups, statutory com-mittees, interdisciplinary teams, steering groups, audit teams and multi-agency projects, we favour a role for managers in developing the thinking and social skills of individuals, and in facilitating their thinking work when they are forced to work in groups.

In the following learning conversation (Box 6.8) we examine some of the problems faced by Sean Fisher, when he was appointed to lead and develop a multi-agency team made up of professionals from different public services.

Box 6.8

EXTRACTS FROM A CONVERSATION: WITH SEAN FISHER 'MULTI-AGENCY MULTI-PROBLEM'

Tony: Tell me how your team was formed?

Sean: In October 1998 we became one of ten national pilot schemes which aimed to develop multi-agency approaches to preventing youth offending. We are made up of three social workers, a teacher, officers from probation and careers services, the police and education welfare, a psychiatric community nurse, a drugs worker and part-time staff.

Tony: Why a multi-agency approach?

Sean: The initiative was driven by the National Audit Office Report *Mis-spent Youth* written in 1997. Multi-agency team working was an example of trying to find 'joined-up solutions to joined-up problems'. It was an attempt to see if education, welfare and criminal justice services could reduce rates of offending.

Tony: What problems did you experience?

Sean: Bringing people together from different professions enabled us to draw on a wide range of experience and access information which was previously difficult to get hold of. Information, for example, from the police con-cerning crime patterns. We are more creative.

Tony: What do you mean by creative?

Sean: When we started, everyone thought that their own approach was the right one. Power struggles and conflict were common. The social workers and the teachers objected to working with a uniformed police officer. Ini-tially the police officer agreed to adopt civilian dress. Eventually she reverted to wearing a uniform – she said she was having an identity crisis! Probation officers challenged social workers. Social workers are committed to welfare and counselling whereas probation ser-vices are driven by evidence-based practices. There is no real 'evidence' that counselling makes any difference to rates of re-offending. We don't use it anymore.

Tony: How did you build a team?

Sean: By getting the right people into the team in the first place. This is not as easy. The for-mation of a multi-agency team can be seen by some managers as an opportunity to get rid of someone. The recruitment processes need to identify the type of people who can and who can't work in a multi-agency team. Many public services are wasting their time on team development exercises when they have the wrong people in the team in the first place. If you can't change the way team members think – and sometimes you can't – then you have to change the team member. I will have to get rid of some people in my team. Some team members resist their new roles.

Tony: How do you deal with that?

Sean: Most team members want to get on with the job and feel frustrated. They do not want to carry passengers. Our performance is being closely monitored. The government expects results. The government has a 'name and shame policy'. We don't want to be seen as poor performers on the pilot scheme. There will be casualties. Despite everyone's best efforts, some people may not be suited to team working. Regular supervision and appraisals are necessary if poor performance is to be identified. You need to tell people when they are not contributing to the team.

Tony: How do you spot a good team worker?

Sean: A Belbin questionnaire can be helpful. For example, it would be good to have a 'Completer–Finisher' in my present team. We have too many ideas people – 'Plants'. But Belbin's questionnaire alone can't be used to identify the right people for the team – it would be impossible to appoint nine people to play all of his team roles. We need flexible people who welcome change; people who can work across boundaries, who know that they have not got all the right answers; people who can step out of the culture of their own profession without feeling vulnerable; people who are fascinated by difference; people who really enjoy learning new things. Such people are rare in public services. We have some very inflexible types.

Tony: Can team development help?

Sean: Yes, but as I have said before, only when you've got the right mix of people. It is important to focus on practical tasks. Act quickly, get people to work together in pairs and threes. Away-days can be useful. Exercises which reveal how the group approaches tasks help to sort out problems. Once you have dealt with practicalities, then you can start to think about clarifying values and developing purposes.

Tony: Has it been difficult to develop a shared sense of purpose?

Sean: It has been a struggle. Different perspectives have been enriching and enraging! I think our purpose is becoming clearer – to prevent re-offending. Having a clear focus, enables us to say 'No'.

Tony: Thanks. Good luck with your team.

GROUP WORK DOESN'T WORK: THE FAILURE OF TEAM WORKING

The difficulties experienced by Sean Fisher are common in many teams. They are made more difficult by the diversity of experience, training and values which people bring to his multi-agency team. We have been asked to look at many situations in which multi-agency team working isn't working. Increasingly, we suspect that the cause is fundamental – group working doesn't work. Teams are often confused, misguided and quite angry. Individuals are not achieving anything like their potential. Leaders fail to lead (Chapter 7). Organizations are pyramids of weak teams. The 'dream team' is nowhere to be seen.[15] We accept, however, that this situation is still an improvement on what preceded it. Many of the steps which we have outlined do help to reduce the difficulties. But it is better, if possible, not to create the difficulties in the first place. Manage people as individuals and not in groups (Chapter 8).

The 'Risky-Shift' in Groups

This concept describes the tendency, highlighted by Stoner,[16] for groups to make decisions that are riskier than those that the members of the group would take on their own. Stoner suggested that when the majority of group members were risk-takers, the group had a tendency to take more risky decisions as a group than they would have been willing to take as individuals. When group members were predominantly risk-averse, they appeared to make more cautious decisions as a group, than they would have taken as individuals. There have been over 300 studies of similar phenomena.[17]

'Group Think' in Groups

Cohesiveness helps groups to survive. In Tuckman's model of group formation, it is cited as one of the hallmarks of a mature, high-performing team. However, Janis's[18] study of a number of American policy disasters revealed some serious negative consequences of group cohesiveness. These disasters included the failure to anticipate the attack on Pearl Harbor in 1941 and the pursuit of the war in Vietnam (1964–67). Janis ascribed these disasters to a phenomenon he called 'Group Think'. Group think is a phenomenon that can occur when the group's need for unanimity and cohesion overrides its responsibilities to do what it is paid to do, in this case to appraise realistically the consequences of alternative courses of action (Box 6.9).

The Holocaust Experiments

Group think can become 'mob think'. There have been many psychological experiments with groups in an attempt to understand how groups of ordinary, non-violent, religious, law-abiding people could perform atrocities and war crimes. In these experiments, the beliefs and values of individuals were assessed prior to putting them into groups. In group situations, these subjects could be persuaded to express agreement with opinions that were contrary to their espoused beliefs and values and to take action based on those opinions, even where such actions involved the infliction of pain and the risk of fatal consequences for other people. In order to reduce the risk of group think, it is necessary for managers to surface and encourage conflict. This often makes the manager, and the group, feel uncomfortable. Perhaps conflict runs against an instinctive preference for control – the very instinct which may have caused the manager to be attracted to management in the first place. Likewise many group members prefer groups that meet their needs for security and belonging (Chapter 7). They like to feel 'comfortable' in their group. The path of least dissent is sought. Decision by consensus is common. Individualism is stifled. The constant search for a middle way leads to mediocre thinking and mediocre performance.

Box 6.9

CHARACTERISTICS OF GROUP THINK

- An illusory sense of unanimity
- An illusory sense of invulnerability
- A tendency for individuals to conform
- A tendency to rationalize and filter evidence to fit preconceptions
- A tendency to simplify, stereotype or ridicule opposing points of view

'I Can't Think!': A More Thoughtful Approach to Group Work

When people come together in a group they feel anxious. The level of anxiety which they report rises with the number of people in the group, until the group reaches a size at which the person feels anonymous. Anxiety levels increase with lack of structure and lack of discipline. Beyond a certain point, which varies from one individual to another, anxiety reduces performance in most tasks, particularly those that involve thinking. Embarrassment, discomfort and an inability to tolerate silence can lead people to break silence impulsively and to fill it with talk that often has little relevance to the task in hand. This is a double jeopardy if the task requires thinking, because 80 per cent of people complain 'I can't think!' while other people are talking. Yet our studies have shown that silences during a two-hour group task rarely exceeded 20 seconds! Despite these and other pitfalls, managers can take a number of steps towards a more thoughtful approach.

WAYS TO MAKE GROUPS WORK – THINKING IN GROUPS

Think before You Group

Never create a team unless team working is essential for the project's success. Before creating a team, consider whether it would be possible to divide the project into tasks that could be delegated to individuals. The work of individuals can be co-ordinated through a series of one-to-one conversations designed to monitor, motivate and coach each individual (Chapters 7, 8, 13 and 14). Cartwheel structures can be effective when the manager at the 'hub' of the wheel uses a conversational approach to management. If you are instructed to use teams, or if you inherit a tradition of team working, do as much work as possible away from the team. Clarify the task to be accomplished and define the objectives that will lead to the completion of the task. Clear terms of reference help to reduce the anxiety of team members when they are brought together. The manager should also think about the knowledge and the experience and skills that the team will require to carry out the task – especially the different kinds of thinking skills that will be required. What roles will need to be played in the team? Is it possible to obtain profiles of potential team members in advance, by using, for example, a questionnaire?

The manager needs to ensure that the group has:

- Time
- Money
- Authority
- Equipment
- Information
- Food and drink
- Accommodation
- Access to key people

Think about Group Procedures

In this phase the manager helps the team to think about boundaries and how the team might set about the task. The manager helps clarify who is responsible for what. Policies and guidelines are set out. A timetable for the task and clear time limits for the length of team meetings help to manage anxiety. The manager may need to open doors and obtain answers that would be denied to individual members of the group. The manager helps to overcome obstacles. Only the manager can remove non-participative passengers, or saboteurs, from the group. This must be done swiftly in the early stages of the life of the group.

Think about Process as well as Progress

The manager must ensure that the group allocates time to think about how it is working. This includes the process as well as the progress of its work. It is time well spent. One way of doing this is to use the forming, storming, norming and performing model of group development – where do we think we are up to? Group roles can be discussed using Belbin's terminology. In an effective team, different people will lead at different times. If the task falters, think about rotating the leadership role. Can someone else take the lead until the next phase of the work prompts further thought about the kind of leadership required? The team needs to think about the type of leadership work that is now needed and allocate that work to one of its members (Chapter 7).

HELPING THE GROUP TO THINK

Help the Group to Remember: Recollective Thinking

This is the kind of thinking that is needed to elicit and take advantage of the group's accumulated knowledge, experience and wisdom and relate it to the task in hand. This is best done by asking individuals to make notes quietly on their own, discuss them with another group member and then pool them in a general discussion. The main points of the discussion should be noted in writing by someone familiar with the problem but not participating in the discussion. Periodically the notes should be read back to the group. The discussion should be free-ranging and at least an hour should be spent exploring hopes, fears, expectations, problems and opportunities. The manager should encourage people to make associations or connections with experiences that other people have reported and to tell their own stories and give their own examples. Try to get people to go back over their anecdotes and share what they learned. Ask them about colours, textures, sounds, even smells and tastes that occur in the stories. Ask them how they felt at the time, as well as what they thought at the time. Give the group encouraging feedback.

Help the Group Make Sense of Experience: Reflective Thinking

It is better to disperse the group for this type of thinking. A break from recollective thinking is advisable. Ideally each group member should be given a copy of the notes taken in the recollective thinking activity. Looking back over those notes, what do they feel now, what do they think now? Any ideas, inspirations, conclusions, learning, any thoughts at all? Get them to give some hand-written notes to the manager. The manager reads everybody's notes and then feeds them back to the group as a composite, without identifying individuals.

Help the Group Apply its Thinking: Predictive Thinking

This is something that groups can sometimes do better together, than as individuals working alone. It involves envisaging what the future situation will be like – a key skill for managers, especially as they become more senior. It involves 'visual' thinking skills, like 'foresight' and 'vision' (Chapter 7). Individual members record their 'view' of the future – what will happen then if we 'do nothing'? They record their predictions anonymously and hand them in to the manager. A composite is fed back to the whole group who then continue their discussion about the future before repeating the process of anonymous recording and feedback. The process continues until there is consensus about what is likely to happen in the future.

Help the Group to Think of New Ideas: Imaginative and Creative Thinking

By creative thinking, we mean thinking of a new way of doing something – a new design, a new service or a new treatment. Thinking creatively may, or may not, involve the use of imagination. Imagining things is an inner world visualization process. We literally conjure up 'images' of things that do not yet exist. Commonly we imagine the problem already solved – the design already working. It is easier to work out *how* to get there, once someone has imagined *what* it will be like when we get there.

Although individuals can be trained to think more creatively working on their own than in a group, most managers will probably obtain more creative ideas if they use 'brain storming' (Chapter 12). The group are asked to sit themselves comfortably, but not so comfortably that they might fall asleep. They are encouraged to relax by contracting and relaxing different sets of muscles, breathing as deeply and slowly as possible between each set of contractions. Most people find it easier to start by contracting and relaxing the muscles in the feet and toes and then working upwards through the calves and thighs, buttocks and abdomen, arms and hands, shoulders and neck, and finally the face and scalp. Always inhale deeply before each muscle contraction and push out as much breath as possible, as slowly as possible, during each relaxation. Allow the slow deep breathing to continue. Electrical activity in the brain will slow down, producing longer brain waves.

The visual systems in the brain can be engaged by inviting the group members to close their eyes and to remember and revisit a favourite scene when they were very relaxed or happy or amused. Encourage them to run the scene backwards and forwards as though it were on a video and to select a favourite scene to hold on a freeze frame. Get them to intensify the colour and to notice how they feel watching that scene now. They can hold that scene in a window, while they bring up another scene and visualize the future situation or scenario in which the creative solution must work.

Encourage them to jot down ideas about things that could be done to improve the predicted scenario – it doesn't matter how outlandish the ideas might seem. Get people to call out their ideas and write them up on a flipchart however strange. Use their words as exactly as possible. Repeat the ideas back as you write them up. Get someone else to note any idea you miss and feed it in whenever the stream of ideas falters – acting like a header tank to maintain the pressure. Keep reading back the whole list quickly and at an accelerating pace – encourage humour, join in the laughter and the fun. Do not allow any negative or evaluative judgement of anyone's ideas at this stage. That will come later. When the pace slows, usually after about 20

minutes, get everyone to take a copy of the list of ideas and then go for a walk – alone or in pairs. When they return write up any extra ideas.

Help the Group Think of Consequences: Empathetic and Ethical Thinking

This involves getting the group to identify key stakeholders (Chapter 4) and then getting them to think about their ideas, as though they were the people affected by their ideas. The object is to get each group member to sense how each stakeholder would feel and what they would think about each of the options. This will also help to identify possible supporters and change agents or people who will resist (Chapter 2). This helps to assess the feasibility of each option, not just its benefits. This is best started by each person thinking on their own and followed by the pooling of thoughts in a collective discussion which the manager can summarize on a flipchart. It is important that actions are ethical, as well as economic, efficient and effective (Chapter 11).

Help the Group to Pick the Best Ideas: Evaluative and Critical Thinking

Critical thinking – challenging the assumptions, logic and the conclusions drawn – contributes powerfully to overall evaluative thinking, but it is not the only basis for evaluation. Evaluative thinking will bring in thinking about what is felt as well as what is thought. It will include what is thought critically by the group members thinking for themselves, but also what is thought by the group members thinking as though they were another person. This should be done individually, using a pre-agreed ranking and scoring system, so that the evaluations of individuals can be aggregated when the group reconvenes. Criteria related to economy, efficiency, effectiveness, feasibility and risk should be agreed together before the group is dispersed (Chapters 10 and 11). The most favoured options should be thought about ethically (Chapter 15).

MANAGING CONFLICT IN AND BETWEEN GROUPS

According to Schmidt,[19] managers spend approximately 20 per cent of their time – one day per week – managing conflict. The ability to manage conflict effectively will have an impact on the manager's performance. Conflict can be thought about in different ways. Mullins[20] defines conflict as 'behaviour intended to obstruct the achievement of some other person's goals'. Buchanan and Huczynski[21] prefer Thomas's idea that conflict is a process in which one party perceives that a second party has frustrated, or is about to frustrate, some concern of the first party. A tentative definition might be 'a struggle between opposing interests, ideas or values'. This avoids saying anything about how conflict is manifested. Intangible manifestations of conflict can be difficult to discern. Amongst high-ranking civil servants, for example, bitter conflicts may be enacted within perfectly civil conversations. Only those experienced in interpreting elaborated codes of etiquette and politeness might detect the underlying hostility.

Not all struggle is conflict. Handy[22] makes a useful distinction between conflict, argument and competition. Argument is a process of resolving differences in order to avoid conflict. Competition, on the other hand, is a process in which opposing parties attempt to gain some prized goal. In most organizations, resources and opportunities are limited and competition produces winners and losers. This does not have to be the case. Competition can be 'win–lose' or 'win–win. In 'win–lose' competitions one person's gain is another person's loss. Skilful managers prefer 'win–win' solutions – solutions in which everybody wins or gains as much as possible. These are sometimes called 'optimal solutions'. Considerable thought must be given to arguments and competitions, if they are not to degenerate into wasteful conflict (Chapter 12). Having said that, is all conflict wasteful?

Different Perspectives on Conflict

The unitary view

This regards conflict as a malfunction. Conflict is undesirable and to be avoided. Organizations should be co-operative structures, designed to achieve agreed objectives. A unitary view is sometimes described as 'happy families'. Consensus is sought. Conflict is avoided. Conflict only arises because of poor communication, badly designed organizational structures, personality factors, inflexibility or external pressures. Peters and Watermann[23] reincarnated this approach in 1982. They claimed that conflict could be avoided by developing a shared culture of openness and trust and through improved communication. Trades unions were, at best, to be tolerated. They were unhelpful because they tended to resolve disagreements through adversarial bargaining. Disney was cited as an example of an organization that was successful, in part, because it took a unitary view of conflict.

The pluralist view

This rejects the notion that different stakeholders in the organization can have the same interests. In particular, it recognizes that the interests of employers and workers conflict. Managers must balance conflicting interests by bargaining. Conflict is seen as a legitimate evolutionary way of bringing about organizational change. Conflict enables change and produces improved effectiveness.

The Marxist view

This sees organizations as arenas in which people battle for limited resources, status, rewards and values. Organizations are theatres in which a class war is fought between owners, managers and workers. Conflict is seen as a necessary and legitimate means of furthering revolutionary change.

Causes of Conflict in Groups

Like a good clinician, a public service manager will seek the causes that lie behind the symptoms of conflict. This may require sensitive enquiry with third parties as well as with those displaying the conflict. Some causes may be minor and easily resolved, for example, conflicts caused by working practices or by patronizing attitudes. Other causes of conflict may be more deeply rooted in the culture of the organization, as when people are asked to act against their values or beliefs (Chapter 15). Cronin and Bryans[24] identified six types of organizational conflict:

1 **Conflict between corporate and individual**
   A primary school teacher may refuse to drill pupils simply to improve the school's position in league tables. In prisons there may be a conflict between retribution and an individual prison officer's desire to rehabilitate offenders.
2 **Conflict between different departments**
   There may be a struggle between departments responsible for building roads and departments responsible for public transport. Sometimes such competition is healthy, sometimes not. Conflict between professional departments and finance departments is common. There is often conflict between clinicians and managers.
3 **Conflict between the formal and the informal**
   In theory, in hierarchical organizations, higher-ranking officers should be able to dictate change affecting lower-ranking employees. In practice, their efforts may be resisted, subverted or even sabotaged, by informal alliances of the lower-ranking employees.
4 **Conflict between managers and managed**
   Grievance and disciplinary procedures are common. Workers may initiate grievance proceedings against managers if they think that they have been victimized or unfairly treated, or if they think that managers have departed from 'custom and practice'. Managers may initiate disciplinary action, claiming that the conduct of a worker is bringing the service into disrepute.
5 **Conflict between task and individual**
   Time off for training may adversely affect the service. The timing of requests for annual leave may not fit in with the workload.

6 **Conflict between individuals**
   This can occur when two people end a close personal relationship, or belong to families who are in dispute with each other.

Conflict in Public Services

In public services, conflict is often seen as deviant behaviour that needs to be controlled and preferably eradicated. However, conflict *per se* is not necessarily good or bad, but it is inevitable. Even if organizations take great care to avoid it, it will still occur.[25] There are positive consequences of conflict:

- The search for new or better ideas
- The clarification of people's views
- The stimulation of creativity and interest
- The opportunity to test capabilities
- The surfacing and resolution of problems

There are also negative consequences of conflict:

- Suspicion and distrust
- Increased turnover of staff
- Resistance rather than team work
- Increased distance between people
- Some people feel defeated and demeaned
- Concentration on individual self-interest[26]

MODELS FOR MANAGING CONFLICT

In 1993 Handy[27] suggested five ways of managing conflict: arbitration, procedure, confrontation, separation and neglect. Thomas[28] suggested that managing conflict in organizations involved two different forms of behaviour: assertion and co-operation. Assertion is concerned with the extent to which individuals or groups aim to satisfy their own needs. Co-operation concerns the extent to which individuals or groups are willing to satisfy the needs of others (Figure 6.3). Thomas's model creates five further possible ways of managing conflict: avoiding, smoothing, competing, compromising and collaborating. That adds up to ten possible ways of managing conflict:

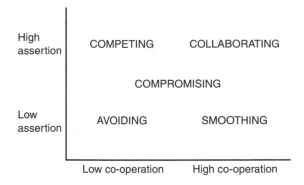

Figure 6.3 Assertion v. co-operation in managing conflict

1 **Avoiding** is characterized by low levels of assertion and co-operation. The conflict is ignored and left unresolved. If only one party does this, then they are likely to be dominated by the more assertive party. Even if the more assertive party gets what they want, the conflict remains because the outcome is unacceptable to the other party. On the face of it, avoidance has little to commend it. However, there may be situations when it is wise to do nothing, or to wait for a more appropriate time. For example, when more important issues are pressing.

2 **Smoothing** is characterized by some degree of co-operation but little assertiveness. Agreement may be reached at the expense of important principles, or by ignoring the real issues. A fragile consensus may result which does not satisfy either party. Smoothing can have advantages. Appearing co-operative and not too pushy can be a way of gaining social capital. This can be traded in at a later date when a favour is required. Smoothing can help relationships with individuals or with other departments. Once relations have been cemented, the co-operative party may be in a position to become more assertive. In the UK, in the 1970s, District Health Authorities were managed through district management teams in which each team member had a veto over any decision. The veto system was aimed at ensuring consensus. In practice it led to failures to resolve important issues.

3 **Competing** is characterized by considerable assertion but little co-operation. One party will win, or the conflict will continue unresolved. The party with most power will eventually force the weaker party to concede. Competing may be the only way of resolving conflict when both parties take entrenched positions. An example of competing to resolve conflict is seen in the way the UK government introduced GP fundholding into the health service. This was opposed by most GPs and by the British Medical Association. Despite strong opposition, the government implemented its unpopular policy and opponents were left with no real alternative.

4 **Compromising** is characterized by a combination of moderate assertion and co-operation. A mutually acceptable agreement is sought. Each party must concede some ground to the other party. This can result in failure to address contentious issues. Most negotiations are likely to involve compromise. In 1999, the decision of the UK government to delay performance related pay for teachers was a compromise.

5 **Collaborating** is characterized by a combination of strongly assertive and positively co-operative behaviour. It aims to produce 'win–win' situations in which all the needs of the different parties are met, i.e. everyone gets what they want. The advantage of this approach is that it encourages all parties to seek creative solutions and to integrate different insights and perspectives. In some situations it may eventually become apparent that it is impossible for all the needs of all parties to be met and this may come to be accepted by both sides. However, starting off by seeking a collaborative solution to conflict fosters goodwill, trust and creativity.

6 **Arbitration** here means inviting a third party to help resolve the conflict. Sometimes the third party may be external. More often it is a senior manager from another department. The

arbitration may be informal or it may follow a formal procedure. In our experience, arbitration works best when the conflict is localized, practical or operational. It does not work well if the conflict is strategic, fundamental or enduring. Changes are usually suspended pending arbitration and so progress is halted. The situation often deteriorates while everyone waits for the arbitration to take place. If a crisis ensues, it often forces panic action which satisfies no one. People feel coerced but think that they have no choice but to accept the new crisis circumstance. There are mutterings about blackmail and of being 'stitched up'. The original conflict remains and the seeds of some new ones have been sown. An organizational game has been set up, in which there will be no real winners. This does not necessarily matter to the players who are only there to play. Service users are the losers.

7 **Procedures** can reduce the risk of conflict or help contain it if it occurs. In combative team sports, rules enable teams to compete safely. This kind of conflict is not a problem provided that the players keep to the rules and abide by the referee's decisions. Procedures are most effective when the types of conflict are predictable. They should be there to help, not hinder, the resolution of the conflict – for the guidance of the wise and the obedience of fools. In public services 'following procedure' can become an end in itself – no longer a means to improving the service.

8 **Confrontation** can be a risky but effective means of resolving conflict. Used badly the conflict may escalate. It is important that confrontation is preceded by, or includes, steps to unearth, clarify and define the issues.

9 **Separation** of the parties involved can be a means of heading off conflict. It can be used to reduce conflict once it has begun. For example, if a manager sees that two members of staff are likely to have different interests, or incompatible styles of working, then making sure that they work separately can prevent conflict.

10 **Neglect** is not recommended by Handy. We think it has a place. Some conflicts are attention-seeking. It is better to ignore the conflict and address the real need being signalled. Intervening can often add unwarranted weight or significance to the issue on which the conflict is being mistakenly focused.

We have looked at ten possible ways of managing conflict, which is only one of the many problems which we create for ourselves every time we attempt to manage people in groups or teams. Besides learning how these problems might be overcome, it may be helpful to understand why they arise and why it might be preferable to manage people as individuals.

GROUPS: THE PROBLEM OF INDIVIDUAL DIFFERENCE

If we are going to manage 'people', we have to accept the dangers implicit in making any kind of general pronouncements about 'people'. 'People' are individuals, all different. One of the points of creating organizations is to take advantage of the differences between people – differences in knowledge, experience and skill. With these differences come other differences – differences in personality, perception and culture. When managers can detect and understand these differences, they are more likely to be able to work out what they need to do to get co-operation and productive effort from each individual person. We will consider these three dimensions of difference: personality, perception and culture.

Differences in Personality

Personality describes the impact we make on other people. There are three main schools of thought about why our personalities differ – the psychoanalytic school, the behaviourist school and the humanist school.

The Psychoanalytic School

This school is dominated by the writings of Sigmund Freud. His model of personality has three parts, the id, the ego and the super ego. The 'id' is a collection of basic animal instincts such as the instinct to fight for food, take flight from danger or to have sex in order to perpetuate one's genes. The super ego is a set of restraints learned from parents, leaders, priests and other authority figures. These restraints change – to socially acceptable forms – the behaviours that would be driven by the 'id' working alone. The 'ego' adjudicates between the instinctive 'id' and the restrictive 'super ego'. According to Freud, the processes of resolving early conflicts between the 'id' and the 'super ego' involves emotional trauma which children do not wish to remember. The memories of such trauma are therefore suppressed. They continue to be held at bay by adults through mechanisms which Freud called defence mechanisms. He called them defence mechanisms because he saw adults using them to defend themselves against painful memories of acute distress which they had suffered earlier, often as children. Common defence mechanisms are projection, rationalization and fixation. In projection, individuals attribute their own motives and feelings to others. When rationalizing, individuals usually feel the need to give a logical (to them) explanation of what they have done. Fixated individuals are rigid and inflexible about rules and procedures, many of which they make up for themselves. Perhaps Freud's major contribution was the idea that our behaviour in the present continues to be affected by memories that we suppress. Because we are not conscious of our suppressed memories, a lot of our behaviour is unconsciously motivated.

The Behaviourist School

This school is dominated by the work of B. F. Skinner.[29] Skinner's hypothesis was that we learn by responding to external stimuli (Chapters 7 and 13).

According to Skinner's stimulus–response model, our personalities are the sum total of all the behaviours that we have learned by responding to all the stimuli we have experienced in our lives. We tend to repeat responses which result in what we regard as a rewarding effect. Repeated responses become habitual and our personality is the sum total of how we habitually behave. By experimenting to find out what each individual regards as rewarding, we can adjust the tasks we delegate, the way we instruct, and the rewards we offer, so as to encourage, or reinforce, the kinds of behaviours we want. So while the psychoanalysts hold out the possibility of understanding why an individual's personality is the way it is, behaviourists hold out the possibility of changing it through 'behaviour modification'. There are limitations to a behaviourist approach in public services. In many public services it is the public servants and not the managers who determine what counts as rewarding (Chapter 7).

The Humanist School

The Humanist School is not dominated by the work of any one person (Chapter 13). The central idea is that each individual has within himself or herself that which is worthy of respect and development. There is an emphasis on self-determination and personal responsibility. Our personalities may have been distorted by the vagaries of parents, teachers and bosses, but we can overcome these distortions by taking personal responsibility for how we feel and act. As we shall see in Chapter 7, Maslow influenced these ideas. In our own conversational approach to developing close relationships with individuals, the notion of immediacy – the valuing of what is happening 'here and now' – owes much to Rogers, who was an influential member of the Humanist School.[30] Because the basic tenets of the Humanist School are hard to test, there is a danger of adopting them as a belief system – almost a religion. To be of value to managers, it is necessary for individuals not only to accept personal responsibility but also to act on it. This requires proficiency in the use of a whole range of thinking skills, not the least of which is the ability to think predictively about the consequence of intended action. Predictive thinking is supported by skills in thinking recollectively, reflectively, imaginatively, creatively and empathetically. These skills are easier to deploy as an individual, perhaps working with one other person. They can be deployed when working in a group, but much skill is required of a manager who expects people in a group to think effectively.

Differences in Perception

Kelly[31] advanced the idea that each individual inhabits an individual world which they 'construct' for themselves (Chapters 2 and 14). That is why individuals do not see things the same way as their managers or their colleagues. Variations of Kelly's original repertory grid have been used by organizations to explore how each person constructs his or her world. Each person's key constructs are different from the next person's. Different key constructs lead to differences in how people perceive events. Technically, a person's perception is the way they select, organize and interpret stimuli. Because people do this differently, one person's perception of the world is different from the next person's perception of the world. The reasons why the perceptions are different might be that they miss, or misconstrue, some of the stimuli. They may selectively (perhaps unconsciously) notice some things but not others. Focused on 'chatting up' one person at a party, we may not notice 90 per cent what is happening around us. 'I only have eyes for you, dear!' Yet we may still overhear our own name in a conversation not meant for our ears, or hear a baby cry in an upstairs room.

The perception we have of events will depend on how much information about the event we can process. This varies also from person to person. People can process between three and seven new chunks of information (Chapter 12). People choose and chunk different quantities of the new information in different ways. This means that people's perceptions of a given event – and any learning they might subsequently take from it – may be entirely different. One way of making sense of the incoming stimuli is to compare the stimuli with material already in the memory to see if it can be recognized as fitting pre-existing patterns or schema. Since each person's memories and schemata are different, then the meanings each individual attaches to the same event are likely to be different.

To summarize, people are sensitive to different stimuli in a situation; they pay selective attention to the stimuli they sense; they process what they pay attention to in different ways; they use different schemata to try to make sense of what they sense; and they are driven by different personal prejudices in what meaning they attach to the stimuli they receive. It is hardly surprising that we can interview 30 people who were in the same room at the time of an incident and be given up to 30 different accounts of what happened. That is why managers need to hold many conversations and exercise much thought, if they are to arrive at a workable consensus about the 'facts'.

Differences in Culture

Our discussion so far – on personality and perception as two dimensions of the differences between individuals – has been based on psychological models of individual differences. People can also think, react and behave differently because of social differences. They may belong to different socio-economic groups, or different ethnic groups. Different groups have different 'norms'. Different norms cause different people to respond differently to the same situation. To say that someone is different is not to say that they are inferior or superior. It is merely to say that their life experiences have not been the same. This is the basis for management practices that attempt to secure fair and equitable treatment for people from different social groups and for legislation concerned with racial discrimination, employment protection and equal pay, and for concerns for the human rights of the disabled, or trades union members, or rehabilitated offenders (Chapter 8). These are all attempts to protect people who are different from exploitation by another dominant group, e.g. white, male or able-bodied groups.

The idea of managing diversity is more positive than legislating against discrimination. Managing diversity goes beyond making negative behaviour illegal. It seeks positively to embrace and value the different personalities, perceptions, experiences and ways of thinking that different people from different groups can bring. There is nothing inherently wrong, right, good or bad in belonging to a particular social group. Academic and mental ability, for example, are more related to the socio-economic group of one's parents rather than one's race. Academically, girls generally outperform boys. Few physical – and only some mental – disabilities present insuperable obstacles to employment. Kandola and Fullerton[32] studied over 500 organizations. They reported improvements in performance when organizations moved from management policies based on grouping people to policies based on managing people as individuals.

In Chapter 8 we look at the adverse (as well as the useful) effects of stereotyping. Stereotyping, which is often unavoidable in fast-moving situations, can be unfair and inefficient. When managers assume that all members of a particular group behave according to their stereotypes, they are showing prejudice. This is undesirable and can be illegal. A prejudice is a type of attitude. People's attitudes are a complex product of what they know and what they feel about what they know. This is determined in part by their individual needs and motivations (Chapter 7). Because their attitudes in turn affect what they notice (and the meanings or constructions they place on what they notice), individual attitudes can be self-reinforcing and difficult to change. It is possible to change attitudes or prejudices through the rational presentation of facts or opinions. Emotional communication can also be effective, especially if it is directed to issues that reflect individual needs and motivations (Chapter 7). A glimmer of hope is our discovery that people will modify their attitudes to make them closer to individuals whom they respect – another example of managers getting better results when they manage people as individuals.

DEALING WITH DIFFICULT PEOPLE

We have seen that managing groups presents many difficulties best avoided by not creating groups and teams in the first place. However, as we have seen, public services managers often have no choice but to work with interdisciplinary teams on multi-agency task groups. The manager's difficulties are compounded by the way many individuals who are fine on a one-to-one basis, become difficult people in a group. In Table 6.2 we offer a conversational approach to dealing with difficult people in groups.

Many individuals do not need the help of a group in order to become difficult. They only need you! We look next at dealing with individuals who are difficult, whether they are in a group or not.

Dealing with Difficult Individuals

Just because individuals resist your ideas for change, it does not necessarily mean they are difficult people. Be open to the possibility that your ideas for change may be dangerous, impractical, ill advised or unethical. In which case, you should be grateful for the courage of those who dare to resist you. Neither are we here concerned with individuals whose performance is poor. We look at how you can raise the performance of poor performers in Chapter 11.

Through over 2000 conversations with managers and the people they manage, we have reported the kinds of difficult people they have encountered. All these difficulties occurred in the spaces between individuals. In that case, both were party to the difficulty. ('It takes two to tango'.) Having said that, if a spectrum of partners reported difficulty when paired with a particular individual X, we defined X as a difficult person. In Table 6.3 we suggest a conversational approach to dealing with difficult people as individuals.

Table 6.2 Dealing with difficult people in groups: a conversational approach

Type	Typical problems caused	Try saying . . .
BUCKPASSERS	Say it's someone else's fault, or someone else's job.	'When did it happen last?' 'Exactly what happened?' 'Why is it that you never take on any work or accept any responsibility?'
WITHHOLDERS	Are unaware of their potential contribution. Seen as lazy, they cause resentment. Their silences raise anxiety, lower energy and lead to withholding by other members.	'What do you suggest?' 'What is the most similar situation you remember?' 'Are you afraid to take on too much?' 'Do you need help with managing your work or time?'
BICKERERS	Keep bringing up past issues or personal hobby horses, or old grudges. They waste time and cause frustration	'These points are very relevant to our purpose today (restate) but these are not . . .' 'We have only X minutes to make good use of these good points.' 'Can you two deal with this other stuff afterwards?'
PERFORMERS	Treat groups as an audience. They play to the gallery, take centre stage, hog the limelight. They constantly seek attention, approval, reassurance and often challenge the leader. They cover up ignorance (or lack of preparation) by making speeches or acting the fool.	'Can I have a private word with you afterwards?' 'What we are actually here to do is . . .' 'Have you actually read the papers?' 'Which part?'
MUMBLERS	Embarrass others, generate impatience and frustration. They make people anxious so that they complete their sentences for them.	'Can people please remain silent until X has finished?' 'Are you saying . . .?'
FRAGMENTERS	Start up second conversations – often at one corner of the table. They create sub-groups and others cannot hear or follow either conversation properly.	'Is what you are saying relevant to X?' 'Can you make that point after Jane has finished?' 'What do you think of Jane's idea?'
WINDBAGS	Take up too much air time – often nervously repetitious or naturally verbose. They slow progress and frustrate other members of the group.	'Let's see what people think about what you've said so far, and then we may need to come back to you.'
OBJECTORS	Always have a 'Yes, but . . .' to everything. Dispiriting and disheartening for others, they lack empathy and spread a defeatist attitude.	'Please replace all "buts" with "and".' 'What is good about this suggestion?' 'What is an interesting possibility here?' 'What is your question?'

Table 6.3 Dealing with difficult people as individuals: a conversational approach

Type	Typical problems caused	Try saying . . .
WHINGERS	Complain, but not to the offending party and without proffering possible solutions, or causing any beneficial catharsis, or venting any widely held feelings. Their wallowing spreads anxiety and undermines others.	'Shall we call up X right now and explain to her what problems she is causing?' 'What would make it better?' 'What would be the first step?' 'If you don't want to discuss solutions, I don't want to hear any more moaning, either to me, or anyone else. Is that clear'
DOOM & GLOOMERS	Have no faith and no hope that anything will ever work out. Failure is inevitable, given their perfectionist criteria of success. The bitterness they spread about past disappointments undermines motivation and morale.	'I need you as a devil's advocate. What might go wrong with X's ideas? You'll want time to really check it through, come back when you're ready, or, even better, when you think you might have a way to improve it.' 'There's no way out, you will have to close down!'
DITHERERS	Procrastinate and waste opportunities. Their indecisiveness precipitates crises and closes down options. Stress is experienced. Help is constantly sought. Rising anxiety disables their thinking.	'Let's brainstorm the possibilities.' 'What are the pluses and minuses?' 'Let's draw a table, so we can see the advantages and disadvantages of each possible decision on your sheet of paper.' 'Which seems to you to have the balance of advantage?'
PLEASERS	Can't say no. They over-commit and under-deliver, rather than risk displeasure by refusing to do things they cannot do. Well intentioned, but not realistic. Often disorganized, they feel terrible when it all gets into a mess.	'You must be feeling pretty bad about this mess.' 'Are you sure you can take on this new thing?' 'How will you tackle it?' 'Who will you get to help you?' 'When will you be able to meet with them?' 'What exactly are you going to do?' 'Have you got a note of that?'
BOASTERS	Need appreciation and will exaggerate their experience or what they know. They can fail unexpectedly or catastrophically when their straw houses collapse. They take up time and become objects of jealousy or irritation. Ignored and isolated, they can redouble their exaggerated claims, living in fear of being shown up, losing face or looking a fool.	'Thank you for your contribution.' 'Who specifically?' 'When exactly?' 'How could you tell it was working, what precisely was different?' 'My own experience was . . .' 'The report showed . . .' 'Thank you for bringing that up, it helps to highlight a need to . . .'

continued

Table 6.3 continued

Type	Typical problems caused	Try saying . . .
PREACHERS	Often experts, they really do know it all. They can use their genuine knowledge and expertise to dominate, control, bore and dispirit others. They demolish newer, contrary ideas,regardless of their merit. If questioned, they often question the motives of the questioner. Often dogmatic and closed-minded, they seem unable to tolerate uncertainty.	'Since we need to meet your criteria for . . .' 'Have we understood you correctly to say . . .' 'Then perhaps, maybe . . .' 'Bear with us for a moment, I was just wondering whether . . .' 'Just supposing for a moment that . . .' 'What do you think might happen if we were to apply your ideas this way?' 'I was wondering if I could ask you to . . .'
INTERRUPTERS	Cut in before other people have finished, often by finishing their sentences for them or, by talking over them in a louder voice, until the first person is reduced to silence. This bullies, disempowers and frustrates others. It engenders anger or depression when used to dominate members of minority groups, or the opposite sex.	'Excuse me, excuse me . . . (repeated until heeded), I think I was/X was still talking.' 'Can we agree that everyone is entitled to finish their sentences?' 'The minimum respect here requires that we do not talk over others.'
BUTTON PUSHERS	Seem to know, consciously, or unconsciously, what to say to make you angry, sad, confused or excited. They seem to bypass your normal thought processes. You just react, often in the same predictable way. It seems you cannot control what happens. Afterwards you feel foolish, or resentful, or depressed.	'Ouch. That hurt.' 'Hey, you did it again!' 'Are you intending to be hurtful?' 'I would like to stop being your victim.' 'You keep picking me up and then putting me down again.' 'Can we work out how to break this cycle?' 'How can you stop yourself from persecuting me?'
NITPICKERS	Will pick you up on the slightest detail, as though they are wanting to pick a fight. They destroy creativity, kill humour and reduce energy. They aggravate, annoy and disturb your concentration.	'At this moment, does it really matter who said what, to whom?' 'I am finding this bickering embarrassing.' 'Are you angry with me about something?' 'You appear to want to pick a fight with someone, what's this all about?' 'Now, children . . .'
FIGHTERS	Love to argue. They find it challenging stimulating, exciting. They relieve their boredom at your expense. They get angry with you when talking about someone else with whom they should feel angry. They ridicule, tease, scapegoat and attack people who are weaker than those on whom they should really vent their feelings.	'Why are you getting angry with *me*?' 'What has this to do with *me*?' 'Stop attacking *me*.' 'Do you realize that you have contradicted everything I have said?' 'What is happening here?' 'Where is this leading?' 'What is it you are trying to say?'
MYSTIFIERS	Use language, terminology or professional jargon to confuse you, or to retain knowledge-based power over you. Some senior managers, consultants, accountants and legal advisers do this.	'Would you mind explaining again what that means?' 'I'll write it down this time.' 'Have I got it down correctly?'

Table 6.3 continued

Type	Typical problems caused	Try saying . . .
LIARS	Distort, withhold or exaggerate the truth to save face, impress others or protect others from pain or embarrassment. They may do it for financial gain or to seek revenge.	'There is probably more than one way of looking at it . . .' 'X has reported it differently . . .' 'We have a difference of opinion here . . .' 'My understanding is that . . .' 'I cannot agree with you on this occasion.'
HARASSERS	Sexual harassment often starts as fantasy and flirtation. If flirtation is not stopped promptly it can get out of hand. Victims can be either sex.	'Are you flirting with me?' 'What are you suggesting?' 'I find you attractive but I do not want to get involved.'
BACKSTABBERS	Can endanger the self-esteem and self-confidence and the performance of others. They engender defensiveness, self-protection and fear of loss of reputation. Trust and mutual helpfulness and learning become difficult.	'I'd like to get X in immediately to give their version of what you are telling me.' 'Why are you telling me this?' 'What is in this for you?'
SPOILERS	Often feel excluded or not 'invited to the ball'. Consciously or unconsciously, they spoil things for those who are. If they can't have it, no one can. They find fault and blemish things they think you value; 'Nice X, pity about the . . . ,' where X is something they know is important to you.	'When I go to see a film for myself, I rarely agree with the critics and they rarely agree with each other.' 'A criticism is an opinion – rarely unanimous.' 'What are you trying to prove?' 'What would it take for you to be 100 per cent pleased with me?'
STIRRERS	Often have dull jobs or dull lives. They get vicarious excitement by stirring up trouble between others and watching the results. They prefer hint, suggestion and innuendo.	'Are you hoping I'm going to be annoyed with X about this?' 'What do you want me to say?' 'Are you trying to create a problem between me and X?' 'I do not wish to discuss X's reaction. That is his business.'
BLOWERS	Like the volcanic hot water springs after which they are named, 'blowers' build up a head of emotional steam and then lose self control and blow. The cycle seems inevitable. As the pressure mounts, it takes less and less to provoke the inevitable explosion. Meanwhile everyone tiptoes around them, walking on eggshells.	'Hello Mr X, hello Mr X, hello Mr X (until you have Mr X's attention). We care, we care . . . we know, we know . . .' 'Let's take a break now and get back together later.' 'What was the final straw for you? How do you know when you are going to get angry?' 'Next time it happens, what is the most useful thing people can do?'

continued

Table 6.3 continued

Type	Typical problems caused	Try saying . . .
JESTERS	Jesters 'jest' to get even, to get attention when they are bypassed or ignored, or to undermine people who oppose their ideas. Not all jesting is intended to be hostile. It can be playful, or used to defuse tension. However, it may be a sarcastic tone, a dismissal or a roll of the eyes. It may take place behind your back. Jesters may make you smile, but through gritted teeth!	'Look, I know you like me really!' 'Excuse me, I missed that, would you just repeat what you said?' 'What does your expression (tone) mean?' 'I don't find that funny.' 'What's the statement behind that quip?' 'How is that remark relevant?' 'Can we have a one-to-one on this later?'
INTRUDERS	Seem to lack respect for your boundaries. They jibe and joke, pass comment and give advice in areas that you think are personal. Often you are so taken aback, so shaken at the intrusion, that you are left fuming but speechless.	'Why do you want to know that?' 'Why is it any concern of yours?' 'I think that this conversation has gone far enough.' 'Can we change the subject, please?' 'This conversation is over.'

Sowing and Reaping
Creating Difficult People

So far we have assumed that some people are just difficult and suggested the kinds of conversations that might reduce the impact of the difficulties that individuals can create. We also said that 'it takes two to tango'. We look now at the kinds of things that managers do, or fail to do, which increase the chances that individuals will become difficult people. It is understandable that managers had a knee jerk reaction when confronted with the kind of behaviour we reported in Tables 6.2 and 6.3. Often a manager's reaction was exactly the kind of reaction that the behaviour may have been unconsciously designed to provoke. The managers' reactions reinforced the difficult behaviour and increased the chance that it would reoccur. A more thoughtful approach was required. The cycle – 'behaviour leading to sought-for reaction' – needed to be broken.

Old familiar feelings

Many difficult people repeatedly recreate the kinds of situations that generate feelings with which they are familiar. It is the old familiar feelings, or the search for them, that provokes the difficult behaviour. Unwittingly, managers can find themselves cast as actors in a play that the difficult person frequently re-stages. Managers may be unaware how frequently they are being rehearsed until they have learned their lines and react on cue! Because of their work role, managers are well placed to be typecast as authority figures with whom the difficult person has had difficulties in the past – people such as parents, or teachers or preachers. A thoughtful approach creates a pause for thought. Do you want to play this part? It can be hard to turn down an offer to play a star role, especially if the role enables managers to re-enact part of their own history, or enables them to re-experience their own familiar feelings: feeling associated, perhaps, with being bullied, or rescued, or being a 'clever girl' or an oldest child who 'should know better'. It is easier for managers to turn down roles in other people's dramas when they are aware of their own histories and their own patterns of behaviour. A manager's self-awareness can be raised through self-development (Chapter 14).

Giving dogs a bad name

When managers expect difficult behaviour to reoccur, it is more likely to do so. Once a dog is labelled a 'bad dog' people are afraid to stroke it. The dog becomes isolated, and feels neglected and unloved. It smells the fear on people and is more likely to bite than to please. This confirms its reputation as a 'bad dog'. If managers call people 'obstructive Luddites', or even just think of people as 'obstructive Luddites', there is a good chance that they will obstruct the implementation of changes. Prophecies about the behaviour of people can be self-fulfilling. This can work in the manager's favour. When managers pause for thought, refuse to react, decline roles that reinforce difficult behaviour and expect behaviour to get *better*, it generally does. This is not an easy thing to do. When confronted with the kinds of difficult behaviour which we report in Tables 6.2 and 6.3, most managers found it hard to say to the difficult person, 'This behaviour is not you' – even when they knew that contradicting the behaviour was far more likely to result in improvement than saying, 'Typical! That's just like you to do that.' The trick is to think beyond the things that an individual does or says, to the individual who is doing or saying. Abhor the sin, but not the sinner. Difficult people are individuals who still have much that is good in them. The challenge is to help them to access, mobilize and express that which is good in them. When individuals are very busy doing good things, they have less time available to do difficult things. Try greeting difficult behaviour with 'That . . . (describe the difficult behaviour) is not like you. You are capable of . . . (describe the more desirable behaviour).

Pausing for thought

A thoughtful approach to handling difficult people creates a pause during which managers can rehearse in their inner worlds, the kinds of outer world conversations they want to have when next they are confronted with behaviour of the kind described in Tables 6.2 and 6.3. Managers can bring out the best in people even when their behaviour is at its worst.

Even with the best intentions, and the most extensive rehearsals, most managers found public criticism hard to handle. Most managers reported loss of face and of loss of control. They felt that their authority had been questioned and their respect undermined. To defend oneself when attacked is instinctive. Yet this understandable reaction nearly always made things worse. The more managers defended and protested, the more credence and importance they seemed to give to their critics. Their critics seemed to revel in the process. The more defensive managers became, the more authority the managers seemed to relinquish. (This seemed to happen whether or not the managers were successful in refuting the criticisms.) We tried to offer managers an alternative to their instinctive self-defence. What we suggested required courage and it did not work every time. However, it proved more successful than when they were drawn into a war of words when dealing with difficult people. We asked managers to take three deep breaths and say: 'Thank you for being honest' or, 'Thank you for taking the time to tell me what you are thinking' or, 'Thank you for caring so much about what is happening'. There is no need for defensive explanation or self justification – just say 'Thank you'.

Idleness makes people difficult

Idle hands make mischief and mischief-makers. Lest we go mad, or die of boredom, most of us structure our idle time either through work, close relationships or distracting activity. If we are at work but there is no real work to do, we form close relationships, create informal groups or ferment distracting activity. Any of these things can make people difficult as far as their managers are concerned.

If managers hoard excess staff and do not increase output, then managers are storing up trouble. They will be creating difficult people who will confront them, sooner or later. In many countries, public service managers are not allowed to dismiss excess staff, or difficult people, especially if their services are owned by the government. There may be no alternative employment available for the excess staff. Unemployment is never popular. Unemployed people may become even more difficult in the community than they are at work – perhaps turning to crime or fermenting political discontent. Government may prefer to have difficult people working in public services where it is easier to keep an eye on them and control their postings. Artificially created work, especially artificially created paperwork, is not demanding. It leaves much energy, especially creative mental energy, under-utilized. In schools, it is often the most able pupils who become disruptive troublemakers when they are not stretched by the school curriculum. Over staffed public service organizations often contain a country's most able and highly educated people. Over staffed public service organizations will breed disruptive and difficult people.

If managers are able to release or transfer people they do not need, they should do so. Often the level of public service that can be provided is limited by funds for consumables (for example, bricks, cement, rail track, X-ray film, school books, fuel, drugs, soap, or even photocopier paper). If the cost of only one annual salary can be 'vired' (Chapter 9), then the remaining staff can often be put to work at an increased level of output. Where managers do not wish to make excess staff redundant, they should still release them for 'training', 'central planning', 'special projects' or 'research'. Consider allowing them to work from home, so that the remaining staff can have proper jobs, proper work rates and proper job descriptions. Most staff would rather do full time worthwhile work, than feel that they were just filling time and wasting their lives. Importantly, they will have less time (and less need?) for difficult behaviour. Managers will create less difficult people.

Dismissing Difficult People

This is a last but necessary resort. Of course it must be done fairly. The procedures for disciplinary action and dismissal are set out in Chapter 8. If people are being difficult people, as opposed to breaking specific organizational rules, then special considerations will apply.

For many difficult people, dismissal will come as a welcome relief from the stress of being difficult. In a new organization, they may not be difficult people – lacking, perhaps, suitable partners for their tango! Managers need not feel bad about dismissing diffi-

cult people. By the time difficult people are dismissed they will, in effect, have dismissed themselves. They will have been given a choice about persisting with their difficult behaviour. They will have chosen to persist and thereby chosen to be dismissed. They will have found a way out of their difficult relationship with their manager, without having to find the courage to resign. They will not have had to take responsibility for leaving. You will have given them someone else to blame. You.

Keeping notes

Managers need to keep a note of the time and place of instances of unacceptable conduct and notes of when they told employees that their behaviour was unacceptable. They should also keep a note of who witnessed the unacceptable conduct. It is the repetition of even seemingly trivial instances of unacceptable behaviour that constitutes a serious breach of discipline meriting dismissal. A written warning should follow the first repetition. Act promptly to save difficult people from unwittingly stepping over a line from which there is no return. Managers must avoid creating the impression that others can become difficult people with impunity. Record facts and seek causes. Agree plans to prevent reoccurrence. If there is a repeat instance, arrange to see the difficult person formally, preferably with your line manager. Let your own manager and the difficult person do most of the talking. Do not interrupt. Having listened to the difficult person, you hope that your boss will say something like: 'You have a choice, either you cease your unacceptable behaviour towards your line manager, or you resign. If you do not resign, you will be dismissed. You are hereby suspended from work for a full day, on full pay. We will all meet again at . . . to receive your decision.' Friends and family of the difficult person will notice this suspension. The suspension will alert them to the difficult person's precarious position and to the need for support. At the appointed time, if the difficult person promises to desist, he or she should be told that there will be no more meetings. Any repetition will be taken as an indication that the difficult person has chosen to leave and they will be asked to resign within forty-eight hours. If their resignation is not received within this time, they will be given notice of termination.

Befriending Difficult People

The difficult person's position is now very precarious. It is to be hoped that the shock of the warning will cause the difficult person to reflect. At this point they need a friend. But how do you befriend a difficult person? Most models of friendship formation assume that people are homogenous. In Chapter 8, we argue that the process of friendship formation should also be based on a conversational exploration of individual difference. There is no universal model that can help us to befriend difficult people. A quick glance at our findings in Tables 6.2 and 6.3 shows that we have identified at least twenty-seven distinct members of the species 'difficult people' and our list is still growing. Of the twenty-seven difficult people we have identified, only one – the 'pleasers' – are likely to welcome a direct offer of friendship. Friendly feelings are not often the feelings most familiar to difficult people – perhaps that is why they are difficult people.

Having said that, each time difficult people change their behaviour in a way that makes them less difficult, it would be helpful if this were noticed, recognized, acknowledged, approved, endorsed and encouraged. These are the sort of things that a friend might do. If the difficult person has few social friends, or workplace friends, consider suggesting a mentor, or a personal development companion (Chapter 14).

Giving Feedback to Difficult People

These new 'friends' will probably find that difficult people find it difficult to hear, let alone take on board, positive feedback. Again, it may be the case that positive feedback does not induce feelings with which difficult people are very familiar. Is that another reason why they are difficult people? For difficult people, positive feedback may have a maximum daily dose. Once they have had their maximum daily dose, extra positive feedback is simply not heard, or not believed, or actively disputed. ('You are only saying that because . . .' 'Well they would say that wouldn't they?'.) Incoming positive feedback can be cancelled out by incoming negative feedback that is often self-administered. This can create a net shortfall against the daily dose, so that further positive feedback can then be accepted. If only a friend were on hand to administer it! Noticing, recognizing, complimenting, and praising in a one-to-one conversation has the advantage of immediately checking that the feedback has been accepted. If the compliment is rejected, it can be immediately re-transmitted, until it appears to have been accepted.

Sending notes

If a difficult person's daily maximum dose of positive feedback has already been exceeded, further positive feedback will be wasted. This is when it can be helpful to send a note. If it is sent on a nice card, it will not readily be binned. The praise or admiration it contains can just sit there, able to be read and re-read until it finally hits the difficult person on a low day and is taken in and absorbed. In our final case study in Chapter 15, we learned that many of Carolyn's staff had made collections of the cards that she had sent them over the previous fifteen years. Some of them had started their relationships with Carolyn as difficult people.

But what if caring conversations, preventative measures, positive expectations, written warnings and all this befriending fail? Let us cut to the chase.

Measure Twice and Cut Once

A good tailor measures twice and cuts once. A surgeon cuts deeply and quickly closes the wound. Difficult people who have defied all remedies and approaches have made their own choice to go. They need to be helped to go quickly and cleanly, so that everybody's wounds can heal. All necessary procedures have been followed. Request their resignation and if you do not get it within forty-eight hours, send a written notice of termination, releasing them immediately. Offer payment for their final period of notice. That will save them embarrassment with their own colleagues and protect the service from sabotage and their clients from ill-will. They can look for another job while still on full pay. Make sure that their final paycheque is not handed over until you have all their files, keys and equipment. It may be necessary for them to come on site to clear their desks. You may decide that they should be accompanied. Call colleagues together as soon as notice has been served and get agreement to your contingency plans. Agree temporary job descriptions. They may become permanent as people realize how much more they can do with one less difficult person around! Do not answer questions about the dismissal, other than to those who have a right to know. Write up the file. Close it and move on.

Who Can't Sack Civil Servants?

In many public service organizations, in many parts of the world, much that we have said here about handling difficult people will be easier said than done. Many public service managers have told us that, in reality, they have few practical powers to dismiss people, let alone employees who are just difficult people. Often they cited cases of when they had attempted to dismiss difficult people, only to have their senior managers refuse to sign the notices of termination. When we followed up these cases, we found that the managers did, in fact, have powers of dismissal. The problem was that their decision to dismiss could not be ratified without putting the organization at risk from litigation. The managers had failed to collect, record and keep proper records. Managers must be able to show that they have tried to have the kinds of conversations that we described in Tables 6.2 and 6.3 and that they have explored their own role in perhaps causing the difficult behaviours they are seeking to eradicate.

When Difficult People Have Connections in Higher Places

In some countries, even after managers had tried talking to difficult people and had tried to break their cycle of difficult behaviour and had followed dismissal procedures and had kept proper records, these records had mysteriously disappeared when the file was sent 'upstairs' for senior management signature. When the manager's own copies were requested, these too mysteriously disappeared. It transpired that the difficult people in question had relatives or friends in high places. We encouraged the managers to start the procedures over again and this time to duplicate their records of incidents of unacceptable behaviour and to keep a duplicate set of records at home. As we expected might happen, within a year there was a change of government. When the new boss arrived, the difficult person's file was waiting on her desk. The difficult person was gone within a week. New brooms often like to set an early example. Keep your own 'difficult people file' up-to-date, secure and handy.

Difficult People as Agents of Change

There is a particular group of difficult people who are very helpful when implementing changes. We call them the 'Big Gs'. They are the Groaners, the Gripers and the Grumblers. They are always very dissatisfied with things the way they are – in fact they never stop complaining about the way things are decided, organized and managed. That's what makes them difficult people. But Big Gs can also provide energy, incentive and reasons for change. If we can link this Big G energy to some excitement (EP) about a proposal that would change things in their preferred direction, then the total energy for change now rises to 3G + EP. When we can see a way to implement the preferred state and, in particular what might be the next step (NS), then we can see how (3G + EP + NS) can be directed towards change. When (3G + EP + NF) is greater than the likely resistance (R) then the change can be implemented. That is, change will take place when:

$$(3G + EP + NS) > R$$

Clearly the more difficult people you have groaning, griping and grumbling, the easier it is to implement changes.

So, difficult people cannot only save managers from making changes that are dangerous, impractical, ill-advised or unethical, they can also help managers to implement changes which are perceived to be safe, sensible, feasible and ethical. Difficult people cannot be handled by putting them into groups. Groups make things worse by providing a ready-made stage on which difficult people can act out their difficulties with a ready-made audience to cheer them on. Difficult people are best managed as individuals, in close one-to-one conversations. In the next chapter we will develop our preference for managing people as individuals when we look at the motivation of people who work in public services.

FINAL THOUGHTS: 'SPINNING THE GLASS DARKLY'

Creating groups and teams heightens anxiety, causes frustration and leads to poor performance. As we have seen, one of the reasons why group work does not work is because people are individuals. When you put them into groups and teams they behave strangely. When they are leaderless, adults regress into infantile behaviour.[33] This is observed in public service organizations, when, for example, a respected leader leaves, and the team then does badly in an inspection. The team takes flight into the past: 'When X was head of department we never . . .' The group idealizes the kind of leader they now need to save them — a saviour. This leads to inaction and dependency on earlier success. If a leader is now appointed from within the group, that person will usually fail. The new team leader is not be able to live up to the group's idealised expectations.[34] Immobilized by dependency and petty squabbles, diversionary issues become substitutes for purposeful action: 'We've got less clerical support than team Y'; 'Z does not pull his weight'. Sometimes the groups will point to an external enemy — 'The head of department does not . . .'; 'All this paperwork is getting in the way of . . .'

Many writers regard such problems as simply a challenge for managers. By understanding group dynamics (Tuckman and Jenson), or by extending a role repertoire (Belbin), or by dealing with the flaws in group-based decision-making (Janis), managers are expected to make teams work. But why bother? Effort is dissipated, energy wasted and stress generated, for what gain? Individuals, or people working in pairs, can do a better job at less cost.

Our focus on managing people as individuals could be misconstrued as promoting an unhealthy individualism which ignores the need for collective action. This is not our intention. Writers such as Lasch[35] have criticized western culture for being obsessed with 'the self'. People must be 'self-centred' and pursue 'self-fulfilment'. Lasch describes this as 'Selfism' — a narcissism — focused on what the individual needs to the exclusion of others. 'Selfism' appears to reject inherited culture on the grounds that it impinges on an individual's autonomy. We believe that managers need to engage with the inherited culture (Chapter 3). We argue for continuity to be considered as well as change. 'Selfism' is detrimental because it signals that 'I' matter most. It opposes volunteering, community leadership and the value of serving others — all values that we associate with the culture of public service.

Faced with the contradiction of having been instructed to build teams from people preoccupied with individual needs, how might we get people to work better together? We have said that we need to do things that meet the needs of individuals and that we need to do things that help to create cohesiveness and maintain the morale of the groups (Chapter 7). There are some things we can do which achieve both simultaneously, such as coaching individuals in the presence of their group or getting each individual to give the group feedback on its process. But management activities that address the needs of the individual and the group simultaneously are rare. Normally the manager must move from one type of activity to another, while keeping both glass plates spinning. If you do not get back to the neglected plate in time, the plate will fall. It will probably smash and the team will cease to work.

Thomas Merton, a modernizing monk, suggests a different approach. In *Thoughts in Solitude* he writes:

> In our age everything has to be a problem ... Ours is a time of anxiety because we have willed it to be so. Anxiety is not imposed on us by force or from outside. We impose it on our world and upon one another from within ourselves. Contradictions have always existed in the hearts of men. We are not meant to resolve all contradictions but to live with them and rise above them and to see them in the light of exterior and objective values which make them trivial by comparison.[36]

We cannot resolve all the contradictions that can disable groups and teams but by creating the silence to be more thoughtful, we can get them into perspective and rise above them.

SUMMARY

- We explored what is meant by a group and identified differences between formal and informal groups. We looked at committees as examples of formal groups.
- We examined how groups are formed, the roles people play, the processes they use, and some unconscious things that happen.
- We tried to explain why many working groups don't work and offered suggestions to public service managers who are obliged to manage multi-disciplinary teams.
- We argued that teams are being created to carry out work that often would be better carried out by individuals.
- We looked at how different personal and professional values, incompatible roles and attitudes, pose particular difficulties when managing multi-agency teams.
- We accept the reality that public services make extensive use of team working. We have suggested a number of interventions

to minimize the disadvantages of team working and to maximize the advantages.
- We examined the causes of conflict.
- We looked at ten ways in which conflict can be managed.
- We looked at what makes us individually different and why managers need to understand individual difference if they are to manage people, preferably, as individuals.
- We identified 27 types of difficult people, the types of problems they can cause and the conversational moves managers can use to deal with them.
- Finally, we wondered whether the anxieties generated when people are brought together in groups might be better tolerated than managed.

THINKING AND LEARNING ACTIVITIES

Activity 1 Self-assessment

1 What is an informal and a formal group? Give three examples of each.
2 List five advantages and five disadvantages of formal groups.
3 Give examples of what might happen at the different stages of group formation.
4 Give examples of the group roles people might play.
5 List the problems managers might encounter while building a multi-agency team.
6 List things a managers can do to make team working more effective.
7 Why is it important for managers to understand how to manage conflict?
8 Using three sentences, summarize the unitary, pluralist and Marxist views of conflict.

9 Give two examples of when conflict in an organization is functional and dysfunctional.

10 How does an understanding of individual difference help managers?

11 Knowing what you know about individual difference, what problems would you expect to encounter at each stage of group development?

12 Briefly describe eight difficult people you might encounter in a working group.

13 Briefly describe twenty difficult people you might encounter as individuals in an organization.

Activity 2 Individual Learning: Visual Thinking

Mental mapping

Take a blank A4 sheet. Skim back over the first section of this chapter. Each time you come to a key idea or section, label it with a few words. Write the label somewhere on your blank A4 sheet and draw a circle round the label. When you come across the next key idea or section, label it and place it on your A4 sheet, close to other ideas to which you think it is related. When you have skimmed through the whole chapter, draw lines between the circles on your A4 sheet, if you think the ideas are connected. If necessary, use a clean sheet of A4 to redraw your diagram so that the connecting lines are clear and the intersections are minimized. Now write verbs, or actions, along all the lines, such as 'which can help with', 'which can be evaluated by'. Keep going until you have a map, diagram or flowchart of how all the ideas in this chapter relate to one another.

Activity 3 Individual Learning: Evaluative Thinking

Group development

Identify five stages in the development of a work group of which you have been a member. Evaluate how well the group negotiated the different stages of the group formation process. Were all stages passed through? How useful do you find the models in this chapter in explaining the group process?

Activity 4 Paired Learning: Critical and Creative Thinking

Is it a group?

Consider the following list:

a) Members of a cricket team
b) An audience at a public lecture
c) People riding on a carousel at a fairground
d) Black people aged between 16–19 years of age
e) A number of young people sheltering at a bus stop

Which of these if any is a group. Why? Discuss your answers with colleagues in a small group. Explore any differences. Are you prepared to modify your views? Why or why not? Is anyone else prepared to modify their views? Why do you think that is?

Activity 5 Group Learning: Reflective Thinking

Using a questionnaire

The diagnosis on page 200 can be used to investigate what stage a group has reached in its development. In your college group, or another group of which you are a member, complete the questionnaire to give an indication of the stage which your group has reached. Answer true or false for each question.

In which section have you inserted most T's? If Section 1, the group is still Forming. If Section 2, the group is still Storming. If Section 3, the group is now Norming and if Section 4, the group is now Performing!

Collate the individual members replies on a flipchart. Is there a consensus about which stage your group has reached? What other factors should characterize a group at this stage? If your group has not yet reached the performing stage, what could be done to move the group on to a further stage in its development? If the group is at the performing stage, what could be done and by whom to improve its performance? By when could this be done? How could you monitor what has been done?

Box 6.10

DIAGNOSING GROUP DEVELOPMENT

Section 1

1 Members are unclear as to group goals.   T F
2 Informal leaders try to direct what the group does but the group is unwilling to follow, or members usually prefer to look to a formal leader.   T F
3 Members are reluctant to say what they think or feel.   T F

Section 2

1 People are prepared to discuss the roles that they and other people play in the group.   T F
2 Members argue a lot about what the group should be doing.   T F
3 On different occasions different people have tried to lead the group.   T F

Section 3

1 Most people in the group are committed to the group's goals rather than their own agendas.   T F
2 Members trust and support one another.   T F
3 Relationships between most group members are friendly. There is a sense of 'togetherness' in the group   T F

Section 4

1 The group is learning to overcome obstacles to achieving its goal.   T F
2 Group members resist being led by any one individual and give the leadership role to different members at different times.   T F
3 People feel comfortable about expressing new ideas and disagreeing with other members without fear of others taking it too personally.   T F

Activity 6 Individual Learning: Reflective Thinking

Your status in your group

Consider the educational institution at which you are studying, or the organization for which you work for and write down:

1 The things that raise your status or standing within it.
2 The things that lower your status or standing within it.
   • How do you rate your standing?
   • Do your colleagues agree with you?
   • Why do these things affect your status?
   • Does it matter to you? If so, why? If not, why?

Activity 7 Group Learning: Predictive Thinking

Formal and informal behaviour in groups

Draw one sociogram (see page 173) that maps the formal relationships and another that maps the informal relationships between the people in the group in which you are studying or the people in your department. When you have done that, use the sociogram to answer:

• Who would you choose to organize a party?
• With whom would you choose to work on a major assignment affecting your course grade, or a major works project where your bonus or promotion depended on getting it done to a high standard on time?

If possible discuss your sociograms with other members of the group. Thinking back over this activity, what do you wonder about?

Activity 8 Individual Learning: Creative and Numerical Thinking

Investigating group effectiveness

Devise a set of criteria and a score card for assessing and scoring a working group on how effective it is. Pilot test your score card on a group and modify your score card in the light of your pilot test. In this activity what worked well, what was interesting and what questions are you left with?

Activity 9 Individual Learning: Reflective Thinking

What's going on?

Consider a significant conflict situation at home, at college, or in the workplace.

- Who was involved?
- How did it make you feel?
- How was the situation resolved?
- What were the causes of the conflict?
- Which perspective on conflict – unitary, pluralist or Marxist – attracts you?

Activity 10 Individual Learning: Reflective Thinking

Going for a win–win solution

In your own organization or an organization with which you are familiar, describe an example of a collaborative win–win solution to a conflict situation. Why was a collaborative solution possible? Can you identify anything about the way that individuals behaved that made a collaborative solution possible?

Activity 11 Individual and Group Learning: Critical and Empathetic Thinking

CASE STUDY: When team working isn't working[37]

'You knew this change was coming in. You knew the service had no choice because of the huge cutbacks. What are you complaining about – you've still got your jobs haven't you?' Samina heard the rising edge in her voice. She stopped herself abruptly. Why couldn't she sound like a 'leader'? Her staff were driving her mad with their petty complaints and negative attitudes.

It always seemed to happen near the end of a team meeting. Perhaps everyone was just tired. Not for the first time Samina felt that these meetings were a waste of time. They hadn't covered any real business. She could understand why there were corridor mutterings about her meetings being a waste of time. They were. She'd introduced them after the restructuring of the Youth and Community Service, but people seemed to resent coming to them. They would never stick to her agenda. She thought that they were just afraid to try anything new.

'I realize that it is difficult getting used to changes and new responsibilities. Perhaps we should look into some training on handling change. Anyway, we've got to

finish now because I've got another meeting. Thank you for coming. I'll send you the agenda for the next meeting as usual'. She left the room hurriedly, before they could start moaning again.

It had been a difficult month since she was appointed as Area Team Manager. Her area comprised four local electoral areas and had a common boundary with Social Services. Recent reductions in local government expenditure had hit the Youth and Community Service. The cuts had led to restructuring of the organization. There had been redundancies. It had all happened very quickly. The remaining staff had been given more responsibility and larger staff teams to manage. Although depressed by the redundancies, Samina was enthusiastic about the new structure and the new responsibilities.

She walked away from the meeting back to her own office where the district training officer, Kevin, was waiting for her. They had arranged a meeting to discuss the training budget and her training plans for next year. Samina had lots of ideas about the training staff needed

– training in management and group work skills. Kevin asked what her staff saw as a training priority. She replied: 'I did try to discuss that with them at one of my meetings, but as usual, they didn't want any training. They never want anything except an excuse to moan.'

She finished her meeting with Kevin as quickly as she could without being rude. It had been a long day and she had promised to visit one of her centres that evening. She decided to put it off. She thought, I'll phone the centre tomorrow and apologize. She would make up for cancelling the visit by having a good chat with the centre manager at the next team meeting. A couple of weeks later Samina was enjoying herself. It was the annual award ceremony for staff who had completed a training course. She felt proud because a number of the staff receiving certificates were staff that she had recruited. At the buffet afterwards she sought them out for a chat.

'I don't know where I'm going wrong these days. I wish all my staff were like you lot. I know I don't see them as often as I would like, but we do have regular team meetings. I'm trying to get them training too – like I did for you – but I can't seem to get them interested. It's like pushing water up a hill.'

'Yes we have heard rumours,' said Andrew. Samina was disturbed.

'Rumours, what rumours?'

'Oh nothing really, you know how staff love to talk – you're a big boss now – people always moan about the boss of any team. You're not one of the team now.'

Samina dropped the subject. She was upset by the thought of people moaning about her behind her back. What had gone wrong? She had tried to involve people and not be an autocratic leader of her team. But still they complained.

Questions

Working on your own, identify and write down what you consider to be the key issues in the case study. Then, working in small groups, discuss your ideas and answer:

1 What do you think Samina could have done before, during and after the area meetings to make them more effective?

2 What do you think was the purpose of the area meetings? Could these purposes have been achieved in other ways?

3 How do you think Samina's status and role changed when she was appointed?

4 In what ways have informal group relationships affected the team?

5 What could Samina do to resolve the conflicts?

6 Make a plan which identifies things you would do to develop Samina's team.

7 Review each of the 27 difficult people described in the text. List the ones Samina might come across.

8 Given the difficult people Samina might come across in her team, plan a possible approach to each of them during the next team meeting.

9 For each of the difficult people she might be able to talk to individually, write a brief 'radio' script of the way the conversation might go.

10 How could the 'moaning' energy be used by Samina?

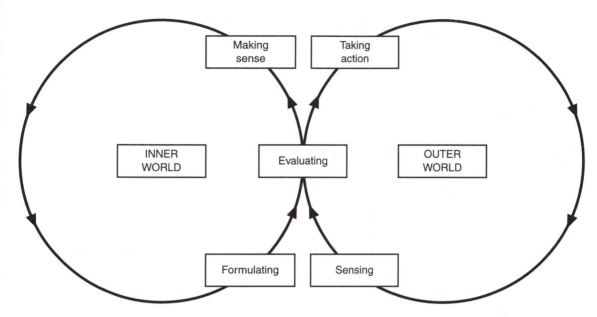

Figure 6.4 The thinking skills of the conversational manager

Activity 12 Individual Learning Review: Reflective Thinking

Inner world thinking

What inner world thinking skills are needed by managers carrying out the work described in this chapter? Have any of the thinking skills you have identified emerged for the first time? If so, add them to your accumulating model of the kinds of thinking skills that you consider to be useful to managers of public services.

What things could you do to develop the thinking skills that you have added to your model? What would be the first step?

Outer world conversations

What outer world conversational skills are needed by managers carrying out the work described in this chapter? Have any of the types of conversational skills you have identified emerged for the first time? If so, add them to your accumulating model of the kinds of conversational skills you think are useful to managers of public services.

What things could you do to develop any of these conversational skills which you have just added to your model? What would be the first step?

Activity 13 Individual Learning: Metacognitive Thinking

Metacognition

Look back through the Thinking and Learning Activities you have been asked to carry out in this chapter. What thinking skills were involved in each of these activities? For each type of thinking, write down how you were learning what you were learning, and how you were learning to think in each of the different ways.

NOTES

1 Robbins, H. and Finley, M. (1998) *Why Teams Don't Work. What Went Wrong and How to Make it Right.* Orion Business Books.
2 Schein, E. (1988) *Organizational Psychology.* Prentice Hall.
3 Gillespie, R. (1991) *Manufacturing Knowledge: A History of the Hawthorne Experiments.* Cambridge University Press.

4 Buchanan, D. and Huczynski, A. (1997) *Organizational Behaviour. An Introductory Text.* Prentice Hall, p. 190.

5 Landsberger, H. A. (1958) Hawthorne Revisited. Cornell University Press.

6 Buchanan, D. and Boddy, D. (1993) *The Expertise of the Change Agent. Public Performance and Backstage Activity.* Prentice Hall.

7 Tuckman, B. and Jenson, N. (1977) 'Stages of Small Group Development Revisited. Groups and Organisational Behaviour'. *Studies*, vol. 2, pp. 419–27.

8 Belbin, M. (1981) *Management Teams: Why They Succeed or Fail.* Heinemann.

9 Buchanan and Huczynski, op. cit., p. 478.

10 French, J. R. P. and Raven, B. H. (1958) 'The Bases of Social Power'. In Cartwright, D. (ed.) *Studies in Social Power Institute of Social Research.* University of Michigan.

11 Moreno, J. L. and Jennings, J. (1960) *The Sociometry Reader.* Free Press.

12 Bales, R. F. (1950) 'A Set of Categories for the Analysis of Small Groups Interaction'. *American Sociological Review*, vol. 15, no. 2, pp. 257–63.

13 Belbin, op. cit.

14 Jung, C. G. (1953) *The Integration of Personality.* Farrar & Ruchart.

15 Robbins and Finley, op. cit., p. 2.

16 Stoner, J. A. F. (1961) 'A Comparison of Group and Individual Decisions Involving Risk'. In Brown, R. (ed.) *Social Psychology.* Free Press.

17 Buchanan and Huczynski, op. cit., p. 281.

18 Janis, I. (1982) *Victims of Group Think: A Psychological Study of Foreign Policy Decisions and Fiascos.* Houghton Mifflin.

19 Schmidt, W. H. (1974) 'Conflict: A Powerful Process for (Good or Bad) Management'. *Review*, vol. 63, Dec., pp. 35–47.

20 Mullins, L. (1996) *Management and Organisational Behaviour.* (3rd edn). Pitman.

21 Buchanan and Huczynski, op. cit.

22 Handy, C. (1993) *Understanding Organisations.* (4th edn). Penguin.

23 Peters, T. and Watermann, R. H. Jr. (1983) *In Search of Excellence: Lessons from America's Best-run Companies.* Harper Row.

24 Cronin, T. P. and Bryans, P. (1983) *Organisation Theory.* Mitchell Beazley.

25 Mullins, op. cit., p. 725.

26 Schmidt, W. H., op. cit.

27 Handy, op. cit.

28 Thomas, K. (1976) 'Conflict and Conflict Management'. In Dunnette, M. D. (ed.) *Handbook of Industrial Psychology.* Rand-McNally, pp. 889–935.

29 Skinner, B. F. (1974) *About Behaviourism.* Knopf.

30 Rogers, C. (1976) *Freedom to Learn.* Charles E. Merrill.

31 See Buchanan D. and Hucznski A. (1997) *Organizational Behaviour. An Introductory text.* Prentice Hall, p. 59.

32 Kandola, R. and Fullerton, J. (1998) *Diversity in Action.* Institute of Personnel and Development, London.

33 Bion, W. R. (1961) *Experiences in Groups.* Tavistock.

34 Morgan, G. (1986) *Images of Organisation.* Sage, p. 216.

35 Lasch, C. (1979) *A Culture of Narcissism.* W. W. Morton.

36 Merton, T. (1979) *Thoughts in Solitude.* Burnes & Oates, p. 83.

37 Our thanks to Sue Bloxham, St Martin University College, Lancaster, on whose story this case was based.

7

MANAGING LEADERSHIP AND MOTIVATION IN PUBLIC SERVICES

A student asked 'What makes a leader?' The teacher replied: 'What determines the strength of a chariot wheel and enables it to carry its load?' The student reflected and said 'Is it not the strength of the spokes?' The Master replied: 'Then why is it that wheels made of identical spokes differ in strength?' The teacher continued, 'A strong wheel is made not only of the spokes, but also of the spaces between them. Strong spokes badly placed make a poor wheel. Good conversation is not only in the quality of what is said, it is also in the silent spaces between the words'.

(Adapted from a Chinese Leadership Tale)

LEARNING OUTCOMES

This chapter will enable the reader to:

- Consider definitions of leadership and understand why leadership is problematic.
- Understand differences between leaders, managers and administrators.
- Critically review the evolution of leadership theories.
- Explore the darker side of leadership.
- Consider a conversational approach to leadership.
- Understand what is meant by motivation.
- Evaluate different approaches to motivating people.
- Consider how a conversational approach to motivation can meet the needs of individuals for warmth, applause and possession.
- Challenge male models of leadership.

INTRODUCTION

In the last chapter we discussed the management of teams. With teams comes the idea of a team leader. A team leader is responsible for the performance of a group. Leadership has been the subject of much research. It is the subject of much literature (for example, Shakespeare: *King Lear* or *Henry IV*; Conrad in *Heart of Darkness*). Autobiographies of business leaders abound. However,

> of all the hazy and confounding areas of social psychology, leadership undoubtedly contends for the top nomination. Ironically, probably more has been written and less is known about leadership, than about any other topic in the behavioural science.[1]

Leaders fascinate, but do we need them? Are good managers, or good administrators, a safer bet? If we do need leaders in public services, can we train them, or are they born? We look at leadership styles and myths. Leadership has a bearing on motivation. Vroom and Deci[2] found that there could be a marked difference between the performance of otherwise matched pairs of employees. They discovered that competence was not sufficient to ensure high performance. People needed to be motivated to use their competence. In the period 1980–2000, there is evidence that many employees in publicly owned public service organizations were demotivated. Public service managers were exhorted to remotivate their staff. We look critically at theories about how this might be done and the role, if any, of leadership.

THE DIFFERENCE BETWEEN LEADERS AND MANAGERS

Leadership is a relationship through which one person influences another. Mullins[3] saw leadership as interpersonal influence directed towards outer world goals. Zaleznik[4] argued that leaders and managers are very different — that they differed in motivation and personal history and in the way they thought and acted. Zaleznik claimed that differences between managers and leaders could be seen in their attitudes towards goals, relationships and their sense of self (Box 7.1).

Differences between Leaders, Managers and Administrators

According to McConkey:[5]

- **Administrators** carry out policies. They do not have much influence. They are concerned with implementation.
- **Managers** are primarily concerned with efficiency and doing things in the right way. They design systems. They seek changes when there is overwhelming evidence that systems are not working.

- **Leaders** are not primarily concerned with doing things in the right way; they are primarily concerned with doing the right things. They spend much of their time trying to clarify vision, purpose and direction. They are creative and receptive to change.

The belief that such differences are not trivial has led to expensive attempts to replace public service administrators with managers, and to imbue those managers with the perceived attributes of leaders, about whom many theories have evolved.

THE EVOLUTION OF THEORIES ABOUT LEADERSHIP

Van Seter[6] provided a useful survey (Box 7.2).

1 The Personality Era

In the personality era, researchers focused on great leaders (not many of them women!). They suggested that people with the same personality traits as those recognized in great leaders could aspire to become great leaders themselves.[7] There are a number of

---

Box 7.1

DIFFERENCES BETWEEN MANAGERS AND LEADERS

- Managers tend to adopt impersonal attitudes towards goals, seeing them as coming from an organizational agenda, rather than from their own desires. Leaders personalize goals.
- Managers tend to solve problems through such things as co-ordination, compromise and coercion. Leaders seek to motivate and create excitement.

- Managers tend to remain emotionally distant in their relationships with other people. Leaders express their emotions and reciprocate the emotions of others.
- Managers often involve themselves with other people in order to control them. Leaders are driven by a profound need to separate themselves from others.

problems with this approach. For example, Byrd[8] collated a long list of personality traits which had been identified in earlier studies of great leaders but found that only 5 per cent of these traits were shared by four or more of the studies! Jenning[9] concluded that 50 years of study had failed to produce one personality trait that could be used to discriminate between leaders and non-leaders. This is not surprising. Leaders such as Mother Theresa, Martin Luther King, Hitler and Gandhi had very different personalities. The approach has little to offer managers seeking to develop their own leadership skills, because it implies that leaders are born and not made.

2 The Influence Era

In the influence era, the analysis moved away from concern with personality traits and focused on analysing the sources from which leaders drew their power. According to Van Seter,[10] this indicated the need for leaders to place a strong emphasis on their power to dominate others. French and Raven[11] identified five sources of power:

- **Reward power:** When the leader is perceived to have resources that can be used to reward subordinates, for example, pay, promotion, or praise.
- **Coercive power:** When the leader is perceived to

be in a position to take punitive action when disobeyed, for example, withholding pay increases or promotion.
- **Legitimate power:** When the leader is perceived to have the right to exercise influence, for example, because of their position in a hierarchy.
- **Expert power:** When the leader is perceived to have special competence in a particular area, such as finance, personnel management or information technology.

3 The Behavioural Era

The behavioural era focused on the identification of behaviour patterns of leaders. One of the most important attempts to categorize the behaviour of leaders was carried out at the Ohio State University by the Bureau of Business Research.[12] The researchers concluded that it is worth thinking about two dimensions of leadership behaviour – consideration and structure. Consideration is the way leaders develop trust, respect and rapport. Structure is a concern to design organizations so that they can achieve their goals. The extent of a manager's concern for 'structure' and 'consideration' combines to produce four possible leadership types (Box 7.3).

The Ohio State research suggested that the last combination – high consideration with high structure – was the combination most likely to be effective. Behavioural research by Lickert,[13] at the University of Michigan, identified two types of leaders: those who were employee-centred and those

---

Box 7.4

FIVE COMMON BEHAVIOURS OF EFFECTIVE LEADERS

1 Delegation of authority
2 Expectation of high standards
3 Avoidance of close supervision
4 Interest in and concern for subordinates
5 Participatory problem-solving

Box 7.5

THREE VARIABLES DETERMINING PREFERRED STYLE

1 **Relationships**: the extent to which leaders are trusted and liked
2 **Task structure**: the extent to which tasks are clearly defined and can be standardized
3 **Position power**: the leader's capacity to exercise influence and authority

---

who were production-centred. Lickert suggested that the best leaders were the ones who were employee-centred but who accepted their responsibility to meet targets. Lickert's study indicated that effective leaders displayed five characteristics (Box 7.4).

In the latter part of the behavioural era there was a dawning realization that leaders do not directly control behaviour in subordinates. They provide conditions and stimuli which increase the chances that such behaviour will take place. There did not appear to be one category of behaviour that led to superior leadership.

4 The Contingency Era

In the contingency era, researchers explored the way in which situational factors helped to determine the kinds of leadership styles and behaviours that were likely to produce effective results. Effective leadership was found to be contingent on a number of factors including behaviour, personality, influence and the situation itself. Different situations required different styles of leadership. Fiedler's[14] contingency model emphasized the importance of placing leaders in situations that suited their preferred style of leadership. According to Fiedler, it was better for managers to change situations to suit their style, rather than to try and change their style to suit the situation. Fiedler suggested that there were three

variables which determined the extent to which a situation would suit a leader's preferred style (Box 7.5).

Potential leaders should assess these three variables in a potential leadership situation. They should ask themselves whether or not they could adopt the style which Fiedler thought would be appropriate. If not, they should investigate whether the situation could be changed. If not, they should go elsewhere. When relationships are good, the task is structured and the leader has much power, then a task-oriented controlling style will be best. When the leader does not have strong relationships and the task structure is unclear, then a more participative approach will be the most effective. According to Fiedler, the best leadership styles for maximizing performance tended to be either coercive or consultative.

Vroom and Yetton[15] identified three possible approaches:

- **Autocratic**: The leader makes decisions alone. The leader may consult with subordinates but only for the purpose of gathering information. The leader may use this information to explain a decision after the event, or to persuade others to accept it.
- **Consultative**: The decision area is discussed with people who have relevant experience. The leader decides, usually in the presence of others.
- **Participatory**: The leader facilitates and tries to achieve consensus.

Contingency approaches are plausible. It seems logical for managers to vary their approach to suit each situation. However, managers claim that they rarely have sufficient time to analyse the situation.

5 The Transactional Era

In the transactional era, the focus was on the importance of the transactions between the leader and the subordinates. Pettigrew and Whipp[16] noted that the transactional leader only intervened when standards were not met. The leader acted as a thermostat for the organization – regulating only when things got too hot or too cold. Pettigrew and Whipp suggested that this reactive approach was appropriate where routine tasks needed to be carried out in a stable environment. However, in times of major change, when the standards were in a state of flux, a reactive transactional approach was not appropriate. John Adair[17] offered a more proactive version of transactional leadership (Figure 7.1). His model required leaders to address three specific sets of needs:

1 **Task needs**: achieving agreed standards on time, within constraints
2 **Group needs**: maintaining collective morale and mutual supportiveness
3 **Individual needs**: identifying and satisfying the needs of individuals

To keep these three sets of needs in balance, the leader must be sensitive to both individual and group dynamics. Addressing the needs of an individual might undermine the morale of the group, or conflict with the achievement of the task.

6 The Cultural Era

Van Seter[18] described the cultural era as an anti-leadership era. 'Leader' was a label attributed to you by those who were led. On this attribution model, if you wish to be considered a leader, then you need to do what leaders do. You need to do the things that leaders do to get tasks achieved on time, to maintain standards, to keep within budgets, to meet the needs of individuals, and to maintain high morale and mutual supportiveness. Pfeffer[19] argued that a leader was primarily a symbol and that the leader's actual performance was of little consequence. Schein[20] went further. He suggested that if a leader could create a culture that favoured the empowerment of self-managing, self-developing groups, then employees would lead themselves.

Leadership – The Story So Far

So far we have seen how leadership theories have progressed from a concern with the leader's personality and interactions with others, to a consideration of situational factors such as power and task. With contingency theories came the idea that leaders might be people with a portfolio of styles and the ability to choose which one to use. In the cultural era the leader was seen as a social construct, based on the attributions of the people who were being led. This leads us to our final model of leadership – transformational leadership. First, we look at leadership from the perspective of a female public service manager. (Box 7.6)

7 The Transformational Era

Chris Reeve seems to be hankering after a more transformational style of leadership. According to Van Seter,[21] transformational leaders must be proactive rather than reactive in their thinking, radical rather than conservative, and open to new ideas. This

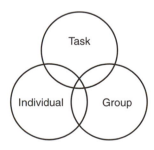

Figure 7.1 Balancing task, group and individual needs
Source: Adair (1983)

Box 7.6

CONVERSATION WITH CHRIS REEVE

(A Senior Female Manager in Education):

'INVISIBLE WOMEN'

Tony: Please talk to me about being a manager.

Chris: As a woman manager, I sometimes feel that I am invisible. One day I was walking down a corridor with a male colleague of the same rank as myself. A more senior manager approached us. He discussed work with my male colleague; I was completely ignored – he didn't even make eye contact. Yet he knew that I was involved in the matters. Women managers have to work hard to be noticed.

Tony: You sound irritated.

Chris: Well yes. I also have to put up with a male-dominated culture that can be very undermining. Overt discrimination and harassment have largely disappeared. Now it is more subtle and insidious. Male managers, for example, often engage in 'harmless' banter. This is often well meaning – affectionate even. It seems to be part of male camaraderie, but it is quite excluding of women. Initial protests are often met with helpful suggestions that we should 'not take things so seriously' – after all it's only a joke! This is very disempowering. The long-term effect is very depressing.

Tony: What can men learn from the way women behave as leaders?

Chris: Most women seem to find it easier than men to give positive feedback. Men find it difficult to deal with their feelings – especially feelings of being hurt. I am not saying that is true of all men. Even when men are sensitive to how they feel, they can find it difficult to express their feelings in a male-dominated culture. We have male managers who can rehearse the rhetoric of being a sensitive male when they are supervising female colleagues, but who then adopt an aggressive style of management with male subordinates. Working in this kind of culture, with few female role models, can put many women off applying for senior management positions.

Tony: But do the women managers behave any differently than the men?

Chris: Yes, for example, men find it easier to tell people what to do. They act as though they have ready-made answers. Men seem to find it difficult to say 'I don't know'. I call it the 'bullshit' factor. Women seem to find it easier to get on a level with their staff without seeing it as weakness. How can men learn anything if they always behave as though they already know everything?

Tony: Anything else?

Chris: I think that women are better at nurturing, encouraging and enabling others. These are the very skills which many public service workers need when dealing with their clients. The use of these skills by male managers is often seen as a sign of weakness, yet I don't think it is realistic to expect staff to value their clients any more highly than they feel valued by their male senior managers.

Tony: Thank you Chris.

approach emphasizes the leader's role as one who motivates others, generating not just compliance, but energetic commitment, to demanding goals. Nancy Roberts[22] suggested that the collective action generated by transformational leaders empowered everyone who participated in the process. According to Tichy and Ulrich,[23] transformational leaders had the capacity to create a shared vision which captured the direction in which an organization needed to move. They were able to communicate this vision and mobilize commitment to it. Bennis asserted:

> to survive the 21st century, we are going to need a new generation of leaders – not managers. The distinction is an important one. Leaders conquer the context – the volatile, turbulent, ambiguous surroundings that sometimes seem to conspire against us if we let them – while managers surrender to it.[24]

Bennis went on to argue that transformational leaders were needed because of their capacity to 'dream the dream', creating a compelling vision of new opportunities, while generating commitment throughout the organization to making the vision real.[25] Tom Peters[26] suggested that an effective vision had the characteristics described in Box 7.7.

Box 7.7

AN EFFECTIVE VISION IS:

- **Inspirational**: clear and challenging
- **Focused**: providing a sense of purpose
- **Future oriented**: while honouring the best of the past
- **Guiding**: providing direction without denying freedom
- **Enduring**: providing a long-term aim without being set in concrete

---

LEADERS, VISION AND CHANGE

We need to evaluate leadership theories in relation to the need to implement changes in public service organizations. On the basis of 12 case studies of senior public services managers, Simpson and Beeby[27] concluded that traditional bureaucratic public service organizations were unlikely to spawn leaders of transformational change. However, they found the concept of transformational change useful. They recognized the importance of:

- Developing a vision of change which captured the attention of the organization
- Communicating the significance of what the organization was trying to do
- Negotiating consensus and commitment

If an agenda for change lacks coherence, then the implementation of discrete changes may fail. According to Kakabadse et al.,[28] a vision is more worthy if it allows for flexibility in how it is to be achieved. It involves defining a desired future. It expresses an optimistic and hopeful sense of what an organization could look like in the future. For Senge,[29] the gap between the vision and the reality leads to creativity. The vision of Moses led his people to the Promised Land; Mahatma Gandhi's vision of a sovereign India led India toward independence; Martin Luther King's vision of racial harmony galvanized civil rights campaigners; Nelson Mandela's vision of a racially united South Africa energized the struggles against apartheid. Do these examples indicate a role for visionary leadership?

Developing a Vision – Bridging the Gap

Charles Handy[30] refers to the 'S curve' as a metaphor for understanding both organizational development and organizational decline. According to Handy, the growth of any successful organization will begin to flatten out at some point (Figure 7.2). Unless the organization can develop a new direction – a new vision for the future – then the organization will go into decline. Handy suggested that this S-shaped

Achievement

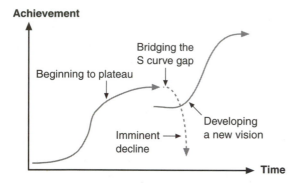

Figure 7.2 Bridging the gap

process was universal. It is mirrored in epic events of history like the rise and fall of the Roman Empire as well as in the ups and downs of individual lives. The reason why decline occurs is because emperors, managers and individuals may be unaware that they have reached a plateau. They are blinded by their success. At this point, according to Handy, countries, organizations and people need to develop new S curves based on a new vision of the future. This process of bridging the S curve gap is depicted in Figure 7.2.

Activity 5, in the Thinking and Learning Activities at the end of this chapter, will enable you to develop a 'vision' of your own future.

Simpson and Beeby[31] rejected the notion that the power to transform an organization should be vested in one person. Pettigrew and Whipp,[32] whose approach appeared to be a combination of the contingent and the transformational, came to the same conclusion. Where the leader's main task was to lead the organization through change, Pettigrew preferred a model of leadership that permeated all levels of the organization. No one person's repertoire of leadership styles is likely to match the complexity of the way organizations change.[33]

The Darker Side of Leadership

Zaleznik[34] reported that leaders had a well-developed sense of self which gave them a strong presence, enabling them to challenge the status quo. We think

that such people would threaten many senior managers in public service organizations. Stable and predictable people are much more likely to be promoted in public service organizations than emerging leaders, whom Zaleznik described as inclined to be dramatic, unpredictable, inconsistent and subject to mood swings. Congar warns that visionary transformational leaders may have a 'dark side' which only becomes apparent in times of crisis. Such leaders are inclined to deny any flaws in themselves or their visions. Leaders can believe too strongly in their own infallibility: 'once a crisis stage is reached, the leader exerts greater personal control and becomes less able to hear the counsel of advisors and staff'.[35] Mrs Thatcher's demise illustrated what can happen when individualistic, vision-driven leaders lose touch with the people they lead.

DO PUBLIC SERVICES NEED LEADERS?

Zaleznik[36] claimed that there was a shortage of good leaders because people no longer had models of good leadership. Bennis[37] also drew attention to this shortage when he asked 'where have all the leaders gone?' Bennis argued that society had created a generation of narcissistic individuals who lacked qualities such as integrity, openness, dedication, magnanimity and humility. Yet these are the qualities needed to restore respect to the role of public servant (Chapter 15). In Britain, in the 1990s, scandals and controversies concerning the management of privatized public services such as gas, water, railways and the prisons resulted in the Nolan and Scott enquiries. These added to Cadbury's concern over corporate governance (Chapter 11). There was a serious erosion in the credibility of public leaders. If public services employees are representative of the societies they serve, and if these societies comprise people who are greedy, self-centred, visionless and attached to the status quo, then we should not be overreliant on models of management which seek to develop leaders from amongst the ranks of public service employees.

Where Have All The Leaders Gone?

During the 1980s, one way in which governments in the UK attempted to make good the leadership of publicly owned public service organizations, was by recruiting senior managers from the private sector. Len Peach was seconded from IBM into the NHS. The boards of NHS Trusts were advised to include managers from the commercial sector. David Lewis, the Director of Prison Services, was recruited from a media business. As outsiders, managers from the private sector were thought less likely to preserve the status quo. Traditionally, public service progression had been via 'upgrading' or 'enhancement'. This required day release or secondment for training. Decisions about who was given training opportunities, 'upgradings' and 'enhancement' were often based on seniority and 'face-fitting' criteria. This encouraged the advancement of those who identified strongly with the existing culture. It was hoped that importing leaders from the private sector might help to dismantle the resulting alliances. The hoped-for benefits failed to materialize. Nameki[38] suggested that any chance of a shared sense of vision between managers and staff was undermined by recruiting leaders from the private sector. The Oughton Report on *Career Management and Succession in the UK Civil Service*[39] found that leaders imported from the private sector lacked sufficiently deep knowledge of public service. Oughton concluded that their approach to change was overly adversarial. The Oughton Report had been expected to endorse the practice of making senior management appointments from outside and to recommend fixed-term contracts. It did not do so.[40]

A CONVERSATIONAL APPROACH TO LEADERSHIP

So there is a shortage of good role models for leaders in public services. Public services employees are drawn from a society that does not equip them well for empowered roles. The private sector is not a hopeful source of recruits. Where next? There are two cases to consider. The case where there is a need for continuity (Case I) and the case where there is a proven need for change (Case II).

Case I: A Need for Continuity

Case I is the case where the economy, efficiency and effectiveness of the organization would benefit from a period of stability and continuity with past practice. Here we prefer approaches based on the competence of managers rather than the inspiration of leaders. The attributes of leadership seem to be in short supply and to be hard to develop in people who do not have them already. There do not seem to be enough natural born leaders to go around. In any event, they often have undesirable characteristics which can show up at times of crisis. Having said that, there are a number of things which leaders *do*, which it would be useful for managers to copy, if they are temperamentally able to do so (Boxes 7.8–7.10).[41]

Case II: A Need for Change

The second case is where managers are faced with a proven need to implement change. The proven need to implement change may have arisen because of technical, economic, market, political, legal, ethical or social forces for change in the organization's environment (Chapter 4), or out of a desire to improve the quality of the service which the organization provides (Chapter 5). For whatever reasons, if the change is a proven necessity, we advocate a conversational approach to the management of change (Chapter 3). So why do we need extraordinary 'transformational leaders' when ordinary managers can adopt an ordinary conversational approach to implementing change? We should not be surprised about this. Figure 7.3 presents the model of the conversational manager. It incorporates the characteristics of 'leadership thinking and leadership acting' which Zaleznik advocated as desirable characteristics of a transformational leader. The sought-after attributes

Box 7.8

A CONVERSATIONAL APPROACH TO LEADERSHIP: THE TASK

- Am I clear about my objectives?
- Does everyone know what their job is?
- Do we have gaps in the skills needed?
- Does everyone know who their boss is?
- Am I clear about my responsibilities?
- Has anyone got too many people accountable?

- What arrangements do I make for continuity?
- Does my work and behaviour set a good example?
- Do I receive information – hard and soft – in order to check progress?
- Have I achieved the tasks set 12 months ago?

Box 7.9

A CONVERSATIONAL APPROACH TO LEADERSHIP: INDIVIDUALS

- Do individuals sign their own letters?
- Are there any controls that I can remove?
- Can I cut down on the checking I do?
- In the case of success, do I acknowledge it and build on it?
- Have individuals got a list of short-term improvement targets?
- Could any individual write my reports to a particular committee?
- Can I increase any individual's accountability for their own work?
- Is the performance of each individual regularly appraised face to face?
- Do I give personal attention to matters of direct concern to individuals?

- Have I made sufficient provision for training or retraining of each person?
- In the case of failure, do I give guidance on improving future performance?
- Do I know enough about individuals to have an accurate picture of their needs?
- Have I agreed with individuals their main responsibilities, expressed as results?
- If, after opportunities for training and development, an individual still does not meet the requirements of the job, do I try to find them a position more closely matched to their capacity – or see that someone else does?

Box 7.10

A CONVERSATIONAL APPROACH TO LEADERSHIP: THE TEAM

- Do I deal with grievances promptly?
- Do I take action on matters likely to disrupt?
- Do I welcome and encourage new ideas?
- Do I brief the team – at least monthly – on likely developments?
- Is there a formal and fair grievance procedure understood by all?
- Is the size of the team correct and are the right people working together?

- Do I agree team objectives with members and make sure they are understood?
- Do I consult the team before taking decisions related to their work or standards?
- Is the team clear as to the working standards expected from them, e.g. time keeping, quality of work, house keeping, safety? Do I enforce those standards?

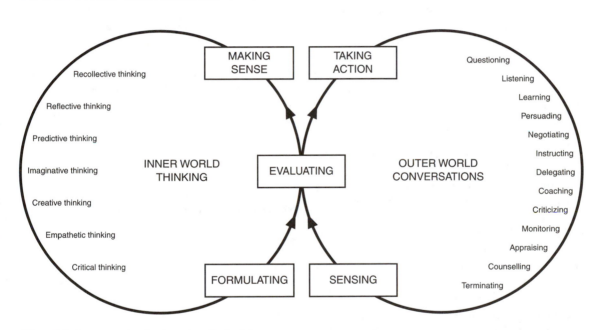

Figure 7.3 A conversational approach to leadership

---

of transformational leaders will automatically manifest themselves in managers using a conversational approach to their work. At the same time the approach will be more balanced. Transformational leaders tend to emphasize prediction, imagination, creativity and empathy. In the conversational approach this is balanced by recollection, reflection, ethics and critical thinking. Transformational leaders tend to practise persuasion, instruction, delegation, appraisal and termination. In the conversational approach these are balanced by questioning, listening, learning, coaching, monitoring and counselling.

The conversational approach is a quieter process and more rounded. Because it delivers change in a more ordinary way, it lacks the inspirational rhetoric that is associated with transformational leadership.

A More Thoughtful Approach to Leadership

Given the existence of less costly, less risky, more readily available ways of getting things done, or changes implemented, the persistency of belief in leaders warrants further thought. Simply because we have a word for something does not necessarily mean it exists. Some things are fantasies constructed in our minds, often borne of a strong desire that they should exist. This is especially true when the thought that they might exist makes us feel less anxious. The idea that there might be a leader helps to allay that anxiety and so the idea is born that a leader will come (Chapter 6). A belief arises that leadership is a real entity. The belief persists despite the failure of our '7 eras' of leadership to yield much tangible evidence of its existence. Hence, perhaps, the difficulties which the researchers have had in defining leadership traits and characteristics.

When a group spawns a leader around whom it can behave cohesively, this is usually received as a positive progressive development – a measure of group 'maturity'. It is equally possible that it may be a measure of group inadequacy – a pathological inability to discuss the anxieties, fears, needs, wants, jealousies, envies and enmities that often arise when people are asked to work in groups. Unfortunately, the more space we devote to discussing theories of leadership, the more credence we give to the idea that leadership is real. People already in leadership positions, or being highly paid for their leadership qualities, have a self-serving interest in funding more studies. This self-perpetuates the assumption that leadership exists. The myth reduces the likelihood that individuals will believe that they are responsible for their own lives and that they can take their own decisions. The more these feelings of dependency are fostered by the leadership myth, the better it suits the vested interests of those already in positions of leadership power. Fearing the consequences (unspecified) of social disorder, we readily collude with myths that preserve our existing order. It is a small step from collusion to delusion. We can easily delude ourselves that we need leaders, that leaders can create order and that leaders can maintain order and that leadership actually exists. To challenge such ideas in many organizations is tantamount to heresy. The consequences for individuals who do challenge the leadership myth can be serious.

Yet leaders themselves often fall victim to their own myth. They are blamed when things go wrong. As long as we have leaders to blame when things go wrong, we will not rectify faults in resource levels, organization design or procedures. If we create a 'follow-my-leader' culture – all pulling in the same direction, having one 'vision', singing from the same hymn sheet – we should not be surprised if people are reluctant to exchange the comfort they may derive from this, for the anxieties of participation. Rather than managers becoming leaders, we are interested in the possibility that managers can help individuals to identify what they really need and can show individuals how some of their needs can be met through their work. This process is called motivation.

MANAGING MOTIVATION

Experiences of Motivation

Symptoms of low motivation include apathy, absence, lateness, inconsistent performance and the avoidance of personal responsibility. In 1996 the BBC included managers' experiences of motivation as part of their series entitled *20 Steps to Better Management*.[42] The things that managers experienced as motivational fell into two categories – positive and negative. Positive motivators included a sense of worthwhile purpose, autonomy, achievement, feeling 'in the know', feeling competent and confident, able to do a good job. Negative motivators were shortage of cash, holidays, status and promotion prospects. Knowledge, skills, abilities, beliefs, values and needs all featured importantly. Conversations involving goal setting, feedback, appreciation and praise were almost always followed by:

- Increased acceptance of personal responsibility
- Increased energy and enthusiasm
- Increased collaboration
- Increased flexibility

Threats were also reported to be motivational in the short term. In the long term threats led to an erosion of good-will and morale generally. Goals and targets were widely held to be beneficial as long as the goals and targets were clear and challenging and their achievement was perceived to be within the control of the person whose goal it was. The experience of managers gave rise to support for checklists of the kind shown in Box 7.11.

Praise and Positive Feedback

Positive feedback and praise may be more motivating for most people, but even for people who prefer positive feedback, there will be a limit to how much they can take before they start to reject it. In order for praise to remain sought-after and valued, it

should be as specific as possible – not generalized platitudes about 'good work' or 'good effort'. Give good reasons and detailed examples to support your good opinion of their work. Giving good reasons models what you expect them to do. Giving detailed examples indicates how much you notice, how much attention you give to them and their work, and thereby how important they and their work must be. Explain how you think that the organization or the clients are benefiting from their efforts.

Checklists and guidelines – however sound the experiences on which they are based – only tell us *how*, but not *why*, a person is motivated. When competence is based only on knowing 'how' without knowing 'why', then when circumstances change the manager will not know that the old 'how' is no longer applicable. One way to understand why checklists and guidelines work is to look at the theories of motivation that underlie them.

Theories of Motivation

Vroom and Yetton[43] classify theories about motivation under five headings:

1 Response theories
2 Drive theories
3 Goal theories
4 Intrinsic–Extrinsic theories
5 Need theories

1 Response theories

Many theories in this cluster refer to the work of Skinner.[44] Skinner developed an 'operant theory', based on the notion of reinforcement. In many experiments on animals, he discovered that when responses are reinforced, for example by reward, then they recur more frequently. When responses are punished, they recur less frequently. By rewarding desired responses and punishing undesired responses, he concluded that behaviour could be controlled or modified. Some of the ideas of scientific management, such as performance related pay, are based on this principle. They seek to link pecuniary rewards or penalties with assessed levels of performance.

Box 7.11

A MOTIVATION CHECKLIST

- Agree challenging targets that are realistic, achievable and within their control
- Be clear about what you expect people to achieve, but don't oversupervise
- Develop individuals to their full potential and don't feel threatened
- Delegate responsibilities, give authority and retain accountability
- Keep people informed, brief directly and avoid the 'grapevine'
- Confront and resolve conflicts as they arise.
- Be tolerant of personal problems

There are a number of difficulties with this approach. It does not recognize intrinsic factors which may motivate people, such as the challenge posed by the job. It assumes that the employees only value the pecuniary rewards. Flynn suggests that: 'Not all public sector employees are motivated primarily by material rewards. Very often they wish to do as good a job as possible.'[45] Employees may be indifferent to the consequences of the threatened punishments. They may perceive attempts to control their behaviour in this way as disrespectful.

2 Drive theories

Hull and Freud[46] are two proponents of drive theories. Drive theories are based on the perception that all behaviour is driven by different urges or drives. For example, Hull argued that all behaviour could be explained on the basis of four drives: hunger, thirst, sex and avoidance of pain. When we experience imbalance or disequilibrium, we are driven by urges which energize our behaviour until our balance or equilibrium is restored. According to drive theory, organisms learn to repeat behaviours and actions that are effective in restoring equilibrium.

Freud's ideas on human drive enabled him to develop a framework for psychoanalysis. At the root of these frameworks is the idea that all human behaviour is motivated by two basic instincts, sex and aggression, and that these two instincts exert their influence at an unconscious level. We are inclined to agree with Vroom and Deci's[47] view that it is difficult to relate drive theories to motivation at work. Whatever the 'basic drives' may be, it is hard to see how they can be used by managers to motivate people who work in public services.

3 Goal theories

In the 1940s, a main proponent of goal theories was Kurt Lewin.[48] He was a psychiatrist and group psychotherapist who worked with soldiers who suffered from post-traumatic stress. Lewin's work was widely taken up by management theorists, particularly in the area of change management (Chapter 2). Lewin relied on Gestalt psychology. The idea of 'Gestalt' refers to a tendency to want to make a unified whole of inner world thinking and outer world actions. For example, when we have business which we regard as unfinished, we experience a tension which drives us to want to finish that unfinished business. The tension persists until the 'Gestalt' is completed. People set themselves goals, or devise plans, so as to decrease the gap between some existing state and some future state that they think is more desirable, i.e. people are motivated to move from perceived initial states to desired future states.

Goals, anticipated outcomes and desired future states are concepts that have been used by managers to try to motivate people to improve their performance. Goal setting was a key component of Management by Objectives as advocated by Drucker,[49] Humble[50] and others. They concluded that specific goals were more motivating than general ones. Motivation was increased by specifying a time by which goals were to be achieved, by reviewing progress towards goal attainment, and by giving employees as much choice as possible about the way in which they thought the goals might best be achieved. Goal theories provide a plausible framework for enabling us to describe the way people move themselves and others towards desired future states. Goal theorists, however, offer no explanation as to why people choose the future states that they desire. Until we understand 'why' people choose their future goals, it is hard to offer managers consistent advice on how they can increase the frequency and speed with which people will move towards them.

4 Intrinsic and extrinsic theories

Intrinsic motivation refers to an innate psychological need for competence and self-determination. The implication is that a great deal of our behaviour at work might be determined by a desire to be proactive in our dealings with the outer world, rather than to be a pawn reacting to the control of other people. Extrinsic motivators are concerned with concrete rewards such as pay and conditions of service.[51] Some writers have suggested that optimal conditions for motivating performance might be a combination of intrinsic and extrinsic motivators.[52] Intrinsic motivators, such as making work more challenging and offering opportunities for personal and professional growth, might be combined with extrinsic motivators, such as good rates of pay, job security and promotion. One problem is that some sources of extrinsic motivation counteract some sources of intrinsic motivation. For example, meeting the requirements of systems designed to monitor achievement often cancels the intrinsic motivation that could come from the achievements themselves.

5 Needs theories

McClelland[53] developed a needs theory in relation to achievement. He postulated that need for achievement is a learned need rather than an innate need. That being so, it should be possible to increase an employee's need for achievement and hence their level of motivation. Following extensive empirical studies, he identified three characteristics of people with high achievement needs:

1 They prefer personal responsibility and control over the completion of tasks.
2 They set moderate achievement goals which pose some risk and challenge but which are not so difficult as to lead to failure.
3 They need clear and unambiguous feedback in order to enjoy the satisfaction of knowing what has been achieved.

McClelland suggested that people could be trained to increase their achievement motivation. Some of the ways managers can do this included:

● Encouraging employees to emulate role models
● Encouraging people to think more positively about themselves

The best known of the needs-based theories of motivation is Maslow's hierarchy of needs.[54] Maslow proposed that human beings were driven by five basic needs which could be represented as a hierarchy ranging from lower physiological needs to higher needs for self-actualization (Figure 7.4 and Box 7.12). Maslow's theory postulated that once a need had been met it was no longer a motivator, and that only a need at a higher level could be a source of motivation.

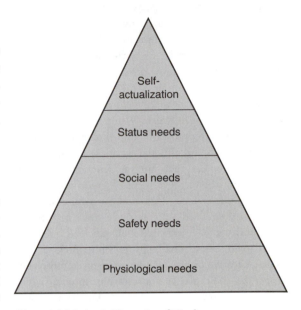

Figure 7.4 Maslow's Hierarchy of Needs

Box 7.12

MASLOW'S HIERARCHY: A DEFINITION OF TERMS

● **Physiological needs**: e.g. the need for food, water, heat
● **Safety needs**: e.g. the need for freedom from pain, physical attack, deprivation, insecurity, chaos and uncertainty
● **Social needs**: e.g. the need for affection, the giving and receiving of love, closeness, friendship and a sense of belonging
● **Status needs**: e.g. the need for self-esteem and the esteem of others – recognition, reputation, respect and reward
● **Self-actualization**: the need to realize fully one's own potential

Maslow's work has been widely adopted by writers on management. Commonly they use Maslow's work to explain why, for example, a manager with a good income may not be motivated by the prospect of higher pay but might be motivated by the prospect of meeting new challenges that would satisfy needs for esteem and prestige. There are a number of problems with the application of Maslow's model to the work of a manager. Work is not the only situation in which people can obtain satisfaction of their needs. A manager cannot control what happens outside work. While managers seek to motivate employees towards higher performance, the employees may obtain satisfaction of their needs through activities that are incidental to, or even counter to, the achievement of improved organizational performance. People may attribute different values to their needs, for example, they may prefer the security of a predictable bureaucratic job to a better paid, more challenging job, which is less secure. Creative or artistic people are often motivated to realize their artistic or creative potential long before their lower needs are met. For some, lower needs for safety or status never become a major source of motivation.

Flynn points out how values and motivation can conflict amongst employees in public service organizations. They are likely to be motivated by a mixture of factors, such as:

> job security and/or a desire to work in an environment where profit is not the primary motive either for themselves or the organization. Or they may feel that what they are doing is 'just a job' to which they have no special commitment. It is very likely that they will have conflicting values which cannot be resolved.[55]

Maslow's model fails to account for changes in people's needs which occur over time, as employees go through life's predictable transitions. Nor is there any explanation for the observed phenomenon that some people seem to have very much more motivatable energy than others.

Motivation Theories: Summarizing the Limitations

Needs-based theories go furthest in alleviating the limitations of response theories, drive theories, goal theories and intrinsic theories when trying to understand motivation in public services. Some residual limitations of needs-based theories have been addressed, in part, by Alderfer,[56] who has condensed Maslow's hierarchy into three groups of needs. Alderfer represents these needs as a continuum rather than a hierarchy. Alderfer's work still has in common with all the theories we have considered so far, a failure to take into account the employee's life outside work. A theory of motivation is needed which helps us to understand why employees become demotivated in public service organizations and which offers us hope that we can still find ways of raising their motivation. We offer a theory of motivation on which we have based our own practice in UK local government, the national health service, higher education and Crown Agency Services in Africa, Malaysia, India and Pakistan.

Addressing the Limitations

Since 1980, we have been in search of a model of motivation which addressed some of the limitations of the theories based on stimulus–response, drive, goals, intrinsic reward and a hierarchy of human needs. Our search has been based on the premise that a person at work will be motivated to move from some existing state to some more desirable state if, on achieving that new state, they think that they will receive something that meets a need which is important to them and which at the moment is not being fully met. Possible changes from the initial to the desired state might include changes in their state of knowledge, or their state of skill, or their level of performance. At its current state of evolution, we have a model that suggests that it may be useful to consider people as having needs of the following types:

- Warmth needs (W type needs – Box 7.13)
- Applause needs (A type needs – Box 7.14)
- Possession needs (P type needs – Box 7.15)

Box 7.13

WARMTH NEEDS ARE ...

Needs for things that are persistent in the absence of their source. They include the need for such things as support, affection, belonging, friendship, acceptance and unconditional positive regard.

Typically, W-type needs can be met at work through such things as personal development programmes, membership of training groups, teams, boards, special project teams, sports teams, research clusters, quiz teams, professional networks, staff associations, co-counselling, informal networks, mentoring and critical friendships.

Box 7.14

APPLAUSE NEEDS ARE ...

Needs for ephemeral things that need constant repetition, replacement and reaffirmation by the source. They include the need for such things as recognition, approval, admiration, gratitude, congratulation, reward, success, positive strokes, achievement and pleasure.

Typically, A-type needs are met through recognition and reward rituals such as league tables, performance related pay, award ceremonies, status symbols, hierarchies of office size, letters and certificates of commendation, performance on training programmes, thank-you notes and mentions in publicity materials, in house magazines and in media coverage.

Box 7.15

POSSESSION NEEDS ARE ...

The need to be able to say 'these things are *mine*'. This need can be met through possessions such as my desk, my parking spot, my body, my office, my car, my department, my wife, my children, my house, my hobby, my career, my space, my ideas, my religion, my beliefs, my values, my faith, my club, my team, my theory, my creativity, my work of art, my song, my poem or my report.

P-type needs at work can be met by allowing people to sign their own reports, letters and memos; to own their own ideas and suggestions; to take personal responsibility; to have authority for decision-making, budgets and spending decisions; to patent designs and inventions in their own name; to put their own names on doors, cabinets and websites.

The needs for warmth, applause and possession can be mapped by using three circles, as illustrated in Figure 7.5. Each circle, or area of need, can then be divided into segments which distinguish between:

1 Needs met through close one-to-one relationships
2 Needs met through activities outside work
3 Needs met through work
4 Needs currently unmet

The relative size of the three empty circles for a particular individual represents the relative driving power of the three areas of need for that individual. The total area of the three circles added together is therefore a representation of that person's total 'neediness' and is a measure of the 'maximum' motivatable energy which might be released if that person could be fully motivated. This maximum motivatable energy differs from one person to another, helping us to understand our experience

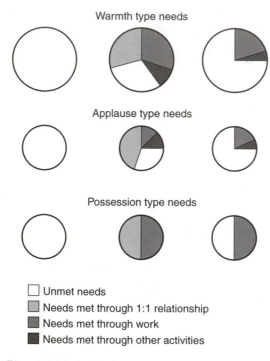

Warmth type needs

Applause type needs

Possession type needs

☐ Unmet needs
◻ Needs met through 1:1 relationship
▩ Needs met through work
■ Needs met through other activities

Figure 7.5 Motivational mapping

that individuals differ, one from another, in how energetic they are. The way in which the relative size of the three circles varies from one person to another helps us to represent our observation that different people are motivated by different types of activity.

The recognition that these needs can be met in many ways other than through work, enables us to account for the way in which a given person's motivation at work can change over time, or quite dramatically following a major life crisis. In the Thinking and Learning section at the end of this chapter, readers are given the opportunity to try out motivational mapping for themselves.

Motivation and Job Satisfaction amongst Public Service Employees

During the 1990s the UK Institute of Health Service Managers reported that pay levels in the health service were too low and that there were insufficient rewards. They concluded that low pay levels had resulted in low morale and made it diffi-

cult to recruit.[57] An empirical study by Keen and Scase came to almost the opposite conclusion: 'Overall, the majority (of middle managers) experienced an increase in their levels of intrinsic satisfaction, related to additional opportunities for exercising personal judgement and discretion as well as opportunities for personal growth.'[58]

This increased level of motivation was attributed to the introduction of devolved management systems and the creation of a performance culture attuned to the notion of continuous improvement. These findings correspond closely to those of Dopson and Stewart,[59] who also identified generally positive attitudes to restructuring within the public services. On the other hand, Scase and Goffee[60] provided evidence of demotivation among public service managers as a result of declining job security and decreased promotion and career opportunities. According to Scase and Goffee,[61] the changes were perceived as a threat by those managers who had seen their careers as a progression of jobs moving up a hierarchy through successive upgradings which would be determined by their seniority or enhanced qualifications. Less hierarchical structures and reduced numbers of management levels removed many of the steps on the public service promotional ladder. Other research concluded that many middle managers were developing an increasingly instrumental attitude to work and were reducing its centrality to their lives:

> Unfulfilled career expectations, together with increasing dissatisfaction and uncertainty associated with programmes of organisational restructuring, have led managers to withdraw psychologically from work and to seek greater personal rewards in their private lives. Managers are no longer prepared to sell themselves to their employing corporations at the expense of their family relationships and personal lifestyles.[62]

Keen and Scase suggested that motivation and job satisfaction could be improved by increasing:

1 Rewards for exceptional performance
2 Opportunities for work-based learning
3 Involvement in the learning and development of others
4 Opportunities for lateral as well as vertical career development

We can conclude that, while opportunities for intrinsic rewards may have increased as a result of decentralization, devolution of responsibility and increased autonomy, extrinsic rewards have diminished, due to reduced prospects for promotion and a general worsening of terms and conditions of employment. These changes have left many public service employees feeling demotivated, insecure and vulnerable. In the next chapter we look at how managers can respond to the needs of staff and the needs of the organization by managing people as individuals.

FINAL THOUGHTS: THE ANDROGENOUS MANAGER

The invisible barrier through which women have to break in order to become senior managers has been described as the glass ceiling.[63] Despite equal opportunities legislation in some countries and policies of positive action in others, the majority of managers in public services are still male. According to Martin Willis,[64] social service departments and probation departments, for example, would need to double the number of their women managers and proportionately reduce the numbers of male managers, in order to reflect the balance of women and men in their departments. Rosner[65] agrees with Chris Reeve that male leaders tend towards command and control while women leaders are good at getting people to channel their own self-interest into the interests of the organization. Rosner also found that women were particularly good at:

- Sharing power
- Sharing information
- Facilitating inclusion
- Not coveting authority
- Encouraging participation
- Giving credibility to others
- Making people feel important
- Enhancing self-worth in others

Rosner argued that in many of their social roles women are supposed to be co-operative, supportive, understanding, gentle and to provide a service to others. Women are expected to derive satisfaction and fulfilment from helping others, including their spouses. Men learn to appear competitive, strong, tough, decisive and in control, whereas women learn to appear co-operative, emotional, supportive and vulnerable. If a command and control style of leadership is inappropriate for progressive, post-bureaucratic, third-wave organizations, then Rosner's findings point to the probability that women would make better leaders of public service organizations than men (assuming we need leaders at all!).

In 1990 Powell carried out a review of research into supposed differences between male and female leaders and came to the following conclusion: 'There is not much difference between the needs, values and leadership styles of male and female managers. The sex differences that have been found are few and tend to cancel each other out.'[66] Oliveres,[67] founder of the European Foundation of Women, disagrees. She thinks that organizations need balanced individuals, who are able to draw from the riches of both their masculine and feminine sides — a case, perhaps, for androgenous managers in public services?

SUMMARY

- We reviewed the history of ideas about leadership under seven headings: the personality era, the influence era, the behavioural era, the contingency era, the transactional era, the cultural era and the transformational era.
- We were interested in leaders in public services. They had undesirable 'dark side' characteristics.
- We favoured solutions based on the competence of conversational managers, rather than the inspiration of hard-to-find leaders. The competence of managers can be enhanced by copying what leaders do.
- An ordinary conversational approach to managing change is preferable to the extraordinary approach of leaders.
- We looked at checklists and guidelines for motivating people at work.
- We examined five theories of motivation to see if we could discover why these guidelines work for some people.
- We assessed the strengths and weaknesses of different theories of motivation.
- We examined levels of motivation amongst public service employees. Extrinsic motivators had been eroded by low pay and job insecurity but intrinsic motivators, such as increased responsibility and devolved budgets, had been increased.
- We proposed a new model of motivation. By having conversations about an individual's need for 'Warmth', 'Applause' and 'Possession', a manager can increase the chances that individuals will motivate themselves.
- Finally, we wondered whether women could bring distinctive and useful attributes to bear on the tasks of leading change in public services.

THINKING AND LEARNING ACTIVITIES

Activity 1 Self assessment

1 Which of the theories on leadership were most meaningful to you and why?
2 In your opinion, would it be a good idea to appoint 'transformational' leaders to senior positions in public service organizations? Give your reasons.
3 In what way are conversational managers more balanced than transformational leaders?
4 There are far fewer female leaders in the public services than there are male leaders. What explanations can you offer?
5 Do you think it is desirable to increase the number of women in leadership positions in public services? Give your reasons.
6 If it were desirable to do so, what could be done to increase the number of women in leadership positions in the public services?
7 Describe the limitations of five models of motivation discussed in this chapter.
8 What evidence is there to suggest that public service employees are demotivated?
9 Which model of motivation do you find most useful in explaining why people might experience demotivation in public services? Give reasons.
10 In what ways does motivational mapping overcome the deficiencies in other theories of motivation?

Activity 2 Individual Learning: Visual Thinking

Mental mapping

Take a blank A4 sheet. Skim back over this chapter. Each time you come to a key idea or section, label it with a few words. Write the label somewhere on your blank A4 sheet and draw a circle round the label. When you come across the next key idea or section, label it and place it on your A4 sheet, close to other ideas to which you think it is related. When you have skimmed through the whole chapter, draw lines between the circles on your A4 sheet, if you think the ideas are connected. Use a clean sheet of A4 to redraw your diagram so that the connecting lines are clear and the intersections are minimized. Now write verbs, doing words, actions, along all the lines, words such as 'which leads to', 'which can help with', 'which is connected to', 'which can be evaluated by'. Keep going until you have a map, a diagram or a flowchart of how all the ideas in this chapter relate to each other.

Activity 3 Paired Learning: Critical and Reflective Thinking

Are you a leader, an administrator or a manager?

Make a list of the characteristics of leaders, managers and administrators. Having compiled the list, identify which attributes of a leader, manager and administrator you think you possess. Ask someone with whom you work or who knows you well, to identify which attributes you possess. Is their perception different? If so, why?

Activity 4 Paired Learning: Evaluative Thinking

What's your style?

There's no one best managerial style. The best one is the one that best suits you under different circumstances. You have to judge what is needed at the time, taking into account the circumstances and the people. Judgement is improved by rehearsal. You can use your 'inner world' as a kind of 'mental laboratory' to test out possible 'styles', possible ways to be in different situations. Consider Table 7.1. Which style comes most easily to you? Give yourself points out of 10 for how well you can imagine yourself carrying off each style of managing. A total score of 70 might be perfect – or would it? Get a colleague to score you. Compare notes and try to understand any discrepancies.

Activity 5 Paired Learning: Creative and Imaginative Thinking

Developing a vision

This is a warm-up exercise to promote relaxation and stimulate the imagination and creative thinking. Get someone to read these instructions aloud:

> Relax and sit with legs comfortably placed on the floor with the upper body well supported without letting it become tense. Close your eyes and visualize a really happy event in your life. Take some time to select and picture the moment. Relive the event, experiencing the pleasant sensations and sense of well-being it is evoking. Recall every moment using all your senses. Notice the colours, noises, smells and tastes. Take a few moments to savour and enjoy the scene.
>
> Now think of something in your life that you would like to improve. A sport, or hobby, something around the house, something you do at work, a relationship – anything that is of real significance to you. Consider it in detail. What is wrong with it at the moment? Don't be harsh on yourself. Acknowledge that faults and limitations are there to be overcome. Piece-by-piece, visualize the improvements that you want to see and gradually build up an image of what the new situation will be like. Evoke the feelings and physical sensations associated with this new situation – sounds, images, feelings and thoughts. For a few moments savour and enjoy what it is like to be living in this future state. Finally, identify at least five things you will need to do to make this vision a reality.
>
> When you are ready, become aware of your body and your surroundings and open your eyes. Begin to move your body and return to everyday awareness.

Discuss with someone else what it felt like to hold, in your inner world, a vision of an improved future state. You do not need to go into details.

Activity 6 Group Learning: Creative and Predictive Thinking

Creating a collective vision

Your task is to build a shared vision as a group. If the group all belong to the same organization, build a vision of your organization as you want it to be in three or four years. If you do not all work in the same organization, then we suggest you work on building a shared vision for the future state of a public service organization with which you are all familiar, for example, a local school or the local police service.

Table 7.1 Management styles

Style	This style is needed when . . .	But beware of . . .
Confronting	• You need to assert yourself • You disagree with somebody • You want to point out inconsistencies • You want to challenge assumptions • An initiative or proposal is needed	• Becoming aggressive, bullying, intolerant, overbearing, domineering
Supporting	• Someone needs help • Someone is talking • You want to be tolerant, open-minded • Someone is trying to speak but is having difficulty finding the words	• Being gullible, allowing yourself to be too influenced by another person
Theoretical	• Relevant theories can be used to explain a situation or to solve problems • You are trying to make generalizations from something that has happened	• Losing touch with real problems • Using theory as an end in itself • Rushing to textbooks and experts • Confusing knowledge with wisdom
Practical	• Something needs to be done • Feasible solutions are required	• Becoming totally pragmatic • Undervaluing thinking • Failing to see patterns • Failing to seek insight
Planning	• You need to make plans, set goals • You need to identify the resources needed to meet your goals • You are preparing budgets • You need to anticipate consequences	• Making grandiose plans that are impractical • Spending all your time thinking about the future, thus avoiding the present
Reviewing	• You want to see how you are doing • You want to see what you have learned • Someone wants an appraisal	• Living in the past, so that you never look to the present or the future • Living on past achievements • Becoming trapped by guilt
Integrating	• You are aware of what is happening • Sensitive to the needs of the situation • Mediating between people in conflict • Balancing theory and practice	• Assuming that you must be in charge • Manipulating people to suit yourself

First, working on your own, create a desired future vision of the organization on which your group has chosen to concentrate. Using flipcharts, paints, art crayons and collage materials, create something to represent the future of the organization. It can be a picture, or a story, or a symbol, or an evocative 'one liner'. Anything that captures the essence of your vision. When each individual has finished, each member of the group will share their images and the visions they convey. When everyone has had a chance to explain their vision, identify the common elements of the vision and then create a composite image that captures the future state vision of the organization you have chosen. If you can't agree on a composite image, do not force people to compromise their opinions. Acknowledge differences and discuss why you cannot achieve a shared vision. Use disagreements as a means of deepening your understanding of why it can be difficult to build a shared vision.

Use Tom Peter's list of the characteristics of effective visions – which is included in the section on transformational leaders – as one way of assessing whether your vision is likely to be effective (Box 7.7). Can you adjust the vision if it does not meet these criteria? If the group has been able to agree on a corporate vision, then we can progress to see how the vision could become a reality.

Activity 7 Group Learning: Critical and Evaluative Thinking

Making a vision a reality

Separate into two groups:

- Pragmatists
- Idealists

The pragmatists will conduct a SWOT analysis of:

- The strengths needed to realize the vision
- The weaknesses which would need to be overcome
- The opportunities which can be built upon
- The threats or problems to be overcome

Without any constraints, the imaginative idealists can come up with ideas which they think might make the vision a reality. This group is invited to be imaginative and creative and not to become engrossed in how these ideas might be implemented. To conclude the exercise, bring the two groups together and let them share their ideas. Try to gain a consensus about the best ideas for making the vision a reality. Record these on a flipchart.

Activity 8 Individual Learning: Thinking and Action

An action learning project

If you are in a position to do so, we suggest that you undertake a project aimed at building a vision for an organization of which you are a part. It could be an organization you work for, or an organization of which you are a member in your leisure time. Introduce the envisioning process by explaining what a vision is and why vision is important. It may be necessary to address any cynicism or answer any or questions participants might have about the value of vision statements. Then work through the same process you have undertaken in Activity 7. The exercise should be ended by gaining practical commitment to implementing the vision. Get participants to refer back to the list of things that need to be done to realize the vision they have collectively developed and ask everyone to draw up an action plan identifying at least five things they will each do in order to translate the vision into reality. Be concrete. For example, 'I will explain the vision to X on Tuesday when we usually meet in his office at 11 am. I will be sitting in the low chair where I can see X and Y and Z out of the window. He will probably say . . . and I will reply . . .' End the exercise by asking participants to share what they have committed themselves to do.

Activity 9 Individual Learning: Evaluative Thinking

What motivates me?

Consider Maslow's Hierarchy of Needs (Figure 7.4). Try to identify things that you do to satisfy these needs. What particular needs in the hierarchy are you concentrating on at this point in your life? What needs in the hierarchy are you neglecting and why? Identify anything that you can do to increase your focus on an area of need that you are neglecting.

Activity 10 Individual Learning: Analytical Thinking

Managing your own motivation

Answer the following questions. Your answers need not be seen by anyone else.

1 What motivates you as a student, at home, or as an employee, if you are employed?
2 What sometimes prevents you doing what you are motivated to do?
3 What would help to reduce the obstacles you have identified in question 2?
4 What is *one* thing you could do to start to change the ideas, thoughts or attitudes or to obtain the necessary resources? What is the first step you will take?
5 What are the activities that leave you with more energy after them than you had before them? For each one, how could you do it one extra time in the coming month? What is the first step you will take to organize that?
6 Who are the people whose conversations usually leave you with more energy than you had before you spoke to them? For each person, work out how you could have one extra conversation with them each month. What will you do to organize that?
7 Go back over each of the steps you are going to take to implement the strategies which you know will increase your self-motivation and picture how things will be after each of your strategies has succeeded. Jot down key words that will help you to keep these pictures in your mind whenever you want to feel more motivated.

Activity 11 Individual Learning: Empathetic Thinking

CASE STUDY: Motivational mapping

The Task

Put yourself in the position of Mr Moody's manager. What would you do to try to motivate Mr Moody?

The Case Information

The following description maps the motivational needs of Mr Moody, at three stages in his life (see Figure 7.6). Mr Moody is a police inspector. In the first motivational map he was 28, with a young family and a large mortgage and much to prove to himself and the world about his talents and ambitions. His possession needs were much greater than his warmth needs. In the second motivation map he is 55 years old, his life is fulfilling and he has relatively few unmet needs. His need for warmth is much greater than his need for possession.

The third map was drawn shortly after Mr Moody suddenly and unexpectedly lost his wife. Before Mr Moody lost his wife, the possibility of motivating Mr Moody was not very great. While Mr Moody was clearly a 'needy' person, the proportion of his needs that were not already met through work, his relationship with his wife and his other activities, was small. It was difficult to tempt Mr Moody to raise his effort or performance. He had little need for whatever his manager might offer in return for increased effort. The loss of Mr Moody's wife changed all that. The pattern of his unmet need changed dramatically and for motivational purposes it is the unmet need that matters. So while we might have thought he would be too depressed and grief-stricken to be very easily motivated, the reverse has proved to be the case. Mr Moody has huge areas of unmet need – for warmth, applause and possession. Some of his outside activities – amateur dramatics, travel, holidays and voluntary work – have reduced, since these activities had been shared with his wife. The needs met by these former activities are now unmet. What is important to Mr Moody's manager is not Mr Moody's total need for warmth, applause and possession, but the proportion of these needs that is not currently met.

In order to motivate Mr Moody, his manager will have to establish a 'psychological contract' between himself and Mr Moody, under which, if Mr Moody agrees to move his performance from some existing state to some desired state, then his manager will arrange for some proportion of Mr Moody's currently unmet need to be met. The question that Mr Moody's manager must think about before talking to Mr Moody is this: 'Mr Moody, if you were to move from your initial state to my desired state, what would you want to receive that would meet a need that is important to you now, but which is currently unmet?'

Mr Moody's manager needs to think empathetically, as though he were Mr Moody. Try to answer the question as you think Mr Moody might answer it.

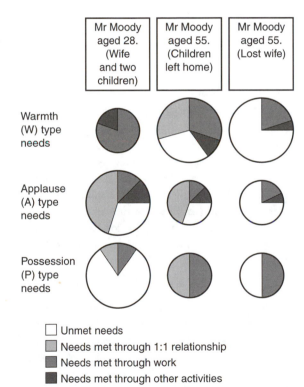

	Mr Moody aged 28. (Wife and two children)	Mr Moody aged 55. (Children left home)	Mr Moody aged 55. (Lost wife)
Warmth (W) type needs			
Applause (A) type needs			
Possession (P) type needs			

☐ Unmet needs
▨ Needs met through 1:1 relationship
▨ Needs met through work
■ Needs met through other activities

Figure 7.6 Mr Moody's motivational map

Activity 12 Individual Learning: Evaluative Thinking

Self-awareness – evaluating models

The model of motivational mapping that we proposed in this chapter may seem plausible, but is it valid? We may never know. What you could know is whether or not you find it useful, or perhaps more useful than existing models of motivation. To do this you could test the model against your experience. Ask yourself the following:

- Does the model cause me to think in new ways?
- Does the model enable me to make predictions?
- Does the model help me to make sense of things?
- Does the model enable me to develop a vocabulary that is capable of supporting discussions with colleagues about needs and motivation?

If the model passes any of the above tests, then the model has some merit. Unlike a scientific theory, the test of a model is utility rather than validity.

Activity 13 Paired Learning: Reflective Thinking

Self-analysis

Re-read our introduction to the W – A – P model and draw a three-circle 'Motivational Map' of yourself. The three circles represent the relative extent of your need for

Warmth, Applause and Possession. Draw a motivational map of yourself when you first started work, or five years ago if you have never had a full-time job. First draw three circles the relative size of which represents the extent of your W – A – P type needs. The larger the circle, the greater the need. Now divide up each circle as if it were a pie chart and use different colours to shade in the different slices of the pie. The size of slice or segment should represent the extent to which a given type of need (W, A or P type) is being met either through work, a close one-to-one relationship, or other non-work activities, or is unmet.

Now repeat the process and draw another W – A – P

motivational map, to represent your motivational needs *now*. Preferably you should draw your motivational maps side by side, so it is easier to spot any change from one period to the next. Now draw a third map to represent your likely motivational needs when you retire.

Review your diagrams with a partner, a close friend or with someone at work. List activities that contribute to needs currently met at work or study. What does this tell you? How might the proportion of your needs met through work or study be increased? With whom could you discuss this: your head of department? Your personnel manager, a coach or a critical friend (Chapters 13 and 14)?

Activity 14 Individual and Group Learning: Projective Thinking

CASE STUDY: The dead-end job

Task

Read the questions and then read the case. Make notes on your answers to the questions. If possible, compare notes with someone else who is doing the activity. If possible, meet up with another pair and agree a composite report which you could present as a foursome, to another foursome. Listen to the report of the other foursome. Make notes with your own foursome. Discuss whether you want to incorporate any of the ideas of the other foursome.

Questions

1 How would you describe Kendrik's motivation?
2 What thoughts and ideas appear to conflict in Kendrik's inner world?
3 Try to guess how you think Kendrik would spend his time during his leave.
4 Can you think of times when you have felt the way you imagine Kendrik is feeling?
5 What happened the last time that you felt that way?
6 Can you describe someone like Kendrik?
7 If you were Kendrik's manager, what kinds of things would you consider doing?

The Case Information

Kendrik woke up with a headache – his third this week. He had not slept well for months. He turned over. He felt better in bed. He did not want to get out until absolutely the last minute – then he would not have time to think about whether or not to go to work. He would set himself another challenge – of catching the train in an even shorter time than yesterday. He did not often miss the train, though he was helped by the fact that it was usually a few minutes late. He tended to rely more and more on the train being late. In any case it was policy in the office to accept that trains running late was an acceptable reason for people arriving late at work. Not that the job was that bad. Secure, reasonable pay – almost certain promotion as you got older – if you kept your nose clean and your head down. He had told himself all this before. The fact was the job was so boring and tiring he never had much energy for anything else at the end of the day – except, perhaps, when there was a match to watch on TV. Then he would work quickly, try to get away promptly and usually try to find a new take-away on the way home and buy something to eat while the match was on. Same old thing, day in day out. Checking the same regulations – putting his initials against the same advice to the same people. They knew the answers anyway, before they asked him. But only he was allowed to initial these answers.

His family worried that his sick days and lateness and lethargy might lose his good job in the advisory service.

He decided to ring in and request three more days' leave – he didn't have much leave left. It seemed such a long time before the end of the year and by then he wouldn't have any leave left for a holiday – not that he would know what to do with it anyway.

Activity 15 Individual Learning Review: Reflective Thinking

Inner world thinking

What inner world thinking skills can you identify in the manager's work described in this chapter? Have any of the thinking skills you have identified emerged for the first time in this chapter? If so, add them to your accumulating model of the kinds of thinking skills that you think are useful to managers.

What things could you do to develop any of the thinking skills that you have just added to your model? What would be the first step?

Outer world conversations

What outer world conversational skills can you identify in the manager's work described in this chapter? Have any of the types of conversational skills you have identified emerged for the first time? If so, add them to your

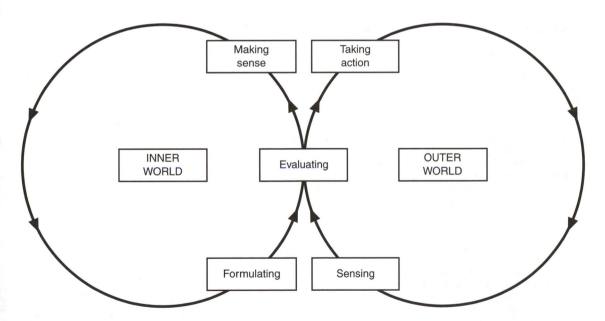

Figure 7.7 The thinking skills of the conversational manager

accumulating model of the kinds of conversational skills you think are useful to managers. What things could you do to develop any of these conversational skills which you have just added to your model? What would be the first step?

Activity 16 Individual Learning: Metacognitive Thinking

Metacognition

Look back through the Thinking and Learning Activities you have been asked to carry out in this chapter. What thinking skills were involved in each of these activities? For each type of thinking, write down how you were learning what you were learning, when you were learning to think in each of the different ways.

NOTES

1 Bennis, W. (1989) 'Leadership Theory and Administrative Behaviour: the Problem of Authority'. In *Administrative Science Quarterly*, vol. 4, p. 259.
2 Vroom, R. H. and Deci, E. L. (1992) *Management and Motivation*. Penguin.
3 Mullins, L. (1989) *Management and Organisational Behaviour*. Pitman, pp. 420–21.
4 Zaleznik, A. (1977) 'Managers and Leaders: Are They Really Different?' *Harvard Business Review*, May–June, p. 76.
5 McConkey, D. D. (1989) 'Are you an Administrator, a Manager or a Leader?'. *Business Horizons*, Sept.–Oct., p. 16.
6 Van Seter, D. A. (1991) 'The Evolution of Leadership Theory'. *Journal of Change Management*, vol. 3, p. 3.
7 See Bowden, A. O. (1927) 'A Study of the Personality of Student Leadership in US'. *Journal of Abnormal Psychology*, vol. 21, pp. 149–60.
8 Byrd, C. (1940) *Social Psychology*. Appleton-Century-Crofts.
9 Jenning, E. E. (1961) *An Anatomy of Leadership: Princes, Heroes and Supermen*. Harper.
10 Van Seter, op. cit.
11 French, J. and Raven, B. (1959) 'The Basis of Social Power', in Cartwright, D. (ed.) *Studies in Social Power*. University of Michigan Press.
12 Fleischman, E. A. and Bass, A. R. (1974) *Studies in Personnel and Industrial Psychology*. 3rd edn. Dorsey.
13 Lickert, P. (1961) *New Patterns of Management*. McGraw-Hill.
14 Fiedler, F. E. (1964) 'A Contingency Model of Leadership Effectiveness', in Berkowitz, L. (ed.) *Advances in Experimental Social Psychology*. Academic Press.
15 Vroom, V. H. and Yetton, P. W. (1973) *Leadership and Decision Making*. Pittsburgh University Press.
16 Pettigrew, A. and Whipp, R. (1992) *Managing Change for Competitive Success*. Basil Blackwell, p. 142.

17 Adair, J. (1983) *Action Centred Leadership*. Gower.
18 Van Seter, op. cit., para. 35.
19 Pfeffer, M. (1977) *Academy of Management Review*, vol. 2, pp. 104–12.
20 Schein, E. H. (1985) *Organisational Leadership and Culture*. Jossey-Bass.
21 Van Seter, op. cit., para. 37.
22 Roberts, N. (1985) 'Transforming Leadership, a Process of Collective Action'. *Human Relations*, vol. 38, p. 11.
23 Tichy, N. M. and Ulrich, D. (1984) in Kimberly, J. R. and Quinn R. E. (eds) *Managing Organizational Transitions*. Dow-Jones-Irwin Illinois.
24 Bennis, W. (1989) 'Managing the Dream'. *Journal of Organisational Change Management*, vol. 7, p. 7.
25 Ibid.
26 Peters, T. and Watermann, R. (1982) *In Search of Excellence*. Harper Row.
27 Simpson, P. and Beeby, M. (1993) 'Transformational Leadership in the Public Sector'. *Management Education and Development*, vol. 24, p. 328.
28 Kakabadse, A. *et al.* (1998) *Success in Sight – Visioning*. Thompson.
29 Senge, P. (1990) 'The Leader's New Work: Building Learning Organisations'. *Sloan Management Review*, vol. 32, no. 1, pp. 7–23.
30 Handy, C. (1994) *The Empty Raincoat – Making Sense of the Future*. Hutchinson.
31 Simpson and Beeby, op. cit., p. 318.
32 Pettigrew and Whipp, op. cit., p. 143.
33 Ibid., p. 144.
34 Zaleznik, A. (1990) 'The Leadership Gap'. *Academy of Management Executive*, vol. 4, no. 1, p. 60.
35 Congar, J. A. (1992) 'The Darker Side of Leadership'. *Harvard Business Review*, Jan.–Feb.
36 Zaleznik, op. cit.
37 Bennis, W. (1989) *Why Leaders Can't Lead*. Jossey-Bass, p. 41.
38 Nameki, M. (1992) 'Creating a Corporate Vision', *Long-Range Planning*, vol. 25, p. 56.
39 *Career Management and Succession in the Civil Service* (1992). HMSO.
40 Bogdanov, V. (1994) 'Can Government Be Run like a Business?' CIFRA, p. 80.
41 Adair, op. cit.
42 *Twenty Steps to Better Management* (1996). BBC Publications.
43 Vroom and Yetton, op. cit.
44 Skinner, B. F. (1974) *About Behaviorism*. Knopf.
45 Flynn, N. (1997) *Public Sector Management*. Prentice Hall.
46 Hull, C. L. (1943) *Principle of Behaviour. An Introduction to Behaviour Theory*. Appleton-Century-Crofts. Freud, S. (1962) *The Ego and the Id*. Norton (Originally published 1923).
47 Vroom, V. H. and Deci, E. L. (eds) *Management and Motivation*. Penguin.
48 Lewin, K. (1951) 'Intention, Will and Need'. In Rapaport, R. N. (ed.) *Organization and Pathology of Thought*. Columbia University Press.
49 Drucker, P. F. (1984) *Management Tasks, Responsibilities, Practices*. Harper Row.
50 Humble, J. W. (1972) *Management by Objectives*. Management Publications.

51 Mullins, L. (1996) *Management and Organisational Behaviour.* Pitman, p. 481.

52 See for example, Porter, L. W. and Lawler, E. E. (1968) *Managerial Attitudes and Performance.* R. D. Irwin.

53 McClelland, D. C. (1961) *The Achieving Society.* N. J. Van Nostrand.

54 Maslow, A. (1943) 'A Theory of Human Motivation'. *Psychological Review*, vol. 50, pp. 370–96.

55 Flynn, op. cit., p. 160.

56 See Buchanan, D. and Huczynski, A. (1997) *Organizational Behaviour.* Prentice-Hall.

57 *Journal of Health Services Managers* (1986), para. 28.

58 Keen, L. and Scase, R. (1996) *Local Government Studies*, vol. 24, no. 4, p. 182.

59 Dopson, L. and Stewart, J. (1990) 'What is Happening to British Management?' *British Journal of Management*, vol. 4, pp. 3–16.

60 Scase, R. and Goffee, R. (1986) 'Are the Rewards Worth the Effort? Changing Management Values in the 1980s'. *Personnel Review*, vol. 15, no. 4.

61 Scase, R. and Goffee, R. (1992) 'Organisational Change and the Corporate Career: The Restructuring of Manager's Job Aspirations'. *Human Relations Personnel Review*, vol. 45, no. 4, pp. 303–85.

62 Scase and Goffee (1992), op. cit.

63 Davidson, M. and Cooper, C. (1992) *Shattering the Glass Ceiling: The Woman Manager.* Paul Chapman.

64 Willis, M. (1990) 'Women and Men in Management', *Insight* (Oct.), p. 20.

65 Rosner, J. B. (1990) 'Ways Women Lead'. *Harvard Business Review*, Dec.–Jan., p. 120.

66 Powell, G. N. (1990) *Academy of Executive Management*, vol. 4, no. 3, p. 69.

67 Oliveres, F. (1991) 'Is It Time to Stop Talking about Gender Differences?', *Harvard Business Review*, Jan./Feb.

8

MANAGING INDIVIDUALS IN PUBLIC SERVICES

One of the symptoms of approaching nervous breakdown is the belief that one's work is terribly important, and that to take a holiday would bring disaster.

(Bertrand Russell 1872–1970, 'Conquest of Happiness')

LEARNING OUTCOMES

This chapter will enable the reader to:

- Trace the development of personnel management from welfare benevolence, industrial relations to employee relations.
- Consider the move from employee relationships to managing individuals.
- Understand the relationship between personnel planning, job analysis, person specifications, recruitment, selection, induction, health and safety, training and termination.
- Understand discipline and grievance.
- Understand the causes of stress and how to develop a stress management programme.
- Consider problems of public service employees who work in 'at risk' situations.
- Understand what is meant by equal opportunities and 'family friendly'.
- Understand how to form close working relationships with individuals at work.
- Reflect on the social entrepreneur.

INTRODUCTION

Public services are delivered by people. Given the large numbers of people involved and the multiplicity of associations, professional bodies and trades unions which represent them, the management of people in public services merits special consideration. Personnel management is that part of management concerned with people at work and their relationships within an enterprise. It seeks to bring together and develop employees who make up an enterprise, enabling each to make their own best contribution to its success. It seeks to provide fair terms and conditions of employment and satisfying work for those employed.[1]

In Chapter 6 we looked at managing people in groups. In this chapter we look at managing people as individuals. We will look at recruitment, induction, appraisal, health and safety, staff welfare, legal matters, grievance handling, discipline and termination of employment. We deal with training in detail in Chapter 13. We highlight aspects of managing individuals that are particularly problematic in public services. For example, we look at the safety of employees who work in situations where they are at risk from their clients and we explore how managers can form close working relationships with staff. We start by looking at personnel management generally, before looking at the particular needs of public services.

FROM WELFARE OFFICERS TO HUMAN RESOURCE MANAGERS

Historical Perspective

Torrington and Hall[2] trace the origins of personnel management to eighteenth-century social reformers who aimed to curb the exploitation and dehumanization of workers in urban factories during the Industrial Revolution. During this period, welfare officers were appointed. Welfare officers dispensed benefits to the least fortunate employees. This trend was continued into the nineteenth century by benevolent employers, leaders amongst whom were Quaker families such as the Cadburys, Rowntrees and Lever Brothers. They set up schemes for unemployment benefit, sickness pay and subsidized housing.

In 1913, an Institute of Welfare Officers was established at the Rowntree factory in York. Personnel management evolved in parallel with management thinking. As we saw in Chapter 1, scientific management spawned work studies which were aimed initially at obtaining a 'fair day's pay for a fair day's work', increasing both the productivity and the financial rewards of employees. Advocates of the human relations school applied behavioural sciences to areas such as selection, training and the motivation of staff. Torrington and Hall[3] refer to the personnel manager in this phase as the 'Humane Bureaucrat'. The personnel manager was learning to operate within a bureaucracy, serving organizational rather than paternalistic objectives, but still committed to a humanitarian role. Public services sought to be 'models of good practice' as employers, even before clearly identifiable personnel functions were established. This is seen as early as 1929. In evidence to the Tomlin Commission, the Civil Services Association boasted that they were passing on their experience so as to provide an 'example' to private employers throughout the country.[4]

Personnel Management

Personnel management evolved in response to the challenges posed by the increased size and complexity of organizations and by the growth of the labour movement. Trades union assertiveness led to an increasing role for personnel managers in industrial bargaining and in negotiating between workers and management. There was a steady growth in the development of consultation mechanisms. Newly established nationalized industries often had a statutory duty to negotiate with trades union representatives. In the UK, the government recognized the importance of the personnel function by encouraging training through university courses in personnel management.

Increasing international competition and anxiety over efficiency and productivity were factors which led to the growth of 'workforce planning' – then called manpower planning. This was concerned with determining what types and quantities of employees were required, both now and in the future, based on current and anticipated trends. On the basis of this information, action could be taken on recruitment, training and retraining, to ensure that supply met demand. As the name implied, this approach tended to view people as resources, to be deployed in the same way as other resources. It led to human asset accounting and skills audits. Both attempted to measure the value of the employee's contribution.[5]

Despite the labour-intensive and complex nature of public services, personnel management was not recognized as a separate management function until the 1970s. Prior to this, the management of the workforce was largely left in the hands of individual departments. In 1972 the Baines Report emphasized the need for public services to develop personnel departments, often called 'manpower services', employing highly graded personnel officers.[6] Baines was ambiguous about where personnel officers should stand in the public service hierarchy. He suggested that they should not be part of the chief officer group. In the UK, following the reorganization of local government in 1974, most authorities appointed personnel officers.

Human Resource Management

The most significant developments in personnel management in the last 50 years came in the 1980s, with the appearance of human resource management.[7] There is no consensus about the exact definition of human resource management. Needle[8] regarded it as an approach to managing people which focused on increasing productivity through greater employee commitment and through the development of skilled, flexible employees and a strong corporate culture (Box 8.1).

The Baines Report recommended the adoption of human resource management in public services. Baines placed a strong emphasis on the development of staff. Unfortunately, this proposal resulted in the creation of centralized and unresponsive personnel services which were obsessed with control.[10] Although it had been emphasized by Baines, scant attention was paid to training. There was little planning on staff matters. The major concern was uniformity in staff policies. The result was a system that was seen as slow, unresponsive and control-oriented. What was lost was the mediating function that had emphasized mutuality and interdependence between management and staff. Torrington and Hall saw human resource management as:

> directed mainly at management's need for human resources to be provided and deployed. Demand rather than supply is emphasized. There is greater emphasis on monitoring and control, than on mediation. It is totally identified with management interests. It is relatively distant from the workforce.[11]

The Situation in Western Europe

The emphasis on the 'manager's right to manage' has led some commentators to view human resource management negatively (Chapter 15). Flynn and Strehl are more enthusiastic. They concluded from a survey of seven western European countries that the development of human resource management was one of the most important contributions to the modernization of public services. They noted that expenditure had increased on training in such areas as leadership skills, performance appraisal and interpersonal skills.[12] They added a cautionary note that in German-speaking countries, legal constraints were impeding change in the way that people were managed in public services. Throughout Europe the growth of human resource management led to the move away from industrial relations to individual employee relations.

Box 8.1

HUMAN RESOURCE MANAGEMENT[9]

- Regards workers as resources to be managed proactively, bringing recruitment, training, appraisal and reward systems in line with corporate goals
- Promotes commitment to, rather than compliance with, corporate goals
- Is carried out by line managers rather than by personnel specialists
- Favours individual rather than collective dealings with staff

---

FROM INDUSTRIAL RELATIONS TO EMPLOYEE RELATIONS

Militancy in Public Services

In the 1970s in the UK, according to Leach,[13] traditional public service approaches to the management of staff began to change for two reasons: organizational change and growing militancy. The 1970s and 1980s were marked by increasing industrial unrest and militancy. Dissatisfaction among local government workers grew. This was due largely to reductions in public expenditure. A National Prices and Incomes Board was appointed which determined that increases in public sector pay levels should be below the rate of inflation. Between 1971–79 public sector pay increased by just 0.1 per cent, compared with 2.2 per cent for the whole economy.[14] Dissatisfaction among employees led to increases in the membership of public service trades unions and increases in industrial conflict. 1970 saw strikes by both dockers and dustmen and a work-to-rule by electrical power workers. In the winter of 1973–74 a state of emergency was called because of the threat of strikes by gas and electricity workers. The UK was forced into a three-day working week. Militancy in the public services included strike action by fire and ambulance services and strikes and overtime bans by members of the National Association of Local Government Officers (NALGO). The fact that emergency services and traditionally non-militant white-collar workers were willing to take industrial action demonstrated the depth of dissatisfaction among employees.

The Rise of Industrial Relations

In the UK the lack of any framework for local bargaining had been highlighted by the Donovan Commission in 1968. New local employee relations mechanisms were put into place and more sophisticated personnel management systems were developed. The National Union of Public Employees (NUPE) and NALGO developed extensive shop steward and employee representation systems for dealing with disputes. Local Joint Consultative Committees were set up to provide a platform for communication between trades union representatives and public service employers. Despite the Labour government's close links with the trades unions, industrial conflict in both the public and private sectors continued. These disputes were predominantly about levels of pay. They reached a climax in the 'Winter of Discontent' in 1978–79. This particularly harsh winter witnessed strikes by lorry drivers and industrial action by sewage workers, dustmen and ambulance workers. Liverpool gravediggers refused to bury the dead. These events ended the Labour government's prospects for re-election.

Curbing Trades Union Power

Mrs Thatcher's government was elected in 1979. She made it a priority to reduce the power of the trades unions, in both the public and private sectors. Mrs Thatcher's first Public Expenditure White Paper, published at the end of 1979, stated that public expenditure was at the heart of Britain's economic difficulties. The Conservative government was committed to reducing inflation and saw public sector pay rises as a major cause. According to Fryer,[15] the Thatcher government thought that it might be easier to impose wage restrictions on the public sector than on the private sector. This led to bitter disputes, cuts in public spending and privatization. Matters came to a head in the early 1980s when striking miners confronted Mrs Thatcher in what became the most sustained industrial dispute in the UK since the General Strike of 1926.

Reducing the power of trades unions was done through legislation, such as the 1984 Trades Union Act, and through organizational changes, such as the move away from national to more local bargaining. Moran[16] has analysed the fragmenting of collective bargaining in the UK prison service. In 1993, the prison service became an executive agency and private companies were invited to provide prison services. Moran identified wide variations in remuneration and terms of employment between private and public prisons. National pay bargaining was seen as an undesirable influence on free-market mechanisms. National pay bargaining rights were taken away from teachers, nurses and midwives and local pay bargaining was introduced. This move dissipated the bargaining power of the unions. Local management of schools (LMS) delegated financial control and staffing to school governing bodies, which now had the power to make decisions about appointments, dismissals and pay.

After the late 1970s, trades union membership began to decline generally. However, in 1992, approximately 72 per cent of UK public service workers were still members of trades unions. Membership ranged from nearly 90 per cent in the railways to around 55 per cent in the fire service and police service. According to Rose and Lawton,[17] human resource management had contributed to this decline.

The Right to Manage

During the 1980s, management reasserted a right to manage which had been lost during the 1970s.[18] Policies were developed that gave public service managers greater control over the workforce. By the mid 1980s most public services had developed policies on redeployment, early retirement and temporary contracts.[19] Having said that, few public services were willing to contemplate compulsory redundancy for full-time permanent employees. Many negotiated 'no compulsory redundancy' policies. Within this overall constraint, local authorities attempted to develop greater flexibility in the management of staff. Changes such as compulsory competitive tendering had a significant impact on working conditions and on the way people were managed in public services (Chapter 4). According to Rigg and Trehan,[20] compulsory competitive tendering introduced a degree of insecurity previously unknown in public services. In order to be competitive, public service employers were forced to accept lower pay. The introduction of fixed-term contracts for senior managers adversely affected job satisfaction and levels of motivation.[21] In 1999 Rose and Lawton[22] warned that short-term contracts and local pay agreements had eroded the ethos of public services.

Human Resource Management and the Ethos of Public Service

The move away from adversarial industrial relations towards management-dominated employee relations was a continuing feature of the management of people in public services until the mid-1990s. However, in 1997 the UK Labour government signed a European Social Charter – a charter which had been rejected by Mrs Thatcher because it emphasized workers' rights. A Low Pay Commission was established to implement a national minimum wage – an idea previously rejected because it would interfere with the free working of the market and Tony Blair said that there was 'no place for militant trades unionism or uncaring management'.[23]

In 1999 Beach and Story[24] suggested that trades unions might have to 'grasp the nettle' of individualism within human resource management. The aim, they thought, should be to develop an approach that would enable employees to embrace the ethos of public services while ensuring that they were treated fairly. One way was to acknowledge that managers needed to manage people as individuals. We turn now to the recruitment and selection of individuals.

RECRUITMENT AND SELECTION

In the western world the context for recruitment at the end of the century was a shortage of skilled labour. This was due, in part, to a declining birth rate. This 'demographic time bomb' had been largely ignored by employers.[25] Box 8.2 outlines the steps involved in recruiting and selecting individuals.

From Job Analysis to Job Description

Job analysis is used to collect and analyse information about the work that needs to be done. This information is used to describe: the kind of tasks that job holders will do, the areas for which they will be responsible, and the person to whom they will be accountable (Box 8.3).

In order to carry out the job as described, a person will need to have certain attributes in terms of education, experience, knowledge, skills and general disposition. This set of attributes is called the *person specification*.

From Job Specification to Person Specification

When defining a person specification, care must be taken to avoid defining too narrowly, or too broadly, the characteristics needed by someone to do the job.

Box 8.2

RECRUITMENT AND SELECTION: THE STEPS INVOLVED

- Reviewing the organization's strategic plan for staffing implications
- Auditing the skill and age profile of existing staff
- Succession planning, allowing for staff turnover
- Describing jobs for which staff will be needed
- Deciding appropriate terms and conditions
- Defining personnel specifications
- Advertising the available posts
- Deciding selection methods
- Communicating decisions

Too narrow a job description may exclude people who would be able to do the job. Over-specifying educational qualifications, for example, may result in the appointment of an overqualified person who will be bored with the job. The two formats most commonly used in public services are the Rogers seven-point plan and the Munro five-point plan. The Rogers seven-point plan includes physique, attainment, intelligence, aptitude, interests, disposition and circumstances. The latter must be handled with care to avoid contravening equal opportunities policies. The Munro five-point plan includes impact on others, qualifications, innate abilities, motivation and adjustment (Box 8.4).

Box 8.3

YOUTH SERVICES OFFICER: JOB DESCRIPTION

Job title	District Team Manager
Division	Life Long Learning
Responsible to	Area Manager
Responsible for	All Team Personnel

Job Purpose

To have oversight of local service delivery, working with and leading a team of full-time and part-time workers and administrative and clerical staff, to provide quality service with responsibility for a budget and most operational matters.

Main Tasks

- Ensure quality, effectiveness and efficiency in the delivery of the service
- Prepare, secure approval for, monitor and review an annual Team Plan
- Allocate and oversee resources in consultation with the Area Manager
- Manage team members and approve plans
- Manage District Administrative staff
- Attend and prepare reports for the District Advisory Committee
- Implement the Staff Development Policy
- Develop close working relationships with relevant services and agencies
- Advise on service developments

Box 8.4

YOUTH SERVICES OFFICER: PERSON SPECIFICATION

Personal Attributes		**Knowledge/Skills/Abilities**	
E = Essential D = Desirable		Knowledge of current issues	E
		Ability to communicate verbally	E
Qualifications		Ability to communicate in writing	E
		Ability to set own work priorities	E
Youth and Community Work	E	Ability to manage and motivate staff	E
Management	D	Financial management and budgetary skills	E
		Ability to work well with limited supervision	E
Experience			
Substantial management of staff	E		
Preparation and monitoring Business Plans	D		
Report writing	E		

The person specification helps to determine the terms and conditions which need to be offered to attract applications from the type of person specified. Increasingly, the terms and conditions offered may include part-time working, short-term contracts and flexible working hours. By 1995, 85 per cent of 249 local authorities surveyed had policies on flexible working.[26] In public services there was an increasing trend towards fixed-term contracts.

Attracting and Selecting Candidates

In order to fill a vacant post, organizations need to attract sufficient numbers of people with the potential to fill the vacancy. Many public services are committed to promoting equal access to employment opportunities, so that the workforce is representative of the community which it seeks to serve. An example would be advertising a post in the language of a local ethnic minority in order to encourage applications from a section of the community which was under-represented in the workforce. A small panel will go through the applications and identify candidates who meet the essential requirements for the job. If there are too many candidates to interview, then those candidates who meet the desirable requirements for the job as well as the essential requirements will be invited to undergo a further selection process.

The Selection Process

Although much criticized, interviews are widely used. Interviews can be one-to-one, sequential or with a panel. Figure 8.1 suggests the sequence in which questions might be asked.

Questions can be planned by considering each aspect of the person specification. Plan to use open questions. Do not use questions that can easily be answered by 'yes' or 'no', unless the candidate's answers are vague, incomplete or inconsistent. Candidates can be asked to describe things they have done, which demonstrate that they possess specific skills and attributes. The open questions used should be the same for all candidates. A balanced interview is more likely if there is more than one interviewer,

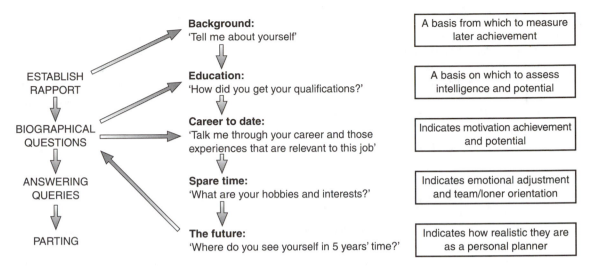

Figure 8.1 An interview sequence

Source: Beardwell and Holden (1994)

in which case, some mutually understood method of scoring each candidate against each aspect of the person specification should be agreed in advance by all the interviewers.

Make sure that candidates are treated as guests from the moment they arrive. The waiting area must be comfortable. Most candidates would appreciate the use of a mirror. Tell them where the nearest toilet is. The setting for the interview should be carefully prepared to ensure that there will be no interruptions or distracting noises. If possible do not interview from behind a desk or table. After establishing rapport (see later), try to get the candidate to talk about themselves, relatively unprompted, from their childhood to the present day. Ask them about their hopes for the future. Take notes. On balance this is better than failing to remember much about the candidate after a day of interviewing. If, however, the candidate starts to talk about something personal that is evidently distressing, put your pen down. The most natural form of prompt is 'Tell me about . . .' followed by a pause. Try not to break this pause for thought. If you only get a short reply, simply repeat their reply with a rising intonation – indicating curiosity and that you wish the candidate to elaborate. Avoid questions that 'lead the witness',

in effect telling the candidate what answer you expect. Do not show disapproval at the candidate's answers or bring them back to the point too sharply if they digress. Some people respond to interview nerves by being over-talkative. Try 'Can you summarize the main points about . . . ?' or 'What were the key events in . . . ?' Check openly through your notes before you let the candidate go, clarifying any points as you do so. Candidates like to feel that the interview was thorough. Tell the candidate about the next step or the next action that will be taken.

Other Methods of Selection

References are an aid to selection, though only as a pointer to eliminating some candidates. No one is likely to ask someone to act as a referee if they do not think that the referee will write something good about them. Individual and group tasks and work-related tests are a better way of providing candidates with an opportunity to demonstrate that they have the ability to do the job. For example, a task that requires a manager to deal with an in-tray containing memos, letters and reports. This type of exercise can be used to assess the candidate's ability to make appropriate decisions under pressure, to deal with difficult situations, to organize and to prioritize. Persistency, energy, motivation and willingness are harder to assess and may be more important. Once someone has been employed, it is easier to develop skills and knowledge than it is to change attitudes or general disposition.

A range of psychometric tests is available. Psychometric tests require trained administrators. The results should be interpreted with the candidates. They remain controversial, particularly when they claim to measure personality. There is evidence that psychometric tests disadvantage candidates from non-European cultures.[27] Tests of aptitude or manual dexterity are also available. Assessment centres often use all of the techniques described here.

Judging the Candidate: Avoiding Perceptual Distortions

The job application and the interview will yield much information about the candidate. This information is used to decide which candidate best fits the job. Every effort must be made to ensure that irrelevant or distorted evidence is screened out. We talk later about the impact of first impressions. Judge intelligence on achievement not on appearance or manner. Do not, for example, rate people wearing spectacles as more intelligent. Be cautious about intelligence tests. They measure only three, or at best four facets of intelligence, whereas Garner[28] has identified seven and Horne and Wootton[29] have identified 17 thinking skills that contribute to intelligent behaviour. Intelligence is a reasonable determinant of eligibility for occupational groups such as manual, clerical, technical, semi-professional, professional and academic, but it does not correlate with performance within them. Do not judge ability to write well from letters of application. People who cannot write will get other people to write their applications. If writing is important to the job, test it on the spot. The best way to judge motivation and likelihood that the candidates will stay is from the questions they ask. Be wary if there is a pattern of unfinished tasks and frequent job changes.

Beware of perceptual distortions that may result in unfounded and unsubstantiated judgement of the candidate. One barrier is stereotyping. Stereotyping involves forming opinions on the basis of a few facts which are interpreted in a biased way. Typically, stereotyping occurs when traits are assumed on the basis of a person's gender, race, nationality, age, accent or class. For example: all women are nurturing; all Germans are hard-working; all Afro-Caribbeans are lazy; all Scots are mean; all accountants are boring, etc.

Another perceptual distortion is known as the Halo Effect. This involves making judgements based on one favourable or unfavourable aspect of the person. For example, an aspect of dress, speech, voice, face or posture. Depending on whether the interviewer likes or dislikes the characteristic, they project a positive or negative 'halo' on to the candidate. Once this halo has been formed, information that confirms the halo will be noted and information that denies it will be filtered out. Interviewers need to be aware that they are likely to give people who are like them a more positive halo than those who are different from them.

Following Through

Every attempted recruitment is a public relations exercise (Chapter 12). All advertising and documentation should be considered as public relations material. Unsuccessful applicants may be negatively disposed to your organization. Do not give them ammunition. Courteous acknowledgements, prompt reports on progress, prompt settlement of expenses claims, and offers of feedback after interviews can all help to avoid negative messages being taken back to the groups to which your candidates belong. You never know when you will next require their services. Public services are highly networked and it does not pay to make enemies, political or professional. Accurate communications with successful candidates are equally important. Unclear arrangements about car parking, office sharing, induction, mentoring and administration generally, quickly dissipate the initial energy and enthusiasm which new recruits usually bring. Documentation concerned with contracts of employment, pension schemes and procedures for handling grievance and disciplinary matters all require specialist handling.

INDUCTION

Induction is the process of ensuring that recruits settle into their jobs quickly, happily and effectively.[30] Induction aims to:

- Familiarize new employees with jobs so that they do not feel out of place
- Ensure employees become efficient rapidly
- Promote commitment to the organization

Induction varies from job to job but certain topics will be of interest to any new employee. These can be discussed using an induction checklist or dealt with in an induction pack. In local government departments which employ large numbers of staff, the personnel section may run an induction programme. However, it is the line manager's responsibility to ensure that the relevant topics are covered. If, for example, a new employee is expected to complete a probationary period, the line manager should explain how this will be assessed and what assistance will be available during the probationary period. Generally, induction includes:

- A tour of the workplace
- Introduction to other managers and staff
- The issue of relevant documentation, e.g. employee handbook, identity pass and rule book
- An explanation of disciplinary grievance and sickness procedure
- Familiarization with telephone and computer systems and with safety procedures

Induction may also be relevant when existing employees transfer to a new job within the same public service organization. Some categories of recruit may have specific induction needs. School leavers, or young people, or new graduates, for example, may lack any experience of full-time paid employment. 'Returner workers' will almost certainly be returning to a changed work environment. A special induction programme may be required to restore their confidence.

Soon after employees have been inducted, they will be expected to perform the duties described in their job description to acceptable levels of performance. In order to do this, training needs may have to be identified and met. We deal with how managers can analyse training needs and design and deliver training and learning programmes in Chapter 14. How managers can measure and manage individual performance is dealt with in Chapter 11. Managing performance may cause difficulties to occur between individual employees and their managers. Procedures for handling grievances or disciplinary matters, must be followed, lest subsequent actions be brought against the organization under civil or industrial law. The following section examines issues that may need to be addressed. Advice must always be sought.

Discipline and Dismissal

Dictionary definitions of discipline refer to training, regulation, a system of obedience and subordination to rules of conduct and orderliness. Discipline implies the regulation of human activity in order to produce controlled performance. Torrington and Hall[31] distinguish between three different types of discipline: managerial discipline, team discipline and self-discipline (see Figure 8.2).

In the UK an Advisory Conciliation and Arbitration Service (ACAS) publishes codes of practice based on an Employment Protection Act (1979). In 1977, in order to encourage employers and employees to manage discipline in a reasonable manner, ACAS published a Code of Practice entitled *Disciplinary Practice and Procedures in Employment* from which we have extracted the features of a good disciplinary procedure (Box 8.5). A misdemeanour should not always result in a disciplinary action. Figure 8.3 describes the stages in deciding if disciplinary action is appropriate. If it is decided to proceed with disciplinary action, then a number of steps must be followed. These are summarized in Figure 8.4.

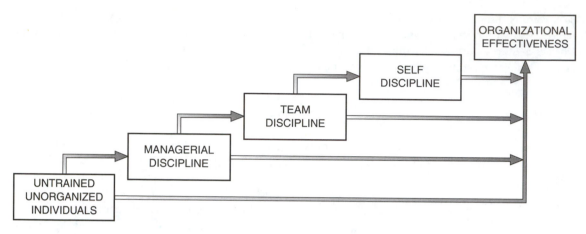

Figure 8.2 Three forms of discipline

Source: Torrington and Hall (1991)

Box 8.5

FEATURES OF A GOOD DISCIPLINARY PROCEDURE

A Good Disciplinary Procedure Should . . .

- Be in writing
- Specify to whom employees need to apply
- Provide for matters to be dealt with quickly
- Indicate disciplinary actions may be taken
- Specify levels of management authority
- Provide for individuals to be informed of complaints against them
- Provide individuals with opportunities to state their case before decisions are taken

- Give individuals the right to be accompanied by a trades union representative or a friend
- Ensure that disciplinary action is not taken until the case has been fully investigated
- Ensure that individuals are given an explanation of any penalty imposed on them
- Provide for a right of appeal and specify the procedures that are to be followed

---

Box 8.6 summarizes the main stages of a formal disciplinary interview.

Grievance Procedures

If discipline is what the organization can do to the employer, then grievance is what the employee can do to the organization. Organizations make mistakes and employees may wish to register a grievance. A grievance is dissatisfaction so strong that an employee raises the matter with senior management or with a trades union representative. Grievances arise for many reasons: changes in working practices, bad decisions, personal attitudes of managers to staff, favouritism, victimization, sexual or racial harassment or abuse. Grievances may be collective – a whole department may feel aggrieved. We are concerned here only with individual grievances. Every

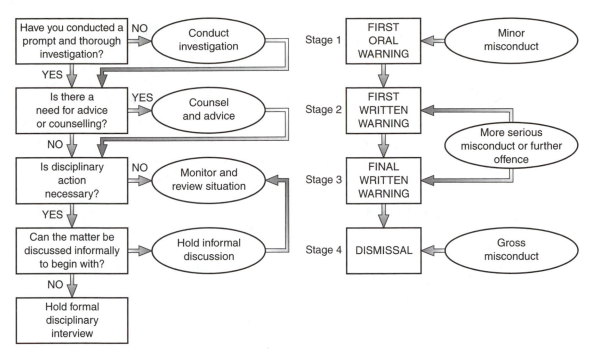

Figure 8.3 Determining whether discipline is necessary   *Figure 8.4* Stages in the formal disciplinary process

---

Box 8.6

CHECKLIST FOR A FORMAL DISCIPLINARY INTERVIEW

Before Interview

- Are all the relevant facts available, including any appropriate statements?
- Confirm in writing the purpose of the disciplinary meeting
- Arrange for a witness of the proceedings to be present
- Look up rules, procedures, previous records
- Define the nature of the complaint
- Clarify options available
- Inform employees of their rights
- Make sure witnesses are available
- Consider any excuses and check their veracity

During Interview

- Introduce people
- Specify the alleged offence
- Listen to employee's version of events
- Ask who, what, when, how, with whom?
- Ask employee what should be done
- Explain what will happen next

After Interview

- Lodge records
- Inform employee of decision in writing
- Inform employees of their right to appeal
- Follow up on sanctions or improvements

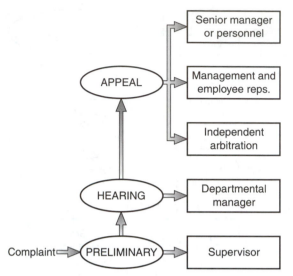

Figure 8.5 Formal grievance procedure

effort should be made to resolve grievances at the lowest possible level. Figure 8.5 summarizes the steps to be followed in a formal grievance procedure.

Box 8.7 summarizes the stages that should be followed in a formal grievance interview.

Managers may need to terminate someone's employment for other than disciplinary reasons. Sometimes, for example, redundancy or redeployment is inevitable.

Redundancy and Redeployment

Under UK employment law, redundancy can take place when an employer:

- Ceases to carry on the business in which the employer was engaged.
- Closes down a workplace.
- No longer requires people with particular skills.
- Needs fewer employees to carry out the same or less work.[32]

Most publicly owned public service organizations try to minimize the need for redundancies. Many have a policy of 'no compulsory redundancy' (Box 8.8).

Redeployment may be by offering alternative employment within the same organization. This may mean an adjustment in salary and may require retraining. Often earnings are guaranteed or salary levels are protected in the new post. If the employee refuses the offer of alternative employment, then the employer can withhold redundancy payments. Sometimes tribunals are used to decide

---

Box 8.7

CHECKLIST FOR A FORMAL GRIEVANCE INTERVIEW

Before Interview

- Check grievance policy and procedures
- Establish nature of dissatisfaction
- Check background information

During Interview

- Discover the nature of the dissatisfaction
- Allow the grievance to be fully aired
- Elicit feelings as well as facts
- Probe all the relevant details

- Ask employee their views
- Do not judge at this stage

After Interview

- Investigate
- Decide action
- Communicate decisions
- Inform about right of appeal
- Monitor attitudes and behaviours
- Check periodically with those involved

Box 8.8

ALTERNATIVES TO REDUNDANCY

- Making use of natural wastage over an extended period of time
- Consulting to generate alternatives
- Part-time working and/or job shares
- Offering early retirement
- Asking for voluntary redundancies
- Not renewing short-term contracts
- Freezing recruitment
- Redeployment

---

whether an offer is suitable and whether a refusal is reasonable.

Redundancy may be necessary when funding for a public service has been withdrawn or cut or when services have been reconfigured and certain jobs no longer exist. Great care must be taken when selecting people for redundancy. In 1994 the European Court of Justice ruled that employers must consult either a recognized trades union or an elected employee representative, if redundancies are compulsory. The Collective Redundancies and Transfer of Undertakings Regulations of 1995 in the UK require employers to consult when 20 or more employees are affected by compulsory redundancy. Many public service organizations have a pre-agreed procedure which sets out criteria for selecting people for redundancy. A common criterion is 'last in first out'. This means that employees with the shortest length of employment will be selected for redundancy first. This may seem fair but one disadvantage of this method is that it may terminate the employment of those with the most up-to-date knowledge and skills.

Individuals who have been selected for redundancy should be told why redundancies are necessary and why they have been selected. Any requirements during the notice period should be explained and redundancy payments should be discussed. Employers are expected to compensate employees when they make them redundant. In the UK, redundancy payments are calculated according to age, length of service and weekly pay. For example, for each year of employment in which the employee was aged 22 or over but was below the age of 41, he or she will get one week's pay. Employees who have worked for more than two years for their employer, and who are to be made redundant, have a statutory right to time off in order to look for other jobs, or to retrain in order to improve their employment prospects. Retirement, especially early retirement on health grounds, may be governed by the rules of pension schemes or superannuation schemes. Finally, where possible, anyone leaving the organization should be interviewed about their experience of working in the organization. It is better if such interviews are carried out by someone other than their line manager.

A common welfare issue that managers are required to manage is stress among their staff. In the next section we consider how managers can prevent excessive stress in the workplace. We begin with an extract from a conversation with Roger Roghton, a social worker who retired early on the grounds of ill health (Box 8.9).

MANAGING STRESS IN THE WORKPLACE

Excessive Stress

Roger's case is not an isolated one. In a five-year study of the effects of organizational change in publicly and privately owned organizations, Worral and Cooper[33] found that public service managers felt under constant pressure to improve performance. According to Philip Cox, an occupational psychologist, stress levels in public services are likely to be

Box 8.9

CONVERSATION WITH ROGER ROGHTON
'A BURNT-OUT CASE'

Tony: Tell me Roger, how did your situation come about?

Roger: I worked for Social Services for 17 years. My caseload was clients who were all mentally disabled and were being resettled in the community. At first I was full of it, I loved it.

Tony: So what went wrong?

Roger: Things started to go wrong when my department introduced 'Total Quality Management'. It started with a big conference which was like some kind of religious revival. Someone from personnel kept on about commitment to the organization and how we would lose our jobs if we weren't committed to quality. An academic gave a speech about change and how normal it was. At the end of the conference we all had to sing 'Simply the best.' It made me puke!

Tony: What happened next?

Roger: Two of my team mates were made redundant. The department had already been broken up into purchasers and providers. This destroyed a lot of close, long-term working relationships. There was a lot of animosity between staff. We felt unsupported and isolated.

Tony: Didn't they go to the union?

Roger: I was the union shop steward. I fought against the redundancies and the changes. Management decided I was a trouble-maker, which wasn't true, actually. My line manager made my life hell. If I was off sick for a day, she would summon me to her office. She would ask me all sorts of questions that were none of her business. Once she suggested that I had drunk too much the night before and was not really ill at all. She was probably right. I couldn't sleep without a drink or a joint. It helped me unwind and relax. I was worried

about work. I was under a lot of pressure. Even though there were only two of us, we still had as many clients as before. More even. It was like a conveyor belt. A never-ending list of people. The job had become unmanageable. I was determined not to let my clients down. No wonder I needed a drink!

Tony: Did you talk to anyone about the workload, or the drinking?

Roger: Not really. They were only bothered about meeting quotas and activity levels. One of my clients died while under my care. I was gutted. I didn't get any support. No counselling, nothing. One night I cracked. I went off duty and never came back. Fifteen years of trying to do a good job, all that training, what a waste. I went on long-term sick. I had a lot of trouble with my stomach. I was diagnosed as having a stomach ulcer. The doctor said it was probably due to stress. He was probably right. He told me that I should stop drinking and stop smoking. That only increased the stress. I felt caught in a vicious circle. I smoked and drank too much because of the stress I was under. Drink and drugs didn't really help – they made things worse – but I could not see this at the time. My relationships also suffered. I must have been awful to live with. I almost lost my partner. We had been together 15 years. I don't know how she stayed.

Tony: What was your organization's policy on stress?

Roger: We all got a leaflet: '100 Ways of Alleviating Stress'. It said things like 'stroke a pet' and 'take five minutes to look at a cloud', 'imagine your worries drifting away'. I might sound angry now. But then, I just swallowed

> my anger and drank. Instead of getting angry, I got depressed. It's a good job I didn't get angry then – no knowing what I might have done to the bastards.
>
> **Tony**: So what did you do?
>
> **Roger**: Personnel did a deal and pensioned me off
>
> sick. They said I was lucky to get such a good deal. I was 36 then and I haven't been able to get social work since then. Who wants a social worker who can't handle stress?
>
> **Tony**: Who do you blame?
>
> **Roger**: Management.

greater than in the private sector because of poorer pay and conditions and poorer management practices.[34] In public services, stress is a major source of lost days at work. In 1999 the Confederation of British Industries (CBI) estimated that stress was the second most common cause of work-related illness. In 1999, stress caused 1 in 5 employees to be absent for a total nationally of 6.7 million working days. The UK Health and Safety Executive[35] estimated that stress-related illness cost £7 billion in 2000.

In November 1994 John Walker, a senior social worker with Northumberland County Council in the UK, won compensation because he had suffered stress at work and his employer was judged to have been negligent. In most countries employers owe a legal duty of care to their employees. In the past this has been interpreted as a duty to protect them from physical hazards, such as exposure to toxic substances or unsafe working conditions. Mr Walker's case extends the duty of care to include protection against threats to their mental well-being, including stress. Mr Walker had suffered a nervous breakdown. On returning to work, no adjustment was made to his workload. He suffered a second nervous breakdown and was subsequently dismissed on the grounds of ill health. Northumberland County Council was deemed to have been negligent because it failed to foresee that Mr Walker's workload was a potential hazard. Mr Walker claimed £200,000 in damages against his former employer.[36] In 2000 the UK High Court awarded Robert McLeod, a former housing officer in Hampshire, £720,000. He claimed that the stress of being bullied by his line manager, a woman, had caused him to have a mental breakdown.

What Is Stress?

The word 'stress' is derived from the Latin word *stringere*, which means to draw tight. Until the eighteenth century it was associated with adversity, hardship or affliction. It was later used by physicists to describe forces exerted on an object causing it to change shape or volume. The changes in shape or volume were called strains. Hence the term 'stresses and strains'.[37] In biology stresses are a pattern of physiological and bio-chemical responses that used to have survival value in prehistoric times. The biological changes associated with stress provided prehistoric people with the extra energy they needed in order to deal with life-threatening situations. The hormones released during stressful experiences prepared them to fight or take flight. Stress is sometimes referred to as the 'flight or fight' response. When the brain perceives immediate threat, it triggers the adrenal glands to secrete stress hormones like adrenaline. Respiration rates increase to provide the blood with more oxygen, the heart speeds up to pump more blood into muscles, sugar pours into the blood to provide extra energy, and muscles tense. Today the immediate threat is unlikely to be from dangerous animals: sabre-toothed tigers and hairy mammoths are only found in museums. The threats today are more likely to be psychological than physical. Modern-day experiences that commonly provoke stress include divorce, sitting exams, meeting deadlines and dealing with aggressive bosses. Despite the fact that these do not pose threats to our physical well-being, the body responds exactly as if they did. The body prepares for fight or flight, but is unable to discharge this surge of energy by engaging in vigorous physical activity. This can result in excessive levels of unrelieved stress and, as we saw in the conversation with Roger the social worker, in a tragic waste of human lives. People with certain types of personality are more prone to suffer from excessive stress.

Personality Type and Stress

Without some stress we would not be sufficiently stimulated to carry out the minimum activities necessary for survival. But at some period in their lives, most people will suffer from excessive stress. Researchers have identified a number of life events that are major causes of excessive stress.[38] At the top of their list is the death of a spouse, moving home, taking out a high mortgage and organizing a family holiday. They also note that poor relationships with managers or supervisors, overwork and under-employment are also sources of stress. Stress may be an inevitable part of life, but certain types of people are more prone to suffer from excessive stress. Friedman and Roseman[39] claim to identify two personality types – Type A and Type B – whose response to stress was different (Box 8.10).

Box 8.10

PERSONALITY AND STRESS

Type A Personalities (More stress prone)	Type B Personalities (Less stress prone)
Restless	Calm
Aggressive	Easy-going
Very alert	Very relaxed
Tense face	Speaks slowly
Moves quickly	Moves slowly
Needs to achieve	Less ambitious
Works quickly	Works steadily
Impatient	Rarely impatient
Competitive	Co-operative

The researchers discovered that Type A personalities were three times more likely to suffer from coronary problems than Type B personalities. Within some industrial and commercial organizations, some characteristics of Type A people are sought after, for example, their ability to work long hours under pressure. In public service organizations, however, Type A people can be dysfunctional. Usually they find it hard to relax or to get their clients to relax. Often they are hostile and impatient, generating stress among colleagues.

Stress, Distress and Positive Stress

Hans Selye[40] distinguishes between 'distress' and 'positive stress'. Distress is the negative condition that occurs in individuals as a result of their being unable to cope with the demands being made on them. When people are happy and efficient and find their work challenging, they are 'positively stressed'. If workloads or responsibilities are increased beyond an 'optimal level, then there is likely to be a deterioration in their performance at work. There is a difference between 'positive stress', which is the excitement experienced by people who expect to succeed, and 'negative stress', which is the fear experienced by those who expect to fail. Managers need to manage the stress experienced by those for whom they are responsible. This requires an ability to identify the symptoms of excessive stress, so that appropriate action can be taken when stress goes beyond optimal levels. The positive and negative effects of stress are illustrated in Figure 8.6.

Stress and Change

In Chapters 2 and 3 we looked at the manager's role in implementing changes in public services. One of the side effects of change is increased stress for the people affected. Horne and Wootton[41] have completed a study of the debilitating effect stress can have on thinking skills and on measured IQ, which can drop by up to 14 points. For those for whom

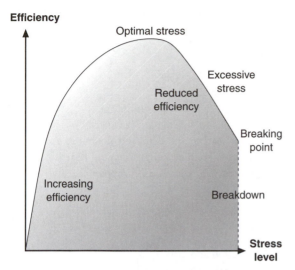

Figure 8.6 The positive and negative effects of stress

The Symptoms of Excessive Stress

According to the Stress Foundation,[42] managers must take seriously any symptoms of excessive stress. These are shown in Box 8.11.

Apart from these physical and psychological symptoms, people who are stressed beyond their optimum level may have difficulty in concentrating when making important decisions. They may hide inadequacy behind lots of activity. They are likely to have higher than average levels of absenteeism.

Combating Excessive Stress

By far the best way of coping with excessive stress is to prevent it. If a job does not suit someone they may experience excessive stress, whereas someone else might find the same job a healthy challenge. You may need to redeploy some staff. By watching carefully for physical and psychological symptoms, managers can learn to recognize excessive stress.

As we saw during our learning conversation with Roger, some people smoke, drink or take drugs, in an attempt to relieve the symptoms of excessive stress. These attempts are self-defeating. They reduce work effectiveness, causing backlogs in work to increase. Since cigarette and alcohol contribute to 25 per cent of deaths and chronic illness, smoking and drinking to relieve stress increase the incidence of stress-related illness. For most people, reducing excessive stress means either changing lifestyle or work style, or changing attitudes and priorities. Lifestyle changes can be brought about through life planning activities (Chapter 14). In the next section we consider a four-stage approach.

stress is likely to turn to 'distress', it can be helpful for them to know in advance how they are likely to feel as a consequence of change. It helps to increase their sense of feeling in control. Feeling out of control is a major contributor to stress. Managers can warn them that the pattern associated with change is likely to be shock, anxiety, denial, blaming, realization, adaptation and acceptance (Chapter 2). People will be able to recognize the stage they are at by the kinds of conversations they find themselves having. Table 8.1 gives typical extracts from the different kinds of 'self talk' associated with different stages of change. The stress which managers generate at each of these stages can be reduced by following the processes described in Chapter 2.

Table 8.1 Using self-talk to track stress during change

Stage	Extracts from typical conversations
Shock	'They must be joking.' 'It can't be true.' 'They are going to do what!'
Realization	'This is going to effect my . . .' 'This will mean that . . .'
Denial	'They'll never get it through.' 'It's impossible, illegal . . .'
Blaming	'It's X's fault.' 'If it wasn't for Y, then . . .'
Adaptation	'Provided that I . . .' 'It could be better if . . .'
Acceptance	'Well at least I'll get . . .' 'If you can't beat them . . .'

Box 8.11

THREE LEVELS OF STRESS: THE SYMPTOMS

Level 1

- Sighing
- Sweating
- Biting nails
- Speeding up
- Talking quickly
- Drumming fingers
- Twitching eyebrows
- Licking and biting lips
- Eating and drinking faster
- Tension in neck and shoulders
- Working at high speed, for long periods

Level 2

- Irritability
- Blurred vision

- Rashes and allergies
- Tension, headaches and migraine
- Insomnia and chronic lack of energy
- Comfort eating and drinking alcohol to excess
- Symptoms such as indigestion and heartburn
- Constipation, diarrhoea, impotence, allergy, eczema

Level 3

- Depression and anxiety
- Physical and mental breakdown
- Palpitations, chest pains, high blood pressure and cardiac problems

A Four-stage Approach to Reducing Stress

Hart[43] suggests that there are basically four approaches to stress management: the physiological approach, the behavioural approach, the psychological approach and the environmental approach. Each of these can be viewed as part of a chain. The different links in the chain combine to generate stress. In order to deal effectively with stress, managers need to understand each link in the stress chain (Figure 8.6).

Physiological Approaches to Stress

According to Hart,[44] this is the most popular approach to handling stress. Various techniques can be used to reduce excessive physiological arousal. These techniques attempt to counteract the biological stress responses we discussed earlier.

For example, one technique involves progressive muscle relaxation. This involves learning a series of exercises aimed at relaxing the body's 16 major muscle groups. By becoming aware of tensions in,

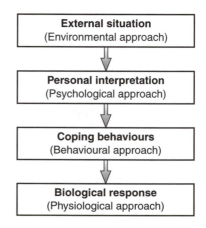

Figure 8.7 The stress chain

for example, the neck and shoulders, people can deliberately reduce tension. This results in feelings of calm. People who find it difficult to relax their muscles may be helped by using bio-feedback machines. Bio-feedback machines provide people with information about how tensed or relaxed their muscles are. By becoming more aware of their physiological responses, people can learn how to control them.

Another way to shift your body from a stressful mode to a calm mode is by practising deep relaxation. Deep relaxation is an easy but powerful way of countering the flight-or-fight response. It takes 5 to 15 minutes. Find a quiet place and sit comfortably. Close your eyes and concentrate your attention on the movement of your breath as it enters and leaves your body. After each exhalation, silently repeat a word or a phrase, allowing yourself to feel calm and relaxed as you exhale. Each time your mind wanders or your concentration is broken, ease your attention back to the smooth and relaxing rhythm of your breathing. Relaxation can increase the ability to concentrate and reduce blood pressure, pulse rate and muscular tension.[45]

Another non-chemical way to reduce physiological stress is to use your imagination. The aim is to project relaxing mental images into your mind's eye. It is possible to use this approach to take several 'mini-mental vacations' during the course of a day by visualizing pleasant and calming scenes. According to Hart,[46] replaying old pleasurable memories, or creating new ones, can decrease blood pressure and adrenaline flow. Finally, any kind of light to vigorous physical exercise, jogging, swimming, weight training or aerobics, for example, is another way to fortify the body against the harmful effects of stress. Box 8.12 summarizes some of the activities we have identified which reduce the biological effects of stress.

The stress management techniques we have described here help to counteract the physiological effects of stress. Used in isolation, they are inadequate. They fail to address the behaviours that caused the stress in the first place.

Box 8.12

PHYSICAL APPROACHES TO REDUCING STRESS

- Joining a gym
- Cycling to work
- Using the stairs – avoid lifts
- Regulating your alcohol intake
- Taking a short nap in the afternoon
- Beginning a yoga or meditation class
- Encouraging lunchtime runs or aerobics
- Taking a physical weekend break
- Avoiding foods high in sugar, salt, white flour, saturated fats or chemical additives

---

Behavioural Approaches to Stress

By managing their time more effectively, people can reduce stress (Chapter 14). Time management is an example of a behavioural approach to managing stress. Behavioural approaches are particularly useful in managing stress that is caused by other people. For example, people who demand your time and try to offload work on you. By being trained to be more assertive – not more aggressive – people can learn to say 'no' to things that might precipitate stressful situations. Good problem-solving skills and decision-making skills can be developed in order to prevent excessive stress (Chapter 12). Box 8.13 summarizes some behavioural techniques.

Psychological Approaches to Stress

Typically, stress originates in a person's external environment. It starts with an event or a situation. External factors leading to stress can include anything bad that happens at work or at home, e.g. delayed deliveries, unco-operative clients. Given the same stressful situation, not everyone reacts with an

Box 8.13

BEHAVIOURAL APPROACHES TO REDUCING STRESS

- Manage your time
- Tackle one thing at a time
- Be assertive and learn to say no
- Allocate time in relation to priorities
- Ask for help and be receptive to it
- Learn to communicate, share problems, avoid isolation, build networks
- Establish objectives and priorities for your working life and your private life

Box 8.14

PSYCHOLOGICAL APPROACHES TO REDUCING STRESS

- Self-reliance
- Reducing perfectionism
- Providing and giving positive feedback
- Accepting you will always be unpopular with someone
- Acknowledging problems as they appear
- Not suppressing feelings, acknowledging them, sharing them with others
- Consulting your values: in the grander scheme of things, does it really matter?
- Catastrophe analysis: what is the worst thing that could happen – could you survive it?

equally stressed response. According to Hart,[47] differences in interpretation will affect the amount of stress a person experiences. How people perceive and then respond to a situation can either increase or decrease stress levels. For example, people who dwell on the negative aspects of a situation experience more stress than people who see the negatives but also try to focus on the positives. There are a variety of psychological approaches to seeing negative experiences in a less stressful way (Box 8.14).

Another way of changing people's perception in order to reduce stress is called 'rational cognitive restructuring'. Rational cognitive restructuring reduces stress by modifying unrealistic expectations and beliefs. Most people hold unrealistic, stress-inducing beliefs, even though they may not be aware of them. For example, people may think 'If I don't receive approval and respect from others, then I'm worthless' or 'If I don't get it right, I'm a total failure'. Another example of a stress-inducing belief is captured in the epigram by Bertrand Russell that opened this chapter:

> One of the symptoms of approaching nervous break-down is the belief that one's work is terribly important and that to take a holiday would bring disaster.
>
> (Bertrand Russell, 'Conquest of Happiness')

A similar psychological approach to stress management is called 'self-statement modification'. Basically this approach involves substituting calming thoughts for stress-inducing thoughts. It teaches people to replace negative 'self-talk' with 'positive self-talk'. This suggests that conversations – either internal dialogues, or preferably conversations with another person – can prevent or reduce stress.

A Conversational Approach to Managing Stress

When you are excessively stressed, not even distressed, the support of others is invaluable. Conversations with others can clarify thoughts, get things off your chest, put things into perspective and enable you to check out:

- 'Is it really this bad or am I just imagining it . . . ?'
- 'Is it really true that . . . ?'
- 'Am I the only one who feels . . . ?'

Other people can confirm, validate, guide or direct you. They may motivate or inspire you. Sometimes they can even lift the depression which can accompany long periods of excessive stress. As a manager, it is helpful to create conversational opportunities for your staff. Staff suffering from excessive stress often find it difficult to take the initiative to create opportunities for themselves. They may be afraid of rejection or a dismissive response if they try to initiate a conversation. Managers should encourage staff to develop mutually supportive networks, rather than rely on one person. Even when people don't need help, they need to invest time in building and maintaining networks in preparation for a time when they might need help.

Advise staff to be specific and factual about their worries and to avoid over-dramatizing their situation. They should make it clear whether they want advice, an opinion, a reaction, an acknowledgement or just a friendly ear. If people approach you and want to talk, take the earliest opportunity to let them talk about what is causing them stress. Do not say 'You are worrying about nothing' or 'Why on earth do you think that?' or 'I don't think you should have done X' or 'That sounds like the time when I . . .' Don't hurry them or interrupt them or finish their sentences for them. Be prepared for silence. Encourage them by using the active listening techniques described later in this chapter.

If they are very stressed, they may retort that they do not have time to talk. Point out that trying to contain the stress in other ways also takes up time. It takes time to go outside for another cigarette, to stop for a 'quick' drink on the way home, to read the newspaper from cover to cover or to flick aimlessly through television channels hoping that something will distract you. Taking time to hold conversations cannot only help people to deal with stress, it is also the process by which close personal relationships are developed. Having even one close relationship has been shown to have beneficial effects on physical as well as mental health.[48]

We have looked at physiological, behavioural, psychological and conversational approaches to managing stress. We turn finally to managing the environment in which the stress is being generated.

Environmental Approaches to Stress

The environmental approach to stress management seeks to create environments that do not generate unnecessary or excessive stress. Examples of environmental approaches to reducing stress might include changing an office layout by re-positioning desks or by changing lighting or colour schemes. Changing management practices or writing clearer job descriptions can also reduce environmental stress factors. 'Feng Shui' might be included as a more recent approach (in the western world) to reducing environmental stress factors. Figure 8.8 describes some of the characteristics of a potentially stressful work environment.

Stress Management: The Business Case

An organization that invests in training in stress management is investing in its human assets. Some accountants fail to value human assets. But, as we saw in the case of Roger, the stressed social worker (Box 8.9), human assets can become financial liabilities when they suffer excessive levels of stress. One feature of public services that can create excessive stress is working alone or in situations where employees are at risk from the public. Public service workers often fear themselves to be at risk from their clients. We turn next to the problem of being a lone worker.

Alone or at Risk

Every day people working in public service organizations are exposed to threats of violence and abuse. Doctors are assaulted in their clinics, social workers and health workers often visit homes where there is domestic violence, youth workers operate in dangerous urban areas, airline workers are outnumbered by drunken passengers. Managers have a duty of care towards individuals who, by the nature of their work, are exposed to the threat of violence or abuse.

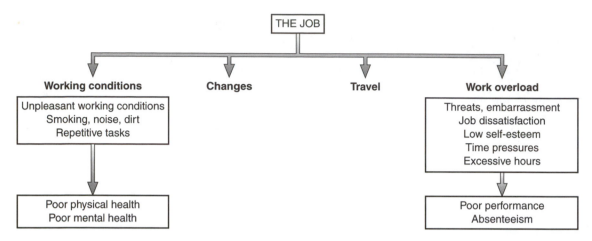

Figure 8.8 Characteristics of a potentially stressful work environment

Source: Furnham (1998)

Guidelines should be developed for the specific conditions under which workers operate (Box 8.15).

If an individual is involved in trauma, then managers should ensure that the individual is debriefed and receives appropriate support, perhaps enabling everyone to learn from the experience so that similar incidents are avoided in the future. Violent incidents can leave people feeling isolated and shocked and thinking 'why me?' Talking over what happened with someone can help the victim come to terms with the experience and may help to prevent long-term distress. It is normal for people to feel very shaken by violence, verbal or physical. Be on the watch for delayed symptoms such as lack of concentration, irritability or loss of confidence. Counselling may also help employees to address problems that are affecting their work.

Counselling in the Workplace

Counselling is a joint activity in which an individual seeks help, support or advice in dealing with personal problems or dilemmas. If counselling is successful, the client will take decisions that enable them to manage their situations. Many public services employ professional counsellors. Professional counsellors provide confidential help when personal problems are affecting performance. Providing counselling in the workplace can reduce stress and absenteeism. Professional counsellors are highly trained. This does not mean that managers cannot use some counselling skills during counselling conversations at work (Box 8.16).[49]

During counselling conversations, managers put

Box 8.15

GUIDANCE FOR INDIVIDUALS WORKING ALONE

- Check for warning signs such as: shuttered shops, fierce dogs, graffiti and toxic waste
- Trust your feelings. If you feel uneasy or scared, heed your intuition
- Always carry and show clients your identification card
- Tell a colleague the time when you expect to return
- Keep your peripheral vision on your surroundings
- As far as possible, avoid provocative behaviour
- Read the signs and stay alert

Box 8.16

COUNSELLING CONVERSATIONS: THE FOUR STAGES

1 **Recollecting**: Getting individuals to tell their own story as fully as possible
2 **Imagining**: Identifying possible solutions to the problems
3 **Evaluating**: Helping individuals choose
4 **Formulating**: Drawing up an action plan of what the client needs to do

---

ment, listening for something to disagree with, and rehearsing what to say.

Having dealt with some of the ways in which the individual welfare of staff can be maintained in the workplace, we now turn to how employees can contribute to ensuring that individuals are treated fairly.

FAIR TREATMENT OF INDIVIDUALS

Legal Aspects of Employment

Legal constraints on the management of organizations are based on a wide range of legislation and case law (Box 8.18).

Here we look particularly at constraints related to the fair treatment of individuals. The equal treatment of individuals, whatever their gender or ethnicity, colour or creed, mental or physical ability, sexual orientation or religion, is an issue, to a greater or lesser degree, in public services throughout the world. In some cases, the argument for equality rests on the pragmatic need to harness all skills and potential of

---

individuals at ease, remove distractions, limit their own talking and avoid interrupting. Box 8.17 identifies some of the skills that are useful in counselling conversations.

During counselling conversations managers should avoid inattentive behaviour, passing judge-

---

Box 8.17

COUNSELLING CONVERSATIONS: SOME USEFUL SKILLS

Attending

- Attending actively to the other person
- Hearing the music as well as the words
- Attaching meaning to the music
- Detecting emotion

Echoing

- Repeating the other person's words exactly

Paraphrasing

- Rephrasing the message accurately

Interpreting

- Suggesting emotions and meanings that might underlie their words

Focusing

- Directing attention to specific issues
- Periodic recounting of the key issues

Planning

- Helping the other person to devise a plan of who needs to do what by when, and to visualize how they will take the first step

---

Box 8.18

TYPES OF LEGAL CONSTRAINT

- **Personnel**: Employment law might extend to minimum wages, sex and racial discrimination, dismissal, hours of work, redundancy payments, or arrangements for the participation of employees in decision-making.
- **Operations**: Laws might place restrictions on the operations of the organization; specifying, for example, the need for healthy or safe working practices or the banning of dangerous substances. Legislation might limit routes for public service vehicles, or the number of hours a public service driver may drive without rest.
- **Marketing**: The sale of goods or services might be restricted by laws relating to their description or advertising.
- **Environment**: Certain operations might be banned because they are damaging to mental health or because they might pollute the air, water or land.
- **Finance**: Nearly all employing organizations have legal obligations to collect taxes.

---

the community. In other cases, the argument derives from moral standpoints based on fairness or human rights. In the UK, certain aspects of the fair treatment of individuals are covered by laws relating, for example, to race relations (Race Relations Act 1976) and sex discrimination (Sex Discrimination Act 1975 and 1986). These laws prohibit discrimination on the grounds of race, sex or marital status (Table 8.2). There are laws that require employers to take a positive approach to employing people with disabilities. Often these can be waived, if employers can demonstrate that the provisions are impractical.

Statutory obligations are often supported by Codes of Practice issued by, for example, the Councils for Racial Equality and Equal Opportunity. These codes of practice are designed to encourage positive action to achieve a composition of the workforce that reflects the composition of the wider community served by the organization. Positive action needs to be distinguished from positive discrimination. Positive discrimination, however well intentioned, is illegal in many countries. If someone was appointed to a post solely on the grounds that their gender or race was currently under-represented, that would be positive discrimination. Positive action, on the other hand, is not normally illegal. It is meant to achieve equality of opportunity. In the UK, for example, specific training was given to Punjabi-speaking women to increase their access to teaching posts in primary schools in the north of England. The UK Local Government Training Board took positive action to provide a national training course aimed at increasing the numbers of women in senior management posts. However, favouring the selection of women over men for the senior posts was illegal. Selection had to be based on

Table 8.2 UK anti-discrimination legislation

Act	Areas covered
Sex Discrimination Act 1975	Sex and marital status
Race Relations Act 1976	Race, colour, nationality or ethnic origins
Equal Pay Act 1970	Male and female work is equal and should be paid equally
Disabled Persons (Employment) Act 1944	Registered disabled persons
Rehabilitation of Offenders Act 1974	Persons with spent convictions
Disability Discrimination Act 1995	Promoting employment of disabled people

individual merit alone. The making of exceptional cases is allowed, for example, when appointing someone to work in a women's refuge, or to projects that target specific ethnic communities. The case that is made must stand up to legal scrutiny.

Implementing Equal Opportunities

In 1994 Leach claimed that despite the rhetoric, the pursuit of equal opportunities in the UK had been largely tokenist:

> It seems that a similar process has happened in the introduction of equal opportunities policies, as occurred with the change in management structures in the 1970s; policies and practices were adopted in a largely symbolic and ceremonial form to ensure external legitimacy, while organisational realities changed little.[50]

Leach acknowledged some changes, such as the appointment of a number of chief executives who were women and a number who were from an ethnic minority. He concluded, however, that the culture of most public services was still one of control by white, male, able-bodied managers.

> Managers faced with financial constraint, particularly those faced with competitive tendering, have argued that they cannot afford expensive policies aimed at equal opportunity. The introduction of an ideology of commercialism has made it easier to argue against a commitment to equality.[51]

The implementation of equal opportunity policies can be made a condition of grant aid or funding or contracts to supply public service organizations. European Social Fund applications require a statement of commitment to equal opportunities to be attached to grant applications. One study[52] has identified four barriers to equality in the employment of women in public services:

- Working hours that are unpredictable
- The absence of facilities such as childcare
- The nature of the relationships with fellow workers
- A style of management that is macho, chauvinistic or aggressive

Box 8.19 suggests some guidelines for implementing equal opportunities policies.

Monitoring Equal Opportunities

Equal opportunities monitoring has become standard practice in many public services. It can be carried out by external bodies, such as a Commission for Racial Equality. Information about the numbers of women, or members of ethnic groups or disabled people who have applied for, been selected, or taken up posts, can be used to assess the relative effectiveness of equal opportunity policies in

---

Box 8.19
GUIDELINES FOR IMPLEMENTING EQUAL OPPORTUNITIES

- The appointment of a senior officer to monitor implementation of the policy
- The adoption of formal statements of commitment to equal opportunities
- Consultation and sharing of information with staff representatives
- Publicizing the statement widely both internally and externally
- Systematic review of policy and regular reporting of progress

- The provision of training in revised employment practices
- Careful communication of the policy to the community
- Oversight of the policy by a committee
- A review of employment policies and practices
- A management duty to apply the policy

different public service organizations. Fowler concluded that successful equal opportunities policies should not be reduced to a set of procedures, but should build equal opportunity thinking into all employment practices, in much the same way as considerations for health and safety have become integrated into all functions of public organizations:

> Good working practices are safe working practices. Safety is not something special which can be added to 'normal' working procedures. It is something for which all managers should accept responsibility and integrate it into their normal work and operations. Similarly, good employment practice is bias-free employment practice – something which can be achieved only if all managers accept responsibility for its achievement as an integral part of their responsibilities as effective managers of the human resource.[53]

Family-friendly Public Services

Research carried out in the UK identified three reasons why organizations needed to develop family-friendly policies:

1 The 'demographic time bomb'. There are fewer school leavers and more elderly people. The workforce will increasingly have responsibilities for caring for dependent elderly adults.
2 By the end of the century, the percentage of women in the workforce had risen to 47 per cent. Women tended to have more responsibilities than men for the care of people outside work, notably children and elderly parents.
3 In most European countries, there is a statutory requirement for the provision for childcare. This is likely to spread. The provision of European funding is increasingly conditional on improved working arrangements for women.[54]

Where employees have difficulty in meeting conflicting demands of work and family, they experience stress. Their performance may suffer and sick leave and absenteeism may increase. If skilled or expensively trained public service employees are forced to leave because they are unable to meet their obligations at home, replacement costs – including costs of recruitment, selection and train-

---

Box 8.20

FAMILY-FRIENDLY EMPLOYMENT

Family-friendly employment recognizes the need for:

- **Childcare support**, such as, workplace nurseries, private nursery places, sponsored childminding, childcare allowances, after-school clubs, holiday play-schemes
- **Flexible working**, part-time job share, career break, term-time and teleworking
- **Care for the elderly**, particularly to deal with crisis situations

---

ing – will be high. The organization needs a good return on its daily investment in staff training and learning. The business case for childcare can be assessed by comparing the cost of replacing an employee with the cost of providing childcare assistance (Box 8.20).

FORMING CLOSER RELATIONSHIPS WITH INDIVIDUALS AT WORK

In this chapter so far we have argued in favour of a movement away from industrial relations and towards employee relations. In Chapter 6 we have already argued against the trend towards managing people in groups and teams. This seems to point to a re-emphasis of the importance of managing people as individuals. We look next at the way one-to-one conversations can be used to help managers form closer relations with individual people at work (Figure 8.8).

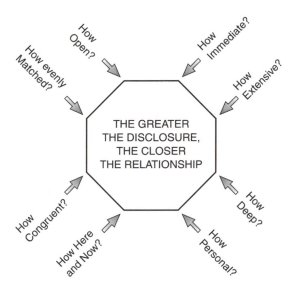

Figure 8.9 A conversational model of relationship formation

A Conversational Approach to Relationship Formation

Our assumption is that the more two people disclose things to each other, the closer their relationship is likely to become. We examine the closeness of a relationship in terms of the disclosure that takes place within it. Our conversational model of relationship formation is shown opposite (Figure 8.9).

The eight components of the model are summarized in Box 8.21.

1 How Immediate is the Disclosure?

The impression created in the first 5 minutes of a conversation between two people can set limits on the communication that can be developed during the remainder of the conversation. We have found, for example, that in 87 per cent of selection interviews lasting 30 minutes or more, the final decision made about a candidate is the same as a tentative decision formed after the first 5 minutes of the interview.

Dress code

If people are shown photographs or silent videos of other people, they give the highest ratings for intelligence, capacity for hard work, reliability and integrity to the people whose dress code is most similar to their own. In the absence of a similar dress code, they give the highest ratings to the most smartly dressed. If you want to be taken seriously as a manager, dress like the most respected manager in

---

Box 8.21

A CONVERSATIONAL MODEL OF RELATIONSHIP FORMATION

1 **How immediate is the disclosure?**
   Making contact, establishing rapport
2 **How extensive is the disclosure?**
   The balance between talking and listening
3 **How deep is the disclosure?**
   Disclosing feelings and opinions
4 **How personal is the disclosure?**
   Disclosures that begin with 'I', not 'you', 'people', 'one', 'they', etc.

5 **How present is the disclosure?**
   Concerned with the here-and-now, rather than the past or the future
6 **How congruent is the disclosure?**
   Verbal and non-verbal messages, consistency and alignment
7 **How matched is the self-disclosure?**
   Self-awareness versus honesty
8 **How open is the disclosure?**
   Trust, secrets and conversational taboos

your organization. The more senior a manager you become, the greater the number of people whose only experience of you is to see what you wear.

Eye contact

During conversation in North America and most western countries you should make eye contact as quickly as possible and hold the eye contact while the other person is talking. Only look away when you are talking or to signal that you wish to say something. Prolonged eye aversion by the other person may indicate that something needs to change in the way the conversation is going. If you can smile at the same time, it will reduce any risk that this will be interpreted as a hostile stare. In western cultures, people who cannot 'look you straight in the eye', or whose eye movements appear 'shifty', are more likely to be distrusted.

This is not true, however, in all cultures. Initial greeting behaviour in Japan, Korea and South Pacific Islands like Fiji, for example, is governed by quite different rituals. It is safer to be reticent than to risk giving offence. Across all cultures a smile during conversation indicates that you are not hostile or critical. In some cases smiling may do more than that. It may communicate liking or even friendliness. People are more likely to like people they think like them. For this reason try not to sit, or stand, where a light shines directly into your eyes. This will cause the pupils in your eyes to contract. It is better for your pupils to dilate, as this is an unconscious signal to the other person that you like them.

Physical contact

Very close relationships between people are signalled by physical proximity during conversation and even by physical contact. This process can be reversed. To the extent that local custom and practice allows, move physically closer to the other person, removing physical barriers like desks or tables. Putting aside papers or drinks, signals a preparedness to develop a closer relationship – physical contact even more so.

The initial possibilities may be limited to hand shakes. Always take the opportunity to offer your hand when it seems appropriate. Maintain the contact as long as seems permissible. Psychologist Bruno Bettelheim said that 'the ability to experience touch as pleasant must precede any human relationship'. Opportunities for tactile communication during initial contact will be limited by culture and by the gender of the other person. With a man, a handshake may be appropriate on the east coast of America; both hands may be gripped in the Middle East; a full body hug may be expected in North Pakistan and Russia; while no contact at all might be offered in Korea. Hand-to-hand contact would not be expected between men and women in a Muslim culture. Appropriate physical contact increases the chances that mental or even emotional closeness will follow in its wake. This might explain, in part, the widespread use of physical outdoor training to accelerate 'bonding' and 'cohesiveness' in multi-disciplinary teams.

Empathetic mirroring

Once initial contact has been made during conversation, try to sense how the other person is feeling. How they are feeling will affect how they are holding their body. If you mirror the way they are holding their body – not too obviously – you can notice how it makes you feel. This may give you a clue as to what the other person is feeling. Try to notice their breathing rate and try to get into the same rhythm. They are more likely to like you and to trust you if they do not feel tense in your presence. Help them to relax.

Once you have mirrored their posture and synchronized with their breathing, you can now slowly relax your posture and slow down and deepen your own breathing. The other person is likely to follow suit. If they are seated with their legs crossed, cross your legs towards them not away from them. Lean slightly towards them, signalling attentiveness and interest in what they have to say. If they follow your lead and lean towards you, the resulting physical closeness will bode well for the closeness you can engender during the conversation. Again you will have to sense the cultural norm. A closed-up posture is the best starting position, because a very open stance may indicate dominance.

Empathetic echoing

During the conversation you should listen actively, maintaining eye contact. When the other person signals that it is your turn to speak, try to speak at a similar volume and speed, using a similar rhythm and intonation as the other person. Slowly increase the speed of your delivery if you want them to feel that you find their ideas exciting and stimulating. If they follow your lead, there will be a mounting sense of chemistry between you. Speak more quietly to increase the sense of being together.

You may notice that the other person has a marked tendency to use visual words, like 'As far as we can *see* . . .', 'It was *clear* to him that . . .', 'That *coloured* his thinking . . .', 'I just *saw* red'. If you reply in the same visual mode, the other person is more likely to feel that you are speaking their language. Other people will be more tonal: '*Sounds* like a good idea . . .', 'It just *rang a bell* for him . . .' etc. Other people will be more tactile: 'It *felt* like he got a *rough* deal and took some *hard* knocks, but I sense that things are going more *smoothly* now', 'We should *feel* our way until it *feels* right'. Using the same verbal mode as another person is sometimes called verbal stroking. In some countries, the stroking is more ritualized than in others. It may involve, for example, a ritual series of enquiries about the health and well-being of family, common acquaintances, or former mutual colleagues.

Making immediate contact with someone makes you an acquaintance. The acquaintance can remain static for years, maintained by periodic ritual exchanges such as 'Hello', 'How are things?', 'What's new?' These rituals relax your muscles, soothe your heart and clear your brain. You should reciprocate them. If you do not, the other person will feel hurt and confused, until they meet someone more courteous.

2 How Extensive is the Disclosure?

To speak or not to speak

In broad terms, the more two people talk to each other, the closer will be their relationship. For some people, the mere fact that they do talk to each other is sufficient for them to say they have a relationship. 'Yes, we get on well – we're never stuck for words – there are never any awkward silences between us.' To be 'not speaking' or 'not on speaking terms' often defines a failed relationship. In the 1960s and 1970s, in unionized industries in the UK, the threat of 'not speaking' was used to coerce individuals. To be snubbed in this way – 'we're not speaking to you' – is experienced as so painful for the individuals against whom it is directed, that they often stay off work or even quit their jobs all together.

Talking about yourself

The negative power of 'not speaking' gives you some insight into the positive power of 'speaking'. But the relationship will not get much closer unless people talk about themselves during conversations: 'Worked with him for years, we chatted all right but I never really got to know him.' The relationship between co-workers can remain as distant as that between acquaintances who keep each other at bay by using well-tried greetings, saying the same thing time after time in the same situations, using empty clichés. Professionals often behave the same way with new clients. They look at the papers not the client. So if you catch yourself or others at work, looking at each other and talking about something other than the task in hand, then the possibility exists of forming a closer relationship.

A clique is a cohesive group of employees who share information about themselves with each other. People not in the clique are not allowed to know. One way to break up cliques is to create opportunities for individual members of the cliques to share information with individuals from outside the cliques. Training events, or structured 'away days' often include getting-to-know-you exercises. These exercises involve individuals disclosing personal information about themselves to other individuals. The fact that such exercises are commonly referred to as 'ice-breakers' is an indication of how cold and distant relationships can be in the absence of disclosure by people of information about themselves. In order to go beyond acquaintanceship, one of you will have to make a different move and the other will need to accept that overture.

3 How Deep Is the Disclosure?

Some people meet up to exchange information – gossip, rumour, jokes, anecdotes, news about a football team, or what was on TV last night. These conversations are not necessarily very deep and the relationships are often not very close. These kinds of conversations help to pass the time when people are afraid of silence, dislike their own company or are easily bored. Some hobby clubs exist primarily so that people can exchange mainly factual information. Regular reunions can serve the same purpose, providing opportunities to exchange anecdotes about past events. Some old soldiers eventually repeat the same anecdotes to anyone who will listen, 'shouldering their crutches to show how fields were won.'[55]

I know, I think, I feel . . .

Disclosures of information alone will not support very close relationships. The relationships will become closer if people in conversation share not only facts, but also what they think about the facts – their opinions – especially if these are strongly held, relating perhaps to their deeply held beliefs. Relationships will be closer amongst people who don't just repeat facts from a television programme about whales, but who also give their opinion on whether or not whales should be killed.

When you are talking to someone, try to imagine that they have an unspoken question in their heads every time you tell them something you know. The unspoken question is 'so what?' Try to answer that unspoken 'so what' question. The relationships might be closer still between people who are prepared to share how they feel about the killing of whales. What emotions do they experience when they think about these things? Emotions are labelled by single words, not whole sentences. The labels need to be more informative than 'I feel bad, glad, sad, mad, OK, fine or nothing'. In practice, it is quite difficult for people to feel 'nothing'. If someone tells you that they feel 'nothing', it usually means that they are unaware of their feelings or are embarrassed by them. Sometimes they do not have the vocabulary to describe their feelings, or simply don't want to reveal or disclose them. Their refusal is a signal to 'back off' – maybe because they do not want as close a relationship as you appear to be offering. The old soldier may prefer not to tell you what it was like to feel cowardly or to experience terror, loneliness or loathing during the war. That would require you to move to a much deeper level of mutual disclosure – to a much closer relationship.

4 How Personal Is the Disclosure?

One way to develop closer interpersonal relationships is to become more personal during the conversation. One way to audit how personal you are in a particular conversation is to notice how frequently you begin sentences with 'I' – '*I* notice that . . . , *I* see that . . . , *I* hear that . . . , *I* think that . . . , *I* feel that . . . , *I* feel pleased, happy, disappointed, annoyed, unimportant, satisfied' etc. as opposed to '*You* notice when . . .', '*One* can see that . . .', '*You* can't just . . .', '*It* is rumoured that . . .', '*Everybody* knows that . . .' This impersonal way of disclosing information gives other people the impression that you do not have any feelings about what is being discussed. This leads your conversations to be experienced as objective, cold, clinical and dispassionate, devoid of energy, motivation or commitment, creating an impression of distance rather than closeness in relationships.

5 How Present Is the Disclosure?

In close relationships people are prepared to talk about 'What I'm feeling now is . . .', 'What I hear you saying is . . .', 'I now think that . . .', 'At the moment I'm wearing my auditing hat and what I'm seeing is . . .', 'I am feeling anxious, tense, stressed, excited, hopeful etc.' Managers more commonly structure their conversations around what has already happened (results, variances, problems, complaints) or around what is going to happen (strategies, plans, changes to next year's budgets, new rules, schedules, action lists, diaries). Both of these kinds of conversations – past and future – are very necessary management conversations, but unless disclosures about present, real-time, here-and-now thoughts and feelings are added to them, these kinds of conversations – that deal only with the past or future – will limit the closeness of the relationships that managers will form.

6 How Congruent Is the Disclosure?

Doing what you say

Conversations are congruent when what you disclose non-verbally is consistent with what you disclose verbally, and when both are well aligned to the disclosures of the other person. Are your disclosures consistent? It is possible for managers to exert considerable conscious control over what they disclose verbally. It is much harder to control non-verbal disclosure, i.e. that which is disclosed through involuntary movements, posturing, gestures and involuntary changes in facial expression or the volume, tone and inflection of the voice. The voice is very sensitive to changes in breathing. The way you breathe changes unconsciously with your emotional state. Your emotional state fluctuates rapidly in response to what you think. And what you think is affected by what you see and hear. If what is communicated non-verbally is not consistent with what is said, the listener may feel vaguely uneasy, but may not be able to articulate their unease, so that it can be explored. If someone experiences unease in several successive conversations with you, they are unlikely to trust you. Distrust makes closeness seem risky and many

people will distance themselves from you. One way to become more aware of your own non-verbal communication during conversation is to observe and categorize the patterns of non-verbal communication used by other people. This has the added advantage that if you can categorize the other person's communications, then you can 'level' with the other person.

'Are you levelling with me?'

Are your disclosures well aligned? The principle behind the idea of keeping disclosures in alignment during conversations is that it is useful to categorize the package of verbal and non-verbal communication being used by the other person as either 'Going one up', 'Going one down' or 'Getting level' and then to adopt a package of your own verbal and non-verbal communication that is aligned with that of the other person. An example of the other person 'going one up' would be when you feel that you are being given advice, warning, reprimand, help or sympathy. It is as though the other person feels superior or more experienced or more knowledgeable or more powerful than you. It feels like they think that they are 'one up' on you. Examples of the other person 'going one down' on you would be if they felt helpless, compliant, dependent, looking for help or approval or forgiveness or if you felt the urge to restrain, moderate or coach their behaviour. When the other person 'goes one down' you might feel superior or more powerful. Examples of well-aligned conversations are illustrated in Figure 8.10.

In other words, if the other person goes 'one down', the complementary move is to go 'one up'. If the other person goes 'one up', the complementary move is to go 'one down'. Management conversations usually start with a lot of see-sawing between 'one up' and 'one down' positions, before both parties to the conversation exhibit a package of verbal and non-verbal communication that indicates that they are both ready to 'level' with each other. When the conversation is 'level', rational problem-solving can take place. Before this state is reached, a purely rational approach to problem-solving will be difficult and more attention will need to be paid to managing the

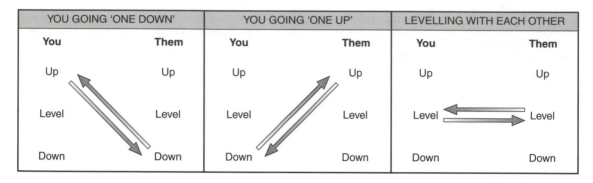

YOU GOING 'ONE DOWN'		YOU GOING 'ONE UP'		LEVELLING WITH EACH OTHER	
You	**Them**	**You**	**Them**	**You**	**Them**
Up	Up	Up	Up	Up	Up
Level	Level	Level	Level	Level	Level
Down	Down	Down	Down	Down	Down

Figure 8.10 Aligning conversations

emotions that are being communicated – verbally and non-verbally – during the conversation. This involves not only getting the other person to recognize, label and express their feelings – but you, as their manager, also need to do the same.

So how do you recognize whether the other person is 'going one up', 'going one down' or 'getting level'? If the disclosures are not accompanied by strong, non-verbal indications of emotion, then just levelling with the other person will usually work. This is the default state (Table 8.3). If there is no indication that the other person is 'going up' or 'going down', try adopting the 'getting level' state. If you are wrong, it will soon become obvious and you can switch to one of the other two states (Tables 8.4 and 8.5).

It is the overall pattern that is diagnostic. Isolated non-verbal behaviours can be misleading. They may have perfectly innocent explanations.

Getting it right

When deciding whether the other person is going one up, going one down or getting level, a way to cross-check whether you have interpreted these clues correctly, is to ask yourself how you feel tempted to respond as the conversation proceeds. For example, if you felt tempted to go 'one up', it is possible that the other person has gone 'one down'. You will be tempted to go one up, either if you feel inclined to criticize, judge or express a strong opinion, or if you feel tempted to comfort, reassure, advise, support, counsel or teach. If you feel drawn to question, to reason, to check, calculate or evaluate then you are being tempted to get level with the other person. You will be tempted to go one down if you feel angry or affectionate or apologetic or if you feel an impulse to entrust yourself or indulge yourself. The temptation to go one down, even as a manager, is

Table 8.3 Getting to a 'level': the clues

Clues	Characteristics
Non-verbal clues:	
Movements	Slow or static
Postures	Erect, or possibly a slight lean towards, but not leaning over you
Gestures	Minimal – level head, good eye contact, regular eye blinking
Expressions	Open face, awake, thoughtful, confident, attentive
Voice	Clear, calm, unemotional enquiring, quizzical
Verbal clues:	
Language	'Let's explore, recap, reconsider, try to . . . , tell me . . .'
	What? How? When? Who? Where? Probability? How much?

Table 8.4 Going 'one down': the clues

Clues	Characteristics
Non-verbal clues:	
Movements	**Either** passive, slouching, squirming and slow
	Or very lively and unpredictable with large-scale movements
Postures	**Either** slumped, head to one side, rigid
	Or big arm movements, waving, thumping
Expressions	**Either** tearful, pouting lip, eyes downcast
	Or looking up from a lowered head, sulky
	Or wide rolling eyes, flirtatious, admiring
Voice	**Either** whining, apologetic, petulant
	Or excited, angry, manipulative, taunting, loud, laughing
Verbal clues:	
Language	**Either** 'can't; won't; don't know; can you help me? It's your fault; you may regret it; I'm afraid that . . .'
	Or 'Gosh', 'wow', expletives, 'I hate, it's my . . .'

Table 8.5 Going 'one up': the clues

Clues	Characteristics
Non-verbal clues:	
Movements	**Either** stiff, immobile, erect, arms folded
	Or slow, relaxed arm movements
Posture	**Either** set chin, puffed chest, arms folded
	Or leaning or bending over
Gestures	**Either** finger pointing, head shaking
	Or touching, patting
Expressions	**Either** scowl, frown, looking down, head tilted slightly back, eyes rolling back, cold, disgusted
	Or smiling, nodding, pleased and sympathetic
Voice	**Either** sneering, clipped, authoritarian, sarcastic, punitive, condescending
	Or gentle, loving, sympathetic, soft, consoling, patronizing, supportive, nurturing, encouraging
Verbal clues:	
Language	**Either** 'don't, must, should, ought, bad, stupid, never, always, because I say so'
	Or 'all right, don't worry', 'I'll help', 'if I were you', 'there there', 'good, come on . . .'

not always to be resisted. It is in this mode that you may be at your most creative.

'It takes two to tango'

You will see from Tables 8.4 and 8.5 that you can choose between two broad patterns of one-up and one-down responses. You may not have as much choice as you might imagine. Many people are very practised at eliciting from others the behaviours and feelings with which they are most familiar. If the behaviours and feelings with which they are most familiar are incompatible with closeness, then, if you want a close relationship with them, you will need to sidestep their invitation to re-enact their old familiar patterns of behaviour.

7 How Evenly Matched Is Disclosure?

If the disclosure of one party to a conversation is generally not evenly matched by the disclosure of the other party, either in the extent of the disclosure or the depth of the disclosure – then the person who has overdisclosed may feel vulnerable, foolishly over-exposed, over-committed, unsafe, dissatisfied, conned or even betrayed. If this occurs and the balance cannot be rectified, the relationship may not only cease to be close, it may break down altogether. A common reason cited by women for breaking off close relationships with men is that the men have failed to match evenly the disclosure of the women, particularly the disclosure of feelings and emotions. Rectifying an imbalance is not always easy. No matter how hard they are trying to match the openness and honesty of the other person, people can only disclose about themselves those things of which they are self-aware. For good self-defensive reasons, some people are less self-aware than others. If such people wish to increase their capacity for sustainable closeness in relationships, they can choose to make increased self-awareness one of their goals for personal development (Chapter 14).

8 How Open Is the Disclosure?

If one party to a relationship senses that there are certain types of conversations that never get pursued, that there are topics that cause the subject to be changed or which evoke unexplained emotion, or lack of it, then they may become obsessively curious or anxious. Fear of the unknown can induce paranoia. 'What's the big secret?' Why is the other person being evasive? Suspicion erodes trust and threatens the closeness of relationships. This threat to closeness in relationships can be insuperable for managers who need to have secrets and knowledge in order to feel powerful. In many public services, especially in the government Civil Service, there is a strong tradition of 'official secrets' and disclosure only on a 'need to know' basis. Many public services are staffed by professionals with strong codes of confidentiality and non-disclosure. Secretiveness limits openness and threatens closeness in relationships. Freedom of Information Acts are intended to produce more open government but they might incidentally increase the possibility of closer working relationships between

those who manage and those who work in public services.

When close working relationships develop into sexual relationships, employees and managers might need to consider some of the consequences.

From intimacy to sex at the office

At one time a comrade was literally someone with whom you shared a room, while a companion was literally someone with whom you shared your bread. Now companions commonly share talk, fun and outings. Companions also share prejudices and advice, as well as fun. Most companions have a certain degree of respect or affection for each other, but some merely seek each other's company to trade insults or to wind each other up. Companions do not necessarily feel responsible for each other's welfare. The relationship is often temporary, perhaps for the duration of a posting or a major project. In this respect, companions are not friends. Friends do not knowingly hurt or criticize each other. If they give advice, it is 'on the level', not from a 'one-up' position. Friends will give help if asked, but generally, only if asked. They do not fuss or meddle. Although friends may back each other up when criticizing other people, they do not criticize each other. Unlike companions, friends may stay together for life.

The closer the relationship, the more self-contained it may become. This may provoke jealousy or envy at home, as well as at work. If there is also freedom from self-serving and self-protection, the relationship has become intimate. Intimate relationships are open, trusting and spontaneous. They are not the same as love. There are three Greek words for love: *philos*, *agape* and *eros*. They can be translated as friendship, affection and desire. The first two kinds of love – friendship and affection – confer benefits in physical and mental health. Problems in the workplace mainly arise with desire – *eros* or erotic love. Some people are nervous about developing closer working relationships at work because they are afraid that they might become sexual. But sexual relationships can arise at any point on the journey towards closeness. Acquaintanceship sex, for example, may occur even before the journey has begun, perhaps at a training event or after an office party. Sex can be an act of spite against a third person. Co-worker sex occurs commonly between workers on the same level. Mutual respect is often a casualty. This makes for awkwardness in working relationships, especially in teams and groups. Formerly good working relationships can be disrupted. The loss of a good working relationship is rarely a price worth paying for casual sex. Admiration sex can be a nice autograph from the admired, but the admired soon tire of signing the same book. Admirers, for their part, soon tire of looking at the same signature.[56] Companionable sex is seen by some as a comfortable way to share expenses and to structure time on business trips, but it is easy to lose a companionable relationship for the price of sexual solace. Good friends may prove harder to come by than good lovers. Having sex can cement a relationship at work but it rarely sets it in concrete. Affairs at work rarely last more than six months.[57] That is still long enough to do irreparable damage to other relationships, inside and outside of work.

Managing individuals – not a cult of individualism

In this chapter we have looked at alternatives to managing through industrial relations (large groups). In Chapter 6 we argued against a trend towards managing through teams (small groups). It would be a mistake to give the impression that we are arguing for a cult of individualism. In fact, we argue strongly against the idea of individuals working independently when they clarify organizational values (Chapter 3), and when they make ethical decisions (Chapter 11). It is true that throughout the book we favour processes that develop in managers the capacity for independent thinking, but this is always to be tested and extended through outer world conversations. Independent thinking (and consequent self-esteem) increases the capacity of individuals to contribute to interdependent relationships with others, at work and in their communities.

FINAL THOUGHTS: SOCIAL ENTREPRENEURS

Public services are increasingly delivered through a network of interdependent organizations. This involves joint working and partnerships. Rigg and Trehan[58] see decentralization as one way these new networks can be developed. In the UK, for example, 'Local Management of Schools' involves decentralizing financial responsibility from Education Authorities to individual schools.[59] Decentralization has repercussions for people who work in public services. Closer working with different agencies and organizations means that public service workers cannot be insular. They need to manage stakeholders who may have different and even conflicting interests. Managers are required to manage not only their own interests but those of the network as a whole. Bids for funding are more likely to succeed if they are joint bids between several agencies. As we shall see in Chapter 10, private finance initiatives encourage partnerships between publicly owned and privately owned organizations. For example, under the provisions of the Private Finance Bill, Bouyguesas, the French construction company, invested £55 million to build a hospital for the North London Health Trust. For the next 30 years the Trust will pay £17 million per year in fees to Bouyguesas.

Enabling Managers

It is difficult for any one agency to address the complex problems faced by organizations that seek to provide public services such as law and order, health, transport, education or training. As we saw in Chapter 1, some people have come to regard local authorities as 'enabling authorities' – enabling private, statutory and voluntary agencies to work together to address community needs. 'Enabling' involves crossing traditional boundaries, such as the boundaries between the courts, police, probation officers, youth workers and teachers, when trying to reduce juvenile crime. This 'enabling' role is complicated by differences in priorities, agendas, interests and cultures. There are no line management structures to resolve these differences.

Emissary Managers

The resolution of these difficulties requires new skills such as the ability to draw up terms of reference and agreements that respect professional boundaries. The public service manager needs to relate closely to political representatives, industrialists, service users and other partners from diverse social, cultural and ethnic backgrounds. This requires the cognitive skill of the political emissary. People who can combine the skills of the enabler and the emissary are referred to by Leadbetter as social entrepreneurs.[60] Working as a social entrepreneur involves high-level thinking and conversational competence. Social entrepreneurs are concerned with finding innovative ways of improving public services. They promote collaborative leadership, encourage cross-boundary working and find new ways of combining both public and private resources to deliver better services. The entrepreneurial public service organization is open and porous in its approach to its environment.[61] Not all public service organizations can depend on secure funding, even if they are publicly owned. Charitable organizations certainly cannot. Privately owned public service organizations are dependent on the vagaries of the capital market and the return they can earn on capital invested or money borrowed. One-off funding has increased, at both national and international levels (Chapter 10). During the 1990s, in the UK, funding opportunities such as City Challenge and the Single Regeneration Budget required local authorities to bid against each other for limited funds. Public service managers had to formulate and promote funding bids which co-ordinated several internal and several external agencies, from both the private and the voluntary sectors. This placed a premium on public service managers who were innovative, creative and risk-taking, who could act as social entrepreneurs.

SUMMARY

- We saw how contemporary personnel management evolved from the concerns of benevolent employers for their workers during the Industrial Revolution.
- We plotted the growth in trade unionism and industrial militancy in public services, leading in many countries to the introduction of legislation to curb trades union power and limit collective bargaining.
- We looked at the move away from managing people through industrial relations to the use of employee relations policies and procedures. We argued for further moves to manage people as individuals, using conversational processes.
- We examined the public service manager's role in recruiting, inducting, disciplining and counselling staff.
- We looked at the special problems of individuals who work alone or who work in 'at risk' situations in public services. We looked at the way this can contribute to other stresses in their lives. We looked at the role of public service managers in minimizing the risk that individuals may suffer excessive stress.
- We examined how managers can formulate, implement and monitor policies designed to achieve equality of opportunity for individuals and to create 'family-friendly' organizations.
- We looked at the way our conversational model of relationship formation can be used to develop close working relationships and even friendships at work.
- Managing people as individuals does not create a cult of individualism. Individuals can serve collective aims. We stress the public service manager's role as a 'social entrepreneur'.

THINKING AND LEARNING ACTIVITIES

Activity 1 Self-assessment

1 What are some differences between managing people in public services today as compared to 100 years ago and 20 years ago?

2 What questions would you nearly always ask during a recruitment interview. Why?

3 What questions would you nearly always ask at induction. Why?

4 What do you think are the differences between professional counselling and a manager engaging in a counselling-style conversation?

5 What causes stress and what can managers do to avoid excessive stress at work?

6 What is the difference between positive action and positive discrimination?

7 How would you make public service organizations more family-friendly?

8 Why is it important to encourage close relationships between people at work?

9 What impedes and what enables people to develop close relationships?

10 What is meant by 'social entrepreneur'?

Activity 2 Individual Learning: Visual Thinking

Mental mapping

Take a blank A4 sheet. Skim back over the underpinning knowledge in section one of this chapter. Each time you come to a key idea or section, label it with a few words. Write the label somewhere on your blank A4 sheet and draw a circle round the label. When you come across the next key idea label it and place it on your A4 sheet, close to other ideas to which you think it is related. When you have skimmed through the whole chapter, draw lines between the circles on your A4 sheet, if you think the ideas are connected. If necessary, use a clean sheet to redraw your diagram so that intersections are minimized. Now write verbs or actions, along all the line, such as 'which leads to', 'which can help with', 'which is connected to', 'which can be evaluated by'. Keep going until you have a map, diagram or flow-chart of how all the ideas in this chapter relate to each other.

Activity 3 Group Learning: Thinking and Action

Recruiting staff

This exercise takes half a day and works best with a group of three learners – A, B and C – sitting in a circle. Referring back to the appropriate section of this chapter, each learner writes out a job description and a person specification for their own job (or their tutor's job if they have no previous employment experience). They then pass these two documents to the person on their left. They then draw up an advertisement and an application form for the job that has been passed to them and again, pass it to the person on their left. Everyone fills in the job application form for the job advertisement in front of them and places it in the centre of the circle by a pre-agreed time.

Applicant A will be interviewed by B and C. B and C retire to plan what questions they will ask. They will use a Monroe five-point plan or Roger's seven-point plan. B and C will need to agree with each other how they will record their rating of applicants' answers. Meanwhile, applicant A retires to work out what seven personal strengths they have in relation to the personal specification. They will use Roger's seven-point plan. Applicant A tries to anticipate how these might be introduced and emphasized during the interview. The interview takes place. The interviewers and the interviewee then give each other feedback. Time permitting, the process is repeated, B being interviewed by A and C, and C being interviewed by A and B.

Activity 4 Individual Learning: Critical Thinking

CASE STUDY: Recruiting a project manager[62]

Jane has been appointed as the new chief executive of a chain of 12 residential care homes which care for people with learning difficulties. Each home provides residential accommodation for 50 young adults aged 18–25. Each home is managed by a unit manager who is responsible for managing staffing, resources and budgets. They liaise with external agencies including health services, social workers, educationalists and officers from housing associations. Care is provided by women working part-time shifts. At the end of her first week, Jane holds a staff meeting in each home to outline her vision for the future of the organization:

> This organization needs to shift its focus. For too long the emphasis here has been on care, not stimulation. All people with learning disabilities, young people in particular, need more than looking after. The focus needs to be on building a learning community where residents grow in confidence, achieve their full potential and have relationships with one another. For some of you, this will mean a shift in focus, a change in your approach as well as a review of your responsibilities. I have every confidence that you will meet this exciting challenge. I want us all to work together to bring about this change. We will need to be flexible, adaptable and committed to a new culture and to creating an environment in which everyone can develop.

After the meeting staff are overheard:

> 'Who does she think she is? Did you hear her going on about commitment and responsibility – what does she think we do now? I've worked my fingers to the bone for this place.'
>
> 'Yeah, I do more than what I'm paid for and I do it well. I'm exhausted when I get home. There's no way that I can do any more. All my residents are clean and well fed. If they want them to be educated as well, they should send them to a school, or hire teachers!'

Jane realizes that she will face major obstacles if she wants to bring about change in this organization. She decides that she needs a project manager to work with her across all 12 homes.

You are required to:

Consider how you would approach the task of recruiting a manager for this role. To refresh your ideas about what a project manager does, turn back to Chapter 3.

Prepare a job description and a person specification for a project manager to work with Jane.

Activity 5 Paired Learning: Creative and Critical Thinking

The role of HRM

Beardwell acknowledges the growth in Human Resource Management in the UK and internationally. It has been adopted by many organizations, including public services:

> In Britain, changes have been driven through local government, education, social work, central government departments and privatized utilities. These changes have had an avowedly market-based agenda attached to them. Human resource management has often been used as an agent of these changes. Indeed it might be said that human resource management often

took on a role as the cutting edge of change in public services. Is this a valid role for human resource management?[63]

How do you imagine that a debate between yourself and Beardwell might continue? Create a radio script for the likely discussion between yourself and Beardwell. Find a partner who is willing to read your part in the script, while you read the response which you have written in the script for Beardwell. At the end of the script reading, allow the discussion with your partner to continue naturally. Afterwards, make some notes on how (if at all) you have been able to accommodate some points of view which you did not hold at the outset.

Activity 6 Individual Learning: Evaluative Thinking and Action

Stress management

Refer back to the list of Type A and Type B characteristics. To which category do you belong? To help you make your selection, consider the following:

- Do you smoke?
- Are you often irritable?
- Do you regularly drink alcohol to excess?
- Do you suffer from dizziness, indigestion, headaches?

If you have answered 'yes' to most of these questions, you may be suffering from excessive stress. Consider the strategies in Section One for reducing stress. Write out your own stress management plan.

Activity 7 Individual Learning: Critical and Creative Thinking

Violence in public services

Think of reasons for and against teaching unarmed self-defence to 'at risk' public service staff. Formally construct a case for or against. Support your case with appropriate examples or evidence.

Activity 8 Individual Learning: Imaginative Thinking

'At risk' from the public

Design a form for reporting a violent incident involving a member of the public. Pay attention to who, where, when and how, and the involvement of other agencies. Draft safety guidelines for an actual or imagined member of your staff who works alone. The guidelines should cover visits to homes or other premises; travel, on foot or by car; the use of taxis or public transport.

Activity 9 Individual Learning: Empathetic Thinking

Post-traumatic stress

Design a debriefing process to be used following a traumatic incident. The process needs to deal with the identification of those at risk from post-traumatic stress; general advice to victims; the warning signs to look for; any help that is available.

Activity 10 Paired Learning: Reflective and Imaginative Thinking

Asking (and answering) good questions

With a partner practise asking and answering the following questions. After each answer the questioner gives the respondent feedback.

1 If you were looking back on a good day at work, what probably would have happened?
2 If you were looking back at a bad day at work, what probably would have happened?
3 If someone who had worked closely with you was asked to give you an honest reference, what would you predict that they would say about your strengths and your weaknesses?
4 Think about a difficult and important decision you once made. Think about whether it was a good decision or not. Share your thoughts and feelings with your partner.
5 If you could live the last 10 years over again, how would you want them to be different?
6 Who, apart from a parent, was the person from whom you have gained most? What was the person like? What did you do to help that person give you what you gained?
7 In the past, what criticisms have hurt you? Did you profit from them?
8 What are the biggest mistakes you have ever made?

Activity 11 Paired Learning: Evaluative and Creative Thinking

The impressions you create

Make a list of things you can see about your partner or a close colleague – hairstyle, dress sense, badges, pens, watch, jewellery, state of shoes, etc. Against each item on the list, make notes of how each of the things you have noticed might be interpreted by a stranger or an interviewer. Give each other feedback.

Activity 12 Paired Learning: Empathetic Thinking

Making eye contact

Make eye contact with your partner. Draw closer until other distractions fade from your field of vision. Sustain eye contact for as long as possible, noticing how you feel and how your impression of the other person changes. Break off. Repeat as often as time allows. Give each other feedback. Try again with a different partner.

Activity 13 Paired Learning: Empathetic Thinking

Making contact

Working with a partner, practise the empathetic mirroring described in this chapter. Between each session, make notes and compare them with your partner's notes. Repeat and try again with as many different partners as time allows.

Activity 14 Paired Learning: Reflective Thinking

Closer relationships through deeper disclosure

Working in pairs, read Steps 3, 4 and 5 of our Conversational Model of Relationship Formation. Sit or stand opposite your partner so that eye contact can easily be made or broken. One partner begins by completing the following three sentences:

- **Sentence 1**. Now I am noticing that . . . (something seen or heard).
- **Sentence 2**. Now I am thinking that . . . (give an opinion).
- **Sentence 3**. Now I am feeling . . . (a single word that captures an emotion).

After one partner has completed the three sentences, the other partner completes sentences 1, 2 and 3. Partners should try slowly to increase the frequency with which they notice things about their partner's appearance, gestures, non-verbal communication or things that they say or appear to be feeling. This forces the pair slowly to focus on each other. The degree of intensity or intimacy of the exchange can easily be regulated by switching attention back to objects or events in the room or to noises from outside. After about 10 minutes, the partners make some notes and discuss their notes with each other. The exercise can then be repeated with different partners.

Activity 15 Paired Learning: Empathetic Conversations

Creating a good first impression

Pair yourself with someone you know little about, preferably a stranger. Sit or stand opposite each other. Partners will receive feedback on the first impressions they make on each other and on the accuracy of the judgements that they make about other people based on first impressions. The partner who starts completes either sentence A or sentence B (see below). Partners should always favour sentence A, unless they need to use sentence B to correct a mistaken impression formed by their partner.

- **Sentence A**: 'I am like you, in that I know about . . . I am thinking that . . . and I am feeling . . .'
- **Sentence B**: 'I am not like you, in that I don't know about . . . I am thinking that . . . and I am feeling . . .'

Having listened actively to what your partner has said, use either sentence A or B as your reply. Where possible, sentence A is to be preferred, but sentence B can be used to correct seriously mistaken assumptions which your partner has made about you. After about 10 minutes, break off and make notes, especially about false impressions you had created in your partner that surprised or alarmed you. Note also any serious errors of judgement that you made about what your partner was thinking or feeling. What misled you? Did you jump to conclusions based on personal bias or prejudice? Share your notes with your partner.

Activity 16 Paired Learning: Empathetic Thinking

Keeping a level head

Read Step 6 in our Conversational Model of Relationship Formation. Have your partner complain to you as though you were the customer service manager of any organization with which you are familiar. The complaint can be based on something real or imagined. As your partner goes through stages of irritation, anger, frustration, exasperation, problem-solving and compromise, try to keep your conversation 'aligned'. After the role play make some reflective notes on the experience and share them with your partner.

Activity 17 Paired Learning: Reflective and Emphatic Thinking

Openness and trust in relationships

This activity is usually only possible with someone with whom you already have a 'safe' relationship, or with whom you have already attempted activities 13–19. Even then it may be helpful to warm up with some physical trust exercises, like being led blind-folded by your partner or being caught by your partner as you allow yourself to fall backwards. Working on your own, you each draw up a list of ten or more topics that you would find it difficult to talk about. Rank them in descending order of horror at the prospect of talking about them. Imagine you have 100 horror points to allocate to the topics, choose the topic which fills you with most horror at the thought of talking

about it and allocate it a good proportion of your 100 horror points. Continue down your ranked list of horror topics until each topic has been allocated at least one horror point and all 100 horror points have allocated.

Decide who is to go first. That person talks for 10 minutes on the topic to which they have allocated the least horror points. The partner practises non-judgmental active listening and keeps the time. At the end of 9 minutes, the person listening says 'You still have one minute left'. At the end of the 10 minutes get up, shake arms and shoulders and walk about for a minute or so. Now reverse roles. There is no need for any further discussion unless someone wishes it. Partners should not ask each other questions about the difficult topic that has been discussed. Another topic from the list can be attempted at another time, as fears moderate and trust develops.

Activity 18 Individual Learning: Visual and Imaginative Thinking

Conversations make a difference every day

Pick one only of the '9 Ways to Improve your Conversational Skills' shown below in Box 8.22. Try to foresee a

---

Box 8.22

NINE WAYS TO IMPROVE YOUR CONVERSATIONAL SKILLS

1 Try to make eye contact with everyone you meet or pass on the way.
2 Be the first to smile and to say hello to people you meet in the car park, the reception and the corridor, as well as in your own place of work.
3 Be the first person to say 'Hello, my name is ... and I don't know (or I have forgotten) your name.' Use names as often as possible during conversations. Use people's names when you say goodbye and whenever you pass on the street or in the corridor.
4 Write down a few short sentences about what you do and practise telling someone what you do. Tell them what you like and don't like about what you do. Don't be afraid to be enthusiastic.

5 Try to find one thing you have in common with people that you meet regularly.
6 Seize any chance you get to help a colleague.
7 Seek advice from someone about something. Let them show off whatever expertise they have.
8 When you are telling someone what you know about a subject, tell them also what you think and feel about the subject. Begin your sentences with 'I'.
9 Decide to have a conversation with a friend, or acquaintance, or a recent contact. Start your quest early in the day. Be sure to talk to them before nightfall.

situation during the following day when you will be able to try it out. Picture the place or the room or the person. What might they be wearing? Concentrate on the colours that are present and make them brighter in you mind's eye. Hear the tone of your voice and the tone of the other person's voice. Notice what other sounds you can hear and how you are feeling now you are trying out the way you have chosen to improve your conversational skills.

Activity 19 Individual or Group Learning: Imaginative and Empathetic Thinking

CASE STUDY: 'Crossing boundaries'[64]

I'd never worked with public servants. So it was quite a milestone when I was seconded from my job with Barclays Bank to be the director of an organization called the Blackburn Partnership. My job was to bring together a partnership – the first town partnership of its kind in the UK – under the umbrella of 'Business in the Community'. I quickly realized that there was an enormous gulf between people and a distinct lack of trust.

I remember the first time the public, private, statutory and voluntary workers sat round the same table. The private sector people sat on one side of the table and the public and voluntary people sat on the other. It was us and them. I tried hard to lighten things, to stop being quite so formal and stuffy. Afterwards, a councillor came up and said that it was the best thing that had happened for a long time. He had never had the opportunity to talk through his problems with people from the private sector. He hadn't appreciated what it must be like to work in a privately owned business. Two weeks later, I had an almost identical conversation with one of the private sector managing directors. It seemed such a bold step for the Council to take in those days. Now the Blackburn Partnership is seen as one of the most successful in the UK. It has attracted a large amount of cash via a successful City Challenge Bid, successful Single Regeneration Bids and European grants.

There is no one reason for our success. It has much to do with forming close relationships, many of which have become close friendships. The Partnership is about relationships and friendships. Through hours of conversations over the years, we have discovered each other's weaknesses and strengths and learned to play to each other's strengths. Gradually, over time, our friendships have flourished in other ways. We go to watch football together – Blackburn Rovers, of course! We eat out together; there are excellent Asian and European restaurants in Blackburn. We meet at each other's offices and at each other's houses. The close relationships blossomed slowly – that's how people are here. We try to build on each other – give added value to each other. Can I help you get what you most want? When we all do it, we all get what we most want. A chief inspector of police said, 'We have realized that we cannot do it alone – we need help. And need to share. A problem shared is often a problem spared.'

Our partnership is genuine. It's not just taken out of a drawer, dusted and produced for the benefit of visitors. It has got better and better over a number of years. These things do not happen overnight. Because we have no personal axes to grind, the partnership can act like a conduit and catalyst. We can harness resources. These days I think the word partnership is used too easily. When I think about how hard we all worked at our individual relationships – to put all those strands in the spider's web, I think the word partner is used too quickly, too readily, too easily – it cheapens the currency. We do not so quickly refer to other personal relationships as 'partnerships' and we should be equally slow to call a working relationship a partnership. Working partnerships require just as much care to develop. We look back and we are proud. We have helped to bring more than £12 million of extra resources to this small East Lancashire town. Blackburn with Darwen is vibrant. We look forward to tomorrow's challenges with confidence. We are always willing to change but only when change is for the better.

Questions

1   Imagine you were the counsellor at the first meeting. What would you have expected the partnership director to believe and value?
2   Imagine you were the managing director, what would you have expected the counsellor to believe and value?
3   What kinds of things do you imagine that the partnership director did or avoided doing, to build his web of close relationships between individuals?
4   What, in this case, was the value of friendship? Who has benefited and how?
5   What might have gone wrong with the idea of a 'town partnership'? What do you imagine helped to prevent it going wrong?

Activity 20   Individual Learning Review

Inner world thinking

What inner world thinking skills can you identify in the manager's work described in this chapter? Have any of the thinking skills you have identified emerged for the first time in this chapter? If so, add them to your accumulating model of the kinds of thinking skills that you think are useful to managers of public services.

What things could you do to develop any of the thinking skills that you have just added to your model? What would be the first step?

Outer world conversations

What outer world conversational skills can you identify in the manager's work described in this chapter? Have any of the types of conversational skills you have identified emerged for the first time? If so, add them to your accumulating model of the kinds of conversational skills you think are useful to managers of public services.

What things could you do to develop any of these conversational skills which you have just added to your model? What would be the first step?

Activity 21   Metacognition

Look back through the Thinking and Learning Activities you have been asked to carry out in this chapter. What thinking skills were involved in each of these activities? For each type of thinking, write down how you were learning what you were learning, when you were learning to think in each of the different ways.

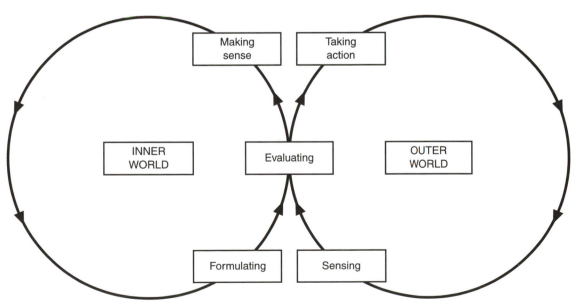

Figure 8.11 The thinking skills of the conversational manager

NOTES

1 Institute of Personnel Management. March (1963).
2 Torrington, D. and Hall, L. (1991) *Personnel Management. A New Approach.* Prentice Hall.
3 Ibid., p. 6.
4 Farnham, D. and Horton, S. (1993) *Managing the New Public Services.* Macmillan, p. 105.
5 Lickert, R. (1967) *The Human Organization: Its Management and Value.* McGraw-Hill.
6 Baines Report (1972) *The New Local Authorities, Study Group on Local Authority Management Structure.* HMSO.
7 Torrington and Hall, op. cit., p. 9.
8 Needle, N. (1989) *Business in Context.* Chapman and Hall, p. 289.
9 Story, J. (1989) 'Human Resource Management in the Public Sector'. *Public Money and Management* (Autumn), pp. 19–24.
10 Leach, S., Stewart, J. and Walsh, K. (1994) *The Changing Organisation and Management of Local Government.* Macmillan, p. 188.
11 Torrington and Hall, op. cit., p. 16.
12 Flynn, N. and Strehl, F. (1996) *Managing Public Services in Europe.* Prentice Hall/Harvester Wheatsheaf, p. 266.
13 Leach *et al.*, op. cit., p. 189.
14 Ibid., p. 189.
15 Fryer, B. (1985) in B. Huw (ed.) *Issues in the Miners' Strike – Digging Deeper.* Verso, p. 69.
16 Moran, P. (1994) in Curwen, P., Richardson, B., Nwankwo, S. and Montanheiro, L. (eds) *The Public Sector in Transition. Case Studies in the Management of Change.* PAVIC Publications, p. 276.
17 Rose, A. and Lawton, A. (1999) *Public Services Management.* Financial Times/Prentice Hall, p. 158.
18 Leach *et al.*, op. cit., p. 190.
19 Ibid., p. 192.
20 Rigg, C. and Trehan, K. (1993) 'The Changing Management of Human Resources in Local Government', in Isaac-Henry, K., Painter, C. and Barnes, C. (eds) *Management in the Public Sector. Challenge and Change.* Chapman and Hall.
21 Fowler, A. (1995) *Human Resource Management in Local Government.* Pitman, p. 131.
22 Rose and Lawton, op. cit., p. 160.
23 Tony Blair (1997) Prime Minister's speech at the Labour Party Conference, Brighton. Reprinted in the *Guardian*, 1 Oct. 1997.
24 Beach, A. and Story, D. J. (1999) 'Individualism and Collectivism', in Ackers, P., Smith, C. and Smith, R. (eds) *The New Work Place and Trades Unionism.* Routledge.
25 Torrington and Hall, op. cit., p. 227.
26 *New Ways to Work* (1995). HMSO.
27 *Sunday Times* (2000), 5 Jan.
28 Garner, H. (1993) *Multiple Intelligences. The Theory and Practice.* Basic Books.
29 Horne, T. and Wootton, S. (2000) *Thinking Skills for Managers.* Kogan Page.
30 Fowler, A. (1990) *A Good Start. Effective Employee Induction.* IAM.
31 Torrington and Hall, op. cit., p. 539.
32 Employment Protection (Consolidation) Act (1978). HMSO.
33 Worrel, C. and Cooper, C. (1998) Report in the UK *Guardian*, 3 Oct.
34 Cox, P. (2000) Quoted in the *Sunday Times*, 16 Feb., p. 5.
35 Ibid.
36 Evans, W. A. (1995) 'Stress Free Work Place'. *People Management*, 20 April, p. 47.
37 Furnham, A. (1997) *The Psychology of People at Work. The Individual in the Organisation.* Psychology Press, p. 317.
38 Selye, H. (1974) *Stress without Distress.* Lippermott.
39 Friedman, M. and Roseman, R. F. (1974) *Type A Behaviour and Your Heart.* Knopf.
40 Selye, op. cit.
41 Horne and Wootton, op. cit.
42 *Understanding Stress* (1987) HMSO.
43 Hart, K. E. (1990) 'Introducing Stress and Stress Management to Managers'. *Journal of Managerial Psychology*, 4, pp. 6–23.
44 Ibid., p. 10.
45 Horne and Wootton, op. cit.
46 Hart, op. cit., p. 18.
47 Ibid., p. 16.
48 Horne and Wootton, op. cit.
49 Egan, G. (1987) *The Skilled Helper.* Kogan Page.
50 Leach *et al.*, op. cit., p. 201.
51 Ibid., p. 202.
52 Fowler, op. cit., p. 117.
53 Ibid., p. 126.
54 IPM (1993) 'Corporate Culture and Sharing. The Business Case for Family Friendly Provision' (leaflet).
55 Goldsmith, O. 'The Deserted Village'.
56 Berne, E. (1981) *Sex in Human Loving.* Penguin.
57 Ibid.
58 Rigg and Trehan, op. cit., p. 87.
59 Hambleton, R. (1987) 'Decentralization – Developments, Objectives and Criteria', in Willmot, P. (ed.) *Local Government Decentralisation and Community.* Policies Study Institute London.
60 Leadbetter, C. (1997) *The Rise of the Social Entrepreneur.* DEMOS, p. 9.
61 Leadbetter, C. and Goss, S. (eds) (1998) *Civic Entrepreneurship.* DEMOS and The Public Management Foundation.
62 Our thanks to Jan Metcalfe for this mini case study.
63 Beardwell and Holden, op. cit., p. 664.
64 Our thanks to Peter Robinson of the Blackburn Partnership.

ROLE FOUR

MANAGING FINANCE AND RESOURCES

Having considered how managers can manage change, manage activities and manage individuals and groups, we consider now how the work of a manager in these roles can be resourced. We deal first with the overall framework of budgeting, highlighting some detailed worked examples in order to develop a command of the accountancy language in which budgets are written. We do this because we think that in order to be able to think numerically, it is first necessary to learn the language. We structure the material in three chapters, budgets (Chapter 9), then resources (Chapter 10) and finally accounting, auditing and performance management (Chapter 11).

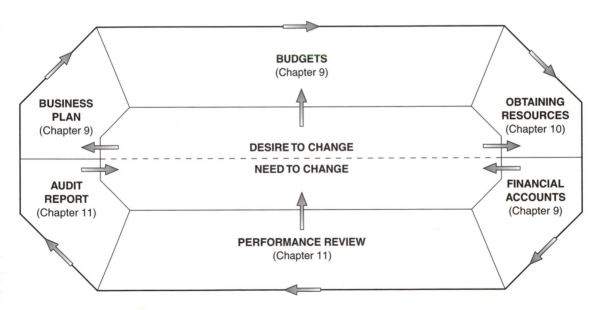

Figure 9.1 Managing finance and resources

9

MANAGING BUDGETS IN PUBLIC SERVICES

Annual income twenty pounds, annual expenditure nineteen pounds, result happiness. Annual income twenty pounds, annual expenditure twenty one pounds, result misery.

(After Mr Micawber in *David Copperfield* (1850) Charles Dickens)

LEARNING OUTCOMES

This chapter will enable the reader to:

- Understand why financial planning is necessary in public services.
- Understand why it is necessary to understand financial language.
- Understand what is meant by a budget, a capital budget, a revenue budget, a budget centre, a budget holder, budgetary control, incremental budgeting, zero-based budgeting, measures of performance and value for money.
- Prepare and 'flex' a budget.
- Understand business planning.
- Prepare a business plan containing a forecast cashflow, estimated profit (or loss) and a projected balance sheet.
- Interpret business plans.
- Adopt a conversational approach to using budgets to motivate staff.
- Anticipate the effect of budgeting on human behaviour.

INTRODUCTION

In public services, managers often write reports that have financial implications. A report proposing to buy a computer system for issuing books in a library might involve not only people in the library but also people in personnel, maintenance and insurance. Nearly all these people will be looking for figures relating to activity and costs. The author of the report will have to put these figures into a form which is recognized and easy to assimilate. This chapter explains the financial language which managers need to use, in order to discuss their plans with other people working in public services. In public services budgeting is necessary because:

- By tradition, many public services work to annual budget cycles in which spending of any kind has to be approved prior to the period in which it is spent.
- Some public service organizations often have no independent sources of revenue, i.e. more activity does not automatically generate more income.
- Where demand for services is rising, then access to those services may have to be rationed. Budgeting ensures that priorities are agreed with key stakeholders.
- Many public services are financed by grants. They have to budget their expenditures within the projections of the income they expect to receive. Politicians may be involved in decisions about priorities.
- The discipline of budgeting enables a framework

of understanding to be developed between the managers responsible for providing a service and the politicians who authorize the resources needed to operate the service. Often politicians will only grant an allocation of resources in response to a 'bid' supported by a budget.[1]

THE PURPOSE OF BUDGETING

The purpose of a budget is threefold:

1 To devise and evaluate short-term plans.
2 To identify budget holders – people to be responsible for their achievement.
3 To allocate the resources between budget holders.

Once we have got an agreed budget, we can use it to co-ordinate, communicate, motivate, control and evaluate the performance of the budget holders. Normally budget holders are senior people in the organization, i.e. the managers. The area for which a budget-holding manager is responsible is often called a budget centre.

Budget Centres

There are generally four types of budget centre: cost, revenue, profit and investment. Cost Budget Centres are normally given a budget level of resources (input) and are required to achieve a planned level of activity (output). In the case of Revenue Budget Centres, the primary measure of performance is the revenue generated (output) as compared to the revenue which was budgeted. Profit Budget Centres are responsible for generating a planned difference between revenue (outputs) and expenditure (inputs). The planned difference may be a surplus (or a deficit) or a profit (or a loss). Finally, Investment Budget Centres are responsible for earning a planned return on the investment made in the centre.

The Manager's Role as a Budget Holder

Managers should only be held accountable for expenditures and revenues over which they can exert con-

siderable control. There are two basic types of control: control over resources (or inputs) and control over results (or outputs). Input controls are the least satisfactory because they do not control the effectiveness of the services, but they are common in public services because outputs or results are often intangible and hard to measure. Figure 9.2 shows the relationship between budgets, budget holders and measures of performance.

Budgetary Control

When managers are exercising budgetary control, most of their conversations will be about variances. A variance is any difference, positive or negative, between a planned budget figure and an actual result. Sometimes the planned budget figure has to be adjusted (or flexed) before the comparison is made. For example, if the number of clients using a drop-in service or a helpline has been greater than expected during a particular period, then the budget

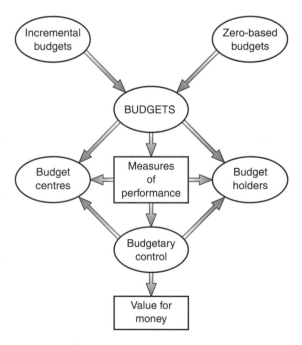

Figure 9.2 Budgets and measures of performance

for the planned level of expenditure for that period may have to be increased proportionally, before being compared with actual expenditure. If, however, the budget is not flexible, i.e. not to be varied with the volume of service usage, then the manager will have to take steps to curtail usage, e.g. by creating waiting lists, rationing or by charging fees, so that the expenditure stays within the planned budget levels.

Preparing the Budget
Incremental vs Zero-based Budgeting

In many public services it is difficult to define a clear relationship between inputs and outputs. In the police service, for example, the relationship between inputs and outputs is not always clear. The budgeted cost of a police force cannot be based on levels of arrests, because levels of arrests will be determined by factors beyond the control of the police, such as levels of crime or willingness to report crime. One

way round this is to use incremental budgeting. In incremental budgeting, last year's budget is taken as the starting point. Last year's budget is increased or decreased by increments, to reflect things that will be different in the coming year. Perhaps new services will come on stream or some will be discontinued. Perhaps the population will increase because of a new housing development. Almost certainly the price index for materials will be expected to rise and wages and salaries may increase. So, under incremental budgeting, next year's budget will be last year's budget, plus or minus the sum total of all the incremental changes expected during the coming year.

One problem with this is that if last year's budget was incorrect – under-resourced or 'padded' or based on inefficient working practices – then the mistakes in last year's budget will be perpetuated by passing them forward again into next year's budget. Incremental budgeting assumes that the demand for the service is stable; that the population being served is not going to be subject to major influx or exodus; that there will be no major change in the technology used; that there will be no major reduction in levels of grant, subsidy or funding; that there is no new category of problem for the clients; that there is no new remit for the service or the way it is delivered; that no political change will impact on support for the service; that there is no new legislation that may increase the demand or constrain the way the service operates or give rise to the need for a whole new service and so on. If we cannot make these assumptions safely, then we may need to create a budget from scratch, from first principles, starting from a zero base. This is called zero-based budgeting.

Zero-based Budgeting

This approach was first reported in the *Harvard Business Review* in 1920, based on a study at Texas Investments. Zero-based budgeting (ZBB) requires the cost of every item in a proposed budget to be justified from first principles. No expense is assumed to be justified. All activities must be justified starting from a 'zero base'. The justification must be linked to the aim or purpose for which the public service

---

Box 9.1

INCREMENTAL BUDGETING

Basis of calculations:

This year's cost	$100,000
This year's activity	20,000 units
Next year's activity	22,000 units
This year's price	100
Next year's price	105
(forecast 5% inflation)	
Last year's unit cost	100
Next year's unit cost target is	97
(target efficiency gain 3%)	

Next year's budget:

$$\$100,000 \times \frac{22,000}{20,000} \times \frac{105}{100} \times \frac{97}{100}$$

$$= \$112,035$$

organization exists, i.e. its mission. An advantage of zero-based budgeting is that resources get allocated according to the priorities of the organization and not according to the priorities of particular 'empire building' managers. Also, managers who have to create and defend their budgets from first principles are more likely to understand and accept them.

On the face of it, zero-based budgeting seems more attractive than incremental budgeting. However, starting from zero, surfacing and making explicit all the assumptions behind the provision of a service is much harder work for the managers than incremental budgeting. But it does mean that the managers have to become involved in the detailed construction of their budgets. With incremental budgeting, even if the conditions are sufficiently stable to make it possible, there is always a danger that the budget will be prepared by someone in the accounts department armed with last year's figures, next year's inflation rate and an efficiency target. This greatly reduces the likelihood that the manager's department will recognize, or 'own' the new budget, let alone achieve it.

During the preparation of a zero-based budget, three questions can be asked, in an attempt to improve value for money:

1 Should this activity be done at all?
2 Do we need to do this much of it?
3 Can the activity be done more cheaply?

Financial Measures of Performance

In Chapter 11 we deal with more general issues of principle concerning the measurement of performance in public services. Here we are concerned with measuring performance in financial terms. How are costs to be attached to some services in a way that is meaningful? Common performance criteria are unit costs, that is, total costs divided by the total numbers of units of activity, i.e.

$$\text{Unit Costs} = \frac{\text{Input Costs}}{\text{Output Units}}$$

Box 9.2

ZERO-BASED BUDGETS

1 State the overall aim or ongoing purpose
2 List the objectives of the activity. These will be different from aims or ongoing purposes in that they will be identifiable activities with completion dates
3 Justify the activity as a use of public or shareholder funds
4 Estimate the cost of the resources that would be needed
5 Say how the desired outcomes or outputs of the service will be evaluated
6 Explain what measures of performance will be used

Comparisons can then be made. Are our unit costs increasing or decreasing compared with former times? How do our unit costs compare with unit costs in other organizations, or with national or international benchmarks (Chapter 5)? The problem with benchmarks is that they assume 'all other things being equal', which they rarely are. However, if the comparisons are not used punitively, they can throw light on possible improvements that might be incorporated into next year's budget. As we shall see in Chapter 11, regulatory bodies, inspectorates and audit commissions regularly publish league tables and other comparators which managers can use as benchmarks. For the moment we want to continue our attempt to understand the accountancy language of budgeting.

Accountancy and Budgets

Accountants who specialize in the preparation and monitoring of budgets are often called management accountants. That is because they exist to help managers. If you are to get the best help from management accountants you will need to be able to speak their language. The starting point for conversations with management accountants is:

> **'A budget is the aims of the service expressed in financial terms.'**

The process of budgeting

If a service is sold or contracted, the starting point will be a revenue budget. Even in non-profit-making organizations there is increasingly an element of 'selling', so this can still prove to be an appropriate starting point. Assuming that a revenue budget is the starting point, the process would be as shown in Figure 9.3.

The policies and requirements of the service and the estimated cost of meeting these requirements must be looked at. Let us suppose that a librarian has selected a brand new computer system, costing £14,300. At present three staff work on the issuing counter, on two separate shifts, an early shift and a late shift. In financial terms, one could say that the present arrangements are costing:

3 people's salaries for the early shift (say £8,000 per person)	£24,000
3 people's salaries for the late shift (same rate of pay)	£24,000
Total salary costs for the year	**£48,000**

Let us suppose that the proposal to buy a new computer is being put forward because the present system is fairly old and approaching the end of its operational life. If a new system is more efficient and speedy than the old one, then the increased efficiency might help to justify the purchase. Assuming that the staffing of the counter desk could be reduced to two people on duty at any one time, a new budget could look like this:

2 people's salaries for the early shift at £8,000 per person	£16,000
2 people's salaries for the late shift at £8,000 per person	£16,000
Total salary costs for the year	**£32,000**

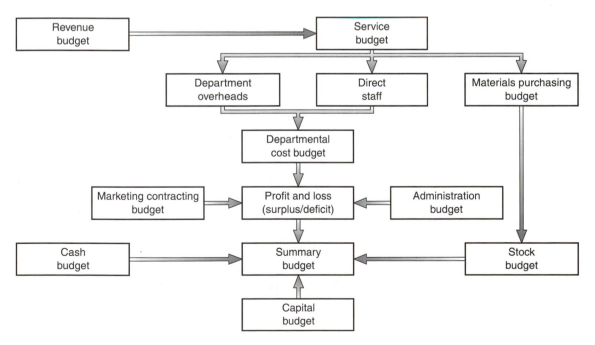

Figure 9.3 The accountancy process in budgeting

The difference between capital and revenue

In the library example we found out that the librarian wants to spend £14,300. This is a one-off item of expenditure. The new computer will last a number of years. It will still be worth something at the end of the year in which the money is spent on it. This kind of expenditure item is called 'capital expenditure'. The benefits from capital expenditure are expected to be long term. The expenditure for the computer is not the same as expenditure on such items as salaries. After someone's salary has been paid all year, at the end of the year there will be nothing tangible to show for it. This type of recurrent commitment is known as 'revenue expenditure'. So, we have two kinds of payments:

- **Revenue payments**: ongoing payments for things that have no residual value at the end of the period in which the payment is made.
- **Capital payments**: for one-off items with a residual value at the end of the payment period .

In drawing up a budget, we distinguish between the budget for revenue expenditure and the budget for capital expenditure. In the case of the library, we would request money for capital expenditure of £14,300, to pay for a new computer system. If this request is granted, it will also affect our revenue budget for staff salaries.

The revenue expenditure budget

If the computer system is purchased by the library, it is estimated that there would be an annual saving amounting to £16,000. Budgeting involves detailed consideration of how the service is to be delivered day-to-day. In this case the library would need one less person per shift. The budget period is usually a period of 12 months – so in this case the saving is a full year's salary of £16,000. This has been calculated as follows:

Present system costs per annum	£48,000
New computer system costs	£32,000
A saving per annum of	£16,000

In public services the largest expenditures are those associated with employing people. They include expenditure on salaries, wages, overtime, insurance, pensions, training costs, etc. Usually the starting point for preparing an estimate of these items is to take the authorized staffing level and to cost out what the total expenditure would be if that level of staff were employed for a full year. Supplies, things used on a day-to-day basis, also need to have money set aside for them in a budget. Again, they need to be costed out based on a price at a particular date. The prices of all items in the budget should be the prices ruling on the same agreed date. Subsequently the components of the budget, once agreed, can be issued for use as a comparator or control against the actual spending. The ability to keep particular items of expenditure within these budgeted amounts may be used as a 'measure of performance' of particular individuals or particular departments. It is common practice in public services to code all spending on a particular kind of item with the same code number. This enables the spending on different categories of items to be collected together under one budget heading so that it can be compared with the intended budgeted expenditure for that item. The comparison of actual spending against the budgeted spending enables the expenditure to be controlled. If the budget turns out to have been wrongly drawn, the budget can be corrected for the following year.

Preparing budget reports for budget holders

Most public service budget reports take the form of computer print-outs intended for the budget holder. They enable actual performance to be compared to the level of spending predicted for a particular point in the financial year. The print-out will identify overspending or underspending under each budget heading. The manager can then work out how to get spending back on target by the end of the year. An example of a budget report is shown in Table 9.1. This is an extract from the account of a fire service.

In the fire service, wholetime pay is for operational personnel, namely the fire officers. The annual

Table 9.1 Budget report of a local fire station

Budget heading	1997/98 revised budget	Virements	TOTAL BUDGET	Projected spend to Jan. 1998	Actual spend to Jan. 1998	Variance O/spend (U/spend)
PAY						
Wholetime						
Wholetime Pay	448,000		448,000	371,400	372,269	369
National Insurance	33,000		33,000	27,500	28,184	684
Overtime			0	0	27	27
Public Holidays			0	0	299	299
National Insurance			0	0	22	22
Total Wholetime	481,000	0	481,000	398,900	400,801	1,401
Administrative & Clerical:						
Administrative Pay	44,500		44,500	37,167	36,734	(433)
Overtime	0		0	0	0	0
National Insurance	3,500		3,500	2,917	2,842	(75)
Superannuation	4,700		4,700	3,917	3,847	(70)
Total Administrative & Clerical	52,700	0	52,700	44,001	43,423	(578)
Other Employee Expenses:						
Other Expenses	0		0	0	0	0
NHS Refunds	800		800	667	459	(208)
Total Other Employee Expenses	800	0	800	667	459	(208)
Total Employees	534,600	0	534,600	443,568	444,683	1,115
Transport:						
Additional Travel			0	0	30	30
Car allowance: Essential users	0		0	0	0	0
Casual	0		0	0	0	0
Lease	5,000		5,000	3,846	4,304	458
Total transport	5,000		5,000	3,846	4,334	488

amount of a full year's pay is shown in the first column. Virement refers to any extra money moved into the budget head after the budget was prepared – virement being a French word meaning transfer. The total budget is in column three. The next column – column four – represents an estimate of how much should have been spent up to this month in the year. Column five shows the money actually spent up to this point. By comparing column five with column four, you find either an overspend (too much having being spent), or the opposite, an underspend. Underspendings are indicated by putting the figures in a bracket. Print-outs such as this are commonly sent to head teachers of schools, departmental heads in colleges, police stations, social services divisional offices, environmental health offices, wards in hospitals, libraries, customs and excise and Civil Service agencies.

Staffing projections are based on an approved staffing list, sometimes called an establishment. The annual spending figure for the budget will be divided equally among the months of the year and the manager will be able to tell from the print-out whether or not they are likely to hit their target by the end of the year.

The budget print-out acts as a trigger for corrective action to be taken, such as freezing the appointment of new staff, altering the staffing mix between full-time or part-time workers, or reducing the level of overtime working.

Non-staffing costs are usually controlled by approving the issue of purchasing orders and by keeping a control over the cumulative total of purchase orders placed, so that money for the whole year is not over-committed. For example, in a school the bursar will keep a control over the purchase of textbooks for each of the subject areas and make sure that predetermined allocations for each department are not exceeded. At the end of the year, the budget reports will be summarized and a narrative report prepared for senior management. In a school situation, the report might be produced for the governors, or be presented to the parents as part of the school's annual report. It is important to sort out budgetary problems as they arise so that embarrassment is avoided at the year-end.

PREPARING A BUDGET: A CASE STUDY IN TOURISM

A Tourism Department wants to open a café on the ground floor of a Visitors' Centre. The director of tourism is concerned about how such a new service will develop and whether turnover will increase sufficiently to generate a satisfactory profit. The director wishes the café to achieve a profit within 18 months of opening. A similar enterprise in a nearby town achieved the following sales:

Sales (total revenue) for 13 weeks   £26,000

Variable costs (mainly the cost of potatoes, fillings and seasonings), represent 40 per cent of the sales revenue. Other expenses are fixed: the amounts shown below are for a period of 3 months:

Cook	£5,200
Assistant cooks	£7,800
Waiting Staff	£6,900
Rent and rates	£5,500
Depreciation	£1,900

In order to prepare a budget, the following approach could be followed:

1 The period we are asked to look at is a full year, so we will need to estimate both revenue (sales) and expenses (costs) for a 12-month period.

2 We are asked to forecast the annual profit or loss.
3 The costs are under two different categories 'variable costs' and 'fixed costs'.

A *variable cost* is one that increases as the turnover or activity increases. For example, the more customers you serve with potatoes, the more money you will have to spend on buying potatoes. Likewise the total costs of buying fillings and seasonings will rise, because more customers means more coleslaw, more salt, more spicy chicken, etc.

A *fixed cost* is one that doesn't rise when the number of customers increases or when customers spend more money. For example, once you have paid rent on a building for a year, that's it. Whether you have more or less customers than you budgeted for doesn't affect the rent you pay. So the rent you pay is regarded as a fixed cost. Bearing in mind that we have to prepare figures for a full year and that we have to show revenue and costs (split into variable and fixed costs), the calculations are set out in Box 9.3.

As the costs are greater than the revenue, the bud-

Box 9.3

AN ANNUAL BUDGET FOR A CAFÉ IN A TOURIST CENTRE

	£
Sales revenue (£26,000 × 4)	104,000
Total revenue for the year	**104,000**
Variable costs:	
(0.4 × 104,000)	41,600
Fixed costs:	
Wages, cooks (4 × 5,200)	20,800
Assistant cooks (4 × 7,800)	31,200
Waiting on staff (4 × 6,900)	27,600
Rent and rates (4 × 5,500)	22,000
Depreciation (4 × 1,900)	7,600
Total costs for the year	**150,800**

geted loss for the enterprise, in its first year, is £46,800. The size of the loss is calculated by taking the revenue of £104,000 away from the costs total of £150,800.

Now What?

When the tourism director receives a budget showing a forecast loss of £46,800 for the first year, the question will arise as to what, if anything, can be done to reduce the loss. Clearly, the café isn't viable on the basis of our initial budget. One way forward is to investigate the effect on the budgeted profit of varying some of the assumptions on which the estimates were based. This procedure is known as 'flexible budgeting'.

Preparing a Flexible Budget

A flexible budget (or a 'flexed' budget) is one in which you develop different scenarios, based on different assumptions, in order to judge whether changes that you are able to make might be beneficial. In the case of the proposed café, we can experiment with different types of assumptions and examine other ways of doing things. For example, using the first draft budget for the café, we can show the effect of increasing the sales by 50 per cent and 100 per cent. If sales were increased by 100 per cent, the existing oven would not cope with the extra volume of food required. A new oven would have to be purchased to cope with a 100 per cent increase in sales. The additional capital expenditure would be:

Acquisition of new oven	£18,000
Fitting and installation of new oven	£2,300
Estimated length of life of new oven	8 years
Residual value of oven after 8 years'	£1,500

If sales increase by 50 per cent, the staff costs for cooking and preparation would remain unchanged, but additional staff would be required for waiting on the tables. This would cost an extra £250 per month. If sales increased by 100 per cent, then the increase in the monthly cost of staff would be £350.

In order to calculate a flexible budget for a full year and forecast the annual profit (or loss) the following approach could be followed:

1 The period we are asked to look at is a full year, so we need to estimate both revenue (sales) and expenses (costs) for a 12-month period.
2 We are asked to forecast the annual profit or loss.
3 We are asked first to assume a 50 per cent increase in sales for the full year and, second, a 100 per cent increase in sales for a full year.
4 If we buy an extra oven to cope with extra demand, that will involve capital expenditure and our budget estimates will have to include an increased allowance for 'depreciation'.

What is Depreciation?

Depreciation is the drop in value, over the course of the year, of any item that is intended to last for a number of years. The most common method of calculating depreciation is the 'straight line method'. This will be illustrated below. First, we collect the information relating to the cost of the asset:

Purchase price of new oven	£18,000
Add on any acquisition or installation costs (i.e. costs associated with getting the equipment into position and ready for use)	£2,300
Total cost of the asset	**£20,300**
Deduct the residual value of the oven	£1,500
Leaving the sum to be depreciated over 8 years	£18,800

Clearly the value of the new oven will reduce, or depreciate, by £18,000 over the next 8 years. In the 'straight line' method of depreciation, we assume that this reduction in value occurs equally during each year of the 8-year life of the oven. In this case, the annual charge can be calculated by dividing £18,800 by 8 years = £2,350. This depreciation charge of £2,350 will be charged against any profits which are made in each of the next 8 years. The basis of the calculation of the annual depreciation charge was:

(Original Costs minus Residual Value) divided by (Expected life of assets in years).

Table 9.2 Flexible annual budget for proposed café

Sales revenue	Original budget	Original budget plus 50%	Original budget plus 100%
Sales	104,000	156,000	208,000
Variable costs (at 40% of sales)	41,600	62,400*	83,200**
Fixed costs			
Cooks	20,800	20,800	20,800
Assistant cooks	31,200	31,200	31,200
Waiting on staff	27,600	27,600	27,600
Additional staff	–	3,000	4,200
Rent and Rates	22,000	22,000	22,000
Depreciation	7,600	7,600	7,600
Extra depreciation			2,350
TOTAL COSTS	150,800	174,600	198,950
NET LOSS	46,800	18,600	
NET PROFIT			9,050

Notes:
*Variable costs increase in proportion to the amount of business, so if sales have gone up by 50%, the variable costs will increase by 50%. The original estimate was £41,600, a 50% increase on that takes £41,600 up to £62,400 (i.e. £41,600 plus £20,800 = £62,400).
**Again, variable costs increase proportionately to the increase in turnover, so if sales increase by 100%, then the variable costs will increase by the same percentage. So, the original estimate of £41,600 plus the same amount again, £41,600, gives a total variable cost of £83,200.

From this flexible budget we observe that with a 50 per cent increase in sales, the café will still run at a loss. If it manages to achieve a 100 per cent increase in sales, we forecast that it will make a profit of around £9,000, but this is dependent on the department of tourism obtaining capital of £20,300 to invest in a new oven.

In the conversation that follows (Box 9.4), we hear from Nancy Bowman, who is head of a Special Needs department. This education service employs 200 staff, 50 of whom are specialist teachers. Her annual budget is $4,000,000.

Box 9.4

EXTRACT FROM A CONVERSATION WITH NANCY BOWMAN 'IF YOU CAN'T COUNT IT, IT DON'T COUNT'

Terry: Nancy, what matters to you most about your work?
Nancy: That the kids learn, that they get better across the whole curriculum, socially and emotionally. That's the bottom line for us.
Terry: But . . .
Nancy: But it's hard to remember that, now

we're part of a Student Services Business Unit. We have 'Financial Commitment Accounting' and Financial Monitoring. Every day I think I must do that finance stuff. My finance file is my most carried about file and the least opened. It's a constant source of guilt feelings. Every day I tell myself I must get to grips with it and every day the needs of the children seem more important.

Terry: It seems hard.

Nancy: No I don't find it hard. I like the idea of creating business units that empower people in the service to innovate – units that can bid for their own projects. There's lots of external funding available for inner city work, for example. It's good to be able to respond to local needs as we come across them without having to go up a long chain to principal officers and down again.

Terry: Sounds great.

Nancy: Yes, doesn't it. But it's not working very well. I'm not keen on having to measure everything, especially financially.

Terry: What do you mean?

Nancy: Look, people have a perfect right to know what we are doing with their money but most people haven't got a clue about special needs education and are not that interested anyway. I get so exasperated when people forget that we are here for the kids – kids with special needs need us. All the inspectors seem to want is figures. Nobody here sees inspections as a proper exercise in accountability. Because of the particular person that heads up the inspections, inspections are seen as politically motivated attacks on the service. Our performance monitoring is turning into a game. All the numbers, including the finances, are our defence against this attack. Because the figures have been 'created' as a defence, when we come to use them ourselves to see if we're getting any better, we can't. We really need two sets of figures, one for us and one for the inspectors – what a waste.

Terry: So, financial monitoring is primarily used to defend yourself against outsiders who do not understand your business?

Nancy: That's not entirely true. The financial stuff is used internally as well. Internally we have been split into a client side and a provider side. The problem for them is that the client side cannot write specifications without our help. Nevertheless, they produce monthly reports on our performance against their faulty specifications. This includes giving us numerical grades for things like flexibility! They do not let us see their reports on our performance, so we could not use them to improve our performance – even if we believed them.

Terry: Why don't you get involved with them in drafting meaningful specifications, then you could make better use of their monitoring?

Nancy: Why make a rod for our own backs?

Terry: What do you mean?

Nancy: If they could get a half decent specification from us, the next thing they would do is to put it out to tender to private contractors. I need that like I need a hole in the head! I already have stress enough being simultaneously accountable to the heads of 500 schools, a committee of politicians, external inspectors for quality and an audit commission for finances. I think I just counted at least four bodies to whom I am accountable. It's stressful enough trying to watch my back from four directions without adding private sector competitors to the list.

Terry: Stressful?

Nancy: Actually, the most stressful thing is when I go home at night and ask 'What did I do today that made things better for any child?' and the answer comes back 'nothing'. Look, I do believe in the need for public services to be accountable ... really I do. But some things can't be measured in money.

Terry: Thank you for taking time out to talk.

BUSINESS PLANNING

Nancy is trying to manage her department in a public service organization which has fully embraced the idea of business planning. Business planning in public services is an approach to putting down on paper, in a single document, an overview of a proposed course of action.[2] A business plan for a training department, for example, might describe the types of users expected, the opening hours, the staffing requirements, the revenue expected and the flow of cash throughout a year. Such a business plan could then be used to calculate measures of performance. For example, the annual figures for revenue and costs could be divided by the number of weeks the training centre was intended to be open; the figures then obtained could then be compared with the actual revenue and costs. Monitoring revenue and costs on a weekly basis enables corrective action to be taken if the actual performance starts to stray away from what was expected in the business plan. Although information in a business plan can be used to help prepare operating budgets, the business plans are more than budgets (Box 9.5).

PREPARING A BUSINESS PLAN: A CASE STUDY

Investment

The Tennessee Tourist Board plans to open a Museum of Appalachian Crafts on January 1. The Tourist Board will invest capital of $100,000 in cash immediately and any additional financial needs will be met by a bank overdraft. The initial setting up of the museum will involve buying exhibits for $95,000 in cash. These exhibits will be depreciated by 5 per cent per year, over the next 20 years, by an equal amount each year.

Entrance Fees

Entrance fees to the museum are expected to generate income of $12,000 for the first two months after opening and $14,000 per month thereafter. One quarter of the visitors pay cash on arrival. Three quarters of the visitors are coach parties. The agents for the coach parties usually settle their bills for admission charges by the end of the month following the visit.

Box 9.5

ITEMS TO COVER IN A BUSINESS PLAN

- **Physical factors**: e.g. availability of buildings, tenure, ownership layout, access
- **Usage**: e.g. opening hours, shift patterns, numbers of estimated users, changes in demand, peaks and troughs of business, staffing levels, use of part-time staff
- **Facilities**: e.g. specialized equipment, consumables, constraints on use
- **Finance**: e.g. estimated levels of costs over a full year (revenue expenditure). Estimates of income over a full year. Estimates of capital expenditure
- **Constraints**: e.g. business planning options considered; whole scheme or part scheme, phasing or staggered start
- **Sources of finance**: e.g. new money initiatives, efficiency savings, self-financing, money from private sector sources, money from overseas grants, sources of borrowing, contingency reserves, endowments or charitable money.[3]

Payroll

The monthly payroll for museum staff will be paid in cash, estimated at $4,500 each month. The landlord of the premises is asking for six months' rent to be paid in advance, at the start of the tenancy on 1 January. The annual rent is $33,000.

Expenses

Normal business expenses, such as electricity, are paid on a monthly budget system, with payments averaging $350 per month. A newly appointed public service manager has been asked to:

1 Prepare a monthly cashflow forecast, on schedules provided by the financial department, for the 4 months ending 30 April.
2 Prepare an estimated profit statement for the 4 months ending 30 April.
3 Prepare a projected balance sheet, as at 30 April.
4 Comment on whether the proposed museum is likely to be profitable in the near future, showing how the estimate of the profit has been arrived at and the assumptions on which the estimate is based.

Method

The new manager will need to prepare three documents: A Cash Flow Forecast, An Estimated Profit and Loss Account and A Projected Balance Sheet, formatted as below.

Monthly Cash Flow Forecast			
Jan.	Feb.	Mar.	Apr.
$	$	$	$

Estimated Profit and Loss Account for the 4 months ending 30 April			
Jan.	Feb.	Mar.	Apr.
$	$	$	$

Projected Balance Sheet as at 30 April			
Jan.	Feb.	Mar.	Apr.
$	$	$	$

- **A Cashflow Forecast** is a monthly chart showing cash received and cash paid out. It is concerned with forecasting the amount of surplus cash (or overdraft) at the end of each month. If the position at the end of any month is negative, this indicates that an overdraft facility will need to be arranged, or that more external funding will need to be introduced as working capital. The size of overdraft required can be found by looking at the position at the end of each month and finding the largest negative figure.

- **An Estimated Profit and Loss Account** estimates the profit (or loss) at the end of the period being considered. This is the surplus (or deficit) after charging all the costs incurred in the period against all the revenue incurred over the same period. (NB the costs of capital items are *not* charged.) Revenue cost are bills which have been paid, plus an estimate of any bills which have not yet been paid, but for which the expense has been incurred in the period being considered.

- **A Projected Balance Sheet** at a future date projects the value of the assets and the expected extent of the liabilities at that future date. It is a snapshot of what an enterprise is projected to be worth, what it is expected to own, and what it is likely to owe, at a particular date.

Cashflow Forecast – Main Features

This is the starting point for the financial section of a business plan. It is a month-by-month chart showing what cash you expect to pay in and what cash you expect to pay out during each month. The timing of receipts and payments is vital. Dates have to be realistic. A cashflow forecast must be comprehensive. Everything has to be shown, including payments for capital items. The cashflow forecast for our museum is shown on the next page. For clarity, receipts have been set out and totalled. Second, underneath the receipts, a separate section has been made out for the payments which have then been totalled. In practice, when keeping ongoing cash records, all cash transactions can be recorded one under the other without

Table 9.3 Craft museum monthly cashflow forecast

	Jan. $	Feb. $	Mar. $	Apr. $
Receipts:				
Capital introduced	100,000			
Admission fees	3,000	3,000	3,500	3,500
Coach parties		9,000	9,000	10,500
Total receipts	103,000	12,000	12,500	14,000
Payments:				
Payroll	4,500	4,500	4,500	4,500
Electricity	350	350	350	350
Purchase of exhibits	95,000			
Rent	16,500			
Total payments	116,350	4,850	4,850	4,850
Balance at start		(13,350)	(6,200)	1,450
Receipts	103,000	12,000	12,500	14,000
Payments	116,350	4,850	4,850	4,850
Balance at end	**(13,350)**	**(6,200)**	**1,450**	**10,600**

separating income and expenditure, just so long as each figure is clearly marked positive (a receipt) or negative (a payment). The cumulative effect of the positive figures less the negative figures is the net cashflow. It can make the end-of-month arithmetic easier if you record the positive figures for receipts in one column, say, 'cash in' and all the negative figures for payments, in another column, labelled, say, 'cash out'. Table 9.3 shows the cashflow forecast for the craft museum.

Taking one month at a time, we have forecast the cashflow for each month by deducting the total payments from the total receipts. In the first month, for example, the payments are higher than the receipts, so there is a negative balance of $13,350 at the end of the month of January. This negative balance then becomes the opening balance for the beginning of February. The position at the end of each month can be calculated by repeating the process. Start with the position at the end of the previous month, add all the receipts and deduct all the payments, to arrive at the new end-of-month position.

Go back to the case study and see if you can trace from where each figure has come. In the preparation of this type of estimated cashflow, almost every figure

used would have been the result of a separate consultation with the staff involved. The calculations can be speeded up by entering the figures into a computer-based spreadsheet, but the principles are the same as those you have just followed. Incidentally, you will have observed that, apart from the first two months when the museum has an overdraft, for the rest of the time it appears to have a positive balance. This reflects the situation in many start-up situations. Help from a bank or other external funding is usually critical in the start-up period, until a regular pattern of money in and money out is achieved.

Estimated Profit and Loss Account – Main Features

An estimated profit and loss account for a particular period is designed to reveal the size of the profit or loss in that period. The profit in a particular period is what is left after we have deducted from the revenue earned in a particular period only those costs that have been incurred as a result of earning that revenue. Expenses that have been incurred to buy capital items, like buildings or equipment, are not deducted, nor are expenses that relate to future

Table 9.4 Working paper calculations to support figures used in museum's estimated profit and loss account

Basis of calculation	Amount $
Income:	
Admission fees 2 months @ $12,000	24,000
2 months @ $14,000	28,000
Revenue from fees estimated @	52,000
Costs:	
Salaries 4 months @ $4,500	18,000
Rent $\frac{4}{12} \times \$33,000$	11,000
Electricity 4 months @ $350	1,400
Depreciation @ 5% per annum	
Annual charge $= 0.05 \times \$95,000 = \$4,750$	
Of which 4 months $= \frac{4}{12} \times \$4,750$	1,583

Table 9.5 Estimated profit and loss account for Craft Museum for 4-month period

	Amount $
Revenue:	
Admission fees	52,000
Costs:	
Salaries and wages	18,000
Rent	11,000
Electricity	1,400
Depreciation	1,583
Total costs	31,983
Net profit	**20,017**

hoped for sources of revenue. Those kinds of expenditure, often called capital expenditure or investment expenditure, appear in the cashflow and in the balance sheet, but not in the profit and loss account.

Often a profit and loss account shows the position after a year's operations. In the case of our craft museum, an estimated profit and loss account is required for the first four months of trading. So, the first stage is to estimate, or guess, the total revenue likely to be earned by the organization or enterprise over the period covered by the account. In Table 9.5 we estimate the total value of admissions over four months to be $52,000. If the estimated costs are greater than the estimated revenue, the profit and loss account will estimate loss. Losses have the effect of weakening and eroding the value of an organization. Profits have the opposite effect, strengthening the organization and allowing it to expand. In a public service organization, the main costs are likely to be people-related costs, salaries, wages, rent, electricity and depreciation. Depreciation is a cost because while the service is being provided, the value of each asset being used is being diminished, through wear and tear and the passage of time. The diminution in value over a particular period of time is charged against the revenue which the organization has generated during

that same period of time. So although depreciation does not appear in the cash budget (because it is not cash actually paid out to someone else), it is legitimate to charge it as a cost against the revenue, in the profit and loss account.

We set out above in Table 9.4 the working paper calculations which support the figures which are required in the estimated profit and loss account for the museum (Table 9.5).

Projected Balance Sheet – Main Features

A balance sheet is a summary of what the organization owns and owes on a particular date. In this respect it is a snapshot at a given moment in time. By comparing successive snapshots, or balance sheets, one can see whether the organization is expanding or contracting, whether or not the value of its assets is growing or diminishing. Table 9.6 sets out the projected balance sheet for the museum at 30 April.

In the case of our Craft Museum, the main fixed assets are the exhibits, to be bought for $95,000. We project their value at the end of four months to be $95,000 minus depreciation of $1,583. We say that the value of the exhibits will have depreciated by $1,583 in four months. We think that the value of the exhibits will decline at the rate of 5 per cent per year.

Table 9.6 Projected balance sheet for museum at 30 April

Assets	Amount $
Fixed assets:	
Exhibits (at cost)	95,000
Less depreciation	1,583
Total fixed assets	93,417
Current assets:	
Debtors	10,500
Prepayments	5,500
Balance at bank	10,600
Total current assets	26,600
Total fixed and current assets	**120,017**
Which came from:	
Capital Account	100,000
P & L Account	20,017
	120,017

Current assets include our bank balance, money owing to us from our customers (in this case the coach tour agents) and also 'owed' to us by our landlord, because we paid six months' rent in advance. On a strict time basis, only four months' rent was due. The landlord is in effect holding for us an advance payment of two months' rent which equals $5,500. This prepayment counts as an asset of the museum, even though it is in the hands of the landlord.

- **The Capital Account** is the accumulated monies that have been invested in the museum project, in this case $100,000.
- **The accumulated P & L Account**, sometimes called the revenue account in public service organizations that are publicly owned, represents the accumulated surplus (or deficit) of all the preceding Profit and Loss Accounts. It is calculated by adding together all previous profit or loss figures. In this case we have only one figure – a profit of $20,017.

READING AND INTERPRETING FINANCIAL ACCOUNTS

Financial accounts, like the balance sheet, the cash-flow and the profit and loss account, can be read like any other account of events. It is like reading any other account or story. It's just that financial stories are written in a rather condensed form of language. Having learned the financial vocabulary and some of the financial grammar (called conventions), you can read or write your own financial accounts.

In the case of our Craft Museum, our forecast cashflow account shows that apart from the first two months, the organization will have sufficient funds for its daily requirements. Difficulties with liquidity – the availability of cash to meet bills as they fall due – will occur in the first two months. We will need treasury funds, or an authorized overdraft from a bank, of at least $13,350 in January. This will then cover us in February when the overdraft should fall to $6,200. After that, we should be self-financing, i.e. able to meet our requirements for cash out of our own earnings.

If our four-month sample is representative, then our estimated profit and loss account shows that the venture as a whole will be profitable. Income estimated at $52,000 will more than cover expenses of $31,983, leaving an estimated surplus or profit of $20,017, over four months. If income falls, any reduction in the estimated level of income will reduce profits by a corresponding amount.

Our projected balance sheet shows the rate of growth in our museum's assets. In four months, it has grown in value from an initial investment of $100,000 to $120,000 after allowing for depreciation. It has grown by $20,17 in four months, so the potential annual growth is three times $20,017, or just over $60,000 per year. That gives us a measure of how much the museum could afford to spend on new purchases next year. For example, the museum could plough its funds back into more exhibits, or extend the car park.

WRITING BUSINESS PLANS

It is important to be aware that the use of financial or business terminology in relation to public services can provoke an adverse reaction, including resistance to any changes being proposed. In situations where new government legislation is forcing the need to implement changes, a business plan can be written and presented to political representatives or community groups, in order to structure the debate, or to help agree priorities. As a result of the discussions, a different form of document – less business oriented – may be prepared and made available through local libraries, or other public places, for public inspection. The way that financial data should be presented in reports about public services is summarized in Box 9.6.

INTERPRETING A BUDGET

The Budgeting Game

An approved business plan can be used as the basis for a discussion with budget holders, or managers of budget centres, about the operational budgets that will need to be met if the approved business plan is to be achieved. Budget holders will then see how they are performing against these operational budgets. Most commonly they will be given a budget report. That is a report that shows the actual income or expenditure to date, compared with what it should be, if the operational budget is to be met by the year end.

Budget reports are usually prepared by people who do this as a regular full-time job. Often they use computers to collect, summarize and analyse the financial information. Items of actual expenditure are compared with the intended expenditure for that item. They may have to do some calculating and estimating to convert the figures in the business plan into monthly budget figures – which is why managers often 'don't know where they get their figures from'. Often 'accounts' use the 'wrong' plan or the 'wrong' version of the plan and so, it is possible for managers to waste much time demanding that 'accounts' justify their figures. As Nancy suggests in her Conversation, this can sometimes turn into 'a game' – providing a smoke-screen to cover up the need for management action. Managers should try to avoid shooting the messenger. The messenger from accounts might be 'right for the wrong reasons'.

Warning Signs

Budget reports are usually issued monthly or quarterly, so that there is plenty of time, if necessary, for corrective actions to be taken before the end of the financial year. Such information is also used to alert public service managers to the need to spend money that has been budgeted for expenditure in the current year. The reason given for this year-end spending frenzy is that otherwise it might be 'knocked off' next year's budget.

Kings and Princes

The final year-end accounts record the actual levels of income and expenditure that have occurred during the previous 12 months. It is sometimes called the actual 'out-turn', i.e. what 'turned out' to be the

---

Box 9.6

FINANCIAL DATA IN PUBLIC REPORTS

The financial data in public reports should be:

1 Referenced and verifiable
2 Made accessible by use of visual aids
3 Consistent with other data
4 Compared with comparable data

actual level of activity, income and expenditure, as opposed to the predicted activity, income and expenditure. The need for end-of-year final accounts arose from the practice of kings and princes in the Middle Ages to entrust their powers of taxation to local landowners, who then had to account for their stewardship of the taxes raised.[3] In the same way today, whether they are financed directly by governments, or through government grants or contracts, or through charitable donation or international aid, or through private shareholder capital, many public services have to account for the way that money has been spent.

Public Audit

Managers' records can be subject to independent public scrutiny by a public auditor or by a regulatory body of some kind (see Chapter 11). Public representatives or public service managers who misuse public funds can be barred from public office, be subject to criminal proceedings, or be required to replace the misused money from their own personal resources. The production of an account of good stewardship represents the final stage of the financial planning process. We began by talking about the need for financial planning in public services. We then drew up a business plan and used it as the basis for setting operational budgets. We then talked about the need to collect information on what was actually happening and compared this with what we hoped would be happening by that stage. Finally, the public service manager must take whatever corrective action is necessary to ensure that the final Annual Account can be audited and certified as evidence of the manager's good stewardship. To end this chapter we consider some of the effects of budgeting on human behaviour and in particular how budgets can be used to motivate people (Chapter 7).

BUDGETS AND MOTIVATION – A CONVERSATIONAL APPROACH

Goal theorists (Chapter 7) consider the motivational. Certainly on our motivational map it could help meet needs for 'applause' and 'possession' (Chapter 7). Hofstede[4] studied the effect of budget pressure on performance. His research revealed that when initial budgets were perceived to be easy, actual performance turned out to be significantly lower than when a budget was set halfway between what was perceived to be easy and what was perceived to be very difficult. When initial budgets were perceived to be very difficult, actual performance again fell to the same low level as when initial budgets had been perceived to be easy. The implication seemed to be that intermediate budgets should be set, because these result in the highest actual performance. These findings do not hold true though if the budget holders are motivated by a fear of failure rather than ambition for success. According to Hofstede, to get the highest achievement with managers who are motivated by fear of failure, rather than ambition for success, it is necessary to set initial budgets that are either very easy or very difficult. If budgets are to be used as a source of motivational pressure in public services, this must be preceded by an assessment of the motivational behaviour of the individuals affected (Chapter 7). Then it can be decided whether to set the initial budgets at levels that are perceived by individuals to be easy or difficult to achieve. In order to use budgets to motivate staff, managers should consider having conversations with their staff around the topics identified in Box 9.7. Remember that initial budgets only motivate some people when they are perceived as challenging. There is always a risk that the challenge might not be fully met.

Box 9.7

A CONVERSATIONAL APPROACH TO BUDGET SETTING

- Talk to budget holders and try to identify if they are ambitious for success, and therefore need budgets of intermediate but achievable level of difficulty, or if they are fearful of failure, and so need very easy or very difficult budgets.
- Ask each first-line manager to create their own draft budget. They might need help from someone in accounts but they should do their own figuring.
- If, subsequently, you cut or change their draft budgets, then discuss the changes with them personally, giving good reasons for your actions.
- Give them a limited variance from budget within which you expect them to decide for themselves what to do about it. Do not interfere unless those limits are breached. Tell them when they achieve positive variance.

- Discuss the need to amend budgets that are set too tightly. If you have to intervene, listen first to the budget holder's explanations and focus the coaching conversation around what can be done to correct the variance rather than placing blame.
- Do not make budget performance the sole basis for appraisal conversations. In the eyes of some budget holders' effort or client satisfaction may merit more appreciation than having no adverse variance against a financial budget.
- Protect your budget holders from demoralizing feedback and pressure from others, especially from staff in the audit or accounts department.
- Remember that it may take several years of conversations – listening, learning, coaching, feedback, appraising and appreciating – before budgeting yields benefits.

FINAL THOUGHTS: 'BUDGET ROUND OR BATTLEGROUND?'

Considering the conflicting purposes for which budgets are commonly used, we should not be surprised when the budget round becomes a battleground. Yes, budgets are about planning to obtain essential supplies, funds, facilities and other resources. Yes, they are also about the delegation of authority over the use of resources and the co-ordination of delegated activities. But in public services, budgets are also about control. Argyris[5] argued that budgets are primarily devices for putting pressure on people to be economical and efficient. This poses an ethical dilemma when it compromises service quality. Resentment between managers and staff is not uncommon. At a departmental level, the annual budget round can turn into a ritual battleground, as departments attempt to settle old scores with other departments. The potential for conflict between the finance department and almost every other department in a public service organization is considerable. Finance departments can become 'budget police'. Unenviably, they have a statutory responsibility to make adverse reports on services that they think are not economic, or not as efficient as other benchmark departments (Chapters 5, 11).

Behind the formal façade of budgeting lies a political process of trading and negotiation, in which managers and departments are competing for resources, power, status and self-serving aggrandizement.[6] Requests for resources are often justified with an ingenuity that reflects years of experience of the relationship between what you ask for and what you get. According to Hofstede, it's a 'game'.[7]

The impact of budgeting is not always in the desired direction. Many managers will blame the budget when their own poor performance is poor. They might claim, for example, that they were never consulted about the level of the budget and that it was unrealistic in the first place. The budget may also be blamed for creating unhelpful pressures and stress, thereby reducing the performance of staff and increasing the disruption caused by absenteeism and sick leave.

In publicly owned public services, budgets must be met within strictly defined cash limits. Most departments will ensure that they spend right up to the limit, for fear of losing resources the following year. According to Coombs and Jenkins,[8] the way that financial performance is reported has an effect on the performance aspirations of both individuals and groups. Financial reporting is a form of feedback, and we saw in Chapter 7 that feedback was an important aspect of motivation and learning. One of the benefits of zero-based budgeting is that it forces managers to be involved in the process. Participation enables managers to have some influence over the levels at which budgets are set. They are then less likely to blame poor performance on the setting of unrealistic budgets over which they have no control.

SUMMARY

- We learned why financial planning was necessary in public services.
- We learned that financial planning involves writing business plans which provide the basis for operational budgets. Operational budgets can either be 'incremental' and based on previous years' expenditure, or 'zero-based', starting from no previous assumptions.
- We examined the relationship between budgets, budget holders and budget centres.
- We learned that whether budgets are capital budgets or revenue budgets, they can provide measures of performance.

- We learned how to flex a budget.
- We learned how to write a business plan starting with a forecast cashflow, followed by an estimated profit and loss account and a projected balance sheet.
- We learned to be circumspect about the use of financial data in annual reports.
- We were encouraged to be proactive in our use of budget reports and to take corrective action in good time to ensure that the final year end accounts reflect good stewardship of a public service.
- We considered a conversational approach to using budgets as a tool for motivating and controlling staff.
- Finally, we warned against perverse behaviour engendered by budgeting.

THINKING AND LEARNING ACTIVITIES

Activity 1 Self-assessment

1 Why is financial planning necessary in public service organizations that are publicly owned?
2 In organizations in which financial planning involves the production of business plans, how can these be used to form operational budgets?
3 Explain what is meant by:
   - Budget holders
   - Budget centres
   - Virement
   - Revenue budget
   - Capital budget
   - Flexible budget
   - Incremental budgets
   - Zero-based budgets
4 What is the difference between an estimate and an out-turn?

5 What is the purpose of the following:
   - a forecast cashflow?
   - an estimated profit and loss account?
   - a projected balance sheet?
6 What precautions would you take when including financial data in public documents and reports?
7 To what good uses can public service managers put budget reports?
8 Of what perverse behaviours should managers be aware in relation to budgetting?

Activity 2 Individual Learning: Reflective Thinking

Control and motivation

When morale is low in a public service organization, the primary concern of the manager is how to motivate staff.

Because of the financial accountability imposed on public service organizations, the primary concern of many accountants involved in budgeting is control. Explore this by talking to staff accounts and to managers in any public service organization.

Activity 3 Individual Learning: Imaginative Thinking

A thought experiment

You are the chief executive of a large public service organization. You have appointed a young, newly qualified management accountant, so that you can develop her approach to budgeting. Write the script of a conversation that you can imagine yourself having with her on her first day.

Table 9.7 Housing revenue account

	1996/97 £'000	1995/96 £'000
Expenditure:		
Repairs & maintenance of council dwellings	3,422	3,561
Rents, rates, taxes and other charges	44	43
Other premises expenses	61	72
Provision for bad and doubtful debts	103	59
Rent rebates – note 2	8,193	8,008
Supervision and management		
– general	1,634	1,569
– specialist support services	1,390	1,363
Capital expenditure charged to revenue	798	775
Capital financing costs – note 4	2,573	2,674
Total expenditure	*18,218*	*18,124*
Income:		
Gross rent income – note 1	11,101	10,753
Housing subsidy – note 3	6,575	6,505
Other rent income (garages, shops and land)	196	188
Charges for services, facilities etc.	464	443
Interest on balances	81	101
Mortgage interest	38	43
Total income	*18,455*	*18,033*
Surplus (deficit) for the year	237	(91)
Balance at beginning of year	775	866
Balance at end of year	1,012	775

Activity 4 Paired Learning: Numerical Thinking

Reading annual accounts

This case study shows the annual account of the activities of a group of managers who were responsible for providing a public housing service (mainly houses, flats and bungalows), during the 12-month period 1996/97. They set the levels of rent and maintained the properties externally. From time to time they improved the properties by rewiring the electrical circuits, renovating the kitchens, or renewing windows. Improvements such as these can be financed by borrowing money, by obtaining grants, by bidding for inner city aid, or by using money obtained from the sale of other properties – called capital receipts. Read through the accounts and notes and then answer the questions at the end of the accounts. Discuss your answers with a colleague. If you disagree on any points, try to understand why this is and see if you can agree a common answer.

Notes to the Housing Revenue Account

1 Gross rent income

This is the total rent income due for the year after allowance is made for voids etc. During the year 1.3 per cent of lettable properties were vacant, in 1995/96 the figure was 1.2 per cent. The average rent was £32.68 a week in 1996/97, an increase of 2.1 per cent over the previous year.

2 Rent rebates/reimbursement of benefit

Assistance with rent is available under the Housing Benefits scheme for those on low incomes. Approximately 72 per cent of the total rents are met from Housing Benefit.

Housing Benefit is administered by the Council and the net cost to the Housing Revenue Account is as follows:

	1996/97 £'000	1995/96 £'000
Rebates given	8,193	8,008
Housing subsidy	6,575	6,505
Net cost to the Council	1,618	1,503

Prior to 31 March 1990 the Government Grant was paid by the Department of Social Security at a fixed percentage of rebates given. Under the new financial regime as explained (in note 3 below), there is no automatic fixed reimbursement of costs.

3 Housing subsidy

From 1 April 1990 the Housing Revenue Account was subject to new rules under the Local Government and Housing Act 1989 as follows:

- **Housing subsidy**: a new housing subsidy was introduced, which means that the level of support does not match that previously available due to the notional nature of the calculation.
- **The 'Ring Fence'**: the rules do not allow authorities to transfer funds from the Housing Revenue Account to the General Fund or vice-versa except under specified conditions. The activities to be included within the Account are also subject to redefinition.
- **Control**: a deficit balance on the Account is not allowed and the format of the Account must also comply with Schedule 4 of the Act.
- **Annual report**: an annual report to tenants must be published detailing housing activities and performance during the year.

4 Capital financing costs

Part IV of the Local Government and Housing Act 1989 requires a minimum revenue provision to be set aside to cover principal repayments. In addition, various other capital financing costs are to be charged to the account set by formula under Part VI of the same Act. These changes took effect from 1 April 1990.

	1996/97 £'000	1995/96 £'000
Minimum revenue provision	473	486
Interest	2,064	2,153
Other items	36	35
Total	2,573	2,674

5 Housing stock

The Council's stock of dwellings (excluding hostel dwellings) at 31 March 1997 was as set out below.

	1919–45	1945–64	After 1964	Total
Low-rise flats	182	668	1,954	2,804
Medium-rise flats	–	464	543	1,007
High-rise flats	–	–	384	384
Houses and bungalows	746	1,167	236	2,149
Total	928	2,299	3,117	6,344

The change in the stock during the year is summarized below.

	1996/97 £'000
Stock at 1 April	6,379
Less sales	33
Less conversions/deletions	2
Stock at 31 March	6,344

6 Rent arrears

During the year 1996/97 rent arrears as a proportion of gross collectable rent (including service charges) increased from 2.6 per cent to 2.9 per cent. The figures are as follows:

	1996/97 £'000	1995/96 £'000
Arrears at 31 March	328,000	287,000
Amounts written off	87,800	57,200
Bad and doubtful debts in Housing Revenue A/c at 31 March	135,000	120,000

This provision has been calculated in accordance with the Housing Revenue Account (Arrears of Rents and Charges) Directions 1990.

Questions

1 Where is income derived from and how much income was generated?
2 What is the cumulative surplus for this year?
3 How does the situation at the end of this year differ from the previous year?
4 What could the authority do to control its costs and raise income?
5 What purpose do the notes that accompany the accounts have?
6 How could the new rules explained in note 3 affect the Housing Department's financial planning?

Activity 5 Individual Learning: Empathetic and Critical Thinking

CASE STUDY: Helsinki City Council Annual Report

Read the enclosed extracts from the 1996 Annual Accounts of Helsinki City Council (Figure 9.4).

Questions

1 What support do you find in the figures for the claims made in the text?
2 Which figures appear inconsistent with the text?
3 If you were a Minister in the Finnish government, to what kind of grant aid application by Helsinki would you be sympathetic?
4 What additional information would you require?
5 Thinking about the presentation of the Helsinki accounts, not the content, how do you think they could be improved?

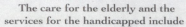
A WIDE RANGE OF SERVICES

Childern's day care
Day care places 23,515
Day care places
per 100 1 – 6 year olds 63
Care for the elderly
Places in sheltered housing 3,318
Places at old people's homes...2,199
Public Health care
Municipal health centres 32
Outpatient visits..................2.9 mill.
Physicians
per 1000 inhabitants..................1,5

SOCIAL AFFAIRS AND PUBLIC HEALTH

Social Affairs and Public Health is the largest sector of the services provided by the City. It affects practically each and every resident of Helsinki. More than half of the employees working for the City work in this sector. Social Affairs and Public Health includes children's day care, care for the elderly and the entire municipal health care system.

Helsinki offers day care to all children under school-age. Most children participate in the activities of day care centres. Parents also have the possibility to receive municipal financial support in order to care for the children under the age of three at home. Due to a relatively long statutory maternity leave most children under the age of one are cared for at home.

The care for the elderly and the services for the handicapped include
– housing services and old-age homes
– service and recreation centres
– home-aid services
– transport aid
The Public Health Care system includes
– maternity and children's clinics
– dental clinics
– mental health clinics
– school nurses and doctors
– various hospital services.
The municipal health centres offer the residents of Helsinki health services free of charge or at very reasonable prices.

EDUCATION AND CULTURE

The City is in charge of the school education, vocational education and adult education, all of them which are known for their high quality. There are 206 comprehensive schools and upper secondary schools in Helsinki. Although the education in most schools is provided in Finnish, there are 27 schools for Swedish-speakers and several other schools operating in other languages such as English, German, Russian and French. Education and school meals are free as is the school material in the comprehensive schools. The Adult Education Centres of Helsinki offer a considerably wide range of possibilities for people willing to develop themselves in different subjects and fields.

The City Library has a well-stocked network of 35 libraries offering not only traditional literary material but also computer services and Internet-stations for the use of the residents.

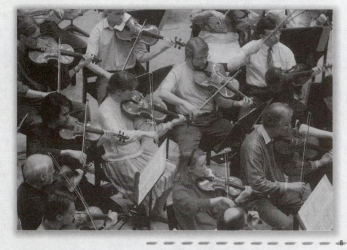

Figure 9.4 Helsinki City Council Annual Report

Source: Helsinki City Council (1996) Reproduced with permission

Helsinki is also proud to offer its citizens a large variety of cultural events and activities. The Helsinki City Museum consists of several different museums specialising in various different areas. Helsinki has its own art museum, which has a considerable collection of Finnish contemporary art. A Modern Art Museum is currently being constructed in the city centre.

The Helsinki City Theatre and the Helsinki Philharmonic Orchestra are well-known cultural institutions, which offer the residents numerous cultural events of high intenational quality. Helsinki takes pride in its new Opera-house as well.

The Helsinki Zoo gives the residents the possibility of observing a vast variety of species in circumstances equivalent to their natural environments.

The City also maintains playing fields, areas for recreation, sports halls, tennis courts and swimming halls. It also organises sports events for both young and old people, runs youth centres, provides club and free-time activities etc.

CITY PLANNING AND INFRASTRUCTURE

The City of Helsinki owns two thirds of the lands inside its boundaries. Helsinki is also a considerable landowner in the surrounding municipalities. The City acquires and sells land in order to ensure ideal conditions for its development. Helsinki also rents land to companies, for housing production, to the industry as well as to private persons. Ecological thinking and environmental consciousness play an important role in

City Library

35 branches
2.1 mill. volumes
0.1 mill. audio cassets and records
9.0 mill. book loans
6.5 mill. users
17.2 loans per inhabitant

Helsinki City Art Museum

49,000 visitors

Helsinki City Museum

70,500 visitors

Helsinki Philharmonic Orchestra

Number of concerts 90
Total audiences 146,800

Korkeasaari Zoo

Number of species 180
Visitors 571,200

Sports and recreation

Recreational areas
and parks ....5,400 ha
Sports halls 35
Swimming halls 13
Boat moorings 9,500

General education

Comprehensive schools 158
Senior secondary schools 48
Students (total) 65,900

Vocational and professional education

Institutions owned by the city 15
Students 12,704

Universities and university-level institutions

Number of institutions 8
Number of students 42,000
% of all students in Finland 31

Educational achievement

% of 15 year olds and over
with comprehensive
School certificate only 40
Intermediate qualification 40
University degree or equivalent 20

City's own housing production

Dwellings completed 623
Dwellings started 1,313
Dwellings renovated...............2,250
FIM 685 million was spent
on housing construction and
renovation during 1996

Housing stock

Dwellings, total 281,400
Rented dwellings owned
by the city 51,000

Land ownership in 1996

City of Helsinki ....122 km² (66 %)
Central government...24 km² (13 %)

city planning. These principles are applied in construction regulation, development and maintenance of the streetwork as well as parks and recreation areas.

The City promotes active cooperation with the enterprises and different organisations in the area as well as the Helsinki Chamber of Commerce and the regional council. Helsinki warmly welcomes enterprises and investors from the other parts of Finland and abroad to take advantage of the City's position as the ideal crossing-centre between the East and the West.

TRANSPORT FACILITIES

The efficient and safe movement of people and goods is ensured by means of effective traffic planning. Helsinki offers excellent harbour facilities. The flow of goods through the Port of Helsinki is constantly on the rise. In April, the City Council approved a plan to establish a new harbour in Vuosaari.

The Port of Helsinki began to use a Portnet system in the spring 1996. The bulk of the information about ships, cargoes and passengers comes through this system. It utilizes information technology in a new way, eases the flow of information between ports and improves safety.

The Port of Helsinki participates in the international, EU-funded Baltic Open Port Communication system. Its goal is to further the ship and cargo traffic in the Baltic Sea region as well as to speed up the area's integration into Europe's traffic network by producing telematics services for harbours and other target groups engaged in foreign trade. These

Figure 9.4 continued

services will cover the different subareas of logistical data flow.

The road network is constantly developed to better serve the increasing needs of transport.

The Helsinki City Transport's fleet includes buses, trams and underground trains. In addition, services are outsourced. The share of public transport is high, reaching almost 70 per cent in the central Helsinki area during the rush hours. The number of tram passengers in particular has risen significantly over the past years.

HOUSING, ENERGY AND WATER WORKS

In 1996 over 2,600 new dwellings were completed in Helsinki. The City also continued to invest considerable amounts in new housing and housing renovation. The main focus in other building construction was set on public service buildings, such as schools.

The City offers electricity, district heating, natural gas and related services to enterprises. Helsinki Energy is one of the largest producers and distributors of electricity and district heating. It has over 300 000 connected clients. Over 90 per cent of the City's housing is connected to

district heating. Helsinki Energy is going international. Expert projects relating to energy systems have commenced in the Baltic countries and nearby areas in Russia.

Helsinki Energy takes constantly into account the over-riding principles environmental consciousness and cost-effectiveness as does the Water Works, responsible for supplying the residents with high-quality drinking water.

The security of the residents is naturally one of the most important objectives for the City's administration. It is not surprising, therefore, that the units of the Rescue Department arrive at the scene of the accident within six minutes from dispatch.

Photo by Jussi Kautto

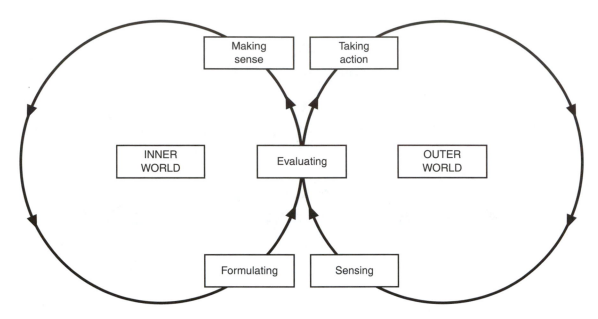

Figure 9.5 The thinking skills of the conversational manager

Activity 6 Individual Learning Review: Reflective Thinking

Outer world conversations

What outer world conversational skills can you identify in the manager's work described in this chapter? Have any of the types of conversational skills you have identified emerged for the first time? If so, add them to your accumulating model of the kinds of conversational skills you think are useful to managers of public services.

What things could you do to develop any of these conversational skills which you have just added to your model? What would be the first step?

Activity 7 Individual Learning: Metacognitive Thinking

Metacognition

Look back through the Thinking and Learning Activities you have been asked to carry out in this chapter. What thinking skills were involved in each of these activities? For each type of thinking, write down how you were learning what you were learning, when you were learning to think in each of the different ways.

NOTES

1   Caulfield, I. and Schulz, I. (1989) *Planning for Change: Strategic Management in Local Government.* Longman.
2   Gray, M. (1992) *Business Planning. Public Finance and Accountability,* no. 10 (April), pp. 12–14.
3   Jones, R. and Pendelbury, M. (1989) *Public Sector Accounting.* Pitman.
4   Hofstede, G. H. (1969) *The Game of Budget Control. Technology and Democratic Society.* Tavistock Publications.
5   Argyris, C. (1953) 'Human Problems with Budgets'. *Harvard Business Review,* pp. 97–103.
6   Hopwood, A. (1974) 'Accounting and Accountancy Behaviour' in *Accounting Age,* p. 64.
7   Hofstede, op. cit.
8   Coombs, H. M. and Jenkins, D. E. (1995) *Public Sector Financial Management.* Chapman and Hall, p. 229.

10

MANAGING RESOURCES IN PUBLIC SERVICES

Money is like a sixth sense, without it, you cannot make complete use of the other five.

(Somerset Maugham, *Of Human Bondage*, 1915)

LEARNING OUTCOMES

This chapter will enable the reader to:

- Understand central government resourcing of public services.
- Present financial proposals and financial information to a lay audience.
- Understand the ways in which public–private finance initiatives operate.
- Identify the main sources of European funding for public services.
- Understand option appraisal, risk assessment and sensitivity analysis.
- Consider people, training, management, inspection and trust as organizational resources.
- Understand why better management needs to precede significant additional resources.
- Consider the impact of financial decisions on people's lives.

INTRODUCTION

Public service managers need to understand the planning cycles which determine decisions about resources for public services. Resources can often be obtained from public funds. It helps to know about the sources of such funds and to act like a 'social entrepreneur' taking an active part in obtaining additional resources for public services (Chapter 8).

Whenever public service managers seek to implement changes, they are expected to be able to answer questions about resource implications. If the resource implications are substantial, they may be expected to produce or assist with the production of business plans, operational budgets and arrangements for monitoring and audit. They may be asked about other possible ways in which the same improvements might be achieved. Senior managers will want to see that other options have been considered and appraised.

We will look at sources of funds and the use of cost benefit analysis, risk assessment and sensitivity analysis in helping to appraise options for the use of these funds.

But money is not enough. We will consider the way other 'soft' resources limit the extent to which services can be improved by injecting more money. The ability to manage operations, while managing change and capital projects is crucial to delivering service improvements.

SOURCES OF FUNDS

Taxes are a major means of financing public services. Taxes also play a complex role in the working of a national economy. They are used to raise monies, to discourage consumer spending and to redistribute wealth. Taxes take many forms. Direct taxes are usually deducted when people are paid wages or salaries. Sales taxes, purchase or value added taxes are paid when money is spent to buy goods or services. Property taxes are levied on owners of dwellings or business premises. Corporation taxes are charged on profits made. Capital gains taxes are calculated when things are sold at a profit. Airport taxes are paid by passengers. Duties are charged when goods are imported and, in some countries, estate duty is assessed when someone dies.

Taxation is not the only means of raising public money. Money can be borrowed, services can be charged for, and capital assets, such as housing stock, can be sold. Charitable donations can come from members of the public, from national lotteries and from business sponsors. There are many European and United Nations funding bodies and many sources of international aid for the provision of public services. We have divided the ways in which funds are raised into five categories: income streams, taxes, private finance, sales of assets and lease-back and the use of derivatives.

1 Income Streams

Finance through existing income streams is most common in privatized utilities such as telephone, electricity, water or postal and broadcasting services. In the case of semi-privatized or 'marketized' services, it may be through pre-authorized increases in external funding limits (EFLs). In some cases it will be through the charging of licence fees, e.g. for using a radio or a TV or for driving a vehicle or for owning a dog. Bridges and roads may be subject to tolls, and fares are usually collected on public transport.

2 Taxes

- **Direct taxes** are levied on incomes, profits and wealth. These include such taxes as income tax, corporation tax and inheritance tax.
- **Indirect taxes** are levied on expenditure. Taxes such as sales tax, purchase tax, value added tax, fuel tax and the excise duties collected on alcohol and tobacco are all examples of indirect taxation.

3 Private Finance

If the public service organization is publicly owned, it can sometimes obtain private finance through joint ventures involving private sector partners. In the UK these are referred to as Private Finance Initiatives. The private partner carries the risk and the public partner provides the income stream.[1]

4 Sales of Assets and Lease-back

In some countries, capital for new services can be raised through the sale of publicly owned assets. These sales might be local – for example – the sale of a city centre railway station or an outdated hospital. A school might sell off part of its sports field for housing in order to finance a new science laboratory. At a national level, sales might involve the privatization of a national airline. Where locally provided public services require new premises, lease-back deals with property developers are not uncommon.

5 Use of Derivatives

There are a variety of strategies involving the use of derivatives to reduce the cost of borrowing or hedge against currency losses when international aid is involved. Derivatives are options or undertakings to buy or sell, loan or borrow money or bonds, in certain currencies at a certain point in the future, at a predetermined rate of interest and at a certain price. In the Thinking and Learning Activities at the end of this chapter, we invite you to consider the funding and resourcing issues confronting public service managers when building a 20 km road/rail link, involving two 6 km sea bridges and an 8 km tunnel, connecting Denmark to Sweden.

PUBLIC EXPENDITURE PLANNING

In 1961 in the UK, the Plowden Committee recommended that:

> Regular surveys should be made of public expenditure as a whole, over a period of years ahead and in relation to prospective resources; decisions involving substantial future expenditure should be taken in the light of these surveys.[2]

Prior to 1961 the UK government had presented both its revenue and its expenditure plans to Parliament at the same time. Following the *Plowden Report*, a delay was introduced between presenting the expenditure plan and presenting the revenue plan to finance the expenditure.[3] In 1992 the UK government decided to bring the presentation of the revenue and spending plans back together again. Coombs and Jenkins[4] saw four main advantages:

1 Ministers would be able to judge expenditure plans in the light of expected income.
2 The early announcement of tax proposals would enable tax payers to plan better.
3 Policies would appear more consistent if linked to financial planning.
4 A more informed debate could take place.

Box 10.1 shows what is contained in the UK annual Budget statement.

PRIVATE FINANCE INITIATIVES

In the UK in 1992, the then Chancellor of the Exchequer, Norman Lamont,[5] announced the introduction of the Private Finance Initiative (PFI). The objective of this initiative was to increase the involvement of the private sector in the financing and management of services that traditionally have been supported by the public purse. It was heralded as a partnership between the public and private sector whereby the private sector could provide a range of commercial and creative skills for the benefit of public services. A PFI panel was appointed to oversee the development of the new initiative. The UK Labour government elected in 1997 quickly made it clear that it intended to develop the PFI. It replaced the PFI panel with a PFI taskforce. The PFI taskforce drew up standard contract conditions and a step-by-step guide to the PFI process. Box 10.2 shows three main types of PFI project.

Examples of Private Finance Initiatives

Most PFI projects are contracted between a public service sponsor such as a Health Service or a University and a consortium of interested private partners such as building contractors, service operators and project financiers. Most PFIs are financed by a combination of 10–15 per cent risk-bearing share capital and 85–90 per cent bank borrowing. Under this type of arrange-

---

Box 10.1

AN ANNUAL BUDGET STATEMENT

- A summary of the main Budget and tax spending changes that have taken place
- An analysis of departmental spending plans for the next three years
- A statement of the government's medium-term financial strategy
- The likely 'out-turn' for public finances in the current year

- A forecast of the likely financial position one year ahead
- The cost of grant relief from taxation to certain groups
- A description of the contributions to revenue
- A short-term economic forecast

Box 10.2

PFI PROJECTS

- **Free-standing** whereby the private sector partner recovers all costs through charges to the user. Examples of this approach included the construction of road bridges such as the one to the Isle of Skye in Scotland.
- **Joint ventures** involve contributions from both the public and private sector but the private sector partner retains overall control. The private sector partner recovers some costs through charging. The government subsidizes the project through loans or equity or the transfer of assets such as land. Normally projects would only be subsidized if they were of social benefit and the costs of providing them could not be fully recovered by charging.
- **Private provision** includes residential care for the elderly, prison services and the provision of kidney dialysis.

---

ment, the private sector company signs a contract with the public sector organization to build a new facility with the agreement that the construction running costs will be recovered almost entirely from charges levied on the end user over the lifetime of the contract. Typically a project has a contract life of 15 to 20 years.

In the UK, the University of Brighton agreed with Dillons book shop to operate the University bookshop and an adjoining café. The University provided the space whilst the contractor provided a full-bookshop service, including linking the bookshop to the University's IT network. In the café, the University specified the catering arrangements and opening times. An initial rent-free period was agreed and subsequent rents were linked to the turnover of the bookshop and café. Another scheme was developed by the University whereby a Housing Association was contracted to develop accommodation to replace unsuitable student housing facilities. The capital financing for this development was arranged by the Housing Association through a combination of their own resources and external borrowing. The arrangement was intended to share risk and be of mutual benefit to all parties. The Housing Association assumed the development and operating risk while the University assumed the occupancy risk.

Many of the older public service organizations have a problem with crumbling infrastructure. Many sewage and water supply pipes are collapsing under the weight of traffic. Bridges are due for renewal. Buildings originally donated by charities are no longer suitable for hospitals or schools. Railways need modern track, signalling and rolling stock. Ferry boats are not up to contemporary safety standards. This work is attractive to the private sector. Although originally intended to provide for both the building and the delivery of public services, in practice in the UK, PFI schemes have been used mainly to build or rebuild the infrastructures rather than deliver services directly. Figure 10.1 summarizes the 14 steps in the PFI process.

Private Finance Initiatives: Benefits and Problems

The benefits to public services include:

- Value for money because the overall cost to the public service will be reduced
- A transfer to the private sector of risks such as escalating costs and delays
- A reduction in public borrowing

The benefits to the private sector include:

- Security of work, which is particularly important during periods of recession
- Long-term cashflow and access to lucrative government contracts

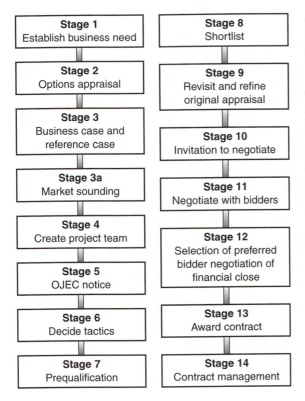

Stage 1 Establish business need	**Stage 8** Shortlist
Stage 2 Options appraisal	**Stage 9** Revisit and refine original appraisal
Stage 3 Business case and reference case	**Stage 10** Invitation to negotiate
Stage 3a Market sounding	**Stage 11** Negotiate with bidders
Stage 4 Create project team	**Stage 12** Selection of preferred bidder negotiation of financial close
Stage 5 OJEC notice	
Stage 6 Decide tactics	**Stage 13** Award contract
Stage 7 Prequalification	**Stage 14** Contract management

Figure 10.1 A step-by-step guide to PFI

The private sector has been criticized for being slow to realize these benefits. According to the UK *Guardian* newspaper (24 June 1998), local authorities did not communicate the benefits of private finance in developing public services.

THE EUROPEAN UNION: RESOURCING

The European Union (EU) has two funds which interest public service managers:

- The European Social Fund (ESF)
- The European Regional Development Fund (ERDF)

The EU collects Value Added Tax (VAT) on the goods and services traded by member states (1.2 per cent of the VAT collected in 1996). Up to 1.22 per cent of each member's Gross National Product (GNP) is also donated to EU funds.

An Office in Brussels

National governments encourage their public service organizations to make their case for a share of EU funds. In order to be on hand to make their case, many public service organizations have set up offices in Brussels and have regional European liaison offices. Over the years these offices have learned how to put together bids that meet European funding criteria. Bids often require detailed research into the social and economic conditions of those areas on whose behalf the bid is made. Information may be required, for example, regarding economic activity, levels of deprivation and the state of the labour market. EU fund managers are concerned that their grants produce sustainable benefits. This is often referred to as 'capacity building'. What they might ask, will be the permanent gain in the skills, knowledge and expertise of a local community? How many hours of vocational guidance, practical training and theory input would each participant in the project receive? In the EU, regional bodies from individual countries must produce and have approved a Single Programming Document containing their proposals for EU funding.

Matched Funding

Monitoring procedures must record all the work that is carried out and account for all the money spent. Money supplied by the EU usually has to be matched by money obtained from other sources, be they public, private or charitable. This is called matched funding. Some EU funding is conditional on the involvement of local people and the production of local Action Plans. These set out how particular social and economic issues will be addressed. One difficulty this creates for public service managers is that the process of getting people together to work on the preparation of an action plan raises their hopes and aspirations. Yet there is no guarantee that the bid will succeed.

The Bidding Process

It is clear that resourcing public services through applications for on–off funding will involve the public service manager in more than just 'number crunching' – though the numbers certainly must be crunched. A range of conversational skills is needed to work across departments and to consult and involve communities. Often creative as well as numerical thinking (Chapter 11) is needed in order to work out ways in which funding criteria can be met. When there are a number of options or projects for which a bid might be made, which one should the public service manager choose? How are the merits of each project option to be appraised? We turn next to option appraisal.

OPTION APPRAISAL

Whenever public service managers seek a significant increase in resources, they are likely to be asked whether or not they have appraised other ways of achieving similar benefits or what greater benefits might be obtained by using the same resources differently. The process used to answer these kinds of questions is called option appraisal. Resources might be requested to support revenue expenditure over a short period – such projects are often termed 'pump priming'. As we saw in the previous chapter, such expenditure is called revenue spending because it will all be spent during the period of the project and there will be nothing tangible of any residual value at the end of the period. When there are things of value that will remain at the end of the project period, like buildings, vehicles, stocks or equipment, this expenditure is called capital expenditure and the project is often called a capital project. In the case of capital expenditure on buildings, the value may persist for 20 years or more. In the case of equipment, the value may persist for only a few years, especially if the equipment is based on computer technology.

If changes which a manager wishes to implement in a public service involve capital expenditure above certain limits, which are often laid down by statute or in financial regulations called Standing Financial Instructions (SFIs), then the funding body will almost certainly want to see an option appraisal. This is an appraisal – primarily in financial terms – of the relationship between the costs and the benefits of different ways of implementing changes in public services.[6] These different ways are the so-called 'options.' The appraisal of each option usually entails cost benefit analysis, risk assessment and sensitivity analysis. Public service managers play a key role in each of these. These processes cannot be carried out by an accountant working in isolation. Where the costs and benefits are expressed in money terms, the problem arises as to what value to put on the money. Clearly, money now is of much more value than money that is to be spent in five years' time. Think of all the interest we would earn on the money if we could hold on to it for five years. Think of all the interest we would lose if we had to wait five years before we started receiving financial benefit from the project. The technique that is used to compare the 'net present values' of monies which will be spent and received at different times during the future life of the project is called 'discounted cashflow'.

Comparing Net Present Values: Discounted Cashflow

Especially where the time periods involved are extensive, the financing body may insist that all cashflow forecasts are produced using Net Present Values (NPVs). This involves discounting (or reducing) the value of monies spent or incomes received by a fixed percentage for each year's delay in spending the money or receiving the revenue. The fixed percentage is usually based on the government's projected inflation rate or the average interest rate that the government expects to pay when borrowing money. This fixed percentage is called the discount rate. Many spreadsheet programs, or pocket calculators, are programmed to allow you to calculate NPVs based on different discount rates. Often government departments or NGOs issue tables of the discount rates to be used. For simplicity, let us suppose that a discount rate of 10 per cent has been set, then 10,000 Rupees which will not be spent or received for two years will have a present Net Present Value (NPV) calculated as follows:

The value in 2 years' time
has been calculated as   10,000 Rupees

The value in 1 year's time, discounted at 10% is

    10,000 less 10% of 10,000

    10,000 less 1000 =   9,000 Rupees

The value now, i.e. the Net Present Value, is

    9,000 less 10% of 9,000 Rupees

    9,000 less 900 =   8,100 Rupees

The example has been simplified to illustrate the principle of Discounted Cash Flow (DCF). All other things being equal, most of us would rather receive a sum of money now rather than wait a number of years to receive it. This is because we would be able to invest the money and receive interest, thereby reducing any loss in its purchasing power as a result of price inflation. DCF calculations, whether using tables or calculators, are simply a way of calculating how much you would need now, assuming you could invest it at the laid down discount rate, in order to be no worse off than if you had waited for your money.

In the following section we recount a conversation with Hassan Patel who has to calculate the Net Present Value of a new irrigation project in The North West Frontier of Pakistan. Hassan is a village health services official near Peshawar, Pakistan.

COST BENEFIT ANALYSIS

When Hassan was trying to compare his various projects, in order to decide which should be given the World Bank support, he could quantify some benefits but not others. On the basis of some things he could quantify – for example, comparing net present values – he got a short list of options. But what to do next? How can the costs and benefits of the different options be compared in order to help decide which options to put forward for funding? The process he is using is called cost benefit analysis. In cost benefit analysis the non-quantifiable benefits of each option can be ranked by key stakeholders who have been asked to help by drawing up a list of desiderata – the benefits desired as a result of implementing changes in the service. Each option to be appraised is then ranked against each of the desired benefits.[7] A total of, say, ten points for each benefit is then allocated between each option, reflecting how well the stakeholder thinks each option will deliver the desired benefits being considered. The pattern of the allocation will follow the order of the ranking, but will not be proportional to it. This allocation to each option is called the option benefit score.

Stakeholders are then asked to weight each desired benefit, according to their relative importance to the stakeholder. Each option benefit score is then multiplied by the weighting of the desired benefit, to produce a list of weighted benefit scores. All the weighted benefit scores of each option are then added together. The options with the highest total weighted benefit scores are the options which that stakeholder perceives as producing the most beneficial changes in the public service. The weighted benefit scores of different groups of stakeholders can be aggregated. Sometimes the scores of different stakeholder groups can be given different weightings. For example, the highest weighting might be given to the service users, or to front-line staff, or to local politicians. The lowest weighting might be given to the finance department!

Software programs are available to 'crunch' all the numbers, if a lot of stakeholders are being consulted. Ranking, rating and weighting benefits and comparing the results with the financial costings described earlier, can inform a debate between key stakeholders about the selection of options for changes in public services.

RISK MANAGEMENT

Implementing changes almost inevitably involves some risk, some uncertainty, some unknown factors.

Box 10.3

EXTRACT FROM A CONVERSATION WITH HASSAN PATEL 'CLEAN WATER FOR THE VILLAGE'

Terry: Tell me how it works here.

Hassan: A Non Governmental Organization has invited proposals for the installation of water treatment and irrigation plants in villages in the areas bordering Afghanistan. Initially, proposals will be short-listed from projects showing the highest Net Present Values. All project proposals must use the same discount table. A discount rate of 10 per cent has been chosen to exceed the current cost of borrowing funds from the World Bank. Later, other intangible benefits, such as population health, employment, technology transfer and the welfare of refugees will be appraised in order to make the final selections.

Terry: What actually happened?

Hassan: In this village, the proposed scheme cost 4,000,000 Rupees and a replacement pump has to be budgeted for in 4 years' time, at a cost of 800,000 Rupees. The intangible benefits of the health gain from treating the water have not been quantified, but I estimate that the value of the rice crop will increase by 1,2000,000 Rupees in year one, rising to a maximum increase of 2,400,000 Rupees in year two. I think that the value of the increased rice production will decline thereafter to 1,200,000 Rupees in year three, to 800,000 Rupees thereafter, as the initial flush of fertility in the soil is exhausted. The residual value of the plant and machinery is assumed to be zero, i.e. its value, so we will write it off.

Terry: Can you give me the numbers?

Hassan: Here's the tabulation for this village: (The table is reproduced below.)

Terry: So you're through to the next round then?

Hassan: Yes, this project has a positive Net Present Value of 471,000 Rupees. Our proposal can go forward to the next round where it will be compared with the NPV of other bids. Final selection will then be made using other benefits, such as health gains and impact on the refugee problem.

Terry: Well, good luck with your bid. Thank you.

| Year | Cash in (Rs000's) | | Cash out (Rs000's) | |
	Actual	discounted	Actual	discounted
Year 5	800	497	0	0
Year 4	800	546	800	546
Year 3	1,200	901	0	0
Year 2	2,400	1,982	0	0
Year 1	1,200	1,091	0	0
Year 0			4,000	4,000
NPV		**5,017**	minus	**4,546 = 471**

But not changing things is sometimes risky too. It is just that we do not usually think to assess the risk of doing nothing. Not all risk is bad. It can excite, challenge and motivate. When assessing risk, it can be useful to distinguish between an estimate of probability that something might go wrong and an estimate of the scale of the consequences, if it did. The probability might have to be assessed by referring to experience elsewhere or by consulting expert opinion. Consequences can usually be predicted on a worst-case basis. The risk of each option might then be assessed by comparing the result of multiplying probability times consequence for each project.

Assessing Your Own Chances

In public services, even a small probability of something going wrong might rule out some options for change, especially if the consequences are politically damaging, or if they threaten life, livelihood or national security. The promotion of public health and safety is the raison d'être of many public services. For example, the Health and Safety Inspectorates, the atomic energy authorities, highway construction, railway transportation, air traffic control, environmental health, water supply and water treatment or food and drug testing, all exist to ensure public safety. Decisions to release criminals, the mentally sick or the mentally disordered often involve finite probabilities of awful consequence. In military applications, the use of computers to model and simulate and assess the chances that certain things will happen is common. The use of computers to assess the chances of disasters occurring is spreading into civilian services such as meteorology, flood control and the prediction of earthquakes, hurricanes and volcanic activity. Computers, in conjunction with mathematical models, have even been used to estimate the likelihood of a riot occurring in a prison.

Sensitivity Analysis

Public service managers can be expected to be familiar with techniques such as sensitivity analysis. Key stakeholders are consulted about the likely range of key variables – the best, worst and the most likely cases. The effect of each condition is calculated. When the effect of even a small error in the predicted value of a key variable produces an unacceptable consequence, then that option may be rejected as too risky – too sensitive to even small errors in the manager's predictions.

Accounting for Inflation

We do not expect public service managers to base their choice of a discount rate on their own estimates of the level of inflation which they expect to occur during the life of a project. It is too difficult to estimate these levels, because the expected rate of inflation in prices of imported materials might be different from the expected rate of inflation in the prices of local materials, which might in turn be different from the expected rates of inflation in public service wages, where these again, might be different from the expected rates of inflation in public service salaries. We suggested the use of a government treasury figure, because the treasury will have attempted to model all these variables. Alternatively, we suggested using the open market fixed interest rate for a public service borrower, over the period of the project. We suggested the latter because it will reflect the money market's view of inflationary prospects. In the case of the Denmark–Sweden road/rail link project, which you will find at the end of this chapter, you would be especially concerned with any likely inflation in the price of steel. The risks here might be better managed through forward contracting – in this case by entering a contract to buy steel at various points in the future, at prices that can be agreed now.

WHICH MORE DO YOU WANT?

More Money?

In manufacturing industry, if only one were given 10 per cent more money, it would be relatively easy to improve productivity, raise quality, or increase production. Public services are different. Politicians, bankers and shareholders tear their hair in frustration at the length of time it seems to take public service managers to gear up services in return for extra money. Even worse, the quality of the services often deteriorates when managers take their eyes off the day-to-day tasks involved in delivering public services. The problem is not the quantity of the money, it is the quality of the management.

More Staff?

Managers cannot provide many extra services without some extra people. Public service managers need to learn to manage the kind of people they can recruit. Many new recruits have little concept of public duty. In many countries, a job in public service no longer carries its former status and security. Idealism born of patriotism or socialism is less available as a call to serve 'the common good'[8] Altruism no longer commands respect amongst the neighbours. Public service managers often recruit from societies whose cultures favour self-serving, rather than the serving of others.[9] Ministers lament, but their pleas go unheeded. People have seen for themselves what one chief inspector can do to a whole generation of teachers. They have heard for themselves what the media mutter about public service workers. In 2001, in the UK *Guardian*, Madeleine Bunting bemoaned the lack of 'a vision of the common good' with which a new generation of public service workers might identify. At the same time John Carvel[10] reported that the UK was short of 10,000 secondary teachers and 110,000 midwives and nurses. Apparently unaware of the ethical implications, UK managers plundered the scarce resources of countries like the Philippines, the West Indies and Zimbabwe, to fill over one-third of the nursing posts in London. Five thousand psychiatrists and other key staff were poached from Spain, along with 70 social workers from South Africa.

More Pay?

Better pay is not the whole answer. By the late 1990s, senior police officials in the UK earned more than lawyers, but much of metropolitan policing was in disarray. Where governments have a more monopolistic hold on a particular professional group, pay levels can become a much more serious threat to the service. In the UK, by 2001 the average pay of a secondary teacher had declined to that of a manual worker. A pay increase of around 30 per cent would have been needed to restore relativity. This money would have been wasted without the development of a more thoughtful and a more conversational approach to the practice of management by governors, head teachers and heads of department. An increase of 45 per cent would have been needed to restore the relative pay of university teachers. Higher calibre university teachers might then have been recruited, but they would not have stayed long if their managers lacked management skill. Better management needs to precede more money. Sue Richards,[11] former civil servant and then Professor of Public Policy at Birmingham University, agreed that the rate of new money needed to be slowed: 'If you overload the system it will collapse.' Senior managers in the police force and in local and national government reported difficulty in managing investments, especially where these involved interagency groups. 'Yes, money matters, especially for pay and conditions, but what matters more is the sense that your life's work is valued.' Trades union leader John Monks said that 'pay is not the only issue'.

More Management?

Shortages of trained staff cannot be solved in the medium term by more money. Existing staff need to be managed more efficiently and more individually. They need to be managed less as groups. The approach of the managers will need to be more thoughtful, more practical, more conversational, less 'strategic'.

More Talk?

Helen Oakley, Assistant Director of Social Services at Stoke-on-Trent, admitted to 'talking the talk' of performance management, while desperately trying to hold on to the public service ethos which first attracted her into social work:

> I still actually want to make things better for those who live on the margins of society. Managers need to be trained to surface those values of public service that can still motivate people to make better use of existing resources, before they bury them under more investment initiatives.

More Inspection?

Many teachers yearn to be left to get on with their teaching. They resent deeply the time they waste filling boxes with documents freshly prepared to satisfy inspectors and assessors. Of course, 15,000 UK teachers were failing their children! Out of 560,000 teachers, 15,000 represented a regrettable 3 per cent; but it was only 3 per cent. How many other professions can boast a 97 per cent level of competence? Yes, it would have been better if the figure were less than 3 per cent, but many public service managers asked whether the money spent on inspection could have been better spent on improving resources, without damaging the morale of the 97 per cent of competent teachers. Many of them left in droves during the 1990s era of OFSTED.

More Training?

As we saw in Chapter 1, the unit of resource for the provision of public services fell dramatically in the period 1980–2000 throughout the world. This was owing to population growth, the increased proportion of the elderly in that population, the progressive erosion of family life, and the spread of infectious diseases like TB and HIV. At the same time as demand rose, the ability of poorer countries, like Madagascar, to fund public services, was ravaged by the demand of richer countries for interest payments on debts. Even in the richer countries, we saw a sometimes politically engendered reluctance to pay taxes for services which might be needed by someone else. The size of the capital injection needed to restore the funding of public services to their per capita levels of the 1970s would exceed the ability of most public service managers to manage and monitor. Training in the implementation of change and the management of projects needs to precede any injection of money on the scale that is required. Extra money distracts attention from the frequent complaint of staff that public service managers lack the cognitive and conversational skills needed to overcome resistance and manage change.

More Trust?

It seems to be a question of trust. The graduate police officer who resented having to spend 2 hours and 14 minutes filling in forms, before anyone was allowed to investigate a telephone call about a child at risk, felt impuned and demotivated by what she experienced as a lack of trust in her judgement of what was needed. Public service managers need to learn how to re-motivate demotivated staff (Chapter 7) and how to build trusting relationships with individuals (Chapter 8). A vicious circle needs to be broken. Head office seems to decide that local services cannot be trusted. Head office then exercises closer control and takes power away from local managers. This weakens local decision-making and lowers the status of local managers. Fewer high-calibre people are attracted to work for the lower local service, so the local service deteriorates further. This deterioration is used by head office to justify its original decision. It exercises even closer control and further weakens local management.

More Thought?

Public service managers must adopt a more thoughtful, more practical, more conversational approach to managing public services. In this book we rarely say 'must', but we do so now. We say 'must' because we have seen the alternative. Private schools, private health insurance, private security guards and private pensions do not buy a society that is free of noise, smog and airborne disease, where the streets are safe for children to play, without fear of kidnapping. The contribution of self-reliance and private savings is not underestimated, but well-resourced well managed public services remain a hallmark of civilized society.

FINAL THOUGHTS: 'THERE'S MORE THAN TWO OPTIONS'

In previous chapters we saw how changes in public services have been driven by financial considerations. In the villages in Pakistan that did not get their clean water projects approved: it is the children and the elderly who are dying now from chronic diarrhoea or worse. In the next chapter Mary Ruebens spells out graphically the consequences for staff and vulnerable members of the community when managers choose the wrong options. Yet there are usually more than two options. It is usually worth a pause for the thought – 'what other possibilities exist?' We think that the benefits of other options should be thought about first. In what other way might the same benefits to stakeholders be obtained? Thinking about benefits to service users avoids wasting time on costing sterile options. For public services, it is rarely appropriate, even if it were practically possible, to attach monetary values to benefits such as the saving of a human life, the furtherance of a human right, the reduction of road rage, or the preservation of the rain forest. We have suggested instead a way in which to orchestrate a debate between the key stakeholders on the relative merits of each option. The methods we have suggested allow the outcomes of the debate to be quantified. This allows different options to be compared. We do not attempt to measure absolute benefits, let alone attach monetary values to them. As we shall see in the next chapter, thinking about what is a 'good' option is not always easy. It takes us into the area of beliefs, values and value judgements. Such judgements demand an approach that goes beyond the science of measurement and quantification.

Time is Money

On the cost side of our cost benefit appraisal, we have advocated the estimation of profit (surplus) and loss (deficit), the projection of growth in the balance sheet (net worth) and the forecasting of the cashflow. The estimated profit and loss account and the projected growth in the net worth of the balance sheet will be of special interest where public services are being provided by private enterprises like Sky TV, or most Greek shipping lines or ferry boats, or where the public services are being provided by privatized but publicly regulated organizations, such as British Telecom (BT) or Virgin Trains, in the UK.

Whether privatized or publicly owned, we think that managers of public services need to be aware of the way in which delays in implementing changes can cost money and affect the viability of projects. We have suggested that the value of all cashflows should be discounted to take this into account and we have argued for the use of Net Present Value (NPV) as the basis for comparing the cost of different options. The costs and the benefits of each option can then be brought together. Options showing the most benefits for the least cost should be short-listed for selection by key stakeholders. It was on this basis that Hassan argued successfully for a clean water project in the village where we spoke to him.

Spreading the Good Works

If there are resources enough to implement more than one change, then an initial tentative allocation could be made by ranking the projects in descending order of their ratio of benefits to cost. The overall benefit of the fund allocation should then be thought about. You might use utilitarian thinking – the greatest good to the greatest number. Sometimes stakeholders will prefer to have you implement a larger number of lower-cost changes, rather than one big change which confers outstanding benefits, but which consumes nearly all of the available resources. In such cases, a public service manager may be advised to give nearly everybody some of what they want, rather than give a relative few nearly all of what they want.

Honest Dealings

A public service manager who is armed with an 'objective' cost benefit analysis is more likely to be able to resist the corrupting influence of those who might seek to abuse their power in order to benefit their own village, their own constituency, their own backyard, or their own back pocket. Public service managers should always be on their guard against those who might be in the pay of those seeking economic power or political influence. Courageous and 'objective' public servants who think for themselves can help to defend society against the kind of corruption that, in the end, undermines the public consensus by which some people in society agree that part of their wealth will be used to provide public services for those who would not otherwise be able to have them.

- The impact of timing and the choice of sources of funding was explored.
- We considered the ways inspection can damage trust and concluded that better management needed to precede extra resources.
- More money will not deliver better public services without better management and better training of managers in the conversational skills needed to motivate people as individuals and not as groups.
- Public service managers were highlighted, as was their important role as stewards of the resources entrusted to them and as guardians of the fragile consensus under which that trust is given.

SUMMARY

- Managers need to know about the wide variety of sources of funds that are available for financing the delivery and development of public services. The public service manager's role in accessing these sources of funding was discussed.
- If public service managers want a large capital grant, or a large sum for initial funding, then the funding body will want to see that they have considered other options and have properly appraised them.
- Our methodology for appraising options adds benefit analysis, risk assessment and sensitivity analysis to estimating costs. It is argued that this is a more 'objective' way of structuring highly subjective questioning, listening and learning conversations with key stakeholders.

THINKING AND LEARNING ACTIVITIES

Activity 1 Self-assessment

1 Define the following terms and give one example of how they might be applied in public services:
   - Net Present Value
   - Discounted cashflow
   - Benefit analysis
   - Sensitivity analysis
   - Risk assessment
   - Cost benefit analysis
2 Explain why discounted cashflow techniques are used in public services.
3 What are the benefits of private finance initiatives?
4 What problems are associated with the use of inspection to secure value for invested money?
5 What training will managers need in order to handle large inward investment and change?
6 In what sense are public service managers stewards?

Activity 2 Individual Learning: Numerical Thinking

Doing a financial appraisal

A public service is carrying out an appraisal of a proposed learning and training resource centre for staff. The following information is available:

	Amount £
Estimated annual costs:	
Premises	16,000
Employees: librarians	33,000
clerical staff (part time)	12,500
Supplies and services	7,900
Estimated annual revenue:	
Income from fines and charges	3,600
Estimated capital costs:	
Purchase of temporary building near town hall	26,000
Computer and index system	14,900

All capital costs are being financed by a loan with interest at 9 per cent per annum. The loan is repayable over 15 years in equal instalments.

1 Set out the estimated staff costs in the first year of operation, based on the above figures.
2 Assuming that the proposed Resource Centre loans 11,000 items to borrowers in its first year of operation, calculate the average cost per item.

Activity 3 Individual or Paired Learning: Numerical Thinking

Taxing time in Australia

The office belonging to the Australian Inland Revenue is currently on split sites. One site has spare land which could be developed; the other has planning permission to add extra floors. Both sites could be sold and a new office built out of town. Relocation to another part of Australia is not practical. Doing nothing would be difficult because the public complain constantly about going to the wrong office or about being shuttled between the two offices. Media and political pressure is being stirred up by complainants. The long list of options includes:

1 Relocate out of town, selling the existing site.
2 Extend the office that has the spare land.
3 Add a floor to the other office.
4 Move elsewhere in Australia.
5 Do nothing.

The short list of options is:

1 Relocate out of town.
2 Extend sideways
3 Add a floor

Costs

The NPVs of each option have been calculated as:

> Option 1: A$21.0 million
> Option 2: A$26.0 million
> Option 3: A$22.0 million

Benefits

Stakeholder top 5 desirable benefits	Stakeholder weighting	Stakeholder average scores		
		Option 1	Option 2	Option 3
No disruption	10	4	4	9
Car parking	8	5	0	9
Access to public transport	1	9	5	1
Room for expansion	2	1	1	9
Better working conditions	7	7	2	9

1 Which option has the highest total weighted benefit score? Which has the lowest?
2 Considering the costs and benefits together, which looks like the 'best' option?
3 What further questions might you want to ask?

Activity 4 Individual or Paired Learning: Numerical Thinking

CASE STUDY: The Sweden–Denmark 'Great Belt'

Working first on your own, read the case study and note down answers to the questions. When you have finished, share your answers with a colleague. Explore differences in opinion and try to come to a consensus about your answers.

The Danish public service road/rail link with Sweden involves Great Belt Contractors building a 6.8 km road bridge; a 6.6 km road and rail bridge across the sea and an 8 km railway tunnel in two parallel lanes. Each component of the project involves different main contractors. By passing a Public Works Act, which opened up the funding possibilities allowable for public works, the savings in finance costs were so great that the envisaged toll charges to motorists were reduced by 20 per cent! Debt repayment was reduced to less than 35 years. The original traffic budget (first forecast in 1988) was based on 14,500 private cars and 2,700 lorries per day when fully utilized.

- *What do you see as problematic so far?*
- *What financial planning prudence would you exercise?*
- *What steps would you take long before the bridge opens?*

At a peak 2,600 Danish citizens are likely to be employed during the construction phase. Once completed, the link will offer continuing employment to 143 maintenance, technical and vessel surveillance personnel – five in a tourist information centre.

Total length of railtrack is 80 km. Total length of steel suspension cables is 1,000 km. 180,000 tons of sheet steel will be used on the two bridges.

- *What occurs to you?*
- *What questions would you like to ask?*

The budget includes a European subsidy of 250 million Danish Kroner at 1990 prices, salary indexed and 300 million Swedish Kronor per year from the Swedish State Railway, starting in January 1991. Not all the contract payments can be made in Danish Kroner. The construction period will span at least two winters in the North Sea.

- *What risks do you foresee and how could you manage them?*

Income budgets have been based on a start-up rate of 10,000 vehicles per day, increasing at 17 per cent per annum thereafter over 20 years. These correspond to the trend growth rates produced by extrapolating the growth of traffic on the ferries with which the toll road and rail bridges will compete.

There is concern that the Swedish Kronir will devalue. The private sector contractor partners have already completed extensive on shore developments in Denmark and Sweden ahead of schedule and their key shareholders are pressing for dividend payments. Repayment of public sector finance is very sensitive to the construction consortia's real rates of interest (actual interest less inflation rates). For example, a 1 per cent increase on the bank overdraft moves the period of debt repayment from 26 to 34 years. Fixed interest loans would be the best protection against rising interest rates and would produce the best chance of low real interest if inflation exceeds the budgeted levels. The quoted rates in Danish Kroner are higher for private sector borrowers and have penalties for early repayment. Currently variable interest rates in Kroner are low and falling. They are barely 2 per cent above the budgeted inflation rate.

- *What funding options occur to you to minimize the repayment period, to pacify the private sector shareholders and to hedge the risks associated with the Danish Kroner?*

Note

Under the Public Works Act you are allowed to borrow in Germany, Switzerland, Japan, France and Belgium. Your European Union loan (5 million Danish Kroner) is available as a 'draw down as you need it' facility, with the European International Bank.

Activity 5 Individual Learning Review: Reflective Thinking

Inner world thinking

What inner world thinking skills can you identify in the manager's work described in this chapter? Have any of the thinking skills you have identified emerged for the first time in this chapter? If so, add them to your accumulating model of the kinds of thinking skills that you consider to be useful to managers of public services.

What things could you do to develop any of the thinking skills that you have just added to your model? What would be the first step?

Outer world conversations

What outer world conversational skills can you identify in the manager's work described in this chapter? Have

any of the types of conversational skills you have identified emerged for the first time? If so, add them to your accumulating model of the kinds of conversational skills you think are useful to managers of public services.

What things could you do to develop any of these conversational skills which you have just added to your model? What would be the first step?

Activity 6 Individual Learning: Metacognitive Thinking

Metacognition

Look back through the Thinking and Learning Activities you have been asked to carry out in this chapter. What thinking skills were involved in each of these activities? For each type of thinking, write down how you were learning what you were learning, when you were learning to think in each of the different ways.

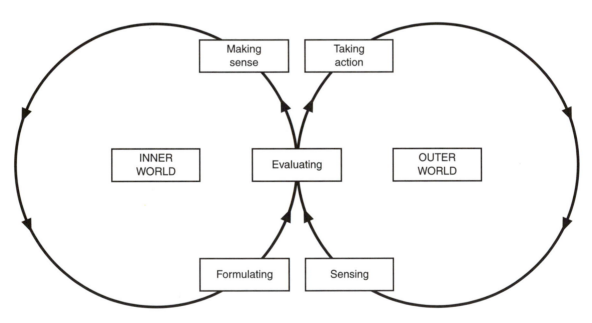

Figure 10.2 The thinking skills of the conversational manager

NOTES

1 Cargill, R. (1991) 'Investing Surplus Funds'. *Public Finance and Accountability*, 13 December, pp. 10–12.
2 *Plowden Report* (1961). HMSO.
3 Lapsley, I. (1986) 'Investment Appraisal in Public Sector Organisations'. *Management Accounting*, June, pp. 28–31.
4 Coombs, H. M. and Jenkins, D. E. (1995) *Public Sector Financial Management*. 2nd edn. Chapman & Hall, p. 229.
5 Chancellor of the Exchequer (1992). Autumn Statement.
6 Henderson, J. (1984) *Appraising Options*. Health Economics Research Unit. Aberdeen University.
7 Sugden, R. and Williams, A. (1978) *The Principles of Practical Cost Benefit Analysis*. Oxford University Press.
8 'The Common Good' (2001) *Guardian*, 27 March.
9 Ibid.
10 John Carvel (2001) *Guardian*, 28 March, p. 2.
11 Sue Richards (2001) *Guardian*, 28 March, p. 2.

11

MANAGING AUDIT, ACCOUNTABILITY AND PERFORMANCE IN PUBLIC SERVICES

A truth that's told with bad intent
Beats all the lies you can invent.
(William Blake 1794)

LEARNING OUTCOMES

This chapter will enable the reader to:

- Understand the role of public audit in ensuring accountability in public services.
- Understand upward accountability and downward accountability.
- Explore stewardship and accountability to conscience.
- Examine the role of ethics and moral reasoning in public services.
- Identify deficiencies in accountability mechanisms in public services.
- Understand what is meant by performance management.
- Understand the need for ethics as well as economy, efficiency and effectiveness.
- Consider the role of Charters and 'Best Value', in setting performance standards.
- Design performance indicators.
- Understand how to implement performance management in public services.
- Understand how to appraise individual performance and how to deal with poor performers.

INTRODUCTION

In the UK, public audit and accountability have been the subject of various reviews.[1] In 1992 the Cadbury Committee reviewed corporate governance. In 1995 the Nolan Committee examined standards of conduct in public life and identified instances of corruption and misbehaviour in local government. In 1997 the third Nolan Report[2] concluded that many people were no longer clear about the standards of conduct expected of people in public services. The old culture of the public sector, seen as a guarantor of probity, was being seriously undermined by the entrepreneurial values of management.[3]

In order to demonstrate that public services are being well stewarded, managers must provide information about how their services are performing. Is the service achieving its targets? Is it meeting identified needs or expectations of quality? Is it giving value for money? In 2000 in the UK, the Labour government was accused of 'performance mania'. The introduction of business-style performance management into public services was criticized as counter-productive and outdated.[4] Yet the fact remains that public services are often paid for from taxation, or supported by public grants. They often benefit from a monopoly created by government. It is right that those with responsibility for managing services should be held accountable to those who fund them and accountable to those for whose benefit the services are provided. In carrying out their duties, public service managers are morally responsible for the performance and the outcomes of those aspects of the service that are under their control.[5] In this chapter we consider how managers can inform their practice with an understanding of social ethics and moral reasoning. We examine ways in which performance is measured at the level of the organization. We explore how managers can try to overcome some of the many difficulties with performance management. Finally, we argue that performance is best improved at the level of the individual. We look in particular at the management of individuals whose performance is poor.

AUDIT AND ACCOUNTABILITY

Accountability is the process of requiring people to account for their actions. Many public service organizations are required by law to provide information to service users, citizens and government. Systems must be in place which define aims and objectives and which monitor how resources have been used to achieve them. Accountability is not simply about apportioning praise or blame. Accountability raises fundamental questions about the purpose and practice of the public service organization. Day and Klein[6] suggested that accountability was the process of constructing an agreed language – a discourse – about the service and about the criteria that should be used to assess it.

Audit and Accountability in Public Services: a Historical Perspective

In the UK there has been a tradition of accountability since 1844, when district auditors were appointed to inspect the accounts of authorities administering the Poor Law.[7] Their job was to ensure that safeguards were in place to prevent fraud and corruption and to ensure that local rates were used for their intended purpose. The purpose of the district audit was to promote proper stewardship of public finances and to help those responsible for the management of public services to achieve economy, efficiency and effectiveness. In the UK, external

audit of public services was carried out by a National Audit Office. This Office audited government departments and public bodies such as the Arts Council. In 1982 an Audit Commission was set up to deal with local government and to provide analysis and advice. In 1990 its remit was extended to cover the National Health Service. The Commission scrutinized every aspect of local government, from the economics of refuse collection and the efficiency of school meals to the effectiveness of police responses to emergency calls. The Commission required NHS Trust hospitals to provide detailed measures of 'activity', such as waiting times and the number of GP referrals.

Since the mid-1980s, new forms of accountability have emerged. The work of Parliamentary Select Committees has been extended to scrutinize the work of central government. A number of specialist 'Offices' have been created to monitor education services and public utilities, even though many of the latter are privately owned organizations. In the UK the office that monitors education services is called OFSTED – the Office for Standards in Education. HMIC – Her Majesty's Inspectorate of Constabulary – scrutinizes the work of the police. OFTEL – the Office for Telecommunications – monitors the work of private organizations like British Telecom and Mercury. Ombudsmen have been appointed to investigate complaints against, for example, planning departments, water companies or the police.

The Role of Audit in Public Services

In the UK the main role of the Audit Commission is to establish whether:

- Accounts have been prepared in accordance with regulations.
- Economy, efficiency and effectiveness have been achieved.
- Proper practices have been followed.[8]

Public services must have adequate mechanisms for internal audit. According to the Chartered Institute of Public Finance Accountants (CIPFA),[9] internal auditors should appraise and report on:

- The suitability and reliability of management information
- The soundness, adequacy and application of internal controls
- The extent to which the organization's assets and interests are safeguarded

Value for Money and Best Value

Value for money in public services is no longer a virtue, it has become a necessity (Chapter 5). Public service managers are required to ensure the best use of limited resources. An audit of value for money should include the steps shown in Box 11.1.

Scandals in Public Services

The level of public service audit in the UK, both internal and external, is partly a response to a series of scandals which occurred in central and local government and in a number of public and privately owned public service organizations. Elsewhere, in Sweden, for example, public service managers enjoy a high degree of autonomy with relatively little political audit or interference.[11] In Swedish public

services the dominant culture is one of trust. This is enabled by policies on openness and transparency. There is a highly developed system of appeals through which Swedish citizens can seek redress against maladministration or injustice. Following the third Nolan Report in 1997, the UK government set down an ethical framework for the conduct of public service employees.[12] Every local authority in England, for example, was required to establish a Code of Conduct for employees and representatives. Complaints that public service employees and elected representatives have breached their code of conduct can be investigated by a Standards Board. If the Standards Board finds that a public servant or a public representative has breached the code, the Board can instigate disciplinary action. The role of auditors and inspectors in public services expanded rapidly during the 1990s. Auditors and inspectors sought to hold managers accountable for their ethical conduct, the efficiency and quality of their services, and the value for money they provided.

ACCOUNTABILITY IN PUBLIC SERVICES

There are many forms of accountability in public services because there are many stakeholders to whom a public service might be accountable (Chapter 4). It is useful to distinguish between upward accountability, sometimes through a political process, and downward accountability, usually to the users of public services.

Upward Accountability

In upward accountability, elected representatives, or representatives of different interest groups, sit on a committee that is responsible for the public service. Public service managers report directly to the committee. Members of public service committees raise their own personal concerns and also raise concerns on behalf of the people they represent. The committees provide a platform for public discourse about the performance and the development of the public

---

Box 11.1

AUDITING VALUE FOR MONEY: THE SEVEN STEPS[10]

1 Obtain past audit reports on the area
2 Check policy objectives have been set
3 Check how performance was measured
4 Appraise intended measurements
5 Review the allocation of costs
6 Note the level of delegation
7 Establish levels of activity
8 Review controls

service. In the case of nationally organized services, such as education and public order, local decision-makers may be accountable to a government minister. In a democracy, these ministers may be responsible to an elected assembly, perhaps via a select committee. Bogdanov[13] has criticized the principle of ministerial accountability for its failure to apply sanctions when ministers breach codes of practice. Technically ministers can be forced to resign, but in practice this happens rarely.

Political Accountability

In a representative democracy, authority to govern is by consent of the people. Consent is given on the condition that those with delegated authority are accountable for its use. Consent is given through periodic voting in referendums or elections. At an election, the electorate often judge a political party on its success in delivering and maintaining public services. Thus elections are a mechanism for making politicians accountable for the provision of public services. They are of limited value. In the UK, on average, only 40–50 per cent of the electorate vote in local elections.[14] Ranson and Stewart[15] are critical of mechanisms of accountability based on periodic voting. They see the electorate as passive. The electorate votes every three to five years and then returns to its respectful place, leaving government to the experts. Table 11.1 indicates the relative levels of

Table 11.1 Voting in elections in the European Union

Country	Average turnout %
Luxembourg*	93
Italy*	85
Belgium*	80
Denmark	80
Germany	72
France	68
Spain	64
Ireland	62
Portugal	60
The Netherlands	54
Great Britain	40

Note: *Compulsory voting in at least some areas.

participation in local elections in countries in the European Union.[16]

Indirect Political Accountability

In Chapter 1 we noted the growth of QUANGOS: non-elected quasi-governmental bodies such as the UK Learning and Skills Councils and Urban and Environmental Development Agencies. There are no mechanisms for direct public assessment of their performance. They do, however, have indirect political accountability to the electorate through ministers who report to Parliament.[17] The Nolan Committee's second report (1996) suggested that more rigorous public audit procedures should be applied to non-elected bodies.[18]

Public Service Accountability in Europe

Public service organizations in countries that are members of the European Union have a supra-national level of accountability. Under the Single European Act (1985) they are required to comply with a range of European directives. These directives came into force in 1987. One directive, for example, is that public services have to purchase from suppliers throughout Europe. Where public services are forced to subject their provision of services to competition, they face competition from organizations in any member state of the European Union. Because the UK has national legislation on compulsory competitive tendering, its public services are open to competition from, say, Germany. But because Germany does not have similar legislation on compulsory competitive tendering, UK public service organizations are not able to compete to supply services in Germany.

Because of the need to be better informed about European regulations and obligations, most UK local authorities now have European liaison units with offices in Brussels. Terry notes:

[L]ocal authority officers now play an important part in negotiations about the setting of common standards for products and equipment in the Community. Standardization issues have been increasingly devolved from

Commission officials to the European standards bodies and access to these is considerably easier for local government representatives.[19]

Accountability to a local councillor, to a central government department, to a European body, or even to an international governmental agency on such matters as the treatment of refugees, terrorists or political detainees, are all examples of upward accountability.

DOWNWARD ACCOUNTABILITY

Participatory Democracy

Public services may be required to account downwards to local citizens or to local people who use the service. In some public services, users are not just consulted, they are actively encouraged to participate in decision-making and in the delivery of services.[20] This is consistent with the ideas on lifelong learning and active citizenship which we discuss in Chapters 13 and 14. In 1998 the UK government produced a consultative paper on Local Democracy and Community Leadership.[21] The paper emphasized the importance of involving local communities in debate and decision-making (Box 11.2).

The Limitations of Downward Accountability

In 1987 Day and Klein[22] found that health authorities were predominantly concerned with their downward accountability to the public. By 1996 Ferlie *et al.*[23] had studied the effects of moving towards private sector models of corporate governance and reported that the new bodies were more concerned about their upward accountability to central authorities than their downward accountability to the public. Ferlie *et al.* concluded that reforms had eroded traditional channels of public accountability. They thought that there was a need to redress the balance by bolstering mechanisms for downward

---

Box 11.2

INVOLVING CITIZENS

- **Opinion polls**: these are usually carried out by experts
- **Conferences**: the issues can be debated live, or via the Internet
- **Focus groups**: intensive discussions held between 12–20 stakeholders
- **People's forums**: up to 1,000 people who are regularly consulted
- **Citizens' juries**: the jurors consider evidence with the aid of experts

---

accountability. Some people thought that it could be done through free market forces.

Markets and Accountability

We saw in Chapter 4 that even though many public service organizations were publicly owned, they were often forced to compete in open markets or in pseudo markets. Prior *et al.*[24] argued that accountability was enhanced by increasing exposure to market forces (Box 11.3).

Ferlie *et al.*[25] took a different view. They studied the effects on UK NHS Trust Boards of increasing the number of business and commercial representatives on the boards. They reported that in the meetings of such boards, the word 'market' was rarely mentioned in relation to accountability. In Chapter 4 we saw that some so-called free markets were not free at all. We saw that competition was often well regulated and that service users had limited choice or no choice at all. To counter these effects, the 1990s saw the emergence of 'charters'.

Box 11.3

MARKET MECHANISMS AND ACCOUNTABILITY

- Market mechanisms extend the range of providers and increase the choice of users
- Privatized services create incentives for people to improve performance
- Market mechanisms force improved quality and value for money
- Users can complain

Box 11.4

CRITICISMS OF CHARTERS[28]

- Service users are not encouraged to have a collective voice
- There is little attention to the rights and responsibilities of the citizen
- Charters mix up legal rights, administrative regulations and managerial promises
- Charters are mostly concerned with the individual user, customer, or client
- Charters claim to empower local service users but directives increase centralization

---

Charters and Standards

As we saw in Chapter 5, Citizen's Charters were developed in the UK during the 1990s, as a means of improving the quality of public services. Such charters were also seen as a means of enhancing downward accountability to the public. These charters stated the standards that the user was entitled to expect and explained how the user might complain if this standard was not achieved. The user's expectations were based on the user's rights as a citizen. According to the Citizen's Charter, citizens had a right to expect that public services would serve the public! Citizen's Charters have come in for a number of criticisms (Box 11.4). Do charters reduce accountability to the level of consumer protection?[26] Certainly they fail to encourage collective criticism. Accountability is seen from the point of view of the individual user. While charters refer to rights, there is little evidence that these are a basis for legal redress. Glaster[27] suggested that the only strength of a charter is its published commitment to action and the ability of some regulatory bodies to publish the extent to which promises have been fulfilled or broken.

Despite criticisms, charters do provide a means of identifying when public services fail to deliver their intended benefits to acceptable standards. Public service organizations have shown an increased willingness to apologize for failures. These apologies do not come cheap. Often they are bought at the cost of millions of dollars of public subsidy, or grant aid. Despite this, the 1996 report on the UK's Citizen's Charter[29] claimed that there had been considerable improvement in the services provided by customs and excise, tax offices and social benefits agencies. It cited achievements on behalf of road and rail users, tenants, victims of crime and customers for water, electricity, gas and postal services. Do charters and the other arrangements for enhancing downward accountability undermine professionals as guardians of standards?

Professional Accountability

Traditionally, professional accountability was linked to the values of the profession – values such as honesty, impartiality and client commitment. Values are developed and conveyed through professional training. Professional training is a prerequisite to practise, for example, as a teacher, a lawyer, a nurse or a doctor. Professional performance is monitored through professional bodies that set and monitor standards. The professional bodies have the right to withdraw a professional's licence to practise. The different inspectorates that we discussed earlier also monitor professional standards. As we saw in Chapter 1, the role and status of the professional have come into conflict with the role of the manager. Gray and Jenkins[30] argued that reforms in the early 1990s undermined the accountability of professionals. High-profile cases of misconduct further undermined confidence in the idea of professional accountability. Can we be certain any longer that professionals will be guided by their conscience about the standards and values of public services? Is accountability to conscience an option worth thinking about?

Accountability to Conscience

Tests of accountability to conscience could include a preparedness to declare an unpopular view, to apologize, to change one's mind, to declare self-interest, to own up to a bias, or to resign on grounds of principle. When public representatives are paid, does that make it too hard for them to resign? We will return to the question of ethics, ethical dilemmas and matters of conscience, but let us first consider the case of Mary Ruebens (Box 11.5). Mary manages hospital services for people with severe behavioural problems. Mary thinks that accountability to conscience must be a component of any scheme to promote more accountable public services.

Box 11.5

EXTRACT FROM A CONVERSATION WITH MARY RUEBENS: 'THE HIDDEN COST OF CARING'

Tony: For what sort of people do you care?

Mary: Among other things, I am responsible for caring for people with learning difficulties and severely challenging behaviour. Often these people have committed horrendous crimes and need to be detained in secure units.

Tony: That must be costly.

Mary: Yes, sometimes I find it hard to justify how much we spend on them. I try telling myself to stop thinking so much and to get on with the job, but actually thinking things through ahead of time helps me to act more quickly when I have to – we often have to respond to emergencies here. It also helps me to feel good about what I'm doing.

Tony: Feel good?

Mary: Underpinning our work here is the value of unconditional positive regard. We do not judge our residents. Whatever they have done, we try to treat them with respect and to give them the best quality of life we possibly can. I have to have unconditional positive regard for people who have raped small children, or who have committed horrible murders. It can be very demoralizing to care for people who do not want to be cared for, who may not even want to live. For example, we have a resident who slashes herself and who will swallow or insert sharp objects into her body. It costs taxpayers £140,000 a year for us to care for her. At the moment she needs an operation to remove a sharp object which she has swallowed. The surgeons are not keen to operate on her because she does not want to live. In the end, she will probably kill herself and I know I will feel awful when she does.

Tony: How can you reconcile spending over £140,000 a year on giving high-quality care for one person who doesn't want it, when that money could improve the lives of many people?

Mary: I was asked the same question by a visitor from Russia. When I went back with him to Russia and saw the problems there, I too wondered whether the values we hold here are a luxury which only the West can afford. Maybe it would be more ethical if I spent some of the money I spend here, helping people in other countries?

Tony: What would your staff feel about that?

Mary: I try to instil the value of unconditional positive regard into all of the staff. If they ever stop believing it, it will be hard to keep the service going. They wouldn't be able to stomach the work, if they didn't believe in it. We discipline staff if they do not treat residents with respect.

Tony: Isn't it hard to justify punishing staff for not respecting people whose behaviour is much worse than the staff you are punishing?

Mary: Yes. My staff are continuously at risk of attack and abuse. Some residents are very manipulative. It is hardly surprising that staff do not live up to our high standards all the time. Still, my approach has to be zero tolerance. Any form of disrespect to residents – no matter how small – attracts swift retribution. Some of my management colleagues think I go too far. For me it is the only way. I cannot weigh up what would be a proportional response to this or that incident. It would be too difficult.

Tony: Where do personal values come into this?

Mary: It helps in this job if you can get clear about personal values. As servants of the public, we do the kinds of things that most members of the public do not want to do for themselves. Even more important than my values as a manager is the need to foster the values of the people who feel drawn to work in public services – people who feel drawn to work at the scene of accidents, clearing up nuclear waste, purifying sewage, putting out fires, manning lifeboats, or who want to care for violent people. We need to get them talking about why they do it. What are their values? We need to get their beliefs out into the open and acknowledge them. That's how we can learn about the values of public service.

Tony: Thank you for sharing your thoughts.

As well as emphasizing accountability to conscience, Mary talks about the manager's role in ensuring professional standards of care. But does accountability to the conscience of individuals, to the ethics of professionals, or to the rights of clients, undermine democratic accountability?

The Democratic Deficit: Accountability and New Managerialism

Ferlie *et al.*[31] argued that New Public Management (Chapter 1) weakened accountability. An increasing number of individuals were appointed to governing bodies of one sort or another, ostensibly for the managerial skills which they could bring. Critics claimed that these appointments were politically motivated and that public services were consequently less accountable to the general public. This practice of appointing, not electing, those who oversee public services such as hospitals, police and universities, can lead to a 'democratic deficit'[32] and to the rise of a 'New Magistracy'.[33] Evidence in the UK NHS, and indications from other public services, pointed to a strengthening of upward accountability and a weakening of downward accountability. This occurred despite considerable rhetoric about increased consumer choice. Ferlie *et al.*[34] argued that whether or not organizations were publicly or privately owned, if they provided public services then they should face tough tests of accountability. In the UK the need for greater control of Non Departmental Public Bodies (NDPBs) was demonstrated by a National Audit

Office report on the working of English Heritage (English Heritage is an NDPB with responsibility for safeguarding England's heritage). The Comptroller Audit General, Sir John Bourne, concluded that there were clear failures in the proper conduct of public business and that events at English Heritage indicated how important it was that chief executives and other senior staff were conversant with all aspects of public accountability.[35]

Self-regulation

The theoretical potential for professional self-regulation is limited by practical leanings towards self-protection. Despite a number of high-profile reports and reviews and considerable attention from the media and politicians, it is by no means clear what the precise future role of public service audit is likely to be. However, there is recognition that some sort of public audit is necessary for the maintenance of high standards of conduct in public life.[36] How then can we square the need for public service managers to improve their own performance through the exercise of professional discretion and self-regulation, while at the same time keeping one eye on their accountability to the public and the other eye on the need to stay within limits that may be determined by the political self-interests of non-executives?

Managerial Accountability and the Concept of Stewardship

Day and Klein[37] maintained that the concept of managerial accountability – sometimes referred to as internal accountability – had its origins in the notion of stewardship. This type of accountability is exercised by managers who are responsible for staff, budgets and the performance of particular aspects of service delivery. We deal with this dimension of accountability in a later section on performance management. Behind the idea that managers might be regarded as stewards is the idea that public service managers exercise power on behalf of the citizens for whose benefit the service is intended.[38] Also implicit is the idea that this power, which they hold

on behalf of citizens, is to be used to help promote the idea of a 'Good Society' (Chapter 4). Ranson and Stewart recognized the value of Inspectorates, Offices and Audit Commissions but thought that they were insufficient. Proper stewardship depends on active citizenship:

> The main guarantee of accounts and accounting lies not in external scrutineers but in open, democratic government. Active citizenship implies a right to know, a right to explanation, a right to be involved and a right to be heard. A sense of stewardship is necessary for its full development.[39]

Aggressive 'take-over wars', insider dealing, fraud, absence of social responsibility, misconduct in public life – such things have fuelled interest in ethics. Public service managers need to be able to think out the ethical principles on which their stewardship is to be based.

ETHICS IN PUBLIC SERVICE

Ethics is the study of the right things to do when our behaviour has an impact on others. Lawton sees ethics as a 'set of principles, a code that acts as a guide to conduct'.[40] There are different sources of ideas about what constitutes ethical conduct. For those who believe in a transcendent God, absolute definitions of right and wrong are often regarded as divinely ordained. The Ancient Greeks considered ethics to be a more practical matter. What we consider to be right and wrong reflects our values. Our values in turn reflect deeply held beliefs. Values in the public domain are not absolute; they are continually contested. Take, for example, the role of prison services. Is their role rehabilitation, or deterrence? Is it prevention or punishment? Should the allocation of resources in education be in favour of the gifted or the deprived? Whose health needs should take precedence – the young, or the elderly? Can we justify the £140,000 per year that Mary Ruebens spends caring for one mentally disordered offender who does not want to live and who is guilty of horrendous crimes? How can public service managers orchestrate debates about questions such as these? Some familiarity with ethical analysis might help. Three terms commonly used in ethical analysis are 'utilitarianism', 'rights' and 'duties'.

Utilitarianism

Utilitarianism is a philosophical principle associated with Bentham (1748–1832) and John Stuart Mill (1806–73). Utilitarianism states that ethical choices are those that produce the greatest good for the greatest number of people. In some situations it can be difficult to calculate what is the greatest good for the greatest number of people. When fluoride is added to public drinking water, is it possible to calculate that the benefit to the many is greater than the health risks to a few? This line of reasoning might lead to the neglect and suicide of Mary Rueben's mentally disordered offenders, because the resources required to care for them could be used to achieve more benefits for more people. This was the line of moral reasoning followed by the Russian who visited Mary's Trust.

Human Rights

The second concept often used in ethical analysis is the concept of rights. The idea of human rights offers an alternative line of reasoning. Any action that violates the human rights of any individual is unethical. According to Irenee Horne, the problem with this approach is that human rights have to be agreed and rights can conflict.[41] One person's right to free speech can disturb another person's right to peace and quiet. How are public service managers to balance individual rights against collective rights? In Mary Rueben's case, the doctors appeared to have made the decision not to operate on a self-harming patient. They had not upheld the 'right' of every patient to healthcare.

Duty of Care

The third concept often used in ethical analysis is the concept of duty. Duties can be ranked in order of

importance. It is then easy to determine ethical behaviour by reference to the higher-ranked duties. Unfortunately, it is hard to get agreement on the rankings. For example, one person might regard paying bills on time as a high-ranking ethical duty; another person might see it as prudent to pay bills only when they receive a final demand for payment. Another line of thinking, which states that we have a duty to act in an ethical way, goes back to the thinking of the German philosopher Immanuel Kant (1724–1804). Kant's famous 'categorical imperative' states that something is not right if it is not right for everybody. Therefore a test that your choice of behaviour is ethical is that you would be happy that the principle you are using should become a universal law. This is the idea that Mary Rueben was unknowingly applying when she said that unconditional positive regard was always right, whatever the circumstances, whatever the consequences.

In trying to orchestrate a stakeholder debate which raises ethical issues, the public service manager should try first to get agreement on the type of ethical principles that are to be invoked. If the manager fails to achieve this, different groups of citizens following different lines of reasoning about ethical issues are likely to come to different, and perhaps conflicting, conclusions.

Ethical Dimensions of Citizenship

The provision of public services continually raises ethical questions. What, after all, do we mean by a 'good' society? What are the characteristics of a 'good' citizen? Should a public service manager be a 'good' citizen working towards a 'good' society? The liberal notion of citizenship, for example, emphasizes the right of individuals to pursue their own interests and to exercise freedom of choice. The 'liberal' citizen may have a duty to respect individuals, but might recognize no obligation to a wider society.

The Civic Tradition

The civic tradition emphasizes participation and belief in a shared common good. Western society has been criticized for an overemphasis on liberalism, to the neglect of community values and the common good.[42] There is a tension between individual and collective morality. One danger of stressing the independence of people, rather than their interdependence, is that what is 'good' becomes more and more a private matter for each individual to decide for themselves. Doherty's research[43] pointed to the danger of promoting a concept of individuality which might deteriorate into a form of selfishness and narcissism (Chapter 6). This would threaten the moral cohesiveness of society. Hill[44] suggested that this tension between an individual and a collective ethic would lead to a renewed search for civic virtue – one that achieved a better balance between individual self-interest and a sense of collective responsibility and duty. According to Ranson and Stewart,[45] a framework of shared moral and political values was needed for any social group to cohere. Many public services are collections of social groups. While accepting their point, we are wary of the imposition of a particular collective ethic. In Chapter 3 we discussed ways in which the beliefs of individuals can be surfaced and adopted as shared values. Public service managers can help their organizations and their communities to define their idea of a 'good society' in ways that are consistent with the diversity of beliefs that are likely to be present in a pluralist community. The challenge to public service managers is to help their communities to formulate ideas about a 'good' society that are compatible with individual freedom.

In Chapter 3 we looked forward to a better balance between individual autonomy on the one hand and adherence to civic values such as cooperation, friendship and fairness on the other. In Chapter 6 we looked at the way ideas on managing groups and teams frequently failed to recognize differences between individuals. In Chapter 8 we said that the nature of these differences between individuals argued for the move away from managing industrial relations and employee relations, to managing people through one-to-one conversations. Perhaps the recognition of individual differences is a precondition of effective interdependent behaviour?

Perhaps a 'good society' is a network of people, each of whom has close one-to-one interdependent relationships with a small number of others. The public service manager's contribution to such a 'good society' could be to adopt a conversational approach to involving them in making decisions about matters that affect the communities to which they belong.[46]

Having audited the performance of a public service and having argued the ethical case for holding the public service manager accountable for that performance, we turn now to the manager's task in maintaining or raising the level of that performance. We will argue that although performance is audited and measured at the level of the organization, a manager's action to improve performance is best taken at the level of the individual.

MANAGING PERFORMANCE: PERFORMANCE MANAGEMENT

According to Blundell and Murdock,[47] performance management can be defined as the process of communicating organizational aims and objectives to all stakeholders, setting performance targets in order to measure the achievement of those aims and objectives, and ensuring that all this activity provides the basis for continual improvement. In order to manage performance, those who delegate tasks to public service managers need to tell the managers what criteria will be used to judge their performance. In public services, such criteria normally relate to the three E's (economy, efficiency and effectiveness). We would also argue for the inclusion of a fourth E for *ethics*, which would in turn incorporate more E's for *equity* – the fair and non-discriminatory treatment of people; *empathy* – the ability to anticipate and accept responsibility for consequences for others; and *ecology* – a concern for environmental impact. Growth in interest in criteria for measuring the performance of public services can be traced to changes identified in Chapter 1 (Box 11.6).

Box 11.6

THE IMPETUS FOR PERFORMANCE MEASUREMENT

- A 'customer' orientation has focused concern on quality and value for money
- Privatization has resulted in the introduction of private sector techniques
- Compulsory Competitive Tendering (CCT) has forced public services to stipulate quantity, quality and costs

---

Box 11.7

PERFORMANCE MANAGEMENT: FOUR QUESTIONS

1 Why measure performance?
2 Who might want to know?
3 What should be measured?
4 How might it be measured?

From Conformance to Performance: The Effect Worldwide

According to Hood,[48] by the 1990s a performance culture dominated public services in Europe, New Zealand, Australia and other OECD countries. By 1996 an increasing emphasis on performance management across Europe was identified by Flynn and Strehl.[49] In their study of seven European countries, they observed that there had been attempts to redirect managerial efforts from conformity to performance. This had necessitated changes in the way organizations had worked. Flynn and Strehl asserted that there needed to be a process by which the purposes of organizations were agreed and their activities and products defined and measured. This assumes that managers are able to organize resources, are committed to targets, and have some reason to achieve them. We invite managers to question the validity of these assumptions, while keeping in mind that public service organizations that fail to set up adequate performance management systems can fall foul of regulatory bodies. In developing a performance management system, it is worth considering the questions in Box 11.7.

WHY MEASURE PERFORMANCE?

When developing performance management systems, it is important that the purpose of measuring performance is clear and is accepted.[50] The purpose of measuring performance in privately owned organizations is generally less complicated than the purpose of measuring performance in publicly owned organizations. In privately owned organizations, shareholders want to know how well their investment is doing. These organizations can use performance ratios to assess how well their assets are being used. The 'bottom line' performance measure is profitability. In publicly owned public services we need additional performance indicators in order to assess how well the organization is achieving its purposes and meeting the standards established for it. Often standards and constraints are laid down by statute, e.g. 'pay all suppliers' bills within six weeks' or 'respond to emergency calls within 4 minutes'. If performance management is used to control and to punish, it will be of limited value. While performance management should lead to the apportioning of blame where blame is due, it should lead also to shared learning and to service improvement. (Chapters 5 and 13) Mayston[51] suggested eight objectives for performance management (Box 11.8).

Box 11.8

WHY MEASURE PERFORMANCE?

- To clarify the organization's objectives
- To indicate potential areas for cost savings
- To enable users to make informed choices
- To evaluate the final outcomes resulting from the organization's activities
- To indicate how well different services contribute to specific areas of policy

- To indicate performance standards when licensing or contracting-out privatized services
- To assist in determining the most cost-effective service levels
- To trigger further investigation and possible remedial action to improve quality

---

WHO MIGHT WANT TO KNOW?

The different stakeholders who might want to know will have different – potentially conflicting – interests and values. In schools, for example, a small average class size may be important for a teacher who believes in individual child-centred learning, but not to an advisor who believes in traditional whole-class teaching. Any stakeholder might want to know how well a public service is performing. Possible stakeholders are shown in Box 11.9.

If performance management is to lead to learning and ongoing service improvement, then internal stakeholders will also want to know. Typical internal stakeholders are shown in Box 11.10.

WHAT SHOULD WE MEASURE?

Measures of performance refer to quantifiable aspects of performance, for example, the cost of delivering services or the number of client contacts. These

---

Box 11.9

ACCOUNTABILITY TO EXTERNAL STAKEHOLDERS

- **Elected representatives** seeking answers to questions raised by their constituents
- **Pressure groups**, e.g. consumer rights, human rights or environmental groups
- **Citizens** informing themselves about the performance of local public services
- **Government departments** concerned to evaluate the benefits of funding

- **Aid agencies** seeking reassurance that grants are being used effectively
- **Inspection agencies** concerned with the quality of a public service
- **Trades unions** concerned about pay
- **Professional bodies** concerned with audit
- **Regulatory bodies** acting as 'watchdog'
- **Auditing bodies**

Box 11.10

INTERNAL STAKEHOLDERS

- Non-executive members of committees
- Chief executive's departments
- Policy analysts and planners
- Performance review panels
- Front-line service staff
- Internal auditors

---

measures often refer to outputs rather than outcomes. This is because some benefits conferred by public services are not easily quantified. The benefits may, however, be implied or indicated, by a chosen measure. In such cases, the measure is called a 'performance indicator'. Increasingly, central government departments specify targets and performance indicators for local public services. For example, in the year 2000 in the UK, central government specified that within one year at least 86 per cent of defence personnel had to receive a dental checkup; that at least 1,750 km of pavement was renewed by the Highways Department; that the ratio of favourable to unfavourable media coverage by the Atomic Energy Authority increased by 43 per cent; and that at least 25 per cent of dealings with the public would be electronic by 2002.[52] Table 11.2 describes some performance indicators that were set for a housing department.

Table 11.2 Examples of public service performance indicators: housing benefit and council tax

Aspect of performance	Indicator
Effectiveness	Reduced overpayment of benefits as a percentage of payments.
Quality	The percentage of claimants who said that staff were helpful.
Efficiency	Percentage of new clients processed within 14 days.
Economy	Administrative cost per claimant.

THE 4 E's OF PERFORMANCE MANAGEMENT

The traditional 3 E's of performance management are Economy, Efficiency and Effectiveness. These three E's alone do not provide adequate measures of performance. We have added a further E for Ethics, embracing Equity, Empathy and Ecology. We deal with each in turn.

Indicators of Economy

- **Economy** is concerned with the input of resources and with ensuring that those resources are procured at the lowest possible cost.

Economy is concerned with how much money is used. Economy is particularly important in relation to public services which are funded through taxation. Treasury budgets are usually cash limited. Consequently, staying within cash limits is a common measure of performance in public services that are funded through taxation. Budgetary reporting systems are used to compare the actual cash spent with the limit set (Chapter 9). For example, if your performance indicator is 'to keep within an annual budget of $10,000 for providing meals in schools' and you have spent $6,000 in the first six months, then you will have to take remedial action if you are to satisfy your performance indicator. You will have to do this even if there are twice as many students in the school as were expected, or even if the price of rice has quadrupled since the budget was set. Indicators set in relation to economy do not take into account demand, usage or inflation. If usage goes up, then unit costs have to be reduced. If prices go up, then quantities have to be reduced to compensate.

Indicators of Efficiency

- **Efficiency** is a ratio. It is concerned with how much output is achieved for a given level of input at a specified level of volume and quality.

Increasingly, public services have to devise ways of measuring their output, for example, the numbers of enquiries handled or the numbers of training hours provided. Going back to our previous example of school meals, if 1,000 meals were planned at a cost of $10 each and only 900 were produced and yet the whole of the $10,000 budget was spent, then the school meals service would have failed to meet its efficiency indicator, because one meal would have cost $10,000 ÷ 900 = $11.11, way over the $10 which was planned. In other words, in order to measure efficiency, the cost of producing one unit of output – one dinner, one enquiry, one training hour, one child's annual education – must be calculated. The cost of educating one child for one year, for example, can be determined by calculating the total costs of staffing and overheads for the year and then dividing this total cost figure by the number of pupils educated during the year. Box 11.11 lists the unit cost of educating one child per annum in four comparable schools. By collating and ranking these figures 'league tables' can be published.

A common way of setting performance standards is to calculate the average cost of producing one unit. For example, in the case of the schools in Box 11.11, the average cost per child per annum is:

$$\$(200 + 250 + 189 + 195) \div 4 = 208.5$$

Schools at or below the average are commended; those above are reprimanded and asked to improve. What a statistical nonsense! It is in the nature of averages that some must be below average! Also, one cannot be sure of comparing like with like. In any case, what does a high or a low unit cost mean? A high cost per pupil might indicate low efficiency, but it might also indicate high quality, i.e. small class sizes or a high ratio of staff to students.

Indicators of Effectiveness

- **Effectiveness** is concerned with impact – does the service achieve its intended purpose? It is concerned with the extent to which services confer the benefits which they are intended to confer.

To continue the example of providing school meals, despite having failed to meet economy and efficiency targets, the school meals service may still have met targets for effectiveness if, for example, it had reduced the learning time lost through malnutrition. In this case, time lost through illness might be relatively easy to measure. Usually, measuring the effectiveness of public services is more problematic. It is often difficult to quantify the intended benefits. The benefits of an intervention by a youth worker may not be seen for a long time. The fact that measurement is difficult does not mean that it should not be attempted. The value of the youth worker's intervention, for example, could be assessed by the young person, or by the wider community, or by a reduction in the levels of juvenile crime. A further problem with measuring effectiveness is that different stakeholders may have different and even conflicting ideas about what they want from the service. Typically, when a planning department puts forward a proposal for a new road, it will be supported by one group of stakeholders and opposed by another. Jackson[53] makes the point that because different stakeholders have different interests in the performance of public services, the stakeholder approach helps to force the question 'whose value for whose money?' Value for money will mean different things to different people. These different perspectives will come into conflict and the conflict will need to be resolved. Value for money is not a value-free

---

Box 11.11

COMPARING UNIT COSTS OF SCHOOLING

Unit Cost = Total Cost ÷ Number
School B = $250 per child per annum
School A = $200 per child per annum
School D = $195 per child per annum
School C = $189 per child per annum

concept! When we consider the interaction between the three E's of economy, efficiency and effectiveness, the problems of interpretation become more complex.

PROBLEMS WITH MEASURING PERFORMANCE

A hospital may be efficient and hit performance indicators concerned with increasing the throughput of patients. This may result in the need for more resources. This will lower the economy of the service. At the same time the re-infection rate may rise with the increased numbers of patients, and an increased number may come back a second time. This in turn raises throughput and efficiency, but reduces economy and effectiveness. This is sometimes called the 'revolving door syndrome'. Another problem is 'Goodheart's Law'.[54] Goodheart was a Bank of England official who tried to find performance indicators that would track inflation. He noted that every time he changed the indicator, its correlation with inflation mysteriously disappeared. Goodheart's Law states: 'Once you make a measurement an instrument of policy, it ceases to tell you what you wanted to know about what you were measuring'. This is because people often act in such a way as to ensure that their performance looks good against the measure however poorly the measure relates to their real performance.

An example of Goodheart's Law was seen in the UK. 'Shortness of waiting lists' was chosen as a performance indicator for NHS hospitals. People quickly worked out that the simplest way to ensure that you performed well against this indicator was to delay taking people onto your waiting list until you were ready to treat them. In many instances the length of the reported waiting lists shortened dramatically but the total lapsed time between when the patient was referred and when the patient was treated was not in fact reduced. Perversely, poor performance was then rewarded by offering extra funds to those hospitals with long waiting lists. If some of the extra funds were then used to pay staff for extra

sessions, and if some were used to pay for contracts with private hospitals who employed the NHS staff privately, then we should not be surprised if, the following year, the NHS waiting lists mysteriously lengthened again!

Comparing Like with Like – Added Value

To be of any value for comparison purposes, performance indicators must compare like with like. For example, if 90 per cent of entrants to a school where the teaching medium is English do not speak English, it is not helpful to compare that school's performance with another school where 80 per cent of entrants arrive already speaking English. Comparisons might be better made between rates of improvement, i.e. where there is some kind of 'base line assessment' and where performance is judged by the amount of value added by an organization to its assessed base line. So the performances of schools, for example, could be judged by comparing the improvements they achieve in relation to their original base line assessment. This approach to measuring performance is sometimes called the 'added-value' approach. Similarly, police services could be compared on the basis of 'clear up' rates, rather than on the basis of the absolute levels of crime. The absolute levels of crime might be affected by factors such as unemployment levels or a breakdown in community values. These are outside the control of the police. Unfortunately, basing police performance on clear-up rates may tempt officers to offer unjustified leniency (or just a caution) in return for an admission of a long string of offences that can then be classed as 'cleared up'. These and other difficulties are not in themselves reasons for not trying to measure the performance of public services. It is a disservice to local communities to dwell too much on the theoretical difficulties of measuring performance.[55] What is more useful is for public service managers to propose practical and creative measures of performance that are appropriate to their local conditions yet which avoid the worst consequences of misleading indicators. Box 11.12 summarizes some of the main problems.

Box 11.12

PROBLEMS WITH PERFORMANCE MEASUREMENT[56]

- The complexity of collecting and interpreting a large source of data quickly
- Defining the objectives of complex services where multiple objectives conflict
- Lack of correlation between overall organizational objectives and specific objectives
- The inexperience of managers in developing and using performance indicators
- Lack of relevant and measurable targets for final outputs and outcomes
- Lack of resources to build up data
- Resistance to time recording by staff
- Lack of staff trained in financial evaluation
- The cost of performance measurement
- Lack of interest

Box 11.13

BEST VALUE: THE PRINCIPLES

- There should be concern for quality and effectiveness as well as for efficiency
- Performance indicators should enable comparison with other service providers
- The planning process should strengthen accountability to the local community
- Performance indicators should relate to things that managers can control
- Auditors should report publicly on whether Best Value has been achieved
- Provision for government intervention if Best Value is not achieved
- Performance indicators should reflect stakeholders' interests
- Competition is not a sufficient test

As we noted earlier in this chapter, the involvement of professional staff is no longer seen as a guarantee of acceptable levels of performance. The language of accountability is frequently the language of accountants and economists. Some attempts have been made to go beyond this by developing performance indicators that determine the volume of services to be offered in relation to the identified need of the population. Other indicators measure the take-up of services. These are welcome developments. Potentially, the concept of 'Best Value' heralds a more coherent and participatory approach to performance management.

'Best Value': A Coherent Framework for Performance Measurement?

A 'Best Value' audit asks 'Could you change and become more efficient?' and 'Does your service meet the needs and aspirations of local people?' Best Value principles are set out in Box 11.13.

Best Value performance indicators should:

- Be meaningful for elected members, tax payers, service users, managers and staff.
- Provide information on the way service users experience service quality.
- Measure the direct impact of the service.
- Provide information about what is delivered.
- Be easily monitored and understood.

Box 11.14 summarizes examples of Best Value performance indicators produced by the Leisure and Cultural Services department of a UK local authority.

Box 11.14

INDICATORS OF BEST VALUE: SOME EXAMPLES

Needs Indicators

1 Recorded evidence of community needs
2 Numbers of people in disadvantaged areas taking part in affordable activities
3 Evidence of equal opportunities monitoring leading to actions to reflect local needs

Economy Indicators

1 Successful economic development bids
2 Examples of support for local groups
3 Choice, description and number of affordable activities benefiting local people

Efficiency Indicators

1 Numbers of citizens benefiting
2 Numbers of new service users benefiting
3 Numbers of community groups benefiting from successful external funding

Effectiveness Indicators

1 Citizens' annual review day
2 User annual satisfaction survey
3 Annual review of quality assurance systems

The Best Value process is one of choosing performance indicators, setting standards, carrying out independent inspections against those standards, and reporting the results. In the UK, Best Value proposals gave wide-ranging powers to government to intervene when the performance of public services failed to meet their standards. Clearly, much depended on the choice and design of good performance indicators. We need to ask whether the choice and design of performance indicators is consistent, comparable, clear, controllable, comprehensive, relevant, complete, motivating, valid, timely, accepted, accessible and integrated.[57]

In 1991 Pollitt[58] reported that the design of performance indicators emphasized economy and efficiency to the neglect of effectiveness. In response to criticisms such as those raised by Pollitt during the 1990s, the UK Audit Commission tried to give a more equal emphasis to all three E's. In addition to economy, efficiency and effectiveness, we think that it is worth thinking about a fourth E, for Ethics – an E that includes equity, empathy and ecology.

E for Ethics

Ethical considerations relate to the inner world and outer world of the organization. Do we treat staff and clients fairly, with equity? Are we causing stress and low morale? Can we empathize? What effect are we having on our environment? What is the impact on ecology? In relation to service users, equity is concerned with equal access to services for people with equal needs.[59] It is possible for public services to score highly on the traditional three E's of economy, efficiency and effectiveness, while failing to meet the needs of the community.[60] Striving for equity requires information about the nature and distribution of need amongst the community that is served by the public service. Information can be obtained through community-based conversations. The information can be used to develop community profiles. Community profiles can be used to decide priorities. Such decisions may involve moral judgements. The values and beliefs of those making such judgements need to be made explicit. If the crew on a public service ferryboat placed a premium on the safety of

Box 11.15

THE DESIGN OF PERFORMANCE INDICATORS: QUESTIONS TO ASK

- **Consistency**: Are the definitions of performance consistent over time and place?
- **Comparability**: Do the PIs compare like with like? For example, does one department measure client satisfaction by counting complaints while another department uses customer surveys?
- **Clarity**: Are PIs simple, clearly defined and understandable by key stakeholders?
- **Controllability**: Is the achievement of PIs within the control of the managers?
- **Comprehensiveness**: Is the choice of PIs determined selectively so that they fail to reflect the overall performance of the organization? For example, have some PIs been chosen because they are achievable while others have been neglected because they might highlight poor performance?
- **Relevance**: Does the PI relate to an aspect of the service that is important to anyone? When a PI has been achieved over a number of years, has a more challenging PI been set?

- **Completeness**: Do the PIs cover economy, efficiency, effectiveness and ethical considerations like equity, empathy and ecology?
- **Motivation**: Do the PIs challenge staff without demoralizing them?
- **Validity**: Is the PI only a correlation with an aspect of the service rather than a cause?
- **Timeliness**: Can failure to meet a PI be identified in time to take corrective action?
- **Acceptability**: Were all relevant stakeholders consulted about the design of the PIs?
- **Accessibility**: Do all stakeholders with a legitimate interest have access to the PI data? Can consumer groups obtain access to information about performance?
- **Integration**: Are the PIs linked to the strategic objectives of the organization? For example, is there a clear link between a strategy to increase representation from ethnic minorities and the PIs set for personnel?

their passengers, who was responsible for the drowning of passengers when the boat set sail with its sea doors open? Was it the crew? Was it the captain? Or was it the managers trying to 'improve their performance' by reducing the time taken to turn the boats around?[61] Having considered what is meant by measuring performance, we now consider in more detail how its improvement might be managed.

HOW CAN WE IMPROVE PERFORMANCE?

Earlier in this chapter we saw performance management defined as communicating the objectives of the

organization to all stakeholders, reviewing performance against targets related to those objectives, and taking action to rectify poor performance. As we saw in Chapter 5, organizations can be viewed as systems that have inputs, processes and outputs. Performance management provides the feedback loop (see dotted line in Figure 11.1). This leads to a view of performance management as being about control, correction and improvement.

Performance Management as Control, Correction and Improvement

In order to understand more about performance management, we can consider separately the com-

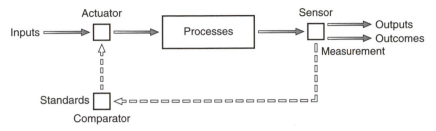

Figure 11.1 A systems view of performance management

ponents of the system described in Figure 11.1. The system has inputs that are controlled by an actuator. Inputs include demands and resources, such as money and materials. Actuators have control over the inputs to the system. Personnel departments, finance managers, receptionists and secretaries purchasing managers are examples of actuators.

The inputs undergo processes that transform them into the services delivered to the public. The process by which schooling is delivered produces outputs such as the daily gain in knowledge and competence of the pupils and the school's growing (or diminishing) reputation. Outcomes are a subset of the outputs. Outcomes refer to benefits (or damage) to the intended beneficiaries of the service. Outcomes are limited by the extent to which potential beneficiaries take up the service outputs. In Figure 11.1 a feedback loop measures the outputs (and the outcomes) of the service and compares these to performance standards. Performance indicators provide specific ways to demonstrate that these standards are being met. In the UK the Best Value initiative provides centrally defined performance standards and encourages public service managers – in collaboration with service users – to develop their own indicators of whether or not those standards are being met. If, following inspection, these standards are not being met, then services are required to take corrective action to meet the standards. In Figure 11.2 we show how a systems model of an organization can be translated into a performance management system for a public service organization. The model in Figure 11.2 embraces different stakeholders, the needs of communities, issues of equity and the role of professional judgement in managing performance.

From Control to Commitment

Performance management does not work well when it relies on mechanistic planning and control. It is important that the use of performance indicators does not relegate the sound judgement of committed public servants. There is evidence to suggest that performance management is more effective within a culture of continuous improvement. Rouse[62] reported that a commitment culture led to greater acceptance of (as opposed to compliance with) performance indicators. A non-threatening, participative environment empowered managers and motivated them to subscribe to the ethos and practice of performance management. Although performance can be, and usually is, measured at the level of the organization, the improvement of performance usually requires managers to take action at the level of particular individuals. Such individuals may include their senior managers or suppliers or purchasers. Most commonly, managers need to take action with their own staff, especially with individuals whose performance is poor.

MANAGING THE PERFORMANCE OF INDIVIDUALS

As we saw in Chapter 8, privatization in the UK was originally designed to reduce the power of trades unions in publicly owned organizations.[63] Privatization also resulted in the incursion of private sector management techniques. One such technique was performance management. An underlying assumption was that the performance of individuals

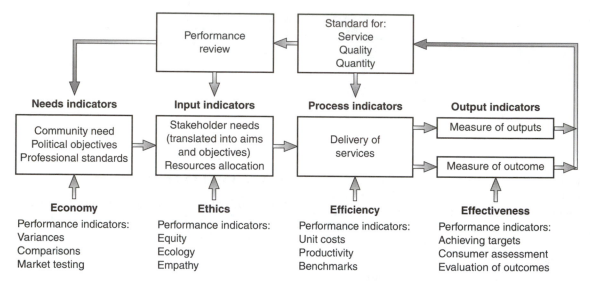

Figure 11.2 A stakeholder model of performance management

in publicly owned public services was poor compared with their counterparts in privately owned public services. Newly privatized public service organizations emphasized the manager's role in rectifying this. Managers began by individualizing contracts of employment. They provided reward packages with private sector type fringe benefits. They initiated performance related pay.[64] Sir Robert Armstrong, then head of the UK Civil Service, hoped that publicly owned organizations would learn from industry and commerce.[65] One of the changes introduced from the private sector was individual performance review – sometimes called performance appraisal. Measuring individual performance in public services proved to be more difficult than measuring individual performance in industry. We will explore some of the reasons for this in our final chapter.

Performance Related Pay

Performance incentives are a common feature of private industry and range from productivity bonuses for manual staff, to performance related pay for managers. In the 1980s Griffiths recommended performance related pay for 800 general managers in the UK NHS. The Griffiths Report emphasized the

setting of individual targets, the appraising of management performance and the rewarding of achievements. Aspects of performance related pay were introduced for most Civil Service managers and for higher-grade local authority managers. In 1989 classroom teachers were included. Performance related pay was seen as a means of motivating managers and improving performance, as well as making public servants more accountable for the way in which they discharged their duties. It remains controversial. In Chapter 7 we identified some reasons why money does not always motivate high performance. Rose and Lawton[66] identified some further advantages and disadvantages of performance related pay in public services (Table 11.3).

Performance related pay tends to reward the people who would have performed well without it. The ranks of poor performers are swelled by adding demotivated and disgruntled, formerly 'average' performers, who have interpreted 'no PRP' as a negative evaluation of their work. The cost of the paperwork and administration of PRP schemes is high and no commensurate benefits have been found in schemes where the PRP element is less than 30 per cent of the pay of the rewarded individual.[67] In public services, where it is not uncommon to find pay related

Table 11.3 Performance related pay in public services

Advantages	Disadvantages
Helps with recruitment and staff retention	Demands management time and specialist skill
Can be adapted to local circumstances	Difficult to establish links with performance
Can create a high-performance culture	Requires precise performance indicators
Devolves responsibility to managers	Demotivates the average employee
Reduces collective bargaining	Potentially divisive and expensive
Encourages flexibility	Distorts appraisal process

costs running at 70 per cent of total costs, assuming one-third of staff would earn PRP, it would increase total costs by about 7 per cent. In most public services this is not affordable.

For PRP to be motivating, staff would need to feel that their performance – or its measure – was within their control. In traditional public service structures, staff rarely have sufficient personal discretion. If pay is motivating at all, its effect is only transient. In the case of PRP, only one-third of the workforce can enjoy this transient effect. For the other two-thirds, the effect is demotivating. In some less traditional public service organizations, such as Mercury telecommunications in the UK, employees are allowed to choose their own reward package. As long as at least 80 per cent is taken in cash, employees can choose extra holidays, pensions, health cover, child-care, car allowance or retail vouchers. These options carry tax and other benefits for the organization and the employee.

Individual Performance Appraisal

Despite little evidence that annual appraisals improve performance, annual appraisals became widespread in public services during the 1990s. Procedures were usually open. Both staff and managers retained copies of the appraisal reports. Performance was measured using specific criteria to indicate the level of performance that had been attained. Usually performance was rated as one of the following:

- Outstanding, superior (highly acceptable)
- Average (fully acceptable)
- Substandard or incomplete (totally unacceptable).

Depending on the performance ratings, some form of reward or some form of improvement action was supposed to be initiated. For the substandard employee, it was intended that appraisal be used to identify training and development needs aimed at performance improvement. Appraisals could also be used as part of a process leading to dismissal or failure to renew a contract. This drew strong criticism. As we have seen, there is a mismatch between the controlling tendencies of many managers and the open culture that would be required for performance appraisal to work.

In Chapter 14 we shall suggest linking appraisal to learning conversations. This brings recollective, predictive, imaginative, creative, empathetic and critical thinking into the process. Appraisal should be seen as a process whereby both the appraisee and the appraiser learn. Managers, for example, can gain insights into their management style and into what motivates their staff. The manager can learn what helps and what hinders staff from carrying out their duties. Rogers thinks that this learning process needs to permeate the whole organization and that the scheme should cover all employees. It is helpful if staff are forewarned about the process and are given questions to think about before the appraisal interview (Box 11.16).

Ideally, written notes addressing the kinds of questions illustrated in Box 11.16 should be returned to the manager before the appraisal interview, so that the manager can give them some prior thought. The conduct of the appraisal is summarized in Box 11.17.

If the individual's performance is poor, this moves

Box 11.16

PREPARATORY QUESTIONS FOR AN APPRAISAL INTERVIEW

- What three things have pleased you most?
- What three things have pleased you least?
- What could your manager do to help you?
- What could your manager do less of?
- What do you wish you had done differently?
- Where do you see yourself in five years?

Box 11.17

CONDUCTING AN APPRAISAL

- Invite appraisee personally, if possible
- Explain the process and the purpose
- Sit alongside appraisee, if possible
- Review the previous action plan
- Ask appraisee for examples
- Let appraisee self-appraise
- Begin and end with praise
- Discuss disagreements
- Discuss training needs
- Agree an action plan
- Summarize learning
- Summarize actions
- End positively

Box 11.18

EVIDENCE OF POOR PERFORMANCE

- Complaints from colleagues
- Benchmark comparisons
- Complaints from clients
- Comparative statistics
- Sickness records
- Unfinished work
- Appraisal notes
- Work sheets
- Time sheets

the manager into the important area of managing poor performance.

IMPROVING THE PERFORMANCE OF POOR PERFORMERS

If through appraisal, or other means, poor performance is suspected, then confirmatory evidence may be needed. Possible sources are shown in Box 11.18.

Before the individual is confronted with apparent evidence of alleged poor performance, managers should compare the actual performance with the levels of performance that were expected. Possible sources of expected performance are suggested in Box 11.19.

Box 11.20 outlines a four-stage process for investigating poor performance.

There may be many reasons for poor performance. Poor performance may not be the fault of the individual whose performance is being assessed. Managers should try to identify extenuating causes of poor performance. Box 11.21 suggests some questions to consider.

Finally, managers need to identify possible actions that can be taken to remedy poor performance. Some of the options available to managers are described in Box 11.22. Failure to remedy poor performance may lead to disciplinary action (Chapter 8).

Box 11.19

SOURCES OF EXPECTED LEVELS OF PERFORMANCE

- Individual briefings, team briefings
- Written instructions, written warnings
- Job descriptions, contracts of employment
- Training courses, away-days, custom
- Professional standards, quality standards, charters, value statements
- Written procedures, manuals, employee handbooks, rule books, official notices

---

Criticisms of Performance Appraisal

There are many difficulties in appraising performance. These are summarized in Box 11.23. Even a well-designed scheme for performance appraisal will fail if there is lack of trust and lack of respect between the appraiser and the appraisee.[69] Many staff fear disciplinary action. This alienates good performers and alerts poor performers to cover their tracks.

As long ago as 1993, Smidt[70] suggested that performance management was not compatible with responsiveness in organizations because it ignored the fact that performance was usually dependent on others. Since then, increased emphasis on multi-agency working and interdepartmental co-operation (Chapter 6) have made formal appraisal schemes increasingly irrelevant.

According to Rogers,[71] performance management creates opportunities for managers to *tell* individuals about ways in which they are not performing well and to *tell* them that failure to improve will result in punitive action. Rogers noted that this 'telling' frequently produced immediate and impressive results, which were short-lived. 'Telling', Rogers discovered, did not engender commitment. It caused time and energy to be wasted on 'game playing', avoidance and dispute. Distorted information became the basis for the design of inappropriate improvement programmes which then failed. Some form of desultory disciplinary action then followed. This was often protracted and rarely conclusive. The result was ill-will between staff and their managers and amongst colleagues who had been called to testify and forced to 'take sides'. Organizational performance then declined to below the levels at which performance management was introduced.

Box 11.20

A CONVERSATIONAL APPROACH TO IMPROVING POOR PERFORMERS

- **Stage 1: Agree the Facts**
  Ask for information about current activity in relation to last year's targets. Ask questions of clarification. Agree the facts. Note dissent or discrepancies to be dealt with later.

- **Stage 2: Interpret the Facts**
  Ask individuals for their feelings, opinions and explanations of the situations revealed by the agreed facts. The aim should be exploration and increased understanding of the situation.

- **Stage 3: Solve Problems**
  Ask individuals to analyse and propose solutions to any problems which are now better understood. Keep them focused on solutions not symptoms.

- **Stage 4: Agree Action Plans**
  Manager helps individual to propose actions. Both should sign a written timetable of who will do what by when, agreeing how it can best be monitored.

Box 11.21

A CONVERSATIONAL APPROACH TO CAUSES OF POOR PERFORMANCE

- **Poor understanding:** Does the individual lack intelligence, education, technical knowledge, proper briefing by manager or clients, or the necessary thinking skills?
- **Poor motivation:** Are unmet needs known? Does the job offer ways of meeting them?
- **Lack of self-confidence:** Does the individual underestimate abilities, overestimate abilities, fear failure or reprisals, have low risk tolerance or a proneness to stress or perfectionism?
- **Clash of values:** Is there a moral, cultural or professional inhibition, or a lack of belief in the probity or value of work? Can the individual think through ethical issues?
- **Victimized:** Is the individual a victim of jealousy, envy or scapegoating, or bullying, harassment, discrimination or prejudice?
- **Abuse of power:** Is the individual a victim of institutional discrimination? (Chapter 8)
- **Domestic difficulties:** Does the individual have responsibilities for children, an elderly parent, a sick or disabled partner or dependant or a difficult domestic situation? (Chapter 8)
- **Health problems:** Does the individual have physical or mental health problems?
- **Transport difficulties:** Has the individual relocated or has transport changed?
- **Physical conditions:** Is performance being affected by lighting, odours, noise, colour, heat, ventilation, photocopiers, computers, clothing, food or drinks?[68]
- **Inadequate training:** Has the individual received adequate training?
- **Poor equipment:** Is the equipment inferior due to lack of investment, sabotage, poor budgeting or poor maintenance work?
- **Poor pay:** Is the individual affected by performance related pay?
- **Poor planning:** Is the individual's management of work and time poor?
- **Poor communication:** Does the individual feel unimportant, powerless, ineffectual, alienated, not 'in the know' and irrelevant?

Box 11.22

DEALING WITH LONG-TERM POOR PERFORMERS: OTHER TACTICS

- **Own management:** Managers contribute to the poor performance through poor management.
- **Improvement plan:** Follow conversational approach (Box 11.20), and agree an action plan to improve performance.
- **Peer pressure:** If the performance assessment scheme is open, colleagues may exert peer pressure on perceived slackers.
- **Training:** Identify training needs (Chapter 13).
- **Removal of alibis:** Remove alibis for poor performance. Remedy legitimate grievances. Resolve external blocks to performance.
- **Seeking help:** Seek help of specialists, e.g. counsellors, trainers or advisors.
- **Transfer:** Transfer individual to a new department, new job or redesigned job.
- **Discipline employee:** When all else fails, invoke disciplinary procedures (Chapter 8).

Box 11.23

PERFORMANCE APPRAISAL: SUMMARY OF DIFFICULTIES

Incompetent Assessors

Managers are the most common assessors of an individual's performance, yet they often lack the specialist knowledge or skills required to make that assessment. Often they have insufficient knowledge of the individual's work to challenge successfully the individual's version of events.

Gaps in Appraisal Scheme

Schemes commonly exclude new recruits, probationers, people on work placement, people due to retire, seconded staff or staff on loan, agency staff, consultants, part-timers, people on short-term contracts and members of multi-agency teams – in other words, a significant proportion of the workforce of a public service organization.

Statistical Nonsense

In order to avoid making waves, or to subvert the system, or to avoid the need for further thought, managers commonly rate the performance of all but a few staff as 'above average'.

'If you can't count it, then it doesn't count!'

'Soft' areas of performance are ignored because they are subjective and hard to measure. Yet they can be the most important part of the job.

The Halo Effect

Managers have pet hates or pet likes. Someone who scores highly on an attribute that is important to the manager is more likely to score highly on other attributes.

Lack of Audit

Often performance appraisals are dominated by target setting and future promises. Relatively little attention is paid to what was promised last time and the lessons that can be learnt.

Formality

Formality brings fear of judgement and defensiveness. Consequently, plans for improvement are based on incomplete or distorted information.

FINAL THOUGHTS: 'THE MORALITY OF MANAGERS'

Can moral judgement and ethical behaviour be learnt? Lawrence Kohlberg thought so. But being able to think ethically does not necessarily mean that you will act morally. Kohlberg[72] identified six stages of moral development which he grouped into three levels (Box 11.24). People are assumed to progress through these stages as a result of personal and social development. Progression however, is not guaranteed.

Kohlberg claimed that the stages were universal. Research carried out by Snary,[73] threw doubts on Kohlberg's claim that all six stages were found in all cultures. In some cultures, Snary failed to find anyone at Stage Five. Gilligan[74] criticized Kohlberg's theory for failing to differentiate between men and women. Despite these criticisms, Trevino[75] claimed that Kohlberg's model could be used to design management development processes. He concluded that:

- Moral education programmes can produce intentional gains in moral development.
- There is a relationship between ethical thinking and ethical behaviour.
- Ongoing learning produces incidental moral development.
- Capacity for moral reasoning increases with age.

Trevino found that a person at a lower level of moral development could have a negative influence on people at a higher level of moral development. He also found that people at a higher level of moral development could develop the ethical thinking and moral behaviour of others.

At the end of this chapter, there are thinking and learning activities which readers can use to develop their capacity for empathetic and ethical thinking. Empathy and ethics are important components of the critical thinking needed to enhance the morality of management.

Box 11.24

MORAL DEVELOPMENT: THREE LEVELS

Level 1: Stages One and Two

Stages One and Two are concerned with pre-conventional morality. Stage One is characterized by a preoccupation with self-preservation and the need to obey whoever is in charge. At Stage Two ethical reasoning is determined by calculating what is in one's own best interests and negotiating this with others. At Stages One and Two, rules and social expectations are external. They are followed because of fear of punishment.

Level 2: Stages Three and Four

Stages Three and Four are concerned with conventional morality. At Stage Three moral judgements are based on pleasing and caring for others and not disappointing or hurting the feelings of people who are close to you. At Stage Four concern is shown for the necessity to enforce moral standards. There is acceptance of the rules and expectations of others, especially those in authority. Most adults reach this stage.

Level 3: Stages Five and Six

Stages Five and Six related to post-conventional morality. The individual questions and challenges rules that fail to meet deeper ethical tests, such as respect for human rights. People regulate their behaviour according to autonomously chosen moral principles.

SUMMARY

- We distinguished between upward and downward accountability. We found that upward accountability was often inadequate. Mechanisms for downward accountability including market competition, and citizen's charters also often failed.
- We discovered tensions between accountability based on consumerism and accountability based on collective responsibility.
- Accountability to one's own conscience is important in public services but it is easily compromised unless managers are practised at resolving moral conflicts.
- We found that mechanisms for accountability are diverse, confusing and inconsistent.
- Audit, accountability and performance management raised ethical questions. If managers are to determine what actions are most likely to contribute to building a 'good' society, they will need greater skills in ethical and empathetic thinking.
- An addition E for Ethics was needed covering Equity, Empathy and Ecology.
- Performance monitoring should tell stakeholders what public service organizations are doing and how well they are doing it. We discovered how indicators based on economy, efficiency and effectiveness are manipulated to give false impressions.
- Best Value was explored.
- We considered what made a good performance indicator and how performance management systems generally failed to raise the performance of organizations.
- We realized that organizations are made up of individuals and we looked at a conversational approach to improving the performance of poor performers.
- We discovered that ethical behaviour can be learned.

THINKING AND LEARNING ACTIVITIES

Activity 1 Self Assessment

1 What do you understand by upward and downward accountability? Give examples of each.
2 What are the strengths and weaknesses of accountability based on conscience?
3 Do market mechanisms strengthen accountability?
4 Summarize the main weaknesses of public services accountability.
5 In what ways could the accountability of public services be improved?
6 Compare the roles of the internal and external auditor in public services.
7 What are the differences between economy, efficiency and effectiveness?
8 Explain why the three E's are not an adequate framework for performance management.
9 How can managers ensure that measures of organizational performance are useful?
10 What is distinctive about performance management in public services?
11 What is problematic about measuring performance in public services?
12 What are the characteristics of a good performance indicator?
13 How can auditors assist public service managers in achieving Best Value?
14 How are performance indicators used in the management of performance?
15 If audit and measurement reveal poor organizational performance, what methods are open to managers to improve the performance of those individuals whose performance is poor?
16 How can managers establish what levels of performance they are entitled to expect?
17 How can managers investigate the alleged poor performance of an individual?
18 What sorts of things might cause an individual to underperform over an extended period?
19 What problems can arise during a performance appraisal?

20 What difficulties are there with performance management generally?

Activity 2 Individual Learning: Visual Thinking

Mental mapping

Take a blank A4 sheet. Skim back over the first section of this chapter. Each time you come to a key idea or section, label it with a few words. Write the label somewhere on your blank A4 sheet and draw a circle round the label. When you come across the next key idea, label it and place it on your A4 sheet, close to other ideas to which you think it is related. When you have skimmed through the whole chapter, draw lines between the circles on your A4 sheet, if you think the ideas are connected. If necessary, use a clean sheet to redraw your diagram so that intersections are minimized. Now write verbs or actions along all the lines, such as 'which leads to', 'which can help with', 'which is connected to', 'which can be evaluated by'. Keep going until you have a map, diagram or flowchart of how all the ideas in this chapter relate to each other.

Activity 3 Individual Learning: Numerical Thinking

Value for money audit

You are a member of an internal audit team in a social welfare department. The following numerical information (Table 11.4) provides a summary of the costs of a community cafe in two different towns. The main areas that you have been asked to audit are: provisions, staff costs, overheads, revenue and management. The Board has specifically requested you to highlight issues that might impact on value for money (VFM). Explain how you would go about a VFM study and suggest ways of improving the service based on the comparative data you have been given. What other data and information might assist you in your task?

Table 11.4 Costs of a community cafe in towns A and B

	Town A		Town B	
	Total cost $	Unit cost cents	Total cost $	Unit cost cents
Provisions	2.1	23	1.8	21
Kitchen staff	3.7	40	3.2	34
Supervision	0.6	7	1.1	8
Administrative staff	0.3	6	0.4	5
Overheads	1.2	13	0.7	9
Gross expenditure	7.9	89	7.2	77
Income from services	2.4	33	3.7	41
Notional income (value of free staff meals)	1.9	21	1.3	15
Net cost of service	**3.6**	**35**	**2.2**	**21**

Activity 4 Paired Learning: Ethical Thinking

Dilemma: a criminal or a moral act?

Heinz, Susan's husband, is dying from terminal cancer. His only hope for survival is a new drug. The pharmacist who developed the drug is charging $10,000 for the treatment. This is 10 times what it cost to produce the drug. Susan has managed to raise $5,000 and has approached her bank to lend her the rest of the money. They have refused her. She approaches the pharmacist and asks him for a discount or a staged payment. He refuses. In desperation, Susan breaks into the pharmacy and steals the drug (after Kohlberg).

Working on your own, make notes on:

1 What, if anything, was right, and what, if anything, was wrong, with what Susan did?
2 Give your reasons for your answers to question 1. (Refer to all stages of Kohlberg's model.)
3 What you think she should have done?
4 Is Susan a 'bad' person?
5 If Susan became a 'bad' person, would she surrender her right to be treated as though she were a 'good' person? (Look back at the Mary Ruebens conversation in Box 11.5.)
6 What would you do if you were in Susan's situation?

If you have a partner, compare your notes and discuss them. On what can you agree? Even on things on which you cannot agree, which of your partner's ideas do you find interesting? Which ideas would merit further discussion? Which of your ideas or your partner's ideas merit further thought on your part?

Activity 5 Paired or Group Learning: Ethical Thinking

Debating a moral dilemma can be challenging, stimulating, fun even! Find a partner or a small group of people who are prepared to help you to think about a moral dilemma. Discuss the following dilemma and see if you can come to an agreed solution to the problem. If you cannot reach a consensus, come up with several possible solutions and identify the Kohlberg stage of moral reasoning to which they most closely relate.

Dilemma: bullying at work

A colleague at work is a female manager. She says that life has become intolerable for her because of the bullying she is receiving at the hands of a senior officer. She has said to you, in confidence, that it is making her feel very depressed and that sometimes she feels like ending her own life. The officer accused of bullying is also your boss and you have a fairly good relationship with him.

What would you do in this situation?

Activity 6 Paired or Group Learning: Ethical Thinking

With a partner or a small group of people, discuss the following dilemma and see if you can find an agreed solution to the problem. If you cannot reach a consensus, come up with several possible solutions and identify the Kohlberg stage of moral reasoning to which they most closely relate.

Dilemma: sexual honesty

You are happily married and you and your partner have a pact to be faithful and a pact to be honest with each other. One night you are a long way from home at a national conference on energy policy. You spend the night sleeping with one of your work colleagues.

Should you confess to your partner?

Activity 7 Paired or Group Learning: Ethical Thinking

Discuss the following dilemma with a partner or in a small group.

Dilemma: kiss and tell?

A manager in the agricultural department has been badly treated by her lover who is a prominent local politician. Soon after he ends their relationship, he is elected to the national assembly. A newspaper offers her $50,000 for her story.

Should she sell her story?

Activity 8 Paired or Group Learning: Ethical Thinking

Dilemma: petty theft

You work for a local education department which has a reputation for treating its staff with great fairness. You are stocking up on stationery equipment for your office. Nobody is around. Would you pilfer paper or pens, or postage stamps that you would normally buy for your personal use?

If you answered 'yes' to this question, would you be prepared to pilfer more expensive items such as computer software which you also needed at home? Would it change your view, if your employer was mean?

Activity 9 Paired or Group Learning: Ethical Thinking

Dilemma: whistle blowing

You discover that one of your colleagues who is responsible for purchasing office furniture and fittings has been requisitioning small items of equipment for personal use. Your two families are very close. You often visit him at his house. On one visit, the door of his study has been left open. You notice that his study is furnished with items that he has requisitioned from work.

What would you say or do? You often depend on him for a lift. Does that affect your decision? He often takes work home at evenings and weekends. Does that change your decision?

Activity 10 Paired Learning: Evaluative Thinking

Dilemma: poor time-keeping

Since being appointed to manage a department, you have noticed that one member of your staff is consistently late for work, yet always leaves on time. The 'quiet word' you had with him about his poor time-keeping has had no effect.

Identify what type of action you would take to address the poor performance of those involved. Write down your ideas and then discuss them with someone else.

Activity 11 Individual or Paired Learning: Empathetic Thinking

Dilemma: bullying

A member of staff has complained to you that her supervisor's behaviour is aggressive and bullying. You have called the supervisor into your office to discuss the matter.

Working initially on your own, identify what type of action you would take to address the poor performance of those involved. Write down your ideas and then discuss them with someone else.

Activity 12 Individual or Paired Learning: Projective Thinking

Dilemma: false expenses

A member of staff has mentioned to you that another member of her team seems to be taking advantage of the expenses process and is claiming for expenses that she has not incurred.

Working initially on your own, identify what type of action you would take to address the poor performance of those involved. Write down your ideas and then discuss them with someone else.

Activity 13 Individual or Paired Learning: Empathetic and Evaluative Thinking

Dilemma: how to get to the bottom of things

A member of your staff has just returned from a week away at a conference on new legislation affecting your service. He says 'There were major implications.' You ask him to call staff together and to give a presentation on Friday. On Thursday, he seems quite agitated. He is uncharacteristically cross with someone from another department.

Working initially on your own, consider the situation outlined above. Identify what type of action you would take. Write down your ideas and then discuss them with someone else.

Activity 14 Individual or Paired Learning: Evaluative and Projective Thinking

Dilemma: poor performance

A member of staff has rung in sick three Mondays in the last six weeks. On your way home on Monday night you noticed him driving through the village where you live. He looked quite well and happy. Prior to this one of his colleagues has complained to you that he is not pulling his weight and that he has been stealing toilet rolls. You decide to confront him about his behaviour at his annual appraisal which is due to take place later in the month.

Working initially on your own, consider the situation outlined above. Write down your answers to the questions and then discuss them with someone else.

1 What would you do to prepare for the appraisal interview?
2 How will you confront him about his behaviour during the appraisal interview?

Activity 15 Individual or Paired Learning: Evaluative and Projective Thinking

Dilemma: letting the team down

You are the manager of a small team. You like everyone to give 100 per cent to their work. You like to think that you set a good example. However, you are frustrated by two members of your team whom you think are lazy. They avoid hard work whenever they can get away with it. You feel that their poor performance is contributing to your team's failure to meet the performance indicators that have been set.

Working initially on your own, write down your answers to the following questions and then discuss them with someone else.

1   What would you do and in what order?
2   How would you hope to arrange, open and close the conversation that would be involved?
3   What questions would you ask?

Activity 16 Paired Learning: Empathetic and Evaluative Thinking

Dilemma: what's going on?

Consider the following two scenarios. Put yourself into the shoes of the people concerned. Make a brief note of your ideas, guesses, musings and speculations about what might be going on in their minds.

- **Scenario 1:** Since returning from her holiday, a normally conscientious member of staff seems to be detached from her job and is uncharacteristically missing deadlines. You have bumped into her in the office corridor and suggested a chat in the canteen at lunch time.
- **Scenario 2:** A member of your team has been off work with a sore wrist. She claims it is a repetitive strain injury. Your doctor is not convinced. You have written to her requesting an interview.

Compare notes with your partner.

Activity 17 Individual Learning: Critical, Numerical and Ethical Thinking

CASE STUDY: Toxic waste

Auditing Performance

You have been recruited as a consultant and are required to analyse the way in which a public service organization handles the disposal of its toxic wastes. You are asked to audit current performance and to come up with recommendations to improve economy, effectiveness and efficiency. You have been invited to comment on other aspects that seem relevant.

The Context

Recently there have been a number of high-profile negative incidents concerning the disposal of the organization's contaminated waste. The waste includes health-threatening materials, pollutants and sharps – things likely to cut or maim others. It is mixed with the waste from offices, kitchens and residential accommodation. The waste disposal contractor has recently been prosecuted for dumping the waste in a disused quarry. Injuries to local school children have been reported in the press. Waste collection and disposal costs the organization approximately $360,000 per annum. The chief executive officer (CEO) regards this as excessive compared to costs incurred by other organizations. The CEO is also concerned that the organization may not be complying with the law. The organization has a five-year contract with its waste disposal contractor. The contract still has three years to run.

Information

A recent government report has indicated that the cost of waste disposal in your country is higher than in comparable countries. The authors of the report think that there is considerable potential for savings. Recent legislation has removed state immunity from prosecution. The legislation extends to all citizens a duty of care in the handling and disposal of waste. All waste disposed by organizations employing more than 25 people must be described and accurate records must be kept of all consignments. Table 11.5 provides information from seven comparable organizations. Your client's figures are in bold.

Produce a report for the CEO covering:

- A summary of how the audit was carried out, including information gathered and the types of people to whom you have talked.
- Your findings and conclusions.
- Recommendations to improve waste management.
- Recommendations for further audit work and the reasons for this.

Table 11.5 Benchmarks for waste disposal

	Toxic waste (kg)	Disposal cost $	Other waste (kg)	Disposal cost $	Total staff	Staff costs $	Other costs $
A	323,750	120,000	700,000	25,000	550	40,000	45,000
B	600,000	150,000	600,000	60,000	750	40,000	60,000
C	900,000	450,000	900,000	18,000	1,000	100,000	80,000
D	700,000	175,000	700,000	21,000	800	80,000	60,000
E	150,000	45,000	400,000	25,000	200	15,000	20,000
F	300,000	90,000	500,000	12,500	400	40,000	45,000
Client	**250,000**	**150,000**	**800,000**	**25,000**	**400**	**130,000**	**45,000**

Answers to the following questions should inform your audit report:

1 What steps would you take in auditing your client's waste disposal activity?
2 What is the average cost for the disposal of toxic and other waste?
3 What will you use as a performance indicator so that it will give you the most useful or reliable basis for comparison between your client and the other sites?
3 Calculate the average cost of staffing.
4 If your client is less economical, or less efficient (or both), are there any indicators in the data as to where to start to investigate the possible causes?
5 What savings could be made if your client achieved the average cost?
6 What performance indicators would you set to improve your client's effectiveness?
7 What recommendations would you make on performance monitoring?
8 What other issues should inform your client's thinking about this matter?
   (NB If you have problems with some of the calculations, turn to the section on handling numerical information in the next chapter.)

Activity 18 Individual Learning Review: Reflective Thinking

Inner world thinking

What inner world thinking skills can you identify in the manager's work described in this chapter? Have any of the thinking skills you have identified emerged for the first time in this chapter? If so, add them to your accumulating model of the kinds of thinking skills that you think are useful to managers of public services.

What things could you do to develop any of the thinking skills that you have just added to your model? What would be the first step?

Outer world conversations

What outer world conversational skills can you identify in the manager's work described in this chapter? Have any of the types of conversational skills you have identified emerged for the first time? If so, add them to your accumulating model of the kinds of conversational skills you think are useful to managers of public services.

What things could you do to develop any of these conversational skills which you have just added to your model? What would be the first step?

Activity 19 Individual Learning: Metacognitive Thinking

Metacognition

Look back through the Thinking and Learning Activities you have been asked to carry out in this chapter. What thinking skills were involved in each of these activities? For each type of thinking, write down how you were learning what you were learning, when you were learning to think in each of the different ways.

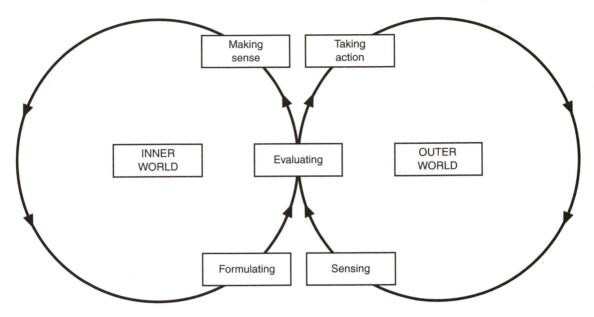

Figure 11.3 The thinking skills of the conversational manager

NOTES

1 Public Accounts Committee (1994) *The Proper Conduct of Public Business.* Session 1993/4 Eighth Report HCP.

2 Third Report of the Committee on Standards in Public Life (1997) London HMSO Local Government in England, Scotland and Wales (July Cmd. 3702).

3 Ferlie, E., Ashburner, L., Fitzgerald, L. and Pettigrew, A. (1997) *The New Public Management in Action.* Oxford University Press, p. 198.

4 The *Sunday Times* (2000), 3 March, p. 6.

5 Thompson, D. F. (1980) 'Moral Responsibility of Officials: The Problem of Many Hands'. *The American Political Review*, no. 74, p. 905.

6 Day, P. and Klein, R. (1989) 'Interpreting the Unexpected: The Case of AIDS in Policy Making in Britain'. *Journal of Public Policy*, no. 9, p. 2.

7 Coombs, H. and Jenkins, D. (1994) *Public Sector Financial Management.* Chapman and Hall, p. 257.

8 Local Government Finance Act (1982) HMSO Section 15, para. 1.

9 CIPFA (1979) *Statements on Internal Audit in the Public Sector.*

10 Coombs and Jenkins, op. cit., p. 262.

11 Flynn, N. and Strehl, F. (1996) *Public Sector Management in Europe.* Prentice Hall, p. 40.

12 *Modernising Local Government* (1998) HMSO.

13 Bogdanov, V. (1996) 'The Scott Report'. *Public Administration*, no. 74, pp. 593–611.

14 Railings, C. and Thresher, M. (1991) 'Local Elections: The Changing Scene'. *Social Studies Review*, vol. 5, no. 4, pp. 163–66.

15 Ranson, S. and Stewart, J. (1994) *Management for the Public Domain. Enabling the Learning Society.* Macmillan, p. 235.

16 Jackson, P. and Lavender, M. (eds) (1996) *Public Service Year Book.* Pitman.

17 Rose, A. and Lawton, A. (1999) *Public Services Management.* FT/Prentice Hall, p. 90.

18 Second Report of the Committee on Standards in Public Life (1996) London HMSO.

19 Terry, F. (1993) 'Managing Relations with the European Commission in Public Service Organisations'. In Isaac-Henry, K., Painter, C. and Barnes, C. (eds) *Management in the Public Sector: Challenge and Change.* Chapman and Hall, p. 166.

20 See Hambleton, R. (1988) 'Consumerism, Decentralisation and Local Democracy'. *Public Administration*, no. 66 (Summer).

21 *Modernising Local Government* (1998) HMSO.

22 Day and Klein, op. cit.

23 Ferlie *et al.*, op. cit., p. 222.

24 Prior, D., Stewart, J. and Walsh, K. (1993) *Is the Citizen's Charter a Charter for Citizens?* Local Govt Management Board.

25 Ferlie *et al.*, op. cit., p. 224.

26 See Hill, D. M. (1994) *Citizens and Cities. Urban Policy in the 1990's.* Harvester Wheatsheaf.

27 Glaster, L. (1995) *Managing Quality in Public Services. Managers' Choices.* Oxford University Press, p. 98.

28 Pollitt, C. (1994) 'The Citizen's Charter. A Preliminary Analysis'. *Public Money and Management.* April–June, pp. 9–14.

29 *The Citizen's Charter Five Years On* (1996) Cmd 3370. London HMSO.

30 Gray, P. and Jenkins, A. (1995) 'From Public Administration to Public Management. Reassessing the Revolution'. *Public Administration*, vol. 73, no. 1, p. 81.

31 Ferlie *et al.*, op. cit., p. 199.

32 Bogdanov, V. (1994) *Local Government and the Constitution.* Kensington Town Hall Solace.

33 See Stewart, J. *et al.* (1992) *Accountability to the Public.* London Everyman Policy Forum.

34 Ferlie *et al.*, op. cit., p. 199.

35 Bourne, J. (1997) *Report of the Comptroller General and General Auditor on the Resignation of the Chief Executive of English Heritage.* London. National Audit Office.

36 Bowerman, M. (1997) 'Public Audit in Public Services', in Jackson, P. and Lavender, M., op. cit., p. 167.

37 Day and Klein, op. cit.

38 Ranson and Stewart, op. cit., p. 237.

39 Ibid., p. 239.

40 Lawton, A. (1998) *Ethical Management for Public Services.* Oxford University Press, p. 145.

41 Horne, I. (1996) 'Defending Values – Promoting Change'. *Human Rights – Philosophical Review.* Bradford University.

42 Ranson and Stewart, op. cit., p. 64.

43 Doherty, A. (1988) 'Personal and Social Education in Vocational Education'. *Values in Education Journal*, vol. 2, pp. 34–48.

44 Hill, D. M. (1994) *Citizens and Cities. Urban Policy in the 1990's.* Harvester Wheatsheaf.

45 Ranson and Stewart, op. cit., p. 67.

46 Horne, T. and Knock, P. (2000) 'Consultation in Public Services'. Research Paper (unpublished) Presented to University of Central Lancashire.

47 Blundell, B. and Murdock, A. (1998) *Managing in the Public Sector.* Institute of Management.

48 Hood, C. (1991) 'Beyond "Progressivism": a New Global Perspective in Public Management'. *International Journal of Public Management*, vol. 19, no. 25, pp. 151–77.

49 Flynn and Strehl, op. cit., p. 12.

50 Flynn, op. cit., p. 113.

51 Mayston, D. (1985) 'Non-Profit Performance Indicators in the Public Sector'. *Financial Accountability and Management*, vol. 1, no. 1. Summer, pp. 51–74.

52 The *Sunday Times* (2000), 3 Feb., p. 5.

53 Jackson, P. (1995) 'Reflections on Performance Measurement in Public Service', in *Measures for Success in the Public Sector.* Public Finance Foundation.

54 McCarthy, S., Bell, L., Brown, R. and Scraggs, S. (1994) 'In Search of the Elusive Outcome Measure'. International conference on Strategic Issues in UK Health Care Management.

55 Audit Commission (1989) *Managing Services Effectively.* Performance Review. HMSO, p. 17.

56 Lawton, op. cit., p. 123.

57 Meekings, A. (1995) 'Unlocking the Potential of Performance Indicators. A Practical Implementation Guide'. *Public Money and Management*, Oct.–Dec., pp. 5–12.

58 Pollitt, C. (1991) *The New Managerialism in the Public Sector.* Blackwell, p. 21.

59 Rose and Lawton, op. cit., p. 241.

60 Flynn, op. cit., p. 142.

61 Connock, P. and James, P. (1995) *Ethical Leadership.* Institute of Personnel and Development.

62 Rouse, A. (1993) 'Resource and Performance Management in Public Service Organisations'. In Isaac-Henry, K. *et al.*, op. cit., p. 68.

63 Bishop, M. and Kay, J. (1988) *Does Privatisation Work?* London Business School.

64 Farnham, D. and Horton, S. (eds) (1993) *Managing the New Public Services.* Macmillan, p. 11.

65 Armstrong, R. (1987) *Future Shape of Reform in Whitehall.* Royal Institute of Public Administration, p. 11.

66 Rose and Lawton, op. cit.

67 Kessler, J. (1996) *Reward Systems in HRM: Critical Text.* Routledge.

68 Horne, T. and Wootton, D. (2000) *Thinking Skills for Managers.* Kogan Page.

69 Maier, N. (1985) *The Appraisal Interview: Objectives, Methods and Skills.* John Wiley.

70 Smidt, S. L. (1993) 'Appraising Performance Appraisal'. *Training and Development.* Nov., p. 11.

71 Rogers, S. (1990) In Clarke, M. and Stewart, J. (eds) *Performance Management in Local Government*, Longmans in Association with LGTB, p. 42.

72 Kohlberg, L. (1973) 'Stage and Sequence: the Cognitive Developmental Approach to Socialization'. In Goslin, D. A. (ed.) *Handbook of Socialization Theory and Research.* Rand McNally.

73 Snary, J. R. (1985) 'Cross Cultural Universality of Social Moral Development: A Critical Review of Kohlbergian Research'. *Psychological Bulletin*, vol. 97, no. 2, pp. 202–32.

74 Gilligan, C. (1979) 'Women's Place in Man's Life Cycle'. *Harvard Business Review*, vol. 49, no. 4.

75 Trevino, L. K. (1992) 'Moral Reasoning and Business Ethics: Implications for Research, Education and Management'. *Journal of Business Ethics*, vol. 4.

ROLE FIVE

MANAGING INFORMATION

In Role One we looked at overcoming resistance and implementing changes in response to the internal and external appraisals which managers carry out in Role Two – Managing Operations. In Role Three we looked at ways in which people could be motivated to implement these changes in groups, or preferably as individuals. In Role Four we looked at ways of obtaining the resources to finance change and looked at ways to overcome the behavioural difficulties of budgeting. We added an E for ethics, an E for empathy, an E for Equity and an E for Ecology to the 3 E's for economy, efficiency and effectiveness, which were used to measure how successfully changes are implemented. A conversational approach to raising the performance of poor performers was outlined.

Success in implementing changes and improving poor performance depends on the quality and timeliness of the information on which decisions are based. We turn now to Role Five, Managing Information. We look at conversational approaches to communication, to managing the media, and to taking complex decisions.

12

MANAGING INFORMATION AND COMMUNICATIONS IN PUBLIC SERVICES

There is no pleasure to me without communication: there is not so much as a sprightly thought comes into my mind but I grieve that I have no one else to tell it to.

(Montaigne 1533–92)

LEARNING OUTCOMES

This chapter will enable readers to:

- Understand the different ways in which information might be communicated.
- Understand techniques for presenting written and spoken information.
- Understand techniques for quantifying and presenting information.
- Understand how information can be managed and mismanaged.
- Understand how to use information for external public relations.
- Identify problems associated with the implementation of IT in public services.
- Consider the implications and potential of IT developments for public services.
- Know how to use a conversational approach to systems design.
- Consider the role of information in rational and complex decision-making.
- Consider how information management can lead to knowledge creation.

INTRODUCTION

Information feeds many kinds of management thinking activities – notably decision-making, problem-solving, planning, predicting, quantifying, evaluating generating and evaluating new ideas. You also need it in order to monitor progress, to keep yourself and your team up to date and to make reports, written or verbal, to those who are entitled to know what you are doing with your time or their money. Often there is too much of it. How do you get the minimum you need, in the form you need it?

Information can either be 'hard' or 'soft'. Hard information is factual and usually verifiable in some way. Examples include income figures, personnel records or statistics about client contacts. It is a helpful but rarely sufficient basis for management decision-making. If only hard statistics about the risk of injury at the office were fed into a computer, the computer might decide that it would be better if everyone stayed at home. Until, that is, you feed it statistics about accidents that occur at home! What is missing is 'soft information' about how your clients would feel if all your staff stayed at home. This kind of 'soft' information is subjective, a matter of judgement or opinion, sometimes based on a 'gut' feeling. 'Soft' information is the kind of information you need when you sit as a member of a parole board or a disciplinary hearing. In this chapter we examine how in public services, information is managed and communicated both internally and externally.

WHY COMMUNICATE

When implementing changes, failures in communication can be costly. It is unlikely that the intended benefits of implementing changes will be fully realized without direct communication, face-to-face, with the employees involved. We recommend – where possible – an individualized conversational approach to communication and the management of change. The different types of conversations that may be involved are set out in Figure 12.1.

Managers do not have a monopoly on wisdom. We cannot afford to waste the knowledge that is held within an organization. Younger people may have become used to being given explanations and having a say, either through their experience at school or through contact with social workers or youth services. They do not leave their skills and expectations behind when they come to work.

Through everyday conversations with managers, staff need to clarify what they are doing and why it is important. Managers need to follow up on their last conversation. The last conversation was probably about the work, but it might have been about an aspect of learning, or a possible new development, or even a personal problem. Conversations can result in improved efficiency, increased effectiveness and greater clarity about the ethical dilemmas that face the service.

WHAT TO COMMUNICATE?

You cannot tell everybody everything. How do you decide what to communicate? Interest is not a good criterion. Things can be interesting but not important. If employees are not interested in things that are

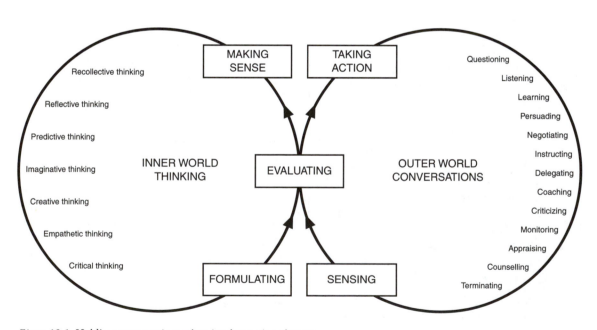

Figure 12.1 Holding conversations when implementing changes

important, that becomes your first task – to engender interest. If something is important but not intrinsically interesting, it will be more difficult to get employees to understand it. But that difficulty should not be shirked. There is little point in having questioning and listening conversations on things people do not understand. Preliminary time may need to be spent coaching until the requisite level of understanding has been achieved (Chapter 13). People do not have to agree with a decision in order to implement it, but they do need to understand it.

Other important conversations relate to making sure that people are clear to whom they are answerable and for what. They need to know how aspects of their work fit into the wider work of the organization. How will the quality of their work be judged? What is safe and unsafe practice? What changes can be made without reference to anyone else? What is this month's top priority? How do people get to be selected for promotion? Where and how to make suggestions to improve things?

HOW TO COMMUNICATE

Information flows around organizations through formal and informal channels. The 'grapevine' is an informal network which is remarkably quick but is subject to distortion and often misses out people, especially managers who do not walk the job. Managers feel disempowered when their staff know more about new developments than they do. The grapevine has no feedback loop to ensure that correct meanings have been attached to what is communicated. The grapevine has advantages and disadvantages, as do all channels of communication. We will consider the advantages and disadvantages of six channels of communication: hierarchy, representation, briefing groups, networks, mass methods and individual conversations (Box 12.1). We will then consider written and verbal communication. We will pay particular attention to the hard language of numerical information. Finally, we will offer a model of the communication process and see if it can help us to understand why there are sometimes barriers to communication.

Box 12.1

SIX CHANNELS OF COMMUNICATION

- **Hierarchy**: Information is imparted upwards and downwards, through a chain of command.
- **Representatives**: Information is given to representatives who are responsible for distributing it to people they represent. Representatives collate response and feed back.
- **Team briefings**: All members of the organization are allocated to a briefing group. Regular written briefs are devised and read out to the briefing groups. There is no debate. Reactions are noted and fed back.
- **Networks**: People with similar interests, or similar backgrounds, or similar status, meet to share experiences. Sometimes they meet to

agree 'best practice'. Often informal networks develop. The activities of such networks are often supported by organizations.
- **Mass methods**: These include notice boards, newsletters, annual reports, recorded messages and e-mail.
- **One-to-one conversations**: In one-to-one conversations we can recognize individual differences between people. We can recognize preferences which individuals might have for the way they receive and interpret information. It is easier to check that one person has received what you sent, heard what you said and understood what you meant.

COMMUNICATION CHANNELS: ADVANTAGES AND DISADVANTAGES

Advantages and Disadvantages of Using the Management Hierarchy

- Senior managers know the reasons for their decisions. They can explain *why* as well as *how*. People will sometimes accept what they don't like if someone senior explains the reasons.
- It increases the authority and standing of managers if they are seen to be 'in the know'.
- Managers should know their staff and be able to couch communications in appropriate language. Subsequently, they can be around – in their departments or on their patch – to deal with questions that people might prefer to raise.
- The cost of bringing staff together.
- Some questions may be asked, but many people are reluctant to look ignorant, foolish or 'not in the know' in front of others.
- Bringing people together in groups raises anxiety (Chapter 6). This makes it more difficult for people to give attention, remember, or think of questions to ask.
- The use of memos, faxes, or e-mails can overcome some of these disadvantages but there is no check that the message sent is understood.

Advantages and Disadvantages of Using Representatives

- It is not so costly in management time – they only have to explain things once.
- Formal contact creates opportunities for informal conversations.
- Creating groups creates problems (Chapter 7).
- Representatives can be reluctant to pass on managers' 'good reasons' with enthusiasm. After all, it is not their job. It's the manager's job.
- The use of representatives for downward communication bypasses junior managers. This reduces their status and disempowers them.

Advantages and Disadvantages of Using Briefing Groups

- The same information can be given to more than one person at once.
- It is more economical and more efficient than individual communication.
- It is not more effective. Not everyone attaches the same meaning to what is said.
- Not everyone will ask questions or seek clarification in a group setting.
- Group reactions and group phenomena are complex and require more interpretation than the body language of individuals (Chapter 6).

The Advantages and Disadvantages of Using Networks

- Quick and self-motivated. Require little support or management time.
- Biased and can lead to sectional self-interest.
- Puts some groups in a privileged position, knowing things that others do not know.
- Can fuel bad feelings between rival groups.
- It annoys managers when they hear things for the first time from the people they are managing.

Advantages and Disadvantages of Using Mass Communication

Notice boards

These should be where people congregate and wait – rest rooms, cafeterias, photocopiers. There should be two separate notice boards, or one clearly divided by coloured tape: one is for urgent or new notices; the other is for notices that are left for reference until their expiry date. It should be somebody's job to manage the board and keep it looking good – free from graffiti and unauthorized notices.

Newsletters

Frequency and flexibility are more important than prestigious production. Four weekly columns, on one side of A4, are sufficient. Reserve approximately one column for new developments or changes, one column for social or learning events, and one column for free personal ads – 'For Sale', 'Wanted', 'Share a flat', 'Rent a house', 'Lift to work'.

Annual reports

These tell the world and the staff what has been achieved during the year, for example, how many clients have been seen how many times, compared with last year. They report on new developments and on achievements that reflect credit on individuals, departments or teams. Pictures of satisfied clients should punctuate the report.

Recorded messages

The messages are pre-recorded on video or audio tapes. By pressing touch buttons, employees can obtain information on a menu of topics, via a telephone helpline.

E-mails

Electronic mail can be sent to all addresses simultaneously announcing, for example, meetings to attend or the need for volunteers for new projects or working groups. We deal later with wider issues related to electronic communication.

- Mass communication is cheap.
- The information transmitted can be controlled.
- It is not possible to ask questions of a notice board, a newsletter, or an annual report, a TV screen or a recorded message.
- Although it is possible to control the message transmitted, it is not possible to check that it has been accurately understood.
- It cannot deal with specifics.

One-to One Conversations

One-to-One conversation is immediate and personal. Queries can be raised and understanding can be checked. However, there is no permanent record of the conversation. In Carolyn's case study (Chapter 15), she often confirmed the main actions points agreed in a conversation, by sending a personal note, often on an attractive card. People are often reluctant to 'bin' personal letters and attractive cards. At Carolyn's memorial service, it became clear that many of her colleagues had kept collections of her notes and cards going back over many years. Sensitive listening to the modulations of tone, volume and pace of speech can greatly aid the attachment of meaning to what is said. One-to-One conversation can make it easier to listen to the music as well as the words. Sometimes the emotional meaning conveyed by the music is as important as the facts.

The Death of Distance

An open line between Australia and Manila enables people in the Philippines to supervise elderly people in Australia. Low orbiting satellites carry mobile phone traffic. Advances in digit compression pack more capacity into existing systems. In 1997 Telecom Finland offered a service enabling people working in public service organizations to talk to one another about what they could each see on their computer screens. In large countries, like Norway, subsidized long-distance calls might help to hold the country together.

Public Service Telecommunications

At the beginning of the new millennium, public telephone services throughout the world were in a situation similar to that which faced public service airlines in the mid-1980s. They faced privatization, deregulation and fierce competition. Fortunately, they were better placed than the airlines to survive it: they had less debt and they owned and controlled the physical networks on which their competitors had to compete. Two out of three people in their global markets still didn't own a telephone. Asia had the fastest rate of growth, adding 25 million lines per year. China alone was adding 14 million lines per year, with plans to increase the rate to 20 million.[1] The Philippines and Venezuela had the highest growth rate for mobile phones. Developing countries like the Solomon Islands and Reunion were able to go straight to advanced digitized telephone systems. Public service telephone organizations in developed countries allowed their historical interests to block their development, while in Chile the state-owned public telephone service was privatized and within three years telephone access doubled and the waiting time fell from ten years to one year.[2] According to Frances Cairncross,[3] other examples abound: Telefonica de España had taken control of the public telephone service in Peru; AT&T built a mobile network in Argentina; Deutsche Telekom built a new system in Argentina; and Australia's Telstra installed pay phones in Vietnam.

These developments allowed developing countries to compete on equal terms with the longer established public telephone services in developed countries. They also helped to slow the migration from rural communities to big cities which were already struggling to maintain their public services. In India 74 per cent of the people lived in villages which had less than 10 per cent of India's telephones.[4] New telephone links to the rural areas brought not only news, education and training but also medical consultation, agricultural advice, entertainment and employment. When people can get these things without uprooting and risking a less pleasant life in a city, they are less likely to migrate to the cities.

Conversations on the Phone

People hate phones when they interrupt their thinking, delay their departures, make them late for their next appointment, add to their stress levels and never stop ringing. People love phones when people know what they are going to say, get to the point, achieve what they want and say goodbye. People hate phoning you if it is hard to find your number, you are always engaged, they have to listen to awful music, they have to repeat the same message each time they are transferred, and when they finally get you, you say that it is 'not your job', 'not your fault' or 'not your problem'. If you want to sound friendly, smile when you are talking. It doesn't matter that the other person can't see you – they can hear the difference. If you don't want to sound bored or uninterested, use the same body language as you would if the caller was in front of you. Tune in to what they want. Are they signalling that they want you to be brisk, chatty or sympathetic? Do they want you to listen, to give advice or to take action? The answers to these questions determine the types of questions you ask them. Probe further with open questions like 'Exactly what happened?' and 'What did you do after that?' Confirm your understanding with questions like 'So you are not happy with . . .' or 'You like . . . but you don't like . . .' Avoid leading questions or more than one question at a time. Then listen to the answers. Try to make sense of them: 'What you seem to be saying to me is . . .' Check that you have got it right: 'Ah, so you are saying that . . .' Formulate a response: 'Right, so what I could do is either X or Y. Which of these would be most helpful to you?' Make notes. Don't interrupt. Summarize from time to time. Pause to indicate it is their turn to speak. Do not break your own silence. Pause after questions to allow the other person time to think about what they are saying. Be thoughtful if you want them to be. If you need to slow the pace, indicate that you would like to make some notes and repeat back to them what you are writing at the speed that you are writing it. Try to treat the caller as an individual. Accept responsibility. Underpromise and try to over-deliver. Try to do more than was asked, sooner than was promised. Call back to see what happened and to enjoy some positive feedback.

If the phone interrupts you, answer it quickly 'Can I ring you back at . . . ?' If you are in a position to give good attention to the caller, say 'Good morning' or 'Good afternoon' and give your name. If it is someone else's phone, you will need a pen and paper. Offer to take a message. You need the caller's name and when and how they can be contacted. Can they say what it is about? Record brief details. Repeat them back to the caller. Double check numbers and the spelling of names. If you notice that the message has not been picked up, call the caller back yourself to explain. Perhaps they would like to speak to someone else. When the caller is on your phone but the call is not for you, be patient. Establish what the caller needs. Explain that they can hold while you find the person they need. Say how long it might take.

If it is a complaint, remember that people whose complaints are well handled are more loyal or satisfied than people who never complain. If they are aggressive, allow them to let off steam. Do not interrupt. Use silence. Do not argue with them. Do not take rudeness personally. If you need to feel more assertive, stand up and continue the call.

If you do not want the phone to interrupt you and it has no voicemail, or if you are on call, ask someone else to take your calls. Be sure to tell them how they can get in touch with you in an emergency. Warn them of likely calls to expect, and if possible, give them enough information to deal with the expected calls. Return the favour another time. Finally, signal when you are intending to end a call. Summarize, smile, say thank you and goodbye. Do not put the phone down until they say goodbye. Last impressions last.

Obscene Conversations

People who make obscene calls are seeking an emotive response. They must be denied what they seek. Do not respond. Put the receiver down and walk away. After a few minutes replace the receiver. Repeat as often as necessary until the caller stops. If it recurs, report it to the police and the network. The network can trace obscene callers and get them arrested. Silent callers should be treated the same way.

Face-to-face Conversations

In Chapters 2 and 3 we discovered that it is much easier to overcome resistance to change through one-to-one conversations. In Chapters 4 and 5 one-to-one conversations provided information on what needed to be changed in order to improve the service.

Without individual face-to-face communication, it is very difficult to build close one-to-one working relationships. In Chapter 8 we saw that managing people as individuals was an important way of overcoming many of the disadvantages of team and group working. In Chapter 7 we saw that close working relationships between individuals could motivate individuals by helping to meet their unmet needs for warmth, applause and possession. Face-to-face conversations can be used to turn experiences into learning (Chapters 13 and 14).

Talking the Job

In each of the chapters in this book the same cycle of management activities has recurred – planning, decision-making, organizing, delegating, motivating and appraising. Each of these steps in the management cycle can benefit from one-to-one conversations. Box 12.2 offers some principles for conversational communication.

Honest Communication in Public Services

Despite rhetoric about democracy, empowerment and openness, public service organizations are political places in which people are rarely entirely honest. Self-serving bias is common. Lying in order to protect oneself or to avoid hurting others is not unknown. People espouse the desirability of open communication but defend their own privacy, while obtaining information about other people in devious ways. When attaching meaning to the information they deviously obtain, they are likely to reframe it so as to make it consistent with some key construct by which they tend to judge others.

Different Strokes for Different Folks

The principles of communication in Box 12.2 are based on the assumption that all people are the same. But they are not. Individuals prefer to communicate

---

Box 12.2

GUIDELINES FOR COMMUNICATION

- **Chunking**: Divide your message into small 'chunks'. Limit each chunk to no more than three new pieces of information. Work with this new information. Make connections with existing knowledge. Give examples. Ask questions. Check acceptance and understanding, before moving to the next chunk of new information. A total of three chunks of nine new pieces of information, is usually the limit of what people can handle at any one time. Their ability to concentrate on what you are saying may be limited to 20 minutes.
- **Empathy**: Put yourself in the receiver's position and anticipate what they will hear.
- **Jargon**: Avoid pitching language too high or the pace too fast.
- **Prejudice**: Be aware that your background or culture can bias the way you interpret.
- **Status**: Be aware that the status of the transmitter distorts communication. Staff commonly read more than was intended into a manager's message.
- **Emotion**: Pay attention to the emotional overtones – emotional music can sometimes be more important than the words themselves.
- **Meaning**: Check what the message has been taken to mean.

---

in different ways. Listening to any one person's use of language usually reveals that they have a preferred type of language. It may be a preference for visual language, for painting verbal pictures, images – 'visions' of the future. Such people talk of 'seeing' their way through things, of things becoming 'clearer', of 'looking' into things, of ideas being less 'hazy', or of their views being 'coloured'. As we saw in Chapter 8, if their manager matches their preferred linguistic mode, the chances of good communication and the achievement of understanding is increased. The problem is that the next person may prefer a different language – 'I *hear* what you are saying', 'That *clicks* with me', 'That *rings* a bell', 'That *sounds* OK'. The important thing is to identify the preferred linguistic mode of individuals rather than to learn 'golden rules' that assume that all people, including all managers, are the same.

Encourage the other person to be precise, as though you were a police officer trying to obtain a witness statement. Ask the other person what they saw or heard. Then ask them what they thought and felt about what they saw or heard.

It is often easier to get people to move from the general to the particular. For example, if you ask managers what motivates their staff, they will usually give you a general answer, but then be willing to support their general opinion by citing specific examples of what motivates particular members of their staff. The art of good communication is to move between what people notice, think, feel and need and what you yourself, notice, think, feel and need. You will need to do this in ways that you feel comfortable with, and to which the other person can respond. These ways will be different for each person: different strokes for different folks.

WRITTEN COMMUNICATION

Writing Reports

Many managers dislike writing reports. Some fear that others will make judgements about their competence, education and intelligence. Yet writing reports is a routine part of the work of most managers in public services. Progress reports for committees, evaluation reports for auditors, feasibility reports for business managers, appraisal reports for funding bodies, all contribute to the information needs of a public service organization. In this section we will consider how to prepare and write a report. A common piece of advice is to 'say what you are going to say, say it and then say what you've said.'

The part of a written report that 'says what you are going to say' is often called a synopsis, or an executive summary. It should be a maximum of one side of A4, double spaced. It should summarize your conclusion and the argument that leads to it. Like a trailer to a film, your synopsis to attract your readers. It must hint at contents that will interest them and motivate them to read the rest of the report. Now that you have said what you are going to say, you need to say it. Begin by setting down the main headings and subheadings. This overview of the report will give you an indication of the time it will take you to write it. Jot down notes for each section. A flow diagram may help you to order your ideas and build a coherent argument. A good way to structure the way you say it is to use questions as the working titles of each section. Eye catching titles can be

added once the report is written. Questions are a good way of avoiding irrelevance. Box 12.3 has sample questions which can be used as working titles for sections.

Once you have determined what you are going to say and used the questions in Box 12.3 to structure your ideas, you need to sum up what you have said. This is a final summary – maximum length one side of A4. This is not a repeat of the initial synopsis which had the goal of tempting the reader to read the report. It has done its job if the reader gets to the final summary! The task of the final summary is to make sure the reader remembers what you consider to be the most important points. Managers are paid to improve things. Without action there will rarely be improvement. It follows that a manager's report will normally have as its purpose the winning of support – moral, permissive or financial – for some actions that have been recommended. The summary must state clearly what benefits will follow if the recommended actions are taken. It must make it clear who needs to take the actions and by when. The first step should be indicated in some detail.

Box 12.3

USING QUESTIONS FOR WORKING TITLES

Why is this report important?

- Who asked for it? Who needs it? What is the background and context?
- What developments make it important?

What is the purpose of writing this report?

- How will we know these aims are served?
- What changes will be noticeable, by whom?

How was the information compiled?

- Why was it compiled this way?
- What other sources were considered?
- What were the main findings?

What can you conclude?

- Of what are you certain?
- What is clearer than it was?

What action do you recommend?

- Reviewing each conclusion in turn, who might now do what, and by when?

Readability

Finally, check the readability of the report. Count the number of words with more than three syllables on a page, and divide the total by the number of lines on the page. For management reports, the score should be three or less. Even for academic or technical reports the score should be 6 or less. Plain language is essential. Short sentences are simpler to construct and easier to understand. Read and re-read the draft report striking out every word you can do without. You can usually remove half the words from an initial draft without losing the meaning. Ask a friend to read the report. When they return the draft to you, ask them to tell you what were the most important three points in the report. Are they the three you intended? If not, you have some re-organizing or re-emphasizing to do.

Putting It in Writing

One of the most important things about putting it in writing is deciding whether or not you should do it at all. First meet the individuals concerned and then, perhaps together, draft a written note of what you agreed. Second choice is to telephone (and then perhaps confirm with a memo or a fax). If the content of the writing is complex or risky, it may be better to send a draft with a suggestion to meet and discuss what has been drafted. If you draft something, you should be clear whether your intention is to instruct, inform, interpret or influence. It takes much longer to plan a memo than to write it. Decide: who is the audience; why are you writing to them; what do they need to know and when they need to know it? Then start. Do not stop to polish the prose until you get to the end. It is easier to redo the logic when you have got to the end.

Internal memos should be less than a page. They can be handwritten. Supporting materials can be attached. Memos should state: To, From, Date, Subject, Content and Signature.

Minutes of meetings should state: Purpose, Date, Time, Place, Chairperson, Attendees, and Apologies from others prevented from attending and the name of the minute taker. They should start by recording the approval of previous minutes and then, item by item, who agreed to do what, by when. They should finish with the date, time and place of the next meeting and the agreed circulation list of the minutes. If possible, the minutes should be checked with someone else who was present before circulation.

E-mails require as much thought and planning as any other written communication. The seductive convenience of the 'reply' function produces managerial mayhem – the antithesis of a 'thoughtful approach to the practice of management'. Message pads, whether desk-based or screen-based, should automatically generate a follow-up copy for your 'bring forward' file. Fax copies will often need to be copied, if you want a permanent copy.

Writing Letters

The image which a letter conveys represents the organization to the outside world. Begin text to the left, leaving a margin of 2.5 cm. Show your reference and their last reference and put the subject heading in the centre. Sign 'Yours faithfully' after 'Dear Sir or Madam', otherwise 'Yours sincerely'. Put your name under your initials and indicate if there are any enclosures (enc.) or copies (cc.) Between the topic heading and your signature, you need to do three things: open by outlining your situation and your reason for writing; elaborate on your reasons for writing and close with a summary and a statement of what needs to happen next.

If there is previous correspondence, begin 'Thank you for letter dated . . .' If the letter is a rejection, give your reasons and make alternative suggestions. If the letter is a complaint, be factual about who, what, when and where; describe the consequences for you and say what you want done about it.

If the letter accompanies a proposal, it should outline the different benefits of the proposal, for each beneficiary. The proposal itself should contain frequent subheadings and plenty of white space. It should be double spaced and have short paragraphs. Make frequent use of the reader's name and answer the reader's question 'what's in it for me?'

Be positive. Write 'when' not 'if'; 'and' not 'but'; 'can' not 'could'. Be active not passive, e.g. 'Please send the forms back' not 'the forms should be submitted to . . .' The proposal can be illustrated using bar charts, pie charts, diagrams and organizational family trees. Keep them simple. Do not rely on colour for clarity because the recipient may not colour copy your proposal for further circulation.

Finally, check your letter. Re-read and strike out every redundant word. If your spelling is suspect, use a spell check. It will not spot all your errors. Proof-reading is more reliable.

Giving a Live Presentation

Having communicated in writing, it is not uncommon for managers to be asked to speak about what they have written. Managers who feel apprehensive or nervous about giving presentations are not alone. Dislike of public speaking is very common yet it is a skill of increasing importance to public service managers as agents of change (Chapters 2 and 3). When we look at public relations later, we deal with presentations on the radio and television. For the moment we will confine our audience to a public meeting, or a gathering of colleagues.

Competence is developed through preparation, practice and rehearsal. Presentations are no exception. To fail to plan is to plan to fail. Consider the purpose of your presentation. Is it to convey information, make recommendations, argue a case, or to persuade? How will you monitor whether or not the purpose of your presentation is being achieved? Allow time in your plan for monitoring the reaction of your audience so that you can change tack if need be. Presentations benefit from dress rehearsal using a live audience. Consider what your audience needs to know. What knowledge and experience of the subject do they have already? How capable are they of understanding the subject? What is their attitude to the subject likely to be? What about their attitude to you? If there is any way to find out in advance? You could begin your presentation by asking 'Has anybody heard of . . . ?', 'Has anyone had a chance to read . . . ?', 'Could I do a quick check to see how many people favour A rather than B?' Questions like these not only give you a quick feel for how well informed your audience is, they also establish contact between you and your audience, helping to break the ice and increasing the chances that they will ask questions later. Questions from an audience are a gift. They are not a threat. They enable you to steer your material towards areas that are of genuine interest to your audience, or to deal with their real doubts and anxieties. If your own questions evoke a response from an individual in the audience, get into conversation with them: 'Oh really, what did you think of it, what interested you about it?'

Think about the room in which your audience will be sitting. Is it a small group room or a conference hall? Is it a quiet room or a busy office? Imagine yourself in it. Where can you anticipate any likely interruptions? How can you reduce the risk of your audience being distracted? If, on arrival, someone offers to monitor their mobile phones, that will be seen as helpful by some and by others as a reminder to turn theirs off.

You will lose your audience if you read to them. Written language and spoken language are quite different. If you must support your argument by referring to a section of a report, extract it and circulate it at the meeting. Allow your audience time to read it there and then. Never assume that people have read your report, even if they have had it in advance and were supposed to read it before they came. Some will not have done so. Be as factual as possible. You will also need to engage the interest of your audience. Think of anecdotes about people that they might recognize. Think of examples with which they might be familiar. Evoke the setting of your example by referring to colours, sounds, sights and smells. Try to paint a verbal picture of the scene you wish them to imagine.

It might be helpful to take along samples, photographs and documents; perhaps a letter from a client. A presentation is an opportunity to communicate things that cannot easily be communicated in a written report. Rehearse it and time it. Try to limit your formal speaking time to 20 minutes. Take as much time as you are allowed to answer questions.

Use the same structure as your written report. That is, 'say what you are going to say, say it, and say what you have said.' You will need to add some things at the beginning and some things at the end. At the beginning find out what your audience know already. At the end finish by thanking the organizers and the audience for their attention and especially for their questions. Mention as many names as you can and illustrate your thanks with genuine examples. Sincerity carries more conviction than rhetoric. If you have strong feelings, let them show.

The setting may require the structure of your presentation to be formal, but your style within those constraints can be conversational. Maintain eye contact with as many people in your audience as possible. Mention as many of them by name as you are able. Do not be afraid to ask again if you have forgotten someone's name. Try to make each point to a separate individual in the audience. One point, one individual conversation.

Handling Questions and Endings

Make sure you understand the question before you deal with it. Questioners are reassured if you note down their questions, preferably on a flipchart. Be sure to note their name next to the question. Deal with each individual's questions before you end. If you cannot do justice to a particular question in 2–3 minutes, briefly outline an answer and indicate the related issues to which the question gives rise. Offer to take up the related issues with the questioner after the presentation. By collecting together clusters of questions, you can save time by answering several at once. Keep some questions in reserve to help bring out points that you wanted to make anyway. If you do not know the answer, say so. If practicable, say that you will find out the answer and get back to the questioner. Some people end their presentation with a question and answer session. This can have drawbacks; for example, the session may be hijacked by a few questioners with axes to grind. They can drain the energy and impact of your presentation. If a question is irrelevant or offensive, answer calmly but briefly. In formal meetings questions are put

through the person in the chair. This enables some to be rephrased or rejected. Do not end with a question. End with thanks and then a summary. Start your summary slowly. Gain speed and momentum. Finish fast and on time. End on an up-beat, emphasizing the three points you most want your audience to remember. Many in your audience will remember only the last three things you said.

VISUAL AIDS

Flipcharts are the cheapest and most effective low-technology aids. For a small round-the-table audience, an ordinary A4 ring file will make an effective flipchart. It can be used flat for an audience of two or three, or it can be made to stand up by bending the covers back on themselves and taping or tying them together. Using two treasury tags is a neat way to do it. For a larger group – a few pre-drawn A1 flipchart sheets can be blue-tacked together or stapled and taped to the back of a chair or to the edge of the table. If a proper flipchart stand is available, a number of sheets in a flipchart pad can be drawn, in pencil in advance and inked over during your presentation. Your audience will not be able to see the pencil but you will. Your charts will look well spaced. Your memory and command of the subject will seem prodigious! One of the disadvantages of using a free-standing, full-sized flipchart is that you may be tempted to spend too much time with your back to the audience, thereby losing eye contact and audibility. Overhead projectors are meant to counter this tendency so do not turn to look at the OHP screen behind you! When preparing OHP slides follow the rule of 7. A maximum of 7 slides, 7 lines per acetate, 7 words per line and a minimum of 7 mms. per letter. Unmounted acetates often curl under the heat from the projector bulb. Use coins to secure the corners. Place the projector on a chair or table slightly to the side of where you are sitting or standing. Cover the slide with white paper. You can easily read the slide through the paper before you uncover it. Again your command of the subject area will seem impressive. You will need to arrive early to check the projector switches and focus. Does it have a spare bulb? If not, is there a back-up projector? If you have a choice, focus the projector high up to one side of you. Four pieces of flipchart paper taped or pinned to a wall will make an impromptu screen. Always turn the machine off whenever you can. The noise and the mesmerizing similarity to a TV screen can make an audience sleepy. Where the projector is computer driven, presentations can incorporate movable graphics and clips of video and audio tape. But beware. Over reliance on a pre-programmed presentation may deprive you of some of the adrenaline that you need if you are to create impact on the hearts as well as minds. Your audience need to take away more than a copy of your slides. Technological talking heads can be impressive but may not carry the conviction of a real conversation with a real public service manager who is genuinely committed to the ideals and values of public service.

Presenting Numerical Information

We have looked at the way in which information can be communicated in public service organizations: the different channels that can be set up and the written and verbal means that can be used to transmit information through those channels. We have looked at the problems of communicating with a live audience and the use of visual aids. There are special techniques for communicating numerical information. The reason why we have chosen to detail them is because we think that it is important for managers to develop their ability to quantify. As we saw in Chapters 3, 4, 5, 9, 10 and 11, the ability to think numerically is as important as the ability to think recollectively, reflectively, predictively, imaginatively, creatively, empathetically, ethically and critically. The need to quantify and to think numerically has turned up already in market planning, service development, quality control, implementing operational change and managing projects, as well as in the more obvious area of budgeting, cost benefit analysis, options appraisal, audit and accounting. Yet many managers in public services appear

number phobic. This can cause them to defer to members of the accounts department or to engineers from the works department. By completing the thinking and learning activities at the end of this chapter, you cannot only improve the way in which you communicate financial information, but you can improve also the numerical thinking on which management evaluation largely depends.

Advocacy and Argument

Advocacy is not negotiation (Chapter 2). In negotiation the object is to reach agreement, in advocacy the object is to win. Your argument must be the one that is finally accepted. Your case must be the case that prevails. Before you start, make sure that victory is likely to be worth the cost of achieving it. Be sure that you could cope with losing. Do your homework. Gather the information that you need but do not air it unnecessarily. Facts can be interpreted in more than one way. Keep your powder dry. Argue only in the presence of decision-makers. The argument should be at a time of your choice. Do not be drawn until you are ready. Deploy facts and figures and reference your sources. Insist on the same from the other side. Speculate about the motivation of their witnesses. It can be advantageous to show emotion but not to lose your temper. Respect your opponent, if not their argument. Make eye contact and adopt an open posture. Start slowly and finish fast. Repetition is frowned upon in written argument but it is essential in a speech. In essays, or papers, repetition comes from re-reading by the reader. A listener cannot re-run your oral argument, so it is essential that you repeat the main planks of an argument, especially its conclusion. The main points, but no new material, should be included in the final summary.

Cultural Differences in Communication

Greville Janner, author of over 50 books on communication, including *Janner's Complete Speechmaker*[5] tells how his friend Jacqueline was born in New York of an Italian mother and a Hungarian father. When she went to live in Holland, she was regarded as harsh, difficult and tactless. Later, living in Israel, Jacqueline was not trusted because she was too diplomatic – too 'nice'. Yet Jacqueline had not changed. It was just that the Dutch were used to less argument and the Israelis were used to more argument than Jacqueline had been brought up to expect in America. In many countries in Europe and South America, confrontation is an expected form of conversation. In Peshawar, where confrontation traditionally carried the risk of tribal vendetta, elaborate ritual greetings and the taking of tea often subsume confrontation.

In Fiji, where unfriendly tribes used to eat each other, it is customary to drink yangona during meetings. Yangona is made from the root of the Kava plant. It is a natural sedative. If the meeting fails to resolve disagreements, everyone falls asleep! Fijians going to North America would be frightened by the level of confrontation there. Many Americans, on the other hand, along with visitors from Japan and Thailand, would be frightened by the levels of confrontation they would find in France and Italy. The French often find consensus boring: we have known them to keep changing the conversation until they find something to disagree about.

Debate or Dialogue?

As we have seen, negotiation is trying to agree. Advocacy is trying to win. Debating, on the other hand, keeps alive the merits of pursuing the truth. But debating can be wasteful and adversarial. Dialogue is less wasteful. In dialogue, the explicit purpose is to convert information into knowledge and experience into wisdom. In 1997 Etzioni[6] proposed that there should be 'rules of engagement' to make communication through dialogue more constructive, especially in cases where people disagreed (Box 12.4).

Perhaps it is time to question the merits of adversarial debate as a way of making academic progress. A more thoughtful approach might recognize that there are usually more than two possibilities. Forcing views to fit into dichotomous camps causes them to be simplified. Sometimes things are not simple. Time spent attacking and defending positions might be better spent on further exploration and research. You do not have to prove somebody else wrong in order to prove yourself right. By moving away from debate towards dialogue (Box 12.4), we can broaden our field of vision and develop more creative ways of challenging received wisdom.

A MODEL OF COMMUNICATION

Communication is an attempt to transmit information in such a way that the recipient understands what the transmitter meant (Figure 12.2). In this model, a transmitter sends a message to a receiver, selecting a channel such as e-mail, fax, telephone or one-to-one conversation. The transmitter chooses the words and the manner in which the message will be encoded. In one-to-one communication, the choice of words, the style of sentence structure, the tone and the loudness of voice are an important part of the way the message is coded. Communication is successful when the feedback confirms that the receiver has understood the message in the way that the transmitter intended.

Box 12.4

DIALOGUE NOT DEBATE

- You do not have to discuss everything
- Deal in conviction not point scoring
- Discuss needs, wants, expectations not rights
- Discuss topics where you may progress

- Do not compromise just to conciliate
- Do not demonize those who disagree
- Do not affront the beliefs of your opponents

Box 12.5

A HYPOTHETICAL CONVERSATION WITH GREVILLE JANNER QC

(Orator, barrister, toastmaster and speaker)

TH: How do you manage to look confident when you're not?

GJ: I do three things – prepare, prepare and prepare. Then I take three deep breaths and look someone in the eye. I do this by turning my head, not by swivelling my eyes.

TH: Is that it . . . ?

GJ: No, next . . . Head up, chin up, weight on heels – or bum if you are sitting – and smile. Look around you while you're smiling. Even if they hate you, someone will smile back. Start a conversation with that person. Ask real individuals in that room, real questions about that room. Ask questions that you are really interested to know the answers to. Then ask rhetorical questions: 'Isn't it good to be here surrounded by . . .' Point things out – objects, sounds, smells – get their attention back into the room with you – then you can begin.

TH: How do you create authority, presence, gravitas?

GJ: Do nothing. Or do very little. Silence gets attention and brings command. The slower you start the better. Giving a speech is not like writing an essay. You have come to make a point and preferably only one point. Link and thread all your stories and examples, facts and figures to that one point. Even jokes should be linked to that same one point. Jokes at your own expense are the most effective. You need to change from stories to facts to examples to visual aids about every 2 minutes to keep the audience awake. If you can change positions in the room, it helps. It stops them developing a fixed focus. You can see their eyes start to glaze over. You are not a hypnotist. You want them to pay attention, not fall asleep.

TH: What about difficult questions?

GJ: 'I wonder if anyone in this room has come across this?' 'Tell us please how did you cope with it?' If no one answers: 'looks like an important question. Perhaps we could talk about it afterwards.' If the question arises because someone has not been listening to you, don't get impatient. That is a wonderful gift – an opportunity to repeat yourself.

TH: What if somebody heckles you?

GJ: Again, a heaven-sent opportunity to repeat yourself! Almost worth planting someone in the audience to be difficult. Say: 'I hope you won't mind if I put the case for the other side!'

TH: How do you appear sincere and believable?

GJ: Keep up the eye contact. Try to catch as many eyes as possible before you finish. Emphasize nouns, not adjectives. 'Ladies and gentlemen, haven't we been lucky to have such a charming, gracious bride?' Emphasize 'bride'. Nouns are hard to disagree about. Emphasizing nouns builds an impression in the mind of the audience that what you say seems generally sincere and believable.

TH: Greville Janner, thank you.

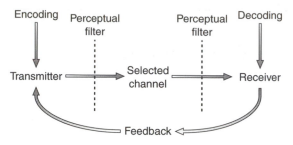

Figure 12.2 A model of communication

Source: After Buchanan and Huczynski

Barriers to Communication

Anything that interferes with any of the steps shown in Figure 12.2 is a barrier to communication. The model shows the presence of perceptual filters. These filters include prejudices, values, frames of reference and past experiences. Figure 12.2 also shows the role of feedback in communication. When we speak face-to-face, it is usually possible to identify non-verbal as well as verbal feedback which indicates whether what is being transmitted is being heard, acknowledged, accepted or understood. Nodding of the head, avoidance of eye contact, the way arms are folded can all provide feedback. In telephone conversations, tone of voice or speed of response can indicate how a message is being received. The richer the information on the feedback loop, the greater the likelihood that the transmitter will persist until a shared understanding has been achieved. There follows extracts from a conversation with an ex-army officer who became the chief executive of a public service organization employing 200 people in the North of England (Box 12.6). Peter Williams was interested in military failures. We have collected here Peter's knowledge of the kinds of failures that can be traced to the mismanagement of information. We were curious to see whether Peter thought there were lessons to be learned for his job as a chief executive of a public service.

Box 12.6

A CONVERSATION WITH PETER WILLIAMS C.E.O.

THE MISMANAGEMENT OF MILITARY INFORMATION

Terry: Why are you interested in history?

Peter: We can learn from history. For example, the study of military history reveals that military mistakes were often followed by a search for someone to blame – 'heads will roll'. This search for scapegoats led to a shortage of information which might be used to prevent the repetition of mistakes.

Terry: and the relevance to public services is . . . ?

Peter: In public services the traditional scapegoats used to be ministers. They were expected to resign following major mistakes. With new managerialism, ministers or directors are far less likely to fall on their swords. They are more likely to seek the resignation of a manager like me.

Terry: How was military information misused?

Peter: Even when people had risked their lives to gather information through reconnaissance or spying, military leaders often put insufficient effort into attaching the right meaning to it. On the whole they undervalued brainwork and analysis. They preferred to leave that to general staff at HQ. Public service managers are similarly sceptical about reports – 'not worth the paper they are written on'. Statistics are dismissed as 'rubbish in rubbish out'.

Public service managers will not spend time trying to see what might be of value in a report despite the trouble someone else has taken to compile it. They prefer to wait until they are told to make changes and then 'freeze' until they get "guidelines".

Terry: What kind of information was lacking?

Peter: Historically, military leaders did not obtain information about the likely level of resistance to their proposed advances. Consequently, their frontal attacks were often repulsed. Wars of attrition followed, often involving protracted periods of inactivity and periodic skirmishes and sabre-rattling. Momentum was lost. Morale was lowered. There was a huge cost in human life.

Terry: Presumably the cost is less now!

Peter: In public services there are similar stand-offs between rival departments. Some departments routinely block proposals by other departments, irrespective of their merit. At meetings they obstruct each other and refuse to give way. Public service managers need the skills of the old political emissaries who carried information between enemies.

Terry: Is the concept of enemies helpful?

Peter: We have enemies within and without. The Vietnam War was an example of the power of the community. Guerrilla warfare can prevail against overwhelming odds when the guerrillas have the support of the people.

Terry: So what is the parallel to public services?

Peter: In public services, some resistance workers seem to survive every reorganization – popping up time and again with different job titles but with the same resistance to change.

Others appear to adopt the ideas of each new manager but in practice they subvert and sabotage. In public services I need information on who is politically allied to whom. I need to control the information that is fed to the local media. I need to keep the support of the community.

Terry: Military lines seem clearer.

Peter: Don't you believe it. Military leaders often failed to guard against mis-information. In public services, managers rarely ask 'how do you know?', 'Who has seen the document?', 'Can we get a copy?', 'Who do we trust to check it out?' Without careful evaluation public service managers are easily duped by the 'spin'.

Terry: Modern warfare is technological.

Peter: You're right, modern warfare is essentially a battle of new technology, much of it information technology. In public services, the rate of adoption of new technology has lagged behind the private sector. Many civil servants disdain computers.

Terry: Does your military training help you to take decisions?

Peter: No. Military leaders are notoriously indecisive – not through lack of skill or courage, but due to information overload. The number of pieces of information that one person can hold is about seven. The number of pieces of new information in a military situation often exceeds this. The same is true of public services. That is why we need to take care how we present information for decision-making. It needs to be 'chunked' and 'visual'.

Terry: Thank you for your time.

MANAGING RELATIONS WITH THE PUBLIC AND THE MEDIA[7]

During the learning conversations with Peter Williams we identified common failings in the military management of information and identified their equivalents in public services. We have explored already how to use conversations to minimize failures in intelligence gathering and 'sensing'. We have looked at the role of inner world thinking in assessing and 'making sense' of the gathered-intelligence. In Chapter 13 on managing learning, we acknowledge that if we are to use inner world reflection to learn from outer world mistakes, then we have to move away from a culture of blame. Peter suggests that building close one-to-one relationships with people who have influence is far more likely to resolve historical differences than mindless obstruction. In Chapter 8 we looked at how that might be done. Peter's final concern is with the role of misinformation and propaganda. It can alienate the public support on which public services depend. Managing the flow of information to the public and orchestrating the struggle for the hearts and minds of their political representatives is the role of public relations. Many of the military failures Peter described were due to failures to manage the flow of information from the front. The enemy got information they shouldn't have had. The generals didn't get the information they should have had. Misreported rumours lowered the morale of the troops. We look now at the need for public service managers to manage the way their services are reported in the press, on TV and on the radio.

Public Relations

The management of public relations should always be for a purpose – towards an end goal. In the case of public services, the end goal of managing public relations might be an enhanced reputation, a more accurately informed workforce and sometimes an increased use of the service, perhaps enabling more resources to be claimed. Requests for more resources often require political backing. This backing may

not be forthcoming if there is widespread public antipathy, or even just apathy. Even if a public service organization makes a good job of managing the internal flow of information to its employees, many employees will still put more store by what they read in the papers or hear on the radio. Favourable media coverage is likely to enhance the pride that employees feel in their service, especially knowing that their family and friends are likely to see or hear it.

Sometimes the outcome of successful media management will be no media coverage. If relations with local journalists and news writers are well managed, then local news desks will respect embargoes, or withhold stories that might prejudice an investigation by customs officers or health officials or which might disturb a hostage negotiation or start a public health scare. Such co-operation has to be earned. There will be many times when you can co-operate with journalists by providing good timely copy, press releases or well-organized photo opportunities, or by making an expert available for comment. A general policy of 'no comment' will be regarded as unco-operative.

It pays to be on good terms with the local media. News editors need news. If you can co-operate with them in good times, by sending them a steady stream of the news they need, they are far more likely to co-operate with you when times are difficult. A national magazine might welcome a feature on a technical advance in your service. A local newspaper might welcome news about success in a quiz league. The key questions are who reads the national magazine and who reads the local paper? What kinds of stories are of interest to these different audiences? Human interest stories about children, animals and heroism are universally popular. Local people will want to read stories about local services, especially services that relate to community safety, food and health hazards, storm and flood risk, local school transport and the risk of accidents to children and old people. However, words like 'first', 'shortest', 'best', 'unique' and 'the only' should be avoided. Journalists rarely have time to corroborate such claims. Extracts from market research or surveys on crime or consumer satisfaction are almost always welcome. They are often taken as a starting point for an investigation, a feature or an interview.

Press releases posted or faxed over the weekend are more likely to be noticed on a quiet Monday morning. During festivals and holiday times there is often a shortage of stories. Writing a weekly column, or a doing a regular radio spot, on 'Health Matters', 'Safety Matters', 'Child Watch', 'Crime Watch', 'Court Cases', 'Tourist Talk' or 'Travel News' can seem attractive, but managers should be sure to have a sufficient supply of good copy. Contributors to regular columns must understand that in the media a deadline is a deadline. A regular feature that becomes irregular will be dropped.

Doing a Press Release

Photographs greatly increase the likelihood that editors will publish information. Photographs greatly increase the likelihood that information, once published, will be read. Photographs should include people – as many as possible. Write names, ages and addresses on self-adhesive labels on the back of the photograph, along with captions. Make sure that people on photographs are representative of the local community and that they are doing something. Avoid chequered patterns on clothing, or in the background, as these can cause difficulties in reproduction. Use 35 mm transparencies for colour. Prints are acceptable if black and white (200 mm × 150 mm is a good size but 250 mm × 200 mm is better). Keep a supply of cardboard-backed envelopes for sending photographs with press releases. Use a digital camera and email if you can.

A press release should be clearly dated, double-line spaced on A4 with a 4 cm margin. The title must attract the sub editor's attention. Make sure the essential message is in the first paragraph because a busy editor will snip off the bottom. Avoid jargon and include quotes. They add credibility. Give the accurate name and title of any person quoted. Indicate the end of the press release with 'ENDS'. A 24-hour contact number should be given as a footnote. If a journalist might need to investigate or interview, write across the top of the press release 'Not for publication before X o'clock on . . .' Managers should have agreed procedures in place for the rapid authorization of press releases. The publication rate is unlikely to be more than 10 per cent, so a steady stream of information needs to be leaving the organization. Keep a record book of press releases and any photographs, so that copies can be ordered from the photographer by members of the public.

A journalist may follow up by phone. Try to provide answers within the journalist's deadline. If the journalist wants an interview, allow double the time requested. Prepare a pack of up-to-date information about the service and have it ready for when the journalist arrives. Offer to be available subsequently to check facts, but bear in mind that some journalists will be offended if you ask to check their finished work.

Even if the news is bad news, be prepared to comment. It will provide a chance to explain and maybe to apologize. Talking to the press should make things better, not worse. Avoiding the press is not a good way to manage the flow of information to the public. Sometimes journalists may agree to treat something as 'off the record'. Agreement to be 'off the record' should be mutual and made prior to what is said. Too much 'off the record' information may waste the journalist's time. Sometimes a journalist may be prepared to quote an anonymous 'spokesperson', but a quote from a named authority will always be preferred. A refusal to comment should be explained. Journalists understand that some matters are subject to legal restrictions, official secrets or confidentiality agreements. Journalists usually understand a desire to protect innocent parties, if the circumstances are explained to them.

Calling a Press Conference

Press conferences are ideal for announcements about restructuring services, about possible mergers, or about major developments. Sometimes calling a press conference is the best way to deal with public panic, a terrorist threat, sleazy scandal, adverse reports, failed inspections, decisions about closures, suspensions, dismissals or demands for resignation. It is important to remember that press conferences are called for the benefit of the press and not as a forum for senior managers. A press reception is a less formal way of getting together with journalists who are interested in your service. Research reports, commission findings, consultative documents and impending legislation are all examples of excuses for calling people together. Ask the advice of the journalists about dates. Check who is planning to attend by phoning 24 hours ahead. Sign in guests and issue name badges. Hosts from the organization should also wear badges showing their roles. Hosts should be few in number. They should be experienced and well briefed. If possible, rehearse your host team the day before. A printed programme should indicate a starting time and a finishing time. If lunch is involved, it should be early, allowing time for busy journalists to get back to their desks. Journalists who were expected to attend but who were prevented, should be sent copies of any material given out on the day.

Doing a TV Interview

TV is no longer the preserve of the professional. Exploding numbers of TV stations, channels and news programmes thirst for material. This creates increasing opportunities for public service managers with something interesting to say to get on the air without having to pay thousands of dollars per minute. Allow one hour of preparation time for each minute of interview time. The interview is unlikely to be more than 2 minutes long. Try to speak to the interviewer the day before. If that is not possible, a research worker is nearly always available. Ask what they would like to know and why. What do they

know already? If they are picking up on a press report, be sure to read it. Who else will be interviewed? Separately or together? What questions do they want to ask? Can the opening topic be agreed? If the programme is not going out live, answers to more possible questions should be prepared. Make sure that each answer makes some points favourable to the service. Consult widely and try to reach consensus on which three points are the most important points for you to make during the interview. Assume that a high proportion of your staff will see the interview. Even if you think the interview was a personal triumph, be prepared to be punctured next day by remarks of the kind 'Pity you didn't make the point that . . .' People do not realize how hard it can be to make even one good point, especially when confronted by a camera and experienced presenters who are out to make points of their own.

Whatever the first question is, your answer should include one, two or preferably all three of your prepared points. In order to stick to their schedule, editors will snip the end of interviews and presenters will interrupt sentences if they are running late. That is why it is important to lead with the punch lines. Create three polished punch lines and try to use them all in the answer to the first question. You might not get another chance. Even if the presenter gives you the chance to repeat your points, the editor may cut them. If you are lucky and your punch line is catchy, it may be picked up as a headline in a later news programme, or in the newspaper the next day.

In their homes many viewers will be eating, or talking to someone else. They will have only half an eye on the television. They may be using the TV as background noise or to relax because they are tired. Not all viewers will be able to follow a complex argument. Try to create verbal pictures. 'I had a phone call from an elderly man this morning. He was sobbing. Your new leg ulcer clinic has given me back my wife after 17 years.' Assume that the viewer is thinking 'so what?' Try to answer the 'so what' questions. Rehearse your punch lines out loud. Keep it simple. Say less and repeat it often. Ask colleagues to brainstorm questions that the presenter might ask. The presenter's questions are likely to be about who, what, when, where, how and why. For each question, work out how you could use it to make one of your own points.

Choose something comfortable to wear. Avoid stripes and checks and the colours red, black or white. Avoid jewellery. Don't have a quick drink to steady your nerves. Don't talk nervously to anyone who will listen. Breathe deeply. Rehearse your lines. Visualize an exciting interview. Picture yourself leaning forward, making eye contact, using simple words, and varying your voice ever so slightly. Visualize smiles all around at the end. One last check in the mirror. A voice will call '30 seconds'. Breathe deeply three times. Smell the heat of the lights, lean forward and look the presenter in the eye. If the presenter tries to cut in before the end of an answer, raise your voice slightly, but be sure to finish within 20 seconds of the attempted interruption. Do not use the presenter's name. It will sound false. Don't try to bluff by using jargon. Many viewers find it intensely irritating. The whole point of giving the interview will be lost if you lose your audience. Try to stick to facts. Avoid phrases like 'It seems to me' or, worse, 'I believe that there may have been times when it might have been more helpful if those involved had been open to the possibility that it might have been more helpful to . . . !' If the presenter introduces surprises, such as adverse film footage, or an unannounced adversary, or a quotation from a leaked report, make it clear to the audience that you think that the presenter is being unfair. Question the presenter about the origin, editing and date of the surprise item. Refuse to be drawn on its contents. 'I do not want to express an opinion on a report I have not read or film footage I have not previously seen.' Usually the last word goes to the presenter. If presenters abuse this by introducing new or erroneous material into a supposed summary, interject with a clear 'That is unfair', 'That is untrue', 'I did not say that.' When the interview ends, remain seated and looking at the presenter, until someone indicates that you are off air. Then smile.

Using Local Radio

In the main, radio listeners are less demanding than TV viewers. They ask only for something interesting to listen to, whereas TV viewers expect to be entertained and preferably amused. Local radio stations are often run on a shoestring compared to regional TV. Consequently, most local radio stations will welcome well-prepared information about local publics services. Preparation for a radio interview is basically the same as for television, but there are a few differences.

Examples and stories that paint a picture are important in TV interviews and are even more important on radio. Surprisingly, radio studios can be more distracting than TV studios, where the bright lights tend to hide most of the production staff. Because there is no visual stimulus for the audience, the presenter will be trying even harder to make the interview pacey and lively and possibly controversial. To keep the colour in your voice, imagine that the microphone is a telephone and that you are having a conversation with a particular listener. Radio presenters will rarely give you more than 20 seconds to answer questions. If the interview is done over the phone at home, keep dogs and young children at bay and turn off the radio![8]

MANAGING INFORMATION TECHNOLOGY

Introducing information technology has been viewed with deep scepticism by some public service managers. It has been perceived as a cause of unemployment and accused of dehumanizing public services. Managers have seen people replaced by computers and many jobs deskilled through automation. In this section we explore problems associated with information technology and offer a conversational methodology for developing information systems. The conversational methodology takes into account both the technical and the social needs of people who use information systems.

The Role of Information Technology in Managing Public Services

Our conversations with Peter Williams underlined the centrality of information gathering and information assessment when managing public services. These are the 'sensing' and 'making sense' activities that feature in our conversational approach to management. Peter highlighted the important role of technology in 'chunking' information into a form which front-line managers can use for decision-making. Attempts to introduce such technology into public services have not always met with success.[9]

In the late 1970s and early 1980s, IT equipment was used to improve administration, rather than to improve decision-making. Subsequently, it was used to co-ordinate dispersed activity. Neighbourhood offices, for example, are of little value to people in the neighbourhood unless the staff have immediate access to centrally held information. On-line computer based information systems provide this. In 1998 the UK government launched a National Grid for Learning. It aimed to provide computer terminals hooked up to the Internet in communities throughout the country. Citizens could access information about public services from computer terminals based in local libraries, post offices, schools, colleges and community centres. In public services, enthusiasm for the increased use of IT is more likely to be found amongst middle managers. Unfortunately their influence is limited. Isaac-Henry discovered that:

> The potential for transforming the organisation by integrating IT strategy with business strategy was neither perceived nor realised. Left to the specialist, much of the emphasis was placed on technical aspects. Lack of managerial awareness and failure to manage the developments were the sources of many problems. By the beginning of the 1990s, the use and management of IT in some public service organisations was in a chaotic state.[10]

These problems were not confined to public service organizations that were publicly owned. According to Buchanan and Boddy,[11] a survey of 400 privately owned British and Irish companies, carried out in the mid-1990s, revealed that only 11 per cent had been successful in their application of Information

Table 12.1 IT: Driving forces and restraining forces

Driving forces	Restraining forces
New developments	Lack of IT awareness
Lower cost of technology	Failure to develop IT
New managerialism	Disorganized acquisition
Government legislation	Lack of specialist skills
Economy and efficiency	Lack of evidence of gains

Source: After Isaac-Henry et al. (1993)

Technology. Most of the problems encountered were not technical. Most of the problems were to do with individuals. There was an over-dependence on external consultants. In order to address these problems, Kearney[12] recommended:

- Recognizing that individuals are the most likely obstacles (Chapter 2).
- Understanding that individual people are key contributors to success (Chapter 8).
- Appointing managers – not IT specialists – as project leaders (Chapter 3).

IT can enable the implementation of useful change. If the change does not improve the service, then it is useless. IT development must be aligned with an overall plan for improving the service. But IT developments can only be aligned with plans for improved service where these plans exist. According to Isaac-Henry[13] in 1991, only 30 per cent of UK local authorities who were engaged in extensive IT development had any kind of service improvement plan with which IT developments could be aligned. When asked why, Sir Ian Bancroft, head of the Civil Service, said:

> A great deal depends on the personal commitment of the Minister in charge of a department as to the amount of time and energy that he is going to give to putting very deep probes into the tasks and manning of his department.[14]

Individuals are needed to champion IT development. They need to understand the potential of IT and have the necessary influence to integrate it into the overall plans for the service.

DEVELOPING ELECTRONIC COLLABORATION

Dennis, Pootheri and Natarajan,[15] writing in 1998, predicted that electronic communication would help to build virtual communities in which members would work together and share a sense of being part of the organization, even if they did not meet in person. However, electronic communications alone cannot create communities. If these means of electronic communication fail to exploit the ideas on relationship formation which we explored in Chapter 8, then it is unlikely that members of an electronic community will develop a compelling need or desire to interact with each other once the novelty of using the new technology has worn off. In 1989, the world wide web made the Internet much more accessible. Originally, the driving force was interest in developing a communications system that would survive a nuclear attack. By 1997, 18 million host computers – the ones that store the information – were connected to the net (http://www.nw.com). Each host computer can account for between one and several thousand users. The Internet is a product of public services – originally public education services. It is publicly financed and, in that sense, it is public property. It grew out of a network which first connected four university sites in the USA. It is now a global network of commercial as well as academic networks. It is linked by leased telephone lines. In 1994 the number of commercial computers linked to the net overtook the number of academic computers. It is designed like a fish net. If one link is disabled, a message can always travel by an alternative route, so that the communications system cannot be disabled by a pre-emptive nuclear strike.

Internet links carry a continuous stream of ones and zeros, broken into individual packets. Each packet is labelled with its destination. At each link in the net, the label is read. If the packet is recognized as having arrived at its destination, it is hooked out. Hooked out packets are reassembled into their correct sequence and decoded into their original message. Packets with unrecognized labels are sent on their way to the next link. Unlike a telephone connection, each link is carrying thousands of messages simultaneously. The packets whizzing round the net carry compressed information about pictures, music, colour and moving images, as well as data and text. The net thus became entertaining and fun to look at, as well as informative. Identical key words or phrases, stored in computers at lots of different places on the net, have been linked together, so that groupings of related documents can be browsed as though they were all in the same place.

The potential of the Internet to support knowledge creation is undoubted. The potential to support real learning communities is something we question in Chapter 13. In 1998 Bill Gates[16] of Microsoft predicted that within ten years no one would notice the Internet. It would just be there – an accepted part of the structure – an integral part of life. He predicted that it would be a reflex to turn on the Intenet for shopping, education, entertainment and communication. The pattern of predictions about information technology has been to overestimate what can be done in two years and to underestimate what can be done in ten. In 1998 we predicted that there would be a backlash against screen-based activities, as people experienced a kind of social starvation. In Chapter 8 we argued that more, not less, face-to-face contact between people was needed. We argued that the formation of close one-to-one relationships was important for personal health and social cohesion, as well as for increased motivation.

Perhaps, like new public roads, the new information highways will bring their own problems. The jams and delays will get worse. According to Frances Caincross,[17] by 1997 the world wide web had already gobbled up two-thirds of the capacity of the Internet. Internet radio exacerbated this, but the ultimate threat was video. While one million bytes of computer memory would by then store a 700 page book, it would hold only 50 spoken words, five A4 photographs or three seconds of video. As with free public services the world over, people got tired of waiting. Since the ongoing cost of using the Internet was generally only the cost of a local call, in places where local calls were 'free' the use of the net was also 'free'. When it costs nothing, subscribers log onto a line and then leave it open all day. After all it is costing them nothing! Hence congestion increased. The longer the delay in getting a connection, the greater the temptation, to stay on line and keep it open – thereby adding to the waiting list.

Easy access and ease of use created its own problems. Sabotage of taxation and social service records and disruption of air traffic control were feared. Security did not keep pace with growth. In 1996 Louise Kehoe[18] reported that there was a 50:50 chance of a system being interfered with in the course of a year. Encryption – the use of codes – was one way to enhance the protection of information stored or in transit, but many governments were wary of allowing communication to be coded.

Bytes with Bite:
The Implications for Public Services

In 1982, there were about 32,000 robots in use in the USA. By the turn of the century there were over 20 million. There has been more information published in the last 30 years than in the previous 5,000 years. The average daily newspaper contains more information than most people would have acquired in a lifetime 200 years ago. The volume of published information doubles every five years. Individuals can access information very quickly. If you take a credit card into a bank in a strange country, they will probably be able to find out if your credit is good within five seconds, even though the information may need to travel over 50,000 miles.

Public services can be run by dispersed individuals who have almost instant access to the information they need to a service. Hence public service organizations could be broken into bits with bytes. They could become flatter and have less layers of management. Faster, though perhaps less thoughtful decisions, can now be made by well-informed individuals who are closer to their clients.

According to Charles Handy, writing in *The Age of Unreason*,[19] less than half of public service users will be in conventional full-time work in the twenty-first century. Many will be in temporary or part-time work. Every year more people will become self-employed. This is likely to be true also for people working for public services. Because client history and other information can be retrieved quickly and remotely from computer files, public service organizations will no longer depend on the memories of long-serving staff. As constantly changing combinations of people come together to carry out projects, trying to write formal job descriptions will be like trying to nail jellyfish! This has affected the way that national broadcasting is organized.

Apart from in the USA, public service broadcasting services used to be publicly owned and usually state controlled. They were commonly financed by public grant or a licence fee. According to Cairncross, the story is similar in Spain and Japan. As technology allows the exact recording for who is watching which channel and for how long, the people who are no longer watching the publicly owned services may demand an end to subsidy.

The proportion of public service work that can be carried out on screens continues to increase. Increasingly this work is carried out in the countries that have high levels of skill and low levels of cost. Public service organizations in Western Europe and America find it cheaper to have patients and old people monitored, security cameras watched, helplines staffed, and routine administration carried out, on screens that are located in Eastern Europe or South-East Asia or in South Africa.

People with common grievances now find it easier to contact one another. They are able to organize and co-ordinate protests against fuel prices, chemical weapons, road building, the spread of nuclear waste or global capitalism. This poses problems for public order and security services.

Education Services:
The End of Universities?

Universities and colleges may become extinct unless they provide global networks of up to date information and interactive certification that information has been understood. Half a dozen universities working together could keep the information on such networks up-to-date. The half dozen with the best international reputations could do it between them. To survive, colleges and universities will have to define a role for themselves which cannot so easily be replicated by a telecommunications network. Universities and colleges must convince governments, employers and students that education is a social process, involving much more than understanding new information. Universities and colleges must convince employers and funding bodies that students need intellectual and social skills and the dispositions that govern their use as lifelong learners and active citizens. Colleges and universities in Australia, New Zealand, Canada, the United States and the United Kingdom, will only continue to be countries of first choice for higher education as long as fluency in written and spoken English continues to enhance earning power. The salary premium paid to people with a command of English will reduce with the improvement of IT systems which can interpret and translate foreign languages.

We have looked at the nature of information and the way it can be communicated orally and in writing, inside and outside the organization, through personal channels and through global computer-based networks. Before we look at the way public service managers can use this information to take decisions, we want to give some thought to the design of the systems that collect and disseminate the information.

A CONVERSATIONAL APPROACH TO SYSTEM DESIGN

Peter Drucker[21] writing in *Post Capitalist Society*, estimated that by the year 2000 no developed country would have more than one-eighth of its workforce employed in the traditional work of making and moving physical goods. In 1991, worldwide spending on information-processing hardware exceeded for the first time the worldwide spending on equipment for industry, mining, farming and construction combined. In the 1990s, the industrial age gave way to the information age. In the United States, two-thirds of the workforce became employed in providing services in which information was the most important component. This called for the design of different kinds of organizations. In the *International Journal of Information Management*, Remenzi, White and Sherwood-Smith[22] argued for a 'post-modern' approach to the design of information systems. We think that a conversational approach can be used to orchestrate a debate between the key stakeholders for whose benefit the information system is to be designed. We think that this debate is necessary for a co-creational approach to the design of information systems:

> [T]ime has run out for IT managers who act like a protected species and who demonstrate a three-fold failure to understand the business, to communicate with colleagues and to deliver cost-effective systems. This has led to a widespread collapse of faith in autonomous IT departments and a need for managers to find other ways to design their information systems.[23]

We think our conversational approach is another way. Our conversational approach involves taking action (to achieve results); sensing the response (to make observations); making sense (to develop meaning) and formulating ideas (to generate plans) on which to take action (Figure 12.1). We can combine this approach with the systems ideas which we introduced in Chapters 5 and 11. A conversational approach to designing an information system involves ten steps (Box 12.7).

Box 12.7

A CONVERSATIONAL APPROACH TO SYSTEMS DESIGN – 10 STEPS

Step 1. Hold outer world conversations to identify the key actors. Who owns the system? Who are its beneficiaries and clients? Who are the unintended victims of its pollution, bad press or reputation? Key actors can include union officials, respected technical experts, founding fathers, editors of local papers, or influential local politicians. Your list of key actors is likely to be divided into:

- Ostensible beneficiaries (usually clients)
- Internal decision-makers (usually managers)
- External influences (usually media politicians)

Step 2. Having refined your list of key actors, you can now hold more specific conversations with representatives of each actor group. What differences do they expect the system to make to the world? How would they be able to tell that it was making this difference? What would change in the world? How could these changes be detected, seen or experienced? How could they make sure that they always detected these changes? Could they measure these changes?

Step 3. Armed with the results of these outer world conversations, retire to your inner world to try to make sense of them. Try to map out what you have learned onto one side of A4, by drawing a map of the system, its subsystems and the wider systems to which it is connected. Show any hierarchy in the relationships between systems, subsystems and wider systems. Show any outside influences that can impact on the system.

Step 4. Still in your inner world, for each of the systems on the systems map you have just drawn, identify the inputs, outputs and measures of performance. Who are the key actors?

Step 5. Return to the outer world for conversations in which you can check out your inner

world thinking with the key actors you have identified. What are the constraints – technological, economic, market, political, legal, ethical and social – on the way resources can be obtained?

Step 6. Back into your inner world. For each of the key actors you have now identified, think empathetically. What does each key actor need to know, by when and how accurately, in order to play their part in the running of the system, if it is to achieve its expected transformation and meet its expected levels of performance? Draw your ideas as a matrix.

Step 7. Take your draft information matrix back into the outer world. Have conversations with the people whose names appear as key actors on the matrix. Is there any information that they can easily do without, or need less frequently or less accurately? How does this information compare with what they have at present? What are the biggest gaps? How crucial do they think the gaps are? How easy or difficult would it be to plug these gaps?

Step 8. Retire to your inner world to consider what changes would be involved in plugging the information gaps. Rank them for desirability, cost, feasibility or likely resistance (Chapter 3). Are there obvious shortlist candidates for the first changes to make? Are there any changes that are desirable and feasible?

Step 9. Back into the outer world, canvass support for candidates on your shortlist of possible changes. Involve key actors in selecting the first change.

Step 10. Implement the selected first change and be sensitive to the impact it makes. The impact can be positive or negative. Examples of positive impacts could be health gains, reduced complaints, reduced staff stress, improved quality of community life, quicker journey times, a better informed public, or people feeling safer. Examples of negative impact could be longer waiting lists, delays in planning decisions, worsened traffic congestion, pollution of rivers, lost mail, increases in car crime, poor quality TV, abuses of human rights, discrimination against minorities, waste of foreign aid, inefficiency of customs officers, rudeness of junior staff, fear of violence, fear of food stuffs, corruption amongst officials, mistrust of the criminal justice system or infringements of free speech. Take what 'sense' you make back to step 3 and continue the iterative conversational approach.

THE ROLE OF INFORMATION IN DECISION-MAKING

One way of viewing the work of managers is to regard them as professional decision-makers. As we discovered in Chapter 6, even when groups are empowered to take decisions they are often reluctant to do so. They are inclined to push individuals into the role of leaders and decision-makers even where none is appointed. Delays in taking decisions can result in delays in providing services, in delays to improving the quality of services, and in delays in addressing ethical issues concerning inequality of provision. The consequences of indecisiveness are so serious that organizations are prepared to pay managers more than they pay others, to take the decisions which others are reluctant to take. Staff are easily demotivated by managers who take the money but do not take the decisions! Managers are paid to assemble information that is relevant to the decisions that need to be taken and to generate and evaluate options based on the manager's analysis of the assembled information. Decision-making benefits from a conversational approach which combines inner world reflective, critical, creative, empathetic and evaluative thinking with outer world conversational skills in listening, learning, persuading and negotiating.

Methods of Decision-making

A useful distinction can be made between 'programmable' and 'non-programmable' decisions. Programmable decisions are decisions that could be worked out by a computer, because the variables are quantifiable and the decision rules are clear and unambiguous. Non-programmable decisions are decisions that could not easily be made by a computer. They are decisions where, for the moment at least, human judgements have to be made. We will distinguish between rational decision-making and complex decision-making and deal with each separately.

Rational Methods of Decision-making: Operational Research

Rational models of decision-making follow a logical sequence of events (Figure 12.3).

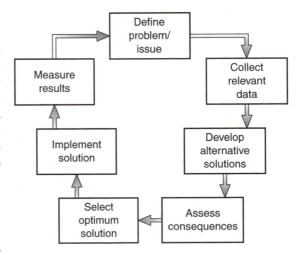

Figure 12.3 A rational model of decision-making

Operational research incorporates numerical and statistical information. The information is fed into a decision-making model of the kind shown in Figure 12.3. In Chapter 10 subjective judgements about the relative benefits of certain public service options were converted into numerical estimates of probability and consequence. Once quantified, information can be used in a rational model of decision-making, but we must not forget the subjective origins of the numbers. Operations research does not take or calculate decisions. It is a tool to assist managers in quantifying and exploring the consequences of possible decisions (Box 12.8).[24]

Decision Trees

Decision trees of the kind shown in Figure 12.4 are helpful when managers need to make a series of decisions, the outcomes of which will affect each subsequent decision. By drawing decision trees, managers can consider the outcomes and consequences of a particular series of decisions. A further step can be added which involves estimating the probability of each outcome and predicting the costs or benefits associated with each.

Brainstorming

Alexander F. Osborne,[25] the director of a New York advertising agency, developed brainstorming in 1939. The technique was originally used to develop creative advertising campaigns. It has since become a common aid to decision-making. There are a number of rules for effective brainstorming:

- No ideas are criticized.
- All ideas must be recorded.
- Groups should be between five and seven people.
- Unconventional ideas are encouraged.
- The group produces as many ideas as possible.
- No idea, no matter how bizarre, is rejected.
- Ideas should be edited after the session.
- The best ideas are put forward for further thought.

Brainstorming rests on a number of assumptions which have been questioned by researchers. First, it assumes that the average person can think up twice as many ideas when working with a group than when working alone. Taylor et al.[26] proved that this was not true. They found that groups in which people brainstormed alone and then aggregated their

---

Box 12.8

OPERATIONAL RESEARCH

1 Formulating the problem in terms of the purpose of the overall system
2 Constructing a mathematical model of the overall system
3 Feeding numerical information into the model to find out 'what would happen if . . .'
4 Selecting a promising model and refining it
5 Setting up a feedback mechanism to measure option outcomes
6 Piloting the promising options
7 Evaluating and refining the model

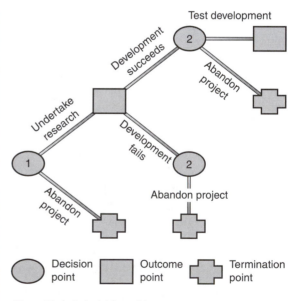

Figure 12.4 A decision-making tree

ideas, performed better than groups that brain-stormed interactively. Second, brainstorming assumes that group thinking and decision-making is better than individual thinking and decision-making. Magin and Richards[27] argued that this was not always the case. They concluded that individuals put less effort into a task when they shared responsibility for outcomes with others. Furnham[28] concluded that the overall research indicated that brainstorming is most often used in situations when individuals properly managed would produce more creative ideas and more effective thinking.

There is evidence to suggest that 'electronic brainstorming' can overcome some of the problems associated with traditional, group-based brain-storming.[29] Electronic brainstorming involves individuals using computer terminals to type their own ideas while having immediate access to the ideas of other group members. This approach encourages increased participation, reduced the anxiety associated with groups, and reduced distractions.

Ethical Decision-making

In Chapter 6 we identified that 'groupthink' can result in unethical decision-making. Here are some guidelines for preventing groupthink when making group decisions.

- Ask one group member to assume the role of critical evaluator who continually raises doubts.
- Managers should not state their position on a decision at the outset.
- Create different groups to work on a decision separately but simultaneously.
- Use external experts to evaluate group processes.
- Appoint a devil's advocate to question the group's decision-making processes.
- When a consensus is reached, encourage the group to re-consider all options one final time before deciding to go with a decision.

Blanchard and Peale[30] propose the following 'ethics check' for decision-makers:

1 Is it legal, i.e. will I be violating the law?

2 Is it balanced, i.e. is it fair to all concerned in the short and the long term?
3 Does it promote win–win relationships?
4 How will it make me feel about myself? Will it make me proud of myself?
5 How will I feel when others become aware that it was my decision?

Problems with Rational Decisions

As we saw in Chapter 1, making estimates and predictions in public services may be difficult. The world in which a public service manager operates may be far from predictable. The value of a particular outcome may be hard to quantify. How would one quantify, for example, the benefits of taking a child into care? Even if such quantification could be attempted, there are usually many different stakeholders whose estimates, predictions and valuations could be considered. Who is to decide? Whose opinions should be taken into account and how are these opinions to be weighed? (Chapter 11) Getting people to estimate probabilities is difficult because the concept itself appears difficult to many people. Many stakeholders struggle to use percentages at all, let alone use them as measures of chance or probability. In public services, many events are unique, one-off and non-repeatable. This makes it difficult to build up a history or database that might be used to improve future estimates. Public services are not like insurance companies which can use data about the number and size of claims to adjust the premiums they charge. Stakeholders in public services sometimes find it easier if you start by asking them what they think the worst case scenario might be and then ask them what they think will actually happen.

Bounded Rationality

Another problem with using a rational model of decision-making in public services is the notion of bounded rationality. Simon[31] pointed out that it is ludicrous to assume that decision-makers will always have all the information they need in order to model all feasible options and outcomes. Information about the consequences of decisions may not be available and only possible to estimate through arbitrary or ill-informed guesswork. The reactions of people affected by the decisions and the consequences of their reactions may be difficult to forecast. Even if all relevant information were available, Simon concluded that the complexity of many decision problems would mean that the decision-maker would be unable to calculate the best course of action. He suggested that the reality of these limitations should be accepted and that decision-makers should just search systematically for feasible options. Decision-making, he thought, should be viewed as a creative rather than a calculative process. Taking this further, Mintzberg[32] encouraged managers to integrate their intuition and insight into complex decision-making. However, he offered no advice to managers as to how this integration might be achieved. Pidd[33] suggested that given our lack of complete certainty over events, decision-makers should give equal weight to both intuition and rationality when making decisions. Again Pidd is less clear about how a manager can learn to develop and use intuition and what thinking

skills might be involved. A conversational approach might help (Figure 12.5).

What's the Problem?

Outer world conversations are used to gather information about the background and the history of the difficulties that are being experienced. It is important to ask what people feel as well as what they think. Making sense of these conversations in the inner world involves recollective thinking, searching for past similar experiences – asking 'when did we feel this way before?' as well as 'when have we thought this way before?' Reflective thinking is involved in searching for a pattern.

Symptoms or Diseases?

Do the things that we sense make *more* sense when they are viewed as symptoms and not the disease? What is the underlying problem about which the decision is needed? Looking back over this information and reflecting, what do we feel now? What do we think now? Thinking projectively into the

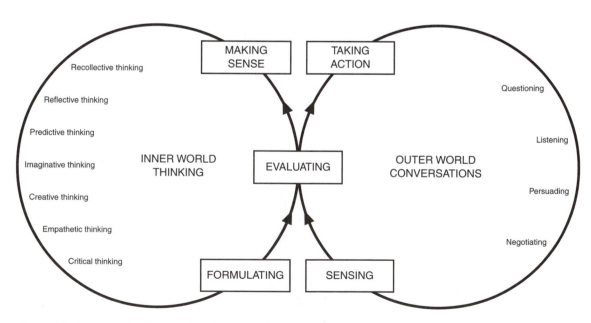

Figure 12.5 A conversational approach to decision-making

future, what is likely to happen if we do nothing? Could we live with any recurrence?

Can we imagine a world in which all these difficulties have been overcome? What would this world look like? What would look different? Who would feel different? Can we think empathetically about their experience of the change – how would it look, sound and feel to them? What would they think about the changed situation?

How to Choose

Of all the possibilities now open to us, what criteria should we use to judge them? How are we to judge feasibility and risk? Make a list of possible options. Looking down our list of possible options, how do we feel? What do we think? Can we imagine how things would be different if we implemented some of the possible decisions on our list? Do any more possibilities occur to us?

Thinking empathetically, what will other people feel and think about these options? Who is likely to support us and who is likely to resist our decisions? Critically evaluating the possibilities, which are the most economical, the most efficient, the most effective and the most ethical? Which ones shall we take out into the outside world in order to hold listening, persuading and negotiating conversations? Do we now have an implementable decision?

Implementing the Decision

Once the decision has been made, instructing, delegating and coaching conversations may need to precede taking action. Monitoring and appraising conversations may then give rise to the need to return to the inner world to make sense of what we sense is now happening in the outer world. Does our decision need to be revised?

In our conversational approach, equal attention was given to what was being felt as well as what is being thought. This is a way to operationalize the advice of Mintzberg and Pidd that we should try to integrate intuition with analysis.

Deciding *not* to Decide: A More Thoughtful Approach

At the moment of decision there should be appropriate mood, motivation and information. If the first two are strong, there is a risk that decisions will be taken impulsively and without sufficient information. We favour a more thoughtful approach. Mood can influence decision-making when it presents as anxiety, excitement or boredom. Anxiety about an impending decision may lead to a pre-emptive decision made to put an end to the anxiety. 'Let's not wait for even more information. Let's decide something!'

Excitement and arousal feed on each other, often leading to a search for fresh experiences of excitement or novel sources of stimulation. Deciding to change something can provide both. We can decide to change, just for a change. Boredom can lead to unpredictable decisions – capricious, whimsical mischievous even – anything to relieve the boredom. Motivation is defined by the need to meet unmet needs for such things as warmth, possession and applause (Chapter 7). If these unmet needs are excessive, the drive to decide can be desperate. Impetuosity and impulse are likely to rule.

Managers are professional decision-makers. They are paid to be thoughtful in their decision-making. In order to curb the impetuosity that threatens their thoughtfulness, they will need to manage their anxiety levels (Chapter 8), manage their motivation (Chapter 7), and manage their need for novelty (Chapter 14). They will need to become self-aware of how all these tendencies to be impulsive may be exacerbated by changes in the manager's circumstances outside work, such as bereavement, profound shock, pregnancy, surgery, influenza, seasonal disorders and the disorientation associated with holidays, strange places and jet lag.

We have looked at how information is gathered and communicated, both personally and electronically, and how it can be used to feed rational and complex decision-making in public services. But 'the end of words is to bring men to knowledge of things beyond what words can utter'.[34] This quotation by Isaac Renington is taken from *Quaker Faith and Prac-*

tice. Throughout this book we have been struck by how many public services owe their origins to the work of charities and religious societies like the Quakers. We have also been struck by how many writers on management draw on the teachings and wisdom of religions. In the last chapter, we shall express some reservations about 'Management as Religion'. In the meantime, in our Final Thoughts, we will take up Renington's idea that words can 'bring men to knowledge'.

FINAL THOUGHTS: KNOWLEDGE BEYOND WORDS

Toffler said 'we live in a knowledge society'.[35] How can public services contribute to the process of knowledge creation? Early in this chapter we saw that some public service organizations can be viewed as hierarchical systems for communicating information. According to Ikujiro Nonaka,

> a critical problem with this paradigm flows from its passive and static view of the organisation. Information processing is viewed as a problem-solving activity which centres on what is given to the organisation – without due consideration of what is created by it.[36]

Nonaka suggests that organizations should be concerned not only with how information is processed, but also with how information can be transformed into knowledge. Unfortunately, in this debate the terms 'information' and 'knowledge' are often used interchangeably. This is confusing. Information and knowledge are not the same (Box 12.9). A flow of information is a flow of messages to which meanings must be attached. Information becomes knowledge when these meanings are anchored to the commitment and beliefs of those who hold and use the information.[37] Environmental scanning (Chapter 4) generates a lot of information. That information only becomes knowledge when it is assessed against the values and beliefs of those in the organization.

The information with which we have been concerned in this chapter has largely been concerned with words and numbers. These only represent the tip of an iceberg of the knowledge which an organ-

ization may possess. Polanyi[39] says, 'We know more than we can tell'. Polanyi classified human knowledge into two types: 'explicit knowledge' and 'tacit knowledge.' Explicit knowledge refers to knowledge that we can transmit through formal language. Tacit knowledge has a personal dimension to it which makes this knowledge hard to formalize and communicate to others. Tacit knowledge connects our inner world to our outer world. It is deeply connected to our inner beliefs and values and to the actions that we take in the outer world. Nonaka suggests that one of the best ways to learn is to make tacit knowledge explicit. The tacit knowledge possessed by employees at all levels of the organization must be valued. Front-line staff are inundated with information and tacit knowledge about the services they deliver and the service users with whom they deal. By valuing this knowledge and encouraging staff to make it explicit, an upward spiral can be created which will enable public service organizations to surface new knowledge about how to improve public services.

Box 12.9

FROM INFORMATION TO KNOWLEDGE[38]

Information	*Knowledge*
Tangible	Intangible
Physical objects	Mental objects
Easily transferable	Learning required
Reproducible	Not reproducible

SUMMARY

- We looked at the communication of 'hard' and 'soft' information.
- We described the advantages and disadvantages of six different channels of communication used in public service organizations. We looked at written reports, letters and memos, making presentations, using visual aids, and presenting numerical information. We looked at the use of the telephone and e-mail and argued for more one-to-one, face-to-face communication.
- Reporting on conversations with an ex-army officer who is now a chief executive of a public service organization, we looked at the way failure to manage information has led to military defeats and is leading to the mismanagement of public services.
- We looked at the role of information management in public relations and examined how to work with different media, including TV, radio and the press.
- We identified some problems for public services associated with the implementation of IT and telecommunications.
- We looked at the way a conversational approach might be used to redesign information systems and take complex decisions in public services.
- We had a Final Thought about how to turn information into knowledge which could improve the quality of services.

THINKING AND LEARNING ACTIVITIES

Activity 1 Self-assessment

1 Make a list of some of the 'hard' information you use every week.
2 What sort of 'soft' information might have improved your decision-making?
3 List the advantages and disadvantages of six channels of communication.
4 On one side of A4, list notes on writing reports, letters and memos.
5 List main points to remember when using telephones.
6 What are the main points to bear in mind when writing a press release?
7 What are the main points to bear in mind when preparing for a TV interview?
8 What are the main points to bear in mind during a TV interview?
9 What differences if the interview is on local radio?
10 What problems do IT developments pose?
11 What are the ten steps in a conversational approach to designing information systems?
12 How can a conversational approach be used to take complex decisions?
13 When can it be better not to take a decision?
14 Write a memo to a junior member of staff about writing letters.
15 Write a memo to a junior member of staff about using the telephone.
16 Write a short report for a middle manager on giving presentations.
17 Write a short report for a junior manager on the use of visual aids.
18 Summarize the main ideas in the section on advocacy and argument.

Activity 2 Individual Learning: Visual and Emotional Thinking

Going soft

What sort of 'soft' information do you use in your job or at college? If you are not employed, choose an area of management you aspire to and imagine what sort of 'soft' information you would use in your job.

Activity 3 Paired Learning: Visual and Numerical Thinking

And the word was made flesh

Compare verbal and written means of communication. Consider, for example, telephones, team working, face-to-face conversations, memos, reports, notices, newsletters. Write brief notes and, if possible, compare your notes with someone else.

Activity 4 Individual Learning: Visual and Numerical Thinking

Norwegian transportation

Soren Glass is a manager responsible for transport and vehicles in a public service organization in Norway. He manages pools of cars, delivery vans, mini buses and heavy transportation vehicles. Some are driven by drivers for whom Soren is responsible. These are used to collect and deliver people and goods in response to requests from other departments. Some are hired on a daily basis by staff from other departments. Some are permanently allocated to senior managers.

Draw a diagram to show the main items of transport information you are likely to receive or need – daily, weekly, monthly and annually. What information will you probably send out and how frequently? For each item indicate its likely source and destination.

Activity 5 Individual Learning: Numerical Thinking

Technology in Belgium

In 1992, when asked how important technology was to their jobs, 500 managers in public services in Belgium responded as follows:

Essential	170
Important	200
Not important	80
Irrelevant	20
Don't know	30

Draw a pie chart that could be used on an OHP to present this data to groups of 50 managers.

How to draw a pie chart using a computer

An Example: Spending allocation in Eindhoven, Holland. The following is the amount in Dutch guilders spent per day, per adult on the electoral role:

Education	56
Social welfare	15
Roads	7
Policing	16
Other	26

Pie charts can be prepared on a PC, using standard spreadsheet software. On the spreadsheet grid, enter the names and percentage levels you want for each category. Click on 'graph' and 'pie'. Check it looks OK on the screen and print it. Select a hatch-pattern or colours if you have got a colour printer.

Drawing a pie chart manually

You will need pencil, ruler, compass and protractor.

- **Step 1**: Add up the total which you want to represented as a 360 degree pie. In our example, it is $56 + 15 + 7 + 16 + 26 = 120$ guilders.
- **Step 2**: Divide the total into 360, to find out how many degrees of the circular pie are needed to represent one guilder. In our example ($360 \div 120$ guilders) we need 3 degrees to represent one guilder.
- **Step 3**: Draw a circle.
- **Step 4**: Draw in slices for each category. In our example, to draw the slice for social welfare, 15 guilders, we will need to use the protractor to mark out 15×3 degrees = 45 degrees on the circle (remember we calculated that we need 3 degrees for each guilder $\times$ 15 guilders = 45 degrees). If we repeat the process for 'roads', we will find we need to measure a slice of $3 \times 7 = 21$ degrees on our circle. Again, use the protractor to work out the size of the pie slice for roads.
- **Step 5**: Repeat until the pie is completely sliced.
- **Step 6**: Shade in the slices and label the pie chart.

Activity 6 Individual Learning: Numerical Thinking

Police services in Holland

In 1992, 500 managers of police services in Holland were asked how they made use of information technology and they replied as follows:

Word processing	25
Business planning	23
Performance monitoring	22
Communication linking	7
Information seeking	2
Other	2
Not at all	419

Represent this information as a bar chart.

How to draw a bar chart

Using a computer

Proceed as above for a pie chart and simply point to 'bar' instead of 'pie' and click on.

Doing it manually

Step 1. Draw a vertical block on the left-hand side of your page. Adjust the length of the clock (or bar) to represent the number in your biggest category. In our case, the biggest category is 25. Choose a scale that is easy to work with, such as 1 mm = 1 police officer.

Step 2. For the next highest category, in our case business planning 23 police officers, draw a vertical block 25×1 mm = 25 mm high. Repeat the process until all categories are represented by vertical blocks.

Step 3. Colour or shade the blocks (bars) and label the bar chart.

Activity 7 Individual Learning: Numerical Thinking

Motoring costs in Germany

A transport manager of a public service organization in Germany has been supplied with the following information and is trying to see if there is any relationship between the annual running costs of the cars and the fleet-buying prices he has been offered. Plot a scatter graph to help see if there is any relationship.

Company	Contract price (DM)	Running costs
Citroën	39,000	3,750
BMW	54,000	4,000
Fiat	12,500	2,300
Lada	13,550	3,000
Nissan	19,500	3,050
Ford	17,450	2,350
Renault	27,000	3,210
Rover	17,500	2,800
Toyota	31,000	2,950

What other 'hard' and 'soft' information might help you decide which car to adopt? If possible, compare your ideas with someone else.

How to draw a scattergraph using a computer

Use a spreadsheet package as before, entering your two variables in adjacent columns. This time, point and click on graph and under options delete the line. What is left – i.e. just the points unconnected to the graph lines – is your scattergraph.

Doing it manually

Use a ruler and pencil to create two lines or scales at right angles to each other, as in Figure 12.6.

We have plotted the combination of pairs of values of average numbers of clients seen by this public service during a particular month, against the salary bill for the service for that same month. It is clear that spending more on staff is not in itself sufficient to increase the number of clients seen in this public service.

**Average no.
clients per day**

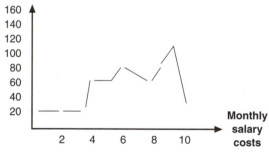

Figure 12.6 A scattergraph

Activity 8 Individual Learning: Numerical Thinking

Ordering stationery in Sweden

You manage a local coastguards office in Sweden. Your stationery store has ten major stock items. Their annual usage and unit value in Swedish Krona is set out below. Use a Pareto curve to help you decide which are the key items whose consumption you should monitor in most detail, most frequently.

	No. of items (Usage per annum)	Value (Krona)
1.	500	210
2.	1,200	240
3.	152	240
4.	148	150
5.	15,000	15
6.	127,600	9
7.	4,270	9
8.	1,100	28
9.	850	28
10.	540	40

How to draw a Pareto curve

- **Step 1**: Rank items in order of value.
- **Step 2**: Work out the total value.
- **Step 3**: Work out the percentage of the total each category of items contributes.
- **Step 4**: Plot the cumulative total contribution against the number of items whose scores contribute.

To create our example, in Figure 12.7 we have listed out the names of 50 staff members in order of the number of complaints made about them by members of the public. We have calculated the cumulative number of complaints as we move down the list of names. We have expressed each cumulative score as a percentage of the total number of complaints. In Figure 12.7 we have plotted the total number of staff needed to generate a given percentage of the number of complaints against the percentage of the complaints that they generate between them. Figure 12.7 shows, not for the first time, that 80 per cent of the complaints are associated with less than 20 per cent of the staff. By relocating, retraining or retiring these members of staff, we could eliminate over 80 per cent of the complaints received from members of the public – greatly enhancing one measure of the quality of service.

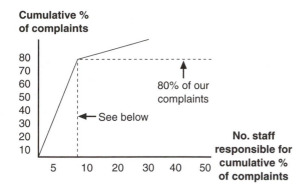

Figure 12.7 Pareto curve

Activity 9 Individual Learning: Numerical Thinking

CASE STUDY: Out of range in Australia

You are a manager in the Australian Ministry of Agriculture and your department has been asked by the treasury to advise on the level of agricultural subsidies for cereal planting to be offered per acre of crop. You need to estimate how many acres should be planted and what level of strategic grain stock should be financed. In the last 30 years, the average yield per hectare, in units adjusted for all known variables except climate, have been 2, 122, 90, 96, 108, 92, 104, 92, 124,103, 129, 114, 117, 102, 84, 96, 127, 1,000, 100, 108, 94, 112, 94, 131, 106, 130, 96, 106, 130, 120 measured in Australian Adjusted Units (AAU's). To help you decide on your advice to the treasury, produce a frequency histogram using a class interval of 10 AAUs. Estimate the most profitable yield of cereals per acre, in any given year, in AAUs.

- What is the range?
- What is the safest figure on which to base the calculation of how many acres to plant?

- What is the most optimistic figure?
- What range of yields would you use in the calculation of acres to be planted?

You could estimate the standard deviation by dividing the range by four. (This makes the assumption that the curve made by the envelope of your histogram is a normal bell-shaped curve.) Compare your estimate of the standard deviation with the standard deviation which you obtain by using a calculator or computer. Would your estimate have been good enough for the purpose of the advice you were asked to give?

Before beginning this exercise you may wish to read the following example of how a histogram was produced by a manager in a fire service.

Dealing with Uncertain Information (Mean, Range, Normal Distributions and Standard Deviations)

In public services, information is often unclear and inconsistent. For example, the following are the times (minutes), which it has taken for a fire service to respond to its last 20 emergency call-outs:

12	20	18	26	22	12	6	6	2	18
14	6	20	24	18	30	14	20	18	16

Do any of these times merit investigation or disciplinary action even? Or do they all lie within 'normal' limits? How could we compare these times with similar data from another fire service? Are all the response times to an acceptable standard? Are the response times acceptable? How can we answer these kinds of question when the figures appear random?

We could work out the average and see how it compares with last year's average, or the average for another fire service. If we add up all the numbers and divide by how many numbers there are, we get to the average of 16.1. If we did this every month we could see whether the average response time was getting slower or faster. Our clients might like there to be less risk – less uncertainty about the range of response times. They might prefer that we had a narrower range of responses, even if the average were not as quick. The range, in our example, is $30 - 2 = 28$. This is not a very good indication of our likely range because either the 30 or the 2, or both, could be freak figures. That means they could lie outside our normal distribution. There is a way to calculate our normal deviation from our mean score which removes the effect of freak figures. This involves the calculation of what is called the standard deviation. Many calculators and computers are programmed to do it very quickly. For a block of figures in cells B to F on a spreadsheet, the command @ AVG B4, F12 will calculate the average of all the figures in the cells between B4 and F12. To get the standard deviation try @ STD (B4, F12).

A good way to estimate a standard deviation is to divide the range by 4. This is because most distributions are bell-shaped. This kind of bell-shaped distribution is symmetrical and the width of the bell at the bottom is usually about 4 standard deviations and this corresponds more or less to the range, especially if you disregard obviously freak values. We could estimate the standard deviation of the response time of our fire service as about 7 minutes (range 28 ÷ 4 = 7).

Another good way to get a feel for the numerical information is to plot a histogram. To do this, divide the range into bands and count how many of your scores fall into each band. Count them in five's by making tally marks and crossing them through diagonally each time you get five. Figure 12.8 is an example.

From the graph we can 'get a feel' for the average. It is about 18 (our calculation was 16.1). Most of the values do seem, in fact, to fall between 11 and 25, which is our calculated mean of 18 plus or minus 7. (Remember, we calculated the standard deviation as: a quarter of the range which was 28 (30 − 2).

The standard deviation does seem to be a good measure of the scatter. We could decide that any response that lay outside the mean, plus or minus one standard deviation, would be worthy of investigation. Too low could indicate a fault in the recording system. Too high could indicate risk of life-threatening delays. In practice, this could mean that too many investigations were triggered. Our fire service data, for example, would have triggered 6 enquiries, because 6 of the response times lie outside a control range of plus or minus 7. Because 'normal' randomness tends to produce a normal distribution curve in which 95 per cent of the

'normal' values are within plus or minus 2 standard deviations of the mean, it is usual only to investigate results that are more than plus or minus 2 standard deviations from the mean. In the case of our fire service, this would suggest a control range of 18 plus 2×7, or 18 plus or minus 14 i.e. a control range of 4 to 32. In which case only one of the response times would have needed to be investigated.

No. responses per bandwidth

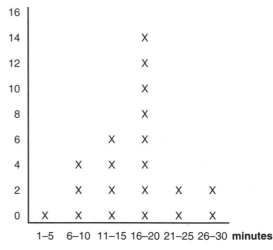

Figure 12.8 A histogram of fire service response times

Activity 10 Individual Learning: Critical and Evaluative Thinking

Confidential information

In an organization with which you are familiar, ask yourself whether you hold any information about individual people. If so, for what purpose is it used? To whom do you disclose it? To what concerns, if any, do the replies you have obtained give rise? What might be done to alleviate your concerns?

Activity 11 Group Learning: Critical and Evaluative Thinking

Information technology

Write down what you consider to be some of the main problems associated with the use of information technology in public services. On a separate sheet of paper write down the potential advantages of increased use of information technology in public services. In small groups share your opinions and weigh up whether the advantages outweigh the disadvantages.

Activity 12 Individual Learning: Recollective Thinking

Computer literacy

What do you think the following terms mean or refer to?

Back up; Bar code; Brand; Bit; Batter; Byte; CAD/CAM; CD ROM, CPS; CPU; Disk drive; DOS; DTP; E–Mail; Fax; Floppy; Hard Disk; Icon; Laptop; Mainframe; Megahertz (MHg); Memory; Menu; Microprocessor; Modem; Mouse; RAM; ROM; Scanner; Software; Spreadsheet; Terminal; VDU; Virus; Word processor.

If you take this test and do not do well, we strongly recommend that you should invest in a basic course in computing which will introduce you to the basic use of word processors, databases and spreadsheets.

Activity 13 Individual Learning: Imaginative Thinking

Criminal attack

In an organization with which you are familiar, ask 'to what kind of criminal attack is your computer system most vulnerable?' What defences could be introduced?

Activity 14 Individual Learning: Analytical Thinking

Designing information systems

Use a conversational approach to design, redesign or suggest improvements to the information systems in use in any public service with which you are familiar. Work through the approach outlined in Box 12.7.

Activity 15 Individual Learning Review: Reflective Thinking

Inner world thinking

What inner world thinking skills can you identify in the manager's work described in this chapter? Have any of the thinking skills you have identified emerged for the first time in this chapter? If so, add them to your accumulating model of the kinds of thinking skills that you think are useful to managers of public services.

What things could you do to develop any of the thinking skills that you have just added to your model? What would be the first step?

Outer world conversations

What outer world conversational skills can you identify in the manager's work described in this chapter? Have any of the types of conversational skills you have identified emerged for the first time? If so, add them to your accumulating model of the kinds of conversational skills you think are useful to managers of public services.

What things could you do to develop any of these conversational skills which you have just added to your model? What would be the first step?

Activity 16 Individual Learning: Metacognitive Thinking

Metacognition

Look back through the Thinking and Learning Activities you have been asked to carry out in this chapter. What thinking skills were involved in each of these activities? For each type of thinking, write down how you were learning what you were learning, when you were learning to think in each of the different ways.

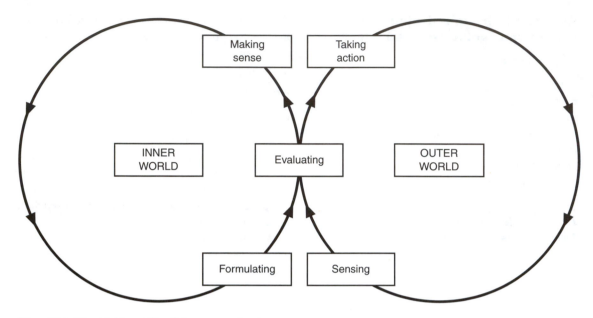

Figure 12.9 The thinking skills of the conversational manager

NOTES

1 'A Revolution in Interaction', *Marketing Quarterly*, vol. 1 (1997), p. 2.

2 World Telecommunications Development Report (1994) ITU, p. 87.

3 Cairncross, F. (1997) *The Death of Distance*. Orion Books, p. 87.

4 Ibid., p. 80.

5 Janner, G. (1998) *Janner's Complete Speechmaker*. Century.

6 Etzioni, A. (1997) *The New Golden Rule. Community and Morality in a Democratic Society*. Profile.

7 For material on public relations, the authors are indebted to Ann Turner, Jo Wilkes and Rosemary Graham of the Lancashire Business School, Dept of Journalism in Preston; David Wragg, press consultant to the Institute of Public Relations; Michael Bland, corporate communications and media consultant to the Institute of Public Relations; and Allison Teaker of Leeds Metropolitan University.

8 See Bland, M. and Wragg, D. (1997) *Effective Media Relations*. Kogan Page. Belsey, A. and Chadwick, R. (eds) (1992) *Ethical Issues in Journalism and the Media*. Kogan Page.

9 Isaac-Henry, K. *et al*. (1993) *Management in the Public Sector. Challenge and Change*. Chapman & Hall, p. 95.

10 Ibid., p. 95.

11 Buchanan, D. and Boddy, D. (1993) *The Expertise of the Change Agent. Public Performance and Backstage Activity*. Prentice Hall, p. 3.

12 Kearney, R. M. (1990) *Barriers to Successful Application of IT*. DTI CIMA. London.

13 Isaac-Henry *et al.*, op. cit., p. 99.

14 Sir Ian Bancroft, House of Commons. Nov. 1991. Evidence.

15 Dennis, Pootheri and Natarajan (1998) 'Early Adopters of Web Groupware'. *Journal of Management Information Systems*. Spring, vol. 14, pp. 65–86.

16 Gates, B. (1998) 'The Web Lifestyle. The World in 1998'. *The Economist*. Feb., p. 118.

17 Cairncross, op. cit., p. 91.

18 Kehoe, L. (1996) *Financial Times*. 3 July.

19 Handy, C. (1993) *The Age of Unreason*. Hutchinson.

20 Cairncross, op. cit., p. 84.

21 Drucker, P. (1993) *Post Capitalist Society*. Butterworth.

22 Remenzi, White and Sherwood-Smith (1997) *International Journal of Information Management*, vol. 17, no. 6.

23 Currie, P. (1991) 'Does the IT Department Have a Future?' *Computer Weekly*. 25 July.

24 Pidd, M. (1996) *Tools for Thinking. Modelling in Management Science*. Wiley.

25 Osborne (1957) *Applied Imagination*. Scribner & Sons.

26 Taylor, D., Berry, P. C. and Bloch, C. H. (1958) 'Does Group Participation When Using Brainstorming Techniques Facilitate or Inhibit Creative Thinking?'. *Administrative Science Quarterly*, vol. 3, pp. 23–47.

27 Magin, B. K. and Harris, R. J. (1980) 'Effects of Anticipated Evaluation on Individual Brainstorming Performance', *Journal of Applied Psychology*, vol. 65, no. 2, pp. 219–25.

28 Furnham, A. (1997) *The Psychology of Behaviour at Work – the Individual in the Organisation*. Psychology Press, p. 494.

29 Gallupe, R. W., Cooper, M. L., Grise, L. and Bastianatti, L. (1994) 'Blocking Electronic Brainstorming', *Journal of Applied Psychology*, vol. 79, pp. 77–80.

30 Blanchard, K. and Peale, N. V. (1998) *The Power of Ethical Management*. Fawcett Crest.

31 Simon, H. A. (1976) *Models of Bounded Rationality: Behaviour, Economics and Business Organisation*. MIT Press.

32 Mintzberg, H. (1976) 'Planning on the Left Side and Managing on the Right', *Harvard Business Review*, vol. 54, pp. 51–63.

33 Pidd, op. cit., p. 62.

34 Isaac Renington (1828) cited in John Bailey (ed.) (1884) *Letters to Isaac Renington*. 3rd edition, pp. 39–40 XVI and in *Quaker Faith and Practice* (1995). Published by the Yearly Meeting of the Religious Society of Friends (Quakers) in Britain.

35 Toffler, A. (1990) *Powershift: Knowledge, Wealth and Violence at the Edge of the 21st Century*. Bantam Press.

36 Ikujiro Nonaka (1994) 'A Dynamic Theory of Organizational Knowledge Creation'. *Organisation Science*, vol. 5, no. 1, p. 15.

37 Ibid.

38 Amidon, D. A. and Skyrme, D. J. (1992) 'Harnessing Knowledge through Socio-technological Fusion'. 12th Annual Conference, Strategic Society. London.

39 Polanyi, M. (1966) *The Tacit Dimension*. Routledge & Kegan Paul.

ROLE SIX

MANAGING LEARNING AND PERSONAL DEVELOPMENT

Increasingly, public service organizations are using learning and personal development programmes as a means of achieving change, enhancing motivation and improving performance. In Chapter 1 we explored the view that bureaucratic organizations under-utilize the intelligence of their employees. According to Heckscher and Donnellon,[1] bureaucratic organizations emphasized the role of a small elite who were portrayed as the brain that sat at the head of the organization – the fount of all knowledge. Employees were expected to follow instructions; they were not expected to think for themselves. But we saw also that third-wave, post-bureaucratic organizations were emerging. These organizations aimed to develop empowered employees who responded rapidly to changing circumstances, and who took the initiative to resolve problems and improve performance. One of the keys to developing responsive, third-wave organizations is employee learning and personal development. Third-wave post bureaucratic organizations are often more rhetoric than reality. Their strategies for learning and personal development are flawed and impractical. In this section we explore how and why people learn; how people learn to think differently; how people learn to think well. How do managers become competent? How do they become agents of their own learning? How can managers enable others to learn and develop? These questions are asked and answered in Chapters 13 and 14.

13

MANAGING LEARNING IN PUBLIC SERVICES

What we have to learn to do we learn through doing.
(Aristotle 384–322 BC *Nicomachean Ethics*, Book II)

LEARNING OUTCOMES

This chapter will enable the reader to:

- Analyse the competencies of high-performing managers and understand why managers need to manage their own learning and the learning of others.
- Consider how management competence and the ability to manage learning can be developed.
- Explore approaches to learning.
- Identify the theoretical flaws and the practical defects of group-based learning and of experiential learning.
- Understand how learning conversations can be used to remedy the deficiencies in experiential learning based on Kolb's model.
- Develop learning organizations.
- Design, deliver and evaluate learning events for others.
- Evaluate practical ways in which work-based learning can be implemented.
- Understand how managers can have coaching and mentoring conversations.
- Explore the tension between learning from mistakes and being accountable.

INTRODUCTION

Throughout the world, public service managers are increasingly required to ensure that their employees continue to learn while at work. Learning is no longer the preserve of education systems. Companies, consultants and publicly funded agencies are offering a wide variety of services to help managers to develop the learning capability of their employees. In some countries a plethora of funding opportunities exist to promote 'lifelong learning', and 'a learning society' to serve their 'knowledge-based economies'.

It is not sufficient that people are better educated or better trained. They need to be better at learning. They need to learn how to learn. The ability to learn and to enable others to learn is a core competence. It requires an extended repertoire of thinking skills. In short, managers need to think about learning and to learn about thinking.

In this chapter we analyse the competencies that public service managers need in order to manage change operations, people, finances, information, their own learning and the learning of others. We explore how these competencies can be developed and the limitations of different approaches. We trace the history of ideas about learning – cognitive, behavioural, humanist and experiential – and use these ideas as a framework for evaluating common approaches to workplace learning. We find that the many common and popular approaches to workplace learning are flawed, resulting in widespread waste of public funds, private investment and human potential. Alarm is raised at the ubiquitous spread into the workplace of group-based experiential approaches to learning. Advantages of group-based experiential approaches are seriously outweighed by the disadvantages which emerge from the evaluation. A conversational approach to learning can address the flaws which the evaluation reveals. In particular, a conversational approach to learning can be used to develop the wide range of transferable thinking skills which managers need to manage change at work. We offer a protocol of the types of conversations that engender learning and that extend people's thinking at work, at school or at play. The role of mentoring and coaching is explained.

In our Final Thoughts we ask how managers can manage the tension between the need to learn from mistakes and the need for employees to accept that they are accountable for the consequences of the mistakes they make. Through the Thinking and Learning Activities we provide opportunities for the reader to practise a conversational approach to workplace learning.

We look first at what managers need to learn — what are the competencies that high performing managers need?

THE COMPETENCE OF MANAGERS

Management competencies are attributes that enable managers to perform tasks to certain standards. Several writers have criticized this concept of competence. According to Handy,[2] for example, it can promote an unhealthy preoccupation with job skills and neglect the need for effective work performance. Managing is not the sequential exercise of individual competencies. Management is a holistic process. How, in any event, do you translate the competence of managers, as assessed against standards, into improved organizational performance? Management competencies must be developed and deployed in ways that are appropriate to changing circumstances, both inside and outside the organization.

Some public service managers perform certain tasks brilliantly by rote. In rapidly changing circumstances, managing by rote is not enough. In rapidly changing circumstances, the kind of competencies that would be of use include: listening and learning; recollection and reflection; prediction and imagination; creativity and empathy. A criticism that Burgoyne makes, is that lists of management competencies rarely include the ability to think ethically:

> If competency approaches are to become a main foundation for management development then ways must be found to expand them and to accommodate the moral and the ethical ... Competent management must involve engaging with and adjusting individual and organisational values.[3]

These views echo the need for ethical thinking which we discussed in Chapter 11. Without the personal competence that is needed to put functional competence into context, the value of functional competence is limited.

None the less, there is a demand from employers and employees for management qualifications that reflect the ability to *do* the job, as opposed to know about the job. Organizations want to know what competencies managers need so that they can recruit people who can *do* the job.

Beyond Competence:
On Becoming a High-performer

Schroder[4] conducted a nine-year research programme in the USA. This study has been replicated and extended in the UK. An important outcome of this research was that 11 attributes constituted a generalizable set of competencies which appeared to distinguish high-performing managers from average-performing managers. The identification of these 11 high-performing competencies (Box 13.1) was based not on career progression, but on identifiable contribution to the performance of the organizations that employed the managers.

Beyond Competence:
On Becoming a Senior Manager

Further research by Kakabadse,[5] based on more than 1,000 senior managers in 740 organizations, identified the competencies needed by senior managers. These included: questioning, listening and learning; recollection and reflection; prediction and imagination; creativity and empathy. Boyatzis[6] described two levels of competence – threshold and superior. To have threshold competency is to have the generic knowledge, motivation, traits, self-image, social roles and skills that are essential to carrying out existing tasks competently. Superior competencies are those needed to be a high performer. Hay recruitment consultancy still seeks many of the original

Boyatzis competencies in candidates for senior posts. Over and above threshold competence, the capabilities that Hay claim lead to superior performance are critical thinking, the ability to make sense of information and extract general principles from it, and the ability to formulate ideas. In addition, Hay look for the ability to persuade, to influence, to create impact and to sense what is going on. Hay's 'customer service orientation' points to the need for empathetic thinking and the ability to create close working relationships.

Beyond Competence: On Becoming a High-performing Senior Manager

Klemp[7] furthered the debate by describing six studies and identifying eight superior performance competencies for senior managers: imaginative and creative thinking; critical thinking; formulation of ideas and concepts; ability to think and learn collaboratively; ability to persuade and influence; ability to communicate with impact; ability to interpret symbolic meanings; and high self-esteem. Klemp claimed that the top-performing senior managers were characterized by the use of cognitive strategies. They mapped a wide area surrounding problem situations, before defining the problem. They usually involved others in the appraising and weighing of options. Such managers saw the goal of thinking as the taking of action in order to influence events in the world.

Box 13.1

HIGH PERFORMANCE COMPETENCIES

Cognitive Competencies
- Information search
- Concept formation
- Conceptual flexibility

Motivating Competencies
- Interpersonal search
- Managing information
- Development orientation

Directing Competencies
- Self-confidence
- Presentation
- Concern for impact

Achieving Competencies
- Proactive orientation
- Achievement orientation

Management Mindsets

Morgan[8] argued that there was a need for managers with 'mindsets' that allowed them to confront, think about and take action on a wide range of issues within and outside their organizations (Box 13.2). Cockerell[9] carried out research on Schroder's eleven competencies and concluded that there was a significant correlation between the presence of high performance competencies in the senior management of an organization and the long term performance of the organizations they were managing.

In summary it appears that threshold competencies can largely be developed through input. High-level or 'superior' competencies are based on a commonly recurring set of thinking and conversational skills. The development of these thinking skills and conversational skills holds out the prospect of moving beyond competence to high performance and we should be concerned with achieving a performance that is beyond competence. Privately owned public service organizations need to outperform organizations with which they compete. They expect a performance from their managers that gives them a competitive advantage, not compliance with a national standard. Publicly owned public service organizations often compete for funding, or put in competitive bids for limited public resources (Chapter 10). Often they vie for public support and ultimately compete for political support (Chapter 8). Sometimes they are forced to put their services out to competitive tender (Chapter 4). Some public services may be required to defend a continuance of their monopoly by showing that their performance exceeds 'benchmarks' provided by comparable organizations in other countries. They may be required to do this by a regulatory body or by an inspectorate (Chapter 11). If their performance is not as high as the 'benchmarks' set by others (Chapter 5), it will be futile to protest that their managers are competent to national standards. The knowledge of the workers and the learning skills of learners are valuable assets of any public service organization. The ability to change and to respond to threats and opportunities requires employees who can learn quickly in the workplace. Everything points to the need for managers to learn about learning.

Why Managers Need to Learn about Learning

Managers in public services are increasingly required to act as coaches and mentors and to ensure that employees develop the knowledge and understanding that underpin a broad range of competencies. Managers have to evaluate the claims of external organizations which offer to run training events for their staff. They are expected to keep themselves learning, growing and developing. In order to choose between the learning programmes on offer for themselves and for their staff, managers need to understand something about learning generally. In particular, they need to understand the possibilities and the limitations of learning in the workplace. For these reasons, we will spend some time looking at the theory of learning.

Thinking and Learning at Work

Ann Widdecombe, former UK Parliamentary Under Secretary of State, introducing the 1994 research

---

Box 13.2

THE MORGAN MINDSET MODEL OF MANAGEMENT

- Proactivity in the implementation of change (Chapters 2 and 3)
- Reading the environment (Chapters 1, 4)
- Leadership and vision (Chapter 7)
- Human resource management (Chapter 8)
- Using information technology (Chapter 12)
- Creativity and learning (Chapters 13, 14)
- Managing complexity (Chapters 2, 3, 15)

report *Thinking and Learning at Work*,[10] said: 'These days employees at every level need to be workers, learners and managers.' In this context, learning involved the acquisition of new skills, knowledge and concepts. The report concluded that most learning, whether it took place inside or outside organizations, was superficial. They discovered that its value perished rapidly, unless the learning process was well designed and well managed. Clearly managers need to know not only about the theory of learning but also about the process of designing and managing learning. The research revealed a common and unjustified assumption that learning would transfer automatically from one context to another, e.g. from college to workplace, or from inside the workplace to outside the workplace, or from one place of work to another place of work. According to the report, the ability to transfer learning cannot be assumed. The researchers discovered that transfer of learning did not take place unless learners were specifically trained in how to transfer learning.

The Need for Explicit Thinking Skills

Much of our everyday existence is conducted on automatic pilot. Getting through the day on automatic pilot can result in unconscious incompetence. Unless this incompetence is surfaced and made conscious, it is hard to make progress. Unconscious incompetence can be particularly acute when we need to learn to think differently, e.g. when a situation changes. The *Thinking and Learning at Work*[10] report concluded that getting systematic control over thought processes was fundamental to improving our ability to learn and to transfer our learning from one context to another. The report highlighted the need for learning activities that prompt the learner to be more thoughtful, more conscious of exact detail, more inclined to reflect, and more able to formulate plans. Learning what to do should involve questions about *how* to think about what to do. The prior education of many learners, the research concluded, did not equip them with the appropriate thinking skills or strategies. Typically, we have found that learners are impulsive. They

begin tasks before they understand them and they close off their thinking prematurely. Consequently, they draw conclusions that are false and exclude options that it would be profitable to explore. Trainers and educators need to work together to devise new learning activities in which the learner feels safe to explore ideas. The tasks set should be multilayered and multi-faceted. Learners must be encouraged to both pose and answer questions. Where problems are presented to learners, the problems should be ill-defined, providing learners with the opportunity to grapple with ambiguity and to identify the key issues for themselves. Learners need a lot of time to work things out, to puzzle over mistakes, and to evaluate their thinking as well as their performance. As we shall see later in this chapter, the use of learning conversations, in the workplace or in schools, colleges or universities, would address most of the concerns raised in the 1993 research on *Thinking and Learning at Work*. First we consider the concept of the learning organization as a vehicle for workplace learning.

Learning Organizations

There is no universally accepted definition of a learning organization and there are few models that help with the practical task of building one. We do not think that organizations learn, though individuals within them might. Pedler, Burgoyne and Boydell have been influential in developing the concept of the learning organization as an organization that facilitates the learning of all its members and continuously transforms itself. (Box 13.3).[11]

Other definitions of 'learning organizations' emphasize the link between learning and doing things differently. Garvin offers the following definition: 'A learning organisation is an organisation skilled at creating, acquiring and transferring knowledge and at modifying its behavior to reflect new knowledge and insights.'[12]

Pettigrew and Whipp[13] attempted to link adaptation through learning to improved organizational performance. They suggested that learning was the key to competitive success and survival. They saw

Box 13.3

THE CHARACTERISTICS OF A LEARNING ORGANIZATION

- Participative policy making: everybody is involved in policy development
- Intra-company learning: people from different teams learn to improve each other's performance
- A learning climate, characterized by experimentation and reflection on experience
- All managers can facilitate experimentation and the reflection
- Self-development opportunities are available to all

the role of knowledge as paramount in creating differential advantage for organizations. Unfortunately, Pettigrew took for granted the will, the skill, the tolerance to risk and the emotional resilience needed to convert knowledge into action. We do not think that will, skill, resilience and risk-taking can be taken for granted. Senge linked learning to motivation: 'The organisation that will truly excel in the future will be the organisation that discovers how to tap people's commitment and capacity to learn.'[14]

In 1994 Beardwell and Holden[15] argued that in order to meet the challenges of quality, continuous improvement, flexibility and adaptability, organizations needed to demand more of their employees than new or enhanced job skills. Beardwell and Holden stress the need for all employees to learn how to develop closer working relationships, to learn how to learn and to learn how to think. They stress the importance of managers being able not only to learn themselves, but also design and manage high-level social and cognitive development in their staff. We welcome their description of a learning organization as an organization in which people can learn to develop closer working relationships, high-order conversational skills and high-order thinking skills. Pedler[16] and his colleagues admit that creating such

an organization is easier said than done. Before we can evaluate some of the practical ways in which this has been attempted, we need to develop a shared understanding of what is meant by learning.

WHAT IS LEARNING?

Ranson and Stewart[17] claim that public service managers must build learning organizations that serve as vehicles for developing a learning society. Without some shared understanding of what is meant by learning, it is not possible to work out how workplace learning can be engendered at all, let alone a learning organization be developed as a vehicle for a 'learning society'. According to Senge, a propensity to learn comes naturally to human beings.

> No one has to teach an infant to learn. In fact, no one has to teach infants anything. They are intrinsically inquisitive, masterful learners. Learning organisations are possible because not only is it our nature to learn but we love to learn.[18]

Unfortunately, Senge offers scant support for his assumption that this childhood love of learning survives into adulthood. Honey[19] suggests that adult learning is more problematic. Most organizations, he says, are unwittingly designed to encourage people to learn unwanted behaviours and practices (see Table 13.1).

Finger and Brand[20] found that the first and the most important step in improving the performance of the Swiss postal service was 'unlearning' unwanted behaviour. They recognized a need to unlearn a dominant administrative and bureaucratic way of doing things. These were great obstacles because they

Table 13.1 Learning – Wanted and unwanted behaviours

Wanted behaviours	Unwanted behaviours
Taking risks	Being cautious
Asking questions	Acquiescing
Suggesting ideas	Rubbishing ideas
Learning from mistakes	Repeating mistakes
Reflecting and reviewing	Rushing around and not thinking

Table 13.2 Blocks to adult learning

Label	Example
Physical	Place, time
Emotional	Fear of insecurity
Situational	Lack of opportunities
Cognitive	Limited learning styles
Expressive	Poor communication skills
Motivational	Lack of willingness to take risks
Perceptual	Not seeing that there is a problem
Intellectual	Limited repertoire of ways of thinking
Cultural	'The way we do things around here is . . .'
Specific	Manager unskilled in learning

generated subservience, fear of risk, perfectionism, fear of conflict and linear thinking.[21] They concluded that a way of transforming public service organizations was through collective learning. This poses many problems. While learning may be natural, some people's experience of learning — at school for instance — is not always a happy one. This may make them reluctant, anxious or unconfident learners. Mumford[22] identified significant blocks to adult learning (Table 13.2).

THEORIES ABOUT LEARNING

Lewin[23] said that there was nothing so practical as a good theory. In 1995 the centre of gravity of predictors of organizational success moved from the exploitation of physical assets to the exploitation of creative thinking and learning. Education and training were no longer just a discretionary means of disposing of unwanted surplus income. Education and training had become a means of survival, as well as a necessary investment in success.

Philosophers have been thinking about the nature of learning for more than 2,000 years. Their theories of learning fall into four main groupings: cognitive (thinking), behavioural (doing), humanist (as above, but including feelings and a social dimension) and experiential (learning through doing, thereby combining the cognitive and the behavioural approaches).

- **Cognitive learning** is inner world learning. It assumes that you can become positive and accurate about the outer world simply by thinking rationally about it.

- **Behavioural learning** is outer world learning. It involves acquiring knowledge about how to *do* things in the outer world. Like cognitive learning, it also assumes that you can be positive about the outer world, but this time through direct observation of what happens when you do things in the outer world. Information acquired through direct observations is empirical data.

- **The humanist approach** to learning involves elements of the cognitive and the behavioural approaches but adds a feeling dimension and a social dimension to learning. It rests on quite different assumptions about learners and the world they inhabit. In the humanist approach, learning is seen as the process of making actual that which is already potential in the learner. The process is sometimes called self-actualization. The learner is the person who achieves this through a feelings-based process of discovery and experimentation. The role of the 'teacher' is to act as a facilitator — an enabler of learning. Frequently this involves offering the learner 'unconditional positive regard' (Chapter 8). Ideas are generated and modified through social interaction.

- **Experiential learning** also combines cognitive and behavioural learning but the contribution of humanist ideas is largely ignored in experiential 'learning cycles' advocated by David Kolb (Figure 13.1),[24] Mumford[25] and others. Important features of John Dewey's original work on experiential learning are also ignored. Reg Revans[26] and others have incorporated humanist constructs of emotional and social learning into their use of experiential learning in groups called action learning sets. Unfortunately, as we discovered in Chapter 6, many of the thinking skills that individuals need in order to process their actions into learning are severely disabled in a group setting.

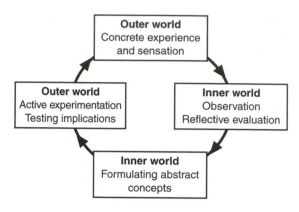

Figure 13.1 The Kolb experiential learning cycle

In order to understand why these experiential models are deficient and how these difficulties can be made good by the use of learning conversations, we review the theories that underpin our ideas about how individuals learn.

THEORIES THAT UNDERPIN IDEAS ABOUT LEARNING

We start with the Greeks – Socrates and his pupil Plato and his pupil Aristotle. Between them, they provided the basic building blocks of the cognitive inner world thinking approach and the behavioural outer world doing approach. We look at the way their ideas have been developed by philosophers down the centuries – philosophers like Descartes, Bacon, Locke, Kant and Hegel. The next fruitful source of building blocks are provided by psychologists, such as Pavlov, Thorndyke, Skinner, Lewin and Piaget. Dewey and Kolb used many of these earlier ideas as building blocks for their theories on reflective learning and experiential learning. From the 1920s onwards, ideas on experiential learning were in turn the focus of work by Freire, Argyris, Schon, Habermas and Kemmis.

By the 1990s, commentators like Jarvis, Johnston, Boud and Wildemeersch had begun to articulate our own doubts about the assumption that learners in general can think reflectively – a key requirement for being able to get around a 'learning cycle'. Others, like Senge, began to pick up the ideas of humanists like Carl Rogers and Bandura and search for ways of developing emotional motivation and empathetic thinking, through one-to-one dialogues in close supportive relationships. By the 1990s, we had developed the use of learning conversations. Learning conversations not only follow the line of our conversational approach to management, they also develop many of the cognitive and social skills that managers need in order to adopt a conversational approach to management.

Workplace Learning: Learning from Experience

The economic pressure on governments to produce a 'learning society' turns up in public services as a pressure on managers to play their part by ensuring that they and their employees engage in 'lifelong learning'. We need a model for learning in the workplace which will help individuals to adapt their existing knowledge and skills as their situations change and which will increase their capacity for learning and thinking. A Conversational Approach to Learning does both. A Conversational Approach to Learning addresses the main deficiencies of the Kolb learning cycle and the main disadvantages of group-based learning.

Learning Conversations: A Conversational Approach to Learning

In the following conversation (Box 13.4) the authors discuss the background to learning conversations and explain how learning conversations – which involve a learner and a critical friend and a coach – can operate in the workplace (or in any other learning situation).

Box 13.4

A CONVERSATION WITH TERRY HORNE

(Director of Masters Programmes in Change Management at the University of Central Lancashire, UK):

'THINKING ABOUT LEARNING ABOUT THINKING'

Tony: Where did your ideas about conversational management come from?

Terry: I started developing a conversational approach to implementing changes in local government, during the reorganization of local government in 1974. In the 1980s, I refined it in health services in the UK and overseas through the Crown Agent Programme. I have used it since 1994 on taught undergraduate and postgraduate programmes. We have evaluation data going back to 1994.

Tony: Why did you develop the idea?

Terry: I noticed that many people had difficulty thinking, let alone learning, in groups. Group work improved the speed and fluency with which students used strengths that they had already, but it rarely developed abilities which they did not have already. Groups provided a good place for people to show off existing skills and to improve their performance with practice. However, groups were not so good at developing thinking capacity. I was interested in how to increase potential as well as how to improve performance.

Tony: So what is a learning conversation?

Terry: A learning conversation is a one-to-one conversation between pairs of people. The pairs can have three different types of conversation.

Tony: What actually happens?

Terry: A learner John, say, has a conversation with a second learner, Jane, say. Jane gets John to remember and describe very accurately an outer world experience – something that has happened, usually at work. So it's something that happened in the past. John has to describe in detail what he thought and felt, as well as what he saw and heard. Jane makes a written record of what John says. She takes it down as if it were going to be used in evidence in a court of law. Jane then brings John to the present time and shows him what she has written down. She asks John to reflect on what he thinks and feels *now*, looking at the written record of what happened *then*. Jane then gets John to envisage an imaginary situation in the future. The situation should have something in common with the experience which John has just recounted – perhaps a similar process, similar task or similar group of people. John will be pressed to use the reflections he has just made to justify actions he would take in the imagined future situation. John is in effect testing, in his inner world, the practicality and consequences of the actions that he is contemplating taking.

Tony: So far, I can see that the learner John has been required to think recollectively about a past experience, reflectively in the present and predictively about some future imaginary situation. Looking at your diagram, what is empathetic thinking?

Terry: That comes next. Jane now thinks aloud about what *she* would have learned, if she had been in John's shoes. She records *what* she would have learned in John's shoes and notes at what point and *how* she would have learned those things.

Tony: So far the first learner, John, has had to use recollective, reflective and predictive thinking. The second learner, Jane, has used empathetic thinking. What about the critical thinking and evaluation that is shown on your model?

Terry: This is where another type of learning

conversation comes in. It is a learning conversation with a 'critical friend' – let's call him Jack. Jane's written record can be used as the subject of a one-to-one conversation with a third learner, Jack – called a 'critical friend'. Every learner should have a critical friend and every learner should be a critical friend. The task of a critical friend in a learning conversation is to give feedback on the quality of recollective observations, the insightfulness of reflections, and the practicality of suggested transfers of learning into future situations. Omissions, poor reasoning or false inferences are pointed out and a revised written record is agreed. This revised record accommodates or rejects the feedback from the critical friend. If feedback from the critical friend is rejected, good reasons for rejection must be recorded. Besides commenting on the written record, Jack, the critical friend, can also comments on Jane's developing skill as a thinking coach i.e. on process as well as content.

Tony: You said that learners can use three different types of learning conversation?

Terry: Yes I did. Firstly, learners, as John, talk about their work experience or an incident or a learning event. They do it recollectively, reflectively and projectively. That's one type of learning conversation. Secondly, learners, as Jane, can coach a learner who is trying to recollect, reflect and project and to make a written record of their own empathetic learning. That's the second type of learning conversation they can have, when they are acting as a coach. Thirdly, the learners have to have learning conversations in which they are the critical friend of another learner – like Jack was – offering positive feedback, critiquing the reasoning, suggesting improvements, making assessments and agreeing action plans. That's the third type of learning conversation. All learners can rotate through all three roles – reflective learner, thinking coach and critical friend – that's how they come to experience three quite different types of learning conversation, involving at least six quite different ways of thinking.

Tony: It sounds complicated.

Terry: It is and that's what makes it a good preparation for life and for work! It is multi-layered and multi-faceted. It is simultaneously social, cognitive and metacognitive.

Tony: Isn't it too complicated for the learners?

Terry: No. I'm always astonished and delighted at how quickly the learning conversations themselves help the learners to cope with complex situations – enabling them to ask and answer complex, multi-faceted questions – the sort of questions that would face them everyday as senior managers. The sort of questions that would face them everyday as lifelong learners.

Tony: Thank you.

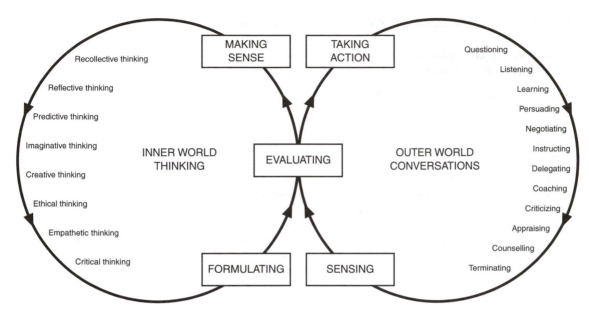

Figure 13.2 The conversational manager

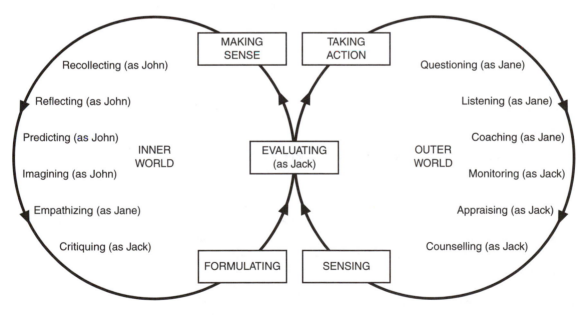

Figure 13.3 A learning conversation

LEARNING CONVERSATIONS

Asking Right Questions
Questioning Right Answers

Socrates bequeathed us his emphasis on seeking questions and questioning answers. Learners do both these things when they act as a thinking coach and when they act as a critical friend. Their main task is to ask helpful questions. This is good preparation for senior management posts. For senior managers, the ability to ask the right questions can be more important than the ability to know the right answers. Junior managers and trainees may need to bear in mind that Socrates is rumoured to have been poisoned because of the awkward questions he was asking! In organizations where the culture is suspicious and insecure, a conversational approach to developing close relationships may need to precede the use of learning conversations, if you are to avoid being stabbed in the back! (See Chapter 8.)

A Critical Friend

Perhaps in an act of self-preservation, Socrates' pupil, Plato warned his own disciples of the dangers of being a questioning critic. He suggested, instead, that they became authorities and teachers. Plato's cognitive approach stressed the useful role of the rational mind in trying to make sense of reality. This is reflected in the basic structure of our conversational model which is characterized by a dynamic relationship between an individual's inner mental world and outer social world. Plato saw thinking as a rational process which involved surfacing and challenging assumptions and using logic to test the reasoning that was used to draw conclusions based on the surfaced assumptions. In our learning conversations, learners subject their inner world reflections to critical evaluation in their inner world, before they formulate plans of action, or formulate questions to ask in their outer world (Figure 13.5).

If you have agreed to reverse roles to give the other person an opportunity to practise their conversational skills as a 'critical friend', then as the 'reflective learner' you could practise the conversational moves in Box 13.6.

Box 13.5

CONVERSATIONAL MOVES FOR 'CRITICAL FRIENDS'

- How is . . . consistent with . . . ?
- How are you able to prove that?
- How is this any different from . . . ?
- Can you explain the relevance of . . . ?
- Do you have evidence to support that?
- How is that connected with what you just said?
- I accept X, what does not seem to follow is . . .
- How do you see that as connected with the original situation?
- You seem very certain of that, can you help me to understand why?

- Can you think of another way to think about that experience?
- Earlier you said X. Can you help me to understand why you now say Y?
- Can you give me a concrete example of how it might work out in practice?
- I have lost the thread, how does that connect to what you were just saying?
- You may be right but I don't quite follow how you got there, please explain.
- What would have to happen before you would reconsider your point of view?

Box 13.6

CONVERSATIONAL MOVES FOR 'REFLECTIVE LEARNERS'

- I always assume that . . .
- I came to this conclusion because . . .
- What do you think about what I have said?
- Is there anything wrong with my reasoning?
- Is there anything you could add to my analysis?
- Here is what I think and here is how I came to think it . . .

- Can you see anything wrong with what I have said so far?
- There is one aspect I would like you to help me think through . . .
- To really understand what it's like for me, try to imagine that you were . . .

A Thinking Coach

In learning conversations in which individuals play the role of 'thinking coach' (Jane in Figure 13.3), the thinking processes they use are similar to those favoured by Socrates. When in the role of 'critical friend' (Jack in Figure 13.3), the approach is more similar to that favoured by Plato. When in a learning conversation as 'reflector' (John in Figure 13.3), the ideas of Aristotle are helpful. Plato's pupil, Aristotle, argued for a more empirical approach. He took as the starting point for his inner world rational thinking, objective observation of what was actually happening in the outer world. He stressed the crucial role of accurate 'sensing' – especially seeing and hearing and describing in detail – as a precursor to the development of inner world ideas. Our conversational model includes these separate activities of 'sensing' and 'making sense'. Useful conversational moves for 'thinking coaches' are found in Box 13.7.

If you have agreed to reverse roles to give the other person an opportunity to practise conversational skills for 'thinking coaches', as the 'reflective learner' you could practise conversational moves as set out in Box 13.6.

Sensing and Making Sense

However, we should not limit ourselves to rational thinking as a way of 'making sense'. Neither should we limit our observations to what individuals see and hear. We include what is thought and felt. Aristotle encouraged individuals to recollect earlier experiences that were similar to the experiences on which they were reflecting. He encouraged them to search their minds for things which they associated with past experiences. The subsequent writings of Bacon (1561–1626) and Descartes (1596–1650) tended to restore the primacy of rational inner world thinking, but Locke (1632–1704) revalidated the dual role of observing the outer world and then reflecting on the observations in one's inner world.

Intuition and Action: Shaping the World

By the middle of the eighteenth century, Kant (1724–1804) had argued that intuition, as well as rational thought, could be used to enrich the process of attaching meaning and 'making sense' of what the observer sensed in the outer world. In 1807 Hegel added a further dimension. In the 'Phenomenology of the Spirit', Hegel asserted that true knowledge about the outer world was only available to those who deliberately – and in a self-aware way – tried to intervene in the outer world and who did so in order to try to shape it. Hegel's ideas are reflected in our conversational model which emphasizes the importance of 'taking action' in the outer world, based on

---

Box 13.7

CONVERSATIONAL MOVES FOR 'THINKING COACHES'

- My concern is . . .
- Why do you say that?
- What do you mean by?
- How would that affect . . . ?
- What can we agree on . . . ?
- What leads you to think that?
- How can you be sure about that?
- I'm sorry I didn't quite follow that.
- OK, so where does that lead us to next?
- What assumptions are we making here?
- Can you just take me through that again?
- Maybe you know something that I don't?

- Have you considered the possibility that . . . ?
- Am I correct that what you are saying is . . . ?
- Can we agree what we know to be the case?
- We appear to have two separate ideas here.
- When you said XYZ, you seemed . . . (state the emotion).
- Is it possible to investigate any of these things?
- You seem to be starting from quite different assumptions, what are they?
- What do we both suspect may be the case, though neither of us can prove it?

---

our inner world thinking, and using the 'action' phase to 'sense' more information about an outer world. In 'making sense' of this new information, our thinking and learning cycle begins once more. If you really want to learn about the world, take action to try and change it! (See Chapter 3.)

Stimulus–Response: Learning through Feedback

In the late nineteenth century, experimental stimulus–response psychology shifted the emphasis firmly back into the outer world. 'Taking action' provided a behavioural 'stimulus' and 'sensing' detected the 'response'. If the evaluation of the response led to a modification of the initial actions, then, according to psychologists like Pavlov and Skinner,[27] learning had occurred. In a slight variation of this stimulus–response learning, Thorndyke explored the idea that learning occurred through a process of trial and error. In stimulus–response learning, the learning manifests itself in outer world behaviour without recourse to thinking. In 1896, in his book *The Reflex Arc Concept of Psychology*, John Dewey began a lifelong fight against the stimulus–response model of learning.

Whose Learning?

Dewey argued that the *purpose* of learning was being overlooked by the stimulus–response psychologists. In a series of publications in 1916 (*Democracy and Education*), and 1938 (*Experience and Education*) and 1946 (*The Philosophy of Education*). Dewey paved the way for the idea of learning from experience. Dewey was concerned then, as we are now, that education and learning might become a means to serve and perpetuate vested interests, rather than a means of giving students the tools to think for themselves.

Thinking for Yourself, as Another: Empathetic Thinking

Dewey thought that this separation of the intellectual from the practical – of inner world thoughts from outer world actions – was the mark of a 'feudal age'. Dewey called for a model of learning that incorporated inner world awareness of the outer world consequences of inner world ideas. It was a plea for the ability to think empathetically – as though you were the person affected by the change. It was a plea to which we responded by adding empathetic thinking to the inner world thinking skills involved in our conversational approach.

Kolb's Mistake

The emotional and motivational dimensions of learning were omitted by David Kolb when he used Dewey's work as the basis of his model of experiential learning. We think that this was a mistake. The Kolb learning cycle does not necessarily involve another person, so there is no outer world challenge to inner world thinking – no challenging of the assumptions, logic or conclusions. No offering of other options and possibilities; no feedback about inconsistencies or failures to take all the information into account. We think that is a major deficiency. Likewise there is no social learning[28] and no social 'applause' to motivate the learner. Nothing to give the learner the energy needed to get round the cycle (Figure 13.4). This was a serious omission.

Kolb's cycle breaks down if any one of the four sequential activities cannot be performed. Each is vulnerable for the reasons italicized in Figure 13.4. The likelihood that any one learner is good enough at all four stages is too low for Kolb's model to justify the common assumption that learners can profit from workplace learning, if only they are given the opportunity to reflect upon it. This false assumption wastes millions of pounds every year that would

be better spent on more effective approaches to learning in the workplace (see later).

A Conversational Approach to Double Loop Learning

Learning conversations address not only the need to learn, but also the need to increase one's skill and capacity for learning (metacognition). This is a concern taken up later by Argyris and Schon[29] who argued for the need for a second learning loop. We think that these concerns are better met by twisting the existing Kolb loop along the axes shown in Figure 13.4. This produces the basic structure for our conversational learning. Clearly, it rests on the same cognitive and empirical credentials as Kolb's cycle but, because the conversational model has two loops which can be used separately, it reduces the number of skills and attributes that a learner needs in order to be able to complete a cycle – either an inner world cycle or an outer world cycle. When the contributory thinking skills and social skills have been separately practised and developed, the two loops can be combined, so that the learner learns to move freely between their inner and outer worlds. If the ability to learn by observation, reflection, conceptualization and experimentation is very low, it is possible to use a conversational approach to separate the inner world and outer world cycles so that the

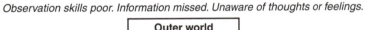

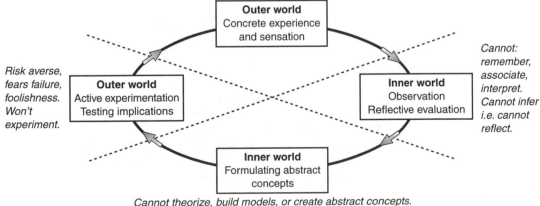

Figure 13.4 The problem with the Kolb learning cycle

knowledge and skill needed to complete an inner world loop can be developed separately from the knowledge and skill needed to complete an outer world loop. In a Kolb learning cycle, the cycle breaks down completely if one of its necessary skills is absent. In a learning conversation, the learner is supported by a ' thinking coach' or 'critical friend' who can help them to complete the learning cycle by using two smaller, separate loops. In the roles of 'thinking coach' and 'critical friend', the learners are developing the skills they need to complete their own learning loops. In a learning conversation, the learner is learning to postpone immediate reactions, to avoid premature closure and the temptation to take action impulsively. They learn to be patient, to wait until observations of the outer world have been clarified and an internal response has been formulated and critically evaluated.

The Kolb Model: Its Adverse Impact on Work-based Learning

During the 1980s, Kolb's model of experiential learning fuelled confidence that employees and placement students could process their workbased experience into learning through a sequential process of reflection, conceptualization and experimentation. As we have seen, this confidence is not supported by an analysis of the learning theories on which the model appears to be predicated. Nor is confidence in Kolbian learning supported by 20 years' experience of trying to get students to think reflectively about their experiences.

Kolb acknowledged the importance of psychologists like Piaget and Lewin. Yet Piaget's work led him to conclude that inner world cognitive structures can only be built up by processing physical and social sensations experienced in the outer world. While Lewin's work was in the Gestalt tradition, stressing the point that individuals must add something to their outer world experience in order for it to 'make sense' to them in their own 'inner world'. Gestalt ideas stress the need for learners to connect their experience to some greater whole. In learning conversations, learners are expected to generalize

from their particular experience to some wider truth – to see their particular experience as part of a larger picture. Depending on the experience that is being recollected and reflected upon, learners are encouraged to project their learning into their wider roles as managers, employees, partners, parent or 'active citizens'.

Knowledge of the Future

For Kolb,[30] learning is emergent and rooted in historical records. This places limitations on the usefulness of Kolb's model to managers or learners faced with an uncertain future. Managers need the thinking skills that will enable them to envisage the future and to rehearse the outcomes and consequences of possible future actions. We are encouraged in this view by Keteljohn[31] who, in an article for the *Financial Times* 'Mastering Management' series, asserted that 'tool boxes are out, thinking is in'. We agree with Keteljohn that management is not about a 'quick fix', no matter how powerful its tools. Management is about coaching people and helping them to learn to think for themselves, not just reflectively, but visually and creatively. Imagination and creativity are needed in situations where today's knowledge, based on yesterday's experience, might not be adequate for tomorrow. That is why learning conversations always involve the use of imagination and the use of predictive thinking skills.

The Naked Emperor

In 1994, Jarvis[32] confirmed what we had already discovered in the 1980s. Namely that, for the majority of potential learners, experience does not readily result in reflective learning. Kemmis[33] had discovered earlier that students find it very hard to reflect on their own. Teachers and trainers who found reflection relatively easy and fruitful for themselves, failed to see, or to admit, that the great majority of their students could not do it. They dug the same hole deeper and their students dutifully told the teachers and trainers what they, the students, were expected to have learned. When asked how they had learned it, their students dutifully said that they had learned it by reflecting on their experience. But our experience, confirmed by Kemmis and Jarvis, was that students were unlikely to have been capable of the reflective learning to which they laid claim. In learning conversations, the learner's capacity to reflect is not assumed, it is explicitly developed through one-to-one conversations.

Learning to Question Answers as Well as Answer Questions

In getting learners to revolve around his cycle, Kolb claimed to have been influenced by revolutionary South American educators such as Freire.[34] Freire had been critical of the 'banking' model of learning, in which teachers deposited knowledge and learners filed, stored and sometimes retrieved it! At the heart of Freire's learning process was 'praxis' – reflection which led to taking revolutionary action in the outer world in order to change it. But Kolb seemed to side-step the passion of the argument which he claimed had influenced him. Importantly, Freire invoked the role of dialogue between learners. We think that it was a pity that Kolb ignored this aspect of Freire's work. Learners need to question answers as well as answer questions. In learning conversations, learners develop conversational skills like listening, appraising and giving feedback. They are learning to question answers as well as answer questions.

Continuous Professional Development

Public services employ a lot of professional workers, such as probation officers, social workers, town planners, community nurses, customs officers, airline pilots, air traffic controllers and water, electricity and gas engineers. Argyris and Schon[35] made extensive studies of how professionals kept up to date. They discovered that professional learning was very technique oriented. They also noted the spread of the idea of the 'reflective practitioner'.[36] We question how much reflective learning takes place, given our experience that less than 15 per cent of our learners can reflect. In 1974 Habermas[37] warned that reflec-

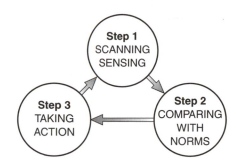

Figure 13.5 Single-loop learning

tive learning on your own would be an astonishing achievement. In a learning conversation the learner is not alone.

Single and Double-loop Learning

Schon thought that work-based learning should not be the learning of subjects. It should be learning about one's own practice as an employee, professional or manager. The recognition of error and its correction is single-loop learning – the sort of learning we saw in the management of quality (Chapter 5). The learner senses what is happening, compares this to some norm or expectation, and then takes action to correct the error (see Figure 13.5).

Instead of an error creating a need only for correction (and self-defence!), the error can be used as the starting point for exploration and discovery, perhaps, of how faulty learning had led to the error in the first place. This is double-loop learning. Figure 13.6 illustrates how this differs from single-loop learning.

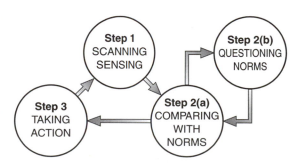

Figure 13.6 Double-loop learning

A Shared Vocabulary

Giddens[38] hoped that double-loop learning would help to make implicit knowledge explicit, so that it could be discussed, shared and disseminated. Argyris and Schon concluded that effectiveness in the workplace is linked to two abilities: the ability to develop ideas of what to do in future situations and the ability to develop close human relationships with fellow workers. 'Thinking coaches' and 'critical friends' often have more faith in their learners than the learners have in themselves. Learning conversations often help learners to integrate emotions as well as thoughts into their learning. Emotion frequently provides the energy and the motivation required to keep the learner learning.

The Energy to Learn

In 1998 we found support for these ideas from Brockbank and McGill: 'Emotions fuel our passions and our behaviours, notwithstanding our espoused rationality. Emotions are a good source of energy for many endeavours, including learning.'[39] The separation of emotions from reason produces a climate of fear and anxiety which militates against the development of the close relationships that are needed to support deep learning.

Using Learning Conversations to Create Learning Organizations

In 1994 Peter Senge[40] took up the cause and used a type of conversational learning which he called a dialogue, to build learning organizations. Peter Senge drew on the writings of a theologian, Martin Buber,[41] a psychologist, Patrick de Maré[42] and a physicist, David Bohm.[43] These Sengian dialogues are not learning conversations as we have defined them. Nigel Laurie,[44] Chair of the Society of Practical Philosophers, has provided us with a critique of Senge's ideas on dialogue. Laurie has also evaluated the practical application of Senge's dialogues. In an unpublished paper, 'Making Dialogue Deliver', presented to the Society of Practical Philosophers in

1998, Laurie reports on his evaluation. Laurie concluded that the practical application of Senge's ideas suffered from 'severe shortcomings', offering 'little practical guidance on what to do at each stage'. Laurie thinks that Senge's difficulties arise because Senge's theoretical underpinnings are flawed and because Senge ignores a history of thinking about learning which stretches back to Socrates.

Socratic Dialogue and Management Learning

Socratic dialogue was adapted for organizational use by Leonard Nelson[45] and by Jos Kessels in Holland. Kessels shares some of Laurie's reservations about Senge's work. We share the concerns expressed by Saran et al.[46] that Socratic dialogue is not informed by what is known about group dynamics. In Chapter 6 we argued that using groups or teams was a difficult way to do many things, including thinking and learning. Some of the difficulties that we have experienced with Socratic dialogue arose, we think, because it was a group process. Do such difficulties occur in the other forms of work-based learning, such as learning sets?

Learning Groups and Learning Sets

Pioneered by Reg Revans,[47] the use of learning sets involves a continuous cycle of individual action and group-based reflection. Learners meet together in sets of 4–6 members. The main function of the set is to review and plan the progress of each person's learning project and to provide social pressure for people to stick to their plans. The group provides an audience before which members perform, using their existing skills. These skills can become more fluent and polished. The self-confident can become more self-confident. But it can be a dire experience for people whose self-confidence on entering the group is low. They can leave the group with even lower self-esteem. We have found little evidence of the development of new skills, such as thinking skills. People get the opportunity to display and fine-tune their existing social skills but, unless the meeting is facilitated along the lines of a therapy group, those with psychological blocks to their performance tend to remain blocked. Normally each member of the set has a mentor. If the mentoring relationship works well, then this is where the most significant learning occurs, i.e. in one-to-one learning conversations.

Workplace Learning in Public Services

Kolb's learning cycle is by far the most commonly used basis for workplace learning. There are other learning cycles in use, but they are usually derivatives and therefore have the same or similar deficiencies. We have serious reservations about approaches to workplace learning that rely on Kolb's learning cycle and its derivatives, or any models that depend on the learners being able to think reflectively, i.e. to recollect accurately, show insight, analyse patterns, draw conclusions, imagine future contexts and then empathize and predict outcomes. Less than 15 per cent of our learners are able to think in all these ways sufficiently well to be able to complete their reflective thinking loops. Neither are we impressed by the use of group-based dialogues – Sengian or Socratic – or by the use of learning sets, unless they are facilitated by someone who can manage group dynamics and who can enable high-level thinking processes in a group situation.

While we have come across isolated learners who can learn well and deeply through self-managed reflective methods and a few ardent adherents to the use of Socratic dialogue or action learning sets, they are a small minority of the learner populations with which we are familiar. There are some people whose learning style is well rounded and balanced – about 15 per cent in our experience. These 'balanced learners' enjoy learning by reflecting on their experience and may even take some action based on their experience. They are outnumbered 6:1 by people who are weak on observation, or reflection, or the ability to conceptualize, or the ability to formulate new ideas, or the preparedness to risk losing control by experimenting. The absence of even one of these capabilities is enough to break the Kolbian learning cycle. That is before we consider lack of motivation

or energy to learn. Either may prevent those who are not otherwise prevented. Just because someone *can* learn reflectively does not mean that they *will*. Equally, we have met evangelical disciples of Senge, Revans and even Socrates. These were often people who loved the performance aspect of working in a group. They were good at it and did it frequently, often playing dominant roles and leading parts. If workplace learning is problematic because managers are unskilled or inexperienced in designing and managing learning, is the answer to make more effective use of local colleges and universities?

The Role of Colleges and Universities in Workplace Learning

Universities used to be reluctant to 'train' undergraduates for work. In 1997 Harvey[48] reviewed UK undergraduate education and concluded that employers could not make up their minds about what they wanted. Consequently, higher education should do more than just respond to the perceived requirements of employers. On the other hand, Harvey recognized that students needed the ability and skill to get a job, to fit in quickly, and to add value effectively. Graduate recruits needed to build a platform of credibility from which they could launch their careers. Pushing new ideas requires self-belief, self-assurance and self-confidence, each of which is associated with the capacity to think for oneself. Unfortunately, much learning in colleges and universities is based on a 'banking' model of knowledge transfer. Public service managers should enquire carefully not only about what the course will teach, but how the learners will learn. If the learning process offered by the college or university is transfer of knowledge followed by assessment to check understanding, then well-designed electronic learning might be more cost-effective (Chapter 11).

Can Workplace Learning Work?

The 1990s saw a number of major studies on workplace learning.[49] The focus of these studies tended to be a triangle composed of a learner, an employer and a college (or a university). Fryer squared the triangle by adding the government.[50] None of these studies mentioned tutors! Nor did they mention coaches or mentors or anyone else who might provide the close one-to-one relationships that are necessary for most learners to learn by recollecting on experiences at work. In 2001 the UK graduate apprenticeship schemes based on a partnership between higher education and employers, offered an opportunity for a more theoretically sound and a more practical approach to workplace learning.

How Adults Learn

In most countries, most of the people at work are adults. In 1984 Knowles[51] concluded that adults needed a learning climate that was relaxed, trusting, warm, collaborative and supportive. In 1996 Lukas Foster[52] had found that groups of people drawn from the same workplace could be tense, suspicious, cool and politically motivated, unless skilfully facilitated. Mumford[53] found similar barriers to learning in 1988. That is why we have argued for a learning process that involves rigorous and disciplined conversations with people with whom some closeness, safety and positive regard have been established. 'Safe' learning conversations respond to Schon's[54] plea for a 'space away from the workplace' – a space relatively free from the very pressures, distractions and workplace risks on which the learner needs to reflect. We share, however, the concerns of Wildemeersch,[55] who sees dangers in a 'romantic curriculum' that over-emphasizes 'learner autonomy', 'student centredness', self-awareness, originality and freedom to choose. Self-directed learning can lead to a self-centredness which militates against good citizenship and the concern which one might have for others and for the wider community. The apparent choice between the rosy glow of a cosy group and the self-centred loneliness of the long-distance learner is a false dichotomy. There are usually more than two possibilities. We favour the intellectual challenge and the critical thinking that are involved in surfacing the work-based theory that underlies the work-based practice. This can come from the use of

disciplined and rigorous one-to-one learning conversations. In some insecure and untrusting places of work, learning conversations may need to be preceded by the formation of trusting and confidential relationships. Chapter 8 describes a conversational approach to developing close relationships at work.

Learners as Individuals

The use of learning conversations responds to Knowles's finding that adult learners need supportive relationships and Schon's finding that adult workers need to feel free from workplace risks. The use of learning conversations avoids the problems of learning in groups and is consistent with the fact that learning can only take place at the level of the individual. Generalized prescriptions and ubiquitous 'big ideas' about how to manage people fail because each manager, and each person to be managed, is different (Chapter 6). We have argued already that managers should move away from managing employees in groups – large or small – and towards managing people as individuals (Chapter 8). Individual learners vary in their starting points, their reasons for learning, their learning styles and their motivation. Their stage of life and their stage in their career development affect their readiness and preparedness to use workplace learning. Sadlington[56] describes the variety of stages of life and career development that can be present in any one group of employees. Schon[57] had earlier identified widely differing starting points for learners related to their self-perceived strengths, weaknesses, motives and expectations. No one model can be right for all people because individuals are different. Kolb's model suits those individuals who have relevant experience, can observe it sensitively with awareness, can recollect their observations accurately, can attach meaning to what they remember, can formulate abstract concepts, and who have the emotional resilience to risk alone the failures that might result from experimentation. There will be some individuals who answer to this description. In our experience they are not numerous.

Learning and Creativity

According to Ken Robinson,[58] creativity is defined as 'imaginative activity fashioned so as to produce outcomes that are both original and of value'. The creative process is driven by the freedom to experiment and enabled by the use of certain skills, knowledge and understanding. Creative achievement often draws on the ideas and successes of others, so that skills in recollection and association are important. Just as different modes of thinking interact in an internal dialogue to produce creative thinking, so creativity can be affected by an external dialogue with others. Traditional education has tended to emphasize verbal and mathematical reasoning, but creative thinking is an essential ingredient of multi-faceted intelligence. Robinson argued that there was a need to recognize the links between learning, creativity, innovation and enterprise. Many public service organizations seek employees who are creative. They want ideas for change that will bring advantages such as success in funding applications, higher rankings in public service league tables, and improvements in service quality at little extra cost. Creative energy often has its origin in an individual's emotional life. Learning conversations add a 'feelings' dimension to learning. They develop empathetic thinking as well as critical thinking. If public service managers choose to involve their local colleges and universities in their programmes of workplace learning, they should satisfy themselves that the models of learning being used are consistent with the way they want their employees to behave when they return to work. Academic life can sometimes be built on the premise that the proper role of reason is the exclusion of emotion!

Emulators and Achievers

Windall and Signitzer[59] discovered that employees who volunteered to attend local colleges or universities for part-time study were not representative of the workforce. They were what Windall called 'emulators and achievers'. Generally speaking, they arrived at the college door with a mindset geared to the acquisition of knowledge. Dwelling on work-based experience was not their style. They were usually looking for facts, other people's ideas and a qualification that would get them an upgrade. The more hopeful discovery which Windall made was that 76 per cent of these people responded well to signals from others. That accords with our experience that this 'mindset' can be changed through learning conversations with tutors, 'thinking coaches' or 'critical friends'.

We conclude this section with a summary of the advantages and disadvantages of the different approaches to work-based learning that we have discussed in this chapter and in particular how they compare to the use of learning conversations (Table 13.3). Having explored the theoretical dimensions of how people learn in organizations, we turn to the practical aspects of implementing learning opportunities. In particular, we look at how a conversational approach to paired learning can be implemented at college, university or in the workplace and how large-scale learning events can be designed and managed.

IMPLEMENTING LEARNING

Designing for Learning: A Conversational Approach

Designing learning events, for skills acquisition, staff development, management development, personal development, or departmental 'away-days' involves conversations to find good answers to five questions:

1 Who needs to learn?
2 What do they need to learn?
3 How will they best learn it?
4 How are the learning methods best facilitated?
5 How will the learning and the learning processes be evaluated?

We shall look at each in turn. The interrelationship between the five questions which are asked during the conversation is summarized in Figure 13.7.

Table 13.3 The three approaches to learning: a comparison of their effectiveness

Characteristics of Effective Learning were found to be	Found in ...		
	Individual learning cycles	Group learning sets	Paired learning conversations
Challenges reasoning	No	No	Yes
Enables internal dialogue	Yes	No	Yes
Makes use of social learning	No	Yes	Yes
Explicitly develops metacognition	No	No	Yes
Cognitive structures explicitly developed	Yes	Yes	Yes
Explicitly develops critical thinking	No	No	Yes
Creates mind laboratory for internal testing	Yes	No	Yes
Makes use of outer world sensory data	Yes	Yes	Yes
Explicitly rehearse simplications for the future	No	No	Yes
Provides immediate stimulus–response learning	No	No	Yes
Avoids impulsive action and premature closure	No	No	Yes
Empathetic learning and thinking explicitly developed	No	No	Yes
Provides 'applause' for motivation and energy to learn	No	Yes	Yes
Develops coaching skills and ability to get others to learn	No	Yes	Yes
Explicitly questions answers as well as answers questions	No	No	Yes
Explicitly provides a confidential safe context for social learning	No	No	Yes
Has idea of praxis – taking action to change the outer world	Yes	Yes	Yes
Explicitly develops imagination, envisioning and creative thinking	No	No	Yes

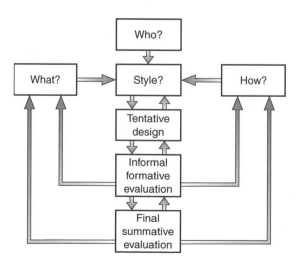

1 Who are the Learners?

What are their jobs, their roles, their backgrounds, their qualifications, their previous experiences of learning, their hopes and fears, their expectations and ambitions, their relationships with each other, their best hopes from this learning event? When talking to adult learners it is useful to bear in mind some of the features of adult learning (Box 13.8).

Figure 13.7 A conversational model of learning design
Source: Horne (1979)[59]

Box 13.8

FEATURES OF ADULT LEARNING

Adult learners are frequently highly anxious, despite having resources and experience which they and others can use. They need to become self-confident, self-reliant learners.

Adult motivation comes from life tasks, problems to be solved, curiosity, a desire to 'better' themselves, or sometimes a need to heal wounds that stem from earlier experiences of learning that were not good.

The atmosphere surrounding adult learning events needs to be informal, warm, collaborative and supportive. Competitiveness between individuals should be minimized.

Learning needs indicate that adults should become more involved in determining what needs to be learned and how it might best be learned.

Learning events can include individualised learning contracts and self-managed investigations. Group tasks should be processed into learning via paired learning.

Evaluation includes individual evidence of participation in the prescribed learning process and evidence of progress against pre-agreed criteria. A proportion of the assessment will need to be reserved in any group activities, to ensure participation by those who 'hate group work'. Formative assessment should be through self, peer and tutor assessment.

2 What Do They Need to Learn? Training Needs Analysis

What is the desired state of their knowledge, skill or attitude? What is the opinion of their line managers, their colleagues or prospective new employers? What do tutors or experts think? What is the learner's existing state with regard to the desired state that has been suggested by others? Who has been consulted? These are some of the questions that a training needs analysis seeks to answer. Training has been defined as:

A planned process to modify attitude, knowledge or skill through learning experiences designed to achieve effective performance. Its purpose is to develop the abilities of the individual and to satisfy the current and future needs of the organization.[60]

Well-trained staff perform better at work. Staff who are offered training report increased levels of motivation. We have already identified a great deal of pressure on public service managers to implement changes (Chapters 1, 2 and 3). Changes can mean that new expertise is required. Public service managers play a key role in forecasting the future skills needs of the organization. Most public services employ training officers who can assist with this task. The development of individual members of staff is an important responsibility of the line manager. Training, learning and personal development cannot be left to training departments. Managers themselves are a primary source of deep learning to aspiring managers. What managers permit and what they reject and the role models they provide, all encourage or discourage learning. Figure 13.8 shows how a training cycle operates. The training cycle in Figure 13.8 in turn feeds into the organization's planning process as illustrated in Figure 13.9.

Training involves providing a range of individual learning experiences directly relevant to work. Education, on the other hand, is concerned with the acquisition of knowledge, skills and values relevant to all aspects of life. Managers will need to be involved in identifying staff training needs. This process is called Training Needs Analysis (TNA). The training received will only be as effective as the

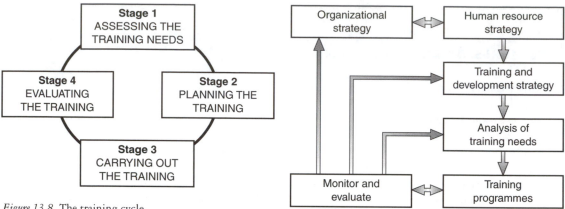

Figure 13.8 The training cycle

Figure 13.9 The relationship between planning and training

training needs analysis on which it is based. Resources are wasted if training needs are not met because they have not been properly analysed, or because training is being used as an inappropriate response to poor performance. Training is not the only solution to problems of poor performance (Chapter 11). Individuals may be prevented from doing their job effectively by unhelpful organizational structures, lack of resources, personal problems, low motivation or by lack of functional or personal competence on the part of their managers. If their managers lack the conversational skills to question, listen and learn or to persuade, negotiate and instruct or to delegate, coach and appraise, then no amount of money spent on training is likely to raise poor staff performance significantly. Training can be used to:

- Meet needs of new practices, or technology.
- Provide solutions to some gaps in performance.
- Introduce new people to the organization.
- Meet specified needs of employees.
- Enable people to cope with change.
- Meet legal and safety requirements.

Three levels of training: organizational, occupational, individual

Boydell[61] suggested three levels:

1 **Organizational**: accommodating structural change
2 **Occupational**: improving performance
3 **Individual**: realizing potential

At the individual level, for example, mentoring, job shadowing, individual supervision or academic study might be appropriate. At the occupational level, professional certification or continuous professional development might be needed. At the organizational level, social events, away-days, cultural workshops, residential weekends or programmes of organization development might be indicated. The starting point for the training needs analysis of an individual is usually an analysis of what that person is expected to do and the attributes that would be helpful in doing it. This is sometimes called job analysis.

Job analysis

Job analysis consists of analysing what is involved in the job, i.e. the main tasks and responsibilities and identifying the skills, knowledge and attitudes required to do the job effectively. Job analysis seeks answers to the questions:

1 What are the organization's goals?
2 In this job, what tasks must be completed?
3 What must the jobholder *do* to complete them?

4 What knowledge, skills or attitudes do job holders need?

Competency-based Training Needs Analysis

Competency-based approaches to TNA reduce uncertainty about the identification of training needs because actual performance can be compared with agreed standards. National vocational standards for managers as a professional group have been established as a result of research by the UK Management Charter Initiative (MCI). This was superseded by the Management Education and Training Organization (METO) and more recently by the National Training Organization for Management and Enterprise. These types of standards are widely used in the UK and the USA and are becoming international standards.

3 How Will They Learn Best?

Having identified learning gaps, what learning activities might best help to fill them? With what learning processes are the learners already familiar? How do they think they have learned effectively before? How have they enjoyed learning in the past? We are likely to have to start with methods they enjoy. Will we need to introduce the learners to new learning methods better suited to bridging the identified learning gap? How good are the learners at observing, analysing, reflecting, theorizing, experimenting or learning by doing? Which of these do they prefer? Are we constrained about what can be offered because of room size, seating or the availability of equipment? Sometimes circumstances dictate that learning events need to be organized and managed for large numbers of people simultaneously. Figure 13.10 provides a plan of what is required for a typical learning event.

How can our assumptions about the learners be checked out before or during the learning event? In

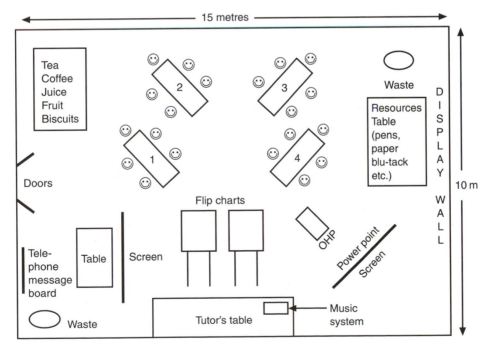

Figure 13.10 Typical room arrangement for a learning event or away-day

---

Box 13.9

POSSIBLE SCHEME FOR AN OPENING SESSION

1 Visual map or summary of first session
2 Ice-breaker
3 Collect hopes, fears and expectations (or present back if collected in advance). Snowball responses by working alone, in pairs, in fours, in groups of eight
4 Clarify roles of tutors and participants
5 Clarify norms, e.g. participation, respect, experiment, honesty, confidentiality
6 Administration
7 Report back of learner's success criteria
8 Relate programme to wider issues
9 Create base teams of 6–8 people. Teams choose names and a motto
10 For a several day residential, each group appoints a representative for committees to deal with refreshments, social programme, morale raising, final night cabaret.
11 Brief teams for their first task
12 Agree time and place for next session

---

an event lasting more than four hours, when are the likely energy peaks and troughs? What could be inserted at the low points? If new information will take more than 20 minutes to present orally, what other methods could be considered? Do we have a plan for opening the event and for explaining the rationale for its design? (See Box 13.9.)

Do we have a plan for closing the event, summarizing its outcomes, looking forward to the future?

(Box 13.10) If there is more than one learning event, these will need to be interspersed with drawing up personal action plans which detail how the new learning is to be applied. These action plans are best done in pairs. Keep to the same pairs if they seem to be working well. All change if they aren't. Create options and alternative routes, to deal with individual agendas. If the programme is to last more than one day, build in team and participant reviews

---

Box 13.10

POSSIBLE SCHEME FOR A CLOSING SESSION

1 Outline agenda for the last session.
2 Pick up carried forward issues, 'parked' items and leftover questions.
3 Positive feedback. Everyone gets one 'rosy glow' – a positive affirmation from each member of their own team. Each team makes an award to each other team (or to each course participant if there are 15 or less).
4 Prioritizing plans. In pairs, prioritize the actions which each planned during the event. Draw up individual action plans. Agree detailed first steps for the top five priority actions. In teams, collate all top actions.
5 Networking and closure. Exchange personal details and confirm how you will maintain contact, if that's what you intend.
6 Individual appreciation. Participants state: 'One thing that I have appreciated about this event was . . .'
7 Give out evaluation forms. Last item is 'The way I'm feeling now is more . . .'
8 Selected feedback from the evaluation forms.
9 A final thank you to the participants.

at the end of each day to fine-tune, or replan, the next day.

Circulate draft learning designs to key stakeholders such as line managers, training officers, chief executives, clients and influential participants. Invite feedback. What pre-course material could be sent to participants to raise awareness and expectation? What follow-up work could be set up and how could it be followed up?

4 What Style of Facilitation?

Learners are likely to present in dependent mode. They are certain to want someone to answer where and when questions. Quite probably they will want what and how questions answered as well. After dealing with where and when, you might prefer to move them from a dependent to a more independent mode of learning. To a mode of learning, for example, in which they decide for themselves what it is important for them to learn in this area, maybe exercising some choice over the types of learning activity. We want them to think for themselves about what is valid, useful and relevant to their

work, to their own situation, and to their preferred way of learning. Our first attempts to move them away from dependence to independence are likely to provoke counter-dependence. This rebellious anger may be expressed as concern that time is being wasted. It might also reflect anxiety about getting things wrong. Whatever its cause, the anger and anxiety will need to be tolerated by the tutor. Individuals will need to be supported with their various difficulties in having to think and learn independently. The greater their involvement in the learning activity, the greater the likelihood that participants will become independent learners, each capable of transferring their learning to new situations (see Figure 13.11).

5 How to Evaluate?

Common methods of evaluation are tests (written and practical), presentations and projects (individual and group), learning logs, vivas, observation and questionnaires. We need to assess what was learned, how important the learning was to the learner, why it was important, and how it was learned. This helps

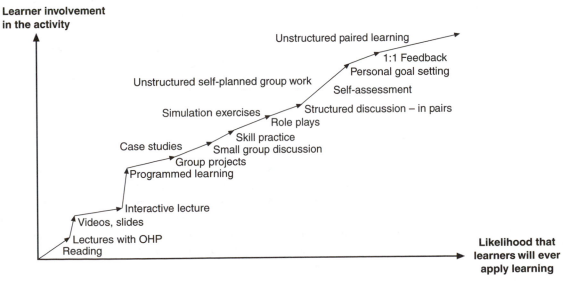

Figure 13.11 Likelihood that learners will apply their learning

Source: Horne and Armstrong (1999)[62]

Box 13.11

CHECKLIST FOR TUTORS

1 If possible, arrive several hours early!
2 Check temperature control, ventilation and lighting. Are the fire exits open?
3 Check rooms and cloakrooms are clean and the toilets are working. Check towels etc.
4 Remove surplus furniture and old flipcharts.
5 Fit fresh flipchart pads. Clean white boards and clear display boards.

6 Check that all audio visual equipment works. Where are the spare bulbs?
7 Arrange all your material on the tutor's table.
8 Double check that refreshments will be available at the times ordered.
9 Arrange furniture. Check seats and tables are clean. Pick up litter found by moving furniture!
10 Begin on time, regardless of who is late.

---

to raise the learner's awareness of how they best learn things that are important to them. Questions about how they think they learned aid their metacognitive thinking. The learners would seem to be the people in the best position to evaluate their learning. However, if the learner is to be assessed for an external qualification, this will not be practical. Where the learning is not qualificatory, the practice of determining and applying criteria for self-assessment and peer assessment will be developmental in itself, especially if it involves peer review and feedback.

Workplace Learning: The Practicalities

Box 13.12 lists 30 methods that can be used to generate learning in the workplace. We will look briefly at what is involved in each and evaluate the advantages and disadvantages of each method. We favour 1:1 methods and will, in the following section, look in detail at the manager's role as a learning coach and mentor. We accept that some learning events need to be for large groups of people learning together simultaneously. We have looked at the practicalities of how such events can be designed and managed. In Table 13.4 we give brief descriptions of many of these methods and summarize the advantages and disadvantages of each.

Box 13.12

DEVELOPMENTAL ACTIVITIES

- Visits, films, feedback, deputizing
- Job swaps, counselling, think-tanks, logs
- Project work, quality circles, guided reading, job shadowing
- Personal development groups, attending conferences and seminars
- Writing reviews, surfing the net, paired learning, chairing meetings

- Interactive videos, writing summaries, internal consulting, action learning sets
- In-house training courses, professional associations, co-option to working parties
- On-the-job coaching, giving presentations, distance learning, external training courses

Table 13.4 Workplace learning: comparing methods

Method	Advantages	Disadvantages
Training departments (Including training centres, staff colleges, purpose-built centres)	Ensures training is convenient. Control over culture, process and content. Signals the legitimacy and the importance of training. Can control the training budget by controlling the allocation to the centre. Can become an informal, safe source of suggestions for improvements.	Under-utilization of centre wastes resources and creates pressure to put on inappropriate training. Training managers build empires. Facilities management requires different skills from those needed by tutors. Training centre staff become insular and isolated from the mainstream culture.
Job swaps (Including deputizing, 'acting up', internal consulting, work shadowing, overseas postings, secondments and placements in other organizations)	Can increase the breadth of experience. Can widen employees' knowledge. Can change perspectives, enhance empathy, generate new ideas and insights – a 'fresh pair of eyes'. Helps employees expand their networks. Fosters links and cross-fertilization between departments.	The idea of on-the-job learning is problematic (see earlier in this chapter). Trainees often given meaningless, undemanding, time-consuming tasks because of the time it would take to train them up to do anything demanding.
Using outside consultants (Includes using them for training, organization development, change implementation. Trainee managers may be attached to an internal consultant or be an internal change agent)	They bring fresh ideas, often from competitive organizations, or from a different sector. They can afford to be more confrontational than internal managers and less inhibited by the risk of upsetting people by speaking the unspeakable. They can be used to train the trainers already working in the organization. They can be used as and when required. They may be more objective – having fewer personal axes to grind.	They can be politically unaware and not versed in the culture of the organization. They are usually expensive. They have no ongoing responsibility. They may undermine internal trainers. They can create dependence, to increase their chances of 'selling on' more work. Temptation to distort problems to fit the consultant's solutions. They can be glib, plausible, charming, entertaining, good talkers, or all talk.
Working parties (Includes membership of teams, co-options, project teams, multi-disciplinary teams, multi-agency work)	Break down barriers between departments, other organizations, agencies or clients. They can be used to train the trainers already working in the organization.	Can disrupt 'normal' departmental working and procedures. Because they lie outside the formal structure, they may have difficulty obtaining access to information, expenses, resources. Lack of clarity about responsibility.
Mentoring (Mentoring is rarely done by line managers – usually be someone senior who 'knows the ropes' – see later)	The senior manager gains as much as the mentor in personal development. Their advice is practical and politically grounded in the organization. They can help resolve difficulties between mentees and their managers.	Senior manager's time is expensive. Mentees may abuse their privileged access to information or use it to up-stage their managers or bypass the normal chain. The mentees may provoke jealousy. Can go against equal opportunities.

continued

Table 13.4 continued

Method	Advantages	Disadvantages
Self-managed seminars (Training staff may provide facilities and administrative support but the content and delivery of training is down to trainees)	Helps to pool experience, or to report on each other's learning. Provides social motivation to learn. Performance anxiety can help to raise energy to learn.	Can degenerate into a moaning session. The only thing shared is ignorance. The only thing you may get support for is existing prejudices and ways of doing things. Group conformity reduces likelihood that anything new will be explored. Only well-established work is considered.
Internal consultancy (Managers are given a role to be available for consultation by other managers on technical or personnel issues)	Managers get the benefit of wider experience. The conversational skills developed by both parties to the consultation. Reduces isolation, fosters a sense of belonging and supportiveness. Aids networking and career planning.	Time-consuming. Distracting. Requires advanced skills from both parties. May degenerate into 'telling how it is' and 'see it my way' scenarios.
Counselling (Includes co-counselling [see Chapter 8]. Deals with personal problems – marital, family, money troubles, physical and mental illness)	Helps to bridge home life and the organization and reduce conflicts. Addresses under-performance due to distractions from personal preoccupations. Makes the organization more humane. Generates gratitude and loyalty. Makes the counselling client feel valued.	It is difficult work to do well. Can create dependency. Confidentiality can give rise to conflicts of interest for the counsellor. Uninterrupted private space can be difficult to find in a busy organization.
Personal development groups (Includes such things as T-Groups, TA Groups, analytic groups. Usually unstructured, characterized by boundaries around membership, duration, confidentiality and preparedness to deal openly and honestly)	Interpersonal as well as intrapersonal issues can be tackled. This type, level and accuracy of feedback are otherwise hard to obtain. The group experience for many can be intense and can bond members together. This may transfer as cohesiveness and mutual support in other working groups. Shared meanings develop along with a common vocabulary that enables complex issues to be diagnosed with an ease not formerly present.	Most managers by nature prefer structure and control and are threatened by unstructured, self-disclosing groups. The erosion of difference between work life and personal life is unacceptable. They need skilful and experienced facilitation. They raise issues for people that may be beyond the scope of the group. Back-up resources are needed. They have a tendency to adopt trendy 'fads' or ideas about management. They can develop a religious zeal.

Not included in Table 13.4, because they merit a special mention, is the role of coaching and mentoring conversations. Coaching and mentoring conversations not only raise performance of staff, they also provide a particularly powerful aid to the personal development of individuals (Chapter 14). We look first at the need to create an environment conducive to coaching

COACHING AND MENTORING

Creating a Coaching Environment

Poor managers, like poor teachers, often feel that they have little to learn from their 'pupils'. The autocratic manager, the person who gives orders and expects them to be carried out, is not likely to make a good coach. Development is a process of partnership in which managers – through superior ability, knowledge or experience – can assist more junior people to develop their confidence and expertise. The partnership will not work where the managers are afraid that the junior people might take their jobs. Managers are more likely to be fearful of this if the organization is in the process of 'downsizing', 'delayering' or 'merging'. Likewise, if the organization is bureaucratic, autocratic and highly structured and dependent for its success on fear and conformity, it is unlikely that many managers will wish to create a situation where free discussion and freedom to learn from mistakes can flourish. Yet freedom and respect are essential for coaching. A good coaching climate cannot be created overnight. It depends on a slow build-up of confidence, following, perhaps, a change in managerial style. Above all, managers who would like to become good coaches must recognize that they may have much to learn and more to practise.

The Characteristics of a Good Coach

Four characteristics of a good coach were identified by Reigal.[63]

1 They are interested in their staff as individuals.

2 They look for potential as well as performance.
3 They are people-centred.
4 They put trust in people.

1 Interested in individuals

To be good coaches, managers will need to extend their conversations beyond 'How are you?' and 'Where are you going for your holiday?' They will have their sincerity doubted, and run the risk of being seen as intrusive. They need to believe that it is legitimate for managers to have a genuine desire to help other people to accomplish goals, to become emotionally mature, to pursue personal ambitions, to foster self-reliance, to develop self-confidence, to show tolerance of others, and to think for themselves.

2 Look for potential

Good coaches assume that people are capable of doing more demanding work than they currently do. They work out with people what new knowledge, experience or practice they need and support them while they get it. With the help of a coach most people are capable of mastering new challenges. Being a partner in helping people to meet new challenges helps managers to learn what further potential people might have. The manager gives thought and takes trouble.

3 People-centred

This does not mean that a good coach is only interested in people and not in managing operations, finance, information and changing. Good coaching is a work-based activity. One of the end-products of good coaching is improved performance in all six of the roles for which a manager is responsible. Coaching is not counselling. At any one time the focus of the coaching is helping someone to perform a specific task better, whereas counselling is usually concerned with personal issues. Personal problems may be affecting performance at work and these problems may come to light during coaching conversations. If this is the case, workplace counselling may be offered (Chapter 8). If counselling is offered, it will be at least one step removed from the issue of work performance. If the issues are recurrent, or deep rooted, the counselling is better carried out by someone other than the line manager. Although good coaches have characteristics in common with good counsellors, such as a concern for people and a desire for people to come up with their own solutions, few managers can realistically promise the 'unconditional positive regard' offered by most counsellors.

4 Trust people

There is a risk element in coaching. Managers cannot know for certain that their staff will perform well. But they should always talk as though they had that certainty. They expect their faith in individuals to be justified by successful outcomes. The best preparation for success is to expect it.

COACHING CONVERSATIONS

The conversational skills of a good coach include listening, sensing and monitoring. Listening skills were an important part of the skills needed in conversations related to negotiation and persuasion (Chapter 2), developing close working relationships, appraisal and counselling (Chapter 8). Listening is difficult because we have the capacity to hear and to think at the same time. Most of us hear what a person is saying, and, unfortunately, while they are still talking, we begin to rehearse what we want to say as soon as they pause for breath – or sooner! Listening during a coaching conversation means not only hearing what is being said but attempting to understand what lies behind what is being said. In Chapter 8 we referred to this as listening to the music as well as the words. The manager needs to think empathetically. Listening is a good starting point for coaching because it helps to determine an 'initial state', a starting point, or an opportunity to stretch the skill or broaden the experience of the other person.

As we shall see when we deal with time management in the next chapter, once the answer to the question 'Does this need to be done?' is 'Yes', the next question is 'Who (besides me) could do it?' This could create a coaching opportunity. Coaching increases a manager's awareness of what people are doing elsewhere, beyond the immediate gaze of supervision, perhaps in other departments, on working groups, or outside of work all together. What skills are people displaying elsewhere? How could these skills be used more widely? The monitoring involved in coaching goes beyond the monitoring of task performance. Coaching aids learning and development in individuals, through 1:1 conversations. Does the person understand *why* something worked and not just *how*? Their understanding can be assessed through conversations in which they rehearse the transfer of their understanding to different and unfamiliar situations. Again this rehearsal needs to be conducted expecting success.

Unlike coaching, mentoring is not done by line managers. There has to be somebody other than your line manager to whom you can talk about the inadequacies of your boss! The brief for the mentor is wider than coaching. Coaching is about improving skills and performance in a particular job. Mentoring is about the person. It is about realizing their potential in their present job and in their future career. Line managers should know when an employee has a mentor and should understand what mentoring means. Mentees, in turn, should encourage their colleagues also to find mentors, as a way of furthering their development. This reduces the risk of the jealous backlash. In the next section we examine a conversational approach to mentoring.

Mentoring Conversations

Mentoring relationships can be of many kinds. They can be restricted to certain topics or to professional or technical matters. They can be private, in that few people know that the mentoring relationship exists. They can be persistent, in that they carry on for many years after the mentee has left the original organization in which they started the mentoring relationship. They can be highly structured with regular diaried meetings that take a high priority, or they can be organized 'as and when'.

A mentoring relationship can be between peers, team members, members of other organizations, friends or strangers. Unlike appraisal, mentoring is not judgemental (Chapter 11). Within the confidentiality of a mentoring relationship, mentees can be more honest than they are likely to be in an appraisal interview – especially if the appraisal is linked to pay. Mentoring is not counselling (Chapter 8). There is no expectation of 'unconditional positive regard' and mentors can be quite directive or self-disclosing, intervening on the part of their mentees in a way that counsellors would never do.

Mentors should have relevant job-related skills and knowledge and be experienced, preferably long-serving, members of the organization. Mentors and mentees must like each other! They should enjoy the master–apprenticeship relationship and have a desire to help for no personal gain. They can work on conversational skills, learning skills, thinking skills, career planning, life planning, the politics of the organization, resolving conflicts, advising on difficult individuals, or tricky situations, technical problems or adjusting to change. According to Alred *et al.*,[64] Gerard Egan's model of the 'Skilled Helper' (Figure 13.12) is widely used as the basis for mentoring relationships in the USA, where mentoring tends to be goal-oriented and focused.[65]

In Stage 1 the mentor creates rapport, listens, asks questions and negotiates an agenda for the rest of the meeting. Time and patience are needed to reduce the risk of premature conclusions and insufficiently informed action plans. Typical questions and statements move from open and wide to specific and focused. For example,

- 'Shall we recap on what you said last time?'
- 'What shall we talk about today?'
- 'What's going on for you?'
- 'What's on top?'
- 'What happened when . . . ?'
- 'X seems to be the key to . . .'
- 'You haven't said much about . . .'
- 'Let's explore that issue shall we?'

In Stage 2 the mentor will be confirming and validating the mentee's strengths, identifying developmental needs, agreeing priorities, giving information and advice and sharing their own experiences. If the advice is resisted, the mentor does not insist and goes back to Stage 1. The kinds of conversational skills needed will be the ones commonly used in listening and giving feedback. For example:

- 'You appear to have some regrets about this.'
- 'Where do you suggest that we start?'
- 'What is there to learn from this?'
- 'That feels like a breakthrough'
- 'Here is some information on . . .'
- 'It's a bit like when I . . .'

In Stage 3 the mentor will be encouraging the mentee to problem-solve, consider options, take decisions, set targets and agree an action plan. The mentor will be using creative, empathetic, ethical and evaluative thinking skills. Since mentors want the mentees to choose the options and own the action plans, they should say as little as possible during Stage 3. The mentor simply prompts the process from option generation, through decision-making, on to action planning.

Figure 13.12 A three-stage model of mentoring

Source: Egan (1994)[65]

Choosing a Mentor

Choose a mentor who is enthusiastic about mentoring. In particular, they should be enthusiastic about mentoring you! Choose someone who will look for the positive in you and who seeks out starting points for growth and development in situations that go wrong. A preparedness to be open and honest and a respect for confidentiality are essential. Empathy helps. In a good mentoring relationship you are entitled to be listened to, to be encouraged, to be challenged, to be given advice, to be helped with your career and, occasionally, to be given 'insider' tips about the organization. If you are lucky, you will get a resonant sounding board and a critical friend – maybe, in the end, a personal friend. Periodically you should compare notes with your mentor about the extent to which each of you is getting your expectations met. You should both expect the relationship to change over time – from getting to know each other, to finding trust, to enjoying working together. If the mentoring relationship needs to end, this should be talked about for several meetings before you agree to part or to become just good friends!

FINAL THOUGHTS: 'LEARNING FROM MISTAKES'

According to Ritchie and Connolly,[66] coaching conversations are being increasingly used in public services. Often they are called supervision. Supervision is common in social work, probation services, teaching, youth work, community nursing and health visiting. Ritchie and Connolly question whether such conversations are entirely appropriate in public services. They note, for instance, that the model of conversation developed by Clutterbuck[67] emphasizes the need for confidentiality. Clutterbuck sees confidentiality as essential to the learning process. Connolly and Ritchie think that the levels of confidentiality suggested by Clutterbuck are unrealistic for public services. According to Morgan,[68] systems of accountability foster defensive behaviour, such as covering up mistakes and concealing non-conformance. When Argyris asked managers what actually happened in their organizations, he found their replies were often couched in diversionary rhetoric, or *post hoc* rationalization. He reported that managers tended to filter out evidence that contradicted 'espoused theories'.[69] To overcome the contradictions between accountability and learning, an approach to management is required which promotes learning as a process of open-ended enquiry.

Morgan's proposals, set out in Box 13.13, pose some difficulties. What, for example, is a legitimate error in a public service? How are high standards of public accountability to be maintained alongside a spirit of open-ended enquiry? The human cost of even a single error in a public service may be unacceptable. In October 1998 it was reported that the publicly owned UK Air Traffic Control Service only narrowly avoided a disaster when a trainee's error resulted in a near mid-air collision of two jumbo jets. In manufacturing, the consequences of a failed

---

Box 13.13

LEARNING AS OPEN-ENDED ENQUIRY

- Do not blame people for errors
- Discourage denying or hiding errors
- Accept deep and challenging questions
- Encourage openness and reflection
- Accept error and uncertainty as normal
- See legitimate errors as sources of wisdom
- Give opportunities for the exploration of differing viewpoints
- Learn from negative experiences – don't attempt to cover them up
- Don't impose budgets or targets. Variances provide only single-loop learning

product or new promotion might only be financial. Even then, the consequences may be recoverable. In public services, the human cost of failure may be irreversible. How can public services be accountable if no one is to be blamed (Chapter 11)? Under the circumstances, the plea by the UK Local Government Training Board[70] that managers should turn all the experiences of their staff into learning may be naïve. Perhaps one way forward is to encourage the spread of learning conversations. In our learning conversations, the 'thinking coach' and the 'critical friend' do not need to have experience that is considered to be 'superior' to the learner in the sense used by the Local Government Training Board. The relationship between a 'thinking coach', a 'critical friend' and a 'reflective learner' can be confidential. It doubles or triples the potential learning when two or three learners take turns to coach and critique each other. While one person is developing their capacity to think for themselves, the other is developing their social skills in listening and questioning. Both sets of skills deepen the ability to learn from mistakes through a conversational approach.

- We explored theories of learning and voiced our concern that work-based learning was often based on models from which significant aspects of the learning process were absent. Kolb's learning cycle, group learning sets and some models of reflective practice seem to be seriously flawed. We tabulated our findings and showed how learning conversations can fill the gaps.
- We tabulated 30 methods of learning with their advantages and disadvantages.
- We looked at the manager's role in getting others to learn through coaching and mentoring.
- Finally, we explored the tensions between learning from mistakes and being accountable for mistakes. Learning conversations can help to resolve these tensions?

SUMMARY

- We analysed the competencies of high-performing managers and concluded that competencies associated with learning and thinking were very important.
- We evaluated competency based approaches to learning and concluded that, despite certain deficiencies, they have enabled employees to learn in the workplace.
- We explored why people failed to learn in the workplace and analysed the pressure to create 'learning organizations'. We questioned their practicability.
- We described learning conversations and explained how they might be conducted in the workplace.

THINKING AND LEARNING ACTIVITIES

Activity 1 Self-assessment

1 Represent the steps in a learning conversation in a diagram.
2 Apply criteria for effective learning to:
   - Self-managed experiential learning
   - Learning in groups
   - Reflective practice
   - Learning Conversations
3 What is wrong with the Kolb Learning Cycle?
4 What is wrong with learning in groups?
5 Why might competency based learning be preferred by an employer?
6 What are the possible advantages and the possible disadvantages of managers authorizing day release of staff to a local college or university?

7 In public services, what is likely to prove difficult about using Morgan's ideas about learning from mistakes and errors?

Activity 2 Individual Learning: Visual Thinking

Mental mapping

Take a blank A4 sheet. Skim back over the first section of this chapter. Each time you come to a key idea or section, label it with a few words. Write the label somewhere on your blank A4 sheet and draw a circle round the label. When you come across the next key idea or section, label it and place it on your A4 sheet, close to other ideas to which you think it is related. When you have skimmed through the whole chapter, draw lines between the circles on your A4 sheet, if you think the

ideas are connected. If necessary, use a clean sheet of A4 to redraw your diagram so that the connecting lines are clear and the intersections are minimized. Now write verbs, or actions, along all the lines, such as 'which can help with', 'which can be evaluated by'. Keep going until you have a map, diagram or flowchart of how all the ideas in this chapter relate to one another.

Activity 3 Paired Learning: Empathic and Emotional Thinking

Conversational feedback

This is an activity for three learners – A, B and C – each having conversations in pairs, observed by the third who then gives verbal feedback supported by written examples. Before the conversations start, read the Case Study entitled 'The Annual Celebration' (Box 13.14 below).

Box 13.14

CASE STUDY: THE ANNUAL CELEBRATION

The economic development department of Bordindi employs 80 people. Their district office is in several temporary buildings near the regional office. This is the place where many of the staff bump into each other every day. Every year in October, people will ask 'where shall we go for our meal this year?' Always they let the same group of people decide. Every year the same people decide on the same format. Every year the same people think that it's too expensive, the same people think it's too large and the same people think it's too long. At the meal, the district officer always makes the same long boring speech and each year everybody says 'never again, we won't ask him again!' The party breaks up and the same informal groups continue the same activities and get into the same bother when they arrive home late. Everyone is expected to attend. The boss thinks that it is good for departmental morale. People think the boss enjoys making his departmental speech. In

fact he finds it a painful duty which he believes is expected of him.

Last year a very public argument broke out between a senior male manager and his female secretary. She felt that the meal was simply a men's night out and that it gave male employees permission to behave badly. Another member of staff felt that the form of the annual celebration excluded many people because of their Muslim religion. In recent years, attempts have been made to address this by only having vegetarian food. Many people had resented paying 'fancy restaurant prices for a load of vegetables'. On the night some had paid supplements for extra side dishes of chicken and meat, causing great offence to the vegetarians. It was a popular belief that the senior manager would mark down anyone who was absent or who did not actively appear to be enjoying themselves.

Divide the time available into three equal phases. Each phase should be between 30–40 minutes. Two-thirds of each phase will be for conversations about any matters that arise out of reading 'The Annual Celebration'. One third will be for feedback from the person who is observing the conversation.

- **First period**: A and B talk and C observes.
- **Second period**: A and C talk and B observes.
- **Third period**: B and C talk and A observes.

Questions

Individually A, B and C should take 5 minutes maximum to jot down answers to five questions:

1 What feeling did you experience when reading the passage and at what points?
2 What do you feel at this moment having read it?
3 What do you think about their annual celebration?
4 What are the root causes of any problems posed by the annual celebration?
5 How would you change things?

Each of the following conversations can address one or more of the above questions.

The role of the observer

You will need to use the observation sheet below (Box 13.15). It identifies things that are helpful when conducting learning conversations. Read the explanations of the terms, before using it to identify examples of when the participants display the 'virtues' shown on the sheet.

Explanation of terms

1 **Respect**: Participants in a learning conversation should have care and respect for the other participant and for the procedures that help to keep the conversation flowing.
2 **Listening**: It is important to convey actively and non-verbally that you are giving your full undivided attention to whoever is speaking. Listen to *how* they are talking, as well as to *what* they are saying.
3 **Equality**: Everybody's contribution should be taken seriously.

4 **Puzzlement**: Be on the alert for anything in the conversation that you might find puzzling – including things you have said yourself. Be prepared to point out your puzzlement to the other person.
5 **Reasonableness**: Be prepared to offer reasons in support of opinions you express, especially if they are queried by others. If the reasons are part of an argument that runs counter to someone else's, try to make your reasons relevant rather than intimidatory or belittling. Avoid 'It's obvious that . . .' or 'Nobody in their right mind would . . .'
6 **Reticence**: This has to do with the avoidance of dogma and a reluctance to become too certain too early in the conversation. It is a preparedness to wait, to muse, to speculate and wonder.
7 **Self-correction**: This presupposes not taking anything for granted, including the validity of your own opinions. It means remaining open-minded, even to the possibility that you may be wrong and that you may change your ideas in the light of what others say.
8 **Truth**: A learning conversation is not so much a search for great eternal truths, but rather a tenacious desire to get to the bottom of things, to get things as

---

Box 13.15

CONVERSATIONAL VIRTUES: OBSERVATION SHEET

1 Respect	9 Questioning
2 Listening	10 Sky hooks
3 Equality	11 Connections
4 Puzzlement	12 Tolerance
5 Reasonableness	13 Collaboration
6 Reticence	14 Transience
7 Self-correction	15 Challenging
8 Truth	16 Other

clear as possible, and a refusal to give up easily when the argument becomes cloudy or tediously.

9   **Questioning**: Participants should adopt a genuinely questioning disposition based on real interest or curiosity. They should not use questions to convey doubt, cynicism or sarcasm. These are not really questions – they are negative statements – sometimes quite aggressive – hiding behind questions. Examples of questions that show genuine interest and which support a learning conversation are 'What do you mean by . . . ?', 'What are your reasons for saying . . . ?', 'What might follow from . . . ?', 'Can you give an example . . . ?'

10   **Sky hooks**: Any idea should be assessed as a potential sky hook – as something on which to hang other arguments – to enable the level of discussion to be pulled upwards until the sky hook can no longer support more weight.

11   **Connections**: Participants should try to show how a new idea or thought they wish to offer is connected with what other people have said before, or with what they themselves have said before. Implications or suggestions for future action should be connected to new learning currently being contemplated. Current learning should, in turn, be connected to some past experience. The past experience should be described in detail, so that all can try to understand the origin of what is being learned.

12   **Tolerance**: A learning conversation should not be judgemental. It should be characterized by infinite (well almost!) patience; an acceptance that people and opinions may vary; a willingness to keep listening; tolerance to allow the other person to finish without interrupting them and an openness to the possibility that one may be wrong.

13   **Collaboration**: A learning conversation is an act of collaboration. A learning conversation is not a competition. It is not about the triumph of one point of view over another. Its purpose is not to impress or to convince another person. The object is to help others to learn and to learn yourself. You are given a rare gift – the chance to hear yourself thinking.

14   **Transience**: Participants should be content to create temporary resting places for any reasonable judgements that are made during learning conversations.

Such judgements can then be revisited on another day. After reflection, hindsight or further insight, these temporary judgements may serve again as renewed starting points – sources of inspiration or of mere learning. Judgements are transient. We should hold them tentatively.

15   **Challenging**: Being non-judgemental and tolerant does not remove the need – the duty almost – to challenge the validity of another person's ideas. This should be done with a sense of searching for what is true, rather than with the idea of putting down the other person.

Activity 4 Paired Learning: Reflective and Empathetic Thinking

On becoming a thinking coach

Choose someone at work, or a fellow student, who agrees to have you coach them on some specific aspect of their work. Set aside at least 20 minutes when you will not be interrupted. If both of you are interested to develop your conversational skills as a 'thinking coach', reverse roles after 20 minutes. The two roles in this activity are 'reflective learner' and 'thinking coach'. Your task as 'thinking coach' is to help the 'reflective learner' to think about a work-based or education-based experience. When the 'reflective learner' is describing his or her experience, try out some of the conversational moves for 'thinking coaches' described in the main text (Box 13.7). Practise using the conversational moves. They may seem awkward at first – like the exercises sometimes used to learn keyboard skills. But you will soon become fluent with familiarity and use.

Activity 5 Paired Learning: Critical and Empathic Thinking

On becoming a critical friend

In the role of 'critical friend', your job is different from that of a 'thinking coach'. The thinking coach's job is to help you think through your workplace or educational experience and to come up with things that you could do differently. The job of the 'critical friend' is to help the 'reflective learner' to test that learning – to have it subjected to critical evaluation – to enable the 'reflective learner' to have their tentative conclusions challenged and assessed. In order to practise being a 'critical friend', you will need to find someone who has reflected on an experience and arrived at some tentative conclusions about it. Set aside at least 20 minutes when you will not be interrupted. Practise using some of the conversational moves for 'critical friends' described in the main text (Box 13.5). They are more challenging and more confrontational than the ones you practised as a 'thinking coach'. They may seem artificial and awkward at first – like exercises used to learn keyboard skills. But you will soon become fluent in using them. If both of you are both interested to develop your conversational skills as a 'critical friend', then reverse roles after 20 minutes.

Activity 6 Paired Learning: Critical and Reflective Thinking

Putting it all together

This is an opportunity for three participants to practise putting together the skills involved in holding learning conversations. There are three roles:

1 **The reflective learner**: thinking about a workplace or a life experience.
2 **The thinking coach**: helping the reflective learner think about the experience.
3 **The critical friend**: reviewing the thinking and learning of the learner.

The first two participants take the role of learner and coach for 40 minutes, while the third participant observes (this is not essential but there is much to be learned from observing the other two). The coach and the critical friend then have a conversation for 20 minutes, while the third participant observes. This one hour sequence is repeated twice more, enabling all three participants to practise all three roles, over a three-hour period. The separate instructions for each role can be found in the main text. With practice and increasing skill, this cycle time for three conversations can be reduced to one and a half hours and then to one hour.

The aim is to be able to do it rapidly, on your feet, without notes, almost unconsciously, becoming aware of your unconscious incompetence, to move through conscious competence and back to unconscious competence.

In your role as reflective learner

You will have a conversation with a thinking coach. Think of an incident that has taken place recently at work or in your life. It should be one that generated strong feelings – preferably your own. Follow the promptings and questioning of your thinking coach who will record your account of what you saw, heard, felt and thought *then*, in the past tense, during the incident. Try to keep the sequence clear – what you noticed, heard, saw, felt and thought. Try to replay the internal dialogue you had with yourself then and make sure that your thinking coach records it as near verbatim as possible.

Next, in the present tense, *now*, read through your coach's account of what happened *then*. How do you feel about the incident now, looking back over the written account of it? If you still have strong feelings about it, describe them and have your coach record them until you feel calm enough to think about the incident again now. Think aloud about your reactions, associations, first thoughts – things or ideas that occur to you. Revisit all the points in the incident when you reported feeling quite strongly (positively or negatively) about what was happening at that time. With hindsight, what do you think about what you did or were doing or were not doing? What about the other key actors in the situation? How do you *now* evaluate what they did, or failed to do then? Be sure you agree with the transcript that your thinking coach is making.

Finally, imagine you are the manager in some situation that has something in common with the incident which you have been recalling. Maybe the problem to be solved might have similar ingredients, or perhaps the people involved might have similar positive or negative characteristics, or perhaps similar processes might be involved, such as instruction, feedback or reprimand. Envisage yourself in that imaginary situation armed with the learning you have gained by reflecting upon your experience. What would you do (or avoid doing) in the new situation? Check, item by item, the reflections that your thinking coach has recorded – what learning can you translate into predictions of actions that you will take (or avoid taking) in a future management situation? Imagine how you will be feeling and what you will be thinking in those envisaged future situations.

In your role as thinking coach

Your role is to ask your reflective learner questions that will help them to think recollectively, critically, predictively and imaginatively, and to make an accurate written record of your learner's recollections, reflections and the learning which your learner proposes to transfer into some future management situation.

On the basis of your written account you are then required to think empathetically, as though you were in the shoes of your learner, and record what *you* would have learned and at what point you would have learned it, if you had been in your reflective learner's shoes. You are then required to inspect your empathetic learning and to attempt to make general statements of the kind 'If I had been in my reflective learner's shoes, then I would have learned XYZ about management, because I can learn about management when ABC.'

You must present your written account of your reflective learner's recollections, reflections and predicted actions and your own empathetic and metacognitive learning to the person who will be playing the role of critical friend. Your task here is to make good use of the challenge, assessment and feedback of your critical friend and to accommodate and assimilate as much of it as you can into your written account of what you have so far learned when acting as a thinking coach.

In your role as critical friend

In your role as a critical friend, you are required to sit down with the thinking coach and the thinking coach's written account of what has been recollected, reflected and predicted. You are required to think critically and evaluatively about the written account of the learning conversation so far. To be critical and evaluative does not necessarily mean that you must be negative. You should start by drawing the thinking coach's attention to aspects of the written account that you find especially pleasing or well observed, or insightful, or concisely recorded, or interesting, or provocative. It is always possible to find some genuine positive features of the thinking coach's work on which you can comment. If you think that there are other issues that could have been explored, invite the thinking coach to consider them now. If you cannot see how certain reflections relate to the record of the recollected incident, ask the thinking coach to explain, making clear any unspoken assumptions. If you think that certain conclusions or implications do not follow from what precedes them in the account, then challenge the reasoning. Ask for concrete examples to check that the learning is understood and ask questions that check that the learning can be transferred to situations with which the thinking coach is unfamiliar.

Activity 7 Individual Learning: Critical Thinking

CASE STUDY: Learning from projects and research

Paul was a manager in the social services department of a UK County Council. Partly responding to outside pressures to do so, and partly reflecting the genuine desire of some of his fellow officers to do so, his department was increasingly 'consulting' other people about the quality of their services. Paul wondered why they were doing this and whether or not consulting was a 'good thing'. He formulated a tentative aim for a research project to explore these questions: 'To identify ways to measure the effectiveness of consultation with service users in a local authority social services department'. In order to find information or literature on the subject, Paul used a 'relevance tree' (Figure 13.13).

A relevance tree starts with an aim at the top of the line and uses lines to show the interrelationships between aspects of the research aim and existing literature.

Desirable for whom?

Paul was immediately submerged under a burgeoning literature on 'stakeholders'. Who were the stakeholders in a County Council Social Services department? How to decide? He needed a method to find out. How could he find out what methods were available? He asked the librarian who told him which books were on the short loan and therefore must be most popular and, presumably, most useful. The most popular were:

- Easterby-Smith, M., Thorpe, R. and Lowe, A. (1991) *Management Research – An Introduction*. Sage.
- Edwards, A. and Talbot, R. (1994) *The Hard-pressed Researcher – A Research Handbook for the Caring Professions*. Longman.
- Guba, E. and Lincoln, Y. (1994) 'Fourth Generation Evaluation'. In Simon, G. and Cassel, C. (eds) *Qualitative Methods and Analysis in Organisational Research*. Sage.

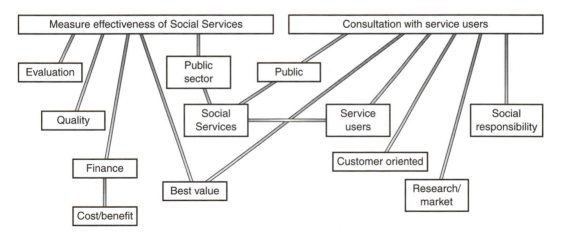

Figure 13.13 Relevance tree for Paul's literature search

- Gummesson, E. (1991) *Qualitative Methods in Management Research*. Sage.
- Crotty, M. (1998) *The Foundation of Social Research*. Sage.

It took Paul the best part of a day to skim-read the reference copies. The language and the terminology were all new to him. He decided that statistical methods would not help him. That greatly simplified his choice. He found Crotty's ideas on qualitative methods helpful, mainly because most of the other writers assumed that he knew what a 'paradigm' was. Paul suspected that they were all using the word 'paradigm' in different ways (just to confuse him!). In any case, he could not understand any of the ways it was being used! He reserved a copy of Crotty for short loan a few weeks ahead and resolved to use it to help him write his methodology chapter. He knew that he would have to write a bit about the methods he was not going to use, in order to explain why he was not going to use them. He photocopied some bits to be going on with. He was particularly hopeful about systems approaches as a way of finding out who his stakeholders might be. He discovered Checkland and got hooked on Checkland's ideas about Soft Systems Methodologies. At closing time the security man threw him out of the library – protesting. It was the best fun he'd had for ages!

One of Checkland's key ideas was ownership. Who owned this idea of consultation – whose project was it? Where had the idea come from in the first place? Who had dreamt it up and why? Whose interests did it serve? What were they getting out of it? What were they really up to? How to find out? It really was very exciting. He felt a bit like an investigator – half detective, half journalist. By now he had dark suspicions about the real motives of some of his stakeholders, but he needed evidence – 'sources', 'Deep Throats', 'documentation' – evidence that would stand up in an academic court. The defending counsel would try to discredit him, saying he was biased. He'd best come clean and declare his political and social allegiances straight away. He thought they ought to know that he was an engineer and a physical scientist by profession, and not a social worker. It might give him more credibility with his assessor, who had a reputation for being a 'quants' man. His project supervi-sor reminded him of his revised aim. How much of this admittedly fascinating investigation was really relevant? What a blessing it was to have a clear aim, time and time again it saved him like Occam's razor. It kept him from the fruitless 'chasing of hares'.

He considered the desirability of performance criteria. Desirable for whom? No, he wouldn't go down that route – the stakeholder route – again. How about thinking about 'Desirability' itself? How does any stakeholder decide whether or not something is desirable – what criteria do they use? 'Do they necessarily use criteria?' his supervisor had asked, unhelpfully. Paul was sure that everyone used criteria (even if they were the wrong criteria). How else could they possibly decide? 'Perhaps you are beginning to get an insight into your paradigm,' his supervisor had said enigmatically, offering to explain himself later. His supervisor suggested that Paul should keep notes of his personal ups and downs with the project. He said that these would come in handy for the final chapter of his report – the one on personal reflections and learning. This would be important in his final assessment.

The task

Assume that a researcher is trying to find answers to the following questions:

1 Why is this research important?
2 What am I hoping to achieve and by when?
3 To what questions do I want to find answers?
4 What possible ways are there to find answers?
5 Which may be the best way to try?
6 Why is it a better way than the others?
7 How will I evaluate the answers?
8 What criteria will I use?
9 How can I work out some criteria?
10 What do I conclude from my evaluation?
11 Based on the conclusions I have drawn, who might benefit by doing what, by when?
12 What am I learning about organizations, management and myself, as I am doing this?

In which parts of Paul's story do you think he might be finding answers to any of these 12 questions?

Activity 8 Individual Learning Review: Reflective Thinking

Inner world thinking

What inner world thinking skills can you identify in the manager's work described in this chapter? Have any of the thinking skills you have identified emerged for the first time in this chapter? If so, add them to your accumulating model of the kinds of thinking skills that you think are useful to managers of public services.

What things could you do to develop any of the thinking skills that you have just added to your model? What would be the first step?

Outer world conversations

What outer world conversational skills can you identify in the manager's work described in this chapter? Have any of the types of conversational skills you have identified emerged for the first time? If so, add them to your accumulating model of the kinds of conversational skills you think are useful to managers of public services.

What things could you do to develop any of these conversational skills which you have just added to your model? What would be the first step?

Activity 9 Individual Learning: Metacognitive Thinking

Metacognition

Look back through the Thinking and Learning Activities you have been asked to carry out in this chapter. What thinking skills were involved in each of these activities? For each type of thinking, write down how you were learning what you were learning, when you were learning to think in each of the different ways.

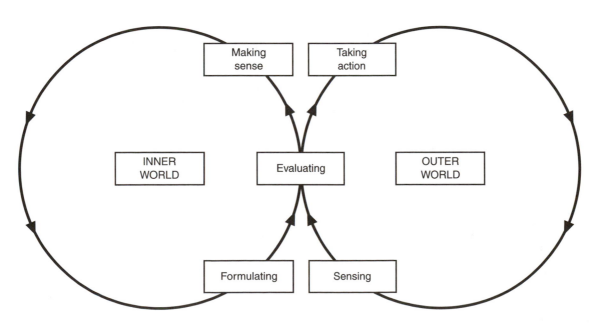

Figure 13.14 The thinking skills of the conversational manager

NOTES

1 Heckscher, C. and Donnellon, A. (eds) (1994) *The Post-bureaucratic Organization. New Perspectives on Organizational Change*. Sage.

2 Handy, C. (1987) *The Making of Managers*. London MSC.

3 Burgoyne, J. (1989) 'Creating the Managerial Portfolio: Building on Competency-based Approaches to Management Development'. *Journal of Management Education and Development*, vol. 20, pp. 56–61.

4 Schroder, H. M. (1989) *Managerial Competence: The Key to Excellence*. Kendall/Hunt, p. 7.

5 Kakabadse, A. (1991) *The Wealth Creators. Top People, Top Teams and Executive Best Practice*. Kogan Page.

6 Boyatzis, R. E. (1982) *The Competent Manager: A Model for Organisational Effectiveness*. Wiley Interstate Sciences.

7 Klemp, G. O. (1980) *Associations of Occupational Competence*. National Institute of Education.

8 Morgan, G. (1988) *Riding the Waves of Change: Developing Managerial Competencies for a Turbulent World*. Jossey-Bass.

9 Cockerill, T. (1989) *Managerial Competence as a Determinant of Organizational Performance*. University of London.

10 Blagg, N. and Ballinger, M. (eds) (1994) *Thinking and Learning at Work*. Great Britain. Employment Department Group.

11 Pedler, M., Burgoyne, J. and Boydell, T. (1986) *The Learning Company. A Strategy for Sustainable Development*. McGraw-Hill, p. 1.

12 Garvin, D. A. (1993) *Harvard Business Review*. July–August, p. 80.

13 Pettigrew, A. and Whipp, R. (1991) *Managing Change for Competitive Success*. Blackwell Business.

14 Senge, P. (1990) *The Fifth Discipline: The Art and Practice of the Learning Organization*. Century.

15 Beardwell, I. and Holden, L. (1994) *Human Resource Management. A Contemporary Perspective*. Pitman, p. 276.

16 Burgoyne (1989), op. cit.

17 Ranson, S. and Stewart, J. (1994) *Management for the Public Domain*. Macmillan.

18 Senge, op. cit., p. 41.

19 Honey, P. (1991) 'The Learning Organisation Simplified'. *Training and Development*, July, p. 30.

20 Finger, M. and Brand, S. B. (1999) 'The Concept of the Learning Organisation Applied to the Transformation of the Public Sector', in Easterby-Smith, M., Burgoyne, J. and Araujo, L. (eds) *Organizational Learning and the Learning Organization. Developments in Theory and Practice*. Sage, p. 136.

21 Ibid.

22 Mumford, A. (1988) 'Learning to Learn and Management Self Development'. In Pedler, Burgoyne and Boydell (eds) *Applying Self Development in Organisations*. Prentice Hall, p. 26.

23 Cited in Buchanan, D. and Huczynski, A. (1996) *Organizational Behaviour: An Introductory Text*. Prentice Hall, p. 178.

24 Kolb, D. (1984) *Experiential Learning: A Source of Learning and Development*. Prentice Hall.

25 Mumford, op. cit.

26 Revans, R. (1983) *The ABC of Action Learning*. Charwell-Bratt.

27 Skinner, B. F. (1974) *About Behaviorism*. Knopf.

28 Bandura, A. (1977) *Social Learning Theory*. Prentice Hall.

29 Argyris, C. A. and Schon, D. (1978) *Organizational Learning. A Theory into Action Perspective*. Addison-Wesley.

30 Kolb, D. A. (1979) *Organizational Psychology*. Prentice Hall.

31 Keteljohn, W. (1996) 'Tool Boxes Are Out, Thinking Is In'. *Financial Times*, 22 March.

32 Jarvis, P. (1994) 'Learning Practical Knowledge'. *Journal of Higher Education*, vol. 18, no. 1, pp. 32–43.

33 Kemmis (1985) 'Action Research and the Politics of Reflection'. In Keogh, R. and Walker, D. (eds) *Reflection: Turning Experience into Learning*. Kogan Page.

34 Freire, P. (1970) *The Pedagogy of the Oppressed*. Penguin.

35 Argyris, C. A. and Schon, D. (1974) *Theory in Practice. Increasing Professional Effectiveness*. Jossey-Bass.

36 Schon, D. A. (1983) *The Reflective Practitioner. How Professionals Think in Action*. Maurice Temple Smith.

37 Habermas. J. quoted in Kermis, op. cit.

38 Giddens, S. (1995) 'The Integrative Principle', *European Journal of Education*, vol. 30, p. 207.

39 Brockbank, A. and McGill, I. (1998) *Facilitating Reflective Learning*. SRHE.

40 Senge, P. (1994) *The Fifth Discipline Field Book. Strategies and Tools for Building Learning Organizations*. Doubleday.

41 Buber, M. (1988) *Knowledge of Man*. Humanities Press International.

42 De Maré, P. (1991) *Koinonia: From Hate through Dialogue to Culture in the Large Groups*. Karnal.

43 Bohm, D. (1985) *Unfolding Meaning*. Foundation House.

44 Laurie, N. (1998) 'Making Dialogue Deliver'. Paper (unpublished) presented to the Society of Practical Philosophers.

45 Nelson, L. (1949) *Socratic Method and Critical Philosophy*. Yale UP.

46 Saran, S., Shipley, P. and Leal, F. (1998) 'Socratic Dialogue. The Dutch Experience'. In *Practical Philosophy*, vol. 1, no. 3.

47 Revans, op. cit.

48 Harvey, J. (1997) *Graduate Work*. Centre for Research into Quality. University of Central England.

49 Brennan, J. and Little, B. (1996) *A Review of Work Based Learning*. DFE.

50 Fryer, R. H. (1997) *Learning for the Twenty-first Century. First Report on Lifelong Learning*. National Advisory Group for Continuous Education and Lifelong Learning.

51 Knowles, M. (1984) *Andragogy in Action*. Jossey-Bass.

52 Foster, L. (1996) *Comparable but Different. Work Based Learning for a Learning Society*. University of Leeds.

53 Mumford, op. cit.

54 Schon, op. cit.

55 Wildemeersch, D. (1989) 'The Principle of Development', in Warner Weil, S. and McGill, I. (eds) *Making Sense of Experiential Learning*. Society for Research into Higher Education.

56 Sadlington, J. (1992) 'Learner Experience: A Rich Source of Learning', in Mulligan, J. and Griffin, C. (eds) *Empowerment through Experiential Learning*. Kogan Page.

57 Schon, op. cit.

58 Robinson, K. (2000) *All Our Futures: Creativity, Culture and Education*. DfEE, p. 4.

59 Windall, S. and Signitzer, B. (1992) *Using Communication Theory*. Sage.

60 Beardwell and Holden, op. cit.

61 Boydell, op. cit. (1989).

62 Horne, T. and Armstrong, R. (1999) *A Seven Year Internal Study of Management Learners.* Lancashire Business School.

63 Reigal, J. W. (1997) *Report on Executive Development.* Bureau of Industrial Relations.

64 Alred, G., Garvey, B. and Smith, R. (1998) *The Mentoring Pocket Book.* Alresford Management Pocketbooks.

65 Egan, G. (1998) *The Skilled Helper. A Problem-Management Approach to Helping.* Brooks/Cole.

66 Ritchie, N. and Connolly, M. (1993) *Management Education and Development*, vol. 24, p. 266.

67 Clutterbuck, D. (1991) *Everyone Needs a Mentor: How to Foster Talent within the Organization.* Institute of Personnel Management.

68 Morgan, G. (1886) *Images of Organization.* Sage, p. 91.

69 Argyris and Schon, op. cit.

70 Clarke, M. (1988) *Going for Better Management.* Local Government Training Board.

71 Pedler, Burgoyne and Boydell, op. cit.

14

MANAGING PERSONAL DEVELOPMENT IN PUBLIC SERVICES

People use less than 0.02 per cent of their intellectual capacity to realize less than 5 per cent of their human potential.

(Einstein)

LEARNING OUTCOMES

This chapter will enable readers to:

- Understand why personal development is important for managers.
- Understand why self-development is the best approach to personal development.
- See connections between personal development, career planning and life planning.
- Relate the development of conversational skills, learning skills and thinking skills to career planning and life planning.
- Improve their time management in order to have time self-development.
- Use a framework for life planning that embraces material, physical, emotional and spiritual well-being, as well as social, intellectual and career development.
- Use a conversational approach to thinking about careers.
- Improve the conversational skills and thinking skills which they identify as relevant to their life plans and career plans.
- Enable the personal development of others.
- Explore postmodern ideas on development.

INTRODUCTION

Early attempts to run personal development programmes for managers often deprived participants of the very attributes that they were trying to develop. The managers became dependent on their tutors. The tutors decided what was best for the managers – what they needed to learn and what was the best way to learn it. Tutors decided what resources were required and what learning processes were to be used. The managers became passive, increasingly looking to their tutors to decide which theories were valid or which techniques were useful. The implicit message was: 'Don't try to decide for yourself – there is always an expert you can ask. You don't need to worry about how you are learning because when you need an update, you can always come back.'

Increasingly, organizations are seeing personal development programmes as a way of enhancing motivation. Only personal development through self-development will enhance the ability and willingness of employees to take responsibility for their own learning. For this reason, the majority of this chapter is designed to support self-development. We have tried to 'suggest' things to the reader. Consequently, we may appear to be prescriptive where this is not intended. The thinking and learning activities at the end of the chapter are designed to help you to decide whether or not our suggestions are useful.

Box 14.1

CHANGES THAT CREATE A NEED FOR PERSONAL DEVELOPMENT

Away from ...	*Towards ...*
One job for life	Many jobs in life
Formal qualifications	Portfolios of lifelong learning
One professional career	Several careers in different professions
Incremental promotions	Leap-frogging based on achievement
Employers offer security	Employees need marketability
Steady career progression	Progression by personal portfolio
Working for one employer	Working for several employers
Sending employees away for training	Employee responsible for own development
Organizational training needs analysis	Self-awareness and self-development

---

WHY DO MANAGERS NEED PERSONAL DEVELOPMENT?

Public service organizations increasingly realize that their staff, professionals and managers need personal development (Box 14.1). It underpins a manager's performance in managing resistance and change, managing operations and activities, managing groups and individuals, managing finance and resources and managing communications and information (Box 14.2).

Box 14.2

MANAGEMENT STANDARDS FOR PERSONAL DEVELOPMENT

1   Demonstrates a proactive concern.
   - Devises and prioritizes personal and organizational objectives
   - Monitors and initiates responses to variances in planned activities
2   Shows sensitivity to the needs of others.
   - Forms close working relationships
   - Wins the commitment of others
   - Presents self positively to others
3   Shows self-confidence and drive.
   - Manages emotional stress
   - Manages learning and development
4   Initiates management of information.
   - Forms and applies concepts
   - Takes decisions

The Personal Attributes of Successful Managers

Early work for the European Foundation for Management Education, at the Centre for the Development of Management, Teachers and Trainers, Lancaster University[1] revealed that 9 out of 11 attributes identified in effective managers were personal attributes. The nine attributes were personal skills and characteristics whose enhancement could only be brought about through a process of personal development. In 1998 Horne and Harrison[2] carried out an analysis of Schroder's[3] nine-year study on high-performing managers. The study revealed that all the attributes of high-performing managers identified by Schroder rested on competencies – mainly cognitive and social competencies – that could best be enhanced through a process of personal development (Table 14.1). This finding echoed our analysis of the work of Kakabadse.[4] Again, we found that the five attributes which Kakabadse identified as distinguishing high-performing managers were personal attributes which could only be acquired through a process of personal development.

When recruiting managers, Hay recruitment consultancy use selection criteria based on the threshold and superior competencies identified by Boyatzis.[5] The superior competencies are personal competencies. A paper presented by Klemp[6] reviewed six studies on management competence and identified the characteristics of high performers as being causal thinking, the ability to conceptualize, the capacity to synthesize, influencing skills, collaborative thinking, self-awareness and the ability to interpret the symbolic meaning of the behaviour of others. Klemp's threshold competencies were a manager's sensitivity to what was going on around them and their ease with the idea of change. Klemp's competencies again signalled the need for personal development – a need echoed by Morgan in *Riding the Waves*

Table 14.1 Analysis of high-performing managers

Attribute	Description of attribute
Information search	Gathers many different kinds of information and uses a wide variety of sources.
Concept formation	Builds frameworks or models or forms concepts, hypothesizes or ideas on the basis of information; becomes aware of patterns, trends, and cause/effect relations by linking disparate information.
Conceptual flexibility	Identifies multiple options in planning; holds different options in focus simultaneously.
Interpersonal search	Uses open questions, summaries and paraphrasing to understand the ideas, concepts and feelings of others. Can comprehend issues and problems empathetically.
Managing interaction	Involves others and is able to build co-operative teams in which group members feel valued.
Developmental orientation	Creates a positive environment in which staff increase awareness of strengths and limitations; provides coaching and developmental resources.
Impact	Uses a variety of methods e.g. persuasion, modelling behaviour, and inventing symbols.
Self-confidence	Takes own 'stand' or position on issues; takes decisions when required and commits self and others; expresses confidence in future success.
Presentation	Presents ideas clearly, with ease and interest so that the audience understands what is being communicated; uses technical, non-verbal and visual aids effectively.
Proactive orientation	Structures the task for the team; implements plans and ideas; takes responsibility for all aspects.
Achievement orientation	Possesses high standards and sets ambitious, risky yet attainable goals; measures progress.

Source: Horne and Harrison (1998)

of Change.[7] Advocating his model for effective performance in managers, Morgan seeks the development in managers of a 'mindset' of attitudes and thinking skills that will enable them to think about and take action on a wide range of issues inside and outside of their organizations.

Personal Development and Employment

There is a fortunate conjunction of the attributes developed through personal development and the attributes sought by employers of graduates. In 1999 Lee Harvey[8] reported that employers valued personal attributes above technical or subject-specific knowledge when employing graduates. The personal attributes they valued included good interpersonal communication, the ability to relate to a wide variety of people and changing situations, the ability to develop close working relationships, and the ability to manage career development. Research by Harvey, Moon and Geall,[9] showed that prospective employers looked for self-awareness, self-assertion, proactivity in the creation and exploration of opportunities, action planning, networking, persuasion and influencing skills, political awareness, ability to cope with uncertainty and a broad repertoire of decision-making and thinking skills. These attributes are not dissimilar to those recommended by Dearing[10] as the 'Key Skills' which need to be acquired by all students during their undergraduate education. The Universities of Manchester, Nottingham and Leeds, in the UK, carried out surveys of their ex-students. The kinds of attributes that had proved to be most valuable to them in their subsequent lives are shown in Figure 14.1. It is important to remember that this map is only a map of the ground to be covered – it is not the ground itself. The map is not the territory. The map indicates the limits of the territory and gives us an idea of possible paths and directions. Only by getting on our feet and walking the paths for ourselves can we find out whether the route is manageable or interesting or leads us to where we want to be.

In 1990 Pedler *et al.*[11] pointed out that self-development makes the learner sovereign. Yet in most organizations, employees are not sovereign. The rights of employees usually lag behind their rights as citizens. In many countries even citizens' rights are sparse. Work organizations tend to be authoritarian. Libertarian ideas such as self-development can create difficulties. We return to these difficulties in our final thoughts at the end of this chapter. In the meantime, let us look at the experiences of Jonathan as he describes his personal development journey.

Jonathan's Story: A Model for Personal Development

What can we learn from our conversation with Jonathan? The decision to give up a 'brilliant career' in the army must have taken a lot of courage. One can imagine the concerns of his family – giving up a 'good job', 'wasting' his education and training. His godfather's role as a mentor was helpful, even if his advice wasn't! His analysis of all the skills and attributes that Jonathan had developed – especially the personal competencies – played an important role in boosting Jonathan, giving him the confidence to talk to people who were already working in training organizations. Jonathan persisted when he was rejected. He made good use of his network of contacts to get his eventual job at the hospital. He developed his own interests and skills, e.g. selling and presenting. When his interest in course design was frustrated, he took the plunge and left. He used personal relationships to minimize the risks. He turned his bankruptcy problem into an opportunity to work abroad. He learned lessons from his weakness in administration. In giving free training to the aid workers, he followed the promptings of his heart. At the time of the interview he was still seeking further challenges, considering an MBA, perhaps through distance learning. Jonathan took personal responsibility and gave up a successful career that he was not enjoying. He deliberately collected developmental experiences that would help him to do something which he could feel worthwhile doing. He persisted when things did not work out.

A conversational model of self-development

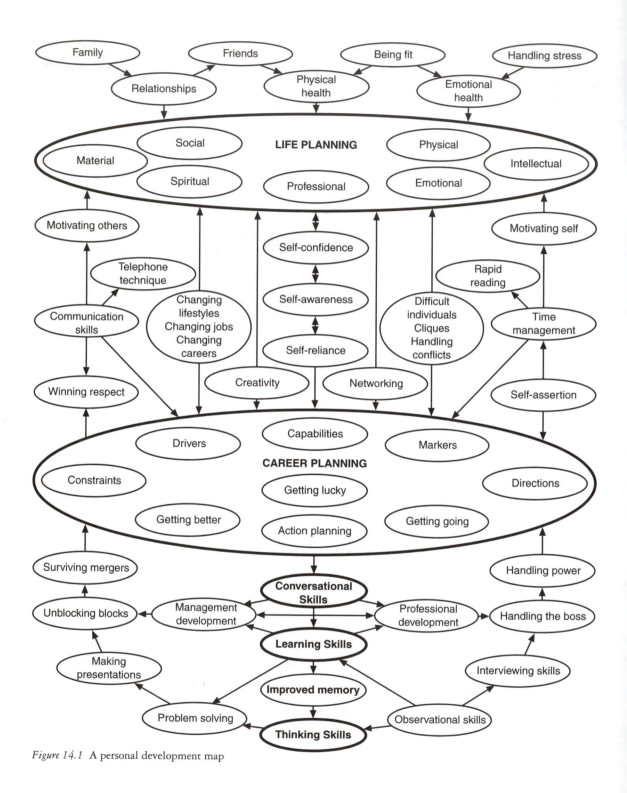

Figure 14.1 A personal development map

Box 14.3

EXTRACT FROM A CONVERSATION WITH JONATHAN

(Jonathan is a self-employed consultant specializing in work with charities)

'FINDING MY HEART'S WORK'

Terry: What did you do when you left?

Jonathan: At university, I'd been in the Officer Cadet Corps, on an army scholarship. When I graduated I signed up. I was quite successful. I got promotion to captain in six years. That was fast-tracking by army standards. I was well tipped for a 'brilliant career' – 'glittering prizes' and all that – but my heart wasn't in it.

Terry: So you quit?

Jonathan: Yes. It was a terrible shock. I'd gone from boarding school to a college in Cambridge, and then into the army without ever having to decide what to do, or how to train for it. Now I was unemployed. I was completely at sea with it all.

Terry: So what did you do?

Jonathan: It was my godfather, actually, who pointed out what a lot of skills I must have picked up along the way at boarding school and then at Cambridge, as well as during my time in the army. Things like rubbing along with other chaps, leadership, taking decisions, issuing orders, solving problems. I wrote it all down and sent copies off to the recruitment agencies and the big-blue chip companies.

Terry: What happened?

Jonathan: Big zero. Nothing. Not a dickey bird. It was terribly disheartening.

Terry: What did you do?

Jonathan: I was interested in getting into training so I started asking around to see if anyone knew anyone already working in training. Finally, I found some people and eventually got a job as a training officer in a hospital.

Terry: Did you enjoy it?

Jonathan: The best part was going around the departments persuading them to release people for training. I got really good at it so they sent me to other hospitals to persuade them to send their staff to us for training. We became the training centre for the whole region! But in the end I got frustrated with being a salesman. I wanted to design and run the training programmes my way. I decided to set up on my own.

Terry: Risky.

Jonathan: Not really. I went with the blessing of the regional director and with some contract work for the regional health authority – enough to start me off. I used to invite him along as a guest speaker. Because I was now a business I could pay him!

Terry: Did you make a lot of money?

Jonathan: No, not really. It seemed like it on paper but my administration and invoicing was awful. I hated filling in claims forms. I was always short of cash. When my car packed up I couldn't afford to replace it! My overdraft got so bad I took a job in Bahrain.

Terry: How was it working in all that heat?

Jonathan: It was brilliant. Best decision I ever took! I set up on my own again but this time with a partner who was good at administration and great fun to work with.

Terry: How did you start with charities?

Jonathan: A fluke really. Bumping into aid workers overseas. Asking them about their work. It always seemed more interesting and more worthwhile than my job – which was just about making money. All their projects needed trained people. They were always short of trained people. I started off running train-

ing courses for them for nothing. Just to help out. Then we got offered a big contract by the World Bank, training aid workers. It was a bit too bureaucratic for my liking but I got to know the development officers of nearly all the big overseas charities. The rest is history. I am really enjoying myself. I could do with more intellectual challenge though. I fancy an MBA.
Terry: We could talk about that sometime!

(Figure 14.2) can help us to map together some of the stages in Jonathan's process of self-development. Jonathan's self-assessment involved a process of inner world thinking and outer world conversations, generating Jonathan's plan for a new life and a new career.

Jonathan's self-development was catalysed by a cash crisis. It involved rehearsing some ideas in his head, checking them out, and modifying them in conversation with others and surfacing his own beliefs. Self-development does not necessarily need to be propelled by a crisis. It can be propelled by a desire to conserve an existing situation that is very satisfactory, or it can be propelled by the sheer joy of feeling that you are still learning and changing. Figure 14.3 represents three things that propel self-development. It's a three-bladed 'propeller': the three blades are Experimentation and Change (seeking growth), Support and Rejuvenation (seeking satisfaction), Fitness and Preparation (seeking survival).

The Attributes of Self-developers

So we have a map of the terrain that you might cover in your self-development, a model of a conversational self-development process you might use, and some ideas about what might propel you to use them. What are the characteristics of those who take up the challenge – who embarks on the journey? How can self-developers be recognized? In Box 14.4 we summarize the attributes of self-developers.

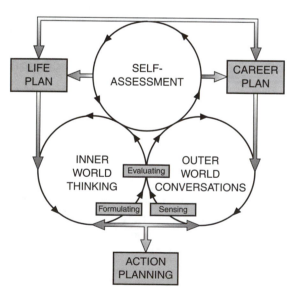

Figure 14.2 A conversational model of self-development

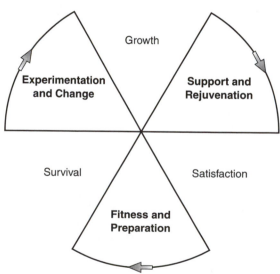

Figure 14.3 A three-bladed propeller of self-development

Box 14.4

THE ATTRIBUTES OF SELF-DEVELOPERS

Self-developers tend to . . .

- Assess their own needs
- Change tack or track if necessary
- See problems as learning opportunities
- Exploit opportunities that are unexpected
- Draw conclusions from general experiences
- Tolerate inconvenience, uncertainty and work
- Try out things even if they feel foolish

- Test out the conclusions they draw or the ideas they have
- Assess their own progress against their own measures of performance
- Take personal responsibility for making things better for themselves and others
- Make their own plans to meet their needs and decide their own measures of performance

When we compare the characteristics of the self-developer in Box 14.4 with the work of a manager in Figure 14.4 it is not hard to see why Harvey Jones, ex-Chairman of ICI, believes that self-development is the best form of management development.[12]

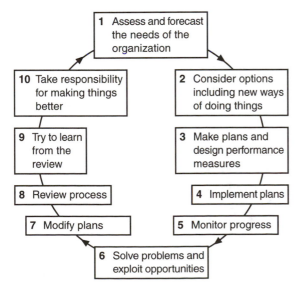

Figure 14.4 The work of a manager: what managers do

PERSONAL DEVELOPMENT SEEN AS A JOURNEY

You have a map of the terrain over which your journey can take you (Figure 14.1), some ideas about the processes you can use to get there (Figure 14.2) and some insight into the kinds of reasons for which you might undertake the quest (Figure 14.3). You have some idea of the kinds of personal characteristics you can expect to develop (Box 14.4) and how this will be helpful for you in your work as a manager (Figure 14.4). Before you begin your journey, it can be useful to choose a companion.

Choosing a Personal Development Companion

A personal development programme is meant to be a period of sustained learning. In Chapter 13 we argued that paired learning was more effective than individual or group-based learning. Thinking and learning activities at the end of that chapter can help you to develop the conversational learning skills you need. While it is perfectly possible to hold learning conversations with yourself, there are many advantages to having a learning companion. It is good to have someone with whom you can share the good and the bad experiences, or with whom you can pool the resources which you will each collect during your times apart. Your companion does not need to be someone who is also engaged in a process of self-development. Your companion can be a more experienced manager. Companions of the opposite sex often offer a different perspective, which can be invaluable. An excellent companion might be someone with whom you have a co-counselling relationship (Chapter 8). Box 14.5 illustrates the kinds of questions you might ask yourself in your search for someone to play the role of personal development companion. Even one positive response is sufficient for someone to be a serious candidate for the role.

Personal development companions rarely start their journey together as soulmates, though that is what they may become. They do not need to be paragons of virtue. It is not a good idea to choose a sexual partner, your boss, or someone with whom you work closely as a colleague or as a client. It should be someone you like. Above all it should be someone you like talking to and who likes talking to you.

A CONVERSATIONAL APPROACH TO PERSONAL DEVELOPMENT

You need to be able to rely on your personal development companion to give you an hour of their time every week. Reciprocal arrangements work well. Book lots of slots, well ahead. Seek out good venues away from phones and other people. Arrange to go on walks maybe. A conversational approach to personal development involves talking about topics of the kind illustrated in Box 14.6.

'What's on Top?'

During 'What's on Top?' time, you can talk uninterrupted about whatever is on the top of your mind – whatever seems important – or carries some kind of emotional charge. Aim to talk for at least 10 minutes. It does not matter where you start. Sometimes it is easier to start in the middle, or with 'I'm feeling . . . and I'm not sure why.' Your companion will not interrupt or comment and will tolerate pauses or awkward silences, until you say 'pass'. They will only comment if you say 'Well . . . ?' Even then they will only comment on what they heard; they will not pass judgement on you.

Box 14.5

FINDING A PERSONAL DEVELOPMENT COMPANION: SOME QUESTIONS TO ASK

- Who could you talk to about the kind of issues raised for you in this chapter?
- Who could you see doing some of the things described in this chapter?
- Who often seems to have and share information with you?
- With whom would you choose to eat?
- Who makes you feel important?
- With whom could you share bad news?
- Who will give you honest feedback?
- Who goads you to 'do something'?
- Who can be enthusiastic?

Box 14.6

A CONVERSATIONAL APPROACH TO PERSONAL DEVELOPMENT: TYPICAL TOPICS

- Something one of you has read, related to an area on the personal development map
- Something one of you has done, related to an area on the personal development map
- A difficult intellectual challenge that one of you has faced since you last met
- An emotionally charged situation that one of you has faced
- Something that is bothering one of you
- 'What's on top?'

Active Listening – The Gift of Silence

The reader may find it useful to reread the sections of Chapter 8 that deal with active listening, empathy and using open questions. At the end of a period of 'active listening' your tongue should be covered in blood – at least metaphorically – from biting it! Resist the temptation to chip in while your companion is talking or, importantly, when they fall silent. Obviously your whole demeanour should convey strongly that you are still interested in what they might go on to say. Try actively to like the person, even if they have just said things with which you did not agree. Try to respect them, even when they have just said something that you thought was stupid. Above all, let them finish. Let them have their say. There may be no one else in their lives who offers them such a priceless gift: the gift of undivided silent attention. Try not to curtail it or to snatch it away almost as soon as you have offered it. At last, when they say 'pass', try to show 'response-ability'.

Response-ability

This is the ability to respond – as opposed to react – to what your companion has said. You might need to pause before formulating a thoughtful response. It is your companion's turn to wait silently. What a gift there is in this silence – a time to reflect and a chance to see their own reflection – a time to listen to the prompting of the spirit – whatever you consider that might be. This will feel unusual because it is unusual! Thoughtful silence is hard to come by, given the busy lives which most managers lead.

Making Statements

When you do respond, do not interrogate your companion. Questions can be very controlling and can limit the other person's options. By social convention, questions carry an expectation that an answer is required. Statements on the other hand, are more self-disclosing and leave the other person free to agree with, disagree with, or ignore your statement.

The exchange is more even-handed, more equal. Try to make your statement empathetic – i.e. a thoughtful guess at what they may be thinking or feeling about what has just been said. The other person can correct you if you have got it wrong. In the process they may become clearer themselves. If the other person becomes distressed, some form of physical contact can be a better acknowledgement than words. Do not be afraid to make confrontational statements of the kind: 'that assumes X and I'm not sure X is true' or 'you said X but then you said Y, X and Y contradict each other' or 'you said that you felt X, but you looked as though you were feeling Y' or 'I don't share your view that . . .' Don't just reject, try to give counter examples: 'What you say about X does not explain the case where . . .' Often questions conceal statements like 'I don't like the sound of X' or ' I don't believe Y'. Try to make these statements explicitly, rather than disguise them as questions. That way your companion has a choice about dealing with (or not dealing with) what you are really saying. In personal development conversations, it is necessary to suspend some social rules governing polite conversation. Despite what we have just said about preferring statements, some questions can be useful.

Asking Questions

The object of the questions is not to make your companion feel inadequate or foolish, but to help your companion to think, and to move the focus of that thinking, e.g. from fantasy to reality, from the abstract to the concrete, from thought to action, from past memories to present ideas, from present ideas to future events.

'Is there a pattern here?', 'So what are you saying?', 'Can you give me an example?', 'When was the last time you felt like this?', 'Is it still happening now?', 'What will you do if it happens again?', 'How will you feel doing that?', 'So what is the first step?', 'When will you take it?', 'Is there anything you need to know, or do, before that?', 'How would you like the situation to be different?', 'What needs to change?', 'What other possibilities are there?',

'What's stopping you from . . .', 'What can you do to minimize what is stopping you?' and so on.

The danger is that you will use such questions to give too strong a steer or lead. Try to be clear about your own motivation. If you fear you have a vested interest, or a bias, or a prejudice, try to own it at least to yourself and preferably to your companion. Finally, summarize what your companion has said will be done and by when. Check out the accuracy of your summary with your companion. Do not add new material or ideas of your own. End with a clear summary of agreed actions and first steps. At the end of the personal development conversation, try to lighten the mood. End on a positive note. Share something that you are looking forward to doing before you meet again.

Making a Difference

Personal development conversations can be tough going but they should also be very rewarding. Personal development is a practical way to realize personal ambitions and the material rewards that come to those who are effective managers. In almost every culture there exists a parable of the talents and the idea of making the best of them for the general good. Personal development is not a competitive sport, it is 'only the fight to recover what's been lost and found and lost again'. Any absurdity we may feel about this has to be set against the good that comes when we make the best of ourselves and when we make some positive difference to the world. Suggestions of what to say and ask during a personal development conversation are found in Box 14.7.

Box 14.7

A CONVERSATIONAL APPROACH TO PERSONAL DEVELOPMENT: THINGS TO ASK AND SAY

1 **Making Sense**
   Offer your interpretation of your partner's conversation so far. 'There appears to be a pattern here . . .', 'It seems that this is not the first time that . . .', 'It seems like a familiar feeling to you . . .', 'I'm wondering what all this means to you?', 'What do you think X is really saying to you?', 'Why do you think these things keep happening?'

2 **Challenging**
   Look for inconsistencies and contradictions in what is said but do not attack or demean. 'A does not appear to be consistent with B', 'A and B cannot be true at the same time', 'You say you feel A but you look B', 'You say you are feeling X but you would like to do Y', 'I feel (saddened, disappointed, alarmed, worried, attacked, disregarded, put down, depressed relieved, hopeful, pleased . . .), when you say . . .'

3 **Illustrating**
   In order to show further interest, deepen your partner's understanding of events, fill in gaps in the pattern and increase the likelihood of spotting further connections, ask for more and more detailed examples. 'Can you think of any more examples?', 'Tell me about that', 'What about the time when . . .', 'You said . . . what exactly did she say?', 'What were her exact words?', 'How did she look when . . . ?', 'Was it like this?', 'I would have felt . . . How did it make you feel?'

4 **Connecting**
   Try to find and get your partner to find connections between the events described and other events which do not, at first appear to be related. 'I'm wondering whether anything similar to this has happened to you before?', 'When did it happen . . . what happened exactly?', 'When was the last time you felt

this way?', 'What happened that time?', 'How do these things usually resolve themselves?'

5 **Supporting**

Show interest, respect and that you have some understanding of what they are thinking and feeling. Sit close and facing them. Nod and smile. 'That seems . . .', 'In your position I would feel . . .', 'That happened to me when . . . and I felt . . .', 'Has that happened before? . . . How did it make you feel then?'

6 **Projecting**

The point of exploring the implications for future behaviours is to test your understanding and interpretation of the present. 'If it is X now, then it seems to me that it will be Y in the future'. This is not an escape from the present. You should return to what is being thought and felt *now* and work out what must be done *now*, to affect the future in some desir-

able way. 'Can you imagine a world in which this will never happen again?' 'What will it be like, what will they see?' 'What will you be able to hear or smell in the background?' Try rehearsing now. 'What is the first thing you must do now?' 'When?' 'Who do you need to phone and when?' 'How will you remember to do that?' 'Have you got the information you need?' 'What else do you need to know?' 'Right, when can we do this now?'

7 **Summarizing**

This involves returning to number 1 and updating the Making Sense stage in the light of all the information you have gained from stages 2–6. End with a quick restatement of how things will be experienced as better when actions are taken.

8 **Reiterating**

This involves going back to any one of stages.

Personal development conversations held on a regular basis with your personal development companion create other opportunities for personal development.

EXTENDING OPPORTUNITIES FOR PERSONAL DEVELOPMENT

Networking

As we saw in the conversation with Jonathan, networking can be very developmental. You meet with people, share information, help each other with jobs, careers and life generally. Networking is also difficult. Spending time talking to people can be boring, awkward and embarrassing. It is also time consuming. Yet by expanding and cultivating a network of contacts, inside and outside your organization, you advance your own interests and perhaps give someone a hand up in life. This can be very rewarding. According to Wellman,[13] agencies specializing in

placing redundant managers attribute 85 per cent of their placements to networking. Begin by tracing people you knew at school or university. Somebody is sure to have a list. Go to reunions. Get a large address book and, besides the usual home and work e-mail addresses and phone numbers, note down birthdays, names of children, areas of interest. If you hear news about someone, drop them a line – the same for condolences. Membership of clubs and societies can be a rich source of contacts. Activities like sport, walking, amateur dramatics or fund-raising cut across many social boundaries. If you belong to a professional institute, attend the meetings. Networking is a numbers game. The more people you know, the greater the chance that you can help somebody.

Keeping a Personal Development Log

An A4 hardback, fixed-leaf notebook works well. Mark off each double page with the week commencing date for each week of the coming year. Your goal is to visit one of the areas on the Personal Development Map (Figure 14.1) each week and record what you discovered and how useful it was. The first follow-up action you intend to take should be recorded in some detail – what, who, when, where and how. Create a box in the margin to tick when it has been done. Create a space also for recording the three most important points that arose from your weekly meeting with your personal development companion. On many competency-based management development programmes you could submit your notebook as a learning log. It will need to be authenticated by others, and to conclude with an ongoing personal development plan (covering life, career and learning development) plus a summary of your most important learnings and how they occurred.

By now you may be wondering how you will find the time to research selected areas on your Personal Development Map, meet with your personal development companion and write up your personal development learning log. This is a good time to look at time management.

TIME MANAGEMENT

According to Ian Fleming,[14] much that can be said about time management is common sense. Time management is not a single skill. Managing time well involves doing lots of things, many of which are tedious. That is why good time management is not common; most of us could manage our time better. The following 12 suggestions are offered to help you manage your time better, so that you have more time available for personal development.

1 Locate the Tasks in One Place – Make One List

Locate all your tasks onto one task list written down the left-hand side of an A4 lined pad. Good places to look for outstanding tasks to be done are: your telephone pad; your incoming mail tray; your boss's action list. Get all the tasks, all located, on your task list. It does not matter about the order. Put vertical columns opposite your task list (Figure 14.5).

2 Eliminate Some Tasks Prioritize those that Remain

Ask 'Does this need to be done at all?' 'Does it contribute to the organization's objectives?' If no, bin it! If yes, 'who besides me could do it?' (Chapter 3). Not all tasks are equally important or equally urgent, or equally high on your boss's agenda. Try using an ABC system for prioritizing tasks (Box 14.8).

Tasks	Priority A, B, C	Estimates (hrs)	Phone	Read	Decide	Discuss	Write	Monday	Tuesday	Wednesday	Thursday	Friday	Week 2	Week 3	Week 4	Other
Available time								3	5	4	4	4	20	20	10	20

Figure 14.5 Allocating work and time

Box 14.8

PRIORITIZATION: THE ABC SYSTEM

For Importance	A = Essential	B = Desirable	C = Marginal
For Urgency	A = Harm if not done	B = As soon as	C = Nothing spoils
For Boss	A = Boss will not negotiate	B = As soon as possible	C = Boss unlikely to notice if not done

In order to rate the importance of tasks, you will need to have criteria. For example, anything that pleases the boss, or produces visible results or reduces stress, might all be A's for you. It is for you to decide your own criteria for rating the importance of tasks. Clients, external or internal, will probably drive your rating for urgency. The boss drives the boss's list. In the longer term, you may be able to develop some shared criteria. Obviously you allocate top priority to your triple A's. (Maybe triple C's should never have got on the list!)

3 Analyse the Tasks
Estimate the Time Needed

Be realistic. If you don't know, guess. Then notice how long it actually takes. In this way you can learn to make more accurate estimates. Analysing the tasks will enable you to group certain types of tasks together. It is better to group your phone calls together and make them all at once at a time that suits you. You can go to the next person on your list, if the first person is engaged. If you ring near the end of the working day, the calls will probably take less time. It enables you to allocate tasks to times best suited, e.g. writing tasks are best suited to times when the timeslots are longer, or less likely to be interrupted. By putting against each item the initials of people you will need to talk to, a quick glance down your list will enable you to pick out all the things you need to deal with when you next talk to them. This avoids repeat phone calls or chasing them to arrange further meetings.

4 Consolidate Your Unallocated Time

Many tasks require single sizeable chunks of time – report writing, for example. Broken time causes inefficient stopping and starting. By renegotiating some of the 'fixed' points that break up your day, it might be possible to consolidate your time into bigger chunks. If you have mid-morning or mid-afternoon meetings, can you send a more junior person for whom the experience would be developmental? You could ask them to prepare a brief summary, or give them limited authority to decide. Offer people appointments near to times they have got to get away – they will be very efficient with your time! Come in early to keep big chunks of early morning time free for your personal work. Feeling you have already got something finished, in the post, will set you up for the day.

5 Allocate the Tasks

When you allocate the task to a particular day or week, transfer the number of hours you have estimated into the column for that day or week. Do not allocate hours unrealistically. If you know from your previous lists that when you have allocated 30 estimated hours into a week, the tasks you have got done rarely exceeded 20 estimated hours, then do not allocate more than 20 hours. If you cannot allocate all your triple A's into the time available, go to your line manager immediately to seek assistance or guidance on reprioritizing your list. At least your case for more time should now be well analysed and

Box 14.9

CHOOSING ASSERTION, NOT AGGRESSION OR DEPRESSION

Aggressive behaviour is when you . . .
Threaten, cajole, ridicule, manipulate and intimidate and try to get your own way regardless of the consequences for others.

And don't . . .
Seek solutions in which everybody wins, having respect for the rights and feelings of others.

Depressive behaviour is when you . . .
Hide or deny your feelings, wish things would turn out your way and hope someone will ask you for your opinion just for once.

And don't . . .
Express how you are feeling, say what you want or draw attention to your needs, for fear of upsetting someone else.

Assertive behaviour is when you . . .
Realize you have rights, state clearly what you would like to happen, and ask for things with some expectations that your request will be granted.

And don't . . .
Violate the rights of others, expect them to guess what you want, and assume that you will be ignored.

well quantified. If your reasonable and well-argued case is not heeded, ask for a three-way meeting to argue the case with your boss and your boss's boss. If the argument is not going your way, do not get angry or depressed, be assertive (Box 14.9).

6 Learning to Say 'No': Being Assertive

If you are being expected to achieve 'triple A' tasks in a timescale that is less than you estimate they will take, you are entitled to have your estimates taken seriously. Unreasonable demands are a source of stress. Employers may be legally liable to compensate you for any damage which such stress causes to your health or your career prospects (Chapter 8).

7 Motivate Yourself

Getting more of the right things done in a given space of time is not only about saying 'no' to ineffective work and allocating time to what is important and urgent, it is also about working faster in the time slots that you have consolidated. Try to work

out how each task can be made to meet your unmet needs for warmth, applause and possession (Chapter 7). Try to work with people who are positive thinking, problem-solving and enthusiastic. Avoid cynics. Enthusiasm is infectious and so is humour. Commit yourself publicly to what you intend to achieve. Fear of losing face is a great spur. Publicize your successes. Success breeds success. Try to get to a finish and have something to show for your efforts – a memo, a report, a photo, a new service, a new job or a new life.

8 Manage Your Energy Levels

The rate at which you can work is limited by the energy your body can make available for work. Most people have energy peaks and troughs in their day. Some people are morning people; some people are night people. These peaks and troughs are determined by the body's bio-rhythms. For most people, the period between 13.00–15.00 can be the lowest energy time of their working day. It pays to know when your own energy levels are likely to be high or low. Don't schedule difficult meetings or tasks for times when your energy levels are likely to be low. Reserve decision-making and important meetings for your peak energy times. The body makes energy available for work by oxidizing the fuel content of the food we eat. The rate at which the body can oxidize food is determined by its metabolic rate. This can be raised through exercise. Keep up your metabolic rate, and hence the energy you have available for work, by having at least 20 minutes vigorous aerobic exercise, three times a week. Use stairs not lifts and walk briskly between buildings and offices. Do not eat carbohydrates at lunchtime or drink alcohol during the day. Avoid caffeine and people who smoke. Have a supply of fresh fruit available. Avoid dehydration and work near an open window, if noise and air quality allow. (For more information on managing your energy levels, see Wootton and Horne (2000) *Thinking Skills for Managers* at www.librapress.com).

9 Deal with Interruptions

Was it really an interruption or was it the kind of thing that you are paid to do? Is what you call an interruption, simply work that you are paid to do straightaway? Do people know the best times to catch you or call you? People hate to be scowled at, to be given short shrift or to be fobbed off. They would much rather know when you prefer to be 'interrupted'. Remember, you are holding up their work and their clients by not talking to them. Make it clear when they can decide things for themselves. If you cannot divert your telephone or have it call-minded, then answer it first ring and ask immediately: 'When would it be a good time to call you back? I am free at such a time.' One in ten times you may have to be interrupted, but at least you have reduced your interruptions by 90 per cent.

If people interrupt in person, despite the fact that you have publicized your 'open door' times, then stand up. People are unlikely to sit down in your office if you remain standing. Ask: 'Have you come to fix a time for later? I have a space tomorrow at . . . or later today.' If they insist that it has to be imme-

diately, work backwards: 'Do you need me to approve something?', 'What is it?', 'Yes, that's fine', or 'What is the reason for . . . ?', 'We'll discuss that later in your office'. By meeting in the other person's office you can control when you leave the meeting.

10 Speed up Your Reading

Before you begin to read ask: 'Is it worth reading?' If so, ask: 'Do I have to read it?' 'Would a more junior person feel privileged to read it, perhaps sending me back the headlines, or recommendations for actions?' If you have to read it, is there a summary? Check the contents list – which parts look interesting? Start with any recommendations. They will probably be at the end. You may be able to accept them outright. If you would like to know the conclusions on which the recommendations are based, flick back a few pages. After reading the conclusions, are you satisfied? If so, move on to your next item of reading. If the conclusions seem suspect, dig deeper, looking for the evidence that supports the conclusions.

It is rare that anything needs to be read from cover to cover. If it does, read the opening and closing paragraphs of each chapter or section, then the first and last sentence of each paragraph. Use your finger to trace a diagonal line across each paragraph – follow your finger tip with your eyes and allow your peripheral vision to pick up any key words. Slowly increase your finger speed until you are reading 300–800 words a minute and still picking up the key words. At 800 words a minute your comprehension may drop to 60 or 70 per cent. At 1,000 words per minute you will still be able to pick up the gist of the content. Slow down for the paragraphs that matter.

11 Reduce Time Wasted in Meetings

If you resent the amount of time you are wasting in meetings, we suggest that you read the part of Chapter 6 that deals with the danger of groups. Try not to create groups yourself. If invited to meetings, ask: 'Could I just receive the papers and a note of any decisions?' If someone must go, ask: 'Who else can I send to bring back a report?' If you must call people together, how about over refreshments, standing around in a rough circle. Say what you have to say. Use a flipchart if you need to illustrate a maximum of three points. Each point can have a maximum of three subpoints. Leave people to discuss the flipchart amongst themselves. Invite them to send you individual comments.

12 Evaluate Your Week

How accurate were your estimates? What is there to be carried forward into next week's plan? Will the priorities change now? Some items, for example, might now need to be upgraded from B to A for urgency. What interrupted your work this week?

LIFE PLANNING

Life has sometimes been compared to a game. Unfortunately, on this analogy, we do not appear to have been given many rules by which to play the game. We often appear to move a random number of squares at a time, towards some unknown end, according to a dice that someone else is throwing! Generally we have little idea why we are playing the game, or what the prize is. Life planning is a way of trying to get some control over the game and some idea of what the prizes might be.

Living Adventurously?

George Fox encouraged the idea that the game should be played adventurously. 'Live adventurously, travelling cheerfully over the earth, greeting that of God in every man.' Helen Keller thought that life was a daring adventure, or nothing at all. Certainly life can be filled with exciting moments and experiences of wonder. Adventure comes when life is approached with enthusiasm, even when it takes us outside our comfort zone. Adventures make our heart race with nervousness and anticipation. Adventures take us to places we have never been before. They give us goose bumps. When we take risks we

value what we fear to lose. One of the attractions of life planning is that it gives us more choice – either to add more adventure to our lives or to make our lives feel less prone to surprises – if that is what we prefer. We do not start life inhibited by fear of failure, or fear of looking foolish. Somewhere along the way we learn these things and our sense of adventure hibernates. We can reawaken our sense of adventure through life planning, if that is what we would like to happen. It is possible to recover the spontaneity we had as children – to delight again in a sudden decision to sky-dive or wind-surf. By responding first to small ideas, you may find your way back to dreaming. You can then plan ways to make your dreams come true. To start with, 'Almost any dream will do'. That song was sung by a group of senior managers at the end of a year-long programme of personal development. At the start of the year, they had discovered that their careers as scientists, engineers, lawyers, managers and accountants had taken some of the colour and warmth out of their lives. Through their own efforts, and through life planning, they were able to rekindle some of the fire they had lost. Slowly they started to build some adventure back into their lives. Whatever you can do or dream you can, begin it now, 'for boldness brings both genius and the power to act' (Goethe).

Planning Your Life: A Conversational Approach

Life planning is a conversation you have with yourself, or with others if they will let you think out loud. There are at least seven areas to talk about when planning your life: Money and Possessions; Health and Fitness; Pleasure and Excitement; Intellect and Learning; Jobs and Careers; Values and Beliefs; Friends and Families. For each of these areas it is useful to make conversational statements of the kind shown in Table 14.2 where X is someone who is, or has been, a very important person to you in your life – someone whose opinion on what you are planning to do would matter to you. In imagining what they will think or feel. Person X need not necessarily still be alive. Parents, grandparents or old

Table 14.2 Life planning: some conversational statements to make

In the past . . .	Here and now . . .	In the future . . .
I have done . . .	I feel . . .	I will do . . .
I have seen . . .	I think . . .	I will see . . .
I have heard . . .	I need . . .	I will hear . . .
I have thought . . .	I want . . .	I will think . . .
I have felt . . .		I will feel . . .
		And
		X will think . . .
		X will feel . . .

teachers, for example, continue to be very significant sources of reference for us, long after they have died.

Now use a spreadsheet to create the matrix in Figure 14.6. Alternatively, you can create one by folding A4 sheets in half and then in half again lengthways and making the creases sharp. Fold the creased strip in half and half again and again press the creases firmly.

A Conversational Approach to Life Planning

When considering each of the seven areas, talk to yourself, or to someone else, about the issues set out below.

- **Money and Possessions**: Think about food, accommodation, clothes, shoes, money. Where do you want to live? How much space do you need? Decoration, the view you would prefer, the environment. Where you would like to travel? The kind of holidays you like, bikes, cars, helicopters, telephones, computers, communications, TV, video, music systems. What sort of work space do you need – comfort, view, equipment? How much free time will you want?

- **Health and Fitness**: Think about diet, strength, stamina, suppleness, speed, shape, energy, co-ordination, confidence, self-concept, skin tone, sports played, exercise, physical recreation. How much tactile contact? Comfort, pain and appearance. Will you need to manage illness or disability – your own or that of others?

- **Pleasure and Excitement**: Think about stability, awareness of feelings, awareness of other people's feelings, ability to label feelings, ability to express feelings, prevailing mood, mood swings, feelings about mother, father, siblings, fears, hopes, wishes, expectations, the way you defend your self and handle conflict. How free, genuine, honest, open and spontaneous are you? How creative do you need to be? What turns you on? How will you keep or add colour in your life?

- **Intellect and Learning**: Think about what kind of abilities you have and how much of each? What is your level of education – generally, specialized and technical. Are you bored or stretched, coasting or under-achieving? How good are you at theorizing, doing practical things, expressing yourself verbally and in writing? How open are you to new ideas? How innovative are you in your thinking? How artistic? How much and how quickly do you read? What kind of things are you studying – formally and out of your own interest?

- **Jobs and Careers**: Think about strengths, talents, training, qualifications, experiences, the effort you are prepared to expend, the importance of success and the fear of failure. How much pressure you can handle? How much stress? What do you need to achieve and for whom? What degree of recognition, responsibility, personal growth is important to you? How senior do you need to be and what rewards will be needed to fund your 'money and possessions'?

- **Values and Beliefs**: Think about religion, nature, political commitment, leading a moral life, your role in the community, spiritual experiences, spiritual places, prayer, meditation, contemplation, quiet times, culture, supernatural forces, extra-sensory perceptions. What are your inner promptings during periods of silence? What creates in you a sense of awe and wonder?

- **Family and Friends**: Think about feeling you belong, warmth in the presence of others, affection, acceptance, acceptance of others, rejection, the importance of sex in your life, feeling an outsider, feeling an insider, extended families, cousins, uncles, aunts – how supportive,

Area / Statement	MONEY POSSESSIONS	HEALTH FITNESS	PLEASURE EXCITEMENT	INTELLECT LEARNING	JOBS CAREERS	FRIENDS FAMILIES	VALUES BELIEFS
IN THE PAST							
I have done …							
I have seen …							
I have heard …							
I have thought …							
I have felt …							
HERE & NOW							
I feel …							
I think …							
I need …							
I want …							
IN THE FUTURE							
I will do …							
I will see …							
I will hear …							
I will think …							
I will feel …							
And							
X will think …							
X will feel …							
FIRST STEPS							
Who							
What							
When							
COMPANION'S COMMENT							
Response to companion							
What actually happened?							
Next step?							

Figure 14.6 A conversational approach to life planning

concerned, interested or welcoming are they? Allegiances and intimate relationships – not necessarily sexual – dependence, independence, interdependence, approachability, popularity, competitiveness, trust, taking risks, confidence, shyness, prejudice, bias, people with whom you feel energetic, inspired, joyful. How much laughter is there in your life? How much love?

Life as the Avoidance of Boredom

The interval between when we are born and when we die can seem a very long time. Unless we build a lot of activity into the journey, for many of us the time will drag. The journey will seem interminable. It will become tedious, boring even. Some thought for the end, and for the possible high and low points on the way, can help to structure the time and reduce the boredom.

CAREER PLANNING: A CONVERSATIONAL APPROACH

The first question to discuss, with yourself or someone else, is 'Do you want to live to work or work to live?' 'A keen interest in a career, however humble, is a real possession during the changing fortunes of time.' (Desiderata 1692). Even if you do decide to live for your job, there are now less and less jobs for life. There is a movement away from the notion of careers as steady progressions through single organizations. One is likely to have to reinvent oneself and have several different careers in a single lifetime. Can these transformations, from career to career, still meet the needs revealed in your life plan?

In 1996 and 1999, Career Development International carried accounts of Doug Counsel's[15] work, at the University of Central Lancashire, into the career strategies of management students and managers in the UK, in Europe, and in developing countries like Ethiopia. Sparrow's[16] definition of a career as advancement within an organization makes it possible to envisage employment policies that are almost cradle-to-the-grave. We favour Clarke's[17] view that: 'There is no such thing as a career path, it is all crazy pathing and you have to lay it yourself!' Life planning is best achieved through taking responsibility for your own life and career planning is best achieved by doing it for yourself. Locke[18] dis-

---

Box 14.10

CAREER DEVELOPMENT

1 Set career goals
2 Create networks
3 Develop an expertise
4 Publicize your success
5 Project the right image
6 Get a mentor or sponsor
7 Be enthusiastic and hard working
8 Use political connections and skills

Box 14.11

CAREER PLANNING: THE 12 QUESTIONS

1 Who am I?
2 What drives me?
3 Time for a change?
4 How good am I?
5 Am I getting enough?
6 What is my potential?
7 Who holds me back?
8 Is this organization bad for me?
9 Have I got the right balance?
10 Why not stay?
11 What next?
12 Can I write it down?

---

covered that the employees with the most successful careers were those who had set career goals for themselves. Without goals and an action plan, it is difficult to develop one's career.[19] Counsel[20] reviewed the ideas of Brandt,[21] Harman,[22] Metz[23] and Hinch[24] and came up with the advice summarized in Box 14.10.

The statements in Box 14.10 can be translated into 12 questions that need to be asked in a conversational approach to career planning (Box 14.11).

Question 1: Who Am I?

Much of what you will need to know emerges when you prepare a life plan. Basically, you need to know what you *want* to do, what you *can* do, and what you feel you *ought* to do. Figure 14.7 shows how these three questions interact to help you decide what you *may* do, you *should* do and what you *need* to do. Answers to all these questions will help you to move your career in a direction that meets more of your needs and wants and better reflects what you feel you ought to be doing with your life.

Alternatively, many public, educational or private agencies run computer-based psychometric tests of your personal interests, preferences and aptitudes.

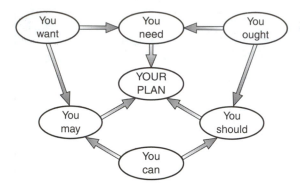

Figure 14.7 Deciding what to do

Source: After Horne and Wootton (2000)

The computer will then list career choices that best fit the results of your test. If the computer list includes your present job or profession, you may decide that you are in the right place for the moment. On the other hand, a change might make your job more enjoyable or enable you to do it better, or enable you to do it somewhere else or during different hours. Do not treat test results as infallible. Use them as a foil to work out what you really think, by agreeing or disagreeing with what the test report says about you. Pay equal attention to doing and being. What do you want to *do* at work? To answer this question, think of activities and verbs to describe the things you want to do. Equally important is what you want to *be* at work (Figure 14.8). To answer this question, think of adjectives to

describe the way you want to be with others at work. What demeanour and disposition do you wish to display at work? You may be content to let your working life speak, but what do you want it to say? To what values do you want it to testify?

Doing often involves skill. Skill involves a little knowledge practised a lot. Being, especially how you are with other people, determines your ability to get other people to share your ideas, or to co-operate with you. It certainly limits your ability to manage.

Question 2: What Drives Me?

In Chapter 7 we looked at how motivational mapping can help with problems of self-motivation, particularly in relation to proactivity, or work rate, or when trying to get more out of your time. The same process can be used here to gain insight into whether you should go or whether you should stay. Your present situation may be in work, out of work, not working, between jobs, part-time or full-time. Do you have unmet needs for warmth, affiliation, belonging, applause, acknowledgement, approval, status, possession, or just the chance to own your own ideas? Are you bored? Does your life plan indicate a need for a change in lifestyle? Is your need for a change outweighed by your need for familiarity – the old familiar feelings you get in your present job, for example? In which case, it might be better to stay, even though your friends and family might find your decision hard to understand.

Question 3: Time for a Change (or a Change for a Time?)

At some time you will reach an age, or a stage, when it feels like it's time for a change. Beware of behaving impulsively at times of transition. It may be true that you need a change, but perhaps only for a short time. Maybe you need a temporary change of scene, or job, while you negotiate a rite of passage or a major life crisis. A secondment, a placement, study leave, career break, intercollation or a year abroad may be all that is needed, provided you can have your old job back again at the end of it. In the event,

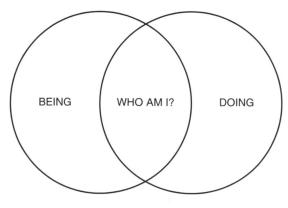

Figure 14.8 Being and doing at work

you may not want to come back. It's good to have a choice. Such considerations may not be relevant in your twenties. Hopefully you have lots of energy, up-to-date qualifications, good health, low commitments and high personal mobility. You can afford lots of moves and some mistakes. If your ultimate ambition is senior management, steer clear of lucrative-sounding consultancy posts and small companies. Larger companies have more learning resources and can better survive the mistakes you will inevitably make. Physical and family constraints may start to become an issue in your thirties. High-flyers will leap-frog your promotion. You will be clearer about what sort of manager you are and what sort of organization suits you. Try to find one you like before you are over forty. After 40, employee moves become harder, unless you are already quite senior. After 50, self-employment is a better bet, especially if your life plan shows a reduction in commitments elsewhere.[25]

Question 4: How Good Am I?

This is a difficult assessment to make. Yet it is very important. If you are too modest, you may not be sufficiently stretched by your work. You may become bored. Boredom is a major contributor to illness. You may resent being managed by people of lower ability than yourself. You may become mischievous. You may be seen as 'over-qualified' and too expensive. You may get the sack! If you overstate your abilities, the risks are less serious. The worst case is that you over-commit yourself and create expectations you cannot realize. You may be disappointed with yourself and become demoralized for a while. Feedback from others can help you to make a more realistic assessment of how good you are. In the end, however good you are, it must be apparent to others, otherwise they will never appoint you, promote you, or trust you to develop. Get feedback from the kinds of people who take the kinds of recruitment and promotion decisions that need to go in your favour. Look for overwhelming encouragement. Anything less may be diplomacy, or damnation with faint praise. Use your mental laboratory to

rehearse yourself in the kinds of situations the senior job will involve. Decide whether you are confident, at ease and happy in these situations.

Question 5: Am I Getting Enough?

No job is intrinsically satisfying. Satisfaction comes from the conjunction of you and the job. What is driving your career? Are you are finding it in this particular job? Job satisfaction is more than being satisfied that you have a job – important though that is. Having a job is second only to the importance of having close relationships. According to Francis,[26] people without either a job or close personal relationships are prone to illness, depression and suicide. Even a job that starts off full of interest and reward can become unsatisfactory. Most jobs have four phases: learning new things, becoming efficient, coasting and decline. Learning new things is a challenge – there are new problems to be solved. As things start to come around the second or third time, we learn tricks that enable us to reach the same standard, or better, with less effort. We become efficient. Eventually it becomes easy – too easy perhaps. We coast. If we don't change jobs, we might take on outside work, or maybe start a new relationship. Finally, we are bored. We are not learning, not developing, not going anywhere. Work has become a routine to be completed with the minimum of effort. We may even feel guilty at how easy it is – money for old rope. It is time to consider moving on.

Question 6: What Is My Potential – the Parable of the Talents?

What do you have that you could give to others? What powers or abilities do you have, from which other people could benefit? Do you feel any responsibility to develop these abilities, or use them for the benefit of others? Are they well developed or are they latent talents? How quickly might they bloom, given encouragement? Often your hobbies or outside interests can give you a clue. According to Francis,[27] it is useful to consider six talents. Consider your talents for expressing yourself, helping others and

---

Box 14.12

CHOOSING A CAREER: MAKING USE OF YOUR TALENTS

A talent for:

1 **Self-expression** is often found in combination with a talent for creativity or artistry or with a desire to share insights with other people.

2 **Being helpful** is often combined with a sense of community or with a desire to improve the quality of other people's lives, through health-care, teaching, religion, social work, therapy or training, for example.

3 **Persuasion** is about getting other people to agree with you. It is often associated with charm, advocacy, coaxing and skills in public relations. It turns up in sales and politics.

4 **Physical prowess** is often born of the joy of moving, doing or physical exertion. Often it turns up in expeditionary or military pursuits and in rural occupations. Mechanization has made this a difficult talent to express.

5 **Science and engineering** is often born of a love of logic or enquiry. This talent turns up in detectives, architects and social scientists.

6 **Management** is born of a liking for order or a need for control. It leads to skills in organizing and co-ordinating. A talent for management often expresses itself as consultancy, teaching or bureaucracy.

---

persuading others and then consider, as well, your physical attributes and your talents for science, engineering and management (Box 14.12).

Question 7: Who Holds Me Back?

Jean-Jacques Rousseau said that man is born free but is everywhere in chains. What is chaining you, holding you back, stopping you from being completely free to choose what to do with your life and career? Is your health up to it? Can you handle the long hours and the stress? Do you have the right qualifications or educational background? Are you too old or too young? Do you have other commitments? How are your self-confidence, self-esteem and self-reliance? Can you think and decide for yourself? Are you in the wrong country?

Question 8: Is this Organization Bad for Me?

Does your present organization, if any, provide you with enjoyable experiences? What are they? Would you be better off in a small owner-managed organization or a partnership? What would be the advantages and disadvantages for you? Would you be better off in a larger, more bureaucratic organization? What might be the advantages and disadvantages for you? Would you be better off in an organization in which most of the employees were highly trained and educated or professionally qualified? Why would you prefer that? Would you be better in an organization that was a loose affiliation of small units? Why? How would you benefit? How about an organization that constantly adapts and changes its form in response to rapid changes in the environment? Would that suit you better? Why do you think it would, or would not? If your organization is old, inflexible, wasteful, impersonal, inhuman or hostile even, and you cannot move elsewhere, you may have to look to your life plan and invest in your life outside your organization to meet your unmet needs. You will have to take the initiative to make things better for yourself. If you think that the senior people in your organization are egotistic megalomaniacs, they are unlikely to make things better for you! If you have your sights set on a new organization, check it out. What stage of evolution has it reached? This is likely to affect the quality of your working life within it.

Organizational climate: talking about the weather

A start-up climate is likely to be chaotic, but full of energy, crisis and new experiences. If it is expanding, there will be growth, travel, long hours and promotion opportunities. Once established, you may find a climate of formality and procedures irksome (or reassuring). If the organization has lost its direction, the climate will be difficult and stressful. People will be thrashing around trying to regain a sense of purpose. Dying organizations are to be avoided. These different stages determine the likely climate of the organization. Ask yourself whether the climate suits you. If the climate doesn't suit you, you have four options: change the climate, leave the organization, put up with it, or change yourself. A conversation about the climate with just one like-minded person might be sufficient to change the way you experience the climate of your organization. Although it seems the least positive option, 'putting up with it' should be considered. Someone may need to 'hang on in there' to keep alive values and ideas that may one day bear fruit when the climate changes. For some this will be the most courageous option — perhaps putting faith in small changes, small groups and quiet processes. Pedler and Boydell[28] illustrated this with an extract from *East Coker* by T. S. Eliot:

> . . . And what there is to conquer,
>   By strength and submission,
>   has already been discovered

Once or twice, or several times,
  by men whom one cannot hope
To emulate – but there is no competition –
There is only the fight to recover what has been lost
And found and lost again and again.

Often there is 'perhaps neither loss nor gain . . . there is only the trying' (ibid.). An organization, as we have said before, is only a collection of people. When their attitudes change, the organization changes. You can change people's attitudes by having conversations with them. The effect of talking to people can spread and spread very rapidly, as we shall see in the case of Carolyn the Conversational Manager (Chapter 15). There are many ways to gain access to people, even in large public service organizations. Access can be obtained through training courses, coaching, mentoring, secondments, social events, clubs, appraisals, consultation, working parties, co-option on to committees, staff meetings, conferences, quality circles or professional associations. The most important thing is to pick one and start having conversations. Conversations help you warm to the task. They help you to find the energy and motivation to survive the 'unpropitious' climate and to do your bit towards changing it. Conversations help you to create 'warm spots' in the organization. In such places ideas germinate, cultures incubate and new thinking spawns. People's attitudes can change and with changing attitudes there comes a change in the climate of the organization — perhaps making the organization good for you. Once there are several such warm spots in the organization, they can spread and spread very rapidly. The place to start is with yourself and with the conversations you can have.

Question 9: Have I Got it Right?

According to Roger Harrison,[29] people need to find the right balance between serving the needs of an organization and serving their own self-interest. Using Harrison's concepts of power, task, role and person, we can classify organizations as autocratic, technocratic, bureaucratic or democratic:

- **An autocratic organization** is one in which what happens is largely determined by one powerful person or a few powerful people.
- **A technocratic organization** is one in which what happens is largely determined by the nature of work being done, or the technology used.
- **A bureaucratic organization** is one in which what happens is largely determined by procedures, often written down, including legislation, guidelines, codes of practice or national agreements with trades unions and professionals.
- **A democratic organization** is one in which the primary concern is for the interests of the people affected by its activities – staff, clients and other community stakeholders.

In Table 14.3 we set out the way in which these four types of organization are likely to serve your interests. Table 14.3 can help you to decide whether or not an organization can provide you with the right balance between meeting its own needs (to co-ordinate, respond and survive) and meeting your needs (for security, worthwhile work and personal development).

Table 14.3 Balancing your needs against the needs of the organization

Type of organization	Consideration of your needs			Consideration of the organization's needs		
	Economic security	Worthwhile work	Personal development	Co-ordination/ control	Respond to environment	Survive threats
Autocratic	LOW At whim of senior managers	LOW Unless you are high in the hierarchy	LOW Unless you are high in the hierarchy	HIGH This is what autocracies are about	HIGH Top controllers short of field intelligence	HIGH People on permanent war footing
Technocratic	HIGH Only while skills are current and relevant	MODEST As long as well aligned to organization's goals	LOW Unless what the organization requires will develop you	HIGH Unless nature of task changes quickly	HIGH Unless nature of task changes quickly	HIGH Unless task changes quickly
Bureaucratic	HIGH Often protected by law or agreement	LOW Work is determined by role	LOW Nearly all activities are predetermined	HIGH By definition this is what bureaucracies are about	LOW Communication up and down slow and inaccurate	LOW The often slow rate of adaptation
Democratic	HIGH This is what people organizations are about	HIGH But you must take the initiative to secure it	HIGH Organizational goals are often driven by people's needs	LOW Consensus is hard to find decisions are difficult	HIGH But can be ineffective due to problems with control	LOW Groups raise anxiety, reduce thinking

Question 10: Why Not Stay Here?

As in any management decision, the option to change nothing should be considered. All things being equal, the 'no change' option is usually the most economical and the most efficient. Change is disruptive and disruption costs stress, time and money. In any event, thinking through the implications of staying where you are will provide a baseline against which other options can be compared. The hoped for benefits of a change will need to well outweigh the costs, because the risks and unknowns associated with moving are considerable.

Are you making the best of your present situation? If you have been there a while, you may have amassed a capital of good-will and familiar relationships. You might miss them when they're gone. A constant preoccupation with future plans – 'over the rainbow' – can result in a failure to live a meaningful life. A meaningful life can only be lived in the present. Today is the first day of the rest of your life. Life is not a rehearsal.

According to Bartholomew,[30] managers at INSEAD, the European School of Business Administration in Paris, revealed that having negative feeling about one's job was a common phase – albeit the phase sometimes lasted a long time. Such phases often arose because work was seen as adversely affecting the quality of life. For the male manager, this phase sometimes persisted until they were in their mid-thirties. Often there followed a second phase, a period of about ten years, characterized by a determination to 'work to live' and not to 'live to work'. There followed a third phase characterized by a return to a more careerist motivation. The INSEAD study found no evidence to support the belief that career success comes only to exploitative workaholics with heart disease! To rejuvenate careers that had turned sour, managers asked:

1 With whom could I have a conversation, if I needed to think something through?
2 With which individuals could I build a closer relationship?
3 What different styles of management could I use?

The most difficult problem cited in the study was when people had a poor relationship with their boss. Often there had been attempts to improve it but they had failed. Internal transfer or temporary secondment had proved the most successful strategy. This was because the study revealed that poor bosses rarely stayed for more than two or three years. Sometimes it can be better to grit your teeth and bear it, rather than wreck your own life and career on account of an incompetent new boss whose influence on your life is likely to be short-lived. Staying where you are does not necessarily mean a passive resignation to the idea that you are stuck there for life. You can use your time to promote your capacity to do something different. How much self-promotion you can engage in will be determined by your personality and by your culture. The balance is hard to strike. Undersell yourself and you will not be noticed. Oversell yourself and you may be guilty of hubris, despised for blowing your own trumpet or grinding your own axe. It helps to be loyal to your organization, to offer help and co-operation with other people's projects, to do some work that is distinctive, to communicate your success, to keep your promises, to be known to senior people in your organization and to let them know that you have ideas for making things better. Volunteer for tasks that have a tangible end product – a new display, a new building, a new service or a new client group. If in the end you decide not to stay, then where next?

Question 11: Where Next?

Where could the next ten years take you? A vision of where you could go with your career in the next decade needs to have a 'wow' factor! When you first think about this idea your whole body should react with a big 'wow!' – 'gosh wouldn't that be wonderful'. Later the idea will need to be detailed. The assumptions on which it is based will need to be tested for practical realism and for consistency with your deeply held beliefs. In trying to surface your ten-year vision, trust your intuition. Note your immediate reaction to ideas as they float through your head or are floated by others in conversation.

Take seriously any to which you have a big 'wow' response. Make a note of them. You can flesh them out later. Do not be too quick with your reality checks. Give your vision time to take shape. Spend time imagining how your new life in this new career might be. Then have conversations with others about how you might get there. Check that there is enough that is new in this move. Without new experiences there may be too little learning. New directions are harder to walk than familiar paths. The stimulus of novelty and the feeling that you are learning help to provide the increased energy that you will need. What's in it for you? If your new career direction benefits mainly other people, you may find it exhausting. You may even become resentful. To what extent are you going to be proud of this new career direction? How will you feel when you tell other people what you intend to do? How would old school friends react? Do you have a son or daughter whose reaction would be important to you? What would a parent or grandparent think, if they were still alive? How do you feel about their reaction? Do you experience sufficient pride and excitement when you imagine yourself telling them about your new life and your new work? Are the next ten years likely to be self-sacrifice? Remember that you may not survive the journey, so the journey itself should be satisfying. To travel may not be better than to arrive, but it must be good enough. It must not be too exhausting. You will need energy for unexpected things on the way – good or bad. You will want to arrive healthy enough to enjoy the fruits of the road! What is this life, if full of care, we have no time to stand and stare!

Finally, take a good look at the height of the peak on which you intend to be perched ten years from now. Do you have a head for such heights? Do you enjoy high wire balancing acts, or do you wish to alight only briefly on your ten-year peak, before soaring off in search of another? If you would like to stay longer and need your peak to feel more stable, then try thinking of it as the top of a pyramid. The higher the pyramid, the broader needs to be its base. Make sure you collect the broad base of experiences which your pyramid needs, if you want to feel safe perched on top of it. If, for example, you are aiming for a senior general management post, you should aim to collect significant periods of operational experience in marketing, quality management, finance and personnel management. This may mean resisting short-term temptations to take highly paid, fixed-term contracts in staff advisory or consultant roles. Personal expenditure has an uncanny way of rising to meet income, so it may be difficult later to take a lower salary in order to broaden your experience base. It may be difficult to re-enter line management after working as a consultant or an academic, whether in your own country or overseas.

Question 12: Are You Now Ready to Write Your Career Plan?

The first eleven steps can get you from a self-assessment of where you are now to some idea about where you might want to be in the future. Turning ideas into reality involves taking action. It can be helpful to set objectives which make it clear who is going to do what by when, and how you will know it has been done. Objectives are like stepping stones, helping to bridge the gap between idea and reality, between thinking and action, especially when the daily tide of events threatens to wash your thinking away. Objectives should relate to desired and feasible changes. Objectives should be so specific that you will know when they have been achieved. By asking, 'How will I achieve this?' about each objective, a more detailed set of objectives will emerge. The process of asking 'How?' and 'Who needs to do this by when?' produces a hierarchy of objectives. Make sure that the first step that needs to be taken is clearly identified and specified. Time, place, who needs to be informed, and who needs to be involved, must all be specified. These objectives are like grappling irons that we throw ahead of ourselves as we climb a mountain. The rope will help to steady us as we climb towards the next ledge, but we still need to plan our route up.

Action planning

Decisions determine directions, but actions determine success. There is an old Chinese saying that a journey of a thousand miles begins with but a single step. It is important that this step is a step in the right direction. It is also necessary to plan who will take it, when and where. In our experience of evaluating the life plans, career plans and operational plans of managers, we have found that if the first step is taken as planned, the project has an 80 per cent chance of completion. If it is not, the chances of completion fall to less than half. For this reason, it pays to think through the first steps in great detail, however trivial they might seem. To paraphrase Shakespeare's Henry V, there is a tide in the affairs of men, that taken at the flood, leads on to fortune and which, if missed, can leave people stranded on the sand banks of their lives and careers. The first step may be a phone call to a friend, or looking up that friend's telephone number. It may be reading an article or a book, or just asking someone 'How do I get hold of a copy?' Who will do it? When? Who else will be there? Where will it be? Which phone? Which desk? What are you likely to see through the window, or smell in the background, as you make that call – as you commit your plan to action?

A good way to set out the necessary steps is to use a Gantt Chart – working backwards from each objective that you have set yourself (Chapter 3). The tactical actions required can be slotted into an action list of the kind that we discussed earlier, under time management. Steps on your life and career plan will automatically carry priority 'A'. Keep a weather eye for signs of things that could blow you off course. Make contingency plans. Do not expect things to go according to plan. Keep reminding yourself of your direction. Set your compass and tack back and forth to take advantage of the wind, or to hold if the tide starts turning against you. Think ahead. Where are possible safe havens – places where you could take shelter during a storm? Storms are likely. Careers, like life, are rarely plain sailing. Be prepared to replan your route, or to reconsider your destination.

Tick every step on your career plan as it comes to fruition. Take time to publicize and celebrate its achievements before you focus on the next step. Check constantly that your career continues to serve the needs of your life. Opportunities of a lifetime can only be taken during the lifetime of an opportunity. There are few cases of people on their deathbed saying 'If only I had spent more time at the office'.

MANAGING PERSONAL DEVELOPMENT OF OTHERS

You may have been persuaded by the argument that personal development should be self-development. You now have a Personal Development Map and a Personal Development Log which you share every week with a Personal Development Companion. Through better time management, you can now find time to develop a new plan for your life and your career. Unfortunately, not all the people for whose personal development managers are held responsible, share our enthusiasm for self-development. For such people, you may need to start by initiating, designing and managing programmes of personal development for them. In the first instance this is not necessarily a bad thing. Too often some managers appoint people, outline their responsibilities and then leave them to sink or swim.

A familiar response, when we asked new staff whether their manager thought they were doing a good job, was 'I suppose I'm doing all right. I guess I'd soon know if I wasn't!' Since managers depend on the performance of their staff, it is surprising that so few managers bother to develop them. Often they assume that staff development is a matter for the personnel department. The majority of managers who accepted that it was their responsibility to develop their staff, offered one or more of three reasons for not doing so: lack of time, shyness and tradition. Many managers felt that today's urgencies had priority over any long-term return there might be from developing their staff. Some managers were shy when it came to offering guidance to other adults. Negative feedback was not found to be the best way to develop most people, though it was effective for some. Manager's need to work out which strokes suit which folks (Chapters 7, 8 and 11). The traditional concept of a manager's role — planning, organizing, directing and controlling — assumes that staff already know how to do the things their managers direct them to do.[31] This assumption is not likely to be valid when the nature of the work is changing. People need to be developed at least as quickly as their work is changing. In 'third-wave' organizations people have more opportunities to apply their own ideas. If their ideas are out of date, they will be of little use.

Setting an Example

We found that staff modelled their approach to personal development on what they observed their managers doing. If their managers attended courses and tried to apply what they had learned, then so did their staff. When managers expected their staff to develop and improve their performance, they generally did.[32] Expectation was a major predictor of success. Coaching conversations greatly increased the chances of success when change was involved (Chapter 3). What worked in managing change seems to work also in changing managers. Building on the ideas developed in Chapter 13, we look at the role of coaching in personal development.

Coaching for Personal Development

Often managers have considerable insight into the strengths and weaknesses of their staff. They are in a good position to help them assess their current state. Managers can also help employees to determine their desired states. Without help and encouragement, few of us dare to dream of very demanding 'desired states' – maybe for fear of never achieving them or of being thought 'above ourselves'. People generally see what *is* and ask 'Why?' George Bernard Shaw saw what *wasn't*, and asked 'Why not?' Managers need to be more like George Bernard Shaw and ask 'Why not?' Once a person's 'initial state' and 'desired state' can be described, it is easier to work out what kind of development activities are needed (Box 14.13).

> ## Box 14.13
> ## POSSIBLE PERSONAL DEVELOPMENT ACTIVITIES
>
> - Visits, films, deputizing, job swaps
> - Counselling, project work, learning logs
> - Quality circles, guided reading
> - Writing reviews, surfing the net, paired learning
> - Training courses, chairing meetings
> - Structured reading, internal consulting
> - Personal development groups
> - Giving presentations, distance learning, working parties

In the previous chapter, we looked at the knowledge and skills that managers needed in order to design and combine the activities in Box 14.13 into programmes of personal development for each member of staff. But who is this person that they are expected to be developing?

FINAL THOUGHTS: 'WHO ARE YOU?'

Some Buddhists teach that enlightenment can only be gained by answering the question 'Who are you?' Perhaps self-development can only be pursued if we have some idea about the 'self' that is to be developed. Are you your body? Are you what you say or do? Are you defined by your job or role in life? Are you a social construct of what other people say or think about you? Trying to answer the question 'Who am I?' is rather like peeling an onion. Each layer reveals another layer. Each new layer presents us with another chance to think differently about who we are.

Are we who we think we are? Is how we think about such a question revealing of who we are? Are we more defined by *how* we think than *what* we think? If so, when our thinking changes, we change. Is self-development about changing the way we think? Ideas about self-development are challenged by the postmodern thinking of deconstructionists like Jacques Derrida. In order to understand postmodern ideas, we must first understand the 'modern' ideas which postmodernists seek to challenge. Typical of 'modern' ideas about self-development is the idea that managers can and should take responsibility for controlling events, including themselves and their own learning. Should inner world development produce outer world results, like improved performance or career advancement? The implicit assumption that outer world results can be controlled is strongly challenged by postmodernists. According to Boyd,[33] 'modern' ideas on liberal education were developed by Vergerios in the fourteenth century. In order to prepare pupils for life in the outer world of 'affairs', Vergerios advocated learning from 'ancient' Roman and Greek texts, alongside 'modern' texts on geometry and arithmetic. Musical culture was to be included alongside a vigorous regime of physical exercise and sport. Daily devotion completed an education designed to develop the 'whole person'. So the antecedents of our map of personal development stretch back over 2,000 years.

Since that time, the quest for a liberal education has suffered many setbacks. According to Bertrand Russell,[34] when the Inquisition made Galileo (1564–1642) recant his theory that the earth revolved around the sun, they stultified science for a hundred years. When Galileo died, his baton was taken up by Newton (1642–1727). Newton founded a Royal Society which agreed the case for generating knowledge through outer world experimentation. Knowledge based on taking action and sensing the results was beginning to assume equal importance with making sense and formulating ideas. It was the beginning of modernism. Some thought that the position of God as the only source of wisdom was challenged by the idea that people could generate knowledge and truth through a process of inner

world reflection on outer world experience. With reduced dependence on an all-knowing God, there came a decline in the authority of organized religion. Nation states asserted their independence of empires founded on religious belief. Democratically elected governments asserted themselves against monarchs who had been installed as 'defenders of the Faith'. The French guillotined their aristocrats. The Americans tipped the Royal emissary into the sea at Boston. The Communists overturned the Russian Tsardom and the Chinese Empire.

Science and technology seemed daily more capable of controlling even the forces of nature. More people must have begun to feel more in control of their lives. The notion of self-development – of being able to take responsibility for yourself and your own learning – emerged. But, say the postmodernists, it was a mistaken notion. Just as Galileo once threatened belief in the centrality of God's place in the universe, so postmodernists now threaten modernist beliefs in the power of people to take action in the world to control their lives and to manage events. According to Fox,[35] Derrida's postmodern deconstructive thinking denies the usefulness of seeking mastery. Whilst we accept what Fox says about postmodernist deconstructionists, we do not accept his implication that self-development is a waste of time. In advocating personal development through self-development, we do not seek mastery – only improvement. Our criteria for improvement are not universal, but personal.

In Chapter 15 we express our own doubts about the pretensions to mastery and control exhibited by managers – in 'the utopian grandiosity of management'. We also accept that the conversational manager operates within a tradition of words – the logocentric tradition, as Derrida called it. It is true that we have argued that improving facility with words can improve outer world conversations and inner world thinking. But we have argued elsewhere[36] that there are many ways in which managers can learn to think that are not dependent on words. It is a Derrida 'Catch 22' that we need words to describe these non word modes of thinking! Derrida might counter, quite rightly, that these words do not mean what they say, nor say what we mean. For Derrida, the primary inner world self is preliterate – before words and beyond words. Kelly[37] appears to support Derrida in the idea that the self is primary, i.e. the self comes first and any subsequent attempts to communicate what it is like fall foul of the limitations and distortions of the words or symbols that we use. For Kelly, our self is no more than the sum total of outer world symbols which are used by other people to construct our 'self'. Kelly, in turn, found some support from Gray, who wrote about a flower 'born to blush unseen and waste its sweetness on the desert air' (Gray's *Elegy Written in a Country Churchyard* 1742). Does this flower actually exist, if we do not or cannot see it? Our model envisages a continual flow between an inner world self and outer world symbols of that self.

Our model sidesteps Derrida's concerns about a starting point. In our continuous cycle it does not matter where you start. In our model, life is *a process of moving between* an inner world, in which symbolic and verbal thinking takes place, and an outer world, in which symbolic and verbal communication takes place. Not all inner world thinking is language dependent and not all outer world communication is language dependent. It is only the process of trying to explain these things that is language dependent. It is the process of sensing, making sense, formulating and taking action that *creates meaning, for ourselves and others*. It is only if we want to share that meaning with others that we may become dependent on language. Although we may be curious, it is not essential to know which of these activities was the original starting point of the process. The process knows no end save death. Death robs us of the possibility of taking action and thereby breaks the cycle.

Managers take action to make the outer world a 'better' place by criteria which they can formulate and modify in their inner world. Public service managers cannot master the world, but their impact on the world is still significant. They make an impact on the world through decisions they take on the feeding of livestock, the modification of genes, the design of buildings, the control of crime, the provision of healthcare, or on the safety of trains and boats and planes. Public service managers need to take their 'selves' seriously.

SUMMARY

- We discovered that the attributes most highly sought by employers were personal attributes.
- We discovered that the attributes which *distinguished* high-performing people from competent people were personal attributes.
- We learned that the attributes needed to apply knowledge and skill were personal.
- We argued that the best process for developing personal attributes was self-development in the context of life and career planning.
- We looked at ways of freeing personal time for life planning and career planning and for the self-development activities that support them.
- We presented frameworks for life planning and career planning.
- We recognized that managers are responsible for their own development and for ensuring that their staff are pursuing programmes of personal development. We have made suggestions for staff who were unable or unwilling to do this through self-development.
- In our final thoughts we explored postmodernist thinking about self-development.
- Finally, we leave you to choose from the 25 self-development activities at the end of this chapter or from over 200 of the other self-managed activities which can be found at the end of each of the previous chapters. All of these activities can be used to further your personal development.

THINKING AND LEARNING ACTIVITIES

Activity 1 Self Assessment

1 Which attributes of an effective manager are personal competencies?

2 Which attributes required for senior management are personal competencies?

3 Which attributes of top-performing managers are personal competencies?

4 Why is self-development best for developing these personal attributes?

5 How does personal development relate to life planning and career planning?

6 How do life planning and career planning relate to each other?

7 Write brief notes on 12 aspects of time management. For each indicate one practical step you could take to improve your own time management.

8 What seven aspects of your life might it be useful to consider when life planning? Write brief notes on what might be involved in considering each aspect.

9 What are your answers to the questions it is useful to ask when planning your career?

10 What activities could you suggest to someone for whose development you were responsible.

Activity 2 Individual Learning: Visual Thinking

Cognitive mapping

Consider Figure 14.1 at the beginning of this chapter. It is a map or schema for personal development. It maps together over 80 topics. Organize the topics into five, six or seven groups. Label your new groupings. On one side of A4, construct a diagram showing the relationships between the groupings that you have created. Where you think that your groupings are influenced by activities in other groupings, connect them with a line. Reorganize your diagram to minimize the crossed lines. Along each line write a short sentence that explains the way one grouping influences another.

Activity 3 Individual Learning: Recollective Thinking

NVQ qualifications: Key Skills

Box 14.14 shows the performance criteria that have to be met to satisfy most NVQ assessments of Key Skills. For each of the Key Skills performance criteria, identify which sections of this book are relevant.

Box 14.14

PERFORMANCE CRITERIA FOR NVQ KEY SKILLS

Self-management

- Working relationships are improved
- Appropriate attitudes are maintained
- Self control is exercised when faced with difficulties
- Work is completed to timetable
- Willingness to seek advice
- Learns new skills

Managing Tasks

- Agreement of others about work is obtained
- Progress monitored and corrective action taken
- Appropriate timetables are developed
- Plans for work are provided
- Deadlines are met

Communicating with Others

- Written communications are accurate
- Spoken communications are clear and lucid
- Style of communication is appropriate
- Communications are effective

Relating to Others

- Working with and relating to others
- Good working relationships are maintained
- Appreciates the role and function of others
- Manner and approach to others are appropriate
- Ability to work well in groups is demonstrated
- Conflict is avoided and help is offered

Applying Knowledge

- Identifies, analyses and resolves problems
- Uses course knowledge in dealing with customers

- Uses knowledge of management
- Uses knowledge to develop new designs
- Can use a systematic approach

Showing Initiative

- Takes the lead when appropriate
- Takes the lead in problem-solving
- Appropriate inventiveness is demonstrated
- Suggestions are made in appropriate ways
- Self-motivation and initiative are demonstrated
- An ability to provide new ideas and draw up plans is demonstrated

Reflection on Own Learning

- Ability to identify what has gone well or badly
- Critical evaluation of previous situations
- Can identify areas for improvement

Activity 4 Paired Learning: Imaginative and Predictive Thinking

Thinking backwards

Managers usually start at the end. With Life Planning the end might be an obituary. Imagine that you have died. Some people who have been very important to you are gathered together. They are reading your obituary. It is a short summary of your life and of the things for which you will be remembered. Look over their shoulders. What do you want to find written there? Make a note of the things you hope will be said about you when your life is over. Discuss your notes with a colleague, or your personal development companion.

Activity 5 Individual or Paired Learning: Recollective and Reflective Thinking

Drawing out your life

Creating a picture, or an image or a visual representation of your experiences can help you to analyse them. It helps you to see patterns. It helps you to project those patterns into the future. Practise by creating a life-graph (Figure 14.9). Draw a horizontal line and label the left end BIRTH and the right end DEATH. Intersect your horizontal line with a vertical line to represent NOW. To the left of your vertical NOW line, use small crosses to note high and low points in your life to date. Position the crosses so that they correspond roughly to the age at which the high and low points occurred. Join the crosses with a lifeline, thus:

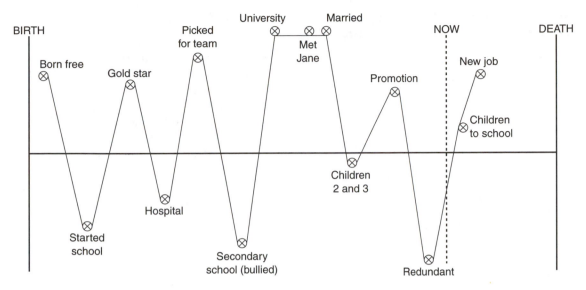

Figure 14.9 Example of a life-graph

Label the high and low points with the life events that were occurring at the time of the high and low points. Make the assumption that the patterns of the past will repeat themselves in the future unless you deliberately intervene. Guess at future highs and lows associated with events you know are almost certain to happen – like the death of a parent or the time the children will probably leave home. Decide if you would like more highs and fewer lows. (It will be difficult to protect yourself from all the natural disasters which beset us. These are a consequence of being human and fallible.) Look back at the kind of events that have produced high points in the past. Is it possible that by taking some actions now, you could increase the chances of adding in more of those sort of high points in the future? If high points in the past were associated with academic achievement, or a part in a play, or an expedition, or a new relationship, or a new job, or the birth of a child, or writing a poem, or finishing a project, or painting a picture, what could you do *now*, that would increase the chances of one or more such events happening again in the future? If you can, discuss your life-graph with another person.

Activity 6 Individual or Paired Learning: Imaginative Thinking

Magic wand

Imagine that you could wave a magic wand and spend two days doing exactly what you wanted! Anyone you want can be there with you. You can be where you like. You can do what you like. The only constraints are that one day must be a 'working day' and the other must be a 'non-working day'. Start with waking up. Describe the room, the shape, the colour, the smells, the sounds. Who else is there? What do you do before leaving for work? What will you drink, eat? How do you get there? By car? What sort of car? Describe the setting and the location of your workplace. Your job title? Is it on the door? Describe the door and your working area. Describe what happens during the rest of the day? What happens at midday? What time do you leave? What will you do after work, during the evening, before you finally fall asleep again? When you wake up next morning, it's a 'non-working day'. You can wake up where you like, with whomever you like. Describe how you will spend your ideal day. Everything is possible. If you are able, compare notes with someone else who has done the same exercise.

Activity 7 Individual Learning: Evaluative and Predictive Thinking

Learning to plan and planning to learn

Planning increases the chances that you will get to know what you want and how to get it. Successful people rely on themselves, not organizations, to give them what they need and want out of life. Avoid waiting e.g. 'until the children go to school' or 'until the children have left home', 'until the mortgage is paid off' or, even worse, 'until I win the Lottery'. Luck favours the prepared mind – the person with a plan. The plan need not limit or constrain you. When you change, your plans change. Life is like a pie (Figure 14.10). When you change the shape of the career slice, you change the shape of the rest of your life – and vice versa.

Answer the questions in the next four sections. They will help you to decide where you are now, where you want to go, and how you can get there. What are your skills, experiences, motivations, interests and constraints? Where would you like to be in one year's time? Who will need to do what, by when, in order to get there? What are the manageable steps? What is the first step? Address each of the four sections now.

Figure 14.10 The interdependency of life and career

Section 1: Personal Values

Each of us places a different emphasis on things that are important in life and at work. The following are some things which you may value. Think about each in turn and rate it on the scale, 1 = low and 10 = high, putting a tick in the appropriate column on Figure 14.11. When you have worked through the list, add other values that are important to you and rate them on the scale.

Now look at those aspects that you have rated highly, particularly those for which you scored 8, 9 or 10. How do these aspects match those which you feel are valued by other people in your life? What is the balance between work and non-work people?

Section 2: Your Present Situation

Write down your answers to the following questions:

1 How is your personal life changing or likely to change in the foreseeable future?
2 How does your present job or occupation relate to things you find satisfying?
3 What is important to you about your present job?
4 Who are you close to in your personal life and family life?
5 What do you dislike about your present job?
6 What do you like about your present job?
7 How do you spend time when not working?
8 What is important to you about your personal life?
9 How are things likely to change in the future?
10 What are the reasons for any changes?
11 Who are your best friends?

Importance Aspect	Low 1	2	3	4	5	6	7	8	9	High 10
Achievements										
Adventures										
Affection										
Being creative										
Competing										
Co-operating										
Family happiness										
Freedom										
Friendships										
Getting on in life										
Health										
Improving the world										
Inner harmony										
Integrity										
Involvement										
Loyalty										
Morality										
Order										
Personal development										
Recognition										
Responsibility										
Self-respect										
Wealth										
Wisdom										

Figure 14.11 Personal values matrix

Section 3: Longer-term Action Plans

```
Goals for the next 1–5 years
(Consider home and work)
1
2
3
4
5
Helping forces                    Hindering forces




Actions: List what has to be done
   When?          How?          By whom?
1
2
3
4
5
```

Figure 14.12 Personal long-term goals and actions

Checklist

- Consider what skills you need and what experiences you need to have.
- Consider what you need to do and what you need to ask others to do.

Section 4: Short-term Action Plans

```
Goals for the next 6 months
(Consider home and work)
1
2
3
4
5
Helping forces                    Hindering forces




Actions: List what has to be done
   When?          How?          By whom?
1
2
3
4
5
```

Figure 14.13 Personal short-term goals and actions

Checklist

- Consider what skills you need and what experiences you need to have.
- Consider what you need to do and what you need to ask others to do.

Activity 8 Paired Learning: Evaluative Thinking

Assessing the need for personal development

This activity is designed to help you assess your needs for cognitive, social and attitudinal development. Start by assessing yourself (Figure 14.14). Then seek out another person who knows you well, and get them to assess you. Compare your assessment with theirs. The next stage is to agree with your companion the first actions you could take. To score your behaviours, estimate how frequently you think that you exhibit the behaviours.

If ...	Score
Never	0
Rarely	1
Sometimes	2
Usually	3
Often	4
Nearly Always	5
Always	6

Cognitive development	Score self	Score peer	Actions that could be taken	When
How frequently do I...				
Build on the contributions of others				
Use analogies and metaphors				
Hold my views tentatively				
Give and ask for reasons				
Develop and use criteria				
Surface assumptions				
Challenge relevance				
Infer consequences				
Make distinctions				
Point out fallacies				
Seek clarification				
Offer alternatives				
Develop concepts				
Hypothesize				
Generalize				
Social development	Score self	Score peer	Actions that could be taken	When
How frequently do I...				
Treat all behaviour as communication				
Pay attention to what is not being said				
Speak out when I have a contribution				
Put argument challenging own view				
Challenge without giving offence				
Hear statements behind questions				
Sense insecurity behind pretence				
Make good use of feedback				
Sense fear behind bravado				
Refrain from monologues				
Keep a group on task				
Support others				
Give feedback				
Listen actively				
Attitudinal development	Score self	Score peer	Actions that could be taken	When
How frequently do I exhibit ...				
Tolerance				
Pluralism				
Defence of freedom				
Sensitivity to situations				
A capacity for self-correction				
Respect for the contributions of others				

Figure 14.14 Matrix for cognitive, social and attitudinal development

Activity 9 Individual Work: Sensing and Making Sense

Finding help

Personal development: sources of help

Personal Development Issue	Look up ...
Relationships, work, family, friends	Chapter 9
Motivating self and others	Chapter 7
Creative thinking and problem-solving	Chapters 2, 4, 13 and 14
Handling groups, cliques	Chapter 6
Rapid reading, improving memory,	D. Rowntree (1997) *Learning to Study*.
observation and study skills	Chapters 7 and 8
Handling power, handling the boss	Chapter 7
Unblocking blocks to performance	Doherty and Horne (2001) 'Managing Development'
Managing personal development	Pearsons FT
Conversational skills	Chapters 2, 8, 12, 13, 14 and 15
Making presentations	Chapter 12
Learning and thinking skills	Thinking and Learning Activities at the end of each chapter
Changing job, career, lifestyle	Chapter 14
Ethical investment (Quaker-funded ethical	EIRRIS, 71 Broadway, London SW8 16Q
sleuths who run ethics checks)	New Ways to Work, 309 Upper St.,
	London N12 TY1

Activity 10 Paired Learning: Conversational Thinking

Choosing a thinking companion

For many of us, thinking is like an internal dialogue which we have in our heads. It is dependent on our internal vocabulary, which may not be very precise. Our grammar and our logic may have become flawed. We may have developed bad habits, sloppy slang and verbal shortcuts, and have forgotten when these shortcuts are unsafe to use. Consequently we get 'bogged down'. We sink into mental quicksand. It can be helpful to think aloud and have someone else point out the flaws in our logic or limit our tendency to ramble haphazardly in our thinking. Someone else can give you a hand out of the quicksand. Sometimes when we struggle on our own, we just sink deeper. But how do we find a good thinking partner? Someone else known to be on a personal development programme would be a good bet. Maybe you can reciprocate. Do not choose a very close friend, or someone with whom you have an intimate relationship. You are looking for someone with an interest in the task. Someone with a respect for you that is independent of the mistakes (or the progress) you will make. Someone with an ability to challenge without giving offence. Someone who will be reluctant to give you advice.

Brainstorm a long list of possible candidates for the role 'thinking companion'. Edit to a short list. Use the considerations outlined above to rank your list. When can you talk to some of the people near the top of your list?

Activity 11 Individual and Paired Learning: Reflective Thinking

Keeping a personal development log

Obtain a fixed leaf book, preferably hard-backed, preferably A4 size. Open each double page and rule it across the middle. In the top left-hand corner insert the date of each Monday for the next year.

Quadrant Q1

Each week, using the top left quadrant only, marked Q1 in Figure 14.15, describe either an incident which you think you handled particularly well, or an incident which you handled not as well as you would have liked. Give the incident a label and enter it in the top right corner of Q1. In the bottom right corner of Q1, enter 'Well' or 'Not Well', depending on how you think you handled the incident. Make sure all your sentences begin with 'I' (I noticed, I saw, I heard, I felt, I thought, etc.). Stay in the past tense. These have to be your personal memories, not hearsay. Do not record the opinions of other people. Imagine you were a police officer and this was an entry in your official notebook. Try to use exact quotations of what people said and how they looked when they said it. Record what you saw them *do* and what you heard them *say*. Imagine you might be cross-examined in a witness box. Only record what you could support with evidence or example. Do not record conjecture or guesswork. Stay in the past tense. Now take a break of some kind. Perhaps have a drink or take a walk.

Quadrant Q2

Now return and re-read what you have written in the first quadrant, about what happened *then*. Thinking about it *now*, what do you notice? What seems strange, odd, surprising, interesting, curious, alarming, exciting or concerning? Record what you notice *now*. Record it in quadrant Q2 of Figure 14.15. Record also what you are feeling now that you are noticing what you are noticing. Feelings should be single words – emotions, not sentences. Sentences are thoughts, judgements or opinions – they are not feelings. If you cannot find a word of the type: bad, glad, sad, mad etc. to describe your feelings or emotion, it is probably not a feeling – you may still be in your head and not your heart! Strong emotions are often associated with a bodily reaction. Check out your body. Do you feel slightly nauseous (fear), sweaty (fear or excitement), butterflies in stomach (nervous), your neck or shoulders tense (anxious), your eyes wide (joy), your mouth open (pleasure or trust), your nose tense (suspicious), your back stiff (stressed), your head bent (dejected) or your eyes downcast (sad)? When you are clear about how you are feeling, notice how you experience that emotion physically in your body. Calibrate your body. Notice how it can keep you informed about your emotions in fast-moving and confusing situations. Having recorded what you are feeling *now*, about what happened *then*, notice next what opinions, views, interpretations you have formed. What meanings do you attach to what happened *then*? How can you make sense of it *now*? What is your understanding of what happened? What explanations could you offer? What might have caused it? What contributed to what happened? What might have prevented it? What helped? What hindered? What, if anything, have you learned? Finally, in the bottom right-hand corner of quadrant Q2 write either 'a lot' or 'not a lot' to record how extensive, important or significant you think your learning is from this incident. Take a break.

Quadrant Q3

Come back and re-read what you have written in quadrant Q2 of Figure 14.1. Re-enter your time machine and project yourself into some future time when, as a manager, you will be in a situation that has some dimension in common with the situation in which the incident took place. Maybe the composition of the group of people will be similar, or the age of the key actors will be the same, or the nature of the discussion will be comparable. Imagine you are there. Envisage the setting, the colours and the people. Listen out for the key word that will be said. What will you do, or do differently, or avoid doing in this future situation? What will you do less of? What will you do more of? What will you say? See yourself doing and saying these things and notice the reactions of the people who are present. Notice how you feel in this future situation and notice yourself thinking how much better things are going. Record the actions (use doing words/verbs) you are taking in this future situation. When is the next most likely time that you will have an opportunity to do these things? Finally, decide how relevant these actions are to improving your ability to manage economically, efficiently or ethically and write either 'very relevant' or 'not very relevant' in the bottom right-hand corner of Q3.

Quadrant Q4

Find someone who is prepared to read Q1, Q2 and Q3 and discuss them with you. Quadrant Q4 is reserved for a summary of the discussion. It could be a friend, a colleague, someone involved in the incident, a line manager, a mentor, a coach or, better still, your regular personal development companion. Finally, write your response to what they have written. Decide how useful the conversation has been to you and write 'useful' or 'not useful' in the bottom right-hand corner of Q3.

Finally, once you have more than 20 entries, you can start looking for generalizable principles – patterns in how you learn, as well as what you learn. You could try

just summarizing the things you learned that were important to you. (Note why you think the learnings were important to you.) For each important learning, note the nature of the incident and whether you learned, for example, by reflection, or by taking action, or by discussion with another person. What helped the reflection? What helped the taking of action?

Activity 12 Paired Learning: Conversational Thinking

Personal development conversations

Ask your personal development companion to listen to you without interruption for 10 minutes. Your PD companion should give you active, undivided attention. Ask your PD companion to watch the time and warn you when you have 2 minutes left. Chapter 13, gives examples of the kind of things your companion, as con-

Date . . .	Incident label		
Q1 **PAST**		**Q3** **FUTURE**	
Past memories I saw . . . I heard . . . I felt . . . I thought . . . Repeat the sequence. (Recollective thinking)		*Future actions* Who? What? When? I will do . . . . when I will avoid . . . . when I will do less . . . . when I will do more . . . . when (Projective thinking)	
I handled this incident:	*well/not well*	This learning will be:	*very relevant/not very relevant*
Q2 **PRESENT**		**Q4** **PD CONVERSATION**	

Looking back on Q1 now . . .
Present feelings and opinions
Right now I am noticing . . .
Right now I am feeling . . .
Right now I am thinking . . .
Repeat the sequence.
 	
(Reflective thinking)
		Written feedback from companion
		• Good is . . .
		   Good is . . .
		   Good is . . .
		• Interesting is . . .
		   Interesting is . . .
		   Interesting is . . .
		• A question is . . .
		<hr>Your response to companion's feedback	

I am learning:	*a lot/not a lot*	This conversation:	*was useful/was not useful*

Figure 14.15 Proforma for possible entries in a personal development log

versational thinker, might say, or the questions they might ask in order to help you think.

Activity 13 Individual Learning: Intuitive Thinking

Beyond sixth sense

The more professionally perfect we become at deploying our skills, the less comfortable our clients and colleagues seem to become. Patients often resent a doctor's perfectly professional manner. Students can be bored or intimidated by immaculate PowerPoint presentations by their teachers. People do not want to be the objects of perfectly honed skill. They want to be more than that. They want spontaneity, humanity, striving and intuition. Each of our six senses is capable of development to a further level. By adding an intuitive level to each of our six senses, we can aspire to Steiner's idea that we have 12 senses.

- To our sense of sight we can add the idea of insight, 'I see what you mean' and foresight, 'I can see problems looming ahead' and dreaming, 'I dream of a time when all our people can . . .' 'I have a dream . . .'
- To our sense of hearing we can add the idea of agreement, 'I'm not sure I'm in tune with what you are saying . . .' or 'I'm not sure I like the sound of that . . .' and of empathy – 'good vibes' and ideas that 'resonate'.
- To taste we can bring judgement, 'They left a bad taste in my mouth'.
- To smell we can add premonition, 'I smell a rat' and suspicion, 'It smells fishy'.
- To touch we an add a sense of inclusion: 'I warmed to them', and exclusion: 'We are being frozen out'.
- To our sixth sense of movement we can add a sense of motivation, 'I feel moved to . . .', 'It's time to move on . . .' and of balance 'He caught me off guard', 'We need to steady down' and 'We need to keep our feet firmly on the ground!'

Figure 14.16 models the development of an intuitive layer to take our six senses to 12 senses. If you want to find out how the different parts of the brain that process information from our senses can be used and developed to support a range of thinking, try reading *Thinking Skills for Managers* (Wootton and Horne 2000) or visit www.librapress.com.

Activity 14 Individual and Paired Work: Analytical and Evaluative Thinking

To see yourself as others see you

How people respond to you is influenced by how you expect them to respond to you. You can learn to control your expectations and so you can learn to influence how people respond to you. Fold an A4 sheet into half and half again and half again. Press the creases and tear neatly into eight strips. On each strip, write down the name of someone you know quite well – from work or college. It can be a friend but preferably not family. Fold the strips so that the names are concealed.

Step 1: Dimensions of difference

Pick two strips at random. Study the two names and decide how these two people differ significantly in character, personality or temperament, e.g. dull – bright; honest – dishonest; mild – aggressive; humorous – serious; reliable – unreliable; political – straightforward

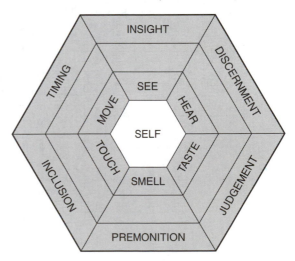

Figure 14.16 Developing intuition

etc. Whatever two words come up, write them on the left-hand side of your folded A4 sheet. Write one word in one box and the other word in another box. Join the boxes with a line divided in six segments (see Figure 14.17). Put the two names back in the hat. Pick two more. It does not matter if some names get picked more than once, or some never get picked. Just take the two names you've picked and think of a way in which they differ – a dimension of individual difference. Again, choose two words that represent the opposite ends of the dimension on which they differ and put the words into the next pair of boxes on the left-hand side of your A4

sheet. Continue the process until you have identified ten or more dimensions on which you tend to distinguish people.

Step 2: How I see myself

Next go to the three columns on the right-hand side of your A4 sheet (Figure 14.17). For the first dimension decide how close to the word in the left-hand box or the right-hand box you would *ideally* like to be. If extreme left, enter number 1 in the column labelled 'ideal'. If extreme right, enter number 6 in the column labelled

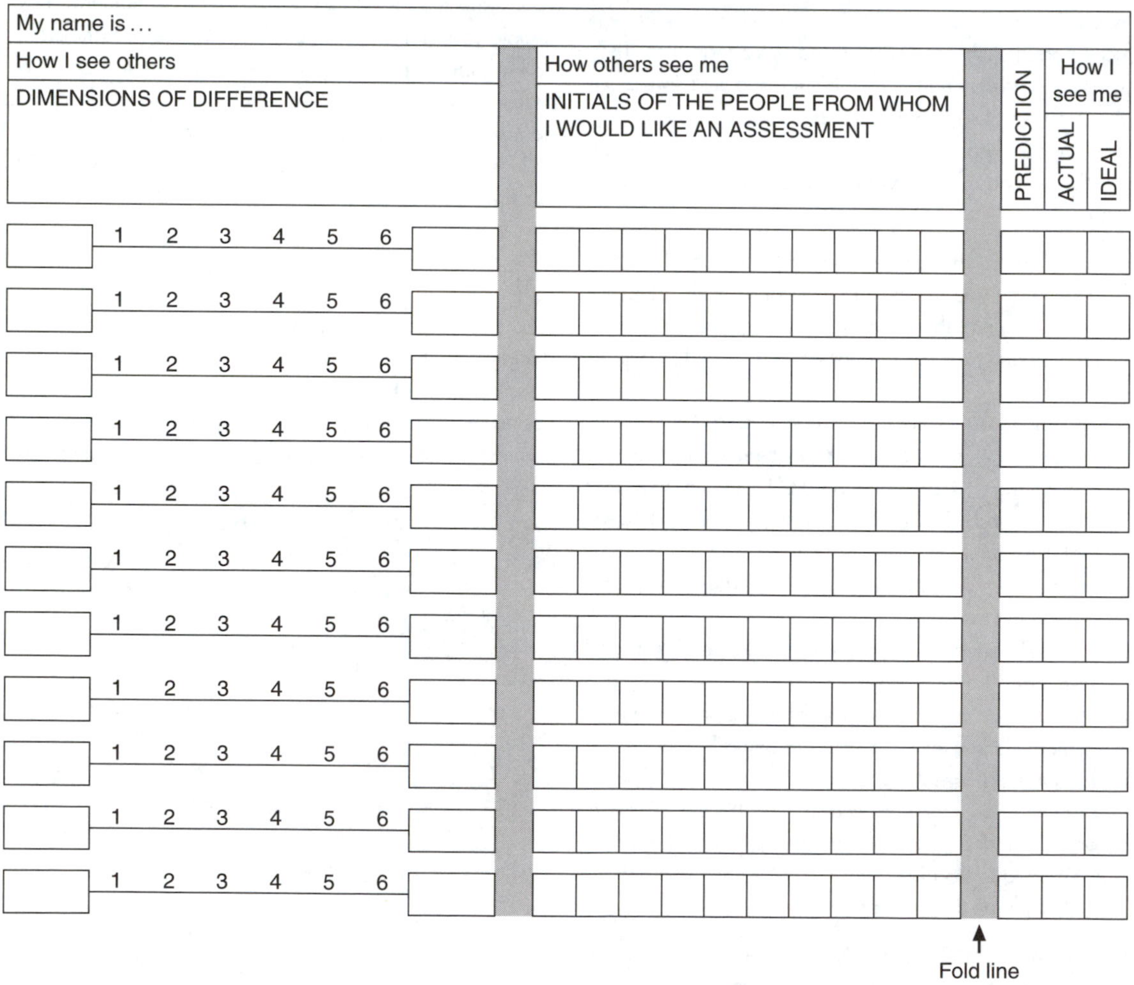

Figure 14.17 Dimensions of individual difference

'ideal'. If somewhere in between, select one of the numbers 2, 3, 4 or 5 to represent how close you would like to be to either end of the dimension. Repeat for each of the dimensions that you originally used to differentiate between the people on your strips of paper. When you have filled in your 'ideal' scores, now decide how you 'actually' are on each of these dimensions and enter your self-assessed scores.

Step 3: How others see me

Now, for each dimension, try to guess how other people would score you. Enter your prediction in the prediction column. Who would be prepared to tell you how they would score you on these dimensions? Send them a copy and ask them to enter their scores in one of the blank columns. If you don't want them to be influenced by your ratings, then fold, or cut, the page along the fold line in Figure 14.17. If you are using the sheet to obtain feedback from a group, ask people to use the empty columns to the right and keep folding their scores out of sight, to avoid influencing the next person. When you get your sheet back, check to see how accurate your predictions were. Do people really see you the way you thought they did? Are there any scores that concern you? Any differences between ideal and actual that would merit thinking about? What is it that you habitually do or say that causes people to score you that way? Ask them.

Activity 15 Individual or Group Work: Analytic and Reflective Thinking

Learning how you learn

In this activity you are trying to find out whether incidents from which you learned a lot have anything in common and, if so, whether you could make use of your findings to increase your chances of learning from future incidents. Working alone, or with a group, write out incidents – usually emotionally charged – that have occurred in the last month or year. Fold them up and chuck them in a hat or pile. Number them as you go. Keep going until you have about 30 incidents in your pile. Get people to call out random pairs of numbers, or draw the slips from the pile, in pairs, at random. Pick as large a

sample of the incidents as you have time to analyse. Construct a repertory grid as shown in Figure 14.17.

Stage 1: constructing the dimensions

Take these three dimensions as a given, i.e.

1 'learns a lot – does not learn a lot'
2 'highly relevant – not very relevant'
3 'this incident was well handled – this incident was not well handled'

To find another 15–20 dimensions that are relevant to you, pair off the incidents at random. Look up each of the paired incidents and try to decide how they differ. Consider separately the incident itself, the process of thinking about it afterwards and the determination to do things differently another time. Each time you identify a dimension of difference, enter it in one of the paired boxes on the left-hand side of your grid (see Figure 14.18). When you have exhausted the important differences between the first pair of incidents, return them to the pile and draw two more. It does not matter if one of the incidents has been drawn before. Repeat the process until the same dimensions are starting to recur or until you have enough dimensions for your analysis.

Stage 2: the analysis

For each incident now consider each dimension. If you think the incident is distinctly nearer the left-hand end of your dimension, score an 'A' in the column for that incident. If you think it is distinctly nearer the right-hand end of your dimension, score a 'C'. If you are unsure, score 'B'. Repeat for each dimension. Move to the next incident and score each dimension A, B or C as before. Continue until all incident columns have either an A, B or C next to each dimension. (The dimensions and the scores in Figure 14.18 are purely for illustration. Your dimensions and scores will be particular to you.)

Stage 3: implications and inferences the regressive syllogism!

Posh words for having a look to see if you can make any sense of your analysis! If you use numerical scoring, and

Dimensions of difference	A B C	Incident numbers	1	5	9	11	12	18	19	28	31	40	42	50	51	52
Learn a lot	A B C	Learn not a lot	A	A	A	C	C	C	B	A	A	A				
Leads to relevant management action	A B C	Not relevant to management actions	A	A	A	C	C	C	B	C	C	C				
Handled well by me	A B C	Not handled well by me	C	C	A	A	A	C	B	A	A	A				
Other people present	A B C	Solitary experience	A	B	C	A	A	C	B	C	C	C				
Pleasant	A B C	Unpleasant	A	B	C	A	A	C	B	A	A	A				
Discussed with manager	A B C	Not discussed with manager	C	C	C	A	A	A	C	C	C	C				
At work experience	A B C	Non-work experience	A	C	C	A	C	A	C	A	B	C				
Discussed with person of opposite sex	A B C	Discussed with person of same sex	A	A	C	C	C	C	C	A	A	A				
Emotional	A B C	Not emotional	A	A	A	C	C	C	C	A	A	A				
Feelings clearly identified	A B C	Unsure how to label emotions	A	A	B	C	C	C	B	A	A	A				
Funny	A B C	Not funny	A	A	C	A	B	C	B	A	A	A				
Feeling relaxed	A B C	Feeling tense and stressed	A	B	C	C	C	B	B	A	A	A				
Feeling safe	A B C	Feeling insecure	A	B	C	C	C	B	B	A	A	A				
Positive optimistic feeling	A B C	Poor expectation of learning	A	A	A	C	C	C	C	A	A	A				
Indoor	A B C	Outdoor	A	B	C	C	B	A	A	B	C	A				
Seared on memory	A B C	Prefer not to remember it	A	A	A	C	C	C	C	A	A	A				
Clear picture	A B C	Unclear picture	A	A	A	C	C	C	C	C	C	C				

Figure 14.18 Learning how you learn

a statistical analysis software package, you can use your PC to test which dimensions are most closely correlated with each other. They will tend to cluster around a few 'key constructs'. That level of sophistication is not essential for our purpose. You are only investigating two dimensions. You want to know if there are commonly recurring conditions which correlate with your experience of learning a lot that is relevant to you, e.g. what correlates with a double A in the first two rows of your analysis in Figure 14.18.

If we take the manager whose analysis has been started in Figure 14.18, even after only 10 incidents have been analysed, it would be possible to pose a number of hypotheses about the way she best learns things that are relevant to improving her management. For example, detailed recollection seems to increase the chances of her learning at all. Having a clear picture of a future application seems to increase the chances of a subsequent application of the learning. She does not need to learn only from her mistakes, she can learn from successes too. The presence of other people does not appear to be essential, nor to preclude learning. (The jury is out until we have analysed more incidents.) Her manager's contribution is not essential – in fact her manager's role appears counter-productive. It does not seem to matter whether the incidents are work based, for them to be a source of learning about management. Reflective discussion with a person of the opposite sex seems to be consistently more productive for this manager than discussion with people of the same sex. Incidents with a high emotional content seem much more likely to produce relevant learning, especially when the emotions have been recognized and labelled and there is a strong expectation that useful learning can be gained. It does not seem to matter either way whether the incident took place indoors or out of doors. Obviously another 20 or so incidents analysed might increase our confidence in some of these hypotheses about the way this manager learns best.

Stage 4: testing the hypotheses

Hypotheses about the way you best learn things that are important to you can be tested once the analysis of the first 20–30 incidents has been completed. The manager

whose initial analysis is illustrated in Figure 14.17 might, for example, decide to ask herself what went well, as well as what went wrong, during her week. She might be more open to the possibility that incidents from her life outside work might be a source of insight into how she could improve her performance. She could stop discussing work-based incidents with her line manager, if this is avoidable. Where possible, she could try to seek out the male colleague who appears to be emerging as a good personal development companion for her. She could scan back over the week and pick out the times when she felt angry, or glad or disappointed, and see what she could learn from these incidents.

Activity 16 Individual Learning: Emotional and Imaginative Thinking

Overcoming fear

Thinking can be used to overcome fear: e.g. fear of sharing your true 'self' with others; fear of making plans (or of announcing them); fear of failure, public or not; fear of letting yourself down (who is it that is always watching over your shoulder?); fear of ridicule; fear of upsetting someone; fear of being shouted at; fear of making someone angry; fear of appearing stupid or unattractive; fear of losing a friend. Fear and lust are two of the driving forces of life. Are you going to make life plans and career plans that are primarily about the avoidance of things of which you are afraid, e.g. fear of wasting your talents, being lonely or not being an eligible partner? If so, that's okay. It's just that it's a good idea to know why you are doing things. Or are you going to overcome as many of these fears as possible, so that you can pursue plans that 'lust' after positive goals?

A 'lust' plan generates more energy than a 'fear' avoidance plan. A 'lust' plan can result in a much more exciting way of life, if excitement is an old familiar feeling which you would like to recover (or a novel feeling which you would like to experience). So, ask yourself 'what is the worst thing that could happen' if you did appear stupid, provoke a row or lose a friend etc. What would it be like? How would you feel? What would the significant people in your life do or think? Could you cope with the worst they might think? Would you survive? You might discover that feeling sad kept you safe when you were small, but that sad feelings are no longer helpful now that you are grown up. You can do without them now. You don't need them. You can let them go. If, however, your catastrophe analysis – 'what's the worst thing that could happen' – confirms that you could not survive feeling sad, then you can take a logical decision not to do things the prospect of which give rise to such feelings. At least you are back in control and not being unconsciously and impulsively driven by fears of unknown consequences.

A common fear is a fear of asking for something. Imagine that you have decided to go ahead and see some people that you need to please or impress. Imagine them reacting favourably. What will you see? How will you be able to tell they are pleased and impressed with you? How will they show it? Really picture it. What will they say? How will they say it? Listen now to the admiring tone in their voices. Who else do you want to be there hovering in the background to see your success? Turn now and look at the kindness and pride in the eyes that are watching over you. Now you can safely 'lust' after whatever success you are no longer afraid to have. Feel the fear and do it anyway!

Activity 17 Individual Learning: Emotional Thinking

Developing willpower and persistence

You are no longer afraid of the consequences, you positively 'lust' to do something, but you lack the willpower or persistence to do it often enough to achieve what you want to achieve.

If you can develop the willpower to do things you *don't want to do*, things you *do want to do* should seem easier. List ten things you really don't want to do. Number them 1 to 10. Ask someone to give you a number between 1 and 10. Whatever it is, do it within the week. Next week ask for a new number.

Turning next, to persistency, choose tasks that might repay the effort of spending 15 minutes a day on them. Here are some examples of tasks that take less than 15 minutes a day – but you must persist – 15 minutes *every* day:

- Learn ten common misspellings every day for a month. Since less than 100 words account for 90 per cent of most people's spelling mistakes, your spelling should be near perfect after a month.
- Listen to a foreign language lesson for 20 minutes, every day, for four months. Most pre-recorded language courses (available from libraries, language centres or mail order) guarantee that you will be 'fluent' in a new language in less than 60 hours (or your money back!). You will develop a conversational command of three new languages in less than a year – 15 languages in 5 years!
- Paint a watercolour a day. It takes less than 15 minutes. You will have a portfolio of 365 paintings inside a year. Create your own gallery and frame some for presents.
- Each day write one page of a novel, perhaps based on your own life. Most novels are less than 365 pages. You could write a book in a year – fiction or non-fiction.
- Paint one silk scarf, or cushion cover, every day. It's fast work. You'll have presents for everyone and some to sell at the village craft fair at the year end.
- Practise a musical instrument for 15 minutes a day. You could reach grade 2 in the piano in a year. You will be able to play pleasing music or songs, so that other people can sing along.
- Unless medically prohibited, three times a week, for 20 minutes, do some form of aerobic exercise to the point of breathlessness. This is sufficient for you to be entering road races within a year. Get sponsored and give the money away to a charity.
- Listen to one movement a day of the symphonies, piano concertos or operas of a classical composer you like. You could become familiar with one composer in two months – six composers in a year.
- Read a poem a day. In 10 years you will have read 36,500 poems – what a treasure!

And you will have learned persistence – what a bonus!

Activity 18 Paired Learning: Emotional Thinking

Finding courage – being brave

Perhaps you have overcome the 'fear', owned the 'lust', developed the persistency, but lack the courage to take a first step. Your PD companion can be a real support here. A public declaration that you will do something is a great spur. Having someone to whom you can report progress is important. The biographies of brave people can be inspirational. Sometimes just a short vignette is sufficient to set an example. Giving yourself a good talking to can be effective (see Activity 20). Try wearing different clothes or change the style or colour of your hair. Start a conversation with a complete stranger every day for a month. There is no point in doing it for longer, because after 30 attempts you will be immune to your fear. It will no longer require courage. You may even find yourself talking to strangers just because you enjoy it!

Activity 19 Paired Learning: Emotive Thinking

Managing emotions

By managing emotions we do not mean suppressing them or even overly controlling them. In fact, they are key to the deployment of many thinking skills. Strong emotions, consistently unidentified or unexpressed, can lead to stress, breakdown or psychosomatic illness. Whereas the ability to label and share strong emotions greatly helps the process of developing close relationships (Chapter 8) and the process of learning from the experience (Chapter 13). So, working with a PD companion, write on 20 separate strips of paper a different word – each word to represent what you both think are strong emotions. (They will all be variants of 'mad', 'glad', 'sad' and 'bad'.) Your partner selects one strip of paper and has to say the sentence 'Well now, what do you think of that?' The way they say the sentence has to convey the feeling represented by the word on the strip of paper. You try to guess the feeling they are trying to convey. You get feedback and the roles are then reversed. Repeat until all the strips have been used. Discuss any difficulties you have encountered. Repeat the exercise using only non-verbal communication. Discuss the results as before.

Activity 20 Individual Learning: Thinking for Yourself

Building self-esteem and self-confidence

At the end of Activity 18, we suggest going public with a general affirmation. For specific things that are undermining your happiness, or undermining the satisfaction you are getting out of your life or your career, you will need to design a much more specific affirmation, e.g. 'I will develop a closer relationship with X' (name X). 'I will be healthier'. (What specific aspect of your health causes you concern?) Let us suppose your concern is self-esteem. Self-esteem is at the root of our ability to learn, the ability to form close relationships, the ability to be assertive, and the ability to manage others. The affirmation will need to be three-pronged, because our image of ourselves is based on what we tell ourselves, what other people tell us, what we imagine other people say about us behind our backs. For example:

- 'I, Tony, am beginning to be pleased with myself as an academic.'
- 'You, Tony, are beginning to be pleased with yourself as an academic.'
- 'He, Tony, is beginning to be pleased with himself as an academic.'

Write out each affirmation in the first, second and third person. You need to find affirmations that work for you. For example,

- 'I, Tony, enjoy writing more each day.'
- 'You, Tony, enjoy writing more each day.'
- 'He, Tony, enjoys writing more each day.'

Try working with . . .

- 'I, Tony, am becoming more talented every day.'
- 'I, Tony, have much more to offer and people are realizing this.'
- 'I, Tony, am getting fitter each day I cycle to work.'
- 'I, Tony, am getting clearer skin and brighter eyes.'
- 'I, Tony, can notice that more and more people are becoming drawn to me.'

- 'I, Tony, am beginning to forgive Terry for . . .'
- 'I, Tony, am getting over my disappointment about . . .'

Find affirmations that are relevant to you. Write them out in each of their three forms – first, second and third person. Dare you read them aloud, or in front of a mirror? You can record them and replay them as you drive to work. You can use them as a wake-up call. Let your personal companion know what you need to hear.

Activity 21 Individual Learning: Creative and Evaluative Thinking

Discovering the skills you have

Down the left-hand side of a sheet of A4, create a list of things you do in a typical month. In Figure 14.19 we make some suggestions of the sort of things we have in mind. Add to it, or just start with your own list. Create four columns, 'Beginner', 'Tradeskill', 'Craftskill', 'Masterskill'. Tick the column that is nearest your own assessment of your level of skill. Tick 'Beginner', if you are still learning the rules and procedures, still learning how to do the elements, or if you spend most of your time being shown and copying someone else. Tick 'Tradeskill', if you can generally do an acceptable job unsupervised. Tick 'Craftskill', if you are able to apply your skills in new and complex situations. You have acquired 'Masterskill' when you have a sense of mission to use your highly developed 'Craftskill' to serve purposes other than just doing the job, e.g. to make a statement, to provide an example, to be an inspiration, to leave a legacy, to create a monument, to give a gift to the community, or to work in the service of others or to respond to the promptings of a spirit within you.

Activity 22 Individual and Paired Learning: Recollective and Visual Thinking

A conversational approach to skills development

In *Managing Yourself*, Pedler and Boydell[38] suggest having an internal conversation with yourself about how you learned a particular skill in the past. Choose one now. Think back to a time before you had this particular skill. What was life like then? Who did you know then that already had this skill? What made you decide you too wanted to develop this skill? What was your motivation or incentive? How did you know what it would be like to have this skill? What helped you to envisage having the skill? Were you able to watch other people using this skill? Who were they and where did you see them using their skill? How did you decide at what level of skill to aim for initially? How did you start to practise? What was it like the first few times? Was it tedious, hard work or fun? Who gave you feedback on how you were doing? Who was always supportive of your efforts and thought it was a worthwhile project? Who applauded your progress and encouraged you to go further? Was this helpful or not? What steps or pattern can you discern in the way you successfully developed your skill? Choose a new skill you want to develop and repeat the pattern. It might involve watching someone else who has the skill you want and then creating an opportunity to practise. You might decide that it helps you when you get feedback – or not.

Now, visualize some future occasion on which you already have the skill you have chosen to develop. See yourself using it. Where are you? Who else is there? How does it feel to have this skill, to be good at it? How will you sustain the effort to get there? What realistically could you expect to achieve this week? By the end of next month? By the end of the summer? Picture yourself with slowly increasing levels of proficiency. How many hours practice will it take? When will you practise? Book possible practice hours into your diary now. To whom will you report or demonstrate your progress? Who will prod you to practise but always be on your side?

Activity 23 Individual Learning: Empathetic Thinking

Developing empathy

At the end of a week, go over, in your head, in reverse order, everything that happened to you. Rewind your internal video, pausing on key emotional incidents. Observe yourself on this mental video. If it appears black and white, fill in the colours. Fill in the details, especially

SKILL	BEGINNER	TRADESKILL	CRAFTSKILL	MASTERSKILL
Fund raising				
Getting fit				
Caring for people				
Massage				
Budgeting				
Listening				
Choosing clothes				
Plumbing				
Aromatherapy				
Selling things				
Photography				
Tasting wine				
Car maintenance				
Foreign languages				
Driving vehicles				
Keeping accounts				
Dressmaking				
Relating to kids				
Writing reports				
Coaching others				
Electrical work				
Organizing parties				
Handwriting				
Planning trips				
Taking minutes				
Creative writing				
Controlling groups				
Parenting				
Woodworking				
Welding metal				
Training animals				
Chairing meetings				
Breeding animals				
Computing				
Graphic design				
Musical instruments				
Kitchen design				
Singing songs				
Designing gardens				
Growing vegetables				
Foreign travel				
Planting trees				
Public speaking				
Telephone selling				
Rodent control				
Exterior painting				
Knitting jumpers				
Painting silk				
Cooking				
Water colouring				
Restoration				
Meditation				
Mountain walking				
Swimming				
Watersports				
Sailing				

Figure 14.19 Proforma for discovering the skills you have

of the other people. Freeze a frame. Turn the sound down and recall how you were feeling. Turn the sound up and notice the intonation and pace at which you were talking. Recall again how you were feeling. What were you thinking? What exactly were the words you were saying to yourself in your head? When it gets hotter, feel the warmth. What could you smell or hear? (Make sure you are sitting upright, as it is easy to fall asleep before you get back to breakfast time!) It is an exercise of willpower, as well as memory, to stay awake until you get right back to the beginning of each day's videotape. If this is too difficult, try writing your day as a story, with yourself as one of the main characters. The main advantage of writing, as opposed to recalling the video backwards, is that you will need to guess what the other characters were feeling and thinking. This will develop greatly your ability to think empathetically.

Activity 24 Individual Learning: Metacognitive Thinking

Metacognition

Look back through the Thinking and Learning Activities you have been asked to carry out in this chapter. What thinking skills were involved in each of these activities? For each type of thinking, write down how you were learning what you were learning, when you were learning to think in each of the different ways.

Activity 25 Individual Learning Review: Reflective Thinking

Inner world thinking

What inner world thinking skills can you identify in the manager's work described in this chapter? Have any of the thinking skills you have identified emerged for the first time in this chapter? If so, add them to your accumulating model of the kinds of thinking skills that you consider to be useful to managers of public services.

What things could you do to develop any of the thinking skills that you have just added to your model? What would be the first step?

Outer world conversations

What outer world conversational skills can you identify in the manager's work described in this chapter? Have any of the types of conversational skills you have identi-

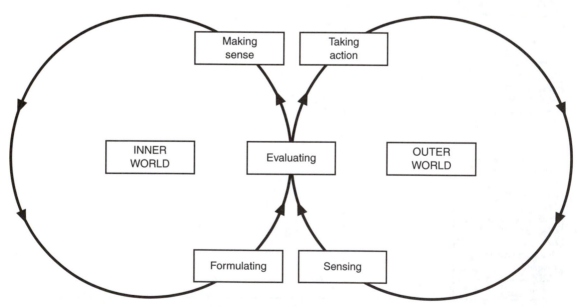

Figure 14.20 The thinking skills of the conversational manager

fied emerged for the first time? If so, add them to your accumulating model of the kinds of conversational skills you think are useful to managers of public services.

What things could you do to develop any of these conversational skills which you have just added to your model? What would be the first step?

NOTES

1 Horne, T. and Draper, J. (1979) 'Attributes of Effective Managers' (internal paper presented at Lancaster University).

2 Horne, T. and Harrison, J. (1998) Internal research paper presented at University of Central Lancashire.

3 Schroder, H. (1989) *Managerial Competence. The Key to Excellence.* Kendall Hunt; Cockerill, D., Hunt, R. and Schroder, H. (1995) 'Management Competencies'. *Business Strategy Review*, vol. 6, pp. 4–35.

4 Kakabadse, A. (1991) *The Wealth Creators.* Kogan Page.

5 Boyatzis, M. E. (1982) *The Competent Manager. A Model for Effective Performance.* Wiley Intersciences.

6 Klemp, G. (1980) The Association of Occupational Competence. National Institute of Education, Washington.

7 Morgan, G. (1988) *Riding the Waves of Change: Developing Managerial Competence for a Turbulent World.* Jossey-Bass.

8 Harvey, L. (1999) Keynote presentation at conference on New Realities – The Relationship between Higher Education and Employment, in Lund, Sweden, August.

9 Harvey, L., Moon, S. and Geall, V. (1997) Report to the Association of Graduate Recruiters.

10 *The Dearing Report* (1997) The National Enquiry into Higher Education. DfEE.

11 Pedler, M., Burgoyne, J., Boydell, T. and Welshman, S. (eds) (1990) *Self Development in Organizations.* McGraw-Hill.

12 Pedler, M. and Boydell, T. (1989) 'Is All Management Development Self Development?' in Beck, J. and Cox, C. (eds) *Advances in Management Education.* Wiley.

13 Wellman, D. A. (1996) *The Making of a Manager.* Kogan Page.

14 Fleming, I. (1995) *The Time Management Pocketbook*, Alresford Press.

15 Counsel, D. (1996) 'Careers in the UK', in *Career Development International.*

16 Sparrow, J. (1994) 'Management in Transition?' In *European Human Resource Management.* Prentice Hall, p. 34.

17 Clarke, P. (1992) *Total Career Planning.* McGraw-Hill.

18 Locke, J. (1984) *Goal Setting: A Motivational Technique that Works.* Prentice Hall.

19 Greenhouse, M. (1987) *Career Management.* Dryden.

20 Counsel, D. (1999) 'Careers in Ethiopia'. *Career Development International*, vol. 4, p. 46.

21 Brandt, E. (1980) 'Inside Moves', *Executive Female*, vol. 12, p. 40.

22 Harman, H. M. (1999) 'Ten Steps to a Successful Career'. In *Management Accountant*, vol. 71.

23 Metz, H. (1990) 'Winning Strategies for Career Management', *Transport and Distribution*, vol. 31, p. 30.

24 Hinch, P. (1992) 'Strategies for Success', in *Public Manager*, vol. 21, p. 5.

25 Bartholomew, F. (1980) *Must Success Cost So Much? A Study of the Careers of 532 European Managers.* Helinford.

26 Francis, D. (1985) *Managing Your Own Career.* Collins.

27 Ibid.

28 Pedler, M. and Boydell, T. (1985) *Managing Yourself.* Collins.

29 Harrison, R. (1972) 'Understanding Organisation Character', *Harvard Business Review.*

30 Bartholomew, op. cit.

31 Katz (1960) 'Towards a More Effective Enterprise', *Harvard Business Review* (September).

32 Stirling Livingstone, A. J. (1990) 'Pygmalion in Management', *Harvard Business Review.*

33 Boyd, W. (1961) *The History of Western Education.* Black.

34 Russell, B. (1946) *A History of Western Philosophy.* Allen & Urwin.

35 Fox, S. (1990) in Pedler, M., Burgoyne, J., Boydell, T. and Welshman, S. (eds), op. cit.

36 Wootton, S. and Horne, T. (2000) *Strategic Thinking for Managers.* Kogan Page. Also at www.librapress.com.

37 See Buchanan, D. and Huczynski, A. (1996) *Organizational Behaviour: An Introductory Text.* Prentice Hall, p. 59.

38 Pedler and Boydell (1985) op. cit.

FINAL THOUGHTS

REVIEWING THE SIX KEY ROLES OF THE COMPETENT MANAGER

- Managing Change
- Managing Operations and Activities
- Managing People
- Managing Finances and Resources
- Managing Information
- Managing Learning and Personal Development

15

MANAGING VALUES – MANAGEMENT AS RELIGION

We are what we repeatedly do. Excellence is not a single act, it is a habit.

(Aristotle 384–322 BC)

LEARNING OUTCOMES

This chapter will enable the reader to:

- End by revisiting ideas set out at the beginning of the book.
- Consider the work of one conversational manager of a public service.
- Revisit the management of values.
- Consider a conversational approach to research.
- Consider ways of making these conversations more thoughtful.
- Surface the assumptions and values that underlie management as an activity.
- Identify and evaluate 'seven deadly sins of management'.
- Surface the values that underlie a conversational approach to management.
- Explore what insights can be gained by viewing management as religion.
- Summarize the book.

INTRODUCTION

In our First Thoughts we looked at general approaches to management in the context of public services. In the main body of the book we divided the underpinning knowledge that managers are expected to have, into that which underpins managing resistance and change; managing operations and activities; managing groups and individuals; managing resources and finance, managing communication and information, and managing learning and personal development. We divided the material up in this way, because knowledge, which underpins competence in these six roles, is assessed for vocational management qualifications. We realize, however, that when we are thinking about what to do, we do not consult a list of competencies. What we do reflects, in part, who we are and, as Aristotle said, 'we are what we repeatedly do. Excellence is not a single act, it is a habit.' Our values and beliefs tell us what we should do; our knowledge and understanding limit what we can do. The Venn diagram in Figure 15.1. illustrates the interplay between desires, needs, capabilities, beliefs and values in determining what managers actually do.

In this last chapter we review the values that are implicit in the things which managers do. This will help managers to think about whether what they do is consistent with the values that underpin the culture of public services. We start by looking at the findings of research by Tony Doherty (1997) into the use of a conversational approach to management by Carolyn Horne.

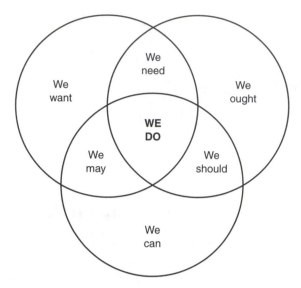

Figure 15.1 Desires, capabilities, needs, beliefs and values

Source: Horne and Wootton (1997)

Box 15.1

CASE STUDY: CAROLYN HORNE – A CONVERSATIONAL MANAGER

The Context

In 1995/96, all providers of primary initial teacher training in England were inspected by the Office for Standards in Education (OFSTED). Teams of inspectors made two separate visits to each of the 68 institutions offering primary initial teacher training. One visit reported on the training provided and the other visit reported on the student teachers' competence to teach. The inspectors used a four-point inspection grading scale:

- Rating 1. Very good: many good features, many outstanding ones
- Rating 2. Good: more good features than sound ones
- Rating 3. Sound: shortcomings, if any, balanced by positive features
- Rating 4. Unsatisfactory: some shortcomings in certain areas

A university college in the north of England was inspected in June 1995 and November 1995. The college was rated '4' (unsatisfactory) in all three areas of inspection. The report concluded its summary of the findings of the inspection:

> On the basis of the inspection evidence, in all areas inspected, the quality of training and students' overall teaching competence do not meet the requirements of Circular 24/89. The training in English and mathematics and ARR does not comply with sections 2.4, 2.6, 3.1, 4.7, and 6.2 of Circular 24/89. At the time of inspection, the university did not have effective quality assurance arrangements in place for the courses inspected.
>
> (OFSTED Publications. London 1996)

If the College failed to pass a re-inspection within 12 months, it would be closed down.

The University

The university in question had taken over the college from a charitable foundation some years earlier. It welcomed the extra student numbers and the funding that came with them. Over the years the former collegiate structures were slowly dismantled and were replaced by the university's own management systems. This brought in its wake the erosion of many of the values of the founder who had given her name to the college. The values of the teachers, and those who trained them, did not sit easily alongside those of the new university managers. Back on its own campus, the university was experiencing severe financial difficulties. The option to sell the college to St Martha's – a church college – was the cheapest option. It was costed at £4,151,000. There would need to be negotiations also about the costs associated with early retirement and a voluntary severance scheme. The sale of the college would also reduce the university's student base by 1,000 students, with a consequent £3 million reduction in income. Negotiations with St Martha's opened in spring 1996. All the time the negotiations dragged on, Carolyn's time was ticking away.

The university finally agreed to a transfer of the failing college to St Martha's in September 1996. Carolyn Horne was immediately seconded from her post, as director of primary initial teacher training at St Martha's, to try and help to save the college from closure. Together with her colleague – a former HMI – she now had only five months to get the college through a re-inspection. She had little time to raise staff and student morale and to help turn around a failing institution.

The Staff

Staff morale and motivation were extremely low. The atmosphere was likened to a state of mourning and bereavement. Lecturers felt that they had let down their students. The staff were demoralized by the takeover and frightened by the personal consequences of being merged with a college that was formerly a rival. Pride would have to be swallowed. They were unsure about their personal future in the new institution. Would they even have a job? All staff felt tarred by the same brush.

There was much questioning of the fairness of the inspection process. It had covered only three areas and did not review areas in which the college was successful. The evidence base for the OFSTED judgements was questioned. Staff felt let down and betrayed by poor management. The last thing they wanted was another new senior manager from a rival college. Carolyn's initial reception was understandably cool and even hostile from some quarters. Carolyn, a Quaker, disliked conflict. She disliked games and politics. She was an emotionally vulnerable person.

The Students

Students were stunned by the failure of the college to pass its inspection. If the college failed the re-inspection and its status as an accredited teacher training agency was withdrawn, it would probably mean that some students at the college would not qualify as teachers. Their future careers were at stake. Students averted their gaze. The bright vibrant displays of student work, which normally characterize a teacher training institution, were absent. To Carolyn, the drabness of the college was ominous.

The Local Community

The college was the most important all-year-round employer in the town. The students brought income into the area. Staff felt that they had not only let down the students but had also failed the local community. The Local Education

Authority had a stake in the college which went back many years. The college had been part of the local authority before going independent and before being taken over by the university. Many of the county's teachers had trained there.

OFSTED

Amongst some of the staff there was a strong feeling that OFSTED had a vested interest in failing the college. They needed a scalp. The chief inspector had made it clear before the national inspection programme that he was unhappy about the quality of teacher training in the UK. He had canvassed readily available support for his views and had been given a considerable budget to prove his point. At the end of his inspection of 68 institutions, he had identified only two possible candidates for failure and one was Carolyn's new college. There was a feeling that he was out to make an example of it.

St Martha's College

Under Carolyn, primary initial teacher training at St Martha's had continued to grow, even through years of cutbacks. From a small church college when she first joined, it now had one of the largest single campus programmes in the country. In its own inspection St Martha's had achieved an 'excellent' rating – a result equalled only by one other institution in England and Wales. Why risk spoiling this record by taking on the failing college? 'If it goes down, we get the business anyhow, we don't need the hassle and headaches of a neglected and outdated college.' Carolyn had watched with dismay the demise of the once highly respected rival college. She knew many of the tutors personally and admired their work. Years earlier she had sent her own god-daughter to this college. She felt angry that a fine reputation had been squandered – in

her view by poor management. She resolved to do all she could to reverse its fortunes in the five months that remained before the re-inspection.

WHAT DID CAROLYN DO?

Staffing

No one was formally asked to leave, but senior staff and heads of departments were invited to take early retirement and/or to seek voluntary redundancy. Carolyn could offer nothing. She had no power to offer guarantees of employment. The uncertainty of the situation led many staff to conclude that severance deals were a much safer bet than Carolyn's belief that she could get them through a re-inspection. NATFHE, the further and higher education union, negotiated severance deals for individual members of staff. Carolyn lacked the basic levers of power and motivation on which most public service managers rely – secure employment and prospects of promotion.

Restructuring

Back at St Martha's, Carolyn gathered together a group of senior managers to whom she could report and, importantly, from whom she could receive support. Feelings were running high at her college. The feelings were mainly negative and often focused on Carolyn as the outsider and as a representative of the new management. She tried to recruit a team to implement the changes that were needed to salvage the college. That was a mistake. There was little enthusiasm for either the team or its task. Many of the experienced senior staff had left. She tried encouraging individuals who had stayed to accept new responsibilities and new job descriptions. Staff were surprised when she invited them to write or modify their own job descriptions. This had never happened before.

Holding Conversations

Slowly the resistance of a few of the staff began to melt. She took up with them quickly and focused on the task; daily individual action plans; daily individual reviews; small steps; small successes; immediate individual feedback; frequent mistakes; ready apologies and a readiness to learn how mistakes had been made. Always the plans and the learning were projected beyond the inspection towards the college as Carolyn saw it in three years' time. Whenever possible she talked to people about the future, what it would be like after they had passed the inspection. Despite private anxieties and private misgivings, she never faltered in her public confidence in her new staff. Even when external pressures intensified because of their lack of apparent progress, she remained positive about even the smallest improvement. She would not discuss the possibility of failing the inspection. She banned the use of the inspection manuals: 'If we act and can show that we are acting on our beliefs about children, about teachers and about education, the inspection will take care of itself. We must think beyond the immediate problems to a new degree programme and not recriminate about past mistakes.'

Carolyn regularly gave positive feedback to her newly appointed staff, but many of them were slow to trust her, slow to respond and even slower to act. Time was running out. Carolyn started to stay late every night, propping open her door, hoping that someone would call in to tell her how they were getting on. For the first two weeks nobody came. She resisted the temptation to check up and supervise. She set up open meetings for all staff but many stayed away. People were still doubtful and mistrustful. She banned cynical remarks and would not entertain political gossip. Little was written down, which frustrated the inspectorate who were pressing for advance copies of documentation. She kept stalling. Occasionally she wrote brief personal notes and e-mails to scotch rumours, or to deal with scare-mongering. She paired people up in mutually supportive relationships. Eventually she gave these pairs tasks to do together. She ran drop-in training events in all the areas identified as weak in the inspection. She did not pretend to know the answers. She tried out ideas which the staff had for improvements and learned with her staff from the mistakes that were made. She held a mock inspection a few weeks before the dreaded real inspection. She declared it fine and set people to work on a development plan for the next three years: 'When the inspectors come, talk to them about your ideas for the future – only discuss the failed inspection if they ask you about it and then be as honest as you can.'

If the re-inspection team did come looking for a scalp they did not find one. Before they left, off the record, members of the inspection team intimated that the college had a fine future ahead of it and that their final inspection report would show an excellent rating in at least two of the areas of the re-inspection!

Carolyn had managed her own anxieties and stress, to which she was personally very vulnerable, partly by talking to her support group at St Martha's. She also talked a lot to her consultant HMI and friend Colin Richards. At home she talked late into the night to her husband, rehearsing conversations for the next day. She thought that planning was an intellectual process but that management was a conversational process. Each night she planned as many conversations as possible with the people on whose performance she depended. In the morning she would rise early and go for a long run as soon as it was light. She claimed that it 'got her brain going' and that solutions to problems she had slept on overnight would often 'pop' into her head as she completed her morning run. She was training for the London marathon.

Once she had been tipped off that the inspection was going to be a success, Carolyn celebrated with her family and decided to resume her evening training runs with her running club. It was on the first evening run that she was hit by a car and killed instantly. At her memorial service Colin Richards said:

> I'm reading a book on management. I'm disappointed with much of it. It's full of platitudes, clichés and management jargon. Ideas like organizational culture and transformational leadership. Terms like that turn off a sceptic like me. However, my attention was taken by at least one quotation in a book by Peter Senge:
>
>> What distinguishes outstanding leaders is the clarity and persuasiveness of their ideas, the depth of their commitment and their openness to continuously learning more. They do not have the answer! But they do instil confidence in those around them that, together, we can learn whatever we need to learn in order to achieve the results we truly desire.

Carolyn was crystal-clear in her ideas; persuasive with a firm sense of purpose. Her commitment to the cause of high-quality education was total. Her willingness to learn from her own experience and from others was humbling. She didn't have the answer, she never pretended to. But she made us all feel confident that together we could learn what we needed, to achieve what we truly wanted, and we did, as was proved by the successful inspection. Peter Senge goes on:

> The ability of such people to be natural leaders, as near as I can tell, is the by-product of a lifetime of effort to develop conceptual and communication skills, to reflect on personal values and to align personal behaviour with values, to learn how to listen and appreciate others and the ideas of others.

Carolyn had amazing conceptual and communication skills. She was one of the most powerful and sensitive listeners I ever met. She even appreciated *me* and my ideas, as well as others and their ideas, but above all her personal values of care, compassion, integrity, steadfastness, determination and love for all her fellow men and women, shone through all she did. She was a truly wonder-full human being.

The sceptic within me has been forced to accept that idea of the transformational leader. Why? Because I have experienced it. Carolyn provided it for me and for so many of us.

CAROLYN THE CONVERSATIONAL MANAGER

In public service organizations, it is common to exclude from the management process everyone except an inner sanctum of 'strategic managers'. Yet Carolyn implemented major changes by having conversations with many people. Seemingly ordinary people. Seemingly ordinary conversations in which choices were made, ideas tested, preferences expressed, minds changed, schemes modified, plots hatched and good reasons given. Carolyn talked to the gardener, the driver, the lady on the switchboard, local teachers, to her much-loved secretary, to the Bursar, to her office supervisor, to governors, to the head of catering, to her friend and colleague Professor Richards and every night to her husband. She had never heard of stakeholder analysis. She did it naturally. Through conversations, she identified good questions and surfaced values on which a strategy should rest. She did not to take it for granted that other people would share her views. She created shared meanings so that matters could be discussed. Professor Richards says Carolyn listened very intently and that, as a result, conversations with Carolyn were intensely energizing. Because she was open to challenge by people whose values were very different from her own, it helped her to surface her own beliefs. That gave her a chance to explain them, or sometimes to change them. Carolyn was a potter. The way she shaped her clay was grounded in an 'intuitive feel' for the public service to which she gave her life. She combined rigorous analysis with creative response. We recognize Carolyn's spirit of exploration, her capacity for quiet reflection and her interest in thinking. In her questioning disposition, her preparedness to challenge embedded assumptions and her use of models, we recognize her concern with the whole as well as the parts.

Carolyn came to conversations with heart and mind prepared, centring herself in the conversation, speaking the truth plainly, listening actively, finding the sense of what was said, waiting silently, writing action minutes, then moving cheerfully over the world, seeking that which was good in everyone.

MANAGING VALUES

At the start of this book, in First Thoughts, we began by exploring what it meant to manage in a public service.

> We shall not cease from exploration
> And the end of all our exploration
> Will be to arrive where we started
> And know the place for the first time.
> (*Little Gidding*, T. S. Eliot)

What is still the same in public services is the same need, day in, day out, to maintain the same routines and to accomplish the same daily tasks. These daily tasks have been going on, day in day out, for more than a century, without the need for professional managers. Yet, during the latter part of the twentieth century, the management of these daily tasks became the work of 'experts'. Managers were employed, and sometimes trained, to organize and regulate much of the activity that took place in public service organizations. Often these managers were led to believe that it was necessary to change the customs and practices and routine habits of the people who worked in there. In Chapters 2 and 3 we explored the idea that if you change what people repeatedly do, you change them. We learned that people change their beliefs, in order to reduce 'dissonance' between their beliefs and things that they are routinely forced to do. If the people who work in a public service organization do change their beliefs, then the culture of the public service organization might also change (Chapter 3). Is that what had happened to the staff at the college which Carolyn was asked to rescue? Is that why Carolyn focused on daily tasks – 'daily lists' – that were consistent with their long-held beliefs about children, teaching and education? Was she attempting to reverse a cultural change that had resulted from the introduction of managerialism? Had the college lost continuity with its long-held educational values?

Managers now exert influence over activities that used to be organized by military authorities, charities or religious orders. Managers now manage our transport, our health, our food chain, our sports and entertainment, exercise, leisure time and lifelong learning.[1] We have discovered that managers work in many different kinds of public service organizations – publicly, privately and charitably owned – and that they carry out a wide variety of roles. Managers have many different kinds of professional and non-professional training – or none at all. Carolyn was a psychologist who had retrained as a teacher. As we saw in Chapter 12, public service managers usually have imperfect information on which to make decisions, under pressure from a plurality of stakeholders. Individual differences between public service managers have made us reluctant to generalize about what all public service managers should do, or avoid doing. Like Carolyn, we prefer a conversational approach to information gathering and testing, in combination with a thoughtful approach to working out what action might be appropriate with the particular people involved in a particular situation.

Ethical Values

Ideas about what managers should do have been unsettled by increased concern about their ethics and an increased awareness of the social and ecological consequences of their decisions (Chapter 11). Increased anxiety has evoked a flood of management prescriptions and 'big ideas'. As we visited each of the six roles that a competent manager must play, we found few 'big ideas' that had any enduring value. Some of the ideas seemed harmful to the service, to their managers or to their staff. Other 'new' ideas, dressed in the language of liberation[2] turned out to be old ideas. Management by objectives becomes performance management leading to downsizing, delayering and outplacement.[3] It was assumed that scientific measurement could result in social improvement, that consumerism could improve public services, and that increasing the proportion of a nation's wealth on which owners of capital could earn a return would lead to a fairer and more civilized society. Why do we have these 'big ideas' about management? Whom do they benefit?[4] How do they relate to what ordinary people do at work?[5] 'Theories' are normally construed as the product of inner world thinking and are generally considered to be separate from 'practice', which is normally construed as part of the outer world of action. In management, practice is generally awarded the higher status, being more 'real'. Theory is more likely to be denounced as 'academic', here used as a term of abuse. Practitioners are proud that their practice is unsullied by theory. Some academics claim virtue in their distance from the world of work.[6] We reject this polarization. We offer a model of management that involves moving from the inner world of ideas to the outer world of practical actions and then back again. Conversational management involves an internal dialogue in which the theories implicit in the proposed outer world practice can be subject to critical evaluation. The evaluation criteria include not only economy, efficiency and effectiveness but also include empathy and ethics – 'How would other people feel about this idea?' and 'Do I think that its outer world practice would be good?' For both of these evaluations – ethical and empathetic – we need some awareness of values.

Scientific Values

Despite the fact that the most taxing problems confronting Carolyn were people problems and problems of low morale, she made good use of her scientific training. Her analysis of the failed inspection was painstaking and her attention to detail was thorough. She encouraged individuals to think beyond the inspection and to contribute to a three-year planning process. Planning, however, sometimes assumes that managers can control the future of their organizations. It is not clear that this assumption is valid. Carolyn, for instance, was subject to the vagaries of UK politics at the time and to the personal agendas of her principal, her advisors and her chief inspector. Planning also assumes that changes in some variables will determine changes in others, i.e. that you believe in determinism. In the 1960s contingency theorists implied that managers had no real choice. What they did was determined by their need to find the 'best fit' with their environment. In 1972 John Child[7] reasserted the possibility of 'real choice'. He claimed that the aims, beliefs and expectations of decision-makers could affect outcomes, within limits set by other determining factors. Child believed in a rational analysis of the internal and external world of the organization. The usefulness of rational approaches has since been disputed.[8] In 1995 Hendry[9] found that many 'rational practices' were in fact contradictory, ambiguous, misunderstood and biased in favour of the ambitions of particular individuals or groups. Because public services are often staffed by a high proportion of scientifically trained technicians and professionals, public service managers frequently varnish their decisions with a glossy coat of rationality. Perhaps they feel that this enhances the credibility of their decisions. Thompson and McHugh[10] have pointed out that rational approaches to management ignore many of the deep-seated problems of organizational life – namely, inequality, conflict, domination, subordination and manipulation. Interviews with Carolyn's staff and colleagues revealed that her conversational approach had forced her to confront many of the problems which Thompson and McHugh fear are commonly ignored.

Political Values

Although many of the problems that concerned Carolyn were 'inner world' and conceptual, she knew that the solutions would have to be implemented in an 'outer world' where the processes would be social. Social difficulties have turned up in each of the six roles of the competent manager that we have considered: managing resistance and change, managing operations and activities, managing groups and individuals, managing finances and resources, managing communication and information and managing learning and personal development. These difficulties are exacerbated by differences between the values held by the managers and the values held by the people they are managing. Carolyn appeared not to compromise her judgements as a professional or her values as an educationalist, but neither did she underestimate the political aspects of being a manager.[11] We think that it is better to surface strong beliefs, because by so doing we give ourselves more choice. We can choose to confirm, challenge or attempt to change our own beliefs or those of other people.

RESEARCHING MANAGEMENT: A CONVERSATIONAL APPROACH

Public service organizations trade in services. They also trade in 'messages'. They try to sell 'messages' of confidence and competence to their clients, the general public, taxpayers and local and central government. They try to keep their employees 'on message'. But employees have conflicting needs (Chapter 7). Conflicting needs threaten the cohesiveness of the organization. The prospect of fragmentation and disorder in turn threatens managers – so much so, that managers introduce rules and procedures. Rules and procedures contribute words and phrases to our vocabulary. The words that we use limit the way we think about what is happening. According to Tony Watson,[12] the frequency with which we use words like customer, competitor and quality affects the way we think. Watson used a con-

versational approach to his research. Conversational approaches to research have a tradition in history (Elizabeth Roberts) and in anthropology (Margaret Mead). Watson combined conversational research with 'discourse analysis'. Discourse analysis is an analysis of the words that people use during conversations or in documents.

In public services there is often more than one kind of discourse. Different sets of words, phrases, statements and expressions are found in rival discourses. One common discourse is a 'developmental' discourse, characterized by words like empowerment, autonomy and learning. Another common discourse is 'business' discourse, characterized by words like efficiency, control and value for money. Competing factions attempt to increase their influence by getting more people to speak their language. Supporters of a 'developmental' culture attempt to colonize the unconverted through conversations about 'growing' the personal skills of 'proactive' people so that they will find work 'empowering' and 'rewarding'. Disciples of a 'business' culture attempt to colonize the unconverted through conversations about 'getting people to do what they are paid for'; about 'monitoring performance, controlling costs and meeting targets'.

Managers as Workers

Watson reports a conversation with a senior manager:

> Do we have to keep doing what someone else decides? . . . I really wonder if we have any values at all . . . what about *my* empowerment? . . . what about *my* personal development?[13]

It is important to note that this is a senior manager talking. He talks as a manager, but also as a worker. He articulates his dissatisfaction as an employee using language that he learned through having conversations as a manager! He recognizes the contradiction between what he has said to others about the organization and the way the organization is treating him. How long can managers go on treating their employees thoughtfully, when they experience their own managers as thoughtless? If staff do not them-selves feel cared about, how long will they care about their clients?

Gary, a manager in an accounts department, believed in the need to change to a 'development' culture. He also thought that the development idea had been cancelled out by the way the change was handled: 'Change has got to be 'because customers require it', not because some swine decided they are going to have a change for their own sake, or for them to make their mark.'[14]

Watson found a widespread view that changes primarily serve the careers of those who introduced them. Tommy was another manager:

> In the last few years we've played four different games – WC, DOC, BIP and TQM – and now we're back to the old one – 'Don't trust management'. Since year dot, the reality is that management have always exploited the workers.[15]

But these workers can be managers too. Managers repeatedly complained of being used. Peter, another manager, saw the pressure on him as coming from outside:

> I don't like inefficiency and it has been right to get rid of slack but, beyond that, always seeing cutting your costs as getting rid of people, will kill us – as a country – not just as an organization.[16]

In many conversations, many managers have expressed views similar to Peter's. The managers have seemed uneasy about appearing to act as agents for outside powers. They spoke of growing mistrust. Ken, a senior manager, said: 'Mistrust is worse than ever it was. There seems to be someone carrying guns around at the highest levels. Overnight you could be without a job.'[17] If this is how managers feel, we can imagine how the workers feel. Maybe not very different, because managers are workers too!

Researching Management Research: Conversations about Conversations

We were fortunate to have conversations about con-versations with Peter Thomas, while he was writing *Strategy Talk*.[18] While Thomas could see that junior

and middle managers needed to have conversations in order to implement strategy, he was very critical of the kinds of conversations senior managers had *about* strategy. He thought that senior managers used 'strategy talk' to mystify their staff, bolster their own positions and justify their seniority and their salaries. The same 'strategy talk' has been used to earn money for consultants, writers, academics and business schools.

In *Strategy Talk*, Thomas classifies their classifica-tions. In doing so, he runs the danger of being drawn into an academic game of 'my model is bigger than your model' – 'my conceptual map maps yours.' Thomas points out that despite having roots in ancient Athens and China,[19] it was not until the 1950s that strategy began to be spoken about in relation to organizations. The term 'strategic man-agement' was not common until the early 1980s.[20] We have followed Thomas's lead in using 'strategic management' as a label for these conversations rather than Corporate Strategy,[21] Strategic Decision Making,[22] or Competitive Strategy.[23]

By 1988 Bowers[24] was complaining that the lan-guage used in conversations about strategy seemed designed to make the conversations incomprehens-ible to the uninitiated. In strategy there is wide-spread confusion about who is doing what, to whom and for what purpose. In Chapter 8 we argued that it was individuals, not organizations, who did things. In 1995 Thomas and McHugh[25] argued that it was a serious error to attribute managers with the characteristics of free agents. We agree with them. Between 1970 and 1990 many attempts were made to group different types of conversations about strat-egy under different headings.[26] Predictably, the next step in the academic game was to classify the classifi-cations. Conversations about strategic management fell into:

- Those that distinguished between what was done and how it was done.
- Those that distinguished between the stages and steps to be taken.
- Those that distinguished between the theories on which each was based.

The theoretical basis for most conversations about strategy is flawed or unclear. Routeau and Seguin[27] would have struggled to categorize our approach to strategy (Chapter 3), because it embraces all three of their categories.

'Stakeholders': Hostages to Whose Fortune?

At a conference in July 1999, Thomas[28] pointed out how language developed for one purpose (i.e. to be critical of management) was being used by managers in ways that served ends other than those originally intended. He cited the 'stakeholder' discourse as an example. During the 1990s we found the idea of 'stakeholders' useful in our conversational approach to designing information systems which made managers of public services more accountable to their stakeholders (Chapter 12). Following a debate between Argenti,[29] Cleaver,[30] Field[31] and Francis,[32] the balance of opinion seemed to be that 'stakeholder management' was a possible route to more responsible management.[33] Unfortunately, this optimistic conclusion was premature. Donaldson and Preston[34] had been concerned that 'stakeholding' did not mean the same thing when used by different people. Ambiguity about the meaning of 'stakeholder' allowed it to be used to sustain injustice. Even worse, according to Thomas, it has been used to damage stakeholder interests, while at the same time giving the impression of supporting them. We are biased in our view that an approach to strategy based on learning to think strategically transcends most of the limitations identified by Thomas. In *Strategic Thinking*, Wootton and Horne[35] identify the basic thinking skills that need to be combined in order to think strategically. In this book – *A Thoughtful Approach to the Practice of Management* – there are thinking and learning activities which develop those basic thinking skills. The role of thinking in strategy can be further explored in *Thinking Skills for Managers* by Wootton and Horne.[36]

More Thoughtful Conversations

In arguing for strategic thinking to be considered as a way of combining a number of basic thinking skills, we are as biased as any authors who hope for fame or fortune from writing. What we write is refracted through a prism of personal experience and personal interest. Having said that, we have tried to build on the work of others, rather than denigrate its authors (even though controversy would have attracted more attention and increased sales!). Routeau and Seguin are guilty of a veiled imputation of self-interest against Mintzberg.[37] Criticisms of motives are hard to defend; they are deeply undermining and often hurtful.[38] Criticism of ideas can be equally thoughtless.[39] Management is a social process and tolerance is required. There is bound to be conceptual confusion, difficulty in prediction, and the use of inductive reasoning.

While Montgomery *et al.*[40] argue for more rigour and objectivity, Mahoney[41] appeals for better conversations. If better conversations are to be more thoughtful conversations, we need to treat others with respect; listen attentively to what they have to say; let them finish their sentences; give good reasons to support our views; hold our own views tentatively; and be open to the possibility that we may be wrong (Chapter 13)! This requires a more thoughtful disposition and militates against prescribing too precisely what managers should do.[42] A more thoughtful disposition points to less haste in arriving at conclusions. Daft and Buenger[43] warn against premature convergence of ideas, based on assumptions that are too narrow. A more thoughtful approach favours plurality and diversity. It favours as much exploration, and widening of the scope of the conversation, as time will allow.[44]

In a conversational approach we are concerned with the practice, not the theory of management. Our test is utility. Ideas are set down, 'not as a rule or form to walk by but rather that in their spirit ye may be guided'.[45] If an idea is helpful, use it. If not, modify or reject it. Practical heuristics are useful. However, care must be taken not to transfer them unthinkingly from one situation to another.

Thought will need to be given. Is the heuristic relevant and applicable to the new situation? Our use of a simplifying heuristic should remind us of the underlying complexity that caused us to need the heuristic in the first place! Just because a management heuristic appears simple, it does not necessarily mean that the thinking behind it was simplistic.

Continuity or Change?

In public services, it is often difficult to balance the need for change against the benefits of continuity. Surfacing beliefs and adopting values can be a useful way of orchestrating a debate about continuity and change. Polarized cultures can result in traditional values losing out. By surfacing beliefs and evaluating their continued relevance, we have been able to reduce the demotivation which often accompanies the exaggerated discrediting of past practices. The values that underpin management, and sometimes their adverse impact on public service organizations, often go undetected. We want to surface some of the values that are implied when managers use the techniques and processes that we have described in this book.

SURFACING MANAGEMENT VALUES

Management as Privilege

We have said that managing is what managers do. We have then described a series of technical competencies that help managers to do what they need to do. This may have created an illusion that management is value free. Where theories have been given to explain 'why' as well as 'how', the theories have usually side-stepped any discussion about the power structures that were needed to give any one person the 'right to manage' another. The word to 'manage' comes from a Latin word which means to break in a horse, i.e. to break its spirit so that it becomes docile and comes to do the bidding of its master! So far, in this book, the 'right to manage' has been a taken-for-granted assumption. Is it a valid assumption? If so,

is it 'right' that it should be so? In capitalist societies, the owners of property and money are thought, by some, to have fostered the emergence and the training of a privileged elite to act on their behalf, defending their interests and adding to their wealth. They are called managers. This privileged elite are usually well paid. It would be surprising, therefore, if managers did not share the beliefs and values of those who have money. Besides, she who pays the piper, generally calls the tune. It can cause problems when public service managers appear to act for their sponsors and seek to increase opportunities for owners of capital to earn a further return on their wealth. Managers do this by supporting the privatization of publicly owned public services and by encouraging public service organizations to buy a proportion of their services from privately owned companies. Managers are often introduced in order to 'help' publicly owned public services to reduce their share of their country's economic cake. Sometimes managers are imported directly from privately owned organizations (Chapter 1). More often people who are already working in the publicly owned organization are trained up as the managers. That happened to Rosie Wakely, at the English National Opera (Box 3.10). Public service staff are often trained to be managers by consultants with 'relevant private sector experience'. Other employees with the 'right management attitudes' are funded, often at public expense, to undergo management training at business schools, where it is hoped that they will acquire some of the values of private sector managers. In such settings, private sector managers can be relied on to express astonishment that their public sector colleagues would allow representatives of the local community to participate in decision-making. What an infringement of the privileged manager's right to manage!

Managers as Professionals

Managers of some public services find it hard to identify with the clients of that service. Managers are likely to have gained membership of the managerial class by espousing the interests and values of the privileged. The clash in values is not obvious because managers often use the language of science (Chapter 12). As we saw in Chapter 3, the notion of management as a science is problematic. Public service organizations are usually too complex to identify controllable variables. Managers who ignore this complexity exhibit thinking that is akin to religious fundamentalism. Presenting management as a science creates the impression that it is a professional process of getting things done through 'human resource management'. The subliminal linking of management to science fosters an illusion of objectivity. Management-as-science is a mystique behind which managers can hide. Managers can hide and hope to be left alone to 'complex decision-making'. When managers hide, there is less risk of them having conversations with people who might like to have a say (Chapter 12).

This self-imposed isolation only serves to increase the anxiety of the managers. The managers become even more anxious about whether staff will comply with their decisions (Chapter 6), and anxiety about compliance can lead to bribery and bullying (Chapters 3, 8 and 11). The values implied by bribery and bullying are not those implied by collegiality or active citizenship! Compliance is usually claimed by managers to be in the interests of clients, funding or public safety. The real motivation is likely to be management anxiety about the consequences of non-compliance, loss of face, or the challenge to their authority. Even senior managers are fearful of the good opinion of their superiors. Management seems to depend on managers being afraid of the people who have more power than they have. In turn, the more powerful people are afraid of losing their power.

Managers as Victims

Representing management as a hierarchy of ascending technical expertise legitimizes the 'right to manage' and with it the right to be a member of a privileged elite. In public service organizations, senior managers devote considerable time, thought and energy to minimizing risks to their security. In order to achieve this, they are not above reducing the

security of others. When managers themselves become the victims of management – through downsizing, delayering and out-placement – they are at least more likely than their staff to be compensated. They are usually redeployed on protected salaries, or retired on enhanced pensions, or made redundant on pre-agreed severance terms – a golden 'goodbye' when they leave, and a golden 'hello' when they are brought back on part-time contracts, or as management consultants. In the 1990s, many managers were victims of human resource management. Performance management was concealed in the velvet glove of new-wave management. New-wave management spoke of decentralization, self-managed teams, creativity, empowerment and contracts that were 'psychological' – not just temporary and part-time.[46]

Managers as People

In Chapter 8 we developed the case for managing people as individuals rather than as groups. We contested the usefulness of generalized prescriptions about managing people, because people display a high degree of individual difference. Since managers are people too, it may be useful to recognize that not all managers are the same. Managers in different functions differ from one another. Even within a given function, managers at different levels differ from one another. Different managers have different concerns, different perspectives, different training and often come from different social backgrounds. Managers in marketing and advertising often tend to have a different personality and disposition from managers in finance and estates. Private sector senior managers are concerned with acquiring capital and making returns on it. Administrative managers are concerned with systems and monitoring. Public service managers are largely concerned with the direction and control of people.[47]

This might explain why generalized management control strategies are not universally successful.[48] Most attempts to refute the generalizability of pronouncements about management seem to come from outside of management. This led Thomas and

Shrivastava[49] to wonder whether ideas about management were ideologically driven.

Management as Ideology

Shrivastava found much management writing to be characterized by reference to 'facts' that were not facts; denials of contradiction; presumptions that the status quo was normal and the pursuit of vested interests. According to Giddens'[50] criteria, most conversations about management are ideological. Most of our conversations with senior managers legitimized existing power structures and inequalities. In particular, the values and actions of senior managers were assumed to be 'good', without regard to their social consequence. The actions that senior managers took were justified as necessary for the organization to survive.[51]

However, survival is a matter of whimsical chance in a system bedevilled by capricious failures and internal contradictions[52] Despite the concerns that Shrivastava[53] first expressed in 1986, many writers since have reinforced the ideological role of management, particularly senior management. According to Thomas,[54] some writers have advocated, without irony, the development of an organizational ideology. Willmott[55] saw this as evolving into a managerial culture. We wondered whether it was more like a religion. In the 1990s, Charles Handy, author of *Gods of Management*, spoke regularly on 'Thought for the Day'. It is a radio programme normally reserved for religious speakers! At the same time, Tom Peters, a management 'guru', was appealing to his disciples in the USA to become 'visionaries'. Huczynski, writing about management 'gurus', is shocked at how taken-for-granted and unchallenged are the fundamental doctrines of management.[56] There are disputes about the best way to learn about management but rarely about its doctrine (Chapter 13). In Chapter 1 we described Carol Kennedy's defence of Frederick Taylor, a Quaker, as a liberal and as a progressive thinker. Her book is called *Guide to Management Gurus*.[57] A guru is a religious teacher!

The Beliefs of Managers

'All great truths begin as blasphemies' (George Bernard Shaw in *Annajanska* 1917). Recognizing the uneasy co-existence in public service organizations of two different types of conversation, of two separate strands of thinking – scientific performance management and new-wave liberal thinking – may help us to understand why staff and professionals in public services are confused about management. The underlying assumptions and beliefs of performance management and the underlying assumptions and beliefs of new-wave liberation management are very contradictory. This makes managers appear incoherent. As a consequence, many people in public service organizations do not trust managers. What people hear managers *say* often sounds inspirational. But what people see managers *do* – measure, rationalize, control and economize – evokes a quite different response. They experience a contradiction between the manager's rhetoric and their reality – between the manager's 'espoused theories' and the manager's 'theories in use'.[58] The rhetoric of managers, about the needs of clients, conflicts with the behaviour of managers, who cover their backs by focusing primarily on the needs of their bosses.[59]

Managers need to surface their beliefs if they are to manage the impact they are having on the culture of the public services for which they are responsible. In Chapter 3 we described how a conversational approach could be used to surface beliefs and to seek their adoption as values. We have discovered that managers everywhere have certain beliefs that are remarkably consistent. We are tempted to call them the seven deadly sins! In Box 15.2 we summarize the seven most commonly recurring management beliefs which we surfaced through learning conversations with over 2,000 managers in the period 1965–2001 (Chapter 13). We found much variation in beliefs from one organization to another, but those that belonged to management were remarkably consistent.

When we discussed the beliefs that we have surfaced with the senior managers of public service organizations, they usually recognized the beliefs

---

Box 15.2

THE 7 MOST COMMONLY HELD BELIEFS OF MANAGERS

Most managers believe that:

1 They can control everything
2 They can make their futures happen
3 All meaningful results can be measured
4 Everyone must accept their decisions
5 People must give account of their actions to anyone who is more senior
6 Managers should extract maximum effort and energy from every individual
7 The interests of individuals are subordinate to the interests of the organization

---

When thoughtfulness is undervalued, criticism suppressed and truth denied, managers become increasingly divorced from reality. It is natural that senior managers should want members of the public to think well of their organization. Their social standing and their pay, depend on its performance. But in some organizations sharing a vision of success is not enough. People are expected to 'live the vision' and to join in the chorus of 'Simply the Best' (Chapter 8). In such organizations, critics are a nuisance. Senior managers tend to reject factual details that are inconsistent with their strategic view. Staff and professionals who do not want to play these organizational games look for jobs elsewhere. Others become cynical about a service quality that is reported each year to be 'continuously improving', on a diminishing unit of resource. Such cynicism can corrode commitment to the point where the only commitment is to finding another job, or to negotiating 'a good deal' in return for early retirement.

that came from the notion of public service. They did not generally recognize, however, the beliefs that appeared to be there because of their management. This could have been due to a number of reasons. Perhaps the presence of these beliefs in the organization was not caused by the presence of the managers. A correlation does not necessarily indicate a cause. Or perhaps the managers in question were unused to being critical of what they repeatedly *do*. But, according to Aristotle, 'we are what we repeatedly do'. People who see and hear what the managers repeatedly do, are therefore entitled to form a view of what managers believe. Those beliefs may be incompatible with their own beliefs. We will examine conflict between the past beliefs which supported public services, and the seven commonly held beliefs of managers, which we summarized in Box 15.2.

Management Beliefs: Grandiose or Utopian?

The seven commonly held beliefs of managers conspire to produce grandiose utopian expectations.

What are Public Service Values?

What are the values of public service which managers might consider preserving? We have been assured that there exists a distinctive tradition of public service characterized by values such as honesty, impartiality, probity, accountability and public interest.[60] We think this may be a myth.[61] During our work in a broad spectrum of public service organizations, we found some cultures that were 'integrative', some that were 'diverse' and many that were 'polarized' (Chapter 3). We also found examples of what Griseri[62] called 'organizational totalitarianism', i.e. organizations in which no cultural differences were tolerated. In totalitarian cultures where there were managers, the culture turned out to be a culture that was woven around the seven common beliefs of managers (Box 15.2). We should not have been surprised. The seven management beliefs reflect a preoccupation with control. In any struggle for cultural supremacy, a management culture is always likely to win. That is not necessarily a 'good' thing!

Harking Back to the 'Golden Age'

Lawton[63] thinks that public servants are harking back to a mythical 'Golden Age'. The 'Golden Age' may well be a myth; that is not the point. The point about myths is that they are stories that people believe. Children who have lost a parent sometimes invent a mythical parent to replace the one they have lost or never had. The mythical parent is almost always idealized. Normally, no amount of reasoning with the child will convince the child that their mythical parent is not real. The child continues to believe in the idealized parent for as long as that belief is serving some useful purpose. We cannot predict how the seven common beliefs of managers might conflict with the culture of a particular public service. For example, there are major differences between the cultures of public service organizations which offer ostensibly the same service, especially when those organizations are located in different countries. Each country may have markedly different economic, political or religious regimes. Even in any one country, there are marked differences between the culture of a television company, a water authority, a public railway and a prison. What we can do is to take the seven commonly held beliefs of managers and ask: 'Are these management beliefs consistent with the values which public services are widely perceived to have in common?' Such public service values include amongst other things a duty to act in the public interest, in 'a spirit which delights to do no evil' (James Naylor, *Quaker Faith and Practice* 1660).

Whistle-blowing in Public Services

Where there is a lack of probity, or a risk of harm, many public servants would see it as their duty to 'blow the whistle'. Managers, however, are likely to see whistle-blowing by public servants as disloyal. Managers often try to anticipate such 'disloyalty' by putting 'gagging' clauses into new contracts of employment. If the contracts are short term, the implied threat is that they may not be renewed.

Even permanent contracts have had 'gagging' clauses inserted, with sanctions for 'bringing the organization into disrepute'. What is good for commerce may not be good for the community. Secrecy is hard to defend when the public service organization is publicly owned. Secrecy conflicts with the idea that citizens have a right to know what is done in their name, with their money, and ostensibly for their benefit.[64] When managers with a high need for control turn up in public services which have a tradition of official secrecy, the conjunction is not a happy one. Protected by official secrecy, managers are able to coerce or intimidate with impunity. Only through such things as 30-year disclosure rules, investigative journalism, a free press, leaked documents, and the 'whistle-blowing' courage of public servants have the power abuses of managers come to light.

Absolute Power Corrupts

In the seven common beliefs of managers, power was a major preoccupation. Power corrupts – the greater the power, the greater the corruption. Absolute power corrupts absolutely.[65] Unfortunately, according to Geoffrey Hunt,[66] even when the concerns of UK whistle-blowers are subsequently vindicated, it does not prevent a powerful and vindictive management elite from closing ranks to exact revenge. Graham Pink, a nurse, was dismissed. Helen Zeitla, a doctor, was made redundant. Chris Chapmann, a university biochemist, lost his job. The known fate of public service whistle-blowers at the hands of their managers is the visible tip of an iceberg of suppression – of critical reports which are 'put on ice'. By the turn of the century, the authors of these critical reports had become so intimidated that documents were more often leaked than published. The number of 'unattributed' press reports increased markedly. Within two years of new management reforms in the NHS, a survey of 50 UK journalists revealed that NHS staff had become too frightened to speak 'on-the-record' about issues like care, fraud or misconduct.[67]

Your Obedient Servant

Obedience follows the use by managers of techniques like organizational review ('you can all re-apply for your existing jobs'), and performance review ('everyone is expected to achieve an above average rating within three years'). Meanwhile managers double-talk their desire for self-starting, self-critical, self-improving, innovative, empowered and liberated workers:

> Managers want employees to develop and employ initiative. Employees are expected to use their initiative and discretion in a disciplined way that is acceptable to management.[68]

'Thou Shalt Have No Other Gods'

It is clear from the seven common beliefs of managers (Box 15.2) that managers think that it is legitimate to organize a public service so that it extracts the maximum possible effort and energy from its staff. This is at odds with the idea that staff are also members of a community where they are expected to be caring parents, close friends, good neighbours, active citizens and lifelong learners! Public servants, whose job it is to guard the health and well-being of others, find it strange that their own managers try to stretch them to the limits of safe working. Managers send them home stressed and with little energy for exercise, hobbies or family life, let alone participating in community politics. 'Thou shalt have no other Gods before me'.[69]

If You Can't Count It, It Doesn't Count

'Outputs' – the results of maximizing return on human inputs – must be measured. But as Rosie, exclaimed in Chapter 3, 'how do you measure the output of art?' (Box 3.10). What is the measurable outcome of a programme of pub poetry, or a mural designed as part of a community arts project? How and what do you measure as the output of a project to preserve the heritage and culture of a minority group? In what units shall managers measure the value of human life, of removing a disfiguring birth-

mark from the face of a child, of improved fitness, of feeling safer on the streets at night, of trusting that water is safe to drink or that food is safe to eat? If managers force their public servants to measure everything, then they may get to know the cost of everything and the value of nothing. Carolyn, our conversational manager, did not even try to measure the self-confidence of a trainee teacher, or the increased self-esteem of their pupils, but she still knew that these were key measures of her performance. In the name of 'customer satisfaction', managers often saddle their staff with impossible standards. Public servants are expected to get everything right, first time, every time, and even better next time!

'But if you're a Senior Manager, it's different . . .'

Meanwhile the senior managers of these near-perfect public services try to make 'least worse' decisions, as soon as they reasonably can, because of the 'turbulent' environment. Even though they readily use the turbulence of the environment to excuse their under-performance, the seven sins of managers reveal a deep belief in their power to control it. They appear to believe they can control others and themselves and the future. They can 'make the future happen'. Charles Handy[70] likens them to gods, pointing again to our emerging suspicion that management might be viewed as a religion.

A CONVERSATIONAL APPROACH TO MANAGEMENT

Underlying Values and Beliefs

Having attempted to surface the assumptions and values implied by the theory and practice of management generally, it behoves us to subject our own conversational approach to the same treatment. It is inherently difficult to avoid self-serving bias when surfacing one's own assumptions and values. 'Well they would say that, wouldn't they?' Even the attempt risks appearing 'holier than thou'. These risks are not trivial but, on balance, it seems better to make the attempt, than not. The result may turn out to be a hostage to fortune. A conversational approach is based on an explicit assumption that people are individuals who are different one from the next. We should not be guided by generalized prescriptions that assume that all managers are the same, and that all managed people are the same (Chapter 8). We have assumed that it is better to manage people as individuals by having conversations with them (Chapters 2, 3, 7, 8, 11, 13 and 14).

Social Interdependence

The conversational approach includes an 'outer world' conversational loop through which managers involve other people in their 'inner world' thinking. This implies a degree of interdependence which is not apparent in the seven common beliefs of managers. The seven common beliefs of managers imply that employees are 'human resources' to be informed, controlled and motivated to exert the maximum effort of which they are capable, in order continuously to improve their performance. In a conversational approach, 'outer world' conversations involve listening, learning, persuading, negotiating, coaching and counselling. These imply a more interdependent relationship. A conversational approach implies that managers will be sensitive to feedback, and will strive to 'make sense' of it through processes of empathy as well as analysis. In a conversational approach, manager 'formulate' adaptive responses and check them out with the people affected before 'taking action'. Final decisions about what changes to implement include an evaluation of the consequences. These consequences are to be evaluated by rational and measurable criteria related to economy, efficiency, effectiveness and by criteria related to empathy and ethics (Chapter 11). In our interdependent conversational approach we seek to get beyond Stephen Covey's[71] 'I' of independence, 'You' of dependence, and the 'Them' and 'Us' of counter-dependence. We think that the idea of independent management learners and independent management

thinkers is illusory and unhelpful. Conversations are necessary. Conversations provide the warmth and applause needed by managers and the people they manage (Chapter 7).

A Culture of Compliance or Speaking Truth to Power?

We think that the need for loyalty and obedience implied by the seven common beliefs of management (Box 15.2) places an onerous burden on someone who works in a public service and who disagrees with what is happening there. In our conversational approach, there is an everyday expectation that managers will give good reasons for proposals and decisions. The conversational approach assumes that these good reasons will be open to question and that proposals are open to alteration. When these kinds of conversations are discouraged or, even worse, suppressed, then staff who are morally sensitive and thoughtful may leave the organization and be progressively replaced by staff who are more compliant. This road leads to public service organizations which are morally and intellectually bankrupt. Alternatively, conversational managers can stay and subvert the worst excesses of externally imposed changes that have no continuity with public service values. In a culture of compliance, employees and other stakeholders are more likely to speak their minds in private one-to-one conversations.

Learning Conversations

Based on the seven common beliefs of management (Box 15.2), there would seem to be little hope of creating an organization in which people can learn from their experience, especially if it involves mistakes (Chapter 13). In any event, it is not clear that the learning would be valued. It may even be the case that up-and-coming learners would be perceived as disruptive threats to a well-controlled organizational machine. People questioning, challenging, negotiating and learning are likely to be viewed with suspicion as potential loose cannons. A conversational approach to learning generates learning for both the manager and the other person. It is a natural by-product of combining inner world thinking with outer world conversations. Thoughtfulness and the learning are both highly valued in a conversational approach to management.

The Practice of Conversational Management

It seems grandiose and overly optimistic to suggest that a thoughtful conversational approach could lighten all the baggage that comes with management. Yet 'we are what we repeatedly do'. Organizations are the sum total of what the individuals within them repeatedly do. The habits of thoughtful conversational management are applicable to the day-in-day-out things that managers do, when they manage change, manage activities, manage people, manage resources, manage information and manage learning. The things that thoughtful conversational managers repeatedly do, run counter to much that is assumed and implied by the seven commonly held beliefs of managers. Thoughtful conversational managers habitually ask people to give reasons or examples. Where reasons or examples are based on past experiences, these are routinely questioned and triangulated against numerical and other information from a variety of sources. Attaching meaning to the 'facts' involves them respecting the different perspectives of a wide variety of individual stakeholders, irrespective of their position in a hierarchy. Thoughtful conversational managers think about things from the other person's point of view. Emerging ideas or assumptions are checked out via outer world conversations. In conversational management there are procedures for weighing feelings and intuition against measurement and scientific analysis. The debate between conflicting perspectives is orchestrated not suppressed. Consensual 'truth' is sought. Bunk is debunked and grandiosity punctured. The result is a more pragmatic, less perfectionist practice than that which is implied by the seven common beliefs of management. In the practice of conversational management, results are achieved in a more honest and more human way.

A Thoughtful Approach to The Practice of Management

We have looked at our assumption that managers are employees and, as people, are different from one another. We have argued for interdependency not individualism. We then looked at the implications of the seven deadly sins of management (Box 15.2). We have compared these beliefs with our more thoughtful conversational approach to management. The implicit assumptions of a more thoughtful conversational approach are summarized in Box 15.3.

Given the fact that many public services trace their origins back to the concerns of early Friends, it is not surprising that many of the assumptions implicit in Box 15.3 are similar to those which underlie the social testimony of the Religious Society of Friends (Quakers). In Chapter 3 we said that cultural management was characterized by a concern for stories and myths, rites and rituals, symbols and ceremonies. According to George Lindbeck,[72] that almost defines management as a religion.

MANAGEMENT AS RELIGION (OR PROFIT FOR THE PROPHETS)

There are more than two ways to think about management as a religion. Just before he died, Kieron Walsh[73] appealed for more balance in the way public services were managed. We have tried to consider the case for preserving continuity with the past values of public service, each time we have considered the need for change in response to some external pressure. 'Do nothing' is routinely added to the list of options to be appraised (Chapter 10). We discovered that unplanned polarization into either a management culture or a public service culture resulted in domination by a management culture (Chapter 3). But the dichotomy may be false: there are usually more than two possibilities. By making the unconscious conscious, and the implicit explicit, management beliefs

---

Box 15.3

THOUGHTFUL CONVERSATIONAL MANAGEMENT: IMPLICIT ASSUMPTIONS

We implicitly favoured:
- Fair treatment and respect for every person irrespective of gender, ethnic origin, sexuality, ability, age or nationality and specifically for prisoners, the elderly, the unemployed, refugees, asylum seekers, victims of crime and the mentally ill.

We implied that each person should have:
- Good health, shelter, employment and the caring concern of their community.
- Explicitly developed thinking skills and explicitly developed conversational skills.

We advocated:
- Learning through conversation.

- Assuming that there is that which is good in every person.
- The development of closer relationships between individuals.
- The non-violent resolution of conflict through conversations.
- Thinking empathetically – as though you were another person.
- As much openness as is possible in the exchange of information.
- Economic structures that serve the planet and the people who live on it.
- Evaluation by ethical criteria as well as economy, efficiency and effectiveness.
- A better balance between working life, citizenship and one-to-one relationships.

---

and public service beliefs can be evaluated. A third way may be found. Managers need to reduce the damage and demotivation that occur when they unthinkingly discredit the history, traditions and beliefs of the people they manage. They need to tread carefully 'lest they tread on our dreams'.[74]

Religious imagery and language have seeped into management. Terms such as values and visions, rites and rituals, ethics and morality, all have a religious flavour. During the 1990s in the UK, teams of senior managers routinely sent themselves off on 'away-days' at monasteries, priories, convents and other spiritual locations. During these 'away-days', managers considered the teachings of 'management gurus' and sought strategic 'renewal'. In this chapter we have relied heavily on management writers like Stephen Pattison, Steve Covey and Charles Handy. All three of them have a religious underpinning to their management writings.

As we saw earlier in this chapter, the underlying belief system of management appears to be uncritically optimistic. Usually managers behaved as though they could control their own thoughts, feelings and behaviour in addition to the thoughts, feelings and behaviour of others. They appeared, at times, to believe that they could control the future and 'make it happen'. Some senior managers of public services had messianic visions of a world benefiting from here to eternity from never-ending improvements in the quality of their services. If religion is a useful metaphor for management, then what sort of religion does it resemble? Is it religious fundamentalism or liberation theology?

Fundamentalism offers certainty in a time of uncertainty. Maybe we would all like to trade in doubts for certainties. The fundamentalist solutions free us from painful encounters with a reality that is changing, upsetting and distressing. If we could 'only believe' in scientific management, we could be 'saved' from the endless process of building up and tearing down, only to begin again. Management fundamentalism provides more certainty about the future and that feels safer. Liberation theology, on the other hand, sees religion as a process in which 'inner world' hopes and visions are constantly engaged in dialogue with a complex, contradictory 'outer world' of suffering, deprivation and oppression. Liberation theology is overtly critical of established religions for aligning themselves with the powerful in society, rather than the weak and the dispossessed. Ruben Alves, a Latin American liberation theologian, explained:

> We are condemned to religion. We may be ashamed of this and clothe our values and dreams in the respectable dress of science. Of one thing I am certain, life is not accompanied by the certitudes and unassailable confidence of the fundamentalists, but by visions, risks, and passions.[75]

Most major religious movements had within them a critical activity that was designed to evaluate the way in which the belief system was interpreted and applied. Sometimes these critical activities have been restrictive and inquisitorial, seeking to suppress new thinking. We hope that those who might take on the role of critical theologians in management as religion, do not follow the inquisitorial tradition. This tends to result in the abortion of new ideas, the premature closure of discussion and the burning of heretics! Liberation theology, on the other hand, has opened up new ways of thinking:

- What sort of a world do we think is out there?
- Whose purposes do we want to serve?
- What makes life worth living?
- Where are we heading?

Readers may recognize the similarity between these theological questions and the questions we have encouraged conversational managers to ask. One reason why we emphasize the importance of managers asking good questions is to try to rescue management from the fate of organized religions which unwittingly serve the interests of those with economic and political power. Uncritical assimilation of management beliefs into public service organizations inhibits and intimidates many public servants. We need public servants who are free to think ill of managers, especially managers of organizations that routinely exploit people, damage their health and despoil the world. If public service organizations can surface their beliefs about public service, they can choose to adopt, as organizational values, those beliefs that they do not wish to see sacrificed to the 'Gods of Management'. It would be good to see public servants with renewed confidence, using that confidence to enrich the belief systems of management, rather than see managers plundering the lexicon of public service for words and ideas that can be used to make management more palatable.

We make claims for conversational management that are hard to substantiate other than through 2,000 conversations on which we have reported and which have informed our text and case histories. We have many success stories in public services and private industry, but these success stories may be myths. Some of the successes reported by people using our conversational approach may have been accidental or coincidental. We have no scientific control groups. Other successes may have been due to correlation with other factors, like the presence of a rare transformational leader (Chapter 7). According to Senge, people who follow leaders often do so because they believe in them as people. This gives ordinary mortals some hope, because, as people, 'we are what we repeatedly do'.

So what is it that people who are regarded as transformational leaders repeatedly do? At Carolyn's college, Professor Colin Richards said that he was sceptical about leaders. Yet it was Colin Richards who said: 'I have been forced to accept the idea of transformational leadership because I have experienced it. Carolyn provided it for me, and for so many others'. Yet Carolyn was not heroic. She was of slender build and quietly spoken. What Carolyn 'repeatedly' did was to have daily conversations with the people on whose performance she relied and then think about them with her colleagues during the day, with her husband at night and on her own before breakfast, on her daily run. She repeatedly did the kinds of things a conversational manager repeatedly does in order to manage activities, manage people, manage resources, manage information and implement changes, through a thoughtful approach to the practice of management.

SUMMARY OF THE BOOK

- In First Thoughts we introduced the six key roles of the competent manager in the context of public services. We considered contradictions in the move from bureaucratic organizations to post-bureaucratic forms of public service organization. Four typologies of public service management were analysed and the impact of change on management over the next twenty years was anticipated. We proposed a conversational approach to management that integrated inner world thinking and outer world conversations.

- In the main body of the book we presented the knowledge that underpins the understanding which managers need to demonstrate in six key roles: managing resistance and change, managing operations and activities, managing groups and individuals, managing finances and resources, managing communication and information and managing learning and personal development.

- In Chapter 2 we analysed theories of change, the nature of change and when change is for the better. We described how managers could use conversations to persuade, negotiate, delegate and counsel individuals.

- In Chapter 3 we explored the strengths and limitations of strategic management and proposed a conversational approach to integrating prescriptive and emergent approaches to managing change. The use of project management techniques as a means of implementing change was discussed. A conversational approach to the management of cultural change was described in detail.

- In Chapter 4 we considered the implications of markets and marketing for public services. We recognized problematic aspects of marketing public services, including the stimulation of limitless demand. We explored the benefits of market research, competitor analysis, vul-

nerability assessment and models for service development. A 5P model of marketing was presented and the relevance of stakeholding and relationship marketing was explored.

- In Chapter 5 we discussed the inspection, control and management of quality and the need for improvements in internal capability. We offered a systemic approach to improving quality in public services.

- In Chapter 6 we looked at the management of groups and the problems associated with managing multi-disciplinary teams and difficult individuals. We looked at the ways conflicts can be managed. We advocated an approach that recognized individual difference and made greater use of one-to-one conversations.

- In Chapter 7, following an analysis of the evolution of leadership theories, we concluded that an overdependence on individual leaders can impede the implementation of changes. We examined theories of motivation and proposed a new model based on meeting individual needs.

- In Chapter 8 we welcomed the move away from industrial relations towards individual employee relations. We examined the personnel and other processes involved in the management of individuals in public services. We considered the management of stress and offered a model for developing closer relationships.

- In Chapter 9 we examined the process of budgeting and drew attention to the behavioural problems to which budgeting can give rise.

- In Chapter 10 we saw how a business case can be made and described a conversational approach to orchestrating a debate between stakeholders.

- In Chapter 11 we examined the management of audit, performance and accountability. We added empathy and ethics to the three E's of economy, efficiency and effectiveness as criteria for assessing performance in public services. We presented a conversational approach to managing poor performers.

- In Chapter 12 we described the nature of information and evaluated ways in which it can be communicated. We described a conversational approach to the design of communication and information systems. The role of information in decision-making and public relations was described.

- In Chapter 13 we analysed theories of learning and questioned the use of reflective learning cycles and group learning sets. We described the use of learning conversations in the workplace. The role of coaching was explained.

- In Chapter 14 we explored the relationship between management development, personal development, career development and self-development. We offered a map and a method

for self-development, including many self-managed learning activities. A conversational approach to personal development was described.

- In Chapter 15 we considered the work of one conversational manager and we evaluated the clash between seven commonly held management beliefs and the values of public service. We argued for the management of continuity as well as the management of change. We surfaced the values underlying a conversational approach to the six roles of a manager: managing resistance and change; managing operations and activities; managing groups and individuals; managing finance and resources; managing communications and information; managing learning and personal development. Finally, we asked what insights could be gained by comparing management to religion.

NOTES

1 Luke, S. and White, P. (1996) In Alvesson, M. and Willmott, H. (eds) *Making Sense of Management*. Sage.
2 Peters, T. (1992) *Liberation Management*. Macmillan.
3 Drucker, P. (1961) *The Practice of Management*. Mercury Books.
4 Kellner, A. (1996) In Alvesson, M. and Willmott, H. (eds) *Making Sense of Management*. Sage.
5 Marsden, R. and Townley, N. (1996) 'The Owl of Minerva', in Clegg, S., Hardy, C. and Nord, W. R. (eds) *Handbook of Organization Studies*. Sage.
6 Peat, R. and Urry, J. (1975) *Social Theory as Science*. Routledge.
7 Child, J. (1972) 'Organisation Structure Environment and Performance', in *Sociology*, vol. 6.
8 Lenz, T. and Lyles (1985) 'Paralysis by Analysis', *Long Range Planning*, vol. 18. Pitzer, R. (1993) *McDonaldization of Society*. Pine Forge. Brunyson, N. (1982) 'The Irrationality of Action', *Journal of Management Studies*, vol. 1.
9 Hendry, J. (1995) 'Strategy Formulation and the Policy Concept', *Journal of General Management*, vol. 20.
10 Thompson, P. and McHugh, E. (1990) Centre for Research in Employment at Work. Lancashire Business School.
11 Pfeffer, M. (1996) in Alvesson and Willmott, *Making Sense of Management*. Sage.
12 Watson, T. (1994) *In Search of Management*. Routledge.
13 Ibid.
14 Ibid.
15 Ibid.
16 Ibid.
17 Ibid.
18 Thomas, P. (2001) *Strategy Talk*. Routledge.
19 Bracker, J. (1980) 'Historical Review of Strategic Management', *Academy of Management Review*, vol. 5.
20 Shendal, E. and Hofer, H. (1979) *A New View of Business Policy*. Little Brown.
21 Ansoff, I. (1965) *Corporate Strategy*. McGraw-Hill.
22 Papdokis, V. and Borwise, P. (1998) *Strategic Decision*. Kluwer.
23 Porter, M. (1980) *Competitive Strategy*. Free Press.
24 Bowers, L. (1976) *Process Research on Strategic Decisions*. Penguin.
25 Thomas, P. and McHugh, D. (1995) *Work Organisation*. Macmillan.
26 Mintzberg, H. (1973) 'Strategy Making in Three Modes', *California Management Review*, vol. 16. Miller, D. and Friesen, H. (1978) 'Archetypes of Strategy Formulation', in *Management Science*, vol. 24. Chaffee, E. (1985) 'Three Models of Strategy', *Academy of Management Review*, vol. 10. Pennings, M. (1998) *The Nature and Theory of Strategic Decisions in Organizational Strategy and Change*. Jossey-Bass. Huff, S. (1990) *Mapping Strategic Thought*. Wiley. Wittington, R. (1993) *What Is Strategy and Does It Matter*. Routledge.
27 Routeau, L. and Seguin, F. (1995) 'Strategy and Organisation

Theories: Common Forms of Discourse', *Journal of Management Studies*, vol. 32.

28 Thomas, op. cit.

29 Argenti, J. (1996) 'Are You a Stakeholder?', *Strategy*, Oct.

30 Cleaver, A. (1997) 'How to Confuse Managers and Staff', *Strategy*, Feb.

31 Field, P. (1997) 'I Am a Stakeholder!', *Strategy*, Feb.

32 Francis, A. (1997) 'No Simple Solution', *Strategy*, Feb.

33 Special Theme (1998) 'The Stakeholding Corporation', *Long Range Planning*, vol. 31 (April).

34 Donaldson, T. and Preston, E. (1995) 'Stakeholder Theory: Concepts, Evidence and Implications', *Academy of Management Review*, vol. 20.

35 Wootton, S. and Horne, T. (2000) *Strategic Thinking for Managers*. Kogan Page.

36 Wootton, S. and Horne, T. (2001) *Thinking Skills for Managers*. Also at: www.librapress.com.

37 Mintzberg, H. (1990) 'The Design School: Reconsidering the Basic Premise of Strategic Management', *Strategic Management Journal*, vol. 11. Mintzberg, H. (1991) 'Learning/Planning a Reply to Igor Ansoff', *Strategic Management Journal*, vol. 12. Ansoff, I. (1991) 'A Critique of Henry Mintzberg', *Strategic Management Journal*, vol. 12.

38 Donaldson, L. (1996) 'Against Organisation Types', in Donaldson, L. (ed.) *For Positions Against Theory*. Sage.

39 Coners, C. (1985) 'Redirecting Research in Business Policy and Strategy', *Strategic Management Journal*, vol. 6.

40 Montgomery, A., Wererfelt, B. and Balakrishnan, S. (1989) 'Strategy, Content and Research', *Strategic Management Journal*, vol. 10.

41 Mahoney, T. (1993) 'Strategic Management and Determinism: Sustaining the Conversation', *Journal of Management Studies*, vol. 30.

42 Zan, L. (1990) 'Looking for Theories in Strategic Analysis', *Scandinavian Journal of Management*, vol. 6.

43 Daft, L. and Buenger, V. (1990) 'Hitching a Ride on a Fast Train to Nowhere'. In Frederick, W. (ed.) *Perspectives on Strategic Management*. Harper Row.

44 Prahalad, C. K. and Hamel, G. (1994) 'Strategy as a Field of Study', *Strategic Management Journal*, vol. 15.

45 From Religious Society of Friends (Quakers) (2001) *Advice and Queries*, Intro.

46 Peters, T. J. and Watermann, R. H. (1982) *In Search of Excellence: Lessons from America's Best Run Companies*. Harper & Row.

47 Story, J. (1985) 'The Means of Management Control', *Sociology*, vol. 19. Buchanan, D. (1986) 'Management Objectives in Technical Change', in Knight, D. and Willmott, D. (eds) *Managing the Labor Process*. Gower. Thomas, P. and Wainwright, D. (1994) 'Gaining the Benefits of Integrated Manufacturing Technology – Who Benefits and How?', *Inter-*

national Journal of Production Economics, vol. 34. Armstrong, P. (1984) 'Competition between Organisational Professionals', in Thompson, K. (ed.) *Work, Employment and Unemployment*. Oxford University Press.

48 Hyman, R. (1987) 'Strategy or Structure: Capital Labour and Control', *Work, Employment and Society*, vol. 1.

49 Shrivastava, P. (1986) 'Is Strategic Management Ideological?', *Journal of Management*, vol. 12.

50 Giddens, A. (1979) *Central Problems in Sociology*. Macmilllan.

51 Henderson, D. (1989) 'The Organisation Strategy', *Harvard Business Review*, Nov.–Dec.

52 Hobsbawn, E. (1998) 'The Death of Liberalism', *Marxism Today*, Nov. Krugman, P. (1998) 'A Desperate Remedy', *Fortune*, July.

53 Shrivastava, op. cit.

54 Thomas, op. cit.

55 Willmott, H. (1993) 'Strength Is Ignorance: Strategy Is Freedom', *Journal of Management Studies*, vol. 30.

56 Huczynski, A. (1993) *Management Gurus*. Routledge.

57 Kennedy, C. (1998) *Guide to Management Gurus*. Random House.

58 Argyris, C. (1991) 'Teaching Smart People How to Learn', *Harvard Business Review*, May–June.

59 Pratchett, L. (1994) *The Public Service Ethos in Local Government*. London CLD Ltd. with ICSA.

60 Ibid.

61 Lawton, A. (1998) *Ethical Management for Public Services*. Oxford University Press.

62 Griseri, P. (1998) *Managing Values. Ethical Change in Organisations*. Macmillan.

63 Lawton, op. cit., p. 65.

64 Ponting, C. (1990) *Secrecy in Britain*. Oxford University Press.

65 Lord Acton (1887).

66 Hunt, G. (ed.) (1995) *Whistle Blowing in Health Services*. Edward Arnold.

67 Ibid.

68 Alvesson and Willmott, op. cit.

69 Handy, C. (1996) *Beyond Certainty*. Arrow Books.

70 Handy, op. cit.

71 Covey, S. (1989) *Seven Habits of Highly Effective People*. Simon & Schuster.

72 Lindbeck, K. G. cited in Patterson, S. (ed.) (1997) *The Faith of the Managers*. Cassell.

73 Walsh, K. *et al.* (1994) in Leach, S., Stewart, J. and Walsh, K. (eds) *The Changing Organisation and Management of Local Government*. Macmillan.

74 Yeats, W. B., 'He wishes for the clothes of heaven'.

75 Alves, R. (1979) in Gebillini, R. (ed.) *Frontiers of Theology in Latin America*. Orbis.

FURTHER READING

Accountability for Performance (2000)
Sir John Robinson, Dr M. Kaul and V. Ayeni
ISBN: 0-85092-641-6

This book sets out best practice on developing and managing institutions for good governance. It looks at policy and practical issues relating to the main institutions in the Commonwealth.

Designing Performance Appraisals: Assessing Needs and Designing Performance (2000)
Edited by Sam Egere and Noella Jorm
ISBN: 0-85092-630-0

Many organizations in public service are under pressure to improve their performance and achieve set goals and objectives. Through case studies in Barbados, Samoa and Tonga this book shows how to measure performance in the delivery of service to the public. It shows how to conduct a needs assessment in the ministries, how to design an appropriate appraisal system, how to train the people who will be using it, and how to integrate it into the public service machinery.

Promoting Good Governance: Principles, Practices and Perspectives (2000)
Sam Agere
ISBN: 0-85092-629-7

This publication focuses on key elements of good governance. It discusses the role of public management in

- Promoting productivity

- Improving performance in the pursuit of efficient, effectiveness, economic growth, sustainable development and social justice.

It looks at the public/private sector interface in the context of developing a meaningful and effective partnership in economic development.

Strengthening Ombudsman and Human Rights Institutions in Commonwealth Small and Island States: The Caribbean Experience (2000)
Victor Ayene, Linda Reif and Hayden Thomas
ISBN: 0-85092-639-4

This book looks at accountability, privatization of government functions, the complaint-handling process, systematic investigations, compliance issues and management concerns. It provides Caribbean case studies placed within a larger international context, illustrating the experience of developing small and island states in general. Issues and strategies relating to human rights protection and promotion in the Caribbean are also explored.

From Problem to Solution (1996)
ISBN: 0-85092-452-9

Current strategies for achieving productive change in the public service.

Working Towards Results: Managing Individual Performance in Public Services (1996)
ISBN: 0-85092-491-X

A closer look at the need for new management thinking and approaches and includes chapters on organizational performance, managing individual performance and the appraisal system.

Introducing New Approaches: Improved Public Service Delivery (1999)
ISBN: 0-85092-564-9

Current economic realities have led many governments to look for methods of service delivery that are more responsive to clients' needs, and more cost-effective. This volume sets out practices which have emerged across the world, emphasizing the choice available.

Better Information Practices: Improving Records and Information. Management in Public Services (1999)
ISBN: 0-85092-582-7

Aims to share best practice in order to: improve records management systems and facilitate the reform process; demonstrate Retention Schedule development; prepare for computerized personnel records; formulate guidelines for using the new system and increase the awareness of senior government officials.

Managing Change: Changing the Role of Top Public Servants (1999)
ISBN: 0-85092-584-3

Reforms in the public administration in almost every Commonwealth country have put tremendous new demands on the men and women at the top levels of the public service. This study is an inquiry into how permanent secretaries around the Commonwealth see their jobs. It is based on extensive conversations and surveys of senior officials in over twenty-five countries.

Strengthening Management Development Institutions: The role of management development institutions in public services (1999)
ISBN: 0-85092-585-1

The Management Development Institutes were established soon after Independence in most African countries. Their role was to provide training, consul-tancy and research services to governments, particularly to the indigenous people who had assumed senior positions in the machinery of state. It offers a very down to earth approach to the issues raised.

Redefining Management Roles: Improving relationships between ministers and permanent secretaries (1999)
ISBN: 0-85092-614-9

The publication highlights problems facing ministers and permanent secretaries in the management and reform of the public service; redefines the role and responsibilities of ministers and permanent secretaries in implementing reform; identifies the policy and administrative boundaries of elected and appointed officials; shares best practices in enhancing the functional relationships through case studies of Britain, Canada and Trinidad and Tobago.

A Profile of Public Services in New Zealand (1995)
ISBN: 0-85092-437-5

Commonwealth member governments have been taking part in a unique mapping exercise, identifying changes in key areas of public service management. The Public Service Country Profile Series sets out the results, country by country, to provide an unprecedented insight into the real managerial and structural changes under way in the public service.

Electronic Governance: Living and Working in the Wired World – the Lessons of Experience (2001)
Professor Thomas B. Riley *et al.*
ISBN: 0-85092-659-9

This book discusses: tools of electronic delivery of government services; modernizing government; E-citizen, E-business, E-government; becoming a wired nation; community access; lifelong learning; smart communities; cyberlaws and regulations; inter-agency co-ordination; electronic benefit transfer; web interactive network of government services; electronic democracy and the changing face of democracy; governance in a wired world; advocacy on-line. It includes case studies from Great Britain, Canada, USA, Singapore, Malaysia and Hong Kong.

Information Technology and Globalisation: Information and Communication Technologies in Public Services (2001)
Edited by R. W'O Okot-Uma, *et al.*
ISBN: 0-85092-517-7

Looks at the role of information and communication technologies (ICTs) in trade and investment in the context of IT and globalization; addresses key issues related to trade and investment, including strategic alliances, smart partnerships and other partnering frameworks; ICT frameworks for accommodating trade and investment are discussed including making the transition to the information superhighway and evolving the national information infrastructure for the digital economy.

Pollution Control and Waste Management in Developing Countries (2000)
Edited by R. W'O Okot-Uma, *et al.*
ISBN: 0-85092-557-6

A comprehensive, practical view of environmental management, recording the experience gained through regional seminars in Africa over several years. The book deals with the following subjects, using real examples to illustrate points made:

- air pollution
- coastal and marine pollution
- managing domestic, industrial, mining, biomedical, nuclear and radioactive waste
- solid waste re-use and recycling
- waste water treatment
- laboratory waste management
- moving hazardous waste between nations.

Citizens and Governance: Civil Society in the New Millennium (1999)
ISBN: 0-903850-20-6

This report in based on the answers thousands of citizens from forty-seven Commonwealth countries gave to these questions:

- What is your view of a 'good society'? To what extent does such a society exist today?
- What roles are best played by citizens and what roles are best played by the state and other sectors in such a good society?
- What would enable citizens to play their role in the development of society more effectively in the future?

Developing Countries and the Millennium Round of the World Trade Organisation (2001)
ISBN: 0-903431-07-7

This report presents the case that developing countries can improve their growth prospects effectively by taking better advantage of multilateral trade rules, and particularly by pressing for rigorous implementation of Uruguay Round commitments and the early launch of a new trade round, focusing on market access issues, reduction in peak tariffs and culminating in a 'single undertaking'.

Developing Countries and the Global Financial System (2001)
Edited by Stephany Griffith-Jones
ISBN: 0-85092-675-0

How will proposed reforms of the global financial system affect developing countries? Do the IMF and World Bank need to find new roles? Can international standards and regulatory bodies operate in such a way that they help rather than hinder development? This book looks at how these and other issues of global governance impact on the developing world.

INDEX